TIBETAN LITERATURE
Studies in Genre

TIBETAN LITERATURE
Studies in Genre

Edited by
José Ignacio Cabezón
and
Roger R. Jackson

Essays in Honor of
Geshe Lhundup Sopa

Snow Lion
Ithaca, New York

Snow Lion Publications
P. O. Box 6483
Ithaca, New York 14851 USA
tel. 607-273-8519

First edition USA 1996

Printed in the United States of America

ISBN 1-55939-044-1 (paper)
ISBN 1-55939-031-X (cloth)

Studies in Indo-Tibetan Buddhism Series
ISBN 1-55939-000-X

Library of Congress Cataloging-in-Publication Data

Tibetan literature : studies in genre / edited by José Ignacio Cabezón and Roger R. Jackson. — 1st ed.
p. cm. — (Studies in Indo-Tibetan Buddhism)
"Essays in honor of Geshe Lhundup Sopa."
Includes bibliographical references and index.
ISBN 1-55939-044-1 (alk. paper). — ISBN 1-55939-031-X (alk. paper).
1. Tibetan literature — History and criticism. 2. Buddhist literature, Tibetan. 3. Tibet (China) — Civilization. I. Lhundup Sopa, Geshe, 1925- . II. Cabezón, José Ignacio, 1956- . III. Jackson, Roger R., 1950- . IV. Series.
PL3705.T53 1995
895'.409—dc20 95-22297
CIP

Contents

Dedication

Geshe Lhundub Sopa (lHun grub bzod pa) was born in the Shang principality of gTsang in western Tibet in 1923. He was ordained a novice monk at the age of nine and entered the famed dGa' ldan chos 'khor Monastery, an institution renowned for having produced some of the most important scholars in the country. In 1941, at the age of eighteen, in order to pursue more advanced studies, he travelled to Lhasa, the capital of Tibet, and was admitted to the gTsang pa House of the Byes College of Se ra Monastery. There he studied under four of the greatest scholar-practitioners of the dGe lugs pa school of Tibetan Buddhism: dGe bshes lHun grub thabs mkhas, who would later hold the position of *dge bkod* both at the Byes College and at the Tantric College of Lower Lhasa, and who would eventually become abbot of the Byes College itself; dGe bshes Ngag dbang rig gsal, an erudite scholar and yogi who was eventually appointed tutor to the young Phur mchog Byams pa rin po che; dGe bshes Ngag dbang dge 'dun, a renowned scholar who would later hold the position of *dge bkod* at the Tantric College of Lower Lhasa; and the former holder of the throne of dGa' ldan (the head of the dGe lugs pa school), Khri zur lHun grub brtson 'grus.

Geshe Sopa quickly gained a reputation as a dedicated and brilliant scholar, and began his teaching career at a very early age. In 1952 he was appointed tutor of the fourth Khams lung sprul sku, and took up residency at the Khams lung Bla brang in the 'Bra ti house of the Byes College. In 1956 he was awarded first position at the Rig chen tshogs glang examinations and then entered the honors, or *lha ram*, class. Before completing his own examinations for the degree of *dge bshes* he was chosen by the Monastery as one of the Dalai Lama's debate examiners during the annual Prayer Festival in 1959.

After the final overthrow of the Tibetan government by Chinese forces in 1959, Geshe Sopa sought political asylum in India. He remained for two months in Assam in a camp that had been set up for Tibetan refugees, and then moved to Dalhousie. In 1962 he sat for the annual *dge bshes* examinations in Buxador, India, one of the principal settlement sites of the Tibetan monastic community in exile, and there he was awarded the degree of *dge bshes* with highest distinction (*lha ram pa*). In that same year, H. H. the Dalai Lama appointed him tutor to three young recognized incarnate monks who had been selected to begin studies in the United States. The four of them settled at the Lamaist Buddhist Monastery in Freewood Acres, New Jersey, where Geshe Sopa would remain for the next five years.

In 1967, Professor Richard Robinson invited Geshe Sopa to join the faculty of the recently formed program in Buddhist Studies at the University of Wisconsin-Madison, making him one of the few Tibetan scholars to hold a regular position at a Western institution of higher learning. Geshe Sopa would make Wisconsin his home. In 1973 he became Assistant Professor of Buddhist Studies, was promoted to the rank of Associate Professor in 1976, and to Professor in 1985. At the University of Wisconsin Geshe Sopa has been the main impetus behind the Tibetan Studies emphasis within the Buddhist Studies Program, where he has taught elementary and advanced courses in Tibetan language, general courses in Buddhist philosophy and specialized doctoral colloquia on a variety of topics in Indo-Tibetan Buddhist thought.

His fame as a teacher and scholar began to attract students from the United States and abroad. Many entered the doctoral program at the University, but an increasing number began to request private instruction. The continued demand for his teachings outside of a formal academic setting led eventually to his founding the Deer Park Buddhist Center, an institution for the study and practice of Buddhism that has been host to some of the most prominent masters of the Tibetan tradition, among them the present Dalai Lama, who in 1981 offered the Kālacakra initiation there. To this day, Geshe Sopa continues to fill this dual role: as the spiritual master of a growing Buddhist community, and as a respected teacher and scholar in an academic setting.

Among his more well-known senior Tibetan students were Lhun grub bstan rgyas and Blo bzang rab rgyas, the latter an extraordinary yogi who lived in meditative retreat in Dharamsala, India, until his death at an early age. dGe bshes Ye shes stobs ldan, another of Geshe Sopa's students, continues to live in meditational retreat in Dharamsala to this day. Many of Geshe Sopa's Tibetan students today hold important positions, both in the Tibetan community and abroad: mKhan zur Blo bzang bstan 'dzin is the retired abbot of the Tantric College of Lower Lhasa in Hunsur, India; dGe bshes Blo bzang tse ring is the present abbot of the Byes College of Se ra in Bylakuppe, India; dGe shes Blo bzang don yod, formerly of Deer Park Buddhist Center, is a peripatetic teacher; dGe bshes sKal bzang rgya mtsho is director of the Manjushri Institute in Ulverston, England; and the late Thub bstan ye shes and his successor and student, Thub bstan bzod pa rin po che, are the founders of the Foundation for the Preservation of the Mahayana Tradition.

Many of the contributors to this volume studied under Geshe Sopa at the University of Wisconsin-Madison. Many of us were fortunate to have had him as our dissertation advisor. Those who have not enjoyed this direct teacher-student relationship have nonetheless profited greatly from his published work and from his example as a vehicle for the cross-cultural exchange of ideas. It is with heartfelt gratitude and respect for his accomplishments as a teacher and a scholar of Tibetan thought that we dedicate this volume of essays to him.

Acknowledgments

We have been helped by many people in the process of preparing this volume. Our first debt is to the contributors, whose enthusiasm both for the idea of honoring Geshe Sopa and of attempting to compile a volume on Tibetan literature has been a great source of support for us. A number of contributors went considerably beyond their "contractual" responsibility of writing articles, by providing us with suggestions and criticism along the way; we want especially to single out David Jackson, Leonard W. J. van der Kuijp and Matthew Kapstein. The volume has been greatly improved as a result of the unusually detailed comments provided us by Snow Lion's two anonymous readers. Dan Arnold has performed a heroic labor by compiling the index. Finally, Susan Kyser of Snow Lion has painstakingly edited the book for style and consistency of conventions; any coherence that it may have is due in no small part to her efforts; any inconsistencies that may remain are the fault of the editors.

The editors also wish to thank their respective institutions and various funding agencies who helped make completion of this work possible. José Cabezón wishes to express his gratitude to the Iliff School of Theology, the Rockefeller Fellowship Program at the Center for the Study of Cultures (Rice University), and the Alexander von Humboldt Stiftung, which made possible a year of research at the Institut für Kultur und Geschichte Indiens und Tibets (Hamburg). Roger Jackson wishes to thank Carleton College for summer and sabbatical support that greatly facilitated work on the volume.

Editors' Introduction

José Ignacio Cabezón and Roger R. Jackson

Tibet and the West

Tibet possesses a literature that stretches back over 1300 years. It is one of the great literary traditions of Asia, in terms of both its size and range of influence. From ancient pillar inscriptions, to manuscripts sealed away in long-forgotten caves, to block-printed texts on every imaginable subject piled high in monastic libraries, the Tibetan corpus numbers tens of thousands of works. It has exercised an abiding influence not only in Tibet itself, but in the larger cultural area at one time dominated by Tibet, which includes Mongolia, Ladakh, Nepal, Sikkim, Bhutan and parts of northern Pakistan, northern India, western China and southern Russia.

In spite of its size and influence, Tibetan literature was largely unknown to either scholars or the public in the West as recently as thirty-five years ago. This is because the period in which expanding Western colonial powers encountered and began to study Asian literary traditions—the eighteenth and nineteenth centuries—coincided with Tibet's systematic (and virtually unprecedented) isolation from the rest of the world. A few intrepid missionaries, adventurers, soldiers and scholars did make their way to "the Roof of the World," and some even reached "the Forbidden City," Tibet's capital of Lhasa. The West's first intimations of the richness of Tibetan literature were derived from the reports of such early figures as the Jesuit father Ippolito Desideri (eighteenth century), the Hungarian linguist and explorer Alexander Csoma de Körös (mid-nineteenth century), and the English soldier L. A. Waddell (early twentieth century). Later, in the 1930s and 1940s, the Russian historian A. I. Vostrikov and the Italian scholar Giuseppe Tucci began to provide the first detailed scholarly accounts of Tibet and its literature. Still, such accounts were few and far between, and until the 1960s Tibet was far less known from its own literature than from its caricatures in Western writing—whether as the inaccessible home of the "ascended masters" celebrated by Theosophists, the utopian Shangri-la of the novel and film *Lost Horizon*, or the land of psychic mysteries detailed in the "autobiographical" writings of T. Lobsang Rampa, who claimed to be a Tibetan adept who had transferred his consciousness into the body of an Englishman.

In the last thirty-five years, all this has changed. Tibetan literature is now better known in the West than ever before. Translations of Tibetan works fill entire shelves in some Western bookstores, and courses on Tibetan religion and culture have become a fixture, rather than a rarity, at many universities. Like the earlier dearth, the present plethora of information on Tibetan literature is attributable to historical circumstance—in this case, the tragic diaspora of Tibetans that began in 1959. In that fateful year, an abortive revolt against the eight-year occupation of the country by the Chinese led to the flight, to India, of Tibet's spiritual and temporal ruler, the Dalai Lama, who was followed into exile by nearly 100,000 of his compatriots. In the ensuing years, while Tibet itself has suffered terrible depredations at the hands of its occupiers, exiled Tibetans have preserved their culture in small communities throughout India and Nepal and, increasingly, in Europe and America. The dispersal of thousands of Tibetans—many of them deeply learned in their own traditions—coincided with the rise, in the 1960s and 1970s, of a fascination among Westerners, particularly the young, with all things Asian. First in Nepal and India, and later in the West itself, contacts between Westerners and Tibetans became increasingly common. One of the fruits of this encounter was a quantum leap in the quantity and quality of Western scholarship about Tibet.

Despite this increase in Western knowledge of Tibetan literature, its study is still, relatively speaking, in its infancy—especially in comparison to the work that has been done on the literatures of India, China and Japan. Only a tiny portion of the vast Tibetan corpus has been translated into or discussed in Western languages, and the works that have been translated are overwhelmingly on religious and philosophical subjects. This reflects the fact that the majority of Tibetologists have been motivated, initially at least, by religious curiosity, and this has, unfortunately, helped create the mistaken impression that Tibetan literature is exclusively religious. Granted, religious works in Tibetan are numerous and influential, and highly valued by educated and simple Tibetans alike, but there is much else in the corpus besides: lyric and epic poetry, at least one novel, and discussions of a wide range of arts and sciences, including grammar, politics, medicine, law, art and architecture, and even erotics. Even among Tibetologists, appreciation of the range and variety of Tibetan literature has grown slowly, and the evidence for it has tended to be published piecemeal, primarily in scholarly articles tucked away in obscure journals or edited volumes.[1] It is a central purpose of this volume to help remedy this situation by bringing together under a single cover a series of essays that will convey at least a sampling of the tremendous range of genres actually represented in Tibetan literature, and convey, too, a sense of our present knowledge of these genres. The volume is less concerned with providing a historical overview of Tibetan literature (since this has been done well elsewhere[2]), but a brief consideration here of its main features and phases may help to contextualize for the reader the accounts of the various genres around which the book is organized.

Features and Phases of Tibetan Literature

Tibetans speak a language that is generally regarded as belonging to the Tibeto-Burman branch of the Sino-Tibetan linguistic group. Though in its present form it is quasi-tonal, it appears in the more distant past not to have had tones, and its relation to its linguistic cousin, Chinese, is probably distant at best.[3] In their legends, Tibetans trace their history back several centuries before the beginning of the Common Era, but insist that they had no written language before the mid-seventh century, when the first of the great nation-building "Dharma Kings" (*chos kyi rgyal po*) of the gYar lung dynasty, Srong btsan sgam po, dispatched his minister, Thon mi Sambhoṭa, to India to acquire a script. Thon mi Sambhoṭa returned with a variant of the Devanagari script in which Sanskrit presently is written, thereby providing Tibetans with a means for recording their oral traditions and translating Indian Buddhist texts. The accuracy of these legends is difficult to assess—both the antiquity of Tibetan civilization and the historicity of Thon mi

Sambhoṭa have been questioned—but, as legends often do, they present us with a kind of "thematic truth" that makes them useful for explanatory purposes. Here, in particular, a number of important facts about the development of Tibetan literature are revealed.

First, like the literature of virtually any other culture that possesses writing, Tibetan literature is marked by the increasing dominance of written over oral forms. Once writing is introduced, the composition of written works seems to increase exponentially from generation to generation; only thus could the Tibetan literary canon have achieved the immense proportions it has. At the same time, it must be noted that the written tradition was preceded by a well-developed oral tradition that included not only the usual repertoire of epic poetry, folk songs and legendary narratives, but also material on such areas as law and politics. What is more, even after the introduction of writing, orality/aurality continued to be an important element of the transmission of Tibetan culture—in part because literacy never became universal, and the unlettered continued to depend on oral forms for the transmission of culture, in part because the Buddhist traditions that came to be so essential to later Tibetan cultural identity were themselves often transmitted orally, and continue to be today, even among the most literate members of the social or religious élite. Indeed, it is an assumption of virtually all Tibetan Buddhist traditions that the most essential religious knowledge is conveyed not through texts, but in oral transmission from master to disciple. Thus, any account of Tibetan literature must balance the observation that from approximately the seventh century onward it is increasingly a written literature, with a recognition of the continuing importance of traditions that stand outside the written corpus and which, though often invisible to the student of written texts, nevertheless influence the written tradition.

Second, like that of the ancient states of Southeast Asia, Tibetan literature is marked by an increasing Indianization, which went hand in hand with the growth of Buddhist influence, to be discussed below. If outside cultural influences on Tibet before the seventh century were varied and relatively insignificant, from that time on, as the gYar lung kings began casting about for sacred symbols and sources of magical power to support their reign, Indian models became increasingly influential. China long has served as a source of various Tibetan secular arts, from gastronomy to woodblock printing, but whether by accident of geography or the design of perspicacious monarchs, it is India that has served as the "motherland" of those cultural elements that are seen by latter-day Tibetans as giving unity and stature to their civilization: a system of writing, Buddhist religion, and knowledge of a wide variety of arts and sciences, most of them directly or indirectly related to religion. If there was resistance to Indianizers during the gYar lung period from those who preferred Chinese or indigenous models, after the twelfth century—when political power devolved upon Buddhist monasteries and the translation of thousands of Indian works into Tibetan was nearing completion—Indian influence became ever more pronounced, and remained so even long after the disappearance of Buddhism from India in the thirteenth century. At the same time, though indigenous traditions often were influenced and altered—or at least overlaid—by new genres and new approaches to old genres that owed much to India, it must be recognized that the degree of Indian influence on literary forms was directly proportional to the social and religious status of the Tibetan literati in question. The greatest Indian influence (at least in the early period) was exercised upon a relatively small—though highly productive—élite, while among those closer to the margins of power and education, indigenous traditions maintained a continuing vibrancy.

Third, to a degree virtually unparalleled in Asia, Tibetan literature is marked by a continual intensification of the influence of religious—especially Buddhist—concerns. This undoubtedly is related to the fact that, unlike in other cultures where Buddhism was a force for political unity and cultural advancement (e.g., Sri Lanka, Burma, Japan), in Tibet the Buddhist monasteries became powerful political and economic institutions as early as the twelfth century, and remained consistently so until 1959. As a result, the élite that is the major source of written literature in any traditional society was in Tibet to a large extent a religious élite, and the works that these literati produced were, unsurprisingly, primarily concerned with that which most interested monks, namely the Buddhist religion. Thus, the frequently repeated observation that (a) the bulk of Tibetan literature is explicitly religious and (b) even forms that are not specifically connected with religion bear its influence, is certainly true. Again, however, we must be cautious about generalizations, for it is clear, too, that just as with literacy and Indianization, "religious" or "Buddhist" influence on a piece of literature often was directly proportional to the author's proximity to the centers of power. Even at the height of Buddhist monastic dominance in Tibet, secular works continued to be composed among the less-educated laity, and non-Buddhist religious works were composed by representatives of the major "alternative" Tibetan religious tradition, Bon.[4] What is more, the Buddhist monastic élite itself was by no means restricted to writing on purely religious subjects, for included in the mass of works translated from Sanskrit were dozens of treatises on secular sciences that proved intriguing to monks either more adventurous or more worldly than their brethren. Furthermore, to the degree that the monasteries came to exercise a variety of mundane powers, reading and writing about such matters inevitably became the concern of at least a portion of the monastic population. Thus, while Tibetan literature is predominantly religious and Buddhist, it is by no means exclusively so.

In short, the development of Tibetan literature is marked by the increasing dominance of written over oral forms, of Indian over indigenous influences, and of religious over secular concerns, but the dominant development never has entirely eclipsed its counterpart—and orality, native themes and styles, and non-religious concerns have continued to find an important place in the literary tradition.

The foregoing discussion has provided a general overview that may help the reader to secure a preliminary foothold in the world of Tibetan literature. It has been framed, however, in terms drawn almost entirely from Western approaches to literary traditions: it assumes that Tibet possesses a "literature," which is divisible into "genres," which may in turn be organized in a variety of ways. If these concepts find no equivalency in Tibetans' ways of articulating their own cultural traditions, we may have to revise the ways in which we discuss "Tibetan literature." In the following two sections, we will attempt to discover just how applicable the terminology of Western literary scholarship is to the Tibetan corpus, and thereby, we hope, expose in greater detail something of the nature of "Tibetan literature."

"Literature" in Tibet

"Literature" is a theoretical construct of Euro-American intellectual culture, and as such it cannot be applied uncritically to other times and places. The English term *literature* of course has no single meaning. Taken most broadly, it simply denotes all material, written or oral, on any of countless subjects. Somewhat more narrowly, it may be regarded as "writings in prose or verse; esp.: writings having excellence of form or expression and expressing ideas of permanent or universal interest" (Webster's: 672a). Most often, though—perhaps because of the basic subject matter treated by university departments devoted to "English" or "Comparative Literature"—it seems to denote verse and prose writings considered of special value that are *not* "factual" in the way that writings on science, history, art, etc., are more apt to be. In short, there is an "imaginative" element to the concept of literature in the West that narrows considerably the range of what may be counted as literary.

If we keep in mind especially this latter, academically dominant notion of literature, and turn to the corpus we have been calling "Tibetan literature," we do not find immediate evidence that such a concept ever has existed among Tibetans. We do encounter the notion of *tsom rig* ("science of composition"), but this primarily refers to practical instruction on literary composition, rather than to the most general collection of texts or to theoretical analyses of the nature or types of literature. Closer, perhaps, is the idea of *rig gnas (vidyāsthāna)*, an abbreviation of the term *rig gnas kyi gzhung*, roughly, "texts of the cultural sciences." The *Bod rgya tshig mdzod chen mo* defines the term *rig gnas* simply as "something that is to be known" (*shes par bya ba'i gnas*) (Krang dbyi sung et al.: 2682). From this vantage point, literature comes to be defined functionally and pragmatically as those texts whose study yields the kind of knowledge worth having. More specifically, literature is the subject matter for a wise person's study, the subject matter that transforms the individual in positive ways. Hence, the great thirteenth-century Tibetan luminary, Sa skya Paṇḍita Kun dga' rgyal mtshan, drawing on Indian tradition, divides all learning into five headings: grammar; dialectics; healing; the outer sciences, consisting of manual arts and techniques; and the inner sciences, covering Buddhist doctrine and practice (see Jackson, 1: 3).

The idea of defining literature in this pragmatic way, as the "texts of that which is to be known" if positive moral transformation is to take place, is not unknown to other Asian cultures. James Hightower, for example, points out that the traditional Chinese view of literature was a didactic one, where literature was seen as "a vehicle for moral instruction" (3).

In modern parlance, the term *rig gnas* is frequently employed as the equivalent of the English word *culture,* referring in some instances to culture in general, in others to classical culture in particular. There is, however, a sense in which the term *rig gnas* means "cultural science," as in Sa skya Paṇḍita's enumeration of the ten *rig gnas* that must be mastered by a "great pandit":

The Five Minor Cultural Sciences

(1) Grammar *(sgra)*
(2) Poetics (*snyan ngag*)
(3) Metrics (*sdeb sbyor*)
(4) Drama (*zlos gar*)
(5) Lexicography (*mngon brjod*)

The Five Major Cultural Sciences

(1) The science of words (*sgra rig pa*), i.e., language
(2) The science of syllogisms (*gtan tshig rig pa*), i.e., logic
(3) The science of healing (*go ba rig pa*), including medicine, alchemy, etc.
(4) The science of "construction" (*bzo rig pa*), including physical sciences, engineering, painting, sculpture, etc.
(5) The science of inner meaning (*nang don rig pa*), i.e., the study of Buddhism (Jackson, 1: 11, n. 17; 3; cf. van der Kuijp, in this volume, p. 393)

It is tempting to consider the idea of the "texts of the cultural sciences," with the pragmatic connotations discussed above, as the closest approximation to the notion of literature found in the West, and to take the ten sciences themselves as a Tibetan taxonomy of the "genres" in the literary canon. It should be clear, however, that while this certainly matches the most general definition of literature as writings on a particular subject, and probably also fits the somewhat narrower demand for verse or prose works of stylistic excellence that treat of important themes, it fits poorly with the predominant modern sense of literature as "imaginative writing." This may be a blessing in disguise, however, for if the concept of "cultural sciences" is treated as a serious alternative to Western criteria of the literary, it frees the student of Tibetan literature to consider possibilities for the verbal arts beyond those delimited by such trinitarian, culturally bound categories as (classically) lyric, epic and drama, or (more recently) poetry, fiction and drama—categories whose limits have come to be recognized even in the West.[5]

Despite the theoretical advantages of taking such a culturally based and pragmatic notion of literature as central to the Tibetans' own conception of the literary, to do so is not unproblematic. The ten "cultural sciences" which then become the basis for the taxonomy of Tibetan literature are not indigenously Tibetan, but of Indian origin.[6] As with much of Indian culture, this division of classical learning (and texts) was imported into Tibet *in toto* and without regard for the extent to which it was truly reflective of the Tibetan cultural experience. For the modern scholar to do likewise, and to accept such a taxonomy uncritically, can only lead to a skewed and unrealistic view of Tibetan literature. For example, in terms of both their number and their importance to Tibetan culture, works dealing with "construction" can only be considered minor—even though the science of construction is counted as a "major" cultural science. Far more important is poetics, which is, however, classified as a "minor" science. And where do royal chronicles (*rgyal rabs*) fit into this schema? What is more, texts on "inner science" (Buddhism)—simply counted as one of five major sciences—in number and bulk exceed those of all the other major and minor sciences combined, and clearly require a separate taxonomy of their own if they are to be arranged comprehensibly. The tradition is not unaware of this fact, and implicit and explicit notions of such a taxonomy may be derived from sources as diverse as the canon of translated Indian scriptures (the bKa' 'gyur and the bsTan 'gyur) and the collected works (*gsung 'bum*) of eminent scholars—but that the indigenous notion of "literature" we are considering does fail to make such a taxonomy at the very least undermines its usefulness as that exact equivalent for the Western concept that we have been seeking.

The fact that there is no *precise* Tibetan equivalent to the Western concept of literature, or that our candidate for such an equivalent, "texts of the cultural sciences," has distinct limitations, does not, of course, allow us simply to conclude that "literature" is a meaningless term in the Tibetan context. To draw such a conclusion is to risk the ethnocentric fallacy whereby works, to qualify as "literature," must conform precisely to the narrowest Western definitions of that term. This, in turn, betrays an essentialist notion of definition that, at least since Wittgenstein, has been found increasingly wanting. Indeed, Wittgenstein's suggestions regarding the "family resemblances" among, e.g., games, may fruitfully be applied to the case at hand: the concept of "cultural sciences" may not meet a Western essentialist's standards for a notion of literature, but it has enough "family resemblances" (e.g., through its attempt to characterize and organize a written canon of knowledge that is of value to human life) that it certainly counts as a concept of literature in the broader senses of the term. Furthermore, of course, it can, by both its similarities to and differences from the Western concept, help to expand our narrower notion of just what it is that "literature" may actually be. In short, the analysis of what constitutes Tibetan "literature" must proceed critically, but not imperialistically, with the recognition that as we discover the literary nature of the Tibetan corpus, the Euro-American concept of literature may itself have to be modified. The notion of Tibetan literature that emerges is therefore the result of a comparative process in which an essentially foreign concept, the idea of "literature" found in the West, is pitted dialectically against those traditional concepts that do exist, and against the reality of Tibetan texts. The result, finally, is a conceptual cross-fertilization whereby Tibetan concepts can enrich and enlarge the Western understanding of "literature," and that still-foreign term then can be applied to the Tibetan corpus in a way that does not violate its integrity, and may, indeed, help to illuminate it from without.

"Genre" and the Organization of Literature

In the West, the concept of "literature" is virtually inseparable from that of "genre," which specifies the types or kinds into which a literary corpus may be organized. The division of a literary corpus into "types" or "kinds" would seem to presuppose some explicit notion of a literary canon, i.e., literature—as Paul Hernadi points out, "knowing what kinds of literature have been possible means knowing a great deal about literature as well" (1).[7] Thus, it should not surprise us that a precise equivalent for the Western notion of "genre" is no easier to find in Tibet than is a precise equivalent for "literature." There appears to be no Tibetan term that conveys exactly the sense that "genre" does in the West. There are, of course, "typology" words, such as *rigs* ("kind"), *sde* ("class") or *rnam pa* ("aspect"), but none of these seems to be used consistently to refer to an abstract notion of literary type in the way that "genre" does.

Nevertheless, even in the absence of a specific terminological equivalent for "genre," we can infer with some certainty that Tibetans were concerned with issues like those of genre-theorists in the West, simply from the fact that—virtually from the beginning of their literary tradition—they have had to organize the increasingly numerous texts that make up the written corpus. To organize is, by definition, to classify, and to classify requires at least the implicit identification of types, hence of "genres." The identification of genres, in turn, may provide a basis for inferring a concept of "literature," even in a culture, such as the Tibetan, that seems not to entertain such a concept explicitly. In any case, our major concern here is primarily to explicate some of the ways in which Tibetans (and scholars of Tibet) have organized Tibetan literature.

In the West, the delineation of genre often was on formal or structural lines) based, e.g., on whether a given work was written in meter or not; then, among metered and unmetered works, other or subsidiary genres might be separated out by their formal characteristics, and so on. Although, as Heather Dubrow points out, "[c]lassical writers tended to emphasize meter as a determining factor.... [N]o one could claim that prosody is the sole determinant of genre in English literature. In some instances it is subject matter that is decisive—witness the epithalamium, which is by definition a poem about a wedding, or the funeral elegy, which is, of course, a poem about death" (5). Dubrow goes on to point out that there may be other bases for genre, such as attitude or tone, but the form- and subject-based criteria seem the most important. These criteria seem to have been present in Tibet, too. Thus, Sa skya Paṇḍita, drawing on discussions in the Sanskrit works of Daṇḍin, analyzes literature into verse, prose, and a combination of the two.[8] This type of genre-analysis is found exclusively in those few Tibetan writers steeped in Indian poetics; far more commonly, it appears that Tibetans have appealed to criteria other than the strictly formal in their attempt to organize their literature, hence implicitly to delineate genres.

Perhaps the most influential of all attempts to organize Tibetan literature is that of the editors of the bKa' 'gyur and bsTan 'gyur, the "canon" of Indian Buddhist works translated into Tibetan. The various editions of the bKa' 'gyur, the "Translation of [Buddha's] Word," will vary in their ordering, or in their number of sectional divisions, but they all include a section designated "Vinaya," which includes various texts on lay and—primarily—monastic conduct, one designated "Tantra," which includes all those texts in which the Buddha (in one or another of his forms) preached the Vajrayāna, and a number of sections that include a variety of *sūtras*, most, though not all of them, Mahāyāna. Thus, the Peking edition is arranged as follows:

I. Tantra (*rgyud*)
II. Prajñāpāramitā (*sher phyin*)
III. Ratnakūṭa (*dkon brtsegs*)
IV. Avataṃsaka (*phal chen*)
V. Sūtra (*mdo*)
VI. Vinaya (*'dul ba*)[9]

There are, of course subdivisions within each of these sections. The Tantra section, for instance, tends to be arranged according to whether the text in question is a *tantra* or a *dhāraṇī*, and *tantras* according to the class of *tantras* to which they have been assigned. In all this welter of divisions and subdivisions, it is difficult to articulate a single organizational principle—other than to observe that there are a number of criteria that seem to be at work: Indian traditions of canonical division (whereby, e.g., Vinaya is separated from the various types of *sūtras*[10]), length (whereby the Ratnakūṭa and Avataṃsaka are separated out chiefly by virtue of their sheer volume) or common subject matter (whereby Prajñāpāramitā is separated from other types of *sūtras*). In the most general sense, it is probably fair to say that the division of the bKa' 'gyur is "subject"-based—*tantras* do differ in topic from the Vinaya, which differs from most *sūtras*—but there seems to be little by way of a theory of genres that we might derive from that division.

The bsTan 'gyur ("Translations of Teachings"), which includes translations of commentaries and synthetic treatises composed principally by Indians, and was first edited and organized primarily by the great polymath Bu ston rin chen grub (1290-1364), is somewhat more uniform than the bKa' 'gyur; in the Peking edition, it is arranged as follows:

I. Hymns of praise (*bstod tshog*)
II. Tantra commentaries (*rgyud 'grel*)
III. Sūtra commentaries (*mdo 'grel*)
  A. Prajñāpāramitā commentaries (*sher phyin*)
  B. Mādhyamika treatises (*dbu ma*)
  C. Cittamātra treatises (*sems tsam*)
  D. Abhidharma (*mngon pa*)
  E. Miscellaneous
  F. Vinaya commentaries and treatises (*'dul ba*)
  G. Tales and dramas (*skyes rabs*)
  H. Technical treatises (*thun mong dang ngo mtshar bstan bcos*)
    1. Logic (*gtan tshig*)
    2. Grammar (*sgra rig*)
    3. Lexicography and poetics (*mngon brjod, snyan ngag*)
    4. Medicine (*sman*)
    5. Alchemy (*gser 'gyur*) and sundry
    6. Supplementary[11]

Here, more than in the bKa' 'gyur, we see an organization of the material that is primarily subject-based: such topics as Mādhyamika, Abhidharma, Vinaya, Logic and Medicine may clearly be distinguished from one another on the basis of the area of human knowledge that they treat. At the same time, subject is not the sole criterion: tales and dramas may treat widely varying subjects, and seem to be set apart as "genres" by virtue of their rather more pronounced "imaginative" elements; by the same token, hymns of praise may vary considerably among themselves, but they all serve a similar religious function.

For understanding the ways in which Tibetans organized their own indigenously produced literature, our best sources are probably the tables of contents (*dkar chag*) of the collected works (*gsung 'bum*) of the more prolific of the great scholars. Thus, the voluminous works of the great Bu ston, mentioned above, can be divided roughly as follows:

I. Tantra commentaries (divided by class of *tantra* and individual *tantras* within each class, as well as by whether the text is an actual commentary or a related text, such as a *sādhana* [meditation ritual], *gtor ma* [offering cake] ritual, fire *pūjā*, etc.)

II. General works on Tantra
III. Guru lineages
IV. Mantra and *dhāraṇī* texts
V. *Maṇḍala* arrangements
VI. *Śāstra* commentaries (on *Abhisamayālaṃkara*, *Tathāgatagarbha*, etc.)
VII. Vinaya commentaries
VIII. Biographies
IX. Texts on Logic
X. History
XI. Memoirs
XII. Replies to inquiries, letters, and advice
XIII. Catalogues[12]

The *gsung 'bum* of Tsong kha pa Blo bzang grags pa (1357-1419), founder of what came to be known as the dGe lugs tradition, includes:

I. Biographies of Tsong kha pa written by disciples
II. Secret teachings on guru yoga
III. Lists of teachings received (*gsan yig*)
IV. Lecture notes collected by disciples
V. Salutations, hymns of praise, letters, brief discourses, prayers, poems, requests, invocations of blessings, etc.
VI. Works on tantra
    A. "The Great [Text on] Stages of the Tantric Path" (*sNgags rim chen mo*)
    B. Tantric commentaries (divided by class and individual *tantra*)
VII. "The Great [Text on] Stages of the Path" (*Lam rim chen mo*)
VIII. Hermeneutics (*Drang nges legs bshad snying po*)
IX. Commentaries on the *Bodhicaryāvatāra*, Logic, Madhyamaka and the *Abhisamayālaṃkāra*, etc.[13]

One of the most systematic arrangements is that of the works of the bKa' brgyud pa master 'Brug pa Padma dkar po (1527-1592), which is divided as follows:

I. Outer sciences
    A. Mundane sciences (medicine, astronomy, poetics, etc.)
    B. History of Buddhism
    C. Biographies
    D. Guides to famous places

II. Inner sciences
  A. Writings on vows and pledges
  B. Works on the Maitreya texts
  C. Stages of the path to enlightenment
  D. Abhidharma
III. Secret sciences: the basic *tantras*
  A. Achieving the root guru's blessing
  B. On various meditational deities and their *tantras* (commentaries, analyses, *sādhanas*, etc., by class and deity)
  C. *Ḍākinī sādhanas*
  D. On *dharma* protectors (divided by Father, Mother or Combined Tantra classes)
IV. Highly secret sciences
  A. The subtle body and completion stage
  . . . .
  D. View, meditation, action and result in the bKa 'brgyud
    1. Mahāmudrā
    2. Six *dharmas* of Nāropa
    3. The one-taste doctrine
    4. Dependent origination
V. Miscellaneous
  A. Hymns of praise
  B. Collected discussions
  C. *Vajra*-songs
  D. Iconography
  . . . .
VI. Polemical works
VII. Miscellaneous advice, lists of teachers and texts, etc.
VIII. Works of aspiration and dedication[14]

The collected works of other masters of different traditions and with different interests may be arranged in other ways, but the three cited above suffice to give us a general picture of the way in which Tibetans organized their own writings. In almost all cases, the organization is by subject-matter, and the various "types" of text into which *gsung 'bums* are arranged are a solid basis on which to compile a list of literary genres accepted in Tibet—if not to solve the more difficult problems (also endemic to Western discussions) of which genres are major and which minor, which classifiable as "genres," which as "sub-genres," which as "types," which as "modes," and so forth.

Though few modern or Western-educated writers have attempted systematically to delineate the genres of Tibetan literature, at least two efforts deserve brief mention. In his *Buddhist Civilization in Tibet*, Tulku Thondup divides the corpus thusly:

I. Religious literature
  A. By origin
    1. Translated from other languages
      a. bKa' 'gyur
      b. bsTan 'gyur
    2. Written by Tibetans [divided into new and old translation school writings, with the writings of each school divided by their arrangement of the doctrine, the *sūtra* and *tantra* texts they study, and the treatises they emphasize]
  B. By subject
    1. Religion
      a. View
      b. Practice
      c. Action
    2. History and biography
    3. Poetic composition and yogic songs
    4. Music, dance, art and architecture
II. Secular literature
  A. History
  B. Grammar
  C. Poetic composition, metrical literature and lexicons
    1. Poetic literature
    2. Metrical literature
    3. Lexicons
    4. Logic
    5. Astrology
    6. Mathematics
    7. Medicine
    8. Geography and Cosmology
    9. Law
    10. Drama
    11. Arts and Crafts[15]

Tulku Thondup's arrangement has the advantage of treating literature according to either its origin or its subject-matter, which increases our appreciation for the different lenses through which genres may be viewed; and his treatment of secular literature is quite detailed.[16] However, his attempt to divide the literature into "religious" and "secular" creates more problems than it solves, since, as we have seen, these two are quite difficult to separate in Tibet; further, his arrangement of religious literature is not nearly as detailed as it should be, given the immense amount of explicitly religious literature produced in Tibet.

A far more detailed arrangement of the literature is contained in Manfred Taube's four-volume *Tibetische Handschriften und Blockdrücke*, whose divisions and subdivisions are too numerous to be listed *in toto*, but whose most important categories are as follows:

I. Canonical texts and commentaries (bKa' 'gyur and bsTan 'gyur)

II. Esoteric Buddhism
   - A. Consecrations and spells (texts on empowerment, consecration, *sādhana*, *maṇḍala*, generating deities in vases, pill-preparation, etc.)
   - B. Offering and devotion (hymns of praise, *gtor ma* prepa ration procedures, fire rituals, tantric feasts, ablution rituals, etc.)
   - C. Prayers and vows (aspiration prayers, blessing invocations, guru lineage invocations, requests to the deceased to return, long-life prayers, blessings, etc.)
   - D. *Guru yoga* texts
   - E. Esoteric teachings (texts on death, after-death, transference of consciousness, Mahāmudrā, six-session *yoga*, stages of Tantra, etc.)
   - F. Non-canonical *dhāraṇīs* and *sūtras*

III. Vinaya exegesis
   - A. Stages of discipline (analyses of vows, moral advice, etc.)
   - B. Particular precepts (*bodhicitta* and refuge ceremonies, confession, one-day precepts, fasting rituals, etc.)
   - C. Exoteric teachings (*Bodhipathapradīpa*-based texts, stages of the path texts, mind-training texts)

IV. Sciences
  A. Logic and epistemology (Prajñāpāramitā, Madhyamaka, Abhidharma, logic)
  B. Linguistic science (grammars, dictionaries, texts on poetics)
  C. Medical science (medicine, pharmacology)
  D. Calculative sciences (texts on astrology, fortune-telling, iconometry)
V. History and geography (biographies, lists of teachings received, letters, catalogues, geographies, etc.)
VI. Songs
VII. Compilations
VIII. Fragments[17]

This is probably the most complete and rationally constructed of the organizational schemes we have surveyed—one could very nearly derive a list of Tibetan literary genres from it—but it too involves omissions (e.g., of tantric commentarial literature, texts on law, music, art, etc.) and some questionable categorical choices (e.g., the placement of stages of the path or mind-training texts under "Vinaya exegesis," or of Prajñāpāramitā under "Logic and epistemology").

Unsurprisingly, then, we find that no scheme for organizing Tibetan literature is entirely satisfactory—any more than any scheme for organizing Western literature is utterly acceptable. Nevertheless, we do see that, even without a precise equivalent to the Western term *genre*, Tibetans, both ancient and modern, implicitly have accepted a concept of genre, which they have articulated in the ways in which they organize either the writings of individual scholars or, less frequently, the literary corpus as a whole. Their delineation of genres is occasionally based on form, occasionally on function, but seems above all to be based on subject-matter, and as the "art" of compiling and organizing bodies of texts developed, the subject-based genres that were coming to be recognized—even in the absence of theoretical discussions of the issues involved—become increasingly clear. Still, the general absence of such theoretical discussions forces us to recall that in analyzing the "genres" of Tibetan literature, we still are applying an essentially foreign notion, and must be modest not only about any particular scheme that we may generate, but about the very process of generating such a scheme, as well. Nevertheless, just as with the concept of "literature," so with genre, a careful, respectful analysis may allow Western perspectives to illuminate the Tibetan material, and the Tibetan material to contribute to the Western discussion of "genre."

A Suggested Typology of Tibetan Literature

It should be evident from the preceding sections that neither "literature" nor "genre" is a concept natural to Tibetan thinkers and writers. There is probably no exact Tibetan terminological equivalent for either notion, and relatively little explicit analysis of the sorts of issues that have preoccupied literary theorists in the West since Aristotle. At the same time, it also should be clear that Tibetans have developed *implicit* notions of both literature and genre—the former perhaps embodied in the concept of "writings on the cultural sciences," the latter inferable from the ways in which Tibetans have sought to organize their literary corpus. It also must be evident, however, that there is no simple or definitive way to articulate either the Tibetan idea of literature or the genres into which that literature may be organized.

We have chosen to organize this volume along the lines of a typology of Tibetan literature that we feel allows both flexibility and a certain amount of precision. Our eightfold typology ignores certain distinctions that often are made in organizing the literature. Recognizing that works in most genres are produced by all the major traditions of Tibetan Buddhism (and Bon), we have ignored "school" lines in devising the broadest categories of our scheme. Feeling that it is too limiting, we also have ignored the divisions employed in both the translated Indian Buddhist canon and many collected works of great scholars, whereby material is organized around such idiosyncratically Buddhist rubrics as Vinaya/Sūtra/Abhidharma, or Sūtra/Tantra. Most importantly, perhaps, we have generally ignored the distinction between religious and secular. We believe that broadly to divide Tibetan literature along these lines is misleading, for at least two reasons: (1) it presents a twofold scheme that is greatly unbalanced, since works of obviously religious literature are far more numerous and bulky than those of secular literature; and (2) given the centrality of religion to Tibetan "cultural sciences," the lines between religious and secular are, in any event, often difficult to determine, given that even apparently secular works often are set within a religious frame, while religious works may incorporate and reflect much that is more secular in nature. Granted, there are some areas of literature that are more exclusively religious or secular than others, and this is reflected in some of our specific divisions; we have, however, eschewed the religious-secular distinction as a general principle.

Our typology, then, is as follows:

I. History and Biography
   A. Historical chronicles (*rgyal rabs*)
   B. Dharma histories (*chos 'byung*)
   C. Religious biographies (*rnam thar*)
   D. Autobiographies/Memoirs
   E. Letters
   F. Lists of teachings received (*gsan yig*)
   G. Guru lineages (*bla ma'i rgyud*)

II. Canonical and Quasi-Canonical Texts
   A. rNying ma canon (*rnying ma rgyud 'bum*)
   B. gSar ma pa canon
      1. bKa' 'gyur
      2. bsTan 'gyur
   C. Bon po canon
   D. Treasure texts (*gter ma*)

III. Philosophical Literature
   A. Tibetan commentaries on Indian canonical material (*'grel pa*)
   B. Doxography (*grub mtha'*)
   C. Collected philosophical topics (*bsdus grwa*)
   D. Debate manuals (*yig cha*)
   E. Polemical texts (*dgag len*)
   F. Treatises on various topics: Abhidharma, Logic and Epistemology, Madhyamaka, Prajñāpāramitā, etc.

IV. Literature on the Paths
   A. Stages of the doctrine (*bstan rim*)
   B. Stages of the path (*lam rim*)
   C. Mind-training (*blo sbyong*)
   D. Vows and pledges (*sdom gsum*)
   E. Treatises on grounds and paths (*sa lam*)
   F. Precept and instruction (*gdams ngag*)
   G. Treatises on various practices: rDzogs chen, Mahāmudrā, Lam 'bras, various tantric deities

V. Ritual
   A. Consecration (*rab gnas*)
   B. Offering rites (*mchod pa*)
   C. Sādhana (*grub thabs*)
   D. Long-life prayers (*zhabs brten*)
   E. Initiation (*dbang bskur*)
   F. Fasting rituals (*myung gnas*)
   G. Fire rituals (*sbyin sreg*)
   H. Death rituals
   I. *Maṇḍala* construction

VI. Literary Arts
   A. Epic (*sgrung*)
   B. Folk songs/poetry (*glu*)
   C. Poetry
      1. Religious poetry (*nyams mgur*)
      2. Ornate poetry (*snyan ngag*)
      3. Songs of praise (*bstod tshogs*)
   D. Novel
   E. Treatises on poetics and composition (*tsom rigs*)

VII. Non-literary Arts and Sciences
   A. Grammar
   B. Law
   C. Medicine and pharmacology
   D. Astronomy/astrology
   E. Mathematics/iconometry
   F. Geography/cosmology
   G. Painting, sculpture, architecture
   H. Drama
   I. Music

VIII. Guidebooks and Reference Works
   A. Itineraries (*lam yig*)
   B. Catalogues (*dkar chag*)
   C. Dictionaries (*tshig mdzod*)
   D. Encyclopedias

We feel that this scheme has the advantage of providing a relatively manageable number of general categories into which most of Tibetan literature's types, genres and sub-genres may comfortably be placed. We have, however, adopted it primarily for heuristic reasons, and recognize that it is not the only, nor necessarily the best, way one could organize Tibetan literature in its entirety.

Quite aside from the question whether the eight general categories we have selected are an adequate reflection of Tibetan literary concerns, there are the more particular problems endemic to genre-schemes everywhere, especially that of particular categorical assignments. We have tried our best to conceive a scheme that is representative and inclusive, but questions about overlap will remain. For instance, long-life prayers are virtually always recited in a ritual context, so we have placed them under this rubric of Ritual; a case could be made, however, that they ought to be under Literary Arts, for they contain some of Tibetan literature's most beautiful and complex poetic statements. Literature on the observance of vows and pledges gives important guidance along the Buddhist path, hence its inclusion in Literature on the Paths; however, these texts contain a great deal of philosophical interest as well, and might well be classed as Philosophical Literature, too. The treatises on various practices included under Literature on the Paths certainly assist adepts in their spiritual path; however, many of these texts entail a ritual dimension that could easily justify their being classed under the rubric of Ritual. Examples certainly could be multiplied, but so they will be in any attempt to organize so vibrant and unwieldy a phenomenon as a literary corpus.

About the Book

Whatever the shortcomings of our scheme, it is our conviction that the essays collected here provide the most wide-ranging and detailed treatment of Tibetan literature ever brought together in one volume. We have sought to represent as many of the important genres of Tibetan literature as we could, and have sought articles from scholars expert in the areas concerned. We gave our contributors the unenviable task of writing essays that would combine deep and accurate learning of the sort required by scholars with a degree of clarity and accessibility that would keep the more general reader interested. We feel that our contributors have succeeded in this difficult balancing act.

We also should say something about what this book is not. Above all—in spite of its range and depth—this book is *not*, nor was it ever intended to be, an encyclopedia of Tibetan literature. There are at least three ways in which it is not an encyclopedia.

(1) It does not include all possible genres, nor, for that matter, every important genre: notable omissions include literature on astrology, initiations, stages of the path (*lam rim*), logic, music and folk songs—topics on which we solicited but were unable to obtain contributions. To this, one could add countless other genres and sub-genres that, for reasons of space, are unrepresented. These include the rNying ma canon, lists of teachings received, death rituals, dictionaries and encyclopedias, *guru*-lineage prayers, and instruction manuals on topics as various as pill-making, *maṇḍala* arrangement or *gtor ma* construction, as well as literature on particular topics of meditation or study, among them the Great Perfection (*rdzogs chen*), Mahāmudrā (*phyag chen*), the Path and Its Fruit (*lam 'bras*), the Three Vows (*sdom gsum*), and Madhyamaka. Further, we have restricted our scope to classical genres, omitting those that may have arisen in a modern context, such as newspapers, magazines or political tracts.

(2) There is some imbalance in the Tibetan traditions on which our authors have chosen to focus—the dGe lugs school is heavily represented, the others less so in proportion either to their historical importance or the bulk of their literary output. This imbalance is in part a reflection of the strength of dGe lugs studies among Tibetologists (especially in America), in part a reflection of our inability to make the volume as large or inclusive as we would have liked.

(3) The individual essays, while usually giving a good sense of the nature and range of the genre under discussion, are not intended to be comprehensive accounts of those genres. Rather, the authors usually focus on particular instances of a given genre—though always against the background of the genre as a general "type." The reason why individual articles are not intended to be comprehensive is simple: our understanding of Tibetan literature still is relatively undeveloped. Even experts on a genre may not have explored the full range of writings available within it; even if they have, space constraints would make such exploration impossible in the present format. As noted earlier, the serious study of Tibetan literature—some pioneering exceptions like Tucci and Stein aside—has only developed in the last thirty years, and there is a great deal still to be learned. Perhaps a decade or more from now, the contributors—or their students—may be able to produce the

sort of encyclopedic coverage of Tibetan literature that is a desideratum, but presently an impossibility.

(4) While individual essays generally follow the pattern just described—exploration of a particular example of a genre against the background of the genre as a "type" of literature—we have chosen not to shape every essay according to a single formula, so the reader will discover exceptions to the pattern. Thus, some essays will range more widely within a genre while some will be highly specific, and some will raise issues of cross-cultural literary analysis while others will not.

So, if this book is neither encyclopedic nor definitive, we hope nevertheless that it will—by bringing together a wealth of material on a range of Tibetan literary genres and types—add considerably to our understanding and appreciation of Tibetan literature, and move us—Westerners and Tibetans alike—toward the day when Tibet's literary achievement will be recognized for the contributions it has made to Asian and world culture.

Notes

1. There are, of course, exceptions, the most notable probably being Vostrikov, Tucci and Stein. In addition, one must acknowledge the painstaking efforts of E. Gene Smith, whose introductions to many of the Tibetan texts he collected for the U.S. Library of Congress PL-480 program are an indispensable resource for all Tibetanists, but, alas, widely scattered and relatively inaccessible. For references to recent work produced in Tibet and China, see below, van der Kuijp, "Tibetan Belles-Lettres," note 1, p. 405.

2. See especially Vostrikov, Tucci , Snellgrove and Richardson, and Stein. The latter contains probably the most succinct and authoritative account.

3. The most authoritative study of the Tibetan language—a topic beyond the purview of this book—is that of Stephan Beyer (1992). Beyer's book also is a treasury of excerpts from Tibetan literature, which he uses for illustrative purposes.

4. The degree to which Bon is or is not indigenous, or the extent of Buddhist influence upon it, cannot be discussed here. Suffice it to say that (a) some aspects of what later came to be called "Bon" almost certainly go back to indigenous Tibetan traditions from a period before the arrival of Buddhism, if not to the very beginnings of Tibetan civilization; (b) some other aspects of

Bon (perhaps the most important) originated outside Tibet, making it very unlikely that it is purely indigenous; and (c) though "latter-day" Bon bears undeniable Buddhist influence—to the point where some have regarded it as a "fifth" Buddhist tradition (alongside the rNying ma, bKa' brgyud, Sa skya and dGe lugs), Bon pos themselves distinguish their tradition clearly from all other Buddhist schools, relying as they do on a different founder than Buddhists (however much gShen rab's story resembles the Buddha's) and on a different set of scriptures (however much they may resemble the Buddhist canon).

5. See, e.g., Hernadi: 34-35.

6. See, e.g., Keith for a taxonomy of Sanskrit literature that strongly resembles the Tibetan one just cited.

7. James Hightower makes a similar point when he states: "When they come to abstract the forms in which literature is written, the lists compiled will be a direct reflection of their concept of literature. And, conversely, the accepted genres will influence the general idea of what the broader abstraction, literature, is" (142-143).

8. See especially the discussion in van der Kuijp. Van der Kuijp interpolates the term "genre" into his analysis and translations, but never supplies a Tibetan equivalent.

9. This listing is drawn from Tulku Thondup (51). For alternative arrangements, see, e.g., Skorupski (especially xiv ff.—sTog Palace) and Robinson and Johnson (272—sNar thang). The sNar thang contains the same divisions, but reverses the places of Vinaya and Tantra; the sTog Palace also places Vinaya first and Tantra last, and subdivides the Prajñāpāramitā and Sūtra sections in such a way that the total number of parts in the canon is doubled to twelve. For discussion of a canonical arrangement that predates either the bKa' 'gyur or the bsTan 'gyur, that of the *lDan kar ma*, see Harrison, in this volume.

10. The classic division of the Indian Buddhist canon is into the "three baskets," the Tripiṭaka (Tib., *sde snod gsum*): Vinaya, Sūtra and Abhidharma.

11. This arrangement is that of Tulku Thondup (52); for another reading of the Peking, cf. Robinson and Johnson: 272.

12. We have based our arrangement on the listing of Bu ston's works in Kanakura et al.: 1-78.

13. Drawn from ibid.: 87-129.

14. Adapted from Lokesh Chandra (1: 26ff.). For a complete list of Padma dkar po's works, see ibid.: 112-128.

15. Adapted from Thondup: 49-72.

16. Cf. that of Sa skya Paṇḍita, cited above.

17. Adapted from Taube: v-vii.

References

Beyer, Stephan
1992 *The Classical Tibetan Language*. Albany: State University of New York Press.

Dubrow, Heather
1982 *Genre*. New York: Methuen.

Hernadi, Paul
1972 *Beyond Genre: New Directions in Literary Classification*. Ithaca: Cornell University Press.

Hightower, James
1965 "The *Wen Hsüan* and Genre Theory." In *Studies in Chinese Literature*. Ed. by John L. Bishop. Harvard-Yenching Institute Studies 21. Cambridge: Harvard University Press.

Jackson, David P.
1987 *The Entrance-Gate for the Wise (Section III): Sa-skya Paṇḍita on Indian and Tibetan Traditions of Pramāṇa and Philosophical Debate*. 2 parts. Wiener Studien zur Tibetologie und Buddhismuskunde, heft 17. Vienna: Arbeitskreis für Tibetische und Buddhistische Studien Universität Wien.

Kanakura, Yensho et al.
1953 *A Catalogue of the Tōhoku University Collection of Tibetan Works on Buddhism*. Sendai, Japan: Tōhoku University.

Keith, A. Berriedale
1920 *A History of Sanskrit Literature*. Oxford: Oxford University Press.

Krang dbyi sung et al.
1984 *Bod rgya tshig mdzod chen mo*. 3 vols. Lhasa: Mi rigs dpe skrun khang.

van der Kuijp, Leonard W. J.
1987 "Sa-skya Paṇḍita Kun-dga' rgyal-mtshan on the Typology of Literary Genres." In *Studien zur Indologie und Iranistik*. Ed. by G. Buddruss et al. Heft 11/12. Reinbek: Verlag für Orientalische Fachpublikationen.

Lokesh Chandra
1963 *Materials for a History of Tibetan Literature*. 3 vols. New Delhi: International Academy of Indian Culture.

Robinson, Richard and Willard Johnson
1982 *The Buddhist Religion: A Historical Introduction*. Third edition. Belmont, CA: Wadsworth.

Skorupski, Tadeusz
1985 *A Catalogue of the sTog Palace Kanjur.* Bibliographia Philologica Buddhica, Series Maior, IV. Tokyo: The International Institute for Buddhist Studies.

Snellgrove, David and Hugh Richardson
1968 *A Cultural History of Tibet.* New York: Praeger.

Stein, R.A.
1972 *Tibetan Civilization.* Tr. J. E. Stapleton Driver. Stanford: Stanford University Press. (New French edition issued, 1988.)

Taube, Manfred
1966 *Tibetische Handscriften und Blockdrücke.* 4 heft. Wiesbaden: Franz Steiner Verlag.

Tucci, Giuseppe
1949 *Tibetan Painted Scrolls.* 2 vols. Rome: Libreria dello Stato.

Tulku Thondup
1982 *Buddhist Civilization in Tibet.* U.S.A. [sic.]: Maha Siddha Nyingmapa Center.

Vostrikov, A. I.
1970 *Tibetan Historical Literature.* [Reprint] Calcutta: Indian Studies Past & Present.

Webster's
1977 *Webster's New Collegiate Dictionary.* Springfield, MA: G. & C. Merriam Co.

Chapter 1

Tibetan Historiography

Leonard W. J. van der Kuijp

If we are to believe later traditions, and there is in my opinion no reason not to do so, the first Tibetan historiographic writings date from Tibet's imperial period (seventh-ninth centuries), which coincided with her relations with the Nepalese, Indians, Arabs, Turks, Uighurs, 'A zha and, above all, Tang China. Only a fragment of this literary corpus, falling into two broad classes, has survived. The first of these constitutes those historical documents that were discovered as late as the beginning of this century in one of the caves of the famous cave-temple complex near the town of Dunhuang in Gansu Province in the People's Republic of China. Recent scholarship generally agrees that the cave housing these manuscripts was sealed sometime after the year 1002, the latest date found in the manuscripts, possibly around the year 1035 (Fujieda: 65), so that the *terminus ad quem* of these undated documents would fall in that year. Of signal importance are especially three untitled manuscripts that are known to English-language scholarship as:

(1-2) *Royal Annals of Tibet* (Bibliothèque Nationale, Paris, Pelliot tibétain no.1288, together with India Office Library, London, Stein no.8212, 187).

(3) *Old Tibetan Chronicle* (Bibliothèque Nationale, Paris, Pelliot tibétain no.1287).

They have been studied in varying degrees of detail by a number of Western, Tibetan, Chinese and Japanese scholars.[1] The first Tibetan to examine these was the great scholar and iconoclast dGe 'dun chos 'phel (1903-1951),[2] who had gained access to these and a few other fragments while in Kalimpong sometime in 1939. As is related by H. Stoddard, his most recent biographer, the French Tibetanist Jacques Bacot visited Tharchin, a Christian missionary of Khunu descent, in Kalimpong and read with him several of these difficult manuscripts in Old Tibetan. Tharchin apparently solicited the help of dGe 'dun chos 'phel, who was able to aid him in deciphering a number of problematic readings. The results of Bacot's studies were published in 1946, but no mention is made there of either Tharchin or dGe 'dun chos 'phel, although he gratefully recorded his philological debt to another Tibetan, namely bKa' chen Don grub.[3] The last tome of a recently published three-volume edition dGe 'dun chos 'phel's works contains *inter alia* three studies of a number of these Tibetan Dunhuang manuscripts. They include a reproduction of the *Royal Annals* with philological notes, an adaptation into Classical Tibetan of the Old Tibetan of the manuscripts of a large portion of a version of the celestial origin of the imperial families and other miscellaneous fragments, and a reproduction of the *Old Tibetan Chronicle*.[4] Some of the results of these initial studies were subsequently incorporated into his incomplete work on Tibetan history, the *Deb ther dkar po* ("White Annals"). He was followed by such recent scholars as Khetsun Sangpo, Khang dkar sKal bzang tshul khrims, rDo rje rgyal po, and Chab spel Tshe brtan phun tshogs.

While most of Tibet's cultural institutions and literary canon derive from India or are based on one or other of her models, a notable exception is the intense preoccupation of Tibet's men of letters with history and historiography. In terms of literary genre, some of Tibet's historiographical writings bear a resemblance to, or are analogous with, the Indian *vaṃśāvalī* ("annals"), but her enormous historiographic literature, including that of biography and autobiography, bears testimony to an approach to history that is different from the Indian one(s) (see Warder, Subhrahmanian). As far as the secondary sources on this large corpus of literature are concerned, the premier study is still the one by A. I. Vostrikov.[5] Now dated in a number of respects, it remains a classic and indispensable treatment of the various literary genres.

Despite the fact that the dissolution of the Tibetan empire seems to have resulted in a virtual cessation of further literary developments for about a century, if we take the Tibetan Buddhist tradition at face value, there is ample evidence for affirming the existence in at least central and eastern Tibet of an unbroken transmission of historiographic texts, or quasi-historiographic documents like family chronicles, throughout this time and into the period of the so-called subsequent propagation, which the Tibetan Buddhist historians generally date to the middle of the tenth century. Indeed, we possess documents that trace the genealogies for such extended families or clans of the 'Khon and rLangs of, respectively, the Sa skya and gDan sa mthil/rTse[s/d] thang monastic principalities.[6] Moreover, some sort of archives may also have been maintained, if only by the scattered descendants of the imperial family. A sample of the kinds of documents that may now lie buried somewhere in the vast collections of the Potala would be a series of "edicts" issued by Khri srong lde btsan (r. 742?-797?), which were preserved in the chronicle by the great sixteenth-century historian dPa' bo gTsug lag phreng ba (1504-1566).[7] By the same token, the two recensions that are now available of the *sBa bzhed*, a virtual biography of the first Tibetan monk, sBa Ye shes dbang po (eighth century), suggest that the original text should by and large be considered a primary source on Khri srong lde btsan and his religious works, in spite of the fact that their transmission is beset with enormous complexity. In his chronicle of Buddhism in Tibet (and much else besides), Nyang ral Nyi ma 'od zer (1124-1192) refers to a number of very early works, in addition to numerous edicts, that have to do with the reign of the latter as well. Their descriptive titles are:[8]

(1) *bKa'i yig rtsis che*
(2) *bKa'i yig rtsis chung*
(3) *bKa'i thang yig che*
(4) *bKa'i thang yig chung*
(5) *rGyal rabs rkyang pa*
(6) *Khug pa*
(7) *Zings po can*
(8) *sPun po*

NYANGb wrongly collapses the titles of nos. 6 and 7, and reads *Khug po zings pa* [sic!] *can*. *NYANGl* has *Yun po* for no. 8, which is due to a misreading of the cursive ligature *sp*, which resembles the graph for *y*. Moreover, the last four would appear to be historiographic texts *per se*, but none of these have been located so far if, indeed, they are still extant. One recension of the *sBa bzhed*, as do Nyang ral and, more elaborately, the chronicles of Buddhism by *lDe'u Jo sras and mKhas pa lDe'u,[9] brings to attention the existence of five early historiographic texts from the imperial period, two of which appear to correspond to nos. 7 and 8 of the above titles. These have been briefly noted in a recent paper by S. G. Karmay.[10]

There are roughly three expressions which, when they occur in book titles, usually indicate that the books in question are historiographic in nature, and all of these are found in writings attested in Tibet for the period covering the eleventh to twelfth centuries, and one which in part may even go back as far as the seventh century. With their probable dates of inception, these are:

(1) *Lo rgyus* ("Records") (eleventh century)
(2) *rGyal rabs* ("Royal Chronology") (eleventh century)
(3) *Chos 'byung* ("Religious Chronicle") (twelfth century)

Due to limitations of space, we shall have to restrict ourselves, with one notable and fairly lengthy exception, to a bibliographic survey of historiographical texts belonging to these two centuries. However, it must be understood at the outset that those philological procedures that are fundamental to other branches of the humanities having to do with texts and their transmission have thus far mostly bypassed inquiries into Tibetan historiography, as they have virtually every other branch of Tibetan studies. Moreover, there are also considerable gaps in the literary corpus of available texts on the present subject. For these reasons, and also in the absence of "critical" texts, some of the remarks that follow are of necessity rather tentative.

Lo rgyus

The first instance of this expression in a historiographic context appears to be the famous but until now inaccessible *Lo rgyus chen mo* ("Grand Annals") by Khu ston brTson 'grus g.yung drung (1011-1075).[11] The expression *lo rgyus*, literally "tidings of year[s]," is only very occasionally best rendered by "annals." It is far more often the case that works with this term in their title do not fulfill what is promised by such a rendition, that is to say, they do not at all give a year-by-year account of their subject-matter, but rather present a narrative of events, historical, quasi-historical, or even ahistorical, in rough chronological sequence. It is well known that later historiographic sources abound in quotations from what appears to be Khu ston's work, although it does not seem to be extant.[12] The fragments indicate that it was largely, if not entirely, written in verse. dPa' bo also often availed himself of this work in his study of Tibet's imperial period, and it functioned, for example, as one of his fundamental sources for information about the decades after Emperor Glang dar ma's assassination in 842 (or 846, the year which he assigns to this event), specifically about the insurrection of 869 against his two sons, 'Od srung and Yum brtan, which spread from central to eastern and northeastern Tibet (see *DPA'1*: 429-430; *DPA'*: 432-433).

rGyal rabs

The expression *rgyal rabs* means something like "account/story of king(s)," and is perhaps best translated by "royal chronicle."[13] As far as the *rgyal rabs* as a specific historiographic genre is concerned, the earliest ones that are presently available were composed by the third and fifth Sa skya pa patriarchs rJe btsun Grags pa rgyal mtshan (1147-1216) and 'Phags pa Blo gros rgyal mtshan (1235-1280).[14] The latter's is dated to the year 1275. In addition to these two, there were also others that were written in the thirteenth century. Possibly dPa' bo but certainly the great Sa skya scholar Mang thos Klu sgrub rgya mtsho (1523-1596), in his study of the chronology of Buddhism in India and Tibet finally completed in 1587, have preserved several fragments of the *rGyal po rabs phreng* by U rgyan pa Rin chen dpal (1230-1309).[15] According to bSod nams 'od zer's hagiography of U rgyan pa, the author wrote this work for Qubilai Khan (r. 1260-1294) as part of his attempt—his hagiographer and disciple states that he was successful—to dissuade the Mongol emperor from invading Nepal. While bSod nams 'od zer does not date this episode, evidence internal to the hagiography suggests that this may have taken place in the 1270s. This is now confirmed by the recent discovery of a thirteen-folio manuscript of U rgyan pa's *rGyal po rabs kyi phreng ba*, which is dated 1278.[16] The still unavailable *rgyal rabs* is the *rGyal rabs dpag bsam ljon shing* of 1286 by the elusive Byang ji ston pa Shes rab 'bum, which so far is first alluded to in Tshal pa Kun dga' rdo rje's extremely influential *Deb gter/ther dmar po* ("Red Book") (see *TSHAL*: 21a; *TSHAL1*: 45, Inaba-Satō: 103; Chen-Zhou: 41). The relevant passage states that his genealogy of Tibet's ruling families was for the most part taken from a summary of Byang ji ston pa's work, which had been written upon his request by a dPag thog pa Rin chen rdo rje or gSer thog pa Rin chen rdo rje.[17]

The *Deb gter/ther dmar po*, the earliest extant Tibetan example of an attempt at writing a global history, has so far been translated into Japanese and Chinese (see Inaba-Satō; Chen-Zhou; and also the papers of Bira, 1964, 1984). To be sure, its scope and the underlying conception of its composition can only be understood against the background of the Mongol conquest of Tibet in 1240 by Ögödei Khan (r. 1229-1241), the subsequent establishment of a central governing body under the 'Bri gung pa and Phag mo gru, and its inclusion into the Mongol empire. Under Qubilai Khan, Tibet became formally part of the Mongol empire in China, and the change of local government in the 1260s, headed this time by Sa skya, together with the preeminent position held by prelates from Sa skya, made it possible for Tibet, as during the imperial period, once again to make an entry onto the stage of world history, albeit this time of course not as a sovereign state, but under Mongol overlordship. The Mongol domination of Tibet from 1240 to 1368 had far-reaching effects on Tibet's religious and political institutions, as well as on the development of the Tibetan language and historiography. One of these was the adoption of numerous Uighur/ Mongol and Chinese loan words. Indeed, the very term *deb gter/ther (gter* and *ther* are homophonous) in the title of Tshal pa's work is an example of such a loan word; in fact, it is its first attestation in written Tibetan. It undoubtedly entered into the Tibetan lexicon from the Mongol *debter* which, in turn, ultimately derives from the Greek via the media of Persian and Old Turkish. While the introductory remarks in both recensions entitle it *Deb gter dmar po*, the chronicle is also known as the *Hu lan deb gter/ther*, where *hu lan* corresponds to Mongol *ula'an/ulaghan*, "red," a title which occurs at the very end of what may have been the original text (see *TSHAL*: 38b; *TSHAL1*: 149; Inaba-Satō: 194; Chen-Zhou: 128).

Tshal pa's notion of historiography is a traditional one, one which in another context Collingwood (257 ff.) has called the "scissors-and-paste" approach to history, characterizing it as "...a kind of history which depends altogether upon the testimony of authorities." Tshal pa not only made use of a number of Indic and Tibetan sources, but also of treatises (originally) in Mongol and Chinese. A case in point of the former is the so-called *Yeke tobčiyan* ("Great/Large Records"), which, though they cannot be identified with any precision, could very well refer to the lost genealogical tables of the Mongol imperial family on which the relevant chapters of the *Yuanshi* are based, or perhaps even to the *Dayuan tongzhi* collection of legal documents.[18] In this connection, we should note that for information on early Sino-Tibetan relations and for the royal/imperial genealogies of the Chinese, Xixia and Mongol empires, bLa ma dam pa, Yar lung pa, the chronicle of 1434 (with a few later interpolations) of sTag tshang pa dPal 'byor bzang po, *alias* Śrībhutibhadra, 'Gos lo tsā ba gZhon nu dpal's (1392-1481) *Deb gter/ther sngon po* of 1476-1478, Paṇ chen bSod nams grags pa's (1478-1554) *Deb ther dmar po gsar ma* ("New Red Annals") of 1538, and dPa' bo depend almost exclusively on the relevant texts in Tshal pa's compilation. Of interest is that dPa' bo contains a translation from a Chinese work on the spread of Buddhism in China which, he takes special pains to specify, is not met with in the so-called *Deb dmar* (see *DPA'2*: 567-572; *DPA'*: 1391-1396). In his remarks that preface the reproduction of this work, he writes that it was first translated from Chinese into Uighur by a Uighur monk called Og zo at the order of Emperor Buyantu (r. 1311 to 1320); subsequently it was rendered into Tibetan in Sa skya Monastery by a Puṇyaśrībhadra (= bSod nams dpal bzang po), who was probably a Uighur as well.[19]

At the outset of the *Deb gter/ther dmar po*, in his statement of intent, Tshal pa writes that what follows is "the first of three *Deb gter dmar po* [texts]"; unfortunately, the other two, if they were ever written, are wanting. However, Dung dkar Blo bzang 'phrin las, the editor of the Beijing recension, does observe that he wrote in addition to other works (which include two biographies) a supplement to a/the *Deb gter/ther dmar po*,[20] a *rgyal rabs* entitled *Deb ther khra po* ("Multicolored Book"), and a catalogue of the so-called Tshal pa bKa' 'gyur, which bore the subtitle of *Deb ther dkar po* ("White Book").[21] Of some interest is of course the use of color terms in the titles (or subtitles) of books. This was unprecedented in Tibetan historiography and is something that is very Mongolian indeed.

Chos 'byung

The third historiographic genre is that of the *Chos 'byung* ("Origin of Buddhism"). The very first of such texts may have been the one written by the eleventh-century scholar Rong zom Chos kyi bzang po of which only a few fragments have surfaced so far.[22] Although the reasons are still far from transparent, it is possible that with the proliferation of various doctrinal cycles a need was felt to place these in historical perspective and thereby legitimate them. In any case we find, starting with the twelfth century, an enormous upsurge of interest in Indo-Tibetan religious history in particular. Unfortunately, only a fraction of the potentially available literary corpus of such texts has been located and published to date. For, while those authored by the bKa' gdams pa masters Phya pa Chos kyi seng ge (1109-1169) and his student gTsang nag pa brTson 'grus seng ge have yet to be discovered, the earliest extant text belonging to this genre is the *Chos la 'jug pa'i sgo* ("Introduction to Buddhism") by the second Sa skya pa patriarch Master (*slob dpon*) bSod nams rtse mo (1142-1182), a work which he completed towards the end of 1167 or the beginning of 1168. The overall approach to its subject-matter and its architecture typifies many subsequent *chos 'byung* texts such as those by *lDe'u Jo sras, mKhas pa lDe'u and Bu ston Rin chen grub, but we do not know whether he was indebted for these to his teacher Phya pa. His work was succeeded by the magnificent text of Nyang ral's *chos 'byung* which, however, bears little resemblance to it in terms of its scope and structure. bSod nams rtse mo's text deals in the main with the life of the Buddha, while Nyang ral principally deals with the religious environment of Tibet's imperial period. The thirteenth century, too, knew of a considerable number of such treatises, the sole information concerning which is owed to a very brief remark by Bu ston as well as potentially to a number of quotations in his own *chos 'byung*. He notes the existence of such treatises by Khro phu lo tsā ba Byams pa'i dpal (1172/73-1236), Chag lo tsā ba Chos rje dpal (1197-1264) and mChims Nam mkha' grags (1210-1285) to which he apparently had access when writing his own well-known work sometime between 1322 and 1326. The present whereabouts of these treatises, if they are still extant, is unknown. As few as two *bona fide chos 'byungs* that probably belong to this century have come down to us, namely those by *lDe'u Jo sras and mKhas pa lDe'u. Ne'u Paṇḍita Grags pa smon lam blo gros' *sNgon gyi gtam* *me tog phreng ba* ("An Account of the Past, A Garland of Flowers") of 1283 (Chab spel, *NE'U*), while often referred to as a *chos 'byung,* styles itself in the introductory lines as a *rgyal rabs*. There is much in the manner in which the subject-matter is treated that is strongly reminiscent of a *chos 'byung,* so that we may characterize it as a text that falls midway between these two other genres.[23]

The *bKa' chems ka khol ma*

Other historiographic texts, that are sometimes styled, or that sometimes incorporate, smaller texts variously called *lo rgyus, rgyal rabs,* or *chos 'byung,* would be a limited number of so-called treasure-texts (*gter ma*) (see Gyatso, in this volume). A case in point is the *bKa' chems ka khol ma,* putatively Srong btsan sgam po's (?-649/50) testament (*bka' chems*), which was allegedly retrieved from a hole in a pillar (*ka khol ma*) by Atiśa (982?-1054?) in ca. 1049. It figures among the earliest such treasure-texts, and a number of particulars of its textual history were delineated by Vostrikov (28-32) and recently by Eimer (1983a). Although two versions were published some years ago, the best recension appears to be the one that was issued a few years ago by sMon lam rgya mtsho on the basis of two handwritten manuscripts, one at the Central Institute of Minorities, Beijing, and one written in silver on dark blue paper that belongs to the library of bLa brang bKra shis 'khyil Monastery in A mdo. In the colophon, the text elicits the following course of its transmission: Atiśa; Bang ston [Byang chub rgyal mtshan]; sTod lung[s] pa [Rin chen snying po] (1032-1116); sPyan snga ba [Tshul khrims 'bar (1033-1103)]; sNe'u zur pa [Ye shes 'bar (1042-1118/19)]; 'Bri gung pa [read here ?"lHa (chen) 'Bri sgang pa"][24]; rGya ma ba; Rwa sgreng pa; dKon [mchog] bzang [po]; rDo rje tshul khrims[25]; "me." Who is this "me"? Obviously, he must be one with strong ties to the bKa' gdams pa school and he must have flourished sometime towards the end of the thirteenth or the beginning of the fourteenth century.

The *bKa' chems ka khol ma* contains a great deal of interest concerning the reign of this first Tibetan religious king, and also contains a number of prophecies in the sixteenth chapter. It served as a primary source for later Tibetan accounts of that period, including, it would appear, the narratives of Thon mi Sambhoṭa's alleged invention of the Tibetan script and the arduous journeys to, and sojourns at, the Nepalese and Chinese courts by the minister mGar sTong btsan yul bzung for purposes of escorting a lady of their ruling houses to Tibet for betrothal to Srong btsan sgam po. Although it is supposed to be the work of the latter, it contains some information which perhaps impeaches the veracity of this imputation. For one, it mentions the date in which he passed away to the exact day and includes a number of prophecies in its sixteenth chapter that most of us would consider to be evidence for much later compilation, since Atiśa is mentioned in them![26]

Of the twelfth and thirteenth century chronicles known to date, the text is only mentioned in the works of Nyang ral and mKhas pa lDe'u. The latter, if he is indeed to be placed in the second half of the thirteenth century, refers to it in passing just prior to his narrative of the building of the Ra sa phrul snang, the gTsug lag khang temple in the center of Lhasa.[27] While he does not explicitly cite it in his account of the life and times of Srong btsan sgam po (although there can be no doubt that he must have used one or another recension of this work) Nyang ral records a few details of its retrieval in the bibliographic remarks at the end of his chronicle.[28] There he writes that the document (*yi ge*) of the *rGyal po bka' chems* was of difficult access, and that Atiśa retrieved three works from a central beam (*gdung bar*) of the Ra sa phrul snang temple, namely the "*bKa' rtsis chen mo* written by the kings, the *Dar dkar gsal ba'i me long* written by the queens, and the *Zla ba'i 'dod 'jo* written by the ministers." He furthermore appears to hold that these three are known together as *rGyal po bka' chems*, which in turn seems to refer to the *bKa' chems ka khol ma*. This might be confirmed by what may be the best recension of the text itself, the first chapter of which states that Atiśa and two assistants excavated three scrolls (*shog dril*) from atop a jug-shaped pillar, or a (hollow) pillar containing a jug within it (*ka ba bum pa can gyi steng nas*), where the first and the third, here noted as the *Zla ba 'dod 'jo* and the *bKa' chems kyi yi ge*, are described as being *lo rgyus*.[29] In addition to these texts, the *bKa' chems ka khol ma* also signals the existence of several other early treatises on which it may be based.[30] A detailed study of this highly significant work, which perforce needs to include a comparative analysis of the various recensions (at least three are known to me) that have come down to us and the various recensions of the *Maṇi bka' 'bum*, is one of the many urgent desiderata in the area of Tibetan historiographic research.

Of course, because *gter ma* texts are considered to date from Tibet's imperial period, many came to be considered crucial sources for this period in later historiographic works. A case in point is Nyang ral's chronicle, for not only is its discussion of the life and times of Srong btsan sgam po largely based on the *bKa' chems ka khol ma*, but Nyang ral also incorporated into it significant portions of the *Zangs gling ma* biography of Padmasambhava, a *gter ma* in its own right, which he himself had retrieved earlier.

As has hopefully become evident, the earliest Tibetan historiographical materials are extremely diverse and, regrettably, to a large extent still unpublished. Investigations into the literary sources used by authors of those texts that are available to us are also in their infancy, as is, consequently, research into the particular ways in which they have made use of them. This renders it particularly difficult to determine the original contributions made by these early authors in terms of how they interpreted them when they were not simply incorporating large portions of their sources into their own work.

Notes

1. A bibliography of non-Tibetan scholars on these texts would take us too far afield; suffice it to mention the following: Bacot et al.; Satō; Wang and Chen; Yamaguchi; Stein (1983-1988).

2. On him, see Stoddard; Stoddard (339) dates his birth to the year 1905. However, he states himself in his *Rgyal khams rig pas bskor ba'i gtam rgyud gser gyi thang ma*, which was not available to Stoddard at the time of her writing the biography, that he reached the age of thirty-two (= thirty-one) in 1934; see *DGE*: 6. This is also the year already given in Macdonald (204).

3. Stoddard: 205-207. This dKa' chen Don grub was most likely the great grammarian and linguist, who is otherwise also known as dKar lebs Drung yig Padma rdo rje (1860-1935). She also writes that, while in Kalimpong, he may have had occasion to get acquainted with S. W. Bushell's translations of the chapters on Tibet in the *Tangshu* and the *Xin Tangshu*, whereupon he contacted a Chinese scholar by the name of Zhang Zhengji with whom he reread (*relut*) the Chinese text to clarify and confirm Bushell's renditions. *DGE1*: 1 states that he completed a manuscript on the history of ancient Tibet from Chinese sources on the twenty-fifth day of the second month of 1943; however, he writes in the colophon, in *DGE1*: 49, that he finished it on the thirtieth day of the tenth month of his fortieth year! The second one is "dated" to the sixteenth day of the third month while at Byang Ku lu ta, and the third is

undated. At the outset of this work, which fills 120 pages, he indicates that he used the translation of a Chinese text from the chapter on Sino-Tibetan relations from Tshal pa Kun dga' rdo rje's (1309-1364) *Deb gter/ther dmar po*, together with the *Tangshu* and the *Zizhi tongjian gangmu*.

4. *DGE1*: 123-204. The last one is dated to the 2480th year after the Buddha's *nirvāṇa*, which seems to be a mistake, for dGe 'dun chos 'phel has elsewhere used 542 B.C.E. and 543/544 B.C.E. as the year(s) of the Buddha's *nirvāṇa*. It is not clear whether this date holds for all three studies.

5. Vostrikov; see also Tucci (1947), and the now dated survey in Hoffmann, which contains many errors of fact and cannot be used with any confidence.

6. The most complete account of the early, pre-eleventh-century fortunes of Sa skya's 'Khon family is found in Yar lung Jo bo Shākya rin chen's *YAR*: 140-144; *YAR1*: 136-139; Tang: 82-84. This work, written in 1376 by a scion of an offshoot of the imperial family that settled in Yar lung, refers severally to "old documents of the 'Khon" when disclaiming other opinions. For the records of the rLangs (together with an analysis of a section), see the literature cited in van der Kuijp (1991: especially 317-321), and now also the translation of the genealogies in Zan la A wang and Wan (1-67), which was not available to me earlier.

7. They were recently studied by Richardson, although his use of *chos 'byung* in the title of his paper is of course anachronistic.

8. *NYANGb*: 460; *NYANGl*: 393; *NYANGm*: 283/3.

9. For these two works, see van der Kuijp (1992).

10. One cannot always agree with his conclusions, however. Of interest is that *LD*: 98 ascribes the *Yo ga lha dgyes can* to a certain sPa sa Bon po, who is not known to me; a sPa ston bsTan rgyal bzang po was the author of an undated history of Bon, for which see *SPA*. S. G. Karmay argues that the correct reading of the title is found in *NYANGb*: 588 [*NYANGl*: 496; *NYANGm*: 361/1], namely, *Bon po yi ge lha dge can*, also known as the *bsGrags pa'i lugs*, holding that Tibet's imperial family descended from heaven.

11. *LD1*: 227 writes that it was co-authored by a certain rGya lha po. It also states that an alternate title of this work is the *Log gnon chen po*, whereas *LD*: 99 writes here merely *Log non chen po*, without mentioning *Lo rgyus chen po*.

12. Of course, the so-called *mdo skor* ("*sūtra*-cycle") of the *Ma ṇi bka' 'bum* collection of apocrypha contains a *Lo rgyus chen mo* (see *MA*: 23-194), but this neither has anything to do with Khu ston's work, nor is it annalistic. For this collection, see Vostrikov: 52-57, and Blondeau.

13. For a discussion and etymology of *rabs*, see Appendice 2 in Stein, 1971: 537-545.

14. For a partial translation of these relatively short works, see Tucci, 1947: 310-316; for their Tibetan texts, see Tucci, 1971: 127-135.

15. See *MANG*: 65, 68.

16. This manuscript is found in the Tibetan library of the Cultural Palace of Nationalities, Beijing, where it is catalogued under no. 002452(8). I am currently preparing an edition and translation of it.

17. The latter, which strikes me as the better reading, is given in *YAR*: 72 [*YAR1*: 72; Tang: 46] and also in *RGYAL*: 246 [*RGYAL1*: 199].

18. *TSHAL*: 14b gives *ye ka thob can*. Both Inaba-Satō (80) and Bira (1964: 73) take this as the name of a text; the reading of *tobčiyan* in Inaba-Satō (86, n. 102) is an oversight. The corresponding text of *TSHAL1* (30) reads *dpe ka thob chen*, which led Bira (1984: 63) to question the veracity of his earlier interpretation. However, Chen-Zhou (27) read part of the phrase as a book-title, namely *tuobuchiyan*, presumably because of the reading *dpe ka*, "book." To be sure, the graphemes for the ligatures *ye* and *dpe* can look deceptively alike in some forms of cursive *dbu med*. The author of *RGYAL*/*RGYAL1* also notes his use of *hor gyi yig tshang*, "Mongol records," for which see *RGYAL*: 249 [*RGYAL1*: 202]. For the *Dayuan tongzhi* collection in Tibet, see van der Kuijp, 1993.

19. Stein (1966: 285, n. 1) was the first to signal this interesting text.

20. See the introduction in *TSHAL1*: *2. This work, the *Deb ther mkhas pa'i yid 'phrog*, is variously styled a *lhan thabs* ("teaching aid") or a *kha skong* ("supplement") to the *Deb gter/ther dmar po*. Dung dkar Blo bzang 'phrin las has seen a handwritten manuscript of this text and states that, while it begins with a survey of the imperial families, it furnishes by and large a history of the ecclesiastics and secular rulers associated with the Tshal/Gung thang estates.

21. Eimer (1983: 11, n. 27) suggested that the *Deb gter/ther dmar po* was "possibly nothing but an historical introduction to the *dkar chag* of the Tshal pa *bKa' 'gyur*." There is a problem with the force of the definite article "the." The anonymous *YIG* (114 ff.) writes that during the tenure of dGa' bde dpal, Grand-governor (*dpon chen*)—better *khri dpon*, "myriarch"—of the Tshal/Gung thang principality, the myriarchy was the seat of an enormous number of religious books; in one locale 13,500 and elsewhere 3,020 volumes. The dates for dGa' bde dpal are probably 1253 to 1310. He is said to have passed away aged fifty-eight (= fifty-seven), and in *DPA'2*: 125 [*DPA'*: 975] we read that in the Iron-Dog year (= 1310) the third Karma pa presided over the monastic community that had gathered [?in Tshal] during the funerary rituals held for him. Oddly, perhaps, no mention is made of a bKa' 'gyur or bsTan 'gyur. The first notice of a bKa' 'gyur occurs in the passage anent Drung chen sMon lam rdo rje, the youngest of dGa' bde dpal's three sons, who had prepared one in 150 volumes; an interlineary note states that this collection was "presently located in dBus gling," a temple that had been founded by dGa' bde dpal. The text then writes that Tshal pa himself had prepared a bKa' 'gyur manuscript comprising 260 volumes which, according to an interlineary note, was also located in dBus gling. The question that needs to be raised of course is the probable relationship of Drung chen's bKa' 'gyur with the one of Tshal pa. In terms of bsTan 'gyurs, *TSHAL1*: 103 [Chen-Zhou: 90] observes that the

third Karma pa consecrated a golden bsTan 'gyur manuscript at Tshal sometime between the end of 1323 and the beginning of the second half of 1324.

22. This work is cited in, for instance, *'DUL*: 253.

23. For an edition and an exhaustively annotated German translation of this work, see Uebach. Another Tibetan version was recently published in *NE'U* in an edition prepared by lDan lhun Sangs rgyas chos 'phel, and it was also recently rendered into Chinese in Wang and Chen (1990).

24. The first reading is quite impossible on chronological grounds. For Lha 'Bri sgang pa, whom I would propose is intended here, see Eimer (1991).

25. Given that Lha 'Bri sgang pa, a descendant of one of Tibet's imperial families, was apparently a close friend of 'Bri gung/khung 'Jig rten mgon po (1143-1217), it is perhaps not entirely out of the question tentatively to identify him as 'Bri gung Monastery's second abbot, whose dates were, according to 'Gos lo tsā ba, 1154 to 1221; see Roerich: 608-609.

26. *BKA'*: 289.

27. *LD1*: 277 gives *bKa' chems*.

28. *NYANGb*: 593-594 [*NYANGl*: 501; *NYANGm*: 363/2].

29. *BKA'*: 4.

30. See, for example, *BKA'*: 235 anent a number of *bka' chems* of the king, in addition to the *Dar dkar gsal ba* and the *Zla ba 'dod 'jo*. *BKA'*: 261 records many fragments (*sil ma*) of *rgyal rabs*. In *BKA'*: 309, reference is made to a *bKa' chems mtho mthong ma* and a *bKa'*[sic!] *khol ma*, and *BKA'*: 313 notes a "biography" or "autobiography" entitled *rNam thar bka' chems gser gyi phreng ba*.

References

Bacot, J., F. W. Thomas and Ch. Toussaint

1940-46 *Documents de Touen-houang relatifs à l'histoire du Tibet*. Paris: Librairie Orientaliste Paul Geuthner.

Bira, Sh.

1964 "Some Remarks on the *Hu-lan deb-ther* of Kun-dga' rdo-rje." *Acta Orientalia Hungarica* 18: 69-81.

1984 "Some extracts from Sh. Damdin's Manuscript Copy of the *Hu-lan deb-ther*." In *Tibetan and Buddhist Studies*, vol. 1, pp. 59-75. Ed. by L. Ligeti. Budapest: Akadémiai kaidō.

bKa' chems ka khol ma

BKA' Ed. by sMon lam rgya mtsho. Lanzhou: Kansu'u mi rigs dpe skrun khang, 1989.

Bla ma dam pa bSod nams rgyal mtshan (probably wrongly attributed to him)

RGYAL *rGyal rabs gsal ba'i me long* [based on the sDe dge print]. Beijing: Mi rigs dpe skrun khang, 1981.

RGYAL1 *rGyal rabs gsal ba'i me long*. Ed. by B.I. Kuznetsov. Leiden: E.J. Brill, 1966.

Blondeau, Anne-Marie

1984 "Le 'découvreur' du *Maṇi bka'-'bum* était-il Bon-po?" In *Tibetan and Buddhist Studies*, vol. 1, pp. 77-123. Ed. by L. Ligeti. Budapest: Akadémiai Kaidó.

Chab spel Tshe brtan phun tshogs et al, eds.

DGE *dGe 'dun chos 'phel gyi gsung rtsom*. Gangs can rig mdzod 10. Lhasa: Bod ljongs bod yig dpe rnying dpe skrun khang, 1990.

DGE1 *dGe 'dun chos 'phel gyi gsung rtsom*. Gangs can rig mdzod 12. Lhasa: Bod ljongs bod yig dpe rnying dpe skrun khang, 1990.

NE'U *sNgon gyi gtam me tog phreng ba, Bod kyi lo rgyus deb ther khag lnga*. Gangs can rig mdzod 9, pp. 3-54. Lhasa: Bod ljongs bod yig dpe rnying dpe skrun khang, 1990.

Collingwood, R.C.

1970 *The Idea of History*. Ed. by T.M. Knox. London: Oxford University Press.

dPa' bo gTsug lag 'phreng ba

DPA'1, 2 *Chos 'byung mkhas pa'i dga' ston*, vols. 1, 2. New Delhi: Delhi Karmapae Chodhey Gyalwae Sungrab Partun Khang, 1981.

DPA' *Chos 'byung mkhas pa'i dga' ston*. Ed. by rDo rje rgyal po. Beijing: Mi rigs dpe skrun khang, 1986.

'Dul 'dzin mKhyen rab rgya mtsho

'DUL *Sangs rgyas bstan pa'i chos 'byung dris lan nor bu'i phreng ba*. Gangtok, 1984.

Eimer, Helmut

1983 "Some Results of Recent Kanjur Research." *Archiv für Zentralasiatische Geschichtsforschung*. Heft 1-6, pp. 3-21. Ed. by D. Schuh and M. Weiers. Sankt Augustin: VGH Wissenschaftsverlag.

1983a "Die Auffindung des *Bka' chems ka khol ma*. Quellenkritische Überlegungen." In *Contributions on Tibetan Language, History and Culture*, vol. 1, pp. 45-51. Ed. by E. Steinkellner and H. Tauscher. Vienna: Arbeitskreis fur Tibetische und Buddhistische Studien Universtat Wien.

1991 "Eine frühe Quelle zur literarischen Tradition: Über die 'Debatte von bSam yas'." In *Tibetan History and Language. Studies Dedicated to Uray Géza on His Seventieth Birthday*, pp. 164-165. Ed. by E. Steinkellner. Vienna: Arbeitskreis für Tibetische und Buddhistische Studien Universität Wien.

Fujieda, Akira

1981 "Une reconstruction de la 'bibliothèque' de Touen-Houang." *Journal asiatique* 269: 65-68.

Hoffmann, Helmut H.R.

1970 "Tibetan Historiography and the Approach of the Tibetans to History." *Journal of Asian History* 4/2: 169-177.

Karmay, Samten G.

1988 "The Etiological Problem of the Yar-luṅ Dynasty." In *Tibetan Studies*, pp. 219-222. Studia Tibetica II. Ed. by H. Uebach and Jampa L. Panglung. Munich: Kommission für Zentralasiatische Studien Bayerische Akademie der Wissenschaften.

van der Kuijp, Leonard W.J.

1991 "On the Life and Political Career of Ta'i-si-tu Byang-chub rgyal-mtshan (1302-1364?)." In *Tibetan History and Language. Studies Dedicated to Uray Géza on His Seventieth Birthday*, pp. 277-327. Ed. by E. Steinkellner. Vienna: Arbeitkreis für Tibetische und Buddhistische Studien Universität Wien.

1992 "Dating the Two Lde'u Chronicles of Buddhism in India and Tibet." In *Études bouddhiques offertes à Jacques May, Asiatische Studien/Études Asiatiques* 46/1: 468-491.

1993 "*Jambhala: An Imperial Envoy to Tibet During the Late Yuan." *Journal of the American Oriental Society* 113/4: 529-538.

*lDe'u Jo sras

LD *lDe'u chos 'byung*. Lhasa: Bod ljongs mi rigs dpe skrun khang, 1987.

MA *Ma ṇi bka' 'bum*. New Delhi, 1975.

Macdonald, A.

1971 "Le Dhānyakaṭaka de Man-luṅs Guru." *Bulletin de l'École Française d'Extrême Orient* 57: 169-213.

Mang thos kLu sgrub rgya mtsho

MANG *Bstan rtsis gsal ba'i nyin byed lhag bsam rab dkar*. Ed. by Nor brang O rgyan. Gangs can rig mdzod 4, pp. 1-251 Lhasa: Bod ljongs mi rigs dpe skrun khang, 1987.

mKhas pa lDe'u

LD1 *Rgya bod kyi chos 'byung rgyas pa*. Ed. by Chab spel Tshe brtan phun tshogs. Gangs can rig mdzod 3. Lhasa: Bod ljongs mi rigs dpe skrun khang, 1987.

mNga' bdag Nyang ral Nyi ma 'od zer

NYANGb *Chos 'byung me tog snying po sbrang rtsi'i bcud*. Manuscript B. Rin chen gter mdzod chen mo'i rgyab chos, vol.6. Paro, 1979.

NYANGl *Chos 'byung me tog snying po sbrang rtsi'i bcud*. Ed. by Chab dpel Tshe brtan phun tshogs. Gangs can rig mdzod 5. Lhasa: Bod ljongs mi rigs dpe skrun khang, 1988.

NYANGm *Chos 'byung me tog snying po sbrang rtsi'i bcud* [*Die Grosse Geschichte des tibetischen Buddhismus nach alter Tradition*.] Ed. by

R.O. Meisezahl. Monumenta Tibetica Historica, Abteilung 1. Band 3. Sankt Augustin: VGH Wissenschaftsverlag, 1985.

Richardson, Hugh E.
1980 "The First Tibetan *Chos-'byung*." *Tibet Journal* 5: 62-73.

Roerich, George, trans.
1979 *The Blue Annals*. New Delhi: Motilal Banarsidass.

Satō, Hisashi
1978 *Chibetto rekishi chiri kenkyū*. Tokyo.

sPa ston bsTan rgyal bzang po
SPA *bsTan pa'i rnam bshad dar rgyas gsal ba'i sgron ma*. In *Sources for a History of Bon*, pp. 498-769. Dolanji: Tibetan Bonpo Monastic Centre, 1972.

Stein, R. A.
1966 "Nouveaux documents tibétains sur le Mi-ñag/Si-hia." In *Mélanges de Sinologie offerts à Monsieur Paul Demiéville*, vol. 1, pp. 281-289. Paris: Presses Universitaires de France.
1971 "Du récit au rituel dans les manuscrits tibétains de Touen-houang." *Études Tibétaines dédiées à la mémoire de Marcelle Lalou*, pp. 537-545. Paris: Adrien Maisonneuve, 1971.
1983-92 "Tibetica Antiqua I-VI." *Bulletin de l'École Française d'Extrême Orient* 72: 149-236; 73: 257-272; 74: 83-133; 75: 169-196; 77: 27-56, 79: 9-17.

Stoddard, Heather
1985 *Le mendiant de l'Amdo*. Paris: Société d'Ethnographie.

Subrahmanian, N.
1973 *Historiography*. Madurai.

Tang Chi'an, trans.
1989 *Yalong zunzhe jiaofa she*. Lhasa: Xizang renmin chubanshe.

Tshal pa Kun dga' rdo rje
TSHAL *Deb ther dmar po, The Red Annals*. Part One. Gangtok: Namgyal Institute of Tibetology, 1961.
1964 *Huran deputura (Hu-lan deb-ther)—chibetto nendaiki*. Trans. by Sh. Inaba and H. Satō. Kyoto.
TSHAL1 *Deb ther dmar po*. Ed. by Dung dkar bLo bzang 'phrin las. Beijing: Mi rigs dpe skrun khang, 1981.
1988 *Hongshi*. Trans. by Chen Qingying and Zhou Runnian. Lhasa: Xizang renmin chubanshe.

Tucci, Giuseppe
1947 "The Validity of Tibetan Historical Tradition." In *India Antiqua*, pp. 309-322. Leiden: E.J. Brill.

1971 *Deb ther dmar po gsar ma. Tibetan Chronicles by bSod nams grags pa*, vol.1. Serie Orientale Roma 24. Rome: Istituto Italiano per il Medio ed Estremo Oriente.

Uebach, H.

1987 *Nel pa Paṇḍita's Chronik Me tog phreng ba*. Studia Tibetica. Quellen und Studien zur tibetischen Lexicographie, Band 1. Munich: Kommission für Zentralasiatische Studien. Bayerische Akademie der Wissenschaften.

Vostrikov, A.

1970 *Tibetan Historical Literature*. Trans. by R. H. Gupta. Calcutta: R. D. Press.

Wang Yao and Chen Jian.

1980 *Dunhuangben tufan/tubo lishi wenshu*. Beijing: Minzu chubanshe.

1990 Translation of Chab spel, *NE'U*. *Zhongguo Zangxue* 1: 108-127. [In Chinese.]

Warder, A. K.

1972 *An Introduction to Indian Historiography*. Bombay: Popular Prakashan.

Yamaguchi, Zuihō

1983 *Toban ōkoku seiritsu-shi kenkyū*. Tokyo.

Yar lung Jo bo Shākya rin chen

YAR *Yar lung chos 'byung*. Ed. by dByangs can. Chengdu: Si khron mi rigs dpe skrun khang, 1988.

YAR1 *Yar lung chos 'byung*. Ed. by Ngag dbang. Lhasa: Bod ljongs mi dmangs dpe skrun khang, 1988.

YIG *rGyal rabs sogs bod kyi yig tshang gsal ba'i me long, sNgon gyi gtam me tog gi phreng ba...*, pp. 79-123. Dharmasala: Library of Tibetan Works and Archives, 1985.

Zan la A wang and Yu Fangzhi, translators

1989 *Langshi jiazu shi*. Ed. Chen Qingying. Lhasa: Xizang renmin chubanshe.

Chapter 2

The Lives of Indian Buddhist Saints: Biography, Hagiography and Myth

James Burnell Robinson

The great religions come down to us by means of a great chain of masters who receive faithfully the teachings from those before them and convey compassionately to those coming after them. The Tibetan schools of Buddhism have been very aware of the importance of these links of tradition. An important feature of Tibetan Buddhism is the authoritative role that representatives of Indian Buddhism have had. Indeed, the Tibetans often portray themselves as transmitters, rather than as originators, of doctrine and practice. As a consequence, the life stories of Indian masters, teachers and saints are zealously preserved by the Tibetans.

Biography and history are genres more characteristic of Tibetan than Indian Buddhist literature and it is Tibetan accounts of the lives of Indian masters that have been most accessible. Tāranātha's *rGya gar chos 'byung* ("History of Buddhism in India") gives accounts of the major Buddhist figures in India, particularly those important in Tibetan teaching lineages. It has been translated into a number of European languages. A biography of the Indian master Nāropa by the Tibetan master lHa'i btsun pa Rin chen rnam rgyal of Brag dkar has been translated by Herbert Guenther as *The Life and Teaching of Nāropa.*

Both of these texts were written by Tibetans. Tibetan translations of Indian biographies are somewhat more rare, and it is a sample of this translated literature that I want to examine here:

the *Caturaśitisiddhapravṛtti*, in Tibetan the *Grub thob brgyad bcu tsa bzhi'i lo rgyus* (*GTGC*) ("The Lives of the Eighty-four Siddhas"). This text, originally written in Sanskrit by the twelfth-century master Abhayadatta, exists now only in Tibetan translation.

There have been three translations of this text into Western languages. The first was a German translation by Albert Grünwedel, *Die Geschichten de vier und achtzig Zauberers aus dem Tibetischen übersetz* (1916). The other two are in English: one my own, assisted by Geshe Lhundup Sopa, published as *Buddha's Lions* (1979); and the other by Keith Dowman, *Masters of Mahamudra* (1986).

The *siddhas* are the figures associated with the rise and transmission of tantric Buddhism in India. A *siddha* is literally "a perfected one," a "perfect master," and there are both male and female *siddhas*. A *siddha* is also one who possesses *siddhi*, a term which means "success," particularly in yoga; it came to be applied to the magical powers which are the signs of yogic success. The *siddhas* then are not only successful in their spiritual quest, but possess magical powers that confirm it. While early Buddhism tended to downplay the role of magic, by the time of the *tantras*, magical powers were very much an item of interest. And the stories of the *siddhas* are notable for the accounts of extraordinary feats which they are said to have performed.

After looking at certain structural elements common to the stories in the *GTGC*, I want to examine some methodological problems raised by these accounts. Although the masters are almost surely historical personages, and these accounts have a historical dimension, this literature is best considered hagiography; beyond even that, we may fruitfully call these narratives "Buddhist myths" which function in both a horizontal and a vertical dimension.

The Stories of the *Siddhas*

At least two types of accounts can be recognized in the eighty-four stories of the *siddhas* collected in the *GTGC*. The more common type is an almost formulaic narration of how individuals in various walks of life achieved high spiritual status, often by taking their daily lives in the world as the basis of spiritual exercise—what the Hindu tradition would call *karmayoga*.

Then there are stories of the great heroes, male and female, of the Buddhist Tantra: people like Virūpa, (the tantric) Nāgārjuna, Kṛṣṇācāri, Kambala, Indrabhūti and his sister Lakṣmīṅkarā and

Ghaṇṭapāda—all of whom figure prominently in tantric lineages. Compared with the first type, these stories are more complex and are often made up of several episodes. Keith Dowman uses a convention of calling the protagonists of the first type *siddhas*, and the figures of the second type *mahāsiddhas* or "great *siddhas*" (xv), though the tradition seems to use these terms interchangeably.

Narratives of the first type follow a certain pattern which, since it is repeated again and again, takes on an almost ritualistic quality (Robinson: 9). The central figure is first introduced by name, caste and country. This name is usually not the name by which the individual was known in ordinary life but a spiritual *nom de guerre* obtained in the course of practice. Lūyipa,[1] for example, broke attachment to the fastidious pattern of eating he had acquired as a prince by eating the innards of fish that fishermen discarded in cleaning their catch. From this practice, he came to be known as *Lūyipa*, a name derived from a Bengali word for fish guts. Śiyalipa, the twenty-first *siddha*, took his name "Jackal-man" from the fact that the howling of jackals was at first an object of fear for him, then an object of meditation. Other names, such as Tantipa ("The Weaver") or Cāmāripa ("The Cobbler") or Kamparipa ("The Blacksmith"), are drawn from their respective occupations, which served as a focus for meditation.

Following the name, the account states the *siddha*'s occupation and caste. While the most famous of the *siddhas* are monks, the majority are laypeople—a notable fact, given that Buddhism has often identified spiritual practice with monasticism. Furthermore, most of the *siddhas* had lowly origins and worked in menial positions. The text is clearly affirming that one can practice the Dharma in any condition of life.

Then follows a short description of a life situation that prompts the protagonist to seek the Dharma. The problems confronting the *siddhas*-to-be are familiar and universal: Kankaripa, the seventh *siddha*, is grieving for his deceased wife; Tantipa is old, senile, and neglected by his family; Kucipa is afflicted with a painful tumor; Medhini is a farmer who is sick and tired of having to work all the time. Still other protagonists are caught up in various self-destructive obsessions: Tantipa is a compulsive gambler; Sarvabakśa is an insatiable eater; Thaganapa is an incessant liar; Mahipa is inordinately proud of his physical strength.

Not all of these life situations that turn the individual from his or her ordinary concerns are unpleasant. Udheli sees the flight of the wild geese and longs to be able to fly with them. Śavaripa is so impressed by a magic arrow that he wishes only to possess its power. Khaḍgapa is a thief who desires a magic sword to make him a better thief. Both positive and negative aspirations as well as life-crises are openings for the *guru* to offer transforming instruction. In some cases, the *guru* himself (occasionally herself) points by his (or her) very presence and example to higher possibilities in the human existence. Confronted with the living results of the Dharma, many protagonists simply surrender themselves and request teachings.

Most *gurus* are wandering ascetics living on what they can beg, sleeping in cemeteries, wearing patched clothes, etc. But the *guru* can also be a superhuman *bodhisattva*. Avalokita appears to the deer hunter Śavaripa and persuades him to abandon his practice of killing. Mañjuśrī appears to a seemingly lazy and dim-witted Bhusuku (Śāntideva) and delivers knowledge and wisdom to him.

Of particular interest is the fact that some of the *gurus* are *ḍākinīs*, the feminine embodiments of wisdom, who appear when needed to provide insight (Govinda: 190ff.). Some appear in dreams and visions, but in several of the stories the *ḍākinīguru* seems to be a human female adept (Robinson: 15).

Once the individual expresses a desire for the Dharma, the *guru* gives two things: initiation and instruction. Initiation, as the name implies, is a ceremony that begins the practice, but it is also seen as communicating an actual spiritual force, without which the student cannot be successful. The tantric systems of the *Guhyasamāja*, the *Cakrasaṃvara*, and the *Hevajra* are all mentioned.

After the initiation, the *guru* gives instruction to the student in terms that relate to his or her immediate situation. Often a worldly occupation or object of concern is used as a vehicle for transcending the world. As a consequence, unlike some other forms of spiritual discipline which require physical isolation, engaging in meditation and living in the world of ordinary human affairs do not exclude each other so long as both are done in the proper way. For example, Kamparipa, a blacksmith who develops a disgust for *saṁsāra* in general and for his work in particular, is told that he should let his inner acts of meditation be like those deeds he did outwardly. The right and left tantric veins should be the bellows, the central channel the anvil and the consciousness the smith. The conceptions should be fuel and his wisdom and insight the shining fire. He should hammer the iron of misery; the result will be the stainless Dharma Body (Robinson: 160).

The student then works for a period of time—twelve years is a common span—and in the end achieves success. There may be some mention of how the *siddha* instructed others or performed some miraculous feat. Finally, he or she goes to the realm of the *ḍākas*, a type of tantric paradise.[2]

Stories of great masters of Tantra are not so easily analyzed. Sometimes we are told the condition in which they achieved enlightenment, other times we are simply given stories that manifest their signs of success. Saraha, a tantric adept, is forced by some Brahmans to justify his drinking wine, a violation of caste restrictions. He undergoes a trial by ordeal, plunging his hand into boiling oil, drinking molten copper and walking on water. Finally, the king simply says, "If anyone who has powers like these drinks wine, then let him drink" (Robinson: 43). Saraha then preaches to the king, who with his court is converted.

The story of Virūpa tells how a monk became a *siddha* through tantric practice. He eats the pigeons of the monastery then resurrects them. When he consumes vast quantities of liquor, he stops the sun to pay the bill. He humbles worshippers of Śiva and overcomes cannibal witches. In the story of Nāgārjuna we are told how he withstands the assaults of demonesses, attempts to change a mountain into gold until dissuaded by Mañjuśrī, helps a cowherder become king, and how he lives for several hundred years. The story of Kanhapa or Kṛṣṇācāri tells of a yogin who had gained all the worldly *siddhis* but found it difficult to put away his pride. Though he did not obtain full success till the end of his life, he was still able to walk on water and change his form from man to wolf. The stories of Ḍombipa and Kambala likewise portray awesome magical power.

The Stories as Biography and History

Like all religious texts, particularly those that deal with an esoteric tradition, these biographies can be read on several levels. I propose three ascending and mutually enriching ways of reading the accounts of the *siddhas*: as history, as hagiography and as myth.

These three approaches do not exclude each other; each has its own particular emphasis and each puts the stories into a particular perspective in the overall context of Buddhism. The historical approach looks for what the texts can tell us about the history of Buddhism in India, particularly the rise of tantric Buddhism. The hagiographic reading focuses upon the religious purposes of a text and how those purposes have affected its transmission and reception. The mythological perspective focuses upon the texts as sacred narrative. Keith Dowman suggests that stories of the siddhas can be read first as edifying tales, second as tantric allegories and symbolic narratives and finally as works that may offer historical insight (xi). Allegorical symbolism is undoubtedly very important here; Govinda, for instance, suggests that accounts of Virūpa stopping the flow of the Ganges and halting the sun are not at all to be taken as descriptions of literal events, but should be understood as descriptions of inner yogic processes (53). But it has been the historical and more strictly biographical levels that have attracted modern scholars, and so it is to these stories as historical narrative that we turn to begin our discussion.

Abhayadatta most likely set down the accounts in the *GTGC* as he had received them, that is, as actual biographical accounts. Tāranātha records similar stories (214-215) in a work intended as history, and while there are those in the Tibetan tradition who look more to the symbolism involved, many simply take these accounts in the same spirit that Americans take the account of Washington crossing the Delaware River in the American Revolution.

While the extraordinary nature of the activities of the *siddhas* requires careful analysis, there is no doubt that, at the very least, we may derive from them certain broad insights into the social conditions of the period. Every account that is passed on reflects its time, if for no other reason than that it has some degree of credibility with its audience. Even if the historical accuracy of certain events and personages may seem suspect to critical scholarly eyes, recurrent motifs probably are quite accurate in mirroring the conditions of the time. For example, the prevalence of lay people in the stories suggests that the *tantras* were reaching out beyond the monastic establishments, which were traditionally the centers of Buddhism. And the fact that several individuals claim that no one would teach them because they were of low caste suggests that, while Buddhism was less tied to ideas of caste than Hinduism was, it did function within Indian caste society and was not completely free of caste prejudice. Both Khaṇḍipa and Kamparipa remark that they had not expected to find a teacher because of their caste status. While the significance of these observations may be modified by further research, these accounts have historical value quite apart from the credibility of specific events.

But be that as it may, the extraordinary feats attributed to these figures play a striking role in the stories and may cause modern readers some perplexity. We are unaccustomed to being told as historical fact that men and women fly by their own power through the air, that they can walk across water or engage in magical duels with witches, to say nothing of stopping the sun to pay one's bar tab. Some degree of skepticism seems in order.

Yet the *siddhas* are not simply products of a religious or literary imagination. Not only do they live in a certain time and place that is often identifiable to some degree, but, more importantly, we have texts attributed to the *siddhas*—someone had to write them. If, for example, Saraha did not write the *Dohās*, the cycle of tantric songs attributed to him, then they were written by someone else to whom we can only give the name "Saraha" (Guenther: 1969). Whether or not Abhayadatta's account of him is true in all its details, somebody in the history of Buddhism likely answered to the name "Saraha." And doctrines and practices do not emerge from thin air; someone has to develop them and someone has to transmit them. In the case of the Tantras, *siddhas* frequently appear in this role. As a consequence, we have little ground to deny *ab initio* that we are dealing with actual historical figures. So we have seemingly real characters who perform seemingly unrealistic deeds.

Western scholars have become increasingly sophisticated in evaluating accounts from other cultures. We examine their sociological function; we may look at them as a reflection of cultural dynamics, as expressions of deep psychological forces or may even consider their value from the point of view of their impact upon individuals and communities. Yet one cannot help but suspect that scholars develop these elaborate and sophisticated analyses precisely because they say in their hearts: of course, we all know that these extraordinary tales cannot be *really* true.

It is not unfair to say that for Western scholars, by and large, any explanation, to count as explanation, is put in terms of purely natural (some would say purely physical) causation and conditions. Anything which cannot be explained at present in purely natural terms simply awaits a natural explanation that will come with future research. As heirs of David Hume, whose essay on miracles (1964: 205-229) has been important in shaping scholarship, we apply a strict canon of probability to historical events. The presumption is that there is no such thing as the miraculous or the extraordinary, though scholars can be very subtle in explaining how any given account came to be. In the final analysis, we are to side with "common sense."

But the rationality of common sense has an inherent limitation; it is by definition founded on the ordinary experience of ordinary people. It is the accustomed and familiar. The accounts of the *siddhas* contain extraordinary happenings but, after all, *siddhas* are extraordinary people. Abhayadatta nowhere claims that walking on water or resurrecting pigeons are events carried out in the normal course of our everyday world. We need not thereby subscribe to the historical truth of these stories but we have to acknowledge the limitations of common sense when used as a criterion of truth. The contemporary historian may well argue that common sense is all we have; but, in the end, it is a cultural postulate and an assumption.

One additional caveat: while such dramatic events as stopping the sun cannot be held literally without our substantially changing the laws of physics, instances of other extraordinary powers and discernments may not be as easily dismissed. Virtually every religion in which practitioners cultivate altered or expanded states of consciousness—that is, the mystical or shamanistic religions—also affirms that those who are successful acquire superhuman powers and perceptions. The *siddha* is only the tantric version of a type found all over the world. While individual religions vary as to their attitude concerning these powers, they affirm that they do exist. In the face of such widespread testimony, some caution is in order before dismissing such claims out of hand.[3]

These Accounts as Hagiography and Myth

Abhayadatta does not seem primarily interested in a history defined by the canons of an empiricist rationality—i.e., just the "facts" in their most plausible form. Rather, he is illustrating a particular tradition through the stories of the *siddhas*. Though he may have intended every story to be history, they may also be taken as symbolic tales in a historical form. Indeed, he might respond to a Western historian by asking what genuine insight anyone gets from mere recitation of facts unilluminated by a spiritual purport.

If we cannot fully grasp what these stories are about by regarding them as straight history or biography, we may consider this genre of religious literature under the fruitful category of hagiography, "writings about holy people." The term emerges from the Christian tradition, where it refers to an account of a saint that is read to the people on the saint's feast day. From this, the term took on a generic meaning of a biographical story presented as historical fact but also designed to convey a religious meaning over and above the historical narration.

While a biography has someone writing a detached and critical account of the major events in the life of a subject, hagiography is concerned first and foremost to illuminate religious truth as exemplified through the lives of extraordinary men and women. This purpose is by no means incompatible with historical accuracy, but holding up a model or illustrating a doctrine shapes the narrative in a way that subordinates mere detail of fact.

The Roman Catholic scholar Hippolyte Delehaye has done much to try to recover the most authentic accounts of the lives of Christian saints (1963). Delehaye defined some of the factors that bear on the transmission of hagiography over time. For example, it is quite common for a link in the chain of transmission of a story to elaborate or refine certain details of an account. The religious purposes and messages are highlighted, other details are suppressed. Complex events are simplified, gaps are filled according to the pious creativity of the transmitter, multiple events and/or characters become conflated and single events and characters can become multiple and circulate independently. So it is with the stories of the *siddhas*. All of these factors come into play, often simultaneously.

To give an example of one such factor, how partially understood elements are provided explanation, we may look at the eleventh *siddha*, Cauraṅgi. The original form of his name was Caturaṅgi, "the man with four limbs," which probably referred to the fact that he practiced a yoga characterized by having four parts. However, in a story similar to the Greek myth of Phaedra and Hippolytus, a young prince who resists his lusty stepmother is sentenced by his father to have his four limbs cut off. By yogic *siddhi*, the prince is able to regain his limbs; hence the name *Caturaṅgi*, which in old Bengali became *Cauraṅgi*. In Sanskrit, this latter name can mean "member of the robbers"—a perplexing name for a yogin and a detail begging for a story to explain it. So we are told some merchants were travelling at night near where Caurangi slept. They woke him up. When he asked who they were, the merchants, afraid that he was a robber, said that they were carrying coal, though in reality they were carrying precious things. Caurangi's curiosity being satisfied, he simply replied: "So be it," and went back to sleep. The merchants discovered the next day that their goods had turned to coal, since Caurangi had spoken "words of truth," a yogic power by which whatever a yogin says comes to pass. They went back to him and begged him to return their original goods. Caurangi denied any unfriendly intent and told them that everything would be as it was before. And so he is called, from this case of mistaken identity, "member of the robbers."

Reading religious biographies as hagiography allows us a richer degree of understanding the process by which this genre comes to be and the dynamics which shape the stories. It bridges the categories of history and symbolic literature; the stories can be presented as true in the spiritual sense and also, for the audience at which they are directed, true in the historical sense as well.

Extending this process one step further, hagiography may be considered a sub-genre of sacred narrative, equivalent to what might be meant by "myth"—a story, sanctioned by a tradition and used to convey what the tradition regards as deep truths. The story may focus on gods, on human beings, on both or may even focus on neither. In contrast to its usage in common parlance, the term "myth" need say nothing about historical accuracy or whether it is true to scientific fact or not.[4]

Mythology in the classical sense has seldom been acknowledged as having an important role in Buddhism, in contrast to Hinduism, for example, which has a particularly rich body of clearly mythological lore. But in this broader sense, Buddhism does indeed have a mythology. Unlike the Hindus and the Greeks, whose myths abound with superhuman beings, gods, *devas*, and spirits, the Buddhists have preferred to populate their mythology with human characters.[5] The life of the Buddha illuminates the origin of the tradition and provides a model for understanding both what it means to be a Buddha and what it means to be a Buddhist.[6]

Using the life of the Buddha as a figure in history to illustrate the Dharma may provide a grounding principle for additional myths—namely, that the lives of others, presented as historical narrative, may further reveal the Dharma. Understanding religious biography as myth allows us to bring Buddhism into structural comparison with other religions, both to highlight the similarities with the other religions and also to bring out the distinctive and unique features of Buddhism. The stories of the *siddhas* have more complex purposes than to serve as mere historical accounts that stand or fall by contemporary empiricist canons alone.

The Horizontal and the Vertical

To summarize: the hagiographical literature about Indian saints is important for the Tibetan tradition because the men and women that it describes are intrinsically worthy of honor by their spiritual success. But their mythic function can be analyzed further into what may be called vertical and horizontal dimensions.

The vertical dimension of myth allows the saints to "humanize" the transcendent; they make the status of an enlightened being accessible to the human level. They give living focus for devotion. They exemplify spiritual triumph in ways understandable to those who still struggle. They give hope in the sense that if they were able to achieve their goal, so might the aspirant who makes the requisite effort. And the symbolic levels of the stories reveal how such a transition may take place. This value is transcendent in the sense that it does not depend upon historical accuracy.

But the horizontal dimension of history is not to be ignored. The claim of these stories to historicity anchors this vertical linking of spiritual success and the ordinary life. The saints represent continuity; they bind the great figures of the past to our own history-bound humanity. They are links in the chain of enlightened beings going back to the Buddha himself, the source of highest wisdom and the supreme teacher in the present age. By their insight and success, the Indian saints guarantee the value of the Dharma and preserve the purity of transmission. They legitimate lineages of spiritual masters living in times closer to our own. The fact that these masters link the present with the sacred past makes their historical existence very important. The alternative is a rupture in the tradition. So this genre derives its value not just from doctrine but also from its affirmation of the sacred in the process of history in which we all live.

Notes

1. Due to the different languages and dialects in which the tantric traditions were transmitted as well as the inevitable textual corruptions, the names of the siddhas have many variations. This paper uses the forms found in *Buddha's Lions*. Both Robinson and Dowman give extensive notes as to variations of names and some of the likely historical backgrounds of the figures.

2. *Ḍāka* is the male form of *ḍākinī*; but the beings thus referred to do not seem to function in the same way as the female forms. The Tibetan form of *ḍākinī* is *mkha' 'gro ma*, literally "sky-walking woman," which can be understood symbolically as those who course in emptiness (Govinda; Guenther, 1963) or perhaps understood more psychologically as a form of yogic ecstasy. The term *ḍāka* most commonly appears in stock phrases such as "the treasure of the *ḍākas*," meaning the *tantras*, or "realm of the *ḍākas*," referring to where the siddhas go when they depart this material realm.

3. A full demonstration of these connections would take us far from the focus of this paper, but the works of Mircea Eliade (1964, 1970) show that the correlation between altered states of consciousness and reputed superhuman abilities is widespread.

4. I am particularly indebted to Smart for this discussion of myth as sacred narrative.

5. The rich Mahāyāna and Vajrayāna pantheon of "cosmic" Buddhas, while very complex in nature, represents divinized abstractions with little or no sacred narrative attached to them. The high bodhisattvas such as Avalokita or Mañjuśrī or Tārā do figure in sacred narrative, but most commonly in the context of the lives of great historical or quasi-historical figures. The bodhisattvas themselves are rarely the central focus of a sacred narrative or myth.

6. For example, Roger Corless's *The Vision of Buddhism* is structured to highlight the way in which the traditional twelve "acts" of the Buddha may serve as a framework for understanding Buddhism as a religion.

References

Abhayadatta

GTGC *Grub thob brgyad bcu rtsa bzhi'i chos skor*. New Delhi: Chophel Legdan, 1973.

Delehaye, Hippolyte

1962 *The Legends of the Saints*. New York: Fordham University Press.

Corless, Roger

1989 *The Vision of Buddhism*. New York: Paragon House.

Dowman, Keith

1985 *Masters of Mahamudra*. Albany: State University of New York Press.

Eliade, Mircea

1964 *Shamanism: Archaic Techniques of Ecstasy.* Translated from French by Willard Trask. New York: Pantheon Books.

1970 *Yoga, Immortality and Freedom.* Translated from French by Willard Trask. Princeton: Princeton University Press.

Govinda, Anagarika

1960 *Foundations of Tibetan Mysticism.* New York: E. P. Dutton.

Guenther, Herbert V.

1963 *The Life and Teaching of Nāropa.* London: Oxford University Press.

1969 *The Royal Song of Saraha: A Study in the History of Buddhist Thought.* Seattle: University of Washington Press

Grünwedel, Albert

1916 *Die Geschichten der vier und achtzig Zauberers aus dem Tibetischen übersetz.* Leipzig: Baessler Archiv.

Hume, David

1964 *Hume on Religion.* Ed. by Richard Wollheim. Cleveland: World Publishing.

Robinson, James

1979 *Buddha's Lions.* Berkeley: Dharma Publishing.

Smart, Ninian

1983 *Worldviews.* New York: Charles Scribner's Sons.

Tāranātha

1970 *History of Buddhism in India.* Translated from Tibetan by Lama Chimpa and Alaka Chattopadhyaya. Ed. by Debiprasad Chattopadhyaya. Simla: Indian Institute of Advanced Study.

Chapter 3

A Brief History of the Tibetan bKa' 'gyur[1]

Paul Harrison

The Indian Background

Sacred texts or scriptures, transmitted either orally or in written form, are common to all the world's religious traditions. In some traditions these texts are relatively brief and unitary, like the Koran, for example. In others they are longer and spring from various sources, but are brought together in a single compilation, as in the case of the Christian Bible. In such instances the resulting collection is known as a canon, which is not one book, but many. These many books, however, share a common identity by virtue of the particular sanctity or authority attributed to them, which sets them apart from other books. Not every work of religious literature is scripture, after all, but only that which for some reason is thought to be especially sacred. For Buddhists, whose canonical literature is extraordinarily prolific, the sacredness of their scriptures depended originally on their utterance by the Buddha, Siddhārtha Gautama. Insofar as we can determine it, the canon[2] transmitted by Gautama's followers after his death consisted of two principal sets of texts, the Dharma or Sūtras (discourses delivered by the Buddha, or in some cases by his disciples, but with his blessing) and the Vinaya (the corpus of monastic regulations, with the various traditions relating to their original promulgation).

Later most schools added a third collection of summaries and systematic restatements of doctrine, the Abhidharma. These three collections or "baskets" (*piṭaka*) were passed down orally for several centuries, and as the Buddhist community split into different ordination lineages and schools, the Buddhist canon or Tripiṭaka ("Three Baskets"), which can hardly have been fixed even in the lifetime of the founder, diverged correspondingly, so that by the beginning of the Common Era there were various "canons" in existence. (Of these only one has survived to the twentieth century relatively complete, but with later modifications that scholars are now beginning to address: the Pāli Canon of the Theravādin school, which was committed to writing in the first century B.C.E.) We are unsure precisely to what extent these collections were ever considered "closed," setting the texts in them apart from others in circulation, but we know that Buddhists worked with very definite ideas about authenticity, about what could be accepted as the word of the Buddha (*buddhavacana*) and what could not (see Lamotte; Ray; Davidson). And we also know that Buddhists of all "Mainstream" schools (on this term see Harrison, 1992b: 45, n. 8) continued to produce works of literature, which caused no problems as far as the borderline between the canonical and the non-canonical was concerned, as long as they were not attributed to the Buddha.

This situation changed around the beginning of the Common Era with the advent of the Mahāyāna, a loose pan-Buddhist movement which, while it may have found more favorable conditions for growth within some Mainstream schools than others, soon overran their sectarian boundaries. To promote the various doctrinal and cultic innovations which were their characteristic concern, the followers of the Mahāyāna produced an enormous number of new texts claiming the status of *buddhavacana*. These then circulated in an uneasy relationship with the canons of the traditional schools, which had in many cases furnished the raw materials for their composition. Although this was in one sense an "anti-canon," co-existing with the Mainstream collections in India while challenging their claims to exclusive authenticity and completeness, this alternative set of scriptures was itself never "closed." Rather, it remained an "open canon," a contradiction in terms evidently occasioned by the need to assign the texts a certain primacy and yet not close the door on further creativity.[3] As for the contents of this "canon," we can only speculate as to what texts were available at any given time or place,[4] but we may assume that most Mahāyānists can hardly have had at their disposal the huge collections of their scriptures we now possess. It is much more likely that, in addition to the traditional canons of the schools they belonged to, they had access to a limited number of Mahāyāna texts, in some cases perhaps to compendia of them. We know of two of these major *sūtra* collections, the *Mahāsaṃnipāta* and the *Ratnakūṭa*, the compilation of which poses difficult historical problems, although some of the texts in them are known to date back to the beginnings of the Mahāyāna. Alongside them we might also place "mega-scriptures" like the *Avataṃsaka* and the various longer versions of the *Prajñāpāramitā* ("Perfection of Wisdom"), one of the most philosophically important productions of the Mahāyāna. Such longer texts and text-compendia may well have done duty as a type of Mahāyāna Buddhist canon.

This situation was further complicated when a new movement known as the Vajrayāna or Tantric Buddhism began to take shape towards the middle of the first millennium. In fact the production of sacred literature simply continued unabated, while the themes addressed changed to suit the needs and tastes of the times. In this new wave of works, which are known as *tantras*, the ritual and iconographical repertoire of Mahāyāna Buddhism was extended, while its doctrines were stretched and remolded so as to harness the power of sexual desire and the potency of sexual symbolism (among other things) in the service of the quest for liberation. Although the *tantras* do indeed qualify as scriptures, given the circumstances of their production and use, a tantric canon was even less likely to emerge than a Mahāyāna canon. By the close of the first millennium, then, towards the end of its life in its homeland, Indian Buddhism was a complex amalgam of three strains—Mainstream, Mahāyāna and Vajrayāna—and it is this multi-layered tradition and its equally complex scriptural heritage which the Tibetans have inherited and passed down to the present day. Without some appreciation of this background, it is impossible to understand the canon which the Tibetans developed.

The Tibetan Translations

Tibetan translations of Buddhist scriptures, mostly Mahāyāna texts, began to be made in the seventh century C.E.; this is the beginning of the *snga dar*, the period of the first diffusion of Buddhism in Tibet. Initially the production of these translations seems to have been a haphazard and irregular business, but significantly the central political authority soon moved to take control of the process. At the beginning of the ninth century, on the instructions of the Tibetan king, a group of Indian and Tibetan scholars devised a new set of guidelines and a new terminology for translating Buddhist texts, intended to be binding on all future translators. Some of the results of this remarkable attempt at literary standardization survive in the bilingual (later multilingual) glossary known generally as the *Mahāvyutpatti*,[5] and in its accompanying volume, the *sGra sbyor bam po gnyis pa* (see Ishikawa). At the same time that new texts were being translated, previous translations were collected and revised by the committee, so that their wording could be brought into line with the new terminology. Lists of works so revised were made, one of which, the catalogue known as the *lDan* (or *lHan*) *kar ma*, has survived.[6] The *lDan kar ma* provides no evidence that there was any move at this time towards setting limits to a Tibetan canon as such, presumably because no Mahāyāna or Vajrayāna canon existed in India. What it does show, however, is that even at this early stage Tibetans were beginning to classify Buddhist literature according to certain principles; and as we shall see, it is this attempt to order the scriptures, rather than to circumscribe them, which is most constitutive of Tibetan canon formation. Thus the *lDan kar ma* starts with *sūtras*, those of the Mahāyāna being followed by those of the "Hīnayāna." The Mahāyāna *sūtras*, which are much more numerous, begin with the Prajñāpāramitā texts, then the works making up the *Avataṃsaka Sūtra*, the *Ratnakūṭa* texts, various individual Mahāyāna *sūtras*, the *Mahāsūtras*, and lastly texts translated from Chinese. The *sūtras* are followed by a small number of treatises, then by *tantras* (*gsang sngags kyi rgyud*) and *dhāraṇīs* (*gzungs*), hymns of praise (*stotra, bstod pa*), prayers (*praṇidhāna, smon lam*) and auspicious verses (*maṅgalagāthā, bkra shis tshigs su bcad pa*). Next comes the Vinaya-piṭaka,[7] followed by *sūtra* commentaries and treatises of various kinds, finishing up with works on logic and revisions and translations in progress. Anticipating subsequent developments, then, we could say that the *lDan kar ma* foreshadows the basic bKa' 'gyur/ bsTan 'gyur division of later times—that *bka'* (the sacred word) comes before *bstan bcos* (the treatises) is after all only logical—and that its "bKa' 'gyur section" follows the basic order Sūtra, Tantra, Vinaya.[8] Within each category works are arranged according to length, with the longer first. Over 700 titles are listed, testifying to the extraordinary level of activity at this time.

This efflorescence of scholarship, the precision and thoroughness of which has rendered the Tibetan translations so valuable to modern Buddhist scholarship, was eclipsed for some time by the political disturbances following the death of King Glang dar ma in 842 and the subsequent collapse of the Tibetan empire, but resumed eventually in the late tenth century with the translation work of Rin chen bzang po (958-1056) and others. Thus began the so-called second diffusion of Buddhism (*phyi dar*), which continued for many centuries, during which translations continued to be made, especially of tantric scriptures, which were still being produced in India. At the same time older versions from the *snga dar* period went on being copied and circulated throughout the greater Tibetan cultural sphere.

The Formation of the bKa' 'gyur

Although none of them has survived, catalogues like the *lDan kar ma* continued to be made, and it was only a matter of time before one of them came to be regarded as definitive, that is, moved from being descriptive—a simple inventory of the holdings of a particular monastery or palace library—to being prescriptive. We can say, in fact, that the formation of the Tibetan canon, or at the very least its shape, can be traced back to the work of cataloguers grappling with the task of imposing some kind of order on the sheer mass of Buddhist literature available to them. When that endeavor was combined with the editorial response provoked by the huge number of copies of individual texts in circulation, each carrying its own peculiar readings, the canon as we know it today was born. It is, however, also likely that the Tibetans were inspired by the Chinese example to attempt a definitive edition of their sacred texts. At any rate we know that at the beginning of the fourteenth century a decisive step was taken at the bKa' gdams pa monastery of sNar thang in gTsang near gZhis ka rtse. An account of this is found in the *Deb ther sngon po* ("The Blue Annals"), written by gZhon nu dpal (1392-1481) in 1476-1478, less than two hundred years after the event. In his sketch of the sNar thang scholar bCom ldan rigs (or rig) pa'i ral gri, gZhon nu dpal tells us (*DTNP*: 410-412) that his accomplishments were such that:

...he had many pupils who were fine scholars, and it is said that two thirds of the canon specialists (*piṭakadhara, sde snod 'dzin pa*) gathered at sNar thang. The great scholar 'Jam pa'i dbyangs was also one of his pupils, but because he once dressed up as a demon and menaced his teacher in the sacred courtyard (?),[9] he was severely reprimanded and no longer allowed to stay with him. Having as a result taken up residence at Sa skya, he received an invitation from the Mongols and became the court chaplain of Buyantu Khan,[10] where he composed a *ṭikā* on the *Pramāṇavārttika* with a summary appended. No matter how many times he sent gifts to bCom ldan through the imperial messengers, the latter displayed no pleasure at all. Finally he sent him a small chest full of ink, with which he was very pleased. bCom ldan also composed sixteen volumes of treatises. The great scholar known as dBus pa Blo gsal was also a pupil of bCom ral and the Reverend 'Jam dbyangs. bCom ral verified the number of sections, the colophons and so on of the sacred word (*bka'*) of the Sugata and also classified the treatises (*bstan bcos*) and then wrote the *bsTan pa rgyas pa,* a treatise which puts them together in their various categories.[11] Later, the Reverend 'Jam dbyangs sent copious quantities of materials. In accordance with his request to dBus pa Blo gsal and others that they make copies of all the sacred word and the treatises in translation (*bka' dang bstan bcos 'gyur ro cog*) and keep them at sNar thang Monastery, dBus pa Blo gsal Byang chub ye shes, the translator bSod nams 'od zer and rGyang ro Byang chub went to great pains to find original exemplars (*phyi mo*) of the sacred word in translation (*bka' 'gyur*) and of the treatises in translation (*bstan 'gyur*)[12] and make good copies of them, after which they were kept in the monastery known as 'Jam lha khang. From these, many copies spread to other places: in Upper Tibet they spread to such places as Grom pa Sa skya and Khab Gung thang, while in Lower Tibet too three copies went also to 'Tshal Gung thang, and three copies to sTag lung and its environs.[13] Bringing the bsTan 'gyur from sNar thang, Bu ston Rin po che[14] removed the duplicates, since the sNar thang one, being the very first, was a collection of whatever exemplars were to be had,[15] arranged in proper order what had not been in any order, and added over a thousand new religious texts, after which it was kept in the monastery of Zha lu. Taking that as his exemplar the teacher Nam mkha' rgyal mtshan[16] made a copy at gZhis kha Rin spungs, which was kept in the Dharma college of rTses thang.[17] This supplied the exemplar for those kept at Gong dkar and gDan sa Thel.[18] All the innumerable copies produced thereafter—the separate copies which Khams pas made and took to Khams, the copies which

> were made using these as exemplars in Khams itself, the copy made by the Chos rje mThong ba don ldan,[19] the copy made in dBus by the Du dben sha ba,[20] the copy made from precious substances at 'Tshur phur by the Chos rje Rang byung ba,[21] the copy made at Byams pa gling by Yar rgyab dPon chen dGe bsnyen pa,[22] the copy in 180 volumes made by gZi Kun spangs pa,[23] right down to when sTag rtse ba,[24] built a fine monastery and made a copy which includes many exemplars obtained later, in addition to the former bKa' 'gyur and bsTan 'gyur—these also came into existence thanks to the Reverend 'Jam pa'i dbyangs, the pupil of bCom ldan rigs pa'i ral gri, and these two in the final analysis owed it all to the grace of rNgog lo tsā ba, who owed it to the grace of the scholars of Kashmir, and ultimately to the grace of the Buddhas.[25]

This account is worth quoting in full for a number of reasons, not least because of the light it throws on the motivation for the compilation of the sNar thang "edition."[26] As gZhon nu dpal tells the story, this particular collection was made only in response to the request, and with the substantial material assistance of 'Jam pa'i dbyangs, whose contribution was therefore pivotal.[27] There is thus a strong suggestion of Chinese influence, since working at the Yuan court 'Jam pa'i dbyangs would no doubt have been influenced by his Mongol patrons' sense of the importance of previous editions of the Chinese Buddhist canon produced under imperial sponsorship, and by their desire to add lustre to this tradition.[28] We know too that sNar thang, like Sa skya, had very close connections with the Mongol rulers of China.[29] Thus the initial compilation of the Tibetan canon may be seen as a distant echo of that well-known process by which the Chinese culturally subverted foreigners who had conquered them by force of arms, and its political implications merit attention. But what is equally interesting about gZhon nu dpal's account, on a more personal and human level, is the implied additional motivation for 'Jam pa'i dbyangs's initiative. Practical jokes often backfire on their perpetrators, but this hair-raising schoolboy prank had spectacular consequences. bCom ral must have given his hapless student such a severe dressing-down that the poor man smarted from it for the rest of his life, engaging in pathetically extravagant attempts to win back his teacher's favor. In this way a brief moment of boyish fun can be seen as the starting point for centuries of sober scholarly activity.[30]

gZhon nu dpal also paints a vivid picture of the veritable explosion of bKa' 'gyur and bsTan 'gyur copies from sNar thang in the fourteenth and fifteenth centuries, as Tibet was swept by what we might call a "bKa' 'gyur craze." But he tells us little about the corresponding flow of copies *towards* that center which preceded the compilation of the "edition." Fortunately the details of that are preserved in the section colophons to the Tshal pa bKa' 'gyur (see below) which have been carried over into the Li thang and other editions.[31] These are documents of capital importance. From them we learn that the Sūtra section of the Old sNar thang was based on over a dozen different *sūtra* collections (*mdo mangs*) from the libraries of Sa skya, gTsang Chu mig ring mo, Shog chung, sPun gsum, Zha lu, and other monasteries, together of course with those held at sNar thang itself. The Tantra section was based on at least five exemplars from Sa skya, Thar pa gling, and sPun gsum, and was arranged according to catalogues compiled by Grags pa rgyal mtshan (1147-1216), 'Phags pa (1235-1280), Rigs pa'i ral gri and others. The Vinaya was based on a manuscript edition compiled by mChims ston Nam mkha' grags pa, abbot of sNar thang from 1250 to 1289, compared against the Vinaya texts of Rung klung shod grog Monastery and others. Nam mkha' grags pa's text had itself been based on the edition made at La stod 'Ol rgod Monastery by Dharma seng ge using copies obtained from bSam yas mChims phu and other monasteries in dBus and gTsang with the help of the teacher and Vinaya specialist (*vinayadhara, 'dul ba 'dzin pa*) Zhing mo che ba Byang chub seng ge during the time of the Vinaya specialist of rGya, dBang phyug tshul khrims 'bar (1047-1131). We see then from these colophons that the sNar thang "edition" was the result of the gathering in of texts from various monastic libraries in gTsang and surrounding areas,[32] and at the same time the culmination of several centuries of collecting and cataloguing activity at a number of centers, including Sa skya.

On some points, however, the testimony of these sources is frustratingly vague. In particular, we do not know whether the scholars of sNar thang took the original manuscripts of all these collections back to sNar thang, or returned home with complete copies of them, or, working from one of their catalogues, copied only those individual works not already in their possession. The *DTNP* gives the impression that bCom ral and his disciples had first worked on the translations of *sūtras* and *śāstras* held at sNar thang, and had written several catalogues, *before* the collection process began, so it is quite possible that they collected selectively and to order. With two or more teams working concurrently, such a procedure is bound to have produced multiple copies of some texts. The *DTNP* enumerates three significant features of the copy of the sNar thang bsTan 'gyur which Bu ston worked on: it was incomplete, it was not in order (at least not to Bu ston's satisfaction), and it contained duplicates. What was true of the bsTan 'gyur is equally likely to have been true of the bKa' 'gyur; it is quite possible that it too contained multiple copies of texts, either different translations of the same text,[33] or different recensions of the same translation. This means that both the sNar thang bKa' 'gyur and bsTan 'gyur may simply have been better arranged collections of high-quality copies, rather than editions in our sense of the word, and that therefore they still required editorial attention.

It is my belief that the initial collection of copies which took place at sNar thang was soon followed by a second phase in the production of the bKa' 'gyur and bsTan 'gyur collections that we know today, and that this phase was carried through in at least two different places.[34] One of these places was Tshal (or 'Tshal) Gung thang Monastery in dBus, where a new edition of the bKa' 'gyur was produced during the years 1347-1351 under the sponsorship of the local ruler, Tshal pa Kun dga' rdo rje, also known as dGe ba'i blo gros (1309-1364). Since the original section colophons of this edition have survived we know a great deal about it. We know, for example, that the texts of the sNar thang "edition," of which three copies were employed, were substantially revised (using the *Mahāvyutpatti* and other such works to standardize the wording), and that their order was also rearranged, with a number of titles being deleted from the bKa' 'gyur because they were deemed to belong to the bsTan 'gyur.[35] A three-volume set of tantric texts translated during the early period (rNying rgyud) was also added. The result is known as the Tshal pa edition. The second center of editorial activity was Zha lu in gTsang. We cannot yet be sure that Bu ston carried out a complete revision of the bKa' 'gyur (as well as the bsTan 'gyur) at Zha lu, but there are indications that he did edit both collections, even though gZhon nu dpal mentions only his bsTan 'gyur edition.[36] However, we have firm evidence that Bu ston worked on substantial portions of the bKa' 'gyur, and that this editorial work was continued by his successors at Zha lu and rGyal rtse (see Harrison, 1994). This aspect of the history of the bKa' 'gyur is rather problematic, but there are good reasons for believing that at some time in the first half of the fourteenth century a Zha lu bKa' 'gyur also came into existence, and that this edition may have been closer to the Old sNar thang than its Tshal pa counterpart, at least in terms of organization. I shall call this edition the **Zha lu ma*, using an asterisk to mark its hypothetical status.[37] Both the Tshal pa and Zha lu editions may well have been based on the same raw materials, but especially in the matter of the deletion of duplicates, different decisions could easily have been arrived at, which would account for much that was to follow.

From this point on our discussion concerns the bKa' 'gyur rather than the bsTan 'gyur, although we should note that the evolution of a basically bipartite canon seems to be a peculiarly Tibetan innovation.[38] (This scheme was also adopted by the Bon pos, whose own canon, divided into bKa' 'gyur and brTen 'gyur, appears to have been systematized in the late fourteenth and early fifteenth centuries (see Kvaerne: 38-39) in imitation of the Buddhist model.) The bKa' 'gyur section of the Tibetan Buddhist canon has in its turn three major divisions: 'Dul ba (Vinaya), mDo (Sūtra) and rGyud (Tantra), thus making it a kind of *tripiṭaka* in itself, arranged according to the three "vehicles" or three different levels of religious avocation (*sdom gsum*): 'Dul ba for "Hīnayāna" (i.e., Mainstream Buddhism), mDo for Mahāyāna, and rGyud for Vajrayāna. To put it like this, however, oversimplifies the picture, because although the 'Dul ba section is comparatively clear-cut, the other two are not. Thus the mDo section, broadly conceived, is broken down into Sher phyin (Prajñāpāramitā texts), Phal chen (the *Avataṃsaka Sūtra*), dKon brtsegs (*Ratnakūṭa* texts), Myang 'das (*Mahāparinirvāṇa Sūtra*) and mDo sna tshogs or mDo mang(s) (miscellaneous *sūtras*) sections, while the rGyud texts are divided, following the classification scheme promoted by Bu ston and others, into four main classes, supplemented in some editions by the rNying rgyud ("Old Tantras") and gZungs 'dus ("*Dhāraṇī* collection") sections.[39] These sections and subsections do not appear in the same order in all editions, partly because of different schemes for classifying the sequence of the Buddha's teachings (see, e.g., Skorupski: xiv-xvii). The same holds true for the order of the individual texts within the sections, especially in the rGyud, where the placing of particular tantric cycles often indicates sectarian preferences.[40] The study of the complicated issues involved here is one way of determining the affiliations of the editions. However, repeated re-arrangements of the bKa' 'gyur make it difficult for us to determine the original order of the Tshal pa and *Zha lu ma editions on the basis of their descendants.

The Later History of the bKa' 'gyur

The Tshal pa and the *Zha lu ma manuscripts are the twin fonts from which most of the later standard editions of the bKa' 'gyur appear to flow, hence the division of the bKa' 'gyur tradition as we now know it[41] into what have been called the "Eastern" and "Western" branches. Identifying this bifurcation, and making a start at sorting out the twists and turns on both sides of the tradition has been the major achievement of recent bKa' 'gyur scholarship, above all that of Eimer (see especially Eimer, 1992), followed more recently by several other scholars. This scholarship brings three basic methods to bear on the problem of determining the affinities of the various accessible editions. The first is to examine Tibetan histories, biographies and the catalogues of these editions (*dkar chag*; see Martin, in this volume) for information relating to their creation; the second is to note carefully the order of sections and individual titles within the editions, since this can also indicate affinities; and the third is to apply classical text-critical technique to the problem, by editing individual texts, i.e., collating as many editions as possible and noting patterns of variants. Given the vastness of the bKa' 'gyur tradition, it is little wonder that these methods have not yet yielded all the answers, and that many problems remain unsolved. At the same time, some progress has been made. What follows is, I hope, a reasonably accurate and reliable reflection of our present state of knowledge.

On the so-called "Western" side of the picture the *Zha lu ma passes from the realm of hypothesis into that of historical fact in the form of the manuscript bKa' 'gyur which was made in 1431 on the order of the ruler Rab brtan Kun bzang 'phags pa (1389-1442) and deposited in the dPal 'khor chos sde Monastery at rGyal rtse.[42] This is known as the Them spangs ma Manuscript. Complete in 111 volumes, it did not include the rNying rgyud collection. There is no doubt that some of its sections were edited by Bu ston and his successors at Zha lu, but the provenance of others is not yet known. Whether the original still exists is a matter of some uncertainty, but there are still several old manuscripts at rGyal rtse, and one of these could be it. The Them spangs ma is extremely important, for it was much copied; during the reign of the fifth Dalai Lama alone (1617-1682), over a hundred copies were made. One such copy was presented to the Mongols in 1671, and now rests in the State Library at Ulan Bator.[43] Another was made during the years 1858-1878 and later donated to the Japanese monk and traveller Kawaguchi Ekai; this is now in the possession of the Tōyō Bunko, Tokyo. These are two recognized copies of the Them spangs ma, but we also have to reckon with the many others which were made, and the copies which were made from them. Into this category fall the London Manuscript bKa' 'gyur, which derives from a manuscript held at Shel dkar chos sde,[44] and the sTog Palace bKa' 'gyur, which was copied from a Bhutanese exemplar (Skorupski).[45] No doubt many more of these copies will eventually come to light. The best general term for all these manuscripts is "the Them spangs ma tradition."

On the other ("Eastern") side of the picture the Tshal pa manuscript provided the basis for the first xylographic or woodblock print of the bKa' 'gyur, the Yongle edition made in Beijing in 1410. At this point the printing technology first invented by the Chinese largely for the purposes of propagating Buddhist literature was enthusiastically adopted by the Tibetans, who were to continue to use it up to the twentieth century, not least to produce ever more editions of the bKa' 'gyur (cf. Snellgrove and Richardson: 160). In Beijing new impressions continued to be taken from the Yongle blocks, and when they wore out, new blocks were prepared, using prints struck from the old blocks as masters. Minor alterations were sometimes made when this was done. In this way were produced the Wanli impression of 1605, the Kangxi impressions of 1684/92, those of 1700, 1717-1720, the Qianlong impression of 1737, and at least one further impression after 1765.[46] But these are not the only offspring of the Tshal pa, for a copy of it kept at the castle of 'Phying ba sTag rtse in 'Phyong rgyas, a copy which must have received further editorial attention, was the basis for the 'Jang Sa tham or Li thang edition in 110 volumes of 1609-1614, which has only recently become available in the West.[47] The same 'Phying ba sTag rtse Manuscript must also have been the basis for some of the sNar thang blockprint of 1730-1732 (on which see below).[48] The Li thang was in its turn the basis for the Co ne edition (107 volumes) of 1721-1731. A convenient term for all these editions is "the Tshal pa tradition."

So far all this looks relatively neat, but in fact we have as yet made no mention of the whole question of what is technically known as "contamination." Contamination occurs when one text is not copied from another in a simple linear progression, but instead mixes readings from two or more exemplars, or "conflates" them. In such a situation parentage is often difficult to trace. The later bKa' 'gyur tradition is in fact bedevilled by contamination, due in part to the great pains the compilers of new editions took to ensure that their text was as sound as possible, which they did by consulting as many reputable old editions as they could lay their hands on. Thus the block-print edition in 104 volumes produced in 1733 at the Sa skya pa monastery of sDe dge, which took as its base text the Li thang, also borrowed readings from the lHo rdzong bKa' 'gyur, a descendant of the Them spangs ma, as well as from a bKa' 'gyur produced by A gnyen pa kshi. The sDe dge xylograph thus represents a conflation of the two main branches of the tradition, as do its later offshoots, the Ra rgya (1814-1820), the Urga (1908-1910) and the Wa ra editions (twentieth century).[49] Similarly, later reprints of the Peking edition often altered the text of the blocks with reference to the Li thang, while the modern Lhasa edition, produced in 1934, is widely known to be a conflation of sDe dge and sNar thang.[50] The sNar thang blockprint edition of 1730-1732, however, is the most unusual case of mixed parentage, since although it takes its texts from at least two separate editions, it does not apparently conflate their readings: text by text, it seems to follow one edition or the other scrupulously. Text-critical research by Eimer and others has only recently enabled us to identify the sNar thang xylograph's two sources: one of them is the 'Phying ba sTag rtse manuscript of the Tshal pa edition,[51] and the other is the Shel dkar copy of the Them spangs ma, on which the London Manuscript was based.[52] What remains to be worked out is which texts it took from which sources, and whether we can identify the point where it switched from one to the other. At this stage it appears that the 'Dul ba section follows the Them spangs ma, while most of the mDo follows the Tshal pa (making the sNar thang in this respect a sister of the Li thang). Evidence for the rGyud section is sparse. We should note, however, that the sNar thang follows the basic order of the Tshal pa editions. The way in which this edition was produced is a good illustration of the care the Tibetan editors took over their work, and of the sophistication of their approach. The same is true of sDe dge. Using these bKa' 'gyurs to edit texts ourselves, we are impressed by the extremely small number of errors which they introduced into the tradition, even though they have complicated our task somewhat by conflating their sources. One other point which needs to be noted in connection with these later printed editions is that the Tibetan canon was never entirely "closed," and that editors of the bKa' 'gyur seem to have had few qualms about adding recently translated or discovered works to existing editions. Texts were still being translated in the seventeenth and eighteenth centuries, albeit not at the prodigious rate of earlier periods.

This picture of the history of the bKa' 'gyur, as complex as it is, may soon need to be revised and elaborated. First of all, new bKa' 'gyurs continue to come to light, some of which do not fit at all well into this scheme. This is, for example, the case with the most recent arrival in the West, the Phug brag (also spelled Phu brag, sPu brag, sPud tra, etc.).[53] In terms of organization this edition, produced ca. 1700, follows neither the Thems spang ma nor the Tshal pa traditions, it contains texts found in no other bKa' 'gyur, and it carries multiple translations of works. Since it has only recently become available, not much text-critical work on individual titles within this collection has been done, but what little research there is suggests an independent tradition, which is sometimes closer to the Them spangs ma, sometimes to the Tshal pa editions.[54] In the second place, studies of the Tibetan *sūtra* translations found at Dunhuang, which date from the eighth to the eleventh centuries, are showing us that at its very beginnings the tradition which was later to become known as the bKa' 'gyur was not at all uniform, but highly contaminated. The Dunhuang collection is in fact a confusing mixture of crude archaic versions and later revised translations, together with texts standing somewhere in between, which must be either half-revised versions or conflations of old and new. If the situation frozen in time by the virtual sealing off of the Dunhuang collection was repeated at other Tibetan book repositories, then it would be surprising if the later history of the bKa' 'gyur did not turn out to be vastly more complicated than this survey might suggest. After all, we must remember that from the earliest times most Buddhist monasteries in Tibet would have possessed their own collections of scriptures, their own Sher phyins, mDo mangs, rGyud 'bums, 'Dul bas, and so on, and that eventually many of these collections must have interacted in one way or another with the systematized bKa' 'gyur tradition sketched in this paper, which was itself derived from various monastic holdings of this type. The resulting pattern of criss-cross lines of descent, mutual influence and exchange is undoubtedly complex in the extreme.[55]

Approaches to the bKa' 'gyur

The historical and text-critical considerations raised above point up some divergences between the modern Western and the traditional Tibetan approach to sacred texts. While there is no denying the great skill and care with which many of the editions of the bKa' 'gyur were produced, the Tibetan editors approached their task from a rather different standpoint. Thus while the sDe dge edition, for instance, was in a loose sense critical, in that it attempted to establish the best text on the basis of at least three witnesses, it lacks the most essential attribute of a proper edition in the Western sense: it has no critical apparatus, by which we mean a set of footnotes recording the variant readings of all the copies of the text used. The sDe dge editors reproduced what they considered to be the best reading, and consigned the rest to oblivion, while a Western critical edition would record every variant of significance, enabling the reader to check the work of the editor, and occasionally to improve upon it. In this respect the bKa' 'gyurs are more like, say, the editions of Shakespeare produced for the popular market, which give their readers no idea at all of the intricate textual problems which underlie them; in both cases the evidence is, as it were, suppressed. Naturally Tibetan scholars were not unaware of the importance of variant readings in bKa' 'gyur editions—there are several works in existence which record them—but in creating new editions they were performing an act of piety as well as scholarship, and piety requires no critical apparatus.[56] Similar considerations apply to their use of the scriptures.

Most modern Western scholars, trained as they are in an academic or scientific approach to texts, view the translations preserved in the bKa' 'gyur (and bsTan 'gyur) as a series of windows through which the historical development of Buddhist thought and practice can be glimpsed. In these translations many texts have been captured which would otherwise have disappeared forever.

They contain information, meanings and messages which Western scholars are concerned to extract and use in the pursuit of their own purposes; they have a content which can be appropriated intellectually. Tibetans are also capable of reading in this fashion, as the prolific nature of Tibetan scholarship indicates, yet at the same time they also believe the texts to be "meaningful" in a further sense. That is to say, they both contain meanings within themselves—in particular, the teachings relating to liberation from suffering—and have meaning or significance in their own right, as symbols of that liberation, the latter sense clearly being dependent on the former. Thus, as complete entities the texts of the bKa' 'gyur are thought to be powerful and transformative, as physical objects when seen or touched or as sounds when uttered or heard, whether or not intellectual understanding takes place. And if one text can be powerful, then the complete set of them, the entire canon, represents a total power source of considerable importance.

This attitude to the bKa' 'gyur is of course linked to tantric notions of sound, to the Buddhist identification of the Buddha with the Dharma, and to ancient Indian beliefs about the magical power of speech which represents the truth. It is the primary force which drives the whole history of the Tibetan canon, rather than any scholarly quest for accuracy, or for the definitive text. Indeed, it renders marginal questions as to the meaning of particular words on a particular page or the relationship between various editions, however important these might be to "those whose burden is books," be they Tibetans or Westerners. How else could one explain the extraordinary proliferation of bKa' 'gyur editions, each one of which consumed substantial resources in the making? It was no small thing to keep an army of calligraphers and carvers at work for years on end, or to furnish them with even the basic materials required for a new woodblock edition, to say nothing of supplying the gold, silver and other precious substances often used to adorn the title pages, covers and bindings of the prints, or to write the manuscript editions in their entirety. In fact, however, the more lavish the resources expended, the greater the merit which accrued to the sponsor of the edition, for naturally the sacred power of the bKa' 'gyur was conceptualized in terms of the Buddhist ideology of merit (*puṇya, bsod nams*). Nor are the political aspects of this ideology and its application any less relevant to the Tibetan situation than they are elsewhere in the Buddhist world. It is no accident that many of the editions we have reviewed were produced by some of the most powerful players in Tibet's turbulent history: Kun dga' rdo rje, Byang chub rgyal mtshan, the fifth Dalai Lama and Pho lha bSod nams stobs rgyal were all important political figures; even 'Jam pa'i dbyangs, whose sponsorship initiated the whole process of systematization, must ultimately have been representing his Mongol patrons. In supplying the funds to create new editions of the bKa' 'gyur on which they could set their own seal, these rulers were no doubt pursuing less "transcendental" purposes as well.

Produced at the behest of the wealthy and powerful, the editions of the canon continued to provide Tibetans from all social strata with a source of merit. To this day, in monastery chapels all over Tibet (if they have been fortunate enough to survive the depredations of the twentieth century), sets of the bKa' 'gyur often flank the central images, with an ambulatory set up beneath them so that, simply by passing under one and around the other, the faithful can worship the books and the images at the same time—the former being a repository of the voice (*gsung rten*), the latter of the body (*sku rten*) of the awakened ones. Indeed, the books are often more worshipped than read, as the thick layers of dust which coat them testify. On special occasions, however, the texts may be recited, teams of readers going through the entire collection, or the bKa' 'gyur of the local monastery may be borne in procession around the fields, so that its power may be applied to the health of the community. This kind of ritual activity, then, is far more common than the kind of reading for sense with which Westerners are familiar (which is of course also practiced in Tibet), yet it is to the attitude which informs it, this intense feeling for the sacredness and power of the bKa' 'gyur as a whole, that we owe the survival of this precious historical resource.

Notes

1. This article is intended as a preliminary sketch of the history of the Tibetan bKa' 'gyur (commonly written: Kanjur), and as a brief introduction to some of the problem areas of this field, our knowledge of which has developed rapidly in the last twenty years. This has been largely due to the researches of Helmut Eimer, who has not only written a substantial number of books and papers on bKa' 'gyur-related topics (see now Eimer, 1992), but has also favored others working in the field, myself included, with constant and unstinting advice and assistance. I would therefore like to thank Dr. Eimer, as

well as all those others whose work has guided me, and I would like at the same time to express my gratitude to Dr. Akira Yuyama and the staff of the International Institute for Buddhist Studies, Tokyo, for providing the excellent working environment in which this article was written, during a Visiting Research Fellowship, November 1991-February 1992.

2. The use of the terms "canon" and "canonical" in the case of Buddhism is highly problematic, and they are employed here only as convenient shorthand. The Buddhist religion has since the death of Gautama lacked the institutional means for establishing any one set of texts as authoritative for the entire tradition, and even on a local level compendia of sacred texts have admitted varying degrees of "openness" to the inclusion of new scriptures. Thus expressions like "the Chinese Buddhist canon" or "the Tibetan Buddhist canon" may convey a misleading impression of fixedness.

3. Certain descriptions of the so-called *bodhisattvapiṭaka* ("canon for bodhisattvas") in early middle Mahāyāna *sūtras* make this quite clear, by defining it in terms of doctrinal criteria rather than text titles.

4. There are a few exceptions to this rule, such as the finds at Gilgit and Dunhuang.

5. Tib. *Bye brag tu rtogs par byed pa chen po*. The date of this work is a matter of some uncertainty, some authorities putting it at around 814 C.E. The edition commonly used is that of Sakaki, but more recently a fine new edition has been prepared by Ishihama and Fukuda.

6. The *lDan kar ma* is a list of scriptures in the palace of lDan kar, for which see, e.g., Lalou. The date of this work is also disputed; one suggestion is 812. Two other catalogues known to have been compiled during this period, the *Phang thang ma* and the *mChims phu ma*, are not extant (see Samten, 1987b: 764).

7. The Vinaya tradition translated into Tibetan is that of the Mūlasarvāstivādins, one of the Mainstream schools. Parts of this Vinaya are also extant in Sanskrit.

8. Note, however, that various commentaries later assigned to the bsTan 'gyur appear beside their "root texts" in the "bKa' 'gyur section."

9. Text: *chos bar sar*. Roerich translates "at the end of a class (evening)," but I can find no support for this interpretation.

10. The Yuan Emperor Renzong, reigned 1311-1320.

11. According to Jampa Samten (1987b: 765), this work was a catalogue of both bKa' 'gyur and bsTan 'gyur. bCom ldan rigs pa'i ral gri also wrote an abridged catalogue for the bKa' 'gyur alone (the *Nyi ma'i 'od zer*) and at least one other catalogue for the two collections. As far as I know, none of these works survives.

12. I have avoided using the terms bKa' 'gyur and bsTan 'gyur here, as this may be something of an anachronism: these collections probably existed as such only after the sNar thang compilation.

13. The abbot of sTag lung, Rin chen 'byung gnas (1300-1361; he was abbot from 1339 onwards), is credited in the *DTNP* with a copy of the bsTan 'gyur

(Roerich: 634), which may have been based on the three copies of the sNar thang sent to sTag lung mentioned above.

14. Bu ston Rin chen grub (1290-1364).

15. From the point of view of Tibetan syntax, this crucial phrase is better taken as a justification for what follows (the lack of order), but this seems less likely from the point of view of sense, so I have followed Roerich's lead and attached it to the preceding clause (concerning the removal of duplicates).

16. For Nam mkha' rgyal mtshan of Rin spungs, a minister in the service of Byang chub rgyal mtshan (cf. next note), see Tucci: 639.

17. Also rTse thang or rTsed thang. This must refer to the edition of the bKa' 'gyur and bsTan 'gyur which Jampa Samten (1987b: 773) says was compiled at rTsed thang in 1362 by Tai situ Byang chub rgyal mtshan (1302-1364), the founder of the Phag mo gru dynasty, and edited by sGra tshad pa Rin chen rnam rgyal, also known as Rin chen rgyal mtshan (1318-1388), the student and successor of Bu ston. According to Samten, this edition was based on the Zha lu bsTan 'gyur (the basis for the bKa' 'gyur is not given, and one wonders whether one was produced at this time). See also Hadano (49), who makes no mention of a bKa' 'gyur; he records the fact that the bsTan 'gyur contained 3,429 works.

18. Also known as gDan sa mThil.

19. The sixth Karma pa (1416-1453).

20. The holder of this title is not identified; Roerich has Dun bden.

21. The third Karma pa Rang byung rdo rje (1284-1339), who according to the *DTNP* (see Roerich: 492), prepared a copy of the bKa' 'gyur and bsTan 'gyur at bSam yas 'Chims phu shortly before his death in 1339. *'Tshur phur* is presumably an alternative spelling of mTshur phu.

22. A patron of the teacher gTsang pa Blo gros bzang po (1360-1423); see Roerich: 693. This copy was probably produced in the early fifteenth century.

23. Not identified. Roerich has gZhi Kun spangs ma.

24. Not identified. This may refer to a local ruler in control of 'Phying ba sTag rtse, where the copy of the Tshal pa bKa' 'gyur on which gZhon nu dpal himself worked was kept.

25. Text also in Ruegg: 22, n. 1. See too the translation in Roerich: 336-339.

26. Not to be confused with the later sNar thang blockprint edition. The so-called Old sNar thang was in manuscript, although one still encounters claims that it was printed.

27. Note also that the Tantra and Vinaya section colophons of the Tshal pa edition (on which see below) also name 'Jam pa'i dbyangs as the author of the sNar thang edition.

28. In fact, a number of editions of the Chinese canon were produced under the Yuan dynasty; the most important of these appeared at the end of the thirteenth century; see Grönbold: 24.

29. See especially Hadano: 78-83. The Sa skya pas also produced several early canonical editions, some of which were used to compile the Old sNar thang (see below).

30. The *Hor chos 'byung* of 'Jig med rig pa'i rdo rje makes it even clearer that the gift of ink which finally did the trick was sent by 'Jam dbyangs for the purpose of copying the canon; see Ruegg: 24, n. 1.

31. For the texts of the colophons in the Li thang bKa' 'gyur see Samten, 1987a. It should be noted that the translations of these important documents in this article (extracts of which are also published with only minor changes in Samten, 1987b) are to be used with circumspection. The syntax of the Tibetan is, it must be admitted, horribly convoluted; cf. Hadano: 71-74.

32. In all cases where the place names can be identified, the monastery concerned is fairly close to sNar thang.

33. This is, incidentally, a standard feature of the Chinese canonical editions, which included all available translations of a text.

34. This section of my account is in the nature of a working hypothesis, and remains to be demonstrated in detail. Because of the highly technical nature of some of the evidence, only a brief sketch of the argument is attempted here. Further details may be found in Harrison, 1994.

35. See Samten, 1987a for the details. As far as we can tell, no bsTan 'gyur was produced at Tshal Gung thang.

36. Unless by *bsTan 'gyur* gZhon nu dpal intended the entire canon, but I think this is unlikely. Bu ston's edition of the bsTan 'gyur was completed in 1334, and his catalogue to it in 1335.

37. Cf. Samten's statement (1987b: 756) that "in 1334...the whole Kanjur and Tanjur were written out again at Sha-lu Monastery based on the Narthang edition." Unfortunately no source is provided.

38. On the later history of the bsTan 'gyur see, e.g., Samten, 1987b and Grönbold.

39. For an excellent study of some of the problems relating to the ordering of the rGyud section, see Eimer, 1989.

40. A well-known example is the pride of place given to commentaries on the *Hevajra Tantra* in the sDe dge bsTan 'gyur, reflecting the position of the Sa skya pa sect, whereas *Kālacakra Tantra* commentaries come first in the Peking bsTan 'gyur, which follows Bu ston's original arrangement and thus reflects the preeminence he assigned to the Kālacakra cycle (see, e.g., Hadano: 36).

41. This qualification is necessary, as the discovery of further editions may well change the picture altogether.

42. See Eimer, 1983, vol. 1: 90-106 and Bethlenfalvy: 6. Although this copy was edited by one Thugs rje dpal, the notices on the Them spangs ma given in the *dkar chags* of several later editions of the bKa' 'gyur indicate that it was based on a copy of the Old sNar thang which Bu ston had edited and for which he had compiled a *dkar chag*. My interpretation of these texts differs

from Eimer's on this essential point, but a full discussion of the problems is out of the question here; cf. Hadano: 74-75 and Harrison, 1994.

43. According to Mongolian tradition this manuscript is in fact the original Them spangs ma, which was itself the personal copy of Bu ston (i.e., our putative *Zha lu ma); see Bethlenfalvy: 6-7.

44. Recent research by Peter Skilling and Jampa Samten puts the date of the London manuscript at around 1712. On its derivation from the Them spangs ma see Harrison, 1994.

45. My own research indicates that the London and Tokyo manuscripts share a common source, which may be the same intermediary copy of the Them spangs ma. The sTog Palace Manuscript carries a slightly different text, suggesting either a different line of descent from the Them spangs ma or direct derivation from the *Zha lu ma; I think the former more likely. Cf. Harrison, 1992a: xxvi-xxviii.

46. The so-called Peking Edition commonly used today is a reprint of the 1717-20 impression, with gaps filled from the 1737 print.

47. See Samten, 1987a. There is some uncertainty as to the exact dates of this edition.

48. The sNar thang blockprint is not to be confused with the Old sNar thang, which was never printed, although this erroneous claim is still to be encountered. Its precise relationship to the 'Phying ba sTag rtse MS has only recently begun to become clear, with my work on several texts in the mDo section (see below).

49. Because of the high quality of its editing—its text usually accords with standard grammar, is seldom unintelligible, and introduces very few new errors into the tradition—the sDe dge has become the most favored and most reproduced bKa' 'gyur this century. From a text-critical point of view, however, the canonization of this edition is less than fortunate, since it is contaminated.

50. Lhasa tends to follow sNar thang more closely. According to Samten (1987b: 779) the editors of the Lhasa also collated a copy of the Them spangs ma, but I have seen no internal evidence to support this.

51. This has been placed beyond all doubt by my own work on the Tibetan text of the *Drumakinnararājaparipṛcchā Sūtra* (Harrison, 1992a), although this conclusion was foreshadowed by my previous research on the *Lokānuvartanā Sūtra* (Harrison, 1992c).

52. The account of this edition by Samten (1987b: 778) explains why this happened. The project began under the sixth Dalai Lama (1683-1705), using the Tshal pa as a basis, but was suspended on his death with only 28 volumes of the Prajñāpāramitā section finished; it was not resumed until bSod nams stobs rgyal, more commonly known as Pho lha or Pho lha nas (1689-1747), took control of Tibet. Pho lha assembled a team of calligraphers and carvers at Shel dkar and completed the edition in 101 volumes. Samten claims that he used a Peking edition to do this, but this cannot be correct. See also Hadano:

63. On the orders of bSod nams stobs rgyal a sNar thang blockprint edition of the bsTan 'gyur was also produced, being completed in 225 volumes in 1742.

53. Now in the possession of the Library of Tibetan Works and Archives, this edition is available in microfiche from the Institute for Advanced Studies of World Religions, New York.

54. My work on the *Druma* (Harrison, 1992a) also indicates that Phug brag is independent, but preserves the same recension of the text found in the Them spangs ma bKa' 'gyurs (London, sTog, Tokyo). Research by Jeffrey Schoening of Seattle into the Tibetan text of the *Śālistamba Sūtra* suggests that the Phug brag is closer to the Tshal pa line. My own initial guess as to the status of the Phug brag was that it might be a descendant of the original Old sNar thang bKa' 'gyur collection, substantially re-arranged, to which new texts have been added. I am now far less sure about this hypothesis.

55. The transmission of the bsTan 'gyur which was also compiled at the beginning of the fourteenth century at sNar thang has been considerably less complicated. To the best of my knowledge, there are five complete editions in existence, all of which apparently go back to Bu ston's substantial revision of the Old sNar thang bsTan 'gyur at Zha lu in 1334. The woodblock prints made in Peking (1724) and sNar thang (1741-1742) are both based on the second enlarged copy of Bu ston's edition made in 1688 at 'Phying ba sTag rtse by the regent Sangs rgyas rgya mtsho. This consisted of 224 volumes, and included over 200 texts translated or discovered since Bu ston's time (see Samten, 1987b: 774). There is also a Golden Manuscript bsTan 'gyur, recently published in Beijing, which is possibly an offspring of the 1724 Peking print. On the other hand, the sDe dge woodblock edition of the bsTan 'gyur (1737-1744) was compiled using a number of manuscripts, some if not all of which were derived from the Zha lu edition (ibid.: 777-778), but it preserves an earlier stage in the development of the tradition: even though it was subsequently enlarged from 209 to 214 volumes, it contains far fewer texts than the Peking or sNar thang prints. The Co ne edition (1753-1773) was based on the sDe dge; complete in 209 volumes, it lacks the later additions. To these must be added the two incomplete editions made at Urga or Ulan Bator (1937) and Wa ra (ca. 1945), both of which are also based on sDe dge.

56. Of course, piety and scholarly punctiliousness are by no means incompatible, but one can easily see how those who produce editions of sacred or authoritative texts for the edification of the faithful may feel awkward about providing copious evidence of human fallibility on every page.

References

Bethlenfalvy, Géza

1982 *A Hand-list of the Ulan Bator Manuscript of the Kanjur Rgyal-rtse Them spaṅs ma.* Budapest: Akadémiai Kiadó.

Davidson, Ronald M.

1990 "An Introduction to the Standards of Scriptural Authenticity in

Indian Buddhism." In *Chinese Buddhist Apocrypha*, pp. 291-325. Ed. by Robert E. Buswell. Honolulu: University of Hawaii Press.

Eimer, Helmut

1983 *Rab tu 'byuṅ ba'i gži: Die tibetische Übersetzung des Pravrajyāvastu im Vinaya der Mūlasarvāstivādins*. Asiatische Forschungen 82. 2 vols. Wiesbaden: Otto Harrassowitz.

1989 *Der Tantra-Katalog des Bu ston im Vergleich mit der Abteilung Tantra des tibetischen Kanjur*. Indica et Tibetica 17. Bonn: Indica et Tibetica Verlag.

1992 *Ein Jahrzehnt Studien zur Überlieferung des tibetischen Kanjur*. Wiener Studien zur Tibetologie und Buddhismuskunde 28. Vienna: Arbeitskreis für tibetische und buddhistische Studien Universität Wien.

Ferrari, Alfonsa

1958 *Mk'yen Brtse's Guide to the Holy Places of Central Tibet*. Rome: Istituto Italiano per il Medio ed Estremo Oriente.

Grönbold, Günter

1984 *Der Buddhistische Kanon: Eine Bibliographie*. Wiesbaden: Otto Harrassowitz.

gZhon nu dpal

DTNP *Deb ther sngon po*. 2 vols. Chengdu: Sichuan minzu chubanshe, 1984, 1985.

Hadano, Hakuyū

1966 "Chibetto-daizōkyō engi [A History of compiling and editing of the Tibetan Buddhist Scriptures, 'Bkaḥ-ḥgyur and Bstan-ḥgyur'], [1]." *Annual of Oriental and Religious Studies/ Suzuki Gakujutsu Zaidan Kenkyu Nempō* 3: 35-83.

Harrison, Paul

1992a *Druma-kinnara-rāja-paripṛcchā-sūtra: A Critical Edition of the Tibetan Text (Recension A)*. Studia Philologica Buddhica, Monograph Series 7. Tokyo: The International Institute for Buddhist Studies.

1992b "Is the *Dharma-kāya* the Real 'Phantom Body' of the Buddha?" *Journal of the International Association of Buddhist Studies* 15/1: 44-93.

1992c "Meritorious Activity or Waste of Time? Some Remarks on the Editing of Texts in the Tibetan Kanjur." In *Tibetan Studies: Proceedings of the 5th Seminar of the International Association of Tibetan Studies, Narita 1989*, pp. 77-93. Ed. by Ihara Shōren and Yamaguchi Zuihō. Narita: Naritasan Shinshoji.

1994 "In Search of the Source of the Tibetan Kanjur: A Reconnaissance Report." In *Tibetan Studies: Proceedings of the 6th Seminar of the International Association for Tibetan Studies, Fagernes 1992,*

Vol. 1, pp. 295-317. Ed. by Per Kvaerne. Oslo: Institute for Comparative Research in Human Culture.

Ishihama, Y. and Y. Fukuda
1989 *A New Critical Edition of the* Mahāvyutpatti: *Sanskrit-Tibetan-Mongolian Dictionary of Buddhist Terminology.* Studia Tibetica 16, Materials for Tibetan-Mongolian Dictionaries, vol. 1. Tokyo: Tōyō Bunko.

Ishikawa, M.
1990 *A Critical Edition of the* Sgra sbyor bam po gnyis pa: *An Old and Basic Commentary on the* Mahāvyutpatti. Studia Tibetica 18, Materials for Tibetan-Mongolian Dictionaries, vol. 2. Tokyo: Tōyō Bunko.

Kvaerne, Per
1975 "The Canon of the Tibetan Bonpos." *Indo-Iranian Journal* 16: 18-56, 96-144.

Lalou, Marcelle
1953 "Les textes bouddhiques au temps du Roi Khri-sroṅ-lde-bcan." *Journal asiatique* 241: 313-353.

Lamotte, Etienne
1947 "La critique d'authenticité dans le bouddhisme." In *India Antiqua,* pp. 213-222. Ed. by F. D. K. Bosch et al. Leiden: E. J. Brill.

Ray, R.A.
1985 "Buddhism: Sacred Text Written and Realized." In *The Holy Book in Comparative Perspective,* pp. 148-180. Ed. by F. M. Denny and R.L. Taylor. Columbia, South Carolina: University of South Carolina Press.

Roerich, George
1976 *The Blue Annals.* Second edition. Delhi: Motilal Banarsidass [originally published in two parts, Calcutta, 1949-1953].

Ruegg, David Seyfort
1966 *The Life of Bu ston rin po che.* Rome: Istituto Italiano per il Medio ed Estremo Oriente.

Sakaki R.
1962 *Honyaku myōgi taishū/Mahāvyutpatti.* Reprint ed. in 2 vols. Tokyo: Suzuki Research Foundation [lst ed. 1916, 1936].

Samten, Jampa, translated with Jeremy Russell
1987a "Notes on the Lithang Edition of the Tibetan bKa'-'gyur." *Tibet Journal* 12/3: 17-40.

1987b "Origins of the Tibetan Canon with Special Reference to the Tshal-pa Kanjur." In *Buddhism and Science,* pp. 763-781. Seoul: Tongguk University.

Skorupski, Tadeusz
1985 *A Catalogue of the Stog Palace Kanjur*. Bibliographia Philologica Buddhica, Series Maior 4. Tokyo: The International Institute for Buddhist Studies.

Snellgrove, David and Hugh Richardson
1968 *A Cultural History of Tibet*. London: Weidenfeld and Nicolson.

Tucci, Giuseppe
1949 *Tibetan Painted Scrolls*. 2 vols. Rome: La Libreria dello Stato.

Chapter 4

The Canonical *Tantras* of the New Schools

Tadeusz Skorupski

The Scope

It was due to certain historical factors[1] and to the formative stages of the Tibetan canon or *bKa' 'gyur*[2] that some tantric texts came to be treated as canonical or authentic and some texts, of uncertain origin, as unauthentic. The tantric texts that were eventually included in the bKa' 'gyur are considered to be authentic or canonical by the new schools (*gsar ma pa*), which began to dominate Tibetan Buddhism from the late tenth century onward. A decisive criterion of textual authenticity was a strict but rather arbitrarily imposed reliance on approved translations of tantric texts executed on the basis of attested Sanskrit or other Indian original sources. Thus, those tantric texts whose Indian origins were unattested or in doubt were excluded from the bKa' 'gyur. A considerable number of such "unauthentic" texts were, however, cherished by the adepts of the Ancient School (rNying ma pa), as is explained in Janet Gyatso's essay in this volume. The present article is concerned mainly with the tantric literature included in the bKa' 'gyur.

The Tantra Section in the bKa' 'gyur

The tantric division comprises several hundred titles in some twenty-two of the 108 volumes of works included in the bKa' 'gyur.[3] These tantric texts represent a variety of works that are different in both length and content, and have diverse titles. The overall length of tantric texts varies considerably. Some are very short, comprising a few folios or even less, but on the whole their length varies between twenty and over one hundred folios, with only a few texts extending over two hundred. Like the *sūtras* the tantric texts are written in the form of dialogues or instructive expositions which are in prose or verse, but most frequently in mixed prose and verse. The *tantras* usually have an opening scene describing the setting and the general assembly surrounding the principal deity. Then, there follow individual sections or chapters that deal with specific topics. There seems to be no apparent logical arrangement within individual texts. Some *tantras* appear to be composed according to a preconceived structure, but in many instances the material is clearly put together in a somewhat disordered manner with the same topics being treated in different sections of the whole text. The principal *tantras* deal with a wide range of subjects that provide the essential instructions for the practice of tantric methods of liberation. Some texts deal with specific topics; others serve as branches, subtexts or elaborations of the major *tantras*. In principle, the totality of esoteric texts is referred to in Sanskrit as *tantra* (Tib. *rgyud*), a term which, like *sūtra*, and having similar literal meaning, came to be employed to distinguish this literary tradition from other Buddhist texts included in the early Tripiṭaka collections or among the Mahāyāna *sūtras*. However, in reality the matter is more complex. The tantric texts bear a number of qualifying terms in their titles. Different texts are named variously as Tantra, "Great Tantra" (*mahātantra, rgyud chen po*), "Root Tantra" (*mūlatantra, rtsa ba'i rgyud*), "Tantra King" (*tantrarāja, rgyud kyi rgyal po*), or again as "Ordinance" (*kalpa, rtog pa*), "Discourse" (*sūtra, mdo*),[4] "Magical Formula" (*dhāraṇī, gzungs*), and "Heroine of Magical Power" (*vidyārājñī, rig pa'i rgyal mo*).[5] These are the most frequently employed terms, but there are several others that are also used in the titles of tantric works. Some of these terms were in existence for a long time before the efflorescence of esoteric literature proper in the eighth and ninth centuries.

The whole Tantra section as such, depending on the particular bKa' 'gyur edition referred to, is named simply "Tantra" (*rGyud*) or "Tantra Collection" (*rGyud 'bum*). However, it is often divided into two major groups called the "Tantra Collection" (*rGyud 'bum*) and the "Formula Collection" (*gZungs 'dus*).[6] Whenever a particular bKa' 'gyur contains only one Tantra section, this single section includes all categories of tantric texts. When it is divided into the two "Collections" noted, the "Tantra Collection" comprises all tantric texts that belong to the four classes of Tantra (see below), those Mahāyāna *sūtras* that are recognized as tantric, magical formulas and all the remaining categories included in the Tantra section of the bKa' 'gyur editions that are not subdivided. The "Formula Collection" comprises over two hundred *dhāraṇīs* and similar texts, including some *sūtras*, that were gathered together because of their particular importance for ritual. The majority of texts included in this collection are also found among the texts in the "Tantra Collection."

The tantric texts contained in the bKa' 'gyur are arranged in a certain (sequential) order which seems to be quite deliberate, but difficult to ascertain with accuracy. However, on the whole the arrangement of individual texts follows the classification of tantric texts into the four classes. Thus, the Tantra section begins with works belonging to the Highest Yoga, followed by those of the Yoga, and finally those of the Action and Performance classes. There also exist further stratifications of works that appertain to a particular group of texts within each Tantra class, but the actual arrangement and sequence of tantric texts are not consistently the same in all editions of the bKa' 'gyur. Furthermore, in some bKa' 'gyur collections, the *tantras* are arranged at the beginning, as the first collection, because they are considered more important than other canonical works, such as the Vinaya or Sūtra collections. In some bKa' 'gyur collections they are placed at the end, as the last collection, which is more in accordance with the historical formation of Buddhist texts.

It is possible to discuss tantric literature without making any particular reference to the bKa' 'gyur. However, since so much effort has been invested by the Tibetan savants in the classification and arrangement of tantric literature in some meaningful manner, it is of importance to the understanding of the complexity and variety of tantric works to be aware of the bKa' 'gyur as the largest repository of such texts.

The tantric texts included in the bKa' 'gyur represent translations predominantly from the Sanskrit but also from the Prakrit, Apabhraṃśa and other Indian languages. A certain number of such texts were translated into Tibetan during the first propagation (seventh-ninth centuries C.E.) of Buddhism in Tibet, and the majority during the second propagation (tenth century C.E. onward).[7] The translation work was done by a number of well-trained Tibetan experts assisted by Indian masters such as Gayādhara, Advayavajra, Jayasena and others. Among the Tibetan translators Rin chen bzang po became the most renowned. But there were many other competent people such as Śākya ye shes or 'Gos lhas btsas who are also ranked very high.

Possible Origins of the *Tantras*

The earliest evidence for the existence of texts with a tantric flavor is frequently sought in the texts of Indian Mahāyāna literature that have sections containing magical formulas. The presence of these formulas, spells and incantations, endowed with certain efficacious powers for the achievement of both worldly and supramundane results, is attested in all periods and forms of Buddhism. However, it is in the late Mahāyāna that such texts began to acquire an important position and serve as inspirations for various practices distinctly different from those of the traditional Mahāyāna. It is not so much the literary genre of the magical texts as such that should be seen as the precursor of tantric texts proper, but rather their spirit and tendency towards magic and occult practices. The exact time, place, and circumstances in which the first tantric texts were produced remain fundamentally unresolved. There exists much speculation and a variety of opinions on the origin of the *tantras*. It is, however, generally assumed and supported by Tibetan sources such as Tāranātha that the tantric texts and practices initially remained a very closely guarded secret in limited circles for several centuries, most likely as an oral transmission, before they became diffused and more readily acceptable to a wider audience of adepts in the eighth-ninth centuries. Such an assumption is further supported by the fact that it was also during that period that numerous commentaries on the *tantras* were written and their authors named.

Tibet was more spiritually inclined toward the tantric tradition than China or Japan, countries in which only selected tantric texts were translated and practiced. The Tibetan tradition received the largest collection of tantric texts and practices, becoming thus the most prominent inheritor in Asia of tantric literature produced in India. A great variety of tantric texts and practices were carried over to Tibet, some surviving both as texts and living traditions, and some only as literary documents. There still continue to exist some salient disagreements in interpretation and precise grading of those texts within individual schools and among the different schools.[8]

The Different *Tantra* Categories

The tantric texts themselves do not provide any specific information with regard to the categories or divisions in which they are to be placed, but they were eventually classified in several different ways, not so much in terms of their literary nature, but rather with regard to the various teachings and spiritual methods advocated for different spiritual adepts or with regard to different Buddha families. One of the common characteristics of all tantric texts is that they focus on one particular deity or groups of deities and incorporate a body of ritual and meditative instructions necessary to achieve spiritual realization in conjunction with those deities. A particular tantric tradition that follows a specific *tantra* or a group of related tantric texts and practices is often referred to as a tantric cycle. There is no clear evidence from Indian sources that the tantric texts were originally classified or grouped in any particular manner. They seem to have been written or compiled in a haphazard manner in different places by individuals or groups of *yogins* who made use of the appropriate mythological and literary lore, and of the various yogic practices that were available to them. In Tibet itself, one of the most widely recognized classifications of the *tantras* accepted by the New Schools is that into four classes. This classification is based on the deliberately stratified levels of spiritual and yogic practices that relate to particular deities and aim to assist the practitioner according to his or her spiritual disposition and aptitude. The four classes of *tantras* are named in ascending order of importance as Action or Ritual (*kriyā, bya*), Performance (*caryā, spyod*), Yoga (*yoga, rnal 'byor*), and Highest Yoga (*anuttara, bla na med pa*). Although there exists evidence that the tantric literature evolved in stages and in different religious centers, and that it contains certain common characteristics—for instance ritual—and although the differentiations among the *tantras* are rather subtle and refined, this classification does serve as a useful point of reference.

In the works of the Action Tantra, the focus is on a wide range of externally performed ritual activities, more so than on internal spiritual exercises. The texts of this class provide instructions on various ritualized activities that are often accompanied by symbols and diagrams. They are predominantly concerned with the worship of deities, offerings and praises, the procurement of worldly and spiritual benefits, the appeasement of diseases and demonic powers, the blessing of images, and the consecrations of their adepts. They also contain instructions for painting deities. The longest text in this class is the "Ordinance of Mañjuśrī" (*Mañjuśrīmūla-kalpa* [or *-tantra*], *'Jam dpal gyi rtsa ba'i rgyud*). Its structure and content contain literary and historical indications that it was compiled over a period of several centuries, with its oldest sections belonging probably to the earliest tantric period. In many ways, it represents a transition between the Mahāyāna *sūtras* and the *tantras*. It contains a mine of information on ritual, the production of images, astrology and some historical events. It also contains long sections that are concerned with Brahmanic deities and magical formulas.

Among the texts included in the Performance Tantra, which focuses on ritual activities in balance with meditative practices, the "Perfect Enlightenment of Mahāvairocana" (*Mahāvairocanābhisambodhi, rNam par snang mdzad chen po mngon par rdzogs par byang chub pa*) is the longest and most important. It is generally considered to be the root text of this class. It provides a fairly coherent and comprehensive exposition of tantric practices in relationship to a set of deities, with Vairocana as the central deity.

The Yoga Tantra texts, which represent an advanced and perfected system of tantric teachings, are predominantly oriented towards meditative and yogic practices. Ritual instructions are also present, but they are not considered essential for the attainment of spiritual perfection. Here, it is a particular set of internal—but also externally ritualized—meditational practices and consecrations that occupy the central position. Within this class, the "Compendium of the Essence of All the Tathagātas" (*Sarvatathāgatatattvasaṃgraha, De bzhin gshegs pa thams cad kyi de kho na nyid bsdus pa*) is the longest and most comprehensive. It comprises a whole range of expositions concerned with the various sets of mystic circles (*maṇḍala, dkyil 'khor*), consecrations and instructions on the stages leading towards enlightenment.

The Highest Yoga Tantra attaches the greatest importance to the control and purification of the mind (*citta, sems*) as the chief agent of all human activities. Among this class, there are several important texts which are particularly valued and followed in Tibet. They are the "Secret Assembly" (*Guhyasamāja, gSang ba 'dus pa*), the "Hail Vajra" (*Hevajra, Kye'i rdo rje*), the "Wheel of Time" (*Kālacakra, Dus kyi 'khor lo*), the group of texts centered on the deity rDo rje 'jigs byed (Vajrabhairava), and the texts belonging to the 'Khor lo sdom pa (Cakrasaṃvara) cycle of which the principal text is the "Short Saṃvara" (*Laghusaṃvara, bDe mchog nyung ngu*).[9] In fact, it is this Tantra class that is recognized among Tibetan new schools as setting forth the most adventurous and efficacious path towards spiritual perfection.

Among the four classes of Tantras, the Action, Performance and Yoga Tantras are also referred to jointly as the lower Tantras. However, it should be remembered that each Tantra category claims superiority for itself in the sense of providing a distinct and complete body of teachings and practices adequate, and indeed unique, for the attainment of the perfect state of enlightenment.

Taking into account the doctrinal elements, literary presentation and the nature of the presiding deities, it is also possible to divide the *tantras* into two major categories, namely those related to the Mahāyāna discourses and those with strong non-Buddhist associations. Since in some *tantras* the literary presentation clearly resembles and overlaps with the later Mahāyāna texts, it is reasonable to assume that such tantric texts, especially those belonging to the first three classes of *tantras*, came into existence in the same or similar religious milieu. It is also among the Mahāyāna texts that some of the earliest literary evidence for the existence of tantric works is to be found. The names of the buddhas and bodhisattvas in such texts are manifestly Buddhist and similar to those in the Mahāyāna discourses. There is, of course, a progressive assimilation of non-Buddhist Indian deities into the Buddhist pantheon, but in a conspicuously subservient role. Among the second category, in particular among the texts belonging to the Highest Yoga Tantra, the non-Buddhist setting and elements predominate. Here, the mythological and literary elements betray strong associations with the Śaivite tantric texts and practices. The buddhas in such texts have little in common with Śākyamuni or his hypostases. They are usually fierce and awe-inspiring manifestations, variously referred to as bDe mchog (Śaṃbara), rDo rje mkha' 'gro (Vajraḍāka), Sangs rgyas thod pa (Buddhakapāla) or 'Jigs byed (Bhairava) and are usually accompanied by attendants of equally terrifying appearances.

The Canonicity of the *Tantras*

The *tantras*, although manifestly apocryphal, are accepted as canonical or "revealed" by the adepts of tantric practices. They constitute the foundation, and indeed, justification for the Buddhist tradition or vehicle known as Mantrayāna, Tantrayāna or Vajrayāna. The term *Mantrayāna* represents historically an earlier alternative name for Vajrayāna and has closer links with the traditional Mahāyāna. The authorship of tantric texts is attributed to Śākyamuni Buddha himself or, more frequently, to various Buddha manifestations who preside as chief deities over their appropriate assemblies and enunciate their particular teachings. So far as the places of such discourses are concerned, the texts belonging to the Action Tantra are said to have been delivered in different localities associated with the mystical families of deities that occupy central positions in particular texts. The Performance Tantra is said to have been enunciated in the Akaniṣṭha heaven and the Yoga Tantra on Mt. Meru. The texts belonging to the Highest Yoga Tantra do not claim for themselves any particular locality, although occasionally the place of enunciation is given. The *Kālacakra Tantra*, for instance, is said to have been disclosed a year or so after the Buddha's enlightenment at a locality called Dhānyakaṭaka. The most frequent location for the discourses of the various wrathful Buddha manifestations is given as the vagina (*bhaga*; usually not translated into Tibetan) of the Vajra-Lady (Vajrayoṣid, rDo rje btsun mo) which is often explained as the Vajra-sphere (*vajradhātu*, *rdo rje dbyings*) or Wisdom (*prajñā*, *shes rab*). The justification for the validity and variety of the tantric texts is largely derived from the tantric reinterpretation of the Buddha's enlightenment and is based on the understanding that buddhahood can manifest itself in many different forms, both peaceful and wrathful. It is the *Compendium of the Essence of All the Tathāgatas* that provides a detailed description of how Śākyamuni attained the state of the tantric enlightenment through instructions and meditative trances (*abhisambodhi, mngon par 'tshang rgya ba*), accompanied by consecrations bestowed by all the buddhas (see Skorupski, 1985).

The Theory and Practice

As already indicated above, the subject matter of tantric texts encompasses a wide range of topics which deal with tantric theory and practice. In essence, the basic doctrinal assumptions are those of the Mahāyāna as propounded by the Madhyamaka and the Yogācāra systems, and in particular the assumption that phenomenal existence (*saṃsāra, 'khor ba*) and the absolute state of spiritual perfection (*nirvāṇa, mya ngan las 'das*) are not two separate entities but rather two contrasting ways in which the mind perceives the nature of things. This dualistic way of perceiving the world is due to the fact that the mind is imperfect and imbued with intellectual and moral impurities.

Taking for granted the doctrinal expositions of the Mahāyāna, the tantric texts represent, however, a radical departure from mere intellectual discourses and traditional practices. They may be viewed to some degree as a mode of protest against, or a reaction to, both speculation and logic as means of explaining and rectifying the human situation. Their main thrust is to provide concrete practical steps towards one's personal deliverance. In order to achieve such a goal, they unveil their own particular methods of meditational and yogic practices, which are cast not as systematic and rationalized expositions, but rather as mystical visions and encounters, and as ritualized and magical activities that are geared towards the inducement of inner experience.

Tantric teachings and practices frequently represent transpositions from the rational expositions of Buddhist doctrines into personified and graded divine manifestations corresponding to various concepts and interacting with phenomena, or into ritualized activities which usually center on cosmic diagrams or mystic circles (*maṇḍala*) in which the deities and ritual implements are given symbolic values. One is to enact such spiritual encounters and ritual exercises in order to gain simultaneously both an insight into the true state of things and spiritual freedom. The encounter with and merging of the phenomenal and transcendental elements is often presented in terms of the cosmic manifestations and activities of buddhahood assumed as being pervasive of all spheres of existence. The steps leading to such an encounter are expressed in terms of particular types of meditation, visualization, tantric vows and consecration performed in connection with a variety of mystic circles, replete with appropriate sets of deities, or by making use, within the body, of the various psychic channels, called veins (*nādi, rtsa*) and nerve-centers, called wheels (*cakra, 'khor lo*) or lotuses, that serve as the foundation for one's spiritual reintegration[10] with the absolute. Tantric practice is thus a particular type of meditation in which one visualizes individual buddha manifestations or sets of deities with whom one attempts to achieve spiritual identity. The visualization of deities can be supplemented by concentration on the movement of trance-inducing winds within the psychic channels of one's body which are guided into the central vein, inducing thus a meditational ecstasy, styled as merging of the winds. Similarly, the practice can focus on the journey of the yogic drop (*bindu, thig le*), most frequently identified with the semen, which represents the thought of enlightenment and gradually descends and ascends through the stratified nerve-centers within the body, culminating its movement in a similar experience of ecstasy.

Along with the specifically tantric types of meditation, which aim not just to eliminate moral and intellectual imperfections but specifically to achieve identification with the absolute, the texts set forth a great number of other important and essential devices, such as bodily postures and hand gesture (*mudrā, phyag rgya*), verbal utterances, a variety of ritual implements, empowerments (*adhiṣṭhāna, byin gyis brlabs pa*) and initiations (*abhiṣeka, dbang bskur ba*), all of which are to help in accelerating the progress towards enlightenment.

The essential tantric practices are often conceived and devised in relationship to the three fundamental aspects or functions of human beings, namely the body, speech and mind. The physical postures and gestures relate to the body. The verbal utterances of different kinds, but in particular the great variety of *mantras* and seed syllables (*bīja, sa bon*) of the visualized deities, relate to the speech faculty, and meditational states correspond to the state of the mind. These three functions are correlated with similar but perfect functions of buddhahood personified and manifested as different Buddhist deities. It is the perfect fusion of the two that leads to the apotheosis of the human. Tantric initiations may be performed as meditational self-consecrations[11] or as externally performed rituals combined with meditation, in which the tantric masters bestow upon their disciples certain esoteric skills. These initiations are said to be endowed with inherent and efficacious powers that are considered essential to the practice and eventual attainment of the final goal.[12] Furthermore, use is made of astrology, magic and any other source of power that can help to advance one's spiritual progress.

The main textual symbology employed in the *tantras* often centers on sets of pairs that represent not just the apparent polarity of phenomenal existence and transcendent reality, but also, and principally, their fundamental nondual (*advaya, gnyis su med*) union. These two factors of spiritual reintegration are referred to as wisdom (*prajñā, shes rab*) and means (*upāya, thabs*), which in tantric texts are often represented as female and male deities embraced in sexual union (*yab yum*). This union may be experienced in meditational visualizations or practiced ritually through the union of the *yogin(ī)* with a human partner. It is also expressed through several other appropriate symbolic pairs, such as emptiness (*śūnyatā, stong pa nyid*) and compassion (*karuṇā, snying rje*), the moon and the sun, the vowels and the consonants, the left and the right psychic veins, the vajra and the bell, and so on.

The actual settings for tantric practices are described as solitary places, isolated trees or forests, temples, haunted cemeteries and various places of tantric power (*pītha, gdan*). The *tantras* do not hesitate to make use of any practice, whether seemingly moral or immoral, that is considered to be conducive to the achievement of a speedy spiritual realization. The lower *tantras* stress morality but occasionally instruct the disciple to contravene conventional morality in order to protect the tantric secrets. The Highest Yoga Tantra makes frequent use of the three fundamental obscurations, namely desire, hatred and delusion, as means of achieving deliverance. The various rituals, consecrations and initiations serve as powerful aids to breaking through the law of moral cause and effect (*karma, las*). The *tantras* assume that apart form the superficial body consisting of the five aggregates, one possesses a subtle body that should be fully developed in order to achieve a perfected *buddha*-body endowed with all the *buddha* attributes. It is the achievement of such a body through meditational, yogic and ritual devices that enables one to gain buddhahood speedily, even within a single lifespan.

The Tantric Language

As already stated, the tantric texts do make use of Mahāyāna terminology, but in general they tend to express their teachings through the use of their own symbols and enigmatic phraseology, which often require special interpretation and the aid of commentaries; this is particularly true of the texts belonging to the Highest Yoga class. The most problematic area for the study of the *tantras* is not so much their general theories and practices, but the language they employ.[13] The technical term for the literary language used by the *tantras* is variously translated as secret, enigmatic, esoteric or more often as intentional or twilight language (*sandhābhāṣā, dgongs pa'i skad*).[14] As already noted, the fundamental difficulty associated with such language is its interpretation. Since it makes use of analogy, double meanings, and rich, and at times far-fetched, symbology, it is difficult to establish the exact significance and meaning of words and whole passages. The deliberate use of intentional language is often justified on the grounds of preserving the secrecy of tantric teachings. It is possible, however, to explain its use as a peculiar mystical language whose intention is not to provide literal and concrete expositions, but to indicate or evoke particular psychic and spiritual trances that are to be attained. The language employed in the three lower *tantras* is fairly comprehensible, although its symbology remains complex. In the case of the Highest Yoga class, the language as such presents a major difficulty. It is in this category that extensive use is made of sexual language and symbology. There is no doubt that sexual symbology serves as a powerful method to express tantric intentions, whether or not the "Western mind" finds such extensive and often very graphic descriptions of sexual activities acceptable in a religious context.

The Highest Yoga Tantra met with little success in China and Japan, whereas in Tibet itself, the *tantras* in general, and the Highest Tantra in particular, were and are highly appreciated. However, it was only after the various objection-inspiring misconceptions were removed and a proper interpretation based on learned commentaries was worked out that they gained widespread acceptance in Tibet.

Notes

1. The decisive factors which had lasting consequences for Tibetan Buddhism were, of course, the religious and political complexities that persisted at the royal court during the early propagation (*snga dar*) of Buddhism in Tibet. The assassinations of Ral pa can (ca. 836 C.E.), and then of Glang dar ma in 842 C.E., led not only to the gradual dissolution of the Tibetan empire, but also to a changed position for Buddhism within Tibetan society. Some of the factors that affected the pattern of Tibetan Buddhism are epitomized by the debate at bSams yas, which produced tangible evidence for the existence in Tibet of different Buddhist traditions. The important thing to remember here is that during the early propagation of Buddhism in Tibet, the monkhood remained, or at least was treated, fundamentally as one community. With the revival of Buddhism and stress on religious lineages and spiritual transmissions during the later propagation (*phyi dar*), there developed a number of individual traditions, some of which succeeded in establishing themselves permanently as separate religious orders. The orders established during this second wave of Buddhism, jointly referred to as the new orders (*gsar ma pa*), are the bKa' brgyud pa, the Sa skya pa, and the dGe lugs pa.

2. Although the general formation of the bKa' 'gyur and its various editions is relatively well documented, there still remains a considerable amount of research to be done to establish the exact stages at which the bKa' 'gyur was compiled and edited. As is well known the decisive work of editing and arranging the bKa' 'gyur was carried out by Bu ston (1290-1364). Appropriate information and references on the formation of the bKa' 'gyur are provided in the article by Harrison in this volume. Much relevant information on the whole position of tantric texts in Tibet is to be found in D. L. Snellgrove's recent book (1987: 426-470); chapter 3 of that work represents a detailed study of the *tantras*.

3. The numbers 108 for the volumes of the bKa' 'gyur and 22 for the volumes of the Tantra section are conventional. The actual number of volumes differs, depending on the particular edition of the bKa' 'gyur.

4. Some important tantric texts proper, such as the "Compendium of the Essence of All the Tathāgatas," are also called *sūtra* texts, and some *sūtras*, such as the "Sūtra of Golden Light" (*Suvarṇaprabhāśa, gSer 'od dam pa*), which contain certain tantric elements, are included in both the Sūtra and the Tantra sections of the bKa' 'gyur. A number of *sūtras* which belong to the Perfection of Wisdom (*Prajñāpāramitā, Pha rol tu phyin pa*) literature are also included in the Tantra section of the bKa' 'gyur. For a list of such texts see Conze (1978: 79-92).

5. The *dhāraṇīs* are occasionally styled in their titles or colophons as both *dhāraṇīs* and *sūtras* and they are enunciated—like the *sūtras*—in different places visited by Śākyamuni Buddha during his lifetime, or in certain mythical localities. The *vidyārājñīs* comprise charms and incantations, and are also called *dhāraṇīs* or *vidyāmantras* (*mantras* of magical knowledge). On occasion,

the term *dhāraṇī* is replaced by *vidyādhāraṇī*, which, it has been suggested, appears to be a fuller form of which the *dhāraṇī* represents an abbreviation. Some *dhāraṇīs* are mere extracts from the important Mahāyāna works such as *Samādhirāja* (*Ting nge 'dzin gyi rgyal po*), *Laṅkavatāra* (*Lang kar gshegs pa*) and other *sūtras*. A fair number of *dhāraṇīs* are frequently named after buddhas, bodhisattvas or Buddhist deities.

6. This division is normally twofold, but some bKa' 'gyurs indicate further divisions. In the sDe dge bKa' 'gyur, for instance, the Tantra section is divided in the following manner: The "Collection of Tantras" (*rGyud 'bum;* Tōhoku Catalogue nos. 360-827 in 20 volumes), the "Old Tantras" (*rNying rgyud*: nos. 828-844 in 3 volumes), the "Commentary on the *Kālacakra*" (*Vimalaprabhā, Dus 'khor 'grel bshad;* no. 845 in 1 volume), and the "Formula Collection" (*gZungs 'dus;* nos. 846-1108 in 2 volumes). The exclusion, or inclusion, of the Old Tantras in some editions of the bKa' 'gyur provides a clear indication that the question of textual authenticity had not been definitely resolved. The Old Tantras refer here to the three volumes of texts excluded from the bKa' 'gyur by Bu ston but included in the *rNying ma'i rgyud 'bum*. The presence of the commentary on the *Kālacakra* also indicates that there exist inconsistencies and disagreements with regard to some texts as to whether they are commentaries written by certain authors or "revealed" Buddha-word.

7. According to a small work entitled *sGra sbyor bam po gnyis pa* ("On Word-Compounds in Two Chapters") and written during the reign of Sad na legs (ca. 800-815 C.E.), the translation of tantric work was prohibited without a special permission; see Simonsson (260-261) and Snellgrove (1987: 442-443). This, and other evidence, indicate that only the accepted translations of tantric texts executed during the first propagation of Buddhism are recorded in the "lDan dkar ma Catalogue" (Lalou: 326-328). The tantric works listed in it are divided into "Secret Mantras" (*gSang sngags;* nos. 316-328), "Great Magical Formulas" (*gZungs chen po;* nos. 329-333) and "Variety of Great and Smaller Formulas" (*gZungs che phra sna tshogs;* nos. 334-436). Without entering into details, it should be mentioned here that the bKa' 'gyur contains the tantric works translated during both propagations of Buddhism in Tibet.

8. Although Tibetan Buddhism inherited the largest collection of tantric texts, and despite being permeated by tantric theories and practices, it does not imply that the *tantras* were accepted without any reservations. See for instance Karmay: 150-162 and note 6 above.

9. At the end of each chapter in the Tibetan version this *tantra* is called *dPal heruka'i nges par brjod pa*. At the beginning of this *tantra* it is said: "Next I shall explain the secret. This will be done in a succinct rather than extensive manner." Perhaps this statement is meant to explain the term "short" (*laghu*) as part of its title.

10. This term has been coined by G. Tucci. See his *The Theory and Practice of the Maṇḍala*, especially chapter 2.

11. According to Abhayākaragupta's *Vajrāvali*, the self-consecration is performed when it is impossible to meet the teacher.

12. An interesting discussion on the efficacy of tantric initiations is to be found in Shinichi Tsuda's thought-provoking article, "A Critical Tantrism" (1978). Per Kvaerne's article (1975) contains much solid information on initiations and related subjects.

13. No doubt some of the tantric practices, especially those of the Highest Yoga Tantra such as the performance of sexual yoga, the use of flesh, blood, excrement, etc., and the apparent defiance of conventional morality, do provoke certain justifiable questions. However, taking into account the basic assumptions and mystical tendencies of the *tantras* and their cultural and religious milieu, it is possible to recognize the validity and the expediency of the tantric methods.

14. Intentional language has been discussed in many publications. One good discussion is chapter 6 of Bharati.

References

Bharati, Agehananda
1975 *The Tantric Tradition*. New York: Samuel Weiser.

Ch'en, Kenneth K. S.
1945-47 "The Tibetan Tripitaka." *Harvard Journal of Asiatic Studies* 9: 53-62.

Conze, Edward
1978 *The Prajñāpāramitā Literature*. Tokyo: The Reiyukai.

Eimer, Helmut
1983 *Some Results of Recent Kanjur Research*. Sankt Augustin: VGH Wissenschaftsverlag.

Fremantle, Francesca
1971 *A Critical Study of the Guhyasamāja Tantra*. Ph.D. dissertation. London: University of London.

George, Christopher S.
1974 *The Caṇḍamahāroṣanatantra, Chs I-VIII*. [Sanskrit and Tibetan Texts with English Translation.] New Haven: Oriental Society.

Imaeda, Y.
1977 "Mise au point concernant les éditions chinoises du Kanjur et du Tanjur tibétains." In *Essais sur l'art du Tibet*, pp. 23-43. Ed. by A. Macdonald and Y. Imaeda. Paris: Librairie d'Amérique et d'Orient.
1981 "Note sur le Kanjur de Derge." *Mélanges chinois et bouddhiques* 20: 227-236.

Karmay, Samten G.
1980 "The Ordinance of Lha bLa-ma Ye-shes-'od." In *Tibetan Studies in Honour of Hugh Richardson*, pp. 150-162. Ed. by M. Aris and A. S. Suu Kyi. Warminster: Aris and Phillips.

Kvaerne, Per
1975 "On the Concept of Sahaja in Indian Buddhist Tantric Literature." *Temenos* 11: 88-135.

Lalou, Marcelle
1953 "Les textes bouddhiques au temps du roi Khri-sroṅ-lde-bcan." *Journal asiatique* 241: 313-353.

Macdonald, A.
1962 *Le maṇḍala du Mañjuśrīmūlakalpa*. Paris: Adrien-Maisonneuve.

Simonson, N.
1957 *Indo-tibetische Studien, die Methoden der Tibetischen Übersetzer untersucht im Hinblick auf die Bedeutung ihrer Übersetzungen für die Sanskritphilologie*. Uppsala: Almqvist & Wiksells Boktryckeri.

Skorupski, Tadeusz
1983 *The Sarvadurgatipariśodhana Tantra: Elimination of All Evil Destinies*. [Sanskrit and Tibetan Texts with Introduction, English Translation and Notes.] Delhi: Motilal Banarsidass.
1985 "Śākyamuni's Enlightenment According to the Yoga Tantra." *Saṃbhāṣā* 6: 87-94.

Snellgrove, David L.
1959 *The Hevajra Tantra*. [Sanskrit Text, Tibetan Version and Commentary, and English Rendering.] 2 vols. London: Oxford University Press.
1987 *Indo-Tibetan Buddhism: Indian Buddhists and Their Tibetan Successors*. London: Serindia.

Tajima, R.
1937 *Étude sur le Mahāvairocanasūtra*. Paris: Maisonneuve.

Tsuda, Shinichi
1974 *The Samvarodaya-tantra (Selected Chapters)*. Tokyo.
1978 "A Critical Tantrism." *Memoirs of the Research Department of the Tōyō Bunko* 36: 167-231.

Tucci, Giuseppe
1961 *The Theory and Practice of the Maṇḍala*. London: Rider.

Chapter 5

Sūtra Commentaries in TibetanTranslation

Jeffrey D. Schoening

Sūtras and Buddhist *Sūtras*

Tibetans translated into Tibetan more than one hundred *sūtra* commentaries. In this essay, we shall make observations about this genre of literature and give some indication as to its value and significance to the Buddhist tradition. For specific examples, we shall refer primarily to the three Indian commentaries to the *Śālistamba Sūtra* (*SJD*). We shall limit our observations to commentaries translated into Tibetan, largely excluding from consideration those written by Tibetans, with the exception of a few of historical importance from ancient Tibet. The *sūtra* genre itself will be mentioned here primarily to contrast Buddhist *sūtra* commentaries with ritual and grammatical *sūtra* commentaries in India. Information derived from this contrast will help us to appreciate the relation of *sūtra* commentaries to *sūtras* in the Buddhist tradition.

In India, Buddhist and Jain *sūtras* formed a distinct genre of literature. This can best be seen by contrasting them with ritual, grammatical, and philosophical *sūtras*. The latter types of *sūtras*, often called "aphorisms," are a prose literature characterized by conciseness of formulation, mnemonic arrangement, and the fact that they are descriptive in nature. They are intended to present succinctly the rules or tenets of a discipline. Because of these *sūtras'* conciseness, commentaries are generally required to make sense of them. *Sūtras* and their commentaries probably began as part of an oral tradition of learning and were later written, though the question is undecided (Gonda: 648). Ritual and grammatical *sūtras* also had rules of interpretation called *paribhāṣā*, which, along with the careful ordering of the *sūtras*, contributed to their brevity. Finally, this literary genre is recognized to be unique to India.

Buddhist and Jain *sūtras* may be called "discourses." Leaving aside the Jain *sūtras*, those of the Buddhists bear little resemblance to ritual and grammatical *sūtras*. Although there do exist philosophical aphorisms in the Buddhist tradition, these are for the most part not known as *sūtras*. Instead, *sūtras*, or in Pāli, *suttas*, are considered by the Buddhist tradition to be the discourses of the Buddha, or at least inspired by the Buddha. These *sūtras* can and do mix verse with prose and, with the development of the Mahāyāna *vaipulya sūtras*, can be vast in size. Each Mahāyāna *sūtra* typically has four parts: a prologue (*nidāna, gleng gzhi*) with an opening formula that gives the time, place, and retinue of the Buddha when the discourse was spoken; an introduction of the topic of the discourse; a discourse or narration containing the bulk of the *sūtra*; and a formulaic conclusion. Because, unlike the ritual and grammatical *sūtras*, Buddhist *sūtras* are not exceedingly concise nor composed primarily for their mnemonic value (though they do contain features suggestive of an oral tradition—formulae and repeating structures), they do not require commentaries, but are more or less in the language of everyday discourse. They are meant as authoritative teachings of Buddhist doctrine that were spoken on a particular occasion, not as systematic summaries of a discipline. Thus, they are intended to be intelligible by themselves.

Therefore, whereas the ritual and grammatical *sūtras* are considered to have had commentaries from their beginning, the same cannot be said for Buddhist *sūtras*. Gonda observes that most ritual *sūtras* have commentaries and that their origin derives from "direct personal instructions of teachers who lived in close community with their pupils"(648). Compare this situation to Vasubandhu's urging anyone who wishes to comment upon a *sūtra* to greatly study, base oneself on study, and to accumulate learning (29a).[1] Vasubandhu, who wrote in the fourth or fifth century C.E., seems to be urging the would-be commentator to become broadly knowledgeable in Buddhist doctrine before writing any commentaries to *sūtras*. In that case, the *sūtra* commentary would not be based upon specific instructions about the *sūtra* passed down from teacher to student, but upon knowledge the commentator has been able to acquire through study, whether in an oral or written tradition, or some combination of both. In such a scenario, the commentary to a *sūtra* could be written any time after the *sūtra* came into existence, but would not accompany the *sūtra* from its origin.

Given the difference between the ritual and grammatical *sūtras* on the one hand and the Buddhist and Jain *sūtras* on the other, we well may wonder how the two literary genres could have the same name. Renou suggests the Buddhist use of the term *sūtra* may derive from the brief phrases that announce a dominant thesis, which is expanded upon and returned to in the large Buddhist *sūtras* (174). For example, the *SJD* begins with Śāriputra asking Maitreya the meaning of the following *sūtra* (and Śāriputra does indeed call the following statement a *sūtra* [*mdo*]) spoken by the Buddha: "*Bhikṣus*, he who sees dependent arising (*pratītyasamutpāda, rten cing 'brel par 'byung ba*) sees the Dharma. He who sees the Dharma sees the Buddha" (116a). The rest of the *SJD* is devoted to answering Śāriputra's question, with primary emphasis on describing dependent arising. In this way the *SJD*, when taken as a whole, can be seen to combine a *sūtra*, the Buddha's brief enigmatic statement, with its commentary, Maitreya's response to Śāriputra's question.

Translated *Sūtra* Commentaries in Tibet

Now let us turn our attention to Tibet. *Sūtra* commentaries were among the early translations into Tibetan. We know this from early catalogues such as the *Lhan* (or *lDan*) *kar ma* (*LKM*), which is preserved in the bsTan 'gyur, "translated treatises," which constitutes one half of the Tibetan Buddhist canon (the other half is the bKa' 'gyur, "translated word [of the Buddha]"; see Harrison and Martin, in this volume). This catalogue, compiled in a Dragon year such as 800, 812, or 824 C.E., after approximately one hundred and fifty years of Tibetan translations of Buddhist texts, is an inventory of treatises stored in the Lhan kar ma Palace in Tibet. Lalou, who has transcribed and indexed the *LKM*, records 736 titles[2] in thirty sections. Section twenty (nos. 514-564) contains the "Commentaries on Mahāyāna *Sūtras*"; section twenty-one (nos. 565-572) contains the "*Sūtra* Commentaries Translated from Chinese" (318). Of these sixty recorded in the *LKM*, approximately[3] half have been preserved in the bsTan 'gyur while the other half have been lost. Thus, fifty percent of the *sūtra* commentaries recorded in the *LKM* did not survive during the dark ages (ca. 840-1040 C.E.) between the early and later propagations of Buddhism in Tibet.

Eventually, Tibetan savants preserved translated *sūtra* commentaries in the bsTan 'gyur. The original Old sNar thang bsTan 'gyur dates back to the early fourteenth century. Bu ston Rin chen grub of Zhwa lu Monastery copied and expanded the bsTan 'gyur in 1335. All of the extant bsTan 'gyurs are descended from the Zhwa lu Monastery bsTan 'gyur and all of them have divided the *sūtra* commentaries into two sections: Prajñāpāramitā (Sher phyin), containing commentaries on the Prajñāpāramitā *sūtras*, and Sūtra Commentary[4] (mDo 'grel), containing commentaries on non-Prajñāpāramitā *sūtras*. Although the *LKM* did not divide the Mahāyāna *sūtras* into these same two sections, it did place the Prajñāpāramitā commentaries first among *sūtra* commentaries. Likewise, the *LKM* placed the Prajñāpāramitā *sūtras* before all other *sūtras*, a tradition continued in many of the extant bKa' 'gyurs.

Each of these two sections of the bsTan 'gyur contains about forty *sūtra* commentaries. However, not all *sūtra* commentaries are found in the Prajñāpāramitā and Sūtra Commentary sections; seven more can be found in the Tantra (rGyud),[5] Cittamātra (Sems tsam),[6] and Miscellany (sNa tshogs) sections. Three of the four *sūtra* commentaries in the Miscellany section are by Tibetans, for this section is reserved for writings of ancient Tibetans, and the fourth lists no author.[7] The compilers of the *LKM* included four or five (see the previous note) of these seven texts among the *sūtra* commentaries, but the editors of the bsTan 'gyur decided to place them in these other sections. Their placement in the Tantra and Cittamātra sections highlights the occasionally arbitrary nature of the classification of treatises as commentaries of *sūtra*, *tantra*, or Cittamātra treatises. For the most part, the Peking and sDe dge bsTan 'gyurs have the same *sūtra* commentaries, with some minor differences as to placement and total number. When the thirty *sūtra* commentaries lost since the compilation of the *LKM* are added to the ninety preserved in the bsTan 'gyur, we get a total of 120. Thus, of the more than one hundred *sūtra* commentaries translated into Tibetan, fewer than one hundred still exist.

One-tenth of the *sūtras* in the bKa' 'gyur, a mere thirty-four, have extant commentaries in the bsTan 'gyur. Eight Prajñāpāramitā *sūtras* have extant commentaries (a ninth whose commentary is lost is recorded in the *LKM*)[8]; approximately twenty-five non-Prajñāpāramitā *sūtras* have commentaries. The non-Prajñāpāramitā *sūtras* include four spells (*dhāraṇī, gzungs*),[9] three cherished recollections (*anusmṛti, rjes su dran pa*),[10] one verse (*gāthā, tshigs su bcad pa*) entitled *Ekagāthā*, one prayer (*praṇidhāna, smon lam*) entitled *Bhadracaripraṇidhāṇarāja*, and sixteen *sūtras* proper, for a total of twenty-five. Thus, *sūtra* in this context seems to mean "the word of the Buddha" (*buddhavacana*) rather than the genre of *sūtras* that have prologues, introductions, lengthy discourses, and conclusions. Seven *sūtras* that received one-third of the extant commentaries include some of the most famous, popular, or important. These are the *Hṛdaya* (with seven commentaries), *Vajracchedikā* (three), *Saddharmapuṇḍarīka* (one), *Bhadracaripraṇidhāna* (six), *Laṅkāvatāra* (two), *Saṃdhinirmocana* (five), and *Aṣṭasāhasrikāprajñāpāramitā* (six). Although all of these *sūtras* have been translated into Western languages, only some of these *sūtras'* commentaries have been analyzed with the results published. One example is Donald Lopez's study of Indian and Tibetan commentaries on the *Heart Sūtra* in which he summarized the seven Indian commentaries and translated two Tibetan commentaries.

Now let us take a closer look at the *sūtra* commentaries themselves. They range in length from several volumes (Haribhadra's *Pañcaviṃśatisāhasrikāprajñāpāramitā*, vols. *ga* to *ca*) to less than a folio (Asaṅga's *Dharmānusmṛtivṛtti*); some are in verse (*Śālistamba[ka]kārikā* [*SJT*]) while most are predominantly prose (Kamalaśīla's *Śālistambaṭika* [*SJGG*]); some discuss several immense *sūtras* (Smṛtijñānakīrti's **Śatasāhasrikāpañcaviṃśatisāhasrikāṣṭādaśasāhasrikātrayasamānārthāṣṭabhisamayaśāsanā*), others only a single verse (Vasubandhu's *Ekagāthābhāṣya*). Some comment upon entire *sūtras* (any of the *SJD* commentaries) and others only on parts of a *sūtra* such as the prologue (Śākya'i blo's **Daśabhūmisūtranidānabhāṣya*) or a chapter (Ye shes snying po's **Saṃdhinirmocanasūtre Āryamaitreyakevalaparivartabhāṣya*). Thus, the commentaries are not homogeneous.

One *sūtra* commentary has been the subject of more commentaries than any one of the *sūtras* themselves. The *Abhisamayālaṃkāra*, a systematic exposition in verse of the Mahāyāna path of deliverance based on the doctrines of the Prajñāpāramitā *sūtras* (in particular, on the *Pañcaviṃśatisāhasrikāprajñāpāramitā*, according to Ārya Vimuktisena) has inspired at least twenty commentaries. Tradition includes the *Abhisamayālaṃkāra*, which has been translated into English by Edward Conze, as one of the Five Treatises of Maitreya, a heavenly bodhisattva, but many scholars attribute the work to Asaṅga, fourth-fifth century C.E. The text has eight chapters, one for each of its eight subjects, which also become the organizing principle for most of its commentaries. The first and dominant subject is the Buddha's omniscience. Because the treatise is very concise, it is difficult to understand without its commentaries, not unlike the ritual *sūtras* of the non-Buddhists. In fact, it has more features in common with the ritual *sūtra* genre than with other Buddhist *sūtra* commentaries: Stcherbatsky describes the *Abhisamayālaṃkāra* as descriptive, summarizing Prajñāpāramitā doctrine and its practice; concise, requiring commentary to be understood; and mnemonic in arrangement (vi, viii). It has also had the most lasting impact of any *sūtra* commentary; it serves as a gateway for the study of Prajñāpāramitā *sūtras* by Tibetan Buddhists of all schools, whose savants have amply added over the centuries to the number of its commentaries. One noteworthy example is gYag ston Sangs rgyas dpal's (1348-1414) eight volume *gYag Ṭik* for the study of the Prajñāpāramitā.

The other *sūtra* commentaries exhibit various commentarial techniques. (Indigenous Tibetan typology of commentary includes, but is not limited to, the *tshig 'grel*, *mchan 'grel*, *don 'grel*, and *dka' 'grel*; see Wilson, in this volume.) Versifications such as the *SJT* summarize their *sūtras* and require commentaries to explain both *sūtra* and versification. Prose commentaries invariably explain the words and phrases of their *sūtras*, again to lesser and greater degrees. Kamalaśīla's *SJGG* comments upon the opening phrase of Buddhist *sūtras*, *evaṃ mayā śrutam ekasmin samaye*:

> In that [connection], by the expression "THUS" (*'di skad; evaṃ*), the compiler, having been supplicated, indicates all the contents of the *sūtra* that come below, in order to avoid disparagement (*skur pa; *apavāda*) and false attribution (*sgro 'dogs pa; *samāropa*).
>
> These two [words], "I HEARD" (*bdag gis thos pa; mayā śrutam*), indicate that I directly heard [the *sūtra* from the Buddha] and did not understand [its meaning]; I myself heard but [what was heard] is not hearsay coming through a lineage from one [person] to another. [It] was merely heard and not understood, because it is impossible that another besides the Buddha [could]

> understand a matter such as this. That also is a cause for inducing belief; otherwise, if an impossible matter were stated, it would not be believed.
>
> "ON ONE OCCASION" (*dus gcig na; *ekasmin samaye*) is joined to the above "heard"; "occasion" [means] either "time" or "gathering [of] the retinue," because of the great difficulty to hear such a precious *sūtra* anytime, anywhere. Also, "on one occasion" is joined to the following "the Blessed One resided"; this indicates that for the sake of infinite disciples, at other times the Blessed One resided at other [places]. (146b)

The next level of organization is for a commentary to follow its *sūtra*'s chapter arrangement or a set of topics for its organizing principle. A twofold example of this is Haribhadra's *Aṣṭasāhasrikāprajñāpāramitāvyakhyābhisamayālaṃkārālokā*, which includes the eight subjects from the *Abhisamayālaṃkāra* and follows the thirty-two chapters from the *Aṣṭasāhasrikāprajñāpāramitā*. More than thirty commentaries are organized along similar principles.

Many *sūtra* commentaries employ five terms in order to introduce their exposition: the "purpose" (*prayojana, dgos pa*), the "text" (*abhidhāna, rjod pa*), the "subject matter" (*abhidheya, brjod par bya ba*), the "connection" (*sambandha, 'brel pa*), and the "purpose of the purpose" (*prayojanaprayojana, dgos pa'i dgos pa*). Broido characterizes these terms as describing "the connection between the whole work and the general purposes for which it was written and is to be studied" (6). As far as he knows, the Indians had no single word for these terms whereas the Tibetans called them *dgos 'brel* ("purpose-connection") (6). Any number of the five terms may be found in a *sūtra* commentary, and they can be found in twenty-five of the commentaries, most often using four of the terms.

The relation of the five terms to the four *anubandhas*, which Huparikar describes as the four requisites at the beginning of a text that explain its purpose, may be quite simple. The Buddhists use the five introductory terms called *dgos 'brel* and certain non-Buddhists use the four *anubandhas* in order to introduce a text and its purpose. Three terms are similar: subject matter (*viṣaya* [non-Buddhist], *abhidheya* [Buddhist]), connection (*sambandha*), and purpose (*prayojana*) (121-122). Not surprisingly, in connection with the five terms, no Tibetan translation of the term *anubandha* is found in any of the *sūtra* commentaries.

Four of the five terms are used in the *SJGS*, a commentary to both the *SJT* and the *SJD*. After quoting and commenting on the verses (*kārikās*) as well as on many of the *sūtra*'s passages, it interprets both texts according to Yogācāra doctrine, thus bringing into question its traditional attribution to Nāgārjuna, who is credited with founding the Madhyamaka in approximately the second century C.E. The *SJGS*, whose organizing principle is the quoted verses from the *SJT*, is, however, encyclopedic in its descriptions of the Eightfold Path and its antithesis, the various realms, their inhabitants, the many localities of rebirth, the five aggregates, the Four Noble Truths, and so forth.

The *SJGS* gives us more information about its four introductory terms than most of the other commentaries that use them. It discusses at some length these four: the connection, the purpose, the text, and the subject matter. The commentary can be said to have a "connection" because it will explain the *SJD* and its *kārikā*; also, it is "connected" with the Buddha and not the works of non-Buddhists. Its "purpose" is—by understanding the meaning of causes and conditions, by realizing that persons and the factors of existence are selfless, and by realizing the absence of grasped and grasper—to become free of the obscurations of defilement and knowledge and so attain the supreme, truly complete buddhahood. Its "text" is the *Śālistamba*, which uses the example of a young rice plant (*śālistamba, sā lu ljang pa*) to link inner and outer dependent arising. Its "subject matter" is dependent arising, which is devoid of an agent and so forth, the understanding of which leads to the abandonment of defilement, the arising of wisdom, and the attainment of the Dharma Body (*dharmakāya, chos kyi sku*) (21b-22b). The omitted term is the "purpose of the purpose." It might also be translated as the ultimate purpose. It is the deeper purpose of the work and, according to Broido, is often more important than the purpose, though dependent upon it (7). However, the *SJGS* appears to combine the "purpose" with the "purpose of the purpose," since the stated "purpose" is so long and concludes with the attainment of buddhahood, a typical "purpose of the purpose."

Another commentarial system is explained in Vasubandhu's *Vyākhyāyukti* (*NR*), a treatise on how to explain and comment upon *sūtras*. He sets out five components to be included in a *sūtra* commentary: the purpose (*prayojana, dgos pa*), concise meaning (*piṇḍārtha, bsdus pa'i don*), meaning of the words (*padārtha, tshig gi don*), connections (*anusaṃdhi, mtshams sbyar ba*), and objections and answers (*codyaparihāradvaya, brgal ba/dang lan gnyis*) (30b). The "purpose" points to the goal or result of the treatise, the "concise meaning" to the meaning and subject of the treatise, the "meaning of the words" explains the concise meaning and so forth, the "connections" explains the order of the words, and the "objections and answers" uphold the treatise's logical and internal consistency. Even though Vasubandhu composed a number of *sūtra* commentaries, Kamalaśīla (late eighth century C.E.) is the author who most explicitly follows Vasubandhu's instructions. The best example is the *SJGG*, in which Kamalaśīla introduces the treatise according to the *NR*'s five components. He organizes the commentary according to a sevenfold concise meaning that conforms to Vasubandhu's directives in the *NR*. Eleven commentaries in all either mention or actually employ this fivefold method. Kamalaśīla wrote three of them: the *SJGG*, the *Avikalpapraveśadhāraṇīṭikā*, and the *Vajracchedikāṭīkā*.

As recorded by the Tibetan tradition, the authors of the *sūtra* commentaries include the greatest luminaries of India: Maitreya, Nāgārjuna, Asaṅga, Vasubandhu, Dignāga, and Śāntideva. However, the authenticity of the authorship of the first two authors is not accepted unequivocally, making Asaṅga the most venerable of the *sūtra* commentary authors credible to most modern scholars. The next oldest author, and most prolific in this category, is Vasubandhu, with nine commentaries. Some of the other authors of *sūtra* commentaries have only a single surviving work: Ārya and Bhadanta Vimuktisena, Dharmakīrtiśrī, Dharmamitra, Kumāraśrībhadra, Jaggatatālar gnas pa, Praśāstrasena, Śrīmahājana, Jñānadatta, Guṇamati, Śīlabhadra, Nyi ma grub, mDzes bkod, rGyan bzang po, and Yuan ts'e (Wen tshegs). Little is known about them. The authenticity of the attribution to later figures from the eighth and ninth centuries C.E. such as Kamalaśīla, Haribhadra, and Vimalamitra, who could have been alive when their works were translated into Tibetan, is more likely.

The *LKM* clearly identifies eight commentaries as translations from Chinese (332). Of these eight texts, only three survive in the bsTan 'gyur: the *Saṃdhigambhīranirmocanasūtraṭīkā* (= Lalou 565 according to Steinkellner [234]), *Saddharmapuṇḍarīkavṛtti* (= Lalou 567), and *Laṅkāvatāravṛtti* (= Lalou 568). Oddly, neither of the authors of the first two commentaries is Chinese: the first is Korean, Yuan ts'e (613-696 C.E.), according to Inaba (105), and the other, Pṛthivībandhu, Sinhalese, according to the colophon.[11] Steinkellner observes that these two treatises display the analytical system used by Tibetans of all epochs to structure their texts, the "divisions" or "sections" (*sa bcad*), a technique he has not been able to find in treatises of Indian origin; he concludes they are of Chinese origin (235).

According to the sDe dge catalogue, important translators of the *sūtra* commentaries include dPal brtsegs rakṣita and Ye shes sde (ca. 812) from the early spread of Buddhism in Tibet. Important translators of the Prajñāpāramitā *sūtra* commentaries include rNgogs lo tsā ba bLo ldan shes rab (1059-1109) and Rin chen bzang po (958-1055) from the later spread. More than forty *paṇḍitas* and translators translated *sūtra* commentaries.

Commentaries and Their *Sūtras*

What does a commentary tell us about its *sūtra*? On the one hand, in a direct manner, it interprets its *sūtra*, the meaning of its words, its purpose, and in some cases its perceived underlying organization. The commentary defends the statements of its *sūtra* or reframes them in a logically defensible manner. It may advance doctrinal positions not explicitly stated in its *sūtra* or be used to debate doctrinal points with contemporaries. Gómez has described a controversy between the proponents of sudden and gradual enlightenment that found expression in Kamalaśila's *Avikalpapraveśadhāraṇiṭikā*. Thus, the commentaries give us insight into the thoughts and contexts of their immediate authors and into the larger tradition of which they are a part. Because *sūtra* commentaries are written after the *sūtra*, not along with it, Eckel's comments on the *Heart Sūtra* commentaries are quite appropriate when he says they do not "yield the 'original' meaning" of the *sūtra* so much as "what a distinctive group of commentators thought it meant" (69). That is not to say that the commentaries are of no value for understanding their *sūtras*. They indeed help the reader to gain an understanding of their *sūtras*, but how are we to know that the understanding gained corresponds to that of the original meaning or that that was the commentator's purpose? We can count far more upon learning about the commentator and the meaning he (all the *sūtra* commentators are men) wished to convey (i.e., his interpretation as we interpet it) as well as the doctrinal issues and the received views of the tradition at his time.

In the relatively unstudied area of *sūtra* commentary, many problems still remain. For example, what was the relationship of the *sūtras* to their commentaries: what determined which *sūtras* received commentaries and which did not? What was the role of *sūtra* commentaries in the Buddhist world: were they written primarily in order for the authors to express their doctrinal views, to explain the *sūtras*, or for some other reason, and who was their audience? How innovative were the commentaries: to what extent did they rely on traditional interpretations of the *sūtras*? How did the Tibetans decide which commentaries to translate?

To summarize, Buddhist *sūtras* and their commentaries preserved in the bsTan 'gyur did not originate contemporaneously; the *sūtra* commentaries came later than their respective *sūtras*. Approximately one-tenth of the *sūtras* in the bKa' 'gyur have commentaries in the bsTan 'gyur, and the bsTan 'gyur has placed them in two sections: Prajñāpāramitā and Sūtra Commentary. The Sūtra Commentary section, which includes commentary upon spells, cherished recollections, and so forth, uses a broad definition of "*sūtra*." From among all the *sūtra* commentaries, the *Abhisamayālaṃkāra* is preeminent; in Tibetan Buddhism it has become the gateway for the study of Prajñāpāramitā. The commentaries employ different commentarial methods, and the authors, though primarily from India, include a Korean, a Sinhalese, and a few Tibetans. Finally, the genre is at least as valuable for what it indirectly tells us about the later tradition and the role of *sūtra* in it as for its interpretations of the *sūtras* themselves.

Notes

1. The Tibetan word translated as "study" and as "learning" is *thos pa*, which literally means "to hear." Nowadays scholars generally translate *thos pa* as "to study," which suggests to the modern reader the image of reading books and not the image of an oral tradition. It is not clear to which form of communication Vasubandhu was referring.

2. Lalou lists two titles under no. 557, so even though Lalou numbers the titles up to 736, the *LKM* actually lists 737 titles.

3. Some uncertainty exists because, while several of the titles in the *LKM* are similar to those in the bsTan 'gyur, the scanty information given in the catalogue makes positive identification difficult.

4. By "Sūtra Commentary" with capital letters is intended a section in the bsTan 'gyur and should not be confused with "*sūtra* commentary" in small letters, which refers to *sūtra* commentaries generally.

5. The Tantra section has two: the *Anantamukhanirhāradhāraṇīvyākhyānakārikā* (= Lalou 551) and the *Anantamukhanirhāradhāraṇīṭikā* (= Lalou 550).

6. The Cittamātra section has one: the **Saṃdhinirmocanasūtre Āryamaitreya-kevalaparivartabhāṣya* (= Lalou 532).

7. The first three commentaries with authors are: sDe dge 4352, *bKa' yang dag pa'i tshad ma las mdo btus pa* by Khri srong lde btsan; sDe dge 4358, *dGongs pa nges par 'grel pa'i mdo'i rnam par bshad pa*, by Byang chub rdzu 'phrul, an alias of Khri srong lde btsan, though Steinkellner follows Bu ston and suggests this text may be the same as Lalou 531 by kLu'i rgyal mtshan (236-241); and sDe dge 4359 (= Lalou 563), *bZang spyod kyi 'grel pa bzhi'i don bsdus nas brjed byang du byas pa* by Ye shes sde. The one commentary without an author is sDe dge 4365, *Don rnam par gdon mi za ba'i 'grel pa*, a commentary on the *Arthaviniścaya Sūtra*.

8. The eight Prajñāpāramitā *sūtras* are: *Śatasāhasrikā*, with four commentaries; *Pañcaviṃśatisāhasrikā*, with six; *Aṣṭadaśasāhasrikā*, with two; *Aṣṭasāhasrikā*, with six; *Sañcayagāthā*, with three; *Vajracchedikā*, with three; *Hṛdaya*, with seven; and *Saptaśatikā*, with two. The *LKM* records two commentaries now lost, Lalou 523 and 524, for the *Nayaśatapañcaśatikā* (331).

9. The four spells are the *Anantamukhasādhakadhāraṇī*, the *Saṇmukhadhāraṇī*, the *Avikalpapraveśadhāraṇī*, and the *Gāthādvayadhāraṇī*.

10. The three cherished recollections, the *Buddhānusmṛti*, the *Dharmānusmṛti*, and the *Saṃghānusmṛti*, are of the Three Jewels: Buddha, Dharma, and Saṃgha.

11. The colophon gives *sing ga la'i slon po sa'i rtsa lag* (Siṅhalese Pṛthivībandhu) as the author.

References

Broido, Michael M.
1983 "A Note on *dgos-'brel*." *Journal of the Tibet Society* 3: 5-19.

Eckel, Malcolm D.
1987 "Indian Commentaries on the *Heart Sūtra*: The Politics of Interpretation." *Journal of the International Association of Buddhist Studies* 10/2: 69-79.

Gómez, Luis O.
1983 "Indian Materials on the Doctrine of Sudden Enlightenment." In *Early Ch'an in China and Tibet*, pp. 393-434. Ed. by W. Lai and L. R. Lancaster. Berkeley: Asian Humanities Press.

Gonda, Jan
1977 *The Ritual Sūtras*. A History of Indian Literature. Vol. 1: Veda and Upanishads. Fasc. 2. Ed. by Jan Gonda. Wiesbaden: Otto Harrassowitz.

gYag ston Sangs rgyas dpal
1985 *g.Yag Ṭīk: The Complete Yig cha for the Study of the Prajñāpāramitā*

Literature. 8 vols. Manduwala, Dehra Dun: Pal Ewam Chodan Ngorpa Centre.

Huparikar, G. S.
1949 *The Problem of Sanskrit Teaching*. Kolhapur City (India): Bharat Book-stall.

Inaba, Shōju
1977 "On Chos-grub's Translation of the *Chieh-shên-mi-ching-shu*." In *Buddhist Thought and Asian Civilization: Essays in Honor of Herbert V. Guenther on His Sixtieth Birthday*, pp. 105-113. Ed. by Leslie S. Kawamura and Keith Scott. Emeryville: Dharma Publishing.

Kamalaśīla
SJGG *Śālistambaṭīkā; Sā lu ljang pa rgya cher 'grel pa*. In the sDe dge bsTan 'gyur, facsimile edition published in Delhi, vol. *ji*, Toh. no. 4001, ff. 145b-163b.

Lalou, Marcelle
1953 "Les texts bouddhiques au temps du roi Khri-sroṅ-lde-bcan." *Journal asiatique* 241/3: 313-354.

LKM *Pho brang stod thang lhan dkar gyi chos 'gyur ro cog gi dkar chag*. In the sDe dge bsTan 'gyur, facsimile edition published in Delhi, vol. *jo*, Toh. no. 4364, ff. 294b-310a.

Lopez, Donald S., Jr.
1988 *The Heart Sūtra Explained: Indian and Tibetan Commentaries*. Albany: State University of New York Press.

Renou, Louis
1963 "Sur le genre du *sūtra* dans la littérature sanskrite." In *Journal asiatique* 251/2: 165-216.

SJD *Śālistambanāmamahāyānasūtra ; Sā lu ljang pa zhes bya ba'i theg pa chen po'i mdo*. In the sDe dge bKa' 'gyur, facsimile edition published in Delhi, vol. *tsha*, Toh. no. 210, ff. 116a-123b.

SJT *Śālistamba[ka]kārikā; Sā lu ljang pa'i tshig le'ur byas pa*. In the sDe dge bsTan 'gyur, facsimile edition published in Delhi, vol. *ngi*, Toh. no. 3985, ff. 18a-20b.

SJGS *Śālistamka[ka]mahāyānasūtraṭīkā; Sā lu ljang pa zhes bya ba theg pa chen po'i mdo'i rgya cher bshad pa*. In the sDe dge bsTan 'gyur, facsimile edition published in Delhi, vol. *ngi*, Toh. no. 3986, ff. 20b-55b.

Stcherbatsky, Th.
1929 *Abhisamayālankāra* [sic] *prajñāpāramitā-upadeśaśāstra: The Work of Bodhisattva Maitreya*. Fasc. 1. Bibliotheca Buddhica 23. Coauthored with E. Obermiller. Osnabrück: Biblio Verlag, 1970.

Steinkellner, E.

1989 "Who is Byaṅ chub rdzu 'phrul? Tibetan and non-Tibetan Commentaries on the *Saṃdhinirmocanasūtra*—A Survey of the Literature." *Berliner Indologische Studien* 4/5: 229-251.

Tohoku

1934 *A Complete Catalogue of the Tibetan Buddhist Canons (Bkaḥ-'gyur and bstan-ḥgyur)*. Ed. by Hakuju Ui, Munetada Suzuki, Yenshō Kanakura, Tōkan Tada. Sendai: Tōhoku Imperial University.

Vasubandhu

NR *Vyākhyāyukti; rNam par bshad pa'i rigs pa*. In the sDe dge bsTan 'gyur, facsimile edition published in Tokyo, vol. *shi*, Toh. no. 4061, ff. 29a-134b.

Chapter 6

Tibetan Commentaries on Indian *Śāstras*[1]

Joe Bransford Wilson

> ...while it is not accurate to say that an interpretation is helplessly dependent on the generic conception with which an interpreter happens to start, it is nonetheless true that his interpretation is dependent on the last, unrevised generic conception with which he starts. All understanding of verbal meaning is necessarily genre-bound.
>
> —E. D. Hirsch[2]

This paper begins an exploration of the application of genre analysis to Tibetan commentaries on Indian exegetical works (*śāstras*). Although here only philosophical works will be considered, the *śāstras*, as extant in translation in the Tibetan Buddhist canon (see below), cover—in Western terms—not only traditional philosophical areas such as metaphysics, epistemology, logic and rhetoric, and cosmology, but also poetics, grammar, monastic discipline, and medicine. (For a more complete discussion, see Bu ston, *DTSCB*: 17a.) Tibetan scholars have been prolific writers of commentaries on the *śāstras*, explaining works such as Vasubandhu's *Abhidharmakośa*, Dharmakīrti's *Pramāṇavārttika*, and Candrakīrti's *Madhyamakāvatāra*. This trend is seen most readily in Sa skya and dGe lugs writers, and less so among bKa' brgyud and rNying ma authors.[3]

The Buddhist Canon

It has been argued that Buddhism does not have a canon in the sense that canon is understood in the Abrahamic religions (Corless: 212-215). It is certainly the case that the Mahāyāna canon was an open one even in India and continues to be so in the Tibetan tradition (Lancaster: 505); this is especially the case in terms of the *gter ma* ("treasure texts"; see Gyatso, in this volume). It is also the case that the Buddhist canon is not seen as an exclusive revelation granted to humans by an extra-human divine being, as is the canonical literature of Judaism, Christianity, and Islam. The principal dissimilarity with the Abrahamic sense of canon, however, stems from the central hermeneutical principle of Buddhism—that the ultimate significance of a scriptural text lies neither in its literal meaning nor in the person from whom it comes, but rather in its ability to generate an awakening to reality (Thurman, 1978; Gómez: 535-536). As Roger Corless succinctly puts it, "The center of Buddhism is not the word of the Buddha, nor even the Buddha. It is bodhi, the enlightened mind.... The text is, in the final analysis, expendable in favor of the practitioner's own bodhi" (213). Corless encapsulates the principle behind the well-known four reliances (*rton pa bzhi*) that are the foundation of Tibetan Buddhist hermeneutics—to rely on doctrines and not on persons, on the meaning of those doctrines in preference to the words, on the definitive meanings in preference to those requiring interpretation, and on nonconceptual wisdom in preference to conceptual knowledge (Thurman, 1978; Hopkins: 425; Thurman, 1984: 113ff.; Gómez: 535-536). This must nonetheless be balanced with the observation that an appeal to a scripture's provenance has been very important, both in India and Tibet. Later Indian and Tibetan Buddhists justified the claim that the Mahāyāna *sūtras* and *tantras* were canonical by citing the claim (made in the texts themselves) that they were the actual teachings of Buddha.

With this in mind, let me offer the following as a tentative minimal definition of "canon": a list or group of texts that are accorded special status because of their perceived authority, an authority attributed either to their source(s) or their transformative ability, but most often to both. Such "transformative ability" in the ultimate sense (in Buddhism) would be salvific: the ability of a text to enable one who hears or reads it to successfully engage in the practice of meditation leading to nonconceptual wisdom realizing emptiness (*śūnyatā*). Less ultimate aims would be the successful practice of morality or the development of compassion. In terms of texts that deal with philosophical issues, a more mundane sort of transformative ability is seen in the explicatory power of an exegetical treatise. In a more traditionally ritual sense, transformative ability may also be seen in the recitation of a text, for example a Prajñāpāramitā *sūtra*, for the sake of alleviating illness.

There was, in Indian Buddhism, a three-part canon, the Tripiṭaka or "three baskets" (see Harrison, in this volume) consisting of the Sūtras (the discourses given by Śākyamuni Buddha during his forty-five year teaching career), the Vinaya (rules of conduct for the monastic community extracted from Śākyamuni's teachings), and the Abhidharma (the "higher teaching," systematic presentations and analyses of Buddha's teachings). Of these two categories of texts, only the first two are actual *buddhavacana* or "words of the Buddha" (see Hirakawa: 509ff.). Thus, even within the most basic canon, the three baskets, there is a hierarchy of privilege, with the Sūtras being accorded more authority than the Abhidharma.

With the rise of Mahāyāna Buddhism, even more *buddhavacana* was recognized—beginning with the Prajñāpāramitā *sūtras* and continuing in the *tantras*—and these were accorded an even higher status than the earlier *sūtras* by followers of the Mahāyāna (see Skorupski, in this volume). Additionally, texts explaining the Sūtra and Vinaya texts were written—the *śāstras* or "exegetical works"—and these also attained canonical status, not only through their explicatory power but also through their authorship by writers remembered by later Buddhists not only as philosophers but also as meditation masters. It is these texts—those current in later Indian Buddhism—that became the basis of the canon of Tibetan Buddhism. *Buddhavacana* became the bKa' 'gyur (literally "Word-translation") and the *śāstras* became the bsTan 'gyur ("teaching/treatise-translation").

It is, therefore, inappropriate to maintain that some of these texts are canonical whereas others are "quasi-canonical." It is more accurate to say that there is a hierarchy of canonical texts in Tibetan Buddhism, with the status of individual less-privileged, lower-ranked texts (for example, the *śāstras*) shifting in dependence on who is doing the ranking.

The Role of *Śāstras* in Tibetan Buddhism

Although *sūtras* are at the core of the scriptural dimension of Chinese Buddhism, this is not the case in Tibetan Buddhism. First, by far the greatest amount of literature is on the *tantras*. Secondly, the literature that is not explicitly tantric is not principally an attempt to explicate the *sūtras* per se, but rather their Indian exegeses (which are included among the *śāstras*; see Schoening, in this volume). Thus, instead of writing commentaries on the Perfection of Wisdom *sūtras* themselves, in most cases Tibetan expositions of the path to awakening as seen in these *sūtras* (an area called by the name "Perfection of Wisdom"—*phar phyin* [*prajñāpāramitā*]) are commentaries on Maitreyanātha's *Abhisamayālaṃkāra* which is itself a commentary on the Prajñāpāramitā *sūtras*. One can thus argue that a typical Tibetan commentarial treatise is actually a sub-commentary, or even a commentary on a sub-commentary.

A look at the Collected Works (*gsung 'bum*) of 'Jam dbyangs bzhad pa (1648-1721) is instructive in this regard. There are many commentaries on *tantras*, none on *sūtras*, and about half of the total number of pages are on non-tantric philosophical subjects, including free-standing works on individual issues and on tenets, and commentaries on Indian *śāstras*. 'Jam dbyangs bzhad pa is a scholar known for his extremely complex *Grub mtha' chen mo* (or "Great Exposition of Tenets")—in which he attempts to avoid the over-generalization characteristic of the tenets (*grub mtha'*) literature through carefully examining his Indian sources book-by-book (instead of school-by-school) and in some cases in terms of the development of an author's thinking from youth through maturity (see Hopkins, in this volume). An examination of his collected works yields the following breakdown. Of a total of 143 separately titled works, 50 are on *śāstras* or tenets, with the remainder covering monastic discipline and monastery regulations, practice of the path to enlightenment, prayers, rituals, liturgies, meditation on the guru as Buddha (*guru yoga*), poetry, lexicography, grammar, history, visionary experience, and biography. There are 26 separately titled commentaries on the tantras of Guhyasamāja, Cakrasaṃvara, and Vajrabhairava, not including his two-part, 400-folio commentary on Vajrabhairava. Of a total of 6,343 folios, only about half are found in non-tantric commentaries on Indian texts. His *śāstra* commentaries include major analyses of Dharmakīrti's

Pramāṇavārttika, the *Abhisamayālaṃkāra* (attributed to Maitreyanātha), Vasubandhu's *Abhidharmakośa*, and Candrakīrti's *Madhyamakāvatāra*. Additionally, he wrote a major commentary on meditation theory (the *dhyānas* and *samāpattis*), a work on the four truths, a work on interdependent arising (*pratītyasamutpāda*)—all part of the perfection of wisdom curriculum—as well as books on hermeneutics and a number of introductory textbooks on philosophy, logic, and allied subjects.

The Fundamental *Śāstras*

'Jam dbyangs bzhad pa's works provide a general overview of the concerns of many Tibetan authors who have devoted themselves, at least in part, to writing on *śāstras*. In his autobiographical *Lectures on Tibetan Religious Culture*, Geshe Sopa speaks of his education at the Byes College of Se ra Monastery near Lhasa. He lists there the five major areas of study—Perfection of Wisdom (Prajñāpāramitā), Middle Way Philosophy (Madhyamaka), Monastic Discipline (Vinaya), Advanced Doctrine (Abhidharma), and Epistemology (Pramāṇa)—and the texts that he studied (Sopa: 42-43; see also Rabten: 47-49):

(1) Maitreyanātha's *Abhisamayālaṃkāra* on Perfection of Wisdom, pertaining to which there are twenty Indian commentaries (the chief of which is by Haribhadra);
(2) Candrakīrti's *Madhyamakāvatāra* on Middle Way philosophy and ontology in general, as well as the works of Nāgārjuna;
(3) Vasubandhu's *Abhidharmakośa* on "advanced doctrine" (although the most accurate doctrine, as perceived by most Tibetans, is that of Candrakīrti's *Madhyamakāvatāra*);
(4) Dharmakīrti's *Pramāṇavārttika* on epistemology.

These texts are at the core of the dGe lugs pa study of *śāstra* literature.

A different set of texts forms the basis of the recent *śāstra* curriculum of the schools of the rNying ma Order: the thirteen great texts (*gzhung chen*) (Tulku Thondup: 81-82).[4] Two are on Vinaya and so will not be treated in this study of *śāstras* on philosophical subjects. The remaining eleven of the great texts are the following *śāstras*:

(1-2) Asaṅga's *Abhidharmasamuccaya* and Vasubandhu's *Abhidharmakośa*—on advanced doctrine;
(3-5) Nāgārjuna's *Mūlamadhyamakakārikā*, Candrakīrti's *Madhyamakāvatāra*, and Āryadeva's *Catuḥśataka*—on the philosophy of Madhyamaka;
(6) Śāntideva's *Bodhicaryāvatāra* on *bodhisattvas'* practice;
(7-11) the five books attributed to Maitreya: the *Abhisamayālaṃkāra*, *Mahāyānasūtrālaṃkāra*, *Madhyāntavibhaṅga*, *Dharmadharmatāvibhaṅga*, and *Uttaratantra* (also known as the *Ratnagotravibhāga*).

There are modern commentaries (of the *mchan 'grel* or annotation type) on some of the thirteen great texts by Mi pham Phyogs las rnam rgyal (1846-1912) and on all thirteen by gZhan phan chos kyi snang ba (1871-1927).[5]

Note that both lists include the *Abhidharmakośa*, the *Madhyamakāvatāra*, and the *Abhisamayālaṃkāra*. Additionally, the *Bodhicaryāvatāra* is a work whose study is important to all lineages of Buddhism in Tibet, although it is not always explicitly included in scholastic curricula.

Criteria for Genre Distinctions

The category of Tibetan philosophical commentaries is too extensive to be considered a genre—in much the same way as theological and philosophical literature in the West: such commentaries comprise a type of literature only in the broadest sense, and those who are unaware of the many significantly different genres seen among commentarial works risk misreading those texts. There are three basic criteria for genre difference in Tibetan commentarial literature, all of which are usually operative in any given text.

(1) Genre in a more clearly literary sense is defined by the style, or format, of the commentary. Three of the more frequently seen formats are annotation commentaries (*mchan 'grel*), critical analyses (*mtha' dpyod*), and general expositions (*spyi don*).

(2) If we define "genre" (following E. D. Hirsch) as "that sense of the whole by means of which an interpreter can correctly understand any part in its determinacy" (86), it is not trivial to say that it is necessary to know, when one is reading a commentary on the *Pramāṇavārttika*, that one is reading an analysis or exposition of that work and not an explanation of the *Abhidharmakośa*. The philosophical jargon of Indian Buddhism is relatively homoge-

neous, with innovation occurring more often in the interpretation of extant terms than in the coining of new ones. Thus, even simple terms (perhaps *especially* simple terms) such as *dravya* (Tib. *rdzas*, "substance" or "substantial entity"), *bhava* (*dngos po*, "thing, phenomenon"), and *nairātmya* (*bdag med*, "lack of self, selfless") are, in important ways, used differently by Dharmakīrti and Vasubandhu, the authors of the above texts.

(3) Finally, and in a sense as a corollary to the second defining criterion, genres are also delimited by perceptions about the primary text brought to it by the author (and the reader, if the reader is a Tibetan who is part of the oral tradition of explication based on that commentary). For better or worse, Tibetan Buddhist philosophers (influenced by tendencies already present in Indian Buddhism) have seen Indian texts not only as products of their authors, but also as the products of normative views of reality associated not only with those authors but with an entire school. The verses of Vasubandhu's *Abhidharmakośa* are thus read as a presentation of the tenets of the Vaibhāṣika school, whereas his autocommentary (that is, the *rang 'grel*—a generic name for a commentary composed by an author upon a text of which he is also the author) is read as a subtle Sautrāntika critique of the Vaibhāṣika position. Thus, from the point of view of a reader who is part of a Tibetan tradition of exegesis (which, historically, have combined both written and oral explanation), a Tibetan commentary on the *Abhidharmakośa* must be read with Sautrāntika and not Mādhyamika expectations.

Thus, the genre of a commentary is defined by (1) the format in which the commentary is written, (2) the basic text upon which it is a commentary or subcommentary, and (3) the school(s) of doctrine associated (by Tibetan writers and readers) with commentary on that basic text.

The first criterion—the style of the commentary—will be discussed in the next section. The second criterion, that the basic text which a commentary explains helps to define the genre into which that commentary should be classified, has three facets. First, as mentioned, whereas the technical language of Buddhist philosophy has, in a relatively conservative way, remained stable, the meanings of the terms have changed over time. (It is an awareness of differences in the application of terminology—that is, in definition [*mtshan nyid*, which, thus, also means "philosophy"]—that is at the basis of the Tibetan taxonomy of Indian Buddhist and non-Buddhist philosophies invoked in the third criterion for genre.) Even such a basic distinction as that between existence as a substantial entity (*dravya*) and existence as an imputation (*prajñapti*) was construed in different ways by Nāgārjuna in the second century, Vasubandhu in the fourth century, and Haribhadra in the eighth century. Secondly, Buddhist writers did utilize different terminology in their works. Some of the terminology that Nāgārjuna inherited from the philosophers of his day was rejected by later writers such as Vasubandhu, along with belief in the existence of the phenomena which that terminology was constructed to describe. Finally, different Indian texts (the bases of the Tibetan commentaries) have different agenda. One of the primary concerns of Vasubandhu's *Abhidharmakośa*, for example, is to locate phenomena according to the "level" at which they are found (that is, in the *kāmadhātu*, *rūpadhātu*, or *ārūpyadhātu*—the Desire, Form, or Formless Realms) and to criticize what it perceives as an over-proliferation of substances in earlier Abhidharma literature. Haribhadra's *Abhisamayālaṃkārāloka*, on the other hand, is concerned primarily with the systematic analysis of paths to enlightenment. Nāgārjuna's *Mūlamadhyamakakārikā* tends to accept without criticism many of the phenomena that Vasubandhu came to question two centuries later, but engages in a radical critique of their mode of existence. Thus, this criterion for defining commentarial genres suggests that the reader ought to approach the commentary in question with an awareness of the agenda of the Indian text that is its basis and of the terminology employed. This is not only a necessary condition for "correct understanding" of the commentary in Hirsch's sense, but is also necessary for recognition of those instances in which Tibetan authors are modifying the agenda and bringing in issues and terminology of their own.

The third criterion for genre implies that a dGe lugs pa commentary on Nāgārjuna's *Mūlamadhyamakakārikā*, for example, should be read—barring internal evidence to the contrary—with the assumption that Candrakīrti's Prāsaṅgika interpretation of Nāgārjuna's Mādhyamika is its normative stance (*rang lugs*, literally "own system"). A Tibetan commentary on the *Abhisamayālaṃkāra*, on the other hand, will normally be based on the interpretive viewpoint of the most influential later Indian commentary on that treatise, the *Abhisamayālaṃkārāloka*, a work written by Haribhadra from what is known in the Tibetan tradition as the Yogācāra-Svātantrika Mādhyamika standpoint.

This is not to say that the twentieth-century reader should uncritically assume that Nāgārjuna's *Mūlamadhyamakakārikā* is, in fact, a work written from the Prāsaṅgika viewpoint. (If nothing else, this is anachronistic, given that the Prāsaṅgika philosophy was constructed by Candrakīrti as a critique of Bhāvaviveka's sixth-century interpretation of Nāgārjuna.) That notwithstanding, the genre consisting of Tibetan commentaries on early Indian Mādhyamika texts such as the *Mūlamadhyamakakārikā* is made of works which, typically, are *themselves* identified as being written from a Prāsaṅgika standpoint. Likewise, the genre of Tibetan commentaries on Prajñāpāramitā—that is, on the *Abhisamayālaṃkāra*—is made up of texts which, at least heuristically, assume a Yogācāra-Svātantrika perspective.

Bu ston's Taxonomy of Commentaries

The first criterion for recognizing a genre within commentarial works is the style or format in which such a work is written. Bu ston, in his *Chos 'byung* ("History of Buddhism") enumerates five main types of subcommentaries (*bka' la mi brten pa'i bstan bcos*) (*DTSCB*: 22a.4-7): (1) extensive commentaries (*rgya cher 'grel ba*) in which both the words and the meaning of the basic text are elaborated; (2) word commentaries (*tshig 'grel*) in which the lexical components of a text (that is, the words or syllables) are explained; (3) commentaries on difficult points (*dka' 'grel*) in which the points in the basic text that are difficult to understand are explicated; (4) commentaries in which the topics of the basic text are condensed into an abbreviated format (*bsdus don gyi 'grel pa*); (5) commentaries merely on the verbal significance of a basic text (*ngag don tsam gyi 'grel pa*).[6] His taxonomy of commentaries (*bka' la brten pa'i bstan bcos*) seems more theoretical and less helpful (*DTSCB*: 22a.7-22b.1): (1) commentaries (such as the *Abhisamayālaṃkāra*) completely presenting the meaning of a single scripture; (2) commentaries which explicate systematically what is scattered (Obermiller: 58); and (3) commentaries (such as Śāntideva's *Śikṣāsamuccaya*) which explicate the meaning of many scriptures.

Bu ston is really speaking of canonical Indian commentaries, whereas our concern is with Tibetan literature. However, there are some clear parallels between genres of Tibetan commentaries and Bu ston's list of subcommentaries. If Tibetan commentaries on Abhidharma (especially on the *Abhidharmakośa*) are examined, examples of four of the five types may be found.

(1) Extensive commentaries are quite common in Tibet; some are called such, while others (at least among the dGe lugs pa) are included in the genre of critical analyses (*mtha' dpyod*). An example of the first is the lengthy two-volume commentary on the *Abhidharmakośa* by the eighth Karma bKa' brgyud patriarch Mi bskyod rdo rje (1507-1554) which is labelled a *'grel pa rgyas par spros pa* ("extensively elaborating commentary") (*CNDGDP*). An example of the second is 'Jam dbyangs bzhad pa's 675-folio commentary on the *Kośa* (*CNDGZK*).

(2) Bu ston's term, "word commentary," is sometimes used by Tibetan writers, but more often seen is the *mchan 'grel* (commentary of annotations). These are commentaries in which the words of a basic text are printed either with small circles under them or in a larger size than the surrounding text, that surrounding text being an expansion on the words and/or syllables of the basic text. gZhan phan's thirteen annotation commentaries have already been noted.

(3) Commentaries on difficult points (*dka' 'grel*) are sometimes seen in Tibetan literature; an Abhidharma example is bSod nams grags pa's (1478-1554) commentary on Asaṅga's *Abhidharma-samuccaya* (*CNKKYP*).

(4) Commentaries which focus on the main points of a text are fairly common. One type is the *spyi don* (presentations of the "general significance" of a basic text). These are not actually abbreviations or condensations of the basic text, however; what makes them "general" is that they do not for the most part engage in the detailed polemical critique seen in their critical analysis counterparts. Thus, rJe btsun pa's *spyi don* on the *Kośa* (*CNDKLS*—labelled in the Library of Congress description a "general introduction") expands considerably on the basic verses of the *Kośa*; rJe btsun pa's textbooks serve as the core of the curriculum of Byes College of Se ra Monastery.

(5) Another type of general commentary is a true condensation of the meaning of the basic text. An example is one of the textbooks used in the sMad College of Se ra Monastery, rGyal dbang chos rje Blo bzang 'phrin las rnam rgyal's verse condensation (*sdom tshigs* or *sdom gyi tshigs su bcad pa*) presentation of the basic verses and autocommentary on the *Kośa* (*CNDMSG*).

I have, in this brief essay, attempted to indicate how genre analysis might be applied to Tibetan commentaries on Indian exegetical works. Such an analysis might include an examination into the ways in which commentaries belonging to different genres elucidate one uncomplicated but significant passage from a basic text. What would need to be examined is the extent to which later commentaries build on earlier works, the extent to which novelty is seen in later commentaries, and—especially—the extent to which application of the three criteria for genre definition is actually necessary for a valid interpretation of the text.

Notes

1. Funding for research necessary to complete this chapter was provided by the Department of Philosophy and Religion and the Faculty Research and Development Fund of the University of North Carolina at Wilmington. The author wishes also to acknowledge the assistance of the late Richard B. Martin, Bibliographer of Buddhism and Curator of the Tibetan Collection at the University of Virginia, without whose labors in cataloging and expertise in bibliographic literature the research presented in the present essay would not have been possible. Conversations with Jeffrey Hopkins (of the University of Virginia) provided insights into some of the aspects of philosophical genre spoken of here, and electronic conversations with Richard Hayes (of McGill University) provided insight into Indian Abhidharma.

2. *Validity in Interpretation*, p. 76.

3. For example, neither Klong chen rab 'byams nor 'Jigs med gling pa—who rank among the most respected scholars in the rNying ma tradition—wrote commentaries on the Indian Buddhist *śāstras*. Their other works, however, refer to *śāstras*, and give evidence of a thorough knowledge of them.

4. The Sa skya and bKa' brgyud schools have similar lists.

5. The Mi pham commentaries are accessible in his collected works; the gZhan phan *mchan 'grel* were published as a set in 1978 in Dehra Dun (India) by D. G. Khochhen Tulku.

6. It is unclear exactly what a *ngag don tsam gyi 'grel pa* would be, other than a commentary that was merely an oral recitation of a text for the sake of transmitting from one generation to the next or a commentary that dwelt on the grammar and syntax of the text.

References

Blo bzang 'phrin las rnam rgyal, rGyal dbang chos rje

CNDLNN *Chos mngon pa mdzod kyi dgongs don gsal bar byed pa'i legs bshad snying po'i snang ba.* Delhi: Mongolian Lama Gurudeva, 1982.

CNDMSG *Dam pa'i chos mngon pa mdzod kyi rtsa 'grel gyi gnas 'ga' zhig phyogs gcig tu bsdebs pa'i sdom gyi tshig su bcad pa rmongs mun sel ba'i sgron me.* Delhi: Mongolian Lama Gurudeva, 1982.

bSod nams grags pa

CNKKYP *Chos mngon pa kun btus kyi dka' ba'i gnad dgrol ba'i dka' 'grel mkhas pa'i yid 'phrog.* Buxa: Shes rig 'dzin skyong slob gnyer khang, 1964.

Bu ston Rin chen grub

DTSCB *bDe bar gshegs pa'i bstan pa'i gsal byed chos kyi 'byung gnas gsung rab rin po che'i mdzod.* In *The Collected Works of Bu-ston*, vol. 24. New Delhi: International Academy of Indian Culture, 1971.

mChims Nam mkha' grags

CNDNG *Chos mngon mdzod kyi tshig le'ur byas pa'i 'grel pa mngon pa'i rgyan.* Buxa, India edition of 1967.

Corless, Roger J.

1989 *The Vision of Buddhism. The Space under the Tree.* New York: Paragon House.

Gómez, Luis O.

1987 "Buddhist Literature: Exegesis and Hermeneutics." In *The Encyclopedia of Religion*, vol. 2, pp. 529-540. New York: Macmillan.

Gyatso, Janet

1986 "Signs, Memory, and History: A Tantric Buddhist Theory of Scriptural Transmission." *Journal of the International Association of Buddhist Studies* 9/2: 7-35.

gZhan phan chos kyi snang ba

CNDSM *Chos mngon pa'i mdzod kyi tshig le'ur byas pa'i mchan 'grel shes bya'i me long.* Sides 7-257 in *Gźuṅ chen bcu gsum gyi mchan 'grel.* Dehra Dun: D. G. Khocchen Tulku, 1978.

Hirakawa, Akira

1987 "Buddhist Literature: Survey of Texts." In *The Encyclopedia of Religion*, vol. 2, pp. 509-529. New York: Macmillan.

Hirsch, E. D.

1967 *Validity in Interpretation.* New Haven: Yale University Press.

Hopkins, Jeffrey
1983 *Meditation on Emptiness*. London: Wisdom.

'Jam dbyangs bzhad pa Ngag dbang brtson grus
CNDGZK *Dam pa'i chos mngon pa mdzod kyi dgongs 'grel gyi bstan bcos thub bstan nor bu'i gter mdzod dus gsum rgyal ba'i bzhed don kun gsal*. In *The Collected Works of 'Jam-dbyaṅs-bźad-pa'i-rdo-rje*, vol. 10. New Delhi: Ngawang Gelek Demo, 1972.

Lancaster, Lewis R.
1987 "Buddhist Literature: Canonization." In *The Encyclopedia of Religion*, vol. 2, pp. 504-509. New York: Macmillan.

Mi bskyod rdo rje
CNDGDP *Chos mngon pa mdzod kyi 'grel pa rgyas par spros pa grub bde'i dpyid 'jo*. New Delhi: Taikhang, 1975.

Mi pham rgya mtsho, 'Jam mgon 'Ju
CNDGGG *Dam pa'i chos mngon pa mdzod kyi mchan 'grel rin po che'i do shal bla gsal dgyes pa'i mgul rgyan*. Dehra Dun: 1971.

Obermiller, E.
1931 *History of Buddhism* (Chos-hbyung) *by Bu-ston: The Jewelry of Scripture*. Heidelberg: Otto Harrassowitz.

Rabten, Geshé
1980 *The Life and Teaching of Geshé Rabten*. London: George Allen & Unwin.

Se ra rje btsun Chos kyi rgyal mtshan
CNDKLS *Chos mngon pa mdzod kyi spyi don dka' gnad legs par bshad pa*. Buxa, India edition of 196?

Sopa, Geshe Lhundup
n.d. *Lectures on Tibetan Religious Culture*. Department of Indian Studies, University of Wisconsin.

Thurman, Robert A. F.
1978 "Buddhist Hermeneutics." *Journal of the American Academy of Religion* 46/1: 19-35.
1984 *Tsong Khapa's Speech of Gold in the Essence of True Eloquence*. Princeton: Princeton University Press.

Tulku Thondup
1987 *Buddhist Civilization in Tibet*. New York: Routledge and Kegan Paul.

Chapter 7

The Literature of Bon

Per Kvaerne

The Bon pos have a vast literature, which non-Tibetan scholars are only just beginning to explore. Formerly, it was taken for granted that this literature was nothing but a shameless plagiarism of Buddhist texts. The last twenty-five years have, however, seen a radical change in the assessment of the entire Bon religion. This has come about above all thanks to the pioneering studies of David L. Snellgrove, who in 1967 made the very just observation regarding Bon po literature that "by far the greater part would seem to have been absorbed through learning and then retold, and this is not just plagiarism" (12). In fact, as Snellgrove also pointed out, Bon po literature is especially important for the light it sheds on pre-Buddhist religious traditions in Tibet (21).

The present essay will be concerned with what is only a part of the vast mass of Bon po literature, viz., the collection of texts which constitutes the bKa' 'gyur of the Bon pos. This is—as is the case with the bKa' 'gyur of the Buddhists (see Harrison, in this volume)—a collection of those texts which are regarded as constituting the authentic and original teachings of the Enlightened One of our age, the latter being, so the Bon pos maintain, not Śākyamuni, but sTon pa gShen rab ("The Teacher gShen rab"). According to Bon po beliefs, sTon pa gShen rab lived long before Śākyamuni and was the ruler of the land of sTag gzig, generally located vaguely to the west of Tibet. From this spiritual center, the universal and eternal doctrine of Bon eventually reached Tibet, passing through the historical but enigmatic kingdom of Zhang zhung in present-day western Tibet.

Bon po tradition holds that the early kings of Tibet practiced Bon, and that consequently not only the royal dynasty, but the entire realm prospered. This happy state of affairs came to a temporary halt during the reign of King Gri gum btsan po (usually counted as the eighth king of the royal dynasty), who persecuted Bon, with the result that a large number of Bon texts were hidden away so that they might be preserved for future generations. As far as Bon is concerned, this was the beginning of the textual tradition styled *gter ma*, "Treasures" (see Gyatso, in this volume), concealed texts which are rediscovered at the appropriate time by gifted individuals known as *gter ston*, "Treasure discoverers."

Although Bon was reinstated by Gri gum btsan po's successor and flourished as before during the reigns of subsequent kings, it was once more persecuted by King Khri srong lde btsan in the eighth century C.E. While Khri srong lde btsan is portrayed in mainstream Tibetan tradition as a devout Buddhist, Bon po sources maintain that his motives for supporting Buddhism were, on the one hand, the belief that he could thereby prolong his life, and on the other, the argument offered by certain individuals at his court, that the Bon po priests, already equal to the king in power, would certainly take over the whole government of the land after his death.

Whatever the truth of the matter may be, both Buddhists and Bon pos agree that during the reign of Khri srong lde btsan, the Bon po priests were either banished from Tibet or compelled to conform to Buddhism. Once again, Bon texts were concealed, to be taken out when the time would be ripe for propagating Bon anew.

Leaving aside the question of whether "later historians have made two persecutions out of what was in fact only one" (Karmay, 1972: xxxiii), it should be noted that the greater part of the Bon po bKa' 'gyur consists of "Treasures" regarded as having been hidden away during the successive persecutions of Bon and duly rediscovered by *gter stons* in the course of the following centuries.[1] Bon pos also claim, reversing the accusation of plagiarism, that many of their sacred scriptures were transformed by the Buddhists into Buddhist texts.[2]

The Bon pos claim that the rediscovery of their sacred texts began early in the tenth century C.E. The first discoveries are said to have been made by chance. Wandering beggars stealing a box from bSam yas in the belief that it contained gold and later exchanging the contents—Bon po texts—for food (Karmay, 1972: 118), has an authentic ring; the same is true of an account of Buddhists looking for Buddhist texts, who, on finding only Bon po texts, simply gave them away (Karmay, 1972: 152). The first real Bon po *gter ston*, however, would seem to be gShen chen Klu dga' (996-1035).[3] His discovery in 1017 of numerous important texts "was preceded by several years of initiatory preparations culminating in a series of visions in which supernatural beings of various kinds revealed the place where the Treasure was hidden" (Kvaerne, 1974: 34).

This is not the place to present the many *gter stons* whose textual discoveries constitute the greater part of the Bon po bKa' 'gyur. This has been done elsewhere (Karmay, 1972; Kvaerne, 1974). Some indications, however, as to when the Bon po bKa' 'gyur was formed must be given. Unfortunately, a precise date cannot at present be ascertained. Nevertheless, it should be noted that it does not seem to contain texts which have come to light later than 1386 (Kvaerne, 1974: 38). I have previously ventured the hypothesis that the Bon po bKa' 'gyur—as well as the Bon po brTen 'gyur[4]—may have been "finally assembled by ca. 1450, which allows ample time for the Bon pos to have felt the need of assembling a canon of their own following the final editing, by Bu-ston and others, of a Buddhist canon in the beginning of the preceding century" (Kvaerne, 1974: 39). While admitting the possibility that the Bon po bKa' 'gyur may, in fact, be more recent still, I would, for the moment, uphold this hypothesis.

We now turn to the bKa' 'gyur itself. A preliminary analysis and title-list was published in 1974 (Kvaerne, 1974) on the basis of a catalogue (*dkar chag*) (referred to hereafter as *KTDG*) by the well-known Bon po scholar Nyi ma bstan 'dzin (b. 1813).[5] This study can be supplemented by the catalogue of Bon po publications preserved in the Tōyō Bunko library in Tokyo (Karmay, 1977). Each publication is carefully described and the contents briefly presented; among the texts thus dealt with are a number to be found in the bKa' 'gyur.

Recently, another and much more detailed catalogue has come to light, composed in 1751 by the great Bon po yogin-scholar Kun grol grags pa (b. 1700) (Karmay, 1990: 148), bearing the title *Zab dang rgya che g.yung drung bon gyi bka' 'gyur gyi dkar chag nyi ma 'bum gyi 'od zer* ("Catalogue of the of bKa' 'gyur of the Profound and Vast Eternal Bon, Rays of Light from One Hundred Thousand Suns") (*ZBKK*). This is an extensive work, one manuscript copy containing no less than 197 folios (although the catalogue proper only commences on fol. 69b). It is a particularly useful work, as it lists not only the titles of the texts, but also provides the headings of each individual chapter of each text.

Both catalogues divide the texts contained in the bKa' 'gyur into categories. In the *ZBKK* they are given as follows:

(1) The Perfect Class of *Sūtras* (*phun sum tshogs pa'i mdo sde*)
(2) The Pure Class of "The Hundred Thousand" (*rnam par dag pa'i 'bum sde*)
(3) The Wonderful Class of *Mantras* (*rmad du byung ba'i sngags sde*)
(4) The Supreme Class of Mind (*bla na med pa'i sems sde*)

The *KTDG* has the same categories, but the "Hundred Thousand" is called "Extensive" (*rnam par rgyas pa*); the third class is designated "Tantras of Secret *Mantras*" (*gsang sngags rgyud*); and the fourth, "The Class of Mental (Teachings) of the Great Perfection" (*bla med rdzogs chen sems phyogs kyi sde*).

mDo, "Sūtras," also includes texts dealing with the discipline and behavior of monks (e.g., *'dul ba, vinaya*). The only text which has been partially translated is the *gZer mig*, the two-volume biography of sTon pa gShen rab in eighteen chapters; a summary of the whole text (Hoffman: 85-96) and a detailed analysis of chapters 10-12 (Blondeau: 34-39) have also been published. Snellgrove has published excerpts from doctrinal sections of the twelve-volume biography of sTon pa gShen rab, the *gZi brjid*, and a detailed paraphrase of the epic story of the latter text has been published by Kvaerne (1986) together with a set of corresponding narrative picture scrolls.

'Bum, literally "Hundred Thousand," corresponds to the Buddhist Prajñāpāramitā literature. So far, this literary corpus has remained entirely unexplored.

sNgags, "Mantras," or rGyud, "Tantras," constitute the basic tantric texts of Bon. This is a vast and complex collection of text, which, like the preceding section, still awaits study.

Sems, "Mind," is the section which deals with the highest philosophical doctrines and meditational practices of Bon. Commonly referred to as the "Great Perfection," this literature has been examined and briefly presented by S. G. Karmay in two chapters of a recent book (Karmay: 201-205, 216-223). The most important textual cycle in this section is probably the *Zhang zhung snyan rgyud* ("The Oral Transmission of Zhang zhung"). Excerpts from this text have been edited, translated, and provided with useful comments by Giacomella Orofino. Several doctoral dissertations dealing with texts from this group are in the course of preparation, so one may hope that our knowledge regarding the "Great Perfection" of Bon will be significantly expanded in the years ahead.

As far as the main scriptural sections are concerned, the Bon po bKa' 'gyur corresponds, on the whole, fairly closely to the various editions of the Buddhist bKa' 'gyur, with two notable exceptions: the Bon po bKa' 'gyur has a separate section for 'Dul ba (Vinaya, monastic discipline), and it has a separate section—the fourth—containing the *rDzogs chen* ("Great Perfection") teachings. The *rDzogs chen* texts of the Buddhists are to be found neither in the bKa' 'gyur nor the bsTan 'gyur, but outside the canon altogether.

It has long been known that manuscript copies of the Bon po bKa' 'gyur existed. Thus, during his expedition to Tibet in 1928, the Russian scholar and explorer George Roerich came across a complete set of the bKa' 'gyur in 140 volumes in Sha ru Monastery, four days' travel northeast of Nag chu rDzong. The whole collection was in manuscript "and had an exceptionally beautiful cursive script.... The front pages bearing the title of the text were invariably painted black and written in gold" (Roerich: 365). The following year, the American scholar J. F. Rock came across another copy of the Bon po canon in the extreme southeastern part of Tibet. In the main temple of the predominantly Bon po Tso so district, situated between Li thang and Lichiang, he found "piled up in a corner of their Lha-khang a manuscript copy of the Bon bKa-hgyur and bsTan-hgyur written on stiff black paper." Unfortunately, Rock was unable to salvage it: "It was an enormous pile, and I could have bought it at the time, but communications were cut, extra transport unavailable, the ferry boat over the Yangtse had been destroyed..." (Rock: 3).

As we have seen, Roerich refers to a set of the bKa' 'gyur in 140 volumes. Whether it really was complete is of course impossible to determine today. The *ZBKK* enumerates 244 volumes, but this may refer to the edition which Kun grol grags pa thought *ought* to be made, rather than to an actually existing edition; the *KTDG* (31) lists 175 volumes, which may be taken to refer to a set of the bKa' 'gyur on which Nyi ma bstan 'dzin based his catalogue.[6] Only a careful comparison of the two catalogues will shed light on this considerable discrepancy.

Besides manuscript copies, there existed two xylographic editions of the Bon po bKa' 'gyur, both prepared in rGyal rong in the extreme east of Tibet in the second part of the eighteenth century. The lay patrons of this gigantic task were the royal houses of the rGyal rong states of Rab brtan and Khro chen, in both cases under the editorship of Kun grol grags pa (Karmay, 1990b). Presumably, the task of carving the wooden blocks was only undertaken after Kun grol grags pa had completed his catalogue in 1751. The editorial colophon of the Rab brtan edition of the *gZi brjid* (which, as we have seen, is part of the mDo section of the bKa' 'gyur) states that the carving of the blocks for the sixteen volumes of the *Khams chen*, a text belonging to the 'Bum section of the bKa' 'gyur, was undertaken in 1766 (Karmay, 1990b). The Manchu conquest of rGyal rong in 1775 and subsequent dGe lugs pa supremacy brought this flowering of Bon po culture to a close, and we may assume that the blocks were already carved by then.[7] No complete set of either of the xylographic editions seems to have survived the Cultural Revolution, although single volumes still exist in Tibet.

Although many individual bKa' 'gyur texts have been and continue to be printed in India by Tibetan Bon pos living in exile, it was long thought that no complete set of the Bon po bKa' 'gyur had survived the catastrophic upheavals of the Cultural Revolution. However, in the early 1980s, a complete manuscript bKa' 'gyur was taken out of its place of concealment in Nyag rong in eastern Tibet. "The printing of a new photoset edition to be based on this manuscript copy of the entire Bon po canon was under way in Chengdu in 1985" (Karmay, 1990a: 147), and was in fact completed within a short space of time.[8] Several academic libraries (Oslo, Paris, Washington, D.C.) already have copies of this set, thus making it possible to undertake a comprehensive study of a vast but hitherto virtually unexplored part of the rich cultural heritage of Tibet.

Notes

1. Bon po *gter stons* have been active until our own times, but their textual discoveries have not necessarily been incorporated into the bKa' 'gyur. See Karmay (1972) and Kvaerne (1974).

2. This charge is expressed as early as the *Gling grags*, dating, as Anne-Marie Blondeau (1990) has shown, from the twelfth century. I am preparing for publication an edition and translation of the *Gling grags*.

3. Dates are given on the basis of the *bstan rtsis*, "chronological table," of Nyi ma bstan 'dzin (b. 1813), published and translated in Kvaerne (1971). Its dates have generally been adopted by those subsequently writing on the history of Bon. Other Bon po sources, however, are based on different calculations. A preliminary study of the *bstan rtsis* of Hor btsun bsTan 'dzin blo gros (1888-1975) has been published (Kvaerne, 1988), and a complete edition and study of the *bstan rtsis* of Tshul khrims rgyal mtshan (b. 1783), composed in 1804, has recently appeared (Kvaerne, 1990). The latter gives the dates of gShen chen Klu dga' as 1116-1155.

4. While the Buddhist collection of commentaries and treatises is styled *bsTan 'gyur*, the Bon pos have adopted, for their collection, the spelling *brTen 'gyur*. The pronunciation would normally be identical, implying the "firmness" (*brten*) of the doctrine.

5. There is no indication in this short text as to when it was composed. However, as Nyi ma bstan 'dzin refers to himself in the colophon as the twenty-second in the "lineage of abbots" (*mkhan rabs*), it must have been written after 1836, the year in which he became abbot of sMan ri Monastery in gTsang (Kvaerne, 1971: 237). The *KTDG* also includes a catalogue of the brTen 'gyur.

6. A breakdown gives the following figures:

	KTDG	*ZBKK*
mDo	62	55
'Bum	91	102
rGyud	18	87
Sems	4	30

7. There is a reference to a xylographic set of the bKa' 'gyur in the autobiography of Kong sprul Blo gros mtha' yas (1813-1899), who passed through rGyal rong in 1846. He reports that in the palace of mKhar shod, he found about one hundred volumes of a printed edition prepared by "the king of Khro skyabs" (he does not say which king) (Schuh: xlix). This probably means that the Khro skyabs king had ordered a set to be printed from the already existing blocks. Sets were printed from the original blocks up to the 1950s. E. Gene Smith (32) refers to the same passage, but gives the impression that the blocks were in the process of being carved in 1846; this must be a misunderstanding.

8. A few years later, a second edition of the bKa' 'gyur was printed in rNga ba (Sichuan Province) in which certain volumes reproduced the xylographic edition. It is reported (1993) that a reprint of the brTen 'gyur is also being prepared in Tibet.

References

Blondeau, Anne-Marie

1971 "Le Lha-'dre bka'-thaṅ." In *Études tibétaines dédiées à la mémoire de Marcelle Lalou*, pp. 29-126. Ed. by A. Macdonald. Paris: Maisonneuve.

1990 "Identification de la tradition appelée *bsGrags-pa Bon-lugs*." In *Indo-Tibetan Studies*, pp. 37-54. Ed. by T. Skorupski. Buddhica Britannica, Series Continua 2. Tring: The Institute of Buddhist Studies.

Francke, A. H.

1924-49 "gZer-myig, A Book of the Tibetan Bon pos." *Asia Major* 1: 243-346; 3 (1926): 321-339; 4 (1927): 161-239; 481-540; 5 (1928): 7-40; 6 (1930): 299-314; New Series 7 (1949): 163-188.

Hoffman, Helmut

1961 *The Religions of Tibet*. London: Allen and Unwin. Translation of *Die Religionen Tibets*. Freiburg: Karl Alber Verlag, 1956.

Karmay, Samten G.

1972 *The Treasury of Good Sayings: A Tibetan History of Bon*. London Oriental Series 26. London: Oxford University Press.

1977 *A Catalogue of Bon po Publications*. Tokyo: Tōyō Bunko.

1989 *The Great Perfection. A Philosophical and Meditative Teaching of Tibetan Buddhism*. Leiden: E. J. Brill.

1990a "Two Eighteenth Century Xylographic Editions of the *gZi-grjid*." In *Indo-Tibetan Studies*, pp. 147-150. Edited by T. Skorupski. Buddhica Britannica, Series Continua 2. Tring: The Institute of Buddhist Studies.

1990b "The Decree of the Khro-chen King." *Acta Orientalia* 51: 141-159.

Kun grol grags pa

ZBKK *Zab dang rgya che g.yung drung bon gyi bka' 'gyur gyi dkar chag nyi ma 'bum gyi 'od zer.* Ms., n.p., n.d., 197 ff.

Kvaerne, Per

1971 "A Chronological Table of the Bon po. The bstan rcis of Ñi ma bstan 'jin." *Acta Orientalia* 33: 205-282.

1974 "The Canon of the Tibetan Bon pos." *Indo-Iranian Journal* 16/1: 18-56; 16/4: 96-144.

1986 "Peintures tibetaines de la vie de sTon-pa-gçen-rab." *Arts asiatiques* 41: 36-81.

1988 "A New Chronological Table of the Bon Religion. The *bstan-rcis* of Hor-bcun bsTan-'jin-blo-gros (1888-1975)." In *Tibetan Studies. Proceedings of the 4th Seminar of the International Association of Tibetan Studies*. Ed. by Helga Uebach and Jampa L. Panglung. Studia Tibetica Quellen zur tibetischen Lexicographie Band 2. Munich: Kommission für zentralasiatischen Studien der Bayerischen Akademie der Wissenschaften.

1990 "A Bon po *bsTan-rtsis* from 1804." In *Indo-Tibetan Studies*, pp. 151-169. Ed. by T. Skorupski. Buddhica Britannica, Series Continua 2. Tring: The Institute of Buddhist Studies.

Nyi ma bstan 'dzin

KTDG *bKa' 'gyur brten 'gyur gyi sde tshan sgrigs tshul bstan pa'i me ro spar ba'i rlung g.yab bon gyi pad mo rgyas byed nyi 'od*. Śata-Piṭaka Series 37, Part II. New Delhi: International Academy of Indian Culture, 1965.

Orofino, Giacomella

1990 *Sacred Tibetan Teachings on Death and Liberation*. Bridgeport: Prism Press. Translation and revision of *Insegnamenti tibetani su morte e liberazione*. Rome: Edizioni Mediterranee, 1985.

Rock, J. F.

1952 *The Na-khi Nāga Cult and Related Ceremonies*, Part I. Serie Orientale Roma 4/1. Rome: Istituto Italiano per il Medio ed Estremo Oriente.

Roerich, George

1931 *Trails to Inmost Asia. Five Years of Exploration with the Roerich Central Asian Expedition*. New Haven: Yale University Press.

Schuh, Dieter

1976 *Tibetische Handschriften und Blockdrucke. Teil 6. (Gesammelte Werke des Koṅ-sprul Blo-gros mtha'-yas)*. Verzeichnis der orientalischen Handschriften in Deutschland Band XI, 6. Wiesbaden: Franz Steiner Verlag.

Snellgrove, D. L.

1967 *The Nine Ways of Bon*. London Oriental Series 18. London: Oxford University Press.

Smith, E. Gene

1970 Introduction to *Kongtrul's Encyclopaedia of Indo-Tibetan Culture*, pp. 1-87. Ed by Lokesh Chandra. Śata-Piṭaka Series 50. New Delhi: International Academy of Indian Culture.

Chapter 8

Drawn from the Tibetan Treasury: The *gTer ma* Literature

Janet B. Gyatso

The rubric *gter ma*, or "Treasure," cannot properly be characterized as representing a genre of Tibetan literature. Texts classified as Treasure are of many different genres; in fact, the range of Treasure genres almost repeats that of Tibetan literature as a whole. Rather, the term *Treasure* refers figuratively to the place from which such a text was drawn. Or more precisely, *Treasure* means that which was drawn from such a place. The place is a treasure cache (sometimes distinguished in Tibetan as *gter kha*, which we may translate as "treasury"); the Treasure is the product extracted. This product is most notably text, but there are also a variety of material objects (*gter rdzas*) which are purported to have been extracted from such treasuries as well.[1] The following, however, will focus upon those Treasures which are textual.

Place in Tibetan Literature and Legitimating Strategies

The fact that the range of Treasure genres competes in breadth with that of Tibetan literature as a whole alerts us to a critical feature of the tradition that needs to be noted from the outset. The various Treasure "cycles" (*skor*) that have been discovered by the Tibetan "Treasure discoverers" (*gter ston*) often constitute complete ritual and doctrinal systems which in an important sense stand on their own. Such cycles of related texts function in their religious milieu as authoritative sets of teachings which amount to challenging alternatives to existing textual systems.

Treasure discovery is still practiced in the twentieth century by contemporary Tibetans in exile, such as Dil mgo mKhyen brtse Rin po che (1910-1991), and even in occupied Tibet, as seen in the outstanding Treasure career of mKhan po 'Jigs med phun tshogs (b. 1933). The tradition seems to have begun in Tibet in the tenth century C.E.[2] The practitioners of this mode of introducing texts have been primarily rNying ma pas and Bon pos; these two groups had much overlap in their Treasure activity.[3] The newer (and, it will be noted, more politically powerful) gSar ma pa schools tend to doubt the Treasures' authenticity (Kapstein, 1989), although there have been discoverers there too (Smith: 10). We need hardly note that Western scholars have also been dubious concerning Treasure claims (Aris, 1989).

The two primary modes of Treasure discovery are the unearthing of what is usually a fragmentary text buried in the ground, statue, or monastery wall (*sa gter*); and the finding of such a text buried in one's mind (*dgongs gter*). In both cases, the discoverer claims that the item found had previously been hidden in that very place at some point in the past. This claim concerning the past is another critical feature of the Treasure tradition, which strictly speaking distinguishes it from the other visionary modes of revealing text in Tibet such as "pure vision" (*dag snang*) and secret oral transmission (*snyan brgyud*) (though not infrequently these labels are used loosely to characterize Treasure as well).

Once discovered, many of the buried Treasure cycles came to be compiled into canons of their own. The early Bon po Treasures were incorporated into the Bon po bKa' 'gyur and brTen 'gyur, which together fill approximately 300 volumes; in fact, Treasures make up nearly all of the former and much of the latter parts of this collection.[4] Per Kvaerne (1974: 39) estimated that the Bon po canon was assembled ca. 1450, approximately 150 years after the compilation of the Tibetan Buddhist canon of the new schools, the bKa' 'gyur and bsTan 'gyur.[5] The Buddhist Treasures were not compiled into a collection of their own until the nineteenth century, when Kong sprul bLo gros mtha' yas edited the *Rin chen gter mdzod* (*RT*), a collection of cycles which in its current edition numbers over one hundred volumes. There are, however, a considerable number of Buddhist Treasures not included in the *RT*, such as the two well-known "historical" cycles, the *Maṇi bka' 'bum* and the *bKa' thang sde lnga*, as well as some of the esoteric sNying thig ("Heart-Sphere") Treasures, some of which came to be classified as Atiyoga *tantras* of the "key instruction class" (*man ngag sde*) and included in the *rNying ma'i rgyud 'bum*.[6] Also not included were cycles that were not available to Kong sprul, as well as some that were not deemed worthy of inclusion.

The subject matter of the Treasure texts, as was already indicated concerning genre, is as broad as that of the rest of Tibetan literature. For the sake of summary, the principal Treasure subjects may be distinguished into two main types: those that purport to recount history and/or hagiography; and those that present religious teachings and practices. In the case of history, the Treasure mode of textual generation performs the important function of offering an arena to recount competing versions of past events, i.e., versions that differ from orthodox or generally accepted versions. As would be expected, such Treasure histories are vulnerable to a charge of forgery; on the other hand, if the conceit of discovery is granted, then the purported age of the text and the status of its original author function to lend authenticity and legitimacy to its narratives.

In the case of religious teachings, legitimacy is claimed by characterizing the "core" of the cycle as a revelation. The Bon po Treasures are often identified as teachings of the founder of Bon, gShen rab mi bo (see Kvaerne, in this volume). In the Buddhist case, Treasure revelations are placed explicitly on a par with the *sūtras* and *tantras* of the more conventional Buddhist canon, and are said to be, in one sense or another, the "word of the Buddha." We shall see below that the very mode in which the Buddhist Treasures are transmitted is characterized as being in consonance with the mode in which the more well-known and accepted teachings of the Buddha were transmitted. The Buddhist Treasures gain legitimacy in particular by explicitly linking themselves with the texts and practices of the "Old Tantras" said to have been translated from Sanskrit, and compiled into what is called the *rNying ma'i rgyud 'bum*, itself a challenging alternative canon to the more conventional canon, the Buddhist bKa' 'gyur with its "New Tantras."[7] In most cases, the Buddhist Treasures are distinct from the Old Tantras in that they present different texts and different visions, but rather than competing with the Old Tantras they complement them, and thus stand together with the Old canon as a joint challenge to the New canon. However, the Buddhist Treasures still maintain an advantage over the canonical Old Tantras by virtue of the position of their discoverer: since the Treasures are received in a "close transmission" (*nye brgyud*), their discoverer has greater proximity to (and by implication, mastery of) the source of his teachings than does a master of the Old Tantras, who has received the texts he is teaching from a "long transmission" (*ring brgyud*), i.e., a succession of masters that stretches back into the distant past.

We have already suggested at least three ways in which the religious Treasure lays claim to authenticity: the exalted status of its original expounder, such as the Buddha; the nature of its doctrines, practices and mode of transmission, which are similar to the more well-known and accepted doctrines, practices and mode of transmission of canonical materials; and the special powers of the Treasure's discoverer. That the powers of the discoverer are of critical concern in the Treasure tradition may be seen particularly in the biographical, and sometimes autobiographical, accounts of the individual discoverers' visionary quests for Treasure. In a series of articles focusing on such accounts from the Buddhist Treasure tradition (1986, 1993, and n.d.), I have shown that the personal struggle to develop the power to find a Treasure, the difficulty in deciphering the cryptic codes and "*ḍākinī* language" in which the Treasure is originally revealed, and the discoverer-to-be's many self-doubts are all necessitated by the nature of the Buddhist myth of the Treasures' previous concealment (see, e.g., Tulku Thondup Rinpoche). Interestingly, this myth makes two legimating moves at once: it harkens back to the authoritative past, and simultaneously sheds positive light on the discoverer in the present.

The Buddhist Treasure myth has come to center upon the activities of Padmasambhava, the eighth-century Indic master credited with introducing tantric Buddhism into Tibet, even though there were a number of earlier traditions regarding the concealings of Treasures in Tibet, most notably those associated with the rDzogs chen teachings of Vimalamitra, another Indian teacher in Tibet during the same period.[8] But by the time of discoverer Nyang ral Nyi ma 'od zer (1124-1192), the myth of the Treasures' origin that stars Padmasambhava and his Tibetan consort Ye shes mtsho rgyal began to dominate the Buddhist Treasure tradition. The predominance of Padmasambhava is probably attributable to the fact that his image as a princely but lay tantric master reflected well the style of the very Tibetans—themselves often lay teachers of the aristocratic class—who were developing what we might call the full-blown Treasure tradition.[9] Nonetheless, in this myth, Padmasambhava is still but a middleman in the dissemination of Treasure, if a very central middleman. The Treasure is most basically transmitted by a primordial *buddha* in a primordial pure land (*rgyal ba'i dgongs brgyud*). Secondarily it is transmitted in signs by the tantric "knowledge holders" (*rig 'dzin brda'i brgyud*), the Indian patriarchs of the rNying ma pa school. Only tertiarily is it taught in verbal form by Padmasambhava, in the eighth-century Tibetan court, "into the ears of persons" (*gang zag snyan khung du brgyud*) (Gyatso, 1986, 1993). Padmasambhava then proceeds to prepare the Treasure teaching for burial. He transmits the teaching in an empowerment ceremony (*smon lam dbang bskur*), during which he specially commissions certain disciples to rediscover it in a future incarnation at a specified time, a commissioning that is assured of fulfillment by virtue of a prophecy Padmasambhava utters to that effect (*bka' babs lung bstan*). Then he appoints powerful protectors to conceal the Treasure from everyone else until the right discoverer comes along at the right time (*mkha' 'gro gtad rgya*). The point is that the wrong person must not discover the Treasure; if he or she does, death will be imminent.[10]

Thus the crucial element in Buddhist Treasure discovery is that the discoverer must prove both to himself and to the world that he is indeed the previously commissioned individual. This is accomplished in a variety of ways, one of which is through signs which demonstrate the blessings of the exalted previous expounders of the Treasure, and another of which is by the discoverer's own spiritual accomplishments, which demonstrate that he or she already mastered the Treasure teachings while studying with Padmasambhava in a past lifetime.

The Discovery of the Buried: History and Implications

The roots of this complex and arcane process of textual transmission may be recognized in the earlier and quite pragmatic Tibetan custom of burying politically sensitive items underground as a means of preventing their destruction. Tibetan histories state, for example, that because of repressive measures taken by anti-Buddhist ministers after the death of the king Mes ag tshoms (ca. 750

C.E.) certain Buddhist texts newly introduced in Tibet such as the *Vajracchedikā Sūtra* were hidden underground, and later retrieved when the next Buddhist king, Khri srong lde btsan, took the throne (*KG*: 308-309; *BC*: 882). But this and other such incidents are not considered to be instances of Treasure transmission.

In some accounts of early Treasure concealment in the Bon po tradition, the reason for hiding texts is also primarily practical. The two principal moments of Bon Treasure burial occur in the wake of the persecutions of Bon during the reigns of (1) the prehistoric Tibetan king Gri gum bTsan po, and (2) Khri srong lde btsan.[11] That this pragmatic view of the need for Treasure burial is still operative in the Bon po tradition may be seen from a recent comment by the contemporary Bon po master bsTan 'dzin rnam dag, who characterized the concealment of texts and objects after the Chinese invasion of Tibet in the 1950s as a third Treasure concealment, on the same order as the previous two (private interview, 1989).

However, at some yet undetermined moment in the development of both the Buddhist and Bon po Treasure traditions, the reasons given for concealment become grounded in the mantic powers of the concealer: rather than trying to protect texts from present adverse conditions, the concealer of Treasure is concerned with the future, which he perceives will be difficult, with special teachings needed. The Treasures that he then hides are specifically formulated to benefit the beings in that future moment. This future-determined motive is especially characteristic of the Buddhist Treasure myth that stars Padmasambhava, although early Bon po sources refer to prophecies of the future as well.[12] In addition to the motive for concealment, the mode of discovery also changes. Rather than digging up an object based on a simple memory or notation of the hiding place, or indeed by accident, as is the case in some accounts of early Bon Treasure discoveries,[13] the act of discovery becomes dependent upon visionary inspiration, the memory of past lives, and especially the compulsion exerted by the prophecy.[14] The contemporary Buddhist Treasure tradition even goes so far as to disallow the accidental discoveries that are sometimes reported in the Bon po Treasure tradition (see Tulku Thondup Rinpoche: 103).

It is also the Buddhist Treasure tradition that, in elaborating the need for, and the mode of, Treasure transmission, was able to utilize incidents in the Indian Buddhist tradition as authenticating precedents. The Buddhist Treasure tradition thereby claims that the mode of Treasure transmission is ultimately to be traced to Indian Buddhism. Indeed, at an early point Buddhism had already allowed the preaching of authentic "*buddha*-word" by individuals other than the Buddha, based either upon the Buddha's inspiration or on those individuals' own realizations (MacQueen). The Tibetan Buddhist expounders of Treasure theory can even cite statements in the *sūtras* that the bodhisattva will hear Dharma teachings from the sky, walls, and trees (*NC*: 511; Dudjom Rinpoche: 743). Buddhist legends concerning visionary receipt of scripture often cited as precedents by the Treasure proponents are Maitreya's revelation of Buddhist philosophical texts to the fourth-century Asaṅga, and Nāgārjuna's retrieval of the Prajñāpāramitā *sūtras* from a *nāga* realm under the ocean. Also noted was the Buddha's prophecy in the thirteenth chapter of the *Pratyutpannasamādhi Sūtra* that this text will "go into a cave in the ground" and 500 years later, in degenerate times, a few beings who have studied with former *buddhas* and who have "brought wholesome potentialties to maturity and planted seeds" will propagate the *sūtra* again (Harrison: 96-108; *YM*: 223-224; *GT*, vol. 2: 448). Further, well known to the Treasure tradition is the rNying ma pa account of the Indian transmission of the Old Tantras of the Mahāyoga bKa' brgyad class, which involves their concealment and later revelation from the *caitya* at Śītavana (*NC*: 111-112; Dudjom Rinpoche: 482-483). In fact, as early as the thirteenth century, the Treasure apologist Guru Chos dbang is finding analogues to Treasure concealment/revealment in virtually the entire history of the Buddhist scriptures, from the transmission of versions of the Vinaya, to that of certain *sūtras*, all classes of the Old Tantras, and even the textual transmission of several Mahāyāna *śāstras* (*GC*: 89-95).

Never mentioned by the Treasure tradition to my knowledge is its close affinity to accounts of text concealment and revelation in Chinese Ling-pao Taoism. For example, the third- to fourth-century "Grotto Passage" tells that Celestial Officials, out of compassion for the suffering beings in a degenerate age, granted special books written in a celestial script which came to be hidden in a casket in Mount Chung to await a future sage. These texts are said ultimately to have been recovered by a Taoist adept (Bokenkamp). We may also note that another frequently mentioned feature of earth Treasure revelation, namely, that it is recovered from the ground in the form of a paper scroll (*shog dril*), suggests Chinese influence as well. Further, the doctrinal and meditative teachings of the rDzogs chen, which many Buddhist and Bon po Treasures propagate, have certain connections with Chinese Ch'an, even if the two are not to be equated (Karmay, 1988: 86-106; Kvaerne, 1983). In particular, the presence of Ch'an passages in the *Blon po bka' thang* (Tucci, 1958; Ueyama) suggests that Treasure may have offered a convenient means to reintroduce Ch'an teachings in Tibet. Such a theory is also implied by Bu ston Rin chen grub, the fourteenth-century scholar and historian who would have been critical of the Treasure tradition and its teachings; he states that when Hva shang Mahāyāna was sent back to China after his loss in debate to the Indian master Kamalaśīla, his books were "hidden as treasure" (*BC*: 890) .

If the Buddhist Treasure tradition itself locates its source in India, and the historian of religion can recognize influences from China as well, the phenomenologist of religion will notice the indigenous Tibetan elements operative in Treasure. We have already noted above that the practice of burying objects in the ground has early Tibetan roots. The significance of retrieving a text out of the Tibetan earth (or mind) should also not be lost on us. This is particularly evident in the Buddhist case, where Indic origin was a critical criterion for a text's inclusion in the bKa' 'gyur and bsTan 'gyur, the Buddhist canon with which Treasure competes. If we bracket, for a moment, the Treasure tradition's own construction of Indian precedent, we may note the thorough-going Tibetanness of the *eidos* of Treasure, i.e., the essentially Tibetan character, or thrust, of a Treasure's claim to fame and importance at the moment it is being presented into the Tibetan world. A Treasure is a text that has not been propagated in India; it was concealed during the period of the Tibetan nation's apogee of military might and golden age of Buddhist practice; it was formulated specifically for this particular moment in Tibetan history; its prophecies in fact describe this moment pointedly; and now this particular Tibetan master has revealed it to Tibet at the proper time.

Whether drawn out of the Tibetan ground or a Tibetan mind, the Treasure stands as a Tibetan product, in this important sense independent of Buddhist and other traditions of Tibet's neighbors. This independence is repeated on the smaller scale, too, within the dynamics of Tibet's internal scene. On this scale, the Treasure is an alternative, and challenge to the religious teachings being propagated in institutionalized, monastic circles. The discoverer himself is an autonomous, maverick figure, typically declaring his independence from received tradition and study; rather, the discoverer focuses on his own mind, his own visions, his own memory of a previous life as Padmasambhava's disciple, his own predestined revelation that he propagates to his own circle of disciples. This recourse to the independent master facilitated by the Treasure tradition underlines the creativity that is thereby made possible. The Treasure itself describes a new vision, and a new system of meditation or ritual. The fact that innovation is made possible by Treasure means that vitality, flexibility, and responsiveness to new situations and needs are maintained in Tibetan religion.

Content and Genres

Here we can only sketch out some of the general features of an enormous landscape. Futher, this overview is limited to Buddhist Treasure; a full study of the Bon Treasure literature, especially when the Bon po canon becomes more readily available, will surely add much to our understanding of the Treasure tradition.

As already indicated, we may make a basic distinction between two major types of Treasure subject matter: (1) the "historical," which in the Buddhist case concerns the introduction of Buddhism to Tibet during the Yar lung dynasty, and (2) religious doctrine and practice.

Again, the first type exemplifies the Treasure tradition's focus upon primarily Tibetan matters. Tibetologists have long recognized that despite certain genuine ancient passages preserved therein, the Treasure narratives are greatly overlaid with myth and fantasy, and are not to be considered as providing historical information (Vostrikov). Nonetheless, the Treasure accounts of the events of the Yar lung dynasty are critical for our understanding of the way that period was retrospectively romanticized and glorified in Tibetans' views of their country's past, as well as the implications of that period for the place of Buddhism in Tibetan society altogether. The Treasures offer some of the most detailed stories of the seventh-century King Srong btsan sgam po, who builds many Buddhist temples to subdue the wild indigenous "demoness" of Tibet, and whose two wives from Nepal and China bring statues of the Buddha; of King Khri srong lde btsan, who invites the Indian Buddhist philosopher Śāntarakṣita and the tantric master Padmasambhava, and builds bSam yas Monastery; of Padmasambhava, who introduces tantric Buddhism in Tibet, and brings under submission Tibet's demons who are transformed thereby into protectors of Buddhism; of the Tibetan teacher Vairocana, who is instrumental in the introduction of rDzogs chen in Tibet; of the great debate between the Indian master Kamalaśīla and the Chinese master Hva shang; and of many other matters at the heart of the founding of Buddhism in Tibet.[15]

The Buddhist Treasures that present these stories, along with much other material, date primarily from the twelfth to the fourteenth centuries. The *Maṇi bka' 'bum* is one of the few Buddhist Treasures that does not deal with Padmasambhava and the period of Khri srong lde btsan, but rather with the hagiography and purported teachings of Srong btsan sgam po. It also presents *sādhanas* for Avalokiteśvara as well as several Indic Buddhist canonical texts connected to the cult of Avalokiteśvara (Macdonald; Aris, 1979: 8-12; Kapstein, 1991; Blondeau, 1984). The *bKa' thang sde lnga* Treasure has five books: the *rGyal po* (Kings), *bTsun mo* (Queens), *Blon po* (Ministers), *Lo paṇ* (Translators and Pandits), and *Lha 'dre* (Gods and Ghosts), and was discovered in stages by O rgyan gling pa in the latter third of the fourteenth century (Blondeau, 1971: 42). These texts focus on the events surrounding Padmasambhava, but contain many other legends as well as passages with historical value, along with such diverse materials as an elaborate and lengthy description of the treasuries of the gYar lung kings in the *rGyal po*, and the Ch'an materials in the *Blon po*, already mentioned.[16] As for the Treasures devoted solely to the hagiography of Padmasambhava, they have been analysed by Blondeau (1980), who found that the Treasure traditions of Padmasambhava's life portray his "miraculous birth" while non-Treasure renditions of his life speak of his "womb birth." The earliest of the Treasure hagiographies of Padmasambhava is the *Zangs gling ma*, discovered by Nyang ral Nyi ma 'od zer (*ZL*); the two best known are the *Shel brag ma*, discovered by O rgyan gling pa (1329-1367) (translated by Toussaint), and the *gSer phreng*, discovered by Sangs rgyas gling pa (1340-1367), which both contain a separate chapter of prophecies of Treasure discoverers. Another major "historical" Treasure is the hagiography of Padmasambhava's Tibetan consort Ye shes mtsho rgyal, discovered by sTag sham rdo rje in the seventeenth century, which recently has been translated into English twice (Dowman; Nam mkha'i snying po).

The second type of subject matter, that which presents religious teachings, *sādhanas*, and rituals, constitutes the content of the majority of Treasure cycles. Once again, let us note that since most Treasures are purported to have been preached by Padmasambhava, these cycles too contain "historical" passages concerning the Yar lung period as well. But the bulk of the cycle is devoted to teachings and practices.

With the exception of several hagiographies of Padmasambhava, biographies of the Treasure discoverers, and texts relating to the structure of the collection, the one hundred plus volumes of the *RT* are comprised of these *sādhana*/ritual cycles. The *RT*'s editor, Kong sprul, has arranged much of the Treasures in this collection according to the nature of the central visualized figure of the *sādhana*/ritual. And since most of the Treasure cycles include several sections which focus upon different figures, Kong sprul saw fit to break these cycles up and insert the parts into their appropriate volumes so as to fit into the general structure according to which he arranged the collection as a whole. Thus the *Rig 'dzin 'dus pa* section of the famed Treasure cycle *Klong chen snying thig* will be found in volume 14 of the *RT* along with sections of other Treasure cycles that focus on a visualization of the interior guru in "peaceful form" as a *nirmāṇakāya*; the *Bla sgrub thig le'i rgya can* section of that same cycle is in volume 17 along with other Treasures presenting *gurusādhanas*; and the rDzogs chen sections of the cycle are in volume 89, in the rDzogs chen portion of the *RT*.

The main organizing principle of the *RT* is the group of the three "inner *tantras*" of the Old canon: the Mahāyoga, Anuyoga, and Atiyoga. The predominance of the first group, the Mahāyoga, in Treasure cycles may be seen from the fact that it occupies volumes 3 to 85 of the *RT*. The Anuyoga is represented by but a few cycles in volumes 85 and 86, and the Atiyoga occupies volumes 86 to 91. [17]

The deities of the Mahāyoga are organized in the *RT* under the three headings of *guru*, *yi dam* (the practitioner's principal deity; Skt. *iṣṭadevatā*), and *ḍākinī*. These headings are further broken down into such standard categories as the external/internal dyad, and the fourfold peaceful/extensive/powerful/wrathful typology of deities. The *gurusādhanas* are exceedingly numerous, occupying fourteen volumes of the *RT*. The *yi dams*, Treasures concerning whom fill thirty-two volumes of the *RT*, are primarily the eight who are classed together in the Mahāyoga *tantras* as the bKa' brgyad. The *ḍākinīs*, comprising five volumes of the *RT*, include a variety of female deities. The Atiyoga Treasures also use some of the same deities in their practices, but there is more emphasis in these cycles on meditative techniques that focus on the nature of the mind. A large variety of techniques are introduced in the Treasures for recognizing that nature, and separate texts that focus on such practices are again organized taxonomically.

When one examines an individual Treasure in one of these categories, one finds that it too is divided into sections, but now at this closer level the organizing principle is no longer deity, and rather is literary genre. This genre-based organization is never strictly determined, but the ideal pattern, if one may say so, consists in what I have called a "core text," and its "surrounding" subsidiary commentarial and ritual texts (Gyatso, 1991). The core text may be couched as a *tantra* or other sort of "root text" (*mūla; rtsa ba*), and it is most likely to represent the revealed Treasure vision or philosophical teaching itself. As such, it will be anonymous, or couched as the words of Padmasambhava, or a buddha, or deity. It is also recognizable by the orthographical device of the *gter shad*—a ༔ separating each line instead of the standard ། used in other forms of Tibetan literature. However, sometimes the *gter shad* is used improperly to mark the subsidiary commentaries and associated rituals as well.

The authorship of the subsidiary texts is often explicitly attributed to the discoverer, or even to a disciple; thus many of the texts included in the *RT* are strictly speaking not revealed Treasures but rather merely based upon them. The principal subsidiary texts are either descriptions of how to perform the empowerment ritual whereby disciples are initiated into the practices of the root text and/or its associated deity, or are *sādhanas* describing how to identify oneself as the deity in visualization meditation (see Cozort, in this volume). But then again, sometimes the revealed core text is itself an empowerment or *sādhana*.

The many other subsidiary genres present the many other types of rituals and liturgies associated with the core revelation, to the point that a typology of Treasure genres will be a typology of Tibetan rituals. Some of these rituals are placed close to their core texts in the *RT*, but others have been gathered in the last portion of the Mahāyoga section, in volumes 64 through 84, which becomes a virtual catalogue of the Treasure rituals that the practitioner of a given cycle may employ as needed or desired. A sampling of some of the genres/rituals included here: construction of *maṇḍalas*; manufacture of ritual hats and costumes; geomantical analysis of a place for its spiritual properties (*sa dpyad*); rituals to appease the human and non-human "owners" of a place in which one intends to practice (*sa chog*); methods to ascertain the disposition of the large being that constitutes the entirety of a place (*sa bdag lto 'phye)*; invocation of blessings (*byin 'bebs*); general meritorious rituals performed between more complex rituals (*chos spyod)*; additional rituals to compensate for ritual transgressions (*bskang bzhags*); techniques for eating bits of paper inscribed with therapeutic mantra letters (*za yig sngags 'bum*); construction of offering cakes (*gtor ma*); mass offering-feast liturgies (*tshogs mchod*); consecration of icons (*rab gnas*); rites for the dead; burnt juniper offerings (*bsang)*; construction of thread-crosses (*mdos*); uses of effigies (*glud*); crop cultivation; weather control; turning back of armies; protective devices against weapons; curing of physiological and psychological disease; extending of lifespan (*tshe sgrub*). Surveying this literature, one realizes how much a Treasure revelation is a starting point for the colorful tantric dramaturgy for which Tibetan religion is so well known. Each discoverer introduces new styles, images, and techniques; many have been accomplished choreographers, painters, sculptors, costume designers.

Several genres that are to be found at some point in the Treasure cycle are a function of the special features that distinguish Treasure from other forms of tantric literature. Most important is the prophecy (*lung bstan*) text, in which Padmasambhava predicts the future discoverer and the moment in history when the Treasure will be revealed. This text (or passage embedded in another text) is the central legimating device of the Treasure; it proves, or attempts to prove, that the cycle was not authored by the discoverer but rather was formulated by Padmasambhava in the past. It also proves that the discoverer is in fact the person who was designated by Padmasambhava for the revelation of this Treasure. A related, distinctive Treasure genre is the certificate (*byang bu;* see Gyatso, n.d.), a curious mini-Treasure discovered prior to the Treasure proper, which may also include prophecies as well as explicit directions on how to find the rest of the cycle. Both the prophecy and certificate are part of the visionary "core" of the Treasure; they inevitably are marked with the *gter shad* device, and are presented as the words of Padmasambhava.

Another important legitimating genre within the religious Treasure is the history of the cycle (sometimes called *lo rgyus*) which may or may not be part of the visionary core. I have identified two main types, one which recounts the transmission of the cycle from its origin in a buddha-land up to its concealment by Padmasambhava, and the other which narrates the events of the discovery (Gyatso, 1993). The account of the transmission of the cycle is often incorporated into the core, and functions to legitimate in much the same way as the prophecy and certificate just discussed.

The second, the account of the discovery, is of particular interest, since it too is meant to legitimate, or to "engender confidence" (*nges shes bskyes pa*) in the Treasure, but it does so on entirely different grounds than do the references to Padmasambhava and his buddha predecessors. Here the reader is presented with an individualistic account of the discoverer's trials and struggles in realizing the revelatory vision. The text recounting this visionary process is often authored by the discoverer. In some instances it is detailed enough to constitute the discoverer's autobiography, or "visionary autobiography," in that what is of concern is the discoverer's visionary career and development as a whole, as well as the events following the climactic revelatory episode, such as his decision to teach and publish the Treasure. Reading these accounts, we can observe quite concretely that the Treasure argument for legitimation is not based solely upon the invocation of the Treasure myth and the discoverer's purported role in the burial of the Treasure centuries earlier. Rather, there is an equal, if not greater, emphasis placed upon a show of honesty and an admission of inadequacies and error, as if such candor and display of self-doubt would also, ironically, engender confidence in the discoverer. The Treasure tradition understands the discoverer ultimately to become a highly realized meditation master capable of "owning" and "controlling" the powerful and esoteric teachings that the Treasure presents; he is not simply Padmasambhava's mailman or delivery boy, as one representative of the Treasure tradition recently put it.[18] The painting of the visions, dreams, and personal qualities in the discoverer's autobiography gives us a picture of an idiosyncratic personality on the way to such mastery, and a sense of the importance of the charismatic individual in the Treasure tradition overall. Here the virtue of creativity reigns supreme.

Notes

1. *GC* lists four main types of material objects that are hidden and then rediscovered as Treasure (81-82), which include wish-fulfilling jewels and auspicious skull-cups, but also such items as entire valleys that are hidden so as to be discovered later by followers of Padmasambhava in order to escape enemies; concealed supplies of water; condensed substances to be mixed into building materials for the construction of temples; hidden forests for building in times of shortage; wealth to buy food for hungry Dharma practitioners; magical techniques to subdue barbarians; and bodily exercises to improve health (81-82). It also discusses the various sorts of icons and images that are concealed as Treasure (87-88). A rare glimpse of Treasure-discovered icons, ritual objects, and scripts may be had from an excellent collection of color photographs published by Tulku Thondup Rinpoche (between pp. 144 and 145).

2. According to Pratz, the discoverer Khyung po dpal dge belongs to the end of the tenth century. The first Bon po discovery of Treasure, by the three Nepalese "*ācāryas*" (Karmay, 1972: xxxiv) is dated in one traditional Bon po chronological table to 913 C.E., although Kvaerne (1974: 38) shows that the first Bon po discoveries by these and other figures cannot have taken place before 1050. Note too that another, earlier Bon po chronological table recently published by Kvaerne (1990) gives dates as much as 240 years later than those of the table published in Kvaerne (1971) which has been followed in most Western studies of Bon prior to 1990. In any case, the history of the development of the Treasure movement needs more research. In particular, the detailed accounts of certain individual Treasure cycles, especially those in the *sNying thig ya bzhi* (e.g., *DZ*), merit close study. Some of the most lengthy and accessible general surveys of the lives of the Buddhist discoverers are the products of the nineteenth and twentieth centuries, for example *GT*, *ND*, *TG*, *NC*. Earlier sources for the lives of the discoverers include the sixteenth-century *SD*, *DL*, and *YM*; the seventeenth-century *SB*; and the eighteenth-century *ST*, as well as the brief "prophetic" summaries of the discoverers' lives in the earlier Treasure hagiographies of Padmasambhava, such as chapter 92 of O rgyan gling pa's *Shel brag ma* (Toussaint: 376-389). Among the many other sources useful for a study of the lineages of the Buddhist Treasure discoverers is the *dkar chag* of the *RT* (vol. 2: 49-617). The *TN*, also of the nineteenth century, is an excellent discussion of the theory and practice of the Treasure tradition. The first non-Treasure-related general history of Tibet known to me that treats the Treasure tradition in depth is *KG* of the sixteenth century (631-661). The earliest survey of the Buddhist Treasure tradition altogether known to me is the thirteenth-century *GC* (see Gyatso, 1994). See also the fifteenth-century *RG*: 48-67. The Bon po tradition preserves several early historical accounts which require further study; see, among others, *Srid pa rgyud kyi kha byang rnam thar chen mo* (Karmay, 1977: no. 61; Karmay, 1972: 196); *'Phrul ngag bon gyi bsgrags byang* (Karmay, 1977: no. 64; Karmay, 1972: 194); *rGyal rabs bon gyi 'byung gnas* (Das; see Karmay, 1972: 194) and *rNam thar chen mo* (Karmay, 1972: 195.) Pioneering work concerning the Bon po Treasure tradition has been done by Anne-Marie Blondeau, Samten G. Karmay

and Per Kvaerne. A promising, heretofore unexamined source concerning Bon Treasure is *gTer gyi kha byang* by sGa ston Tshul khrims rgyal mtshan (fourteenth century), a manuscript in 45 folios, reportedly being translated currently by Tenzin Wangyal and Ramon Pratz.

3. An important study of an early example of the cross-pollination between the Buddhist and Bon po Treasure traditions is Blondeau, 1984. See also Blondeau, 1971, 1985, 1987, and especially 1988 concerning the inclusion of Bon po materials in the *RT*. The fact that there have been numerous discoverers who have revealed both Bon and Buddhist Treasures is well known. See Tulku Thondup Rinpoche, Appendix 1, assessing the relationship from a Buddhist standpoint.

4. Note that the spelling of the second section of the canon differs from that of the Buddhist bsTan 'gyur (Kvaerne, 1974: 23).

5. If we are to follow the *bstan rtsis* of Tshul khrims rgyal mtshan (Kvaerne, 1990) the date of the editing of this canon would be after 1475, the death date of Shes rab rgyal mtshan according to this source. See also Kvaerne, in this volume.

6. Concerning the *rNying ma'i rgyud 'bum*, see n. 7. Regarding the sNying thig literature, see n. 8.

7. See Gyatso, 1981: 233-250 for a descriptive analysis of the *Grub thob thugs tig* Treasure of 'Jam dbyangs mkhyen brtse'i dbang po (1820-1892), noting the many assertions, in the colophons of the various texts of that cycle, of association with one or another of the Old Tantras. The *rNying ma'i brgyud 'bum* is currently available in several editions which differ substantially in content and order. It is usually said to have been compiled first by the fifteenth-century Ratna Gling pa, but there is evidence of its existence in some form prior to him, at least as early as the time of 'Gro ba mgon po Nam mkha' dpal, son of Nyang ral Nyi ma 'od zer (1136-1204). Franz-Karl Ehrhard is currently preparing a detailed historical study of the *rNying ma'i rgyud 'bum*.

8. Vimalamitra's Tibetan student, Nyang ban Ting 'dzin bzang po, was said to have concealed these teachings after the master went to China. The discoverer was gNas brtan lDang ma lhun rgyal (eleventh century), who proceeded to transmit the material to lCe btsun Seng ge dbang phyug, one of the first accomplished Tibetan Buddhist yogis, and to others. This sequence of events narrated in the colophon of *RR*: 100.696-698. Another, more detailed account is to be found in *DZ*: 163-169 et seq. See also Roerich: 191 et seq. Regarding Vimalamitra, see Davidson: 9-10. Another significant non-Padmasambhava Treasure is the *Maṇi bka' 'bum*, supposedly the teachings of Srong btsan sgam po (seventh century). *KG*, vol. 1: 625, lists these Treasure concealers in addition to Padmasambhava: [Ye shes] mTsho rgyal, Khri srong lde btsan, Mu tig btsan po, sNubs Nam mkha' snying po, sNyags [Jñānakumāra], Vairocana, sNa nam rDo rje bDud 'joms, and sNubs Sangs rgyas ye shes.

9. One of the principal architects of which was Nyang ral, himself a tantric master belonging to an old Tibetan aristocratic family. Nyang ral's account of

the life of Padamsambhava is the *Zangs gling ma* (*ZL*). Regarding the development of the hagiographies of Padmasambhava, see Blondeau, 1980.

10. The great majority of Treasure discoverers were men, as far as we know. One female discoverer was Jo mo sMan mo (thirteenth century; see Dudjom Rinpoche, vol. 1: 771-774). In this article I have primarily used the male pronoun to refer to the discoverers.

11. For an extended narrative of both these incidents see Karmay, 1972, which is a translation of the *Legs bshad mdzod*, an early twentieth-century history of the Bon po tradition that draws extensively on such early Bon po sources as the twelfth-century(?) *sGrags byang* and fourteenth-century(?) *Srid rgyud*. See Karmay's comments (xxxiii) suggesting "the possibility that later Bon po historians have made two persecutions out of what was in fact only one." Note that no Treasures are said to have been discovered after the first persecution abated; the first Bon po Treasure discovery is that of the Nepalese "*ācāryas*."

12. Most of the discoveries recounted in *Legs bshad mdzod* (Karmay, 1972) are framed by prophecies quoted from the *Srid rgyud*. The so-called *rGyal rabs bon gyi 'byung gnas* is another relatively early Bon po account that also refers to the appointing of Treasure protectors and the making of prayers for the future discovery (Das: 43 and 50). The Treasure tradition as a whole is labelled in that text as "the manner in which the Bon teachings increased due to the force of [previous] prayers" (Das: 56).

13. The most famous is the discovery by the "three *ācāryas*" (Karmay, 1972: 116 seq.) but note that even this account is preceeded by the claim that it happened "[t]hrough the power of the prayers of Dran-pa Nam-mkha'." The Treasure discovery by the three hunters (Karmay, 1972: 124) also appears to be understood to have been accidental, and lHa dgon finds Treasures based upon an oral tradition originating with his great-grandfather's assertion that texts were hidden in that place (Karmay, 1972: 125). But see n. 12 above. It is interesting to note that whereas Karmay, discussing the Bon po Treasure tradition, suggests that those discoveries made by unlettered men or that were accidental argues for their authenticity (1972: xxxvi-xxxvii), the Buddhist Treasure tradition in its fully developed form would not regard such an accidental event as an authentic discovery of Treasure for precisely that reason.

14. Namkhai Norbu, a current Treasure discoverer who propagates both Buddhist and Bon po teachings, attributes specifically to the Buddhist tradition of Padmasambhava the development of what he characterized as the "precise" technique whereby prophecy compels and determines the later recovery; private interview, 1990. The same view was expressed by mKhan po 'Jigs med phun tshogs, one of the foremost Treasure discoverers operative in Tibet today; private interview, 1993.

15. Some of these Buddhist legends have been found to be based upon earlier Bon po ones: See for example Blondeau, 1971: 33 et seq.; 1975-76: 118.

16. See Thomas: 264-288 for an English translation of parts of the *rGyal po* and *bLon po*, and Laufer for a German translation of the *bTsun mo*.

17. For rDo grub chen's typology of the content of Treasure cycles, see Tulku Thondup Rinpoche: 116-125.

18. mKhan po tshe dbang, speaking of 'Jigs med gling pa in the introduction to an empowerment ritual to the *Yum bka'* given by the fourth rDo grub chen Rin po che in New York City in July 1989.

References

Aris, Michael

1979 *Bhutan: The Early History of a Himalayan Kingdom.* Warminster: Aris and Phillips, 1979.

1989 *Hidden Treasures and Secret Lives: A Study of Pemalingpa (1450-1521) and the Sixth Dalai Lama (1683-1706).* London: Kegan Paul International.

bDud 'joms 'Jigs bral ye shes rdo rje

NC *Gang ljong rgyal bstan yongs rdzogs kyi phyi ma snga 'gyur rdo rje theg pa'i bstan pa rin po che ji ltar byung ba'i tshul dag cing gsal bar brjod pa lha dbang gyul las rgyud ba'i rnga bo che'i sgra dbyangs.* In *Collected Works,* vol. 1. Kalimpong, 1979. [Translated in Dudjom Rinpoche.]

Blondeau, Anne-Marie

1971 "Le Lha-'dre bKa'-thaṅ." In *Études tibétaines dédiées à la mémoire de Marcelle Lalou,* pp. 33-126. Paris: Adrien-Maisonneuve.

1975-76 In *Annuaire de l'École Pratique des Hautes Études,* 84. V^{e} section, pp. 109-119.

1980 "Analysis of the Biographies of Padmasambhava According to Tibetan Tradition: Classification of Sources." In *Tibetan Studies in Honour of Hugh Richardson,* pp. 45-52. Edited by Michael Aris and Aung San Suu Kyi. Warminster: Aris and Phillips.

1984 "Le 'Découvreur' du Maṇi Bka'-'bum était-il Bon-po?" In *Tibetan and Buddhist Studies Commemorating the 200th Anniversary of the Birth of Alexander Csoma de Körös,* pp. 77-123. Edited by Louis Ligeti. Budapest: Akadémiai Kiadó.

1985 "Mkhyen-brce'i Dba'-po: La biographie de Padmasambhava selon la tradition du Bsgrags-pa Bon, et ses sources." In *Orientalia Iosephi Tucci Memoriae Dicata.* Edited by G. Gnoli and L. Lanciotti. Rome: Istituto Italiano per il Medio ed Estremo Oriente.

1987 "Une Polémique sur l'authenticité des *Bka'-thaṅ* au 17e siècle." *Silver on Lapis: Tibetan Literary Culture and History,* pp. 125-160. Edited by Christopher I. Beckwith. Bloomington: The Tibet Society.

1988 "La controverse soulevée par l'inclusion de rituels bon-po dans le 1988 *Rin-chen gter-mjod.* Note préliminaire." In *Tibetan Studies, Proceedings of the 4th Seminar of the International Association for Tibetan Studies,* pp. 55-67. Edited by Helga Uebach and Jampa L. Panglung. Munich: Kommission für Zentralasiatische Studien Bayerische Akademie der Wissenschaften.

Bokenkamp, Stephen R.
1986 "The Peach Flower Font and the Grotto Passage." *Journal of the American Oriental Society* 106/1: 65-77.

Bu ston Rin chen grub
BC *bDe bar gshegs pa'i bstan pa'i gsal byed chos kyi 'byung gnas gsung rab rin po che'i mdzod*. In *The Collected Works of Bu-ston*. Ed. by Lokesh Chandra. New Delhi: International Academy of Indian Culture, 1971.

Byang bdag bKra shis stobs rgyal
SD *gTer brgya'i rnam thar don bsdus gsol 'debs*. In *RT*, vol. 2, pp. 1-31.

Dargyay, Eva M.
1977 *The Rise of Esoteric Buddhism in Tibet*. Delhi: Motilal Banarsidass.

Das, Sri Sarat Chandra, ed.
1915 *Gyal Rab Bon-Ke Jun Neh*. Calcutta: Bengal Secretariat Book Depot.

Davidson, Ronald M.
1981 "The Litany of Names of Mañjuśrī." In *Tantric and Taoist Studies in Honour of R. A. Stein*, pp. 1-69. Ed. by Michel Strickmann. Brussels: Institut Belge des Hautes Études Chinoises.

Dowman, Keith
1984 *Sky Dancer: The Secret Life and Songs Of The Lady Yeshe Tsogyel*. London: Routledge and Kegan Paul.

dPa' bo gtsug lag phreng ba
KG *Chos 'byung mkhas pa'i dga ston*. Beijing: Mi rigs dpe skrun khang, 1986.

'Dul 'dzin mKhyen rab rgya mtsho
DL *Saṅs rgyas bstan pa'i chos 'byuṅ dris lan nor bu'i phreṅ ba*. Gangtok: Dzongsar Chhentse Labrang, 1981.

Dudjom Rimpoche, Jigdrel Yeshe Dorje
1991 *The Nyingma School of Tibetan Buddhism*. Translated by Gyurme Dorje and Matthew Kapstein. 2 vols. Boston: Wisdom.

Guru bKra shis Ngag dbang blo gros/ dByangs can dga' ba'i blo gros
GT *bsTan pa'i snying po gsang chen snga 'gyur nges don zab mo'i chos kyi 'byung ba gsal bar byed pa'i legs bshad mkhas pa dga' byed ngo mtshar gtam gyi rol mtsho*. 5 vols. Written 1807-1813. Published by (Dilgo) Jamyang Khentse, n.p., n.d.

Guru Chos dbang
GC *gTer 'byung chen mo*. In *The Autobiography and Instructions of Guru Chos-kyi-dbaṅ-phyug*, vol. 2, pp. 75-193. Reproduced from a manuscript in the library of Lopon Choedak. Paro: Ugyen Tempai Gyaltsen, 1979.

Gyatso, Janet

1981 "The Literary Transmission of the Traditions of Thang-stong Rgyal-po: A Study of Visionary Buddhism in Tibet." Ph.D. dissertation. Berkeley: University of California.

1986 "Signs, Memory and History: A Tantric Buddhist Theory of Scriptural Transmission." *Journal of the International Association of Buddhist Studies* 9/2: 7-35.

1991 "Genre, Authorship and Transmission in Visionary Buddhism: The Literary Traditions of Thang-stong rGyal-po." In *Tibetan Buddhism: Reason and Revelation*, pp. 95-106. Edited by Ronald M. Davidson and Steven D. Goodman. Albany: State University of New York Press.

1993 "The Logic of Legitimation in the Tibetan Treasure Tradition." *History of Religions* 33/1: 97-134.

1994 "Guru Chos-dbang's *gTer 'byung chen mo:* An Early Survey of the Treasure Tradition and Its Strategies in Discussing Bon Treasure." In *Tibetan Studies: Proceedings of the 6th Seminar of the International Association of Tibetan Studies, Fagernes 1992*, pp. 275-287. Ed. by Per Kvaerne. Oslo: The Institute for Comparative Research in Human Culture.

n.d. "The Relic Text as Prophecy: The Semantic Drift of *Byang-bu* and its Appropriation in the Treasure Tradition." *Tibet Journal*, Rai Bahadur T. D. Densapa Special Commemorative Issue.

Harrison, Paul

1990 *The Samādhi of Direct Encounter with the Buddhas of the Present: An Annotated English Translation of the Tibetan Version of the* Pratyutpanna-Buddha-Saṃmukhāvasthita-Samādhi-Sūtra. Tokyo: The International Institute for Buddhist Studies.

Kapstein, Matthew

1989 "The Purificatory Gem and Its Cleansing: A Late Tibetan Polemical Discussion of Apocryphal Texts." *History of Religions* 28/3: 217-244.

1991 "Remarks on the Maṇi Bka' 'bum and the Cult of Avalokiteśvara in Tibet." In *Tibetan Buddhism: Reason and Revelation*, pp. 79-94. Ed. by Ronald M. Davidson and Steven D. Goodman. Albany: State University of New York Press.

Karmay, Samten G.

1972 *The Treasury of Good Sayings: A Tibetan History of Bon*. London: Oxford University Press, 1972. [Translation of the *Legs bshad mdzod*.]

1977 *A Catalogue of Bonpo Publications*. Tokyo: Tōyō Bunko.

1988 *The Great Perfection: A Philosophical and Meditative Teaching of Tibetan Buddhism*. Leiden: E. J. Brill.

Kong sprul Blo gros mtha' yas, ed.

RT *Rin chen gter mdzod*. 111 vols. sTod lung mtshur phu redaction, with supplemental texts from the dPal spungs redaction and other manuscripts. Reproduced at the order of the Ven. Dingo Chhentse Rimpoche. Paro, Bhutan: Ngodrup and Sherab Drimay, 1976.

TG *Zab mo'i gter dang gter ston grub thob ji ltar byon pa'i lo rgyus mdor bsdus bkod pa rin chen baiḍūrya'i phreng ba*. In *RT*, vol. 1: 291-759.

Kun bzang nges don klong yangs

ND *Bod du byung ba'i gsang sngags snga 'gyur gyi bstan 'dzin skyes mchog rim byon gyi rnam thar nor bu'i do shal*. Dalhousie, India: Damchoe Sangpo, 1976.

Kvaerne, Per

1971 "A Chronological Table of the Bon Po: The Bstan Rcis of Ñi Ma Bstan 'Jin." *Acta Orientalia* [Copenhagen] 32: 205-282.

1974 "The Canon of the Tibetan Bonpos." *Indo-Iranian Journal* 16: 18-56; 96-144.

1983 "'The Great Perfection' in the Tradition of the Bonpos." In *Early Ch'an in China and Tibet*, pp. 351-366. Edited by Whalen Lai and Lewis R. Lancaster. Berkeley: Berkeley Buddhist Studies Series.

1990 "A Bonpo *bsTan-rtsis* from 1804." In *Indo-Tibetan Studies*, pp. 151-169. Ed. by Tadeusz Skorupski. Buddhica Britannica Series Continua 2. Tring: The Institute of Buddhist Studies.

Laufer, B.

1911 *Der Roman einer tibetischen Konigin*. Leipzig.

Macdonald, Ariane

1968-69 In *Annuaire de l'École Pratique des Hautes Études*. IVe section, pp. 527-535.

MacQueen, Graeme

1981-82 "Inspired Speech in Early Mahāyāna Buddhism." *Religion* 11: 303-319; 12: 49-65.

Nam mkha'i snying po

1983 *Mother of Knowledge: The Enlightenment of Ye-shes mTsho-rgyal*. Translated by Tarthang Tulku. Berkeley: Dharma Publishing.

Nyang ral Nyi ma 'od zer

ZL *sLob dpon padma'i rnam thar zangs gling ma*. Beijing: So khron mi rigs dpe skrun khang, 1987.

Ratna Gling pa

RG *gTer 'byung chen mo gsal ba'i sgron me*. In *Selected Works of Ratna-gliṅ-pa*, vol. 1, pp. 1-215. Tezu, Arunachal Pradesh: Tseten Dorje, 1973.

rDo grub chen 'Jigs med bstan pa'i nyi ma
TN *Las 'phro gter brgyud kyi rnam bshad nyung gsal ngo mtshar rgya mtsho*. In *The Collected Works (Gsuṅ 'bum) of Rdo-Grub-Chen 'Jigs-Med-Bstan-Pa'i-Ñi-ma*, vol. 4, pp. 377-447. Gangtok: Dodrup Chen Rinpoche, 1975. [Translated in Tulku Thondup Rinpoche.]

Rig 'dzin Kun grol grags pa
ST *Sangs rgyas bstan pa spyi yi 'byung khung yid bzhin nor bu 'dod pa 'jo ba'i gter mdzod*. In *Three Sources for a History of Bon*, pp. 197-552. Dolanji: Khedup Gyatso, 1974.

Roerich, George N.
1949 *The Blue Annals*. 2 vols. Calcutta: Royal Asiatic Society of Bengal.

RR *De bzhin gshegs pa thams cad kyi ting nge 'dzin dngos su bshad pa ye shes 'dus pa'i mdo theg pa chen po gsang ba bla na med pa'i rgyud chos thams cad kyi 'byung gnas sangs rgyas thams cad kyi dgongs pa gsang sngags gcig pa'i ye shes rdzogs pa chen po don gsal bar byed pa'i rgyud rig pa rang shar chen po'i rgyud*. In *The Tibetan Tripitaka, Taipei Edition*, vol. 56, pp. 46-100. Taipei: SMC Publishing, 1991.

Smith, E. Gene
1970 "Introduction" to *Kongtrul's Encyclopaedia of Indo-Tibetan Culture*, pp. 1-78. Ed. by Lokesh Chandra. New Delhi: International Academy of Indian Culture.

Sog bzlog pa Blo gros rgyal mtshan
YM *sLob dpon sans rgyas gñis pa padma 'byuṅ gnas kyi rnam par thar pa yid kyi mun sel*. Thimphu: The National Library of Bhutan, 1984.

Thomas, F.W.
1935 *Tibetan Literary Texts and Documents Concerning Chinese Turkestan*, pt. 1. London: Luzac.

Toussaint, G.C.
1933 *Le dict de Padma. Padma thaṅ yig*. Paris: Bibliothèque de l'Institut des Hautes Études Chinoises.

Tucci, Giuseppe
1958 *Minor Buddhist Texts*, Part II. Rome: Istituto Italiano per il Medio ed Estremo Oriente.

Tulku Thondup Rinpoche
1986 *Hidden Teachings of Tibet: An Explanation of the Terma Tradition of the Nyingma School of Buddhism*. London: Wisdom. [Includes English translation of *TN*.]

Ueyama, Daishun

1983 "The Study of Tibetan Ch'an Manuscripts Recovered from Tun-huang: A Review of the Field and Its Prospects." In *Early Ch'an in China and Tibet*, pp. 327-350. Ed. by Whalen Lai and Lewis R. Lancaster. Berkeley: Berkeley Buddhist Studies Series.

Vostrikov, A.I.

1970 *Tibetan Historical Literature.* Trans. by Harish Chandra Gupta. Calcutta: Indian Studies, Past & Present.

Zab bu gdan sa pa Karma mi 'gyur dbang gi rgyal po

SB *gTer bton brgya rtsa'i mtshan sdom gsol 'debs chos rgyal bkra shis stobs rgyal gyi mdzad pa las de'i 'brel pa lo rgyus gter bton chos 'byung*. Darjeeling: Taklung Tsetrul Rinpoche Pema Wangyal, 1978.

Zhang ston bKra shis rdo rje (?)

DZ *rDzogs pa chen po snying tig gi lo rgyus chen mo*. In *sNying thig ya bzhi of Klong-chen-pa Dri-med-'od-zer*, vol. 9 (*Bi ma snying thig*, part 3), pp. 1-179. New Delhi: Trulku Tsewang, Jamyang and L. Tashi, 1970.

Chapter 9

The Tibetan Genre of Doxography: Structuring a Worldview[1]

Jeffrey Hopkins

In the Tibetan cultural region (which stretches from Kalmuck Mongolian areas near the Volga River in Europe where the Volga empties into the Caspian Sea, through Outer and Inner Mongolia, the Buriat Republic of Siberia, and through Bhutan, Sikkim, Ladakh, and parts of Nepal) the genre of doxography called "presentations of tenets" (**siddhāntavyavasthāpana, grub mtha'i rnam bzhag*) mainly refers to delineations of the systematic schools of Buddhist and non-Buddhist Indian philosophy. In this context, "philosophy" is, for the most part, related to liberative concerns—the attempt to extricate oneself and others from a round of painful existence and to attain freedom. Focal topics and issues of these schools are presented in order to stimulate metaphysical inquiry—to encourage development of an inner faculty that is capable of investigating appearances so as to penetrate their reality.

The basic perspective is that the afflictive emotions—such as desire, hatred, enmity, jealousy, and belligerence—that bind beings in a round of uncontrolled birth, aging, sickness, and death are founded on misperception of the nature of persons and other phenomena. Thus, when one penetrates the reality of things and this insight is teamed with a powerful consciousness of concentrated meditation, the underpinnings of the process of cyclic existence can be destroyed, resulting in liberation. Also, when wisdom is further empowered through the development of love, compassion, and altruism—and by their corresponding actions—the wisdom consciousness is capable of achieving an all-knowing state in which one can effectively help a vast number of beings.

Because of this basic perspective, namely that false ideation traps beings in a round of suffering, *reasoned* investigation into the nature of persons and other phenomena is central to the process of spiritual development, though it is not the only concern. Systems of tenets, therefore, are primarily studied not to refute other systems but to develop an internal force that can counteract one's own *innate* adherence to misapprehensions. These innate forms of ignorance are part and parcel of ordinary life. They are not just learned from other systems, nor do they just arise from faulty analysis. Thus, the stated aim of studying the different schools of philosophy is to gain insight into the fact that many of the perspectives basic to ordinary life are devoid of a valid foundation. This leads the adept to then replace these with well-founded perspectives. The process is achieved through (1) first engaging in *hearing* great texts on such topics and getting straight the verbal presentation, (2) then *thinking* on their meaning to the point where the topics are ascertained with valid cognition, and (3) finally *meditating* on the same to the point where these realizations become enhanced by the power of concentration so that they can counteract innate tendencies to assent to false appearances.

Since it is no easy matter to penetrate the thick veil of false facades and misconceptions, it became popular in the more scholastic circles of India to investigate not just what the current tradition considered to be the best and final system but also the so-called lower systems. This provided a gradual approach to subtle topics that avoided their being confused with less subtle ones. Within such an outlook, a literary genre that compared the views of the different schools of thought developed in India and became even more systematized in Tibet. That the primary concern was indeed with developing the *capacity* to appreciate the profound view of a high system of philosophy is evidenced by the amount of time actually spent by students probing the workings of the so-called lower schools. Since the philosophies of those schools were appreciated, they were studied in considerable detail.

Because of the need to get a handle on the plethora of Buddhist systems, the genre of "presentations of tenets" assumed considerable importance in Tibet. The main Indian precursors were texts such as the *Tarkajvālā* ("Blaze of Reasoning") by Bhāvaviveka[2] (500-570 C.E.?) (Ruegg: 61) and the *Tattvasaṃgrahakārikā* ("Compendium of Principles") by the eighth-century scholar Śāntarakṣita with a commentary by his student Kamalaśīla (see Jha). Both Śāntarakṣita and Kamalaśīla visited Tibet in the eighth century and strongly influenced the direction that Buddhism took there.

In Tibet, the genre came to be more highly systematized, the presentations assuming a more developed structure.[3] Some of these texts are long; for instance, a lengthy text entitled *Theg pa mtha' dag gi don gsal bar byed pa grub pa'i mtha' rin po che'i mdzod* ("Treasury of Tenets, Illuminating the Meaning of All Vehicles") (*GTRD*) was written by the great fourteenth-century scholar Klong chen rab 'byams[4] (1308-1363) of the rNying ma school of Tibetan Buddhism. Another, the *Grub mtha' kun shes nas mtha' bral grub pa zhes bya ba'i bstan bcos rnam par bshad pa legs bshad kyi rgya mtsho* ("Explanation of 'Freedom from Extremes through Understanding All Tenets': Ocean of Good Explanations") (*GTKS*), was authored by the great fifteenth-century scholar sTag tshang lo tsā ba Shes rab rin chen (b. 1405) of the Sa skya school. The latter criticized many of the views of the founder of the dGe lugs pa school, Tsong kha pa Blo bzang grags pa (1357-1419), as being self-contradictory. sTag tshang's text in turn gave rise to the most extensive text of this genre in Tibet; the *Grub mtha'i rnam bshad rang gzhan grub mtha' kun dang zab don mchog tu gsal ba kun bzang zhing gi nyi ma lung rigs rgya mtsho skye dgu'i re ba kun skong* ("Explanation of 'Tenets,' Sun of the Land of Samantabhadra Brilliantly Illuminating All of Our Own and Others' Tenets and the Meaning of the Profound [Emptiness], Ocean of Scripture and Reasoning Fulfilling All Hopes of All Beings") (*GTCM*), also known as *Grub mtha' chen mo* ("Great Exposition of Tenets"),[5] by 'Jam dbyangs bzhad pa'i rdo rje ngag dbang brtson grus (1648-1721), is written in large part as a refutation of sTag tshang lo tsā ba Shes rab rin chen. 'Jam dbyangs bzhad pa's text is replete with citations of Indian sources but is written, despite its length, in a laconic style (unusual for him) that can leave one wondering about the relevance of certain citations. Perhaps this was part of the reason why the eighteenth-century Mongolian scholar lCang skya rol pa'i rdo rje (1717-1786)—whose reincarnation 'Jam dbyangs bzhad pa, then an old man, helped to find—composed a more issue-oriented text of the same genre entitled *Grub pa'i mtha'i rnam par bzhag pa gsal bar bshad pa thub bstan lhun po'i mdzes rgyan* ("Clear Exposition of the Presentations of Tenets, Beautiful Ornament for the Meru of the Subduer's Teaching") (*GTDG*).[6] After 'Jam dbyangs bzhad pa passed away, his reincarnation, dKon mchog 'jigs med dbang po (1728-1791), became lCang skya's main pupil. In 1733, dKon mchog 'jigs med dbang po wrote an abbreviated version of these texts, entitled *Grub pa'i mtha'i rnam par bzhag pa rin po che'i phreng ba* ("Presentation of Tenets, A Precious Garland") (*GTRP*) (see Sopa and Hopkins, 1990).

In this sub-genre of brief presentations of tenets are earlier texts such as the *Grub mtha'i rnam gzhag* ("Presentation of Tenets") (*GTNZ*) by rJe btsun Chos kyi rgyal mtshan (1469-1546), the *Grub mtha' rgya mtshor 'jug pa'i gru rdzings* ("Ship for Entering the Ocean of Tenets") (*GTGD*) by the second Dalai Lama dGe 'dun rgya mtsho (1476-1542), the *Grub mtha'i rnam bzhag blo gsal spro ba bskyed pa'i ljon pa phas rgol brag ri 'joms pa'i tho ba* ("Presentation of Tenets, Sublime Tree Inspiring Those of Clear Mind, Hammer Destroying the Stone Mountains of Opponents") (*GTTB*) by Paṇ chen bSod nams grags pa (1478-1554), and the *Grub mtha' thams cad kyi snying po bsdus pa* ("Condensed Essence of All Tenets") (*GTDP*) by Co ne ba Grags pa bshad sgrub (1675-1748).[7] A medium-length presentation of tenets that also treats the other schools of Tibetan Buddhism in a biased fashion was written by lCang-skya's biographer and student, who was also a student of dKon mchog 'jigs med dbang po, Thu'u bkvan Blo bzang chos kyi nyi ma (1737-1802). His text is called *Grub mtha' thams cad kyi khungs dang 'dod tshul ston pa legs bshad shel gyi me long* ("Mirror of the Good Explanations Showing the Sources and Assertions of All Systems of Tenets") (*GTSM*).

Most likely, authors such as dKon mchog 'jigs med dbang po chose to write concise texts so that the general outlines and basic postures of the systems of tenets could be taught and memorized without the encumbrance of a great deal of elaboration. Sometimes, the brevity itself makes the issues being discussed inaccessible, but, at minimum, it provides a foundation for the student, who can memorize these short texts and use them as a locus for further elaboration. The aim clearly is to provide an easy avenue for grasping issues that revolve around the nature of persons and phenomena according to a traditional system of education.

Format

dKon mchog 'jigs med dbang po's text is exemplary of the genre. It presents the principal tenets of Indian schools, both Buddhist and non-Buddhist, treating six renowned non-Buddhist schools very briefly and then focusing on the four Buddhist schools and their main sub-schools. In the order of their presentation (the list of Buddhist schools represents an ascent in order of estimation) these are:

- NON-BUDDHIST SCHOOLS
  - Vaiśeṣika (Bye brag pa) and Naiyāyika (Rig pa can pa) (Particularists and Logicians)
  - Sāṃkhya (Grangs can pa) (Enumerators)
  - Mīmāṃsā (dPyod pa ba) (Analyzers or Ritualists)
  - Nirgrantha (gCer bu pa) (The Unclothed, better known as Jaina [rGyal ba pa])
  - Lokāyata (rGyang 'phan pa) (Hedonists)
- BUDDHIST SCHOOLS
  - Hīnayāna (Lesser Vehicle)
    - Vaibhāṣika (Bye brag smra ba) (Great Exposition School) 18 sub-schools
    - Sautrāntika (mDo sde pa) (Sūtra School)
      - *Āgamānusārin (Lung gi rjes 'brangs) (Following Scripture)
      - *Nyāyānusārin (Rigs pa'i rjes 'brangs) (Following Reasoning)
  - Mahāyanā (Great Vehicle)
    - Cittamātra (Sems tsam pa) (Mind Only School)
      - *Āgamānusārin (Lung gi rjes 'brangs) (Following Scripture)
      - *Nyāyānusārin (Rigs pa'i rjes 'brangs) (Following Reasoning)
    - Mādhyamika (dBu ma pa) (Middle Way School)
      - Svātantrika (Rang rgyud pa) (Autonomy School)
      - Prāsaṅgika (Thal 'gyur pa) (Consequence School)

The division of Buddhist philosophy into four schools is itself largely an artificial creation. For instance, the so-called Vaibhāṣika school is, in fact, a collection of at least eighteen schools that never recognized themselves as belonging to a single, overarching school. Also, their tenets are so various (some prefiguring Great Vehicle schools) that it is extremely difficult to recognize tenets common to all eighteen; thus, rather than attempting to do so, the Tibetan doxographers set forth representative tenets as explained in the root text of Vasubandhu's *Abhidharmakośa* ("Treasury of Manifest Knowledge") (see Shastri, Poussin) as if these constituted the general tenet structure of such an overarching system, even though they are merely *typical* of assertions found in these eighteen schools. This pretended amalgamation of many schools into one is a technique used to avoid unnecessary complexity that might hinder the main purpose of this genre of exegesis—the presentation of an ascent to the views of systems considered to be higher. Hence, in the Vaibhāṣika school there *is* a wide variety of opinion, a wide range of views some of which differ greatly from the kind of short general presentation that dKon mchog 'jigs med dbang po gives. Strictly speaking, even the name "Vaibhāṣika school" should be limited to followers of the *Mahāvibhāṣā*, an Abhidharma text that was never translated into Tibetan.

Also, the division of the Sautrāntika school into those following scripture and those following reasoning is highly controversial. The former are said to follow Vasubandhu's own commentary on his *Abhidharmakośa*, in which he indicates disagreement with many assertions of the Vaibhāṣika school as presented in his own root text. The latter—the Proponents of Sūtra Following Reasoning—are said to be followers of Dignāga and Dharmakīrti who (despite the fact that Dignāga and Dharmakīrti do not assert external objects) assert external objects—objects that are different entities from the consciousnesses perceiving them. Again, neither of these groups saw themselves as sub-divisions of a larger school called the Sautrāntika.

Similarly, the two sub-divisions of the Cittamātra school are those following scripture, who depend on the writings primarily of Asaṅga and his half-brother Vasubandhu (after the latter converted to Asaṅga's system), and those following reasoning, who depend on what is accepted to be the main system of Dignāga's and Dharmakīrti's writings. Again, it is unlikely that these two groups perceived themselves as being sub-schools of a larger school. Rather, the groupings are the results of later schematizations that are based on similarities between their systems but are committed to the accepted dictum that there are only four schools of tenets.

Also, the names of the two sub-divisions of the Mādhyamika school—the Autonomy school and the Consequence school—were, as is clearly admitted by Tsong kha pa and his followers, never used in India. Rather, these names were coined in Tibet in accordance with terms used by Candrakīrti in his writings. Thus, the very format of the four schools and their sub-divisions does not represent a historical account of self-asserted identities but is the result of centuries of classification of systems in India and Tibet. Its purpose is to give the scholar a handle on the vast scope of positions found in Indian Buddhism.

Given this situation, the format of four schools can be seen as a horizon that opens a way to appreciate the plethora of opinions, not as one that closes and rigidifies investigation. In Tibet, students are taught this fourfold classification first, without mention of the diversity of opinion that it conceals. Then, over decades of study, students gradually recognize the structure of such presentations of schools of thought as a technique for gaining access to a vast store of opinion, as a way to focus on topics crucial to authors within Indian Buddhism. The task of then distinguishing between what is clearly said in the Indian texts and what is interpretation and interpolation over centuries of commentary becomes a fascinating enterprise for the more hardy among Tibetan scholars. The devotion to debate as the primary mode of education provides an ever-present avenue for students to challenge home-grown interpretations, and affords a richness of critical commentary within the tradition that a short presentation of tenets does not convey.

Topics

In dKon mchog 'jigs med dbang po's text, each Buddhist school is treated under four major topics, the last having numerous subdivisions:

1 Definition
2 Subschools
3 Etymology

4 Assertions of tenets
 Assertions on the basis
  Objects: the two truths, etc.
  Object-possessors (i.e., subjects)
   Persons
   Consciousnesses
   Terms
 Assertions on the paths
  Objects of observation of the paths
  Objects abandoned by the paths
  Nature of the paths
 Assertions on the fruits of the paths

First, for general orientation, a reader is given a definition of the school, its sub-schools, and an etymology of its name. Then the tenets of the school are introduced. The topics considered under the heading of "assertions of tenets" reveal the soteriological orientation of the inquiry. The assertions are divided into three categories—presentations of the basis, the paths, and the fruits of the path. The presentation of the basis refers to assertions on classes of phenomena, which provide the *basis* for practicing the spiritual *paths*, which, in turn, produce attainments, the *fruits of the path*. It is clear from this order that the reason for philosophical learning about phenomena is to enable practice of a path that can transform the mind from being mired in a condition of suffering to being enlightened in a state of freedom.

The general structure of basis, paths, and fruits probably takes its lead from the emphasis in texts of the Mādhyamika School on three coordinated sets of twos:

(1) the two truths—conventional and ultimate—which are the basis
(2) the two practices—method and wisdom—which are the paths
(3) the two Buddha Bodies—Form Bodies and Truth Body—which are the final fruits of the path.

According to the Great Vehicle as described in these texts, taking as one's *basis* conventional truths, one practices the *paths* of method—love, compassion, and the altruistic intention to become enlightened as well the compassionate deeds that these induce—in dependence upon which one achieves the *fruit* of the Form Bodies of a buddha. Also, taking as one's *basis* ultimate truths, one practices the *paths* of wisdom—especially the realization of the final status of persons and phenomena, their emptiness of inherent existence—in dependence upon which one achieves the *fruit* of a Truth Body of a buddha. This threefold format of basis, path, and fruit that finds its main expression in the Great Vehicle seems to have supplied the structure for the genre of presentations of tenets for both the Lesser Vehicle[8] and the Great Vehicle.

Objects. Within the section on the basis, the emphasis on the two truths in all four schools derives from the fact that the two truths are a prime subject in the tenets of what is considered to be the highest school, the Mādhyamika. As Gung thang dKon mchog bstan pa'i sgron me (1762-1823),[9] who was the chief student of dKon mchog 'jigs med dbang po, says, the prime way that the Vaibhāṣika school and the Sautrāntika school delineate the meaning of the scriptures is by way of the Four Noble Truths, whereas the Cittamātra school accomplishes this through the doctrine of the three natures and the Mādhyamika school through the doctrine of the two truths (see *DN*: 80, 235). Thus, the emphasis given in this presentation of tenets to the four schools' delineations of the two truths derives from the system that the author and his tradition have determined to be the highest, the Mādhyamika school. This is not to say that the two truths are not important topics in all four schools, for they are; rather, the two truths are not *the* central topic in the other schools in the way that they are in the Mādhyamika school.

Object-Possessors. Having presented a school's assertions on objects, the text considers object-possessors, or subjects. Object-possessors are treated as being of three types—persons (since they possess objects), consciousnesses (since they are aware of objects), and terms (since they refer to objects).

One might wonder why there is a section on persons if Buddhist schools advocate a view of selflessness. In this Tibetan delineation of Indian schools of Buddhism, the term "self" in "selflessness" refers not to persons but to an over-reified status of phenomena, be these persons or other phenomena. Consequently, even though it is said that *in general* "self" (*ātman, bdag*), "person" (*pudgala, gang zag*), and "I" (*aham, nga*) are coextensive, in the particular context of the selflessness of persons "self" and "person" are not at all coextensive and do not at all have the same meaning.

In the term "selflessness of persons," "self" refers to a falsely imagined status that needs to be refuted, and "persons" refers to existent beings who are the basis with respect to which that refutation is made. All of these schools, therefore, believe that persons exist. They do not claim that persons are mere creations of ignorance.

A question between the schools concerns the nature of the person. According to dKon mchog 'jigs med dbang po and his dGe lugs pa predecessors, all schools except the Mādhyamika Prāsaṅgika posit something from within the bases of designation of a person as being the person. In contrast, the Prāsaṅgika school holds that even though a person is designated in dependence upon mind and body, the person *is* neither mind nor body, being just the I that is designated in dependence upon mind and body. Following the lead of Candrakīrti, recognized by most as the founder of the Prāsaṅgika school, dKon mchog 'jigs med dbang po identifies how in the other schools some factor among the five aggregates (forms, feelings, discriminations, compositional factors, and consciousnesses) is considered to be the person when sought analytically. The Vaibhāṣikas, in general, are said to hold that the mere *collection* of the mental and physical aggregates is the person, whereas some of the five Saṃmitīya subschools are said to maintain that all five aggregates are the person—dKon mchog 'jigs med dbang po's suggestion being that, for them, *each* of the five aggregates is the person (although the absurdity of one person being five persons would seem difficult not to notice). Another subschool, the Avantaka, is said to assert that the mind alone is the person.

Similarly, in the Sautrāntika school, the Followers of Scripture are said to assert that the continuum of the aggregates is the person, whereas the Followers of Reasoning are said to maintain that the mental consciousness is the person. In the Cittamātra school, the Followers of Scripture hold that the mind-basis-of-all (*ālayavijñāna, kun gzhi rnam par shes pa*) is the person, whereas the Followers of Reasoning assert that the mental consciousness is. Again, in the Autonomy school, both Yogic Autonomists and Sūtra Autonomists are said to assert that a subtle, neutral mental consciousness is what is found to be the person when it is searched for among its bases of designation.

For the most part, dKon mchog 'jigs med dbang po's delineation of what these schools assert to be the person is a matter of conjecture and not a reporting of forthright statements of these schools' own texts. Though it is clear that most of these schools (if not all) accept that persons exist, it is by no means clear in their own literature that they assert that something from within the bases of designation of a person is the person. Rather, it would seem that, as presented in Vasubandhu's commentary on the ninth chapter of his *Abhidharmakośa*,[10] persons are merely asserted to be non-associated compositional factors (*viprayuktasaṃskāra, ldan min 'du byed*) and thus an instance of the fourth aggregate, compositional factors, without a specific identification of any of the five aggregates that are a person's bases of designation as the person. For instance, one could quite safely say that there is not a single line in the whole of Indian Cittamātra literature that explicitly asserts that the mind-basis-of-all is the person. Rather, such an assertion is deduced from the fact that Cittamātrins Following Scripture (that is to say, the followers of Asaṅga) assert that the mind-basis-of-all travels from lifetime to lifetime carrying with it the karmic predispositions established by earlier actions. Bhāvaviveka, on the other hand, seems openly to assert that the mental consciousness is the person, when, in response to a challenge, he says that if the opponent is attempting to establish for him that consciousness is the person, he is proving what is already established for him (see Hopkins, 1983: 695-696). In any case, the emphasis of the dGe lugs pa treatises on identifying, for each of these schools, what, from among the five aggregates, the person is comes from their acceptance of Candrakīrti's claim to a *unique* assertion that nothing from among them is the person.

Thus, it can be seen that the very structure (basis, paths, and fruits) and the choice of topics (such as the two truths and assertions on the person) do not altogether arise from prime concerns within each school, but are brought over from focal issues in other schools, particularly those considered to be higher. That topics of prime concern in the "higher" schools dominate to some extent the presentation of the tenets of all four schools is natural, given that the main aim is to draw readers into realizing the impact of the views of the "higher" systems. This genre never seeks to give isolated presentations of these schools' views or a predominantly historical account.

Consciousnesses. The main focus of the tenets concerning consciousness is to identify the different types of minds in terms of misapprehension and correct apprehension. The purpose is to provide a psychological structure for the therapeutic paths that cause a person to proceed gradually from misconceived notions about the nature of persons and other phenomena to states of mind that can counteract innate misconceptions. The liberative directionality of the overall enterprise informs the course of the discussion, the main interest being to separate correctly perceiving from improperly perceiving consciousnesses and to identify the difference between conceptual and non-conceptual consciousnesses. The latter, when they realize selflessness, are considered to be more powerful for overcoming obstructions to liberation and to full enlightenment.

The topics of consciousness are presented in their richest detail in the chapter on the Sautrāntika school, specifically the Sautrāntika Following Reasoning; correspondingly, the topic of terms is discussed most fully in the chapter on the Vaibhāṣika school. Thus, in many respects such books are to be read cumulatively, bringing over to another system those assertions that, although they come from a different system, are concordant with its outlook. The book does not always make clear what is to be carried over and what is not; such information is, however, supplied by the oral tradition, i.e., by a competent teacher.

Paths. Having presented a general outline of phenomena, the basis, dKon mchog 'jigs med dbang po presents the various schools' tenets on the spiritual paths which are founded on their respective assertions about the basis. The paths are described in terms of (1) the main objects of meditation, (2) the main misconceptions that are abandoned through such meditation, and (3) the layout of the paths.

In all four schools, paths are presented for hearers (*śrāvaka, nyan thos*), solitary realizers (*pratyekabuddha, rang rgyal*), and bodhisattvas. It might seem, at first reading, to be surprising that even the Lesser Vehicle schools—the Vaibhāṣika and Sautrāntika schools—should have paths for bodhisattvas, since bodhisattvas are associated primarily with the Great Vehicle. However, a distinction is made between philosophical schools, which are divided into Lesser Vehicle and Great Vehicle, and practitioners of paths, which also are divided into Lesser Vehicle and Great Vehicle. The philosophical schools are divided in this way according to whether they present a selflessness of phenomena (Great Vehicle) or whether they do not (Lesser Vehicle). Since the Great Vehicle tenet systems—the Cittamātra and Mādhyamika schools—present a selflessness of phenomena in addition to a selflessness of persons, they also speak of "obstructions to omniscience" (*jñeyāvaraṇa, shes sgrib*), these being what prevent simultaneous and direct cognition of all phenomena as well as their final nature. The Lesser Vehicle schools, on the other hand, make no such claims even though they present buddhahood as having an omniscience which can *serially* know anything, but not simultaneously.[11]

Even though the Lesser Vehicle schools—the Vaibhāṣika and Sautrāntika schools—do not present a path leading to simultaneous and direct knowledge of all phenomena, they do speak of the path of a bodhisattva proceeding to buddhahood when they relate how Śākyamuni Buddha, for instance, became enlightened. Similarly, the Great Vehicle schools—Cittamātra and Mādhyamika—speak, not just about how bodhisattvas proceed on the path but also about how hearers and solitary realizers, who are Lesser Vehicle practitioners, proceed on the path. In the latter case, the Great Vehicle schools are not reporting how the Lesser Vehicle schools present the path, but how the Great Vehicle schools themselves present the path for those beings—hearers and solitary realizers—whose prime motivation, unlike that of bodhisattvas, is, for the time being, not the welfare of others but their own liberation from cyclic existence. Therefore, it is said to be possible for someone who is, for instance, a Prāsaṅgika Mādhyamika doctrinally to be a Lesser Vehicle practitioner by motivation, in that the person has decided for the time being to pursue his or her own liberation first before becoming primarily dedicated to the welfare of others. Also, it is possible for someone who is, for instance, a Vaibhāṣika to be a Great Vehicle practitioner in terms of motivation, having become dedicated to achieving the enlightenment of a buddha in order to be of service to all beings.

Fruits of the Paths. The three types of paths—hearer, solitary realizer, and bodhisattva—have different results or fruits. The first two lead to liberation from cyclic existence, whereas the last leads to buddhahood, a state free from both the obstructions to liberation from cyclic existence and from the obstructions to the omniscience of a buddha, as described in the respective systems.

Conclusion

Though one of the purposes of such presentations of tenets undoubtedly is to create a hierarchical structure that puts one's own system at the top, this genre of literature functions primarily to provide a comprehensive worldview. Its presentations, ranging from the phenomena of the world through to the types of enlightenment, give students a framework for study and practice as well as a perspective for relating with other beings. The worldview that emerges is of individuals bound by misconception in a round of suffering and mired in afflictive emotions counterproductive to their own welfare, but also poised on a threshold of transformation. The uncontrolled course of cyclic existence is viewed as lacking a solid underpinning; it is ready to be transformed into a patterned advance toward liberation. The starkness of the harrowing appraisal of the current situation of multilayered pain stands in marked contrast to the optimistic view of the development that is possible. Such optimism stems from a perception that the afflictive emotions and obstructions that are the cause of misery are not endemic to the mind, but are peripheral to its nature and thus subject to antidotal influences that can remove them. The hierarchical presentation, fortified with reasoned explanation, itself inculcates the basic posture that the power of reason can penetrate the false veils of appearance and lead to a liberative reality. Presentations of tenets are founded on confidence in the mind's ability to overcome tremendous obstacles to the point where love, compassion, and altruism can be expressed in effective, continuous activity, and, therefore, they do more than just structure Indian Buddhist systems; they structure practitioners' perception of their place in a dynamic worldview.

Notes

1. This article is based on the introduction to Part Two of Sopa and Hopkins (1990), which is a revised second edition of Sopa and Hopkins (1976).

2. This is Bhāvaviveka's commentary on his *Madhyamakahṛdaya* ("Heart of the Middle"). For a partial English translation of the latter (ch. III.1-136), see Iida. For an excellent history of Indo-Tibetan Buddhism, see Snellgrove.

3. For more discussion on this genre of Tibetan literature, see Mimaki (1-12) and Ruegg's foreword to Nyima.

4. Also known as Klong chen dri med 'od zer.

5. For an English translation of the beginning of the chapter on the Consequence School, see Hopkins, 1983.

6. For a translation of the Sautrāntika chapter, see Klein, 1991; for commentary on this, see Klein, 1986. For a translation of the Svātantrika chapter, see Lopez. For a translation of part of the Prāsaṅgika chapter, see Hopkins, 1987.

7. For a list of other such brief texts, see the Bibliography (xlvi, etc.) and Introduction (5-12) in Mimaki, 1982.

8. The term "Lesser Vehicle" (*hīnayāna, theg dman*) has its origin in the writings of Great Vehicle (*mahāyāna, theg chen*) authors and was, of course, not used by those to whom it was ascribed. Substitutes such as "non-Mahāyāna," "Nikāya Buddhism," and "Theravādayāna" have been suggested in order to avoid the pejorative sense of "Lesser." However, "Lesser Vehicle" is a convenient term in this particular context for a type of tenet system or practice that is seen, in the tradition about which I am writing, to be surpassed—but not negated—by a higher system. The "Lesser Vehicle" is not despised, most of it being incorporated into the "Great Vehicle." The monks' and nuns' vows are part of the Lesser Vehicle, as is much of the course of study; years of study are dedicated to Epistemology (*pramāṇa, tshad ma*), Manifest Knowledge (*abhidharma, chos mngon pa*), and Discipline (*vinaya, 'dul ba*), which are mostly Lesser Vehicle in perspective.

9. He wrote two biographies of dKon mchog 'jigs med dbang po.

10. See Poussin: 254 for the person as imputedly existent (*btags yod*) and Poussin: 259 for the person as compounded.

11. As is reported in *GTCM* (*kha*, 7b), one of the eighteen subschools of the Great Exposition school, the One Convention school (Ekavyavahārika, Tha snyad gcig pa), uses the convention of one instant of a buddha's wisdom realizing all phenomena. 'Jam dbyangs bzhad pa says that they employ this convention for a buddha's one mind realizing all phenomena; he thereby suggests that this school did not actually hold that a buddha has such simultaneous knowledge. 'Jam dbyangs bzhad pa may be explaining away a discrepancy in a system that emerged for the sake of easy classification.

References

Dalai Lama II, dGe 'dun rgya mtsho

GTGD *Grub mtha' rgya mtshor 'jug pa'i gru rdzings*. Varanasi: Ye shes stobs ldan, 1969.

dKon mchog 'jigs med dbang po

GTRP *Grub pa'i mtha'i rnam par bzhag pa rin po che'i phreng ba*. In *The Collected Works of dkon-mchog-'jigs-med-dbaṅ-po*, vol. 6, pp. 485-535. New Delhi: Ngawang Gelek Demo, 1972. For a critical edition: K. Mimaki. "Le *Grub mtha' rnam bźag rin chen phreṅ ba* de dKon mchog 'jigs med dbaṅ po (1728-1791)." *Zinbun* 14: 55-112. The Research Institute for Humanistic Studies, Kyoto University, 1977.

Grags pa bshad sgrub, Co ne ba

GTDP *Grub mtha' thams cad kyi snying po bsdus pa*. Delhi: Mey College of Sera, 1969.

Gung thang dKon mchog bstan pa'i sgron me

DN *Drang nges rnam 'byed kyi dga' 'grel rtsom 'phro legs bshad snying po'i yang snying*. Sarnath: Guru Deva, 1965.

Hopkins, Jeffrey

1983 *Meditation on Emptiness*. London: Wisdom.

1987 *Emptiness Yoga*. Ithaca: Snow Lion.

Iida, Shotaro

1980 *Reason and Emptiness*. Tokyo: Hokuseido.

'Jam dbyangs bzhad pa'i rdo rje ngag dbang brtson grus

GTCM *Grub mtha'i rnam bshad rang gzhan grub mtha' kun dang zab don mchog tu gsal ba kun bzang zhing gi nyi ma lung rigs rgya mtsho skye dgu'i re ba kun skong/ Grub mtha' chen mo*. Musoorie: Dalama, 1962.

Jha, G.

1937-39 *The Tattvasaṃgraha of Śāntirakṣita with the commentary of Kamalaśīla*. Gaekwad's Oriental Series, vols. 80 and 83. Baroda: Oriental Institute.

Klein, Anne C.

1986 *Knowledge and Liberation: Tibetan Buddhist Epistemology in Support of Transformative Religious Experience*. Ithaca: Snow Lion.

1990 *Knowing, Naming, and Negation*. Ithaca: Snow Lion.

Klong chen rab 'byams

GTRD *Theg pa mtha' dag gi don gsal bar byed pa grub pa'i mtha' rin po che'i mdzod*. Gangtok: Dodrup Chen Rinpoche, 1969(?).

lCang skya rol pa'i rdo rje

GTDG *Grub pa'i mtha'i rnam par bzhag pa gsal bar bshad pa thub bstan lhun po'i mdzes rgyan*. Varanasi: Pleasure of Elegant Sayings Printing Press, 1970.

Lopez, Donald S., Jr.

1986 *A Study of Svātantrika*. Ithaca: Snow Lion.

Mimaki, Katsumi

1982 *Blo gsal grub mtha'*. Kyoto: Université de Kyoto.

Nyima, Geshé Ngawang

1970 *Introduction to the Doctrines of the Four Schools of Buddhist Philosophy*. Leiden, n.p.

Paṇ chen bSod nams grags pa

GTTB *Grub mtha'i rnam bzhag blo gsal spro ba bskyed pa'i ljon pa phas rgol brag ri 'joms pa'i tho ba*. Buxador, n.d.

Poussin, Louis de La Vallée
1923-31 *L'Abhidharmakośa de Vasubandhu*. Paris: Geuthner.

rJe btsun Chos kyi rgyal mtshan
GTNZ *Grub mtha'i rnam gzhag*. Bylakuppe: Se-ra Byes Grwa-tshaṅ, 1977.

Ruegg, David Seyfort
1981 *The Literature of the Madhyamaka School of Philosophy in India*. Wiesbaden: Otto Harrassowitz.

Shastri, Swami Dwarikadas, ed.
1970 *Abhidharmakośa & Bhāṣya of Ācārya Vasubandhu with Sphuṭārtha Commentary of Ācārya Yaṣomitra*. Bauddha Bharati Series 5. Banaras: Bauddha Bharati.

Shes rab rin chen, sTag tshang lo tsā ba
GTKS *Grub mtha' kun shes nas mtha' bral grub pa zhes bya ba'i bstan bcos rnam par bshad pa legs bshad kyi rgya mtsho*. Thimphu: Kun bzang stobs rgyal, 1976.

Snellgrove, David L.
1987 *Indo-Tibetan Buddhism: Indian Buddhists and Their Tibetan Successors*. Boston: Shambhala.

Sopa, Geshe Lhundup and Jeffrey Hopkins
1990 *Cutting Through Appearances: The Practice and Theory of Tibetan Buddhism*. Ithaca: Snow Lion.
1976 *Practice and Theory of Tibetan Buddhism*. London: Rider.

Thu'u bkvan Blo bzang chos kyi nyi ma
GTSM *Grub mtha' thams cad kyi khungs dang 'dod tshul ston pa legs bshad shel gyi me long*. Sarnath: Chhos Je Lama, 1963.

Chapter 10

bsDus grwa Literature[1]

Shunzo Onoda

Texts of the *bsdus grwa* genre were some of the most influential works of Tibetan philosophical literature, since more than any other genre of text they determined how scholastics in the predominant dGe lugs pa tradition of Tibetan Buddhism reasoned and conceptualized. The term *bsdus grwa* or *bsdus rwa* originally probably meant *bsdus pa slob pa'i sde tshan gyi grwa* or "the schools or classes in which [primary students] learn *bsdus pa* or summarized topics [of logic or dialectics]." Later, the term was etymologized as *rig pa'i rnam grangs du ma phyogs gcig tu bsdus pa'i grwa*, or "the class where many arguments are summarized together."[2] In modern usage, the term has both a general and a more restricted meaning. *bsDus grwa* in its broad sense means the introductory course or classes in dialectics, which consist of the three categories: *bsdus grwa* (in the narrow sense; ontology), *blo rigs* (epistemology) and *rtags rigs* (logic). Without mastering these basic stages, a student cannot advance any further in the dGe lugs pa tradition of Tibetan Buddhist scholasticism.

The *bsDus grwa* Course in Modern Monastic Colleges

Although there exist a few differences in the dGe lugs pa monastic curricula among different colleges, in the main there are five principal subjects to be taught, which are known as the "five books" (*po ṭi lnga*): (1) Pramāṇa (*tshad ma*), (2) Prajñāpāramitā (*phar phyin*), (3)Madhyamaka (*dbu ma*), (4) Vinaya (*'dul ba*), and (5) Abhidharmakośa (*mngon mdzod*). Each of these subjects is divided into small classes (called *'dzin grwa*), and by advancing through these classes—a process which takes at least ten years—one can finally attain the degree of *dge bshes* (see Newland, in this volume).

Here we should remark that the last four of these five subjects, i.e., Prajñāpāramitā, Madhyamaka, Vinaya and Abhidharmakośa, are studied in direct dependence upon original Indian texts (*rgya gzhung*). As for Pramāṇa, however, the initial study by dGe lugs pa monks is undertaken exclusively on the basis of the native Tibetan *bsdus grwa* literature, rather than Indian texts, and at this initial stage the subject of study is commonly called *bsdus grwa* or *rigs lam*, instead of *tshad ma* (*pramāṇa*: Indian Buddhist logic and epistemology) properly speaking.

All monastic universities are composed of a number of *grwa tshang*, or self-supported colleges, and most of these colleges have a few *khang tshan*, or regional houses. Students live in *khang tshans* associated with their native place, and during the school term they attend their appointed class (*'dzin grwa*) in the *grwa tshang*. One year is divided into seven or eight school terms. Apart from the two terms of mid summer and mid winter, lessons are held inside the college.[3]

Three Stages of *bsDus grwa*: *bsDus grwa*, *Blo rigs* and *rTags rigs*

As we have said, the course of *bsdus grwa* can be divided into the following three stages: *bsdus grwa* (in the narrow sense), *blo rigs* and *rtags rigs*. Roughly speaking, these three treat of ontology, epistemology and logic, respectively. This threefold classification is sometimes expressed as the study of "objects" (*yul*), "subjects" (*yul can*), and "the ways to cognize objects" (*yul de rtogs pa'i tshul*). The precise contents of *bsdus grwa* texts are not completely uniform, but these texts do nonetheless share a corpus of principal subjects or "lessons" (*rnam bzhag*).

Let us now briefly examine the contents of *bsdus grwa, blo rigs* and *rtags rigs* by focusing on a few representative subjects. The first stage of the primary course is *bsdus grwa* in its narrow sense, generally comprised of three lessons. The first, which is common to all colleges, is known as "*kha dog dkar dmar*," which literally means "white and red colors." Some colleges even assign a separate class (*'dzin grwa*) to the subject. At this stage, students learn about the notion of pervasion or entailment (*khyab pa*), as occurs, for example, between white color and color itself—the former entailing the latter. Similarly, students learn to differentiate between general propositions involving pervasions, such as "whatever is red must be a color" (*dmar po yin na kha dog yin pas khyab*), and those involving specific topics (*chos can*), such as "take as the topic, red; it is a color" (*dmar po chos can kha dog yin*) (see Tillemans: 286).

In the next class, called *gzhi grub* (literally, "established bases"), students are introduced to some ontological notions construed more or less in accordance with the system of the Indian Sautrāntika school, especially as it is portrayed by Dharmakīrti. Here again, students pay special attention to the inclusions and differentiations holding among the key concepts.

After completing this initial class, students proceed to the next, where they learn more abstract and theoretical notions. At this level, schemata necessary for logical thinking such as concept (*ldog pa*, literally "isolate"), cause and effect (*rgyu dang 'bras bu*), genus and species (*spyi dang bye brag*), relations and contraries (*'brel ba dang 'gal ba*) and definition and definiendum (*mtshan nyid dang mtshon bya*) are introduced and examined.[4] In the last class of this first stage, students learn to use the *thal 'gyur* (*prasaṅga*) argumentation form, i.e., "consequences" or "reductio ad absurdum" (see Onoda, 1986, 1988) and other logical operators such as "implicative negations" and "non-implicative negations" (*ma yin dgag dang med dgag*). In short, the purpose of this first stage, i.e., *bsdus grwa* as more narrowly conceived, is not only to introduce students to basic theoretical schemata, but also to allow them to acquire the practical mastery of debating techniques which will be indispensable for more advanced dialectical study.

When a student has finished the initial stage of *bsdus grwa* classes, he is allowed to proceed to the next stage, i.e., *blo rigs*, which is largely concerned with epistemological matters. The main subjects are the classifications of cognition in terms of "valid and invalid means of cognition" (*tshad ma dang tshad min*), "conceptual and non-conceptual cognition" (*rtog pa dang rtog med*), "self-awareness and other-awareness" (*rang rig dang gzhan rig*) and "mind and mental factors" (*sems dang sems byung*). These classifications in turn frequently admit of sub-classifications. For example, invalid means of cognition (*tshad min*) is divided into five: subsequent cognition (*dpyad shes*), true presumption (*yid dpyod*), inattentive cognition (*snang la ma nges pa*), doubt (*the tshom*), and erroneous cognition (*log shes*). Valid means of cognition (*tshad ma*) is divided into two: direct perception (*mngon sum gyi tshad ma*) and inference (*rjes su dpag pa'i tshad ma*). It should be noted that this type of sevenfold division of cognition (*blo rigs bdun du dbye ba*) is said to have originated with Phya pa Chos kyi seng ge (1109-1169) (see van der Kuijp, 1979).

The last stage, *rtags rigs* (see Onoda, 1981), introduces an Indian type of logic centered around the elaboration of the threefold criteria—the so-called *tshul gsum* (or *trairūpya*)—which enables one to distinguish between correct, or valid, logical marks (*rtags yang dag*) and those which are invalid, or more literally are pseudo-marks (*rtags ltar snang*).

These three types of texts—*bsdus grwa*, *blo rigs* and *rtags rigs*—teach students the practical applications of disputation or debate (*rtsod pa*). One of the main reasons why adepts of such a training are called *mtshan nyid pa* is that they pay special attention to terms and definitions (*mtshan nyid*), memorizing them and analysing them for inconsistencies, insufficiencies and redundancies. A further reason as to why this preliminary training is so indispensable is that the school manuals (*yig cha*) for advanced classes such as Prajñāpāramitā and Madhyamaka are written in the special style and format which we find in *bsdus grwa* texts. This format, where arguments are presented largely by means of *prasaṅgas* (*thal 'gyur*), was christened *thal phyir*, or "sequence and reason," by Stcherbatsky (55), who maintained that it probably had its origins with Phya pa Chos kyi seng ge (see Jackson, 1987: 152, n. 28; cf. van der Kuijp, 1983: 294, n. 220).

The *bsDus pa* as Predecessor to *bsDus grwa* Literature

Both the conventional style and contents of the so-called *bsdus grwa* literature are widely said to have originated with the eighteen *bsdus grwa* subjects of Phya pa Chos kyi seng ge. According to A khu rin po che's list of rare books, Phya pa wrote two Pramāṇa summaries: one entitled *Tshad [ma'i] bsdus [pa] yid kyi mun sel* (*MHTL* 11805) and the other *Tshad ma'i bsdus pa yid kyi mun sel rang 'grel dang bcas pa* (*MHTL* 11804). Probably one was a verse work and the other was its autocommentary. According to Śākya mchog ldan (1428-1507), Phya pa wrote not only these Pramāṇa summaries but also an *dBu ma bsdus pa* ("Madhyamaka Summary"). Aside from Phya pa, other scholars of gSang phu Monastery are also said to have written texts entitled *bsdus pa*. For instance, rGya dmar ba Byang chub grags who was a student of rNgog lo tsā ba (1059-1109) is said to have written several *Tshad ma'i bsdus pa* (*MHTL* 11810).[5] gTsang nag pa brTson 'grus seng ge (twelfth century) wrote an *dBu ma'i bsdus pa*. Chu mig pa (thirteenth century) who was an abbot of gSang phu Upper Monastery, also wrote a *Tshad ma bsdus pa* (*NTTR*: 453). Even among the works of 'U yug pa (thirteenth century) of the early Sa skya pa we can find the title *bsDus pa rigs sgrub*, though this may simply be an abridgment of his famous Pramāṇa work. Although we cannot be sure about the contents of these works until the texts themselves appear, the term *bsdus pa* in their titles probably can be translated as "Summary." But as noted above, such a term was not used only for Pramāṇa summaries in the early period (twelfth to thirteenth centuries).

According to Klong rdol bla ma (1719-1794/5),[6] Phya pa summarized Pramāṇa theories into the following eighteen subjects in his *Tshad ma'i bsdus pa yid kyi mun sel*:

(1) white and red colors (*kha dog dkar dmar*)
(2) substantial phenomena and conceptual phenomena (*rdzas chos ldog chos*)
(3) contraries and non-contraries (*'gal dang mi 'gal*)
(4) genus and species (*spyi dang bye brag*)
(5) related and unrelated (*'brel dang ma 'brel*)
(6) difference and non-difference (*tha dad thad* [= *tha dad*] *min*)
(7) positive and negative concomitances (*rjes su 'gro ldog*)
(8) cause and effect (*rgyu dang 'bras bu*)
(9) the three times (*snga bcan bar bcan phyi bcan*)
(10) definition and definiendum (*mtshan mtshon*)
(11) [*prasaṅgas*] with multiple reasons and multiple predicates (*rtags mang gsal mang*)
(12) exclusionary negations and determinations (*dgag pa phar tshur*)
(13) direct and indirect contraries (*dngos 'gal rgyud 'gal*)
(14) equal pervasions (*khyab mnyam*)
(15) being and non-being (*yin gyur min gyur*)
(16) negation of being and negation of non-being (*yin log min log*)
(17) cognizing existence and cognizing nonexistence (*yod rtogs med rtogs*)
(18) cognizing permanence and cognizing real entities (*rtag rtogs dngos rtogs*)

The great scholar Sa skya Paṇḍita Kun dga' rgyal mtshan (1182-1251), in his *Tshad ma rigs pa'i gter*, criticised many of Phya pa's theories, showing how the latter's ideas differ from those of Indian Buddhist philosophers, who for Sa paṇ were the only source of authentic Buddhism. Sa skya Paṇḍita's criticisms relied predominantly on Dharmakīrti's own texts, with the result that after Sa paṇ, the theoretical focus of Pramāṇa studies in Tibet slowly but gradually shifted away from Phya pa's so-called Tibetan style to Sa skya Paṇḍita's more Indian-based orientation. Nonetheless, on the practical level, most dGe lugs pa and to some extent even Sa skya pa scholars continued to practice Phya pa's style of logic, debating on such typical Phya pa subjects as substantial and conceptual phenomena (*rdzas chos ldog chos*), even though some were aware that such subjects were simply Tibetan in origin.[7] Especially in the dGe lugs pa school, with the establishment of the big monastic universities, it was the *bsdus grwa* tradition propagated by Phya pa that continued as the primary practice for beginners in dialectics.

Later gSang phu and dGe lugs pa *bsDus grwa* Literature

About three centuries after Phya pa's activity, mChog lha 'od zer (1429-1500),[8] who occupied the abbatial seat of gSang phu just as Phya pa had previously done, composed the manual known as the *Ra bstod bsdus grwa.* This text was widely used as the beginner's manual not only in the dGe lugs pa monasteries but also, it is said, in one or two Sa skya pa seminaries (such as at modern Na-lendra). mChog lha 'od zer wrote this text mostly based on Phya pa's tradition but also adopted a few elements of Sa skya Paṇḍita's position.[9]

Even after the three major dGe lugs pa monasteries in the Lhasa area had developed their own sets of debate manuals (*yig cha*), the *Ra bstod bsdus grwa* was still used by dGe lugs pa monks when they began their basic Pramāṇa studies. Another famous *bsdus grwa* text, the *bTsan po bsdus grwa*, was written at the Ra bstod college of gSang phu by gSer khang pa Dam chos rnam rgyal (seventeenth century), who served as the twenty-first abbot of the Ra bstod college, i.e., fourteen abbots later than mChog lha 'od zer (Vostrikov: 61) (see Onoda, 1989c, 1991). Unfortunately, since the text is lost, we know only the subject headings in the *bTsan po bsdus grwa*, but they can be seen to exhibit a close resemblance to those of mChog lha 'od zer's work.[10]

The *bTsan po bsdus grwa* was written in response to a request from Ngag dbang 'phrin las lhun grub (1622-1699). The word "bTsan po" stands for "bTsan po no mon han," which was the honorific title of Ngag dbang 'phrin las lhun grub, the teacher of the celebrated dGe lugs pa author of scholastic manuals 'Jam dbyangs bzhad pa'i rdo rje (1648-1721), who in turn served as the teacher of Sras Ngag dbang bkra bshis (1678-1738), author of the influential *Sras bsdus grwa* used in 'Bras spungs sGo mang College. So, in short, we can say that Ngag dbang 'phrin las lhun grub was probably the person who served as the link between the 'Jam dbyangs bzhad pa tradition of *bsdus grwa* and the *bsdus grwa* tradition which had been handed down at gSang phu Monastery since Phya pa Chos kyi seng ge.

It is as yet unknown how many *bsdus grwa* texts Ngag dbang 'phrin las himself actually wrote, but we are informed (van der Kuijp, 1989: 16) that he wrote a *bsDus grwa'i rnam bzhag cha tshang ba'i rig gnas legs bshad bang mdzod* (Smith: 70), which has the following six subjects:

(1) pervasions (*khyab mtha'*)
(2) negation of being and negation of non-being (*yin log min log*)
(3) cause and effect (*rgyu 'bras*)
(4) definition and definiendum (*mtshan mtshon*)
(5) genus and species (*spyi bye brag*)
(6) substantial phenomena and conceptual phenomena (*rdzas ldog*)

It should be noted that in the *Complete Works* of 'Jam dbyangs bzhad pa'i rdo rje there is a *bsdus grwa* text entitled *Kha dog dkar dmar*,[11] which has exactly the same six subjects as Ngag dbang 'phrin las lhun grub's shorter work. Here then is possible further confirmation of the relationship between the gSang phu lineage of *bsdus grwa* studies of Ngag dbang 'phrin las and that of sGo mang College.

The *Complete Works* of 'Jam dbyangs bzhad pa'i rdo rje has four other titles which are concerned with *bsdus grwa*:[12]

(1) Presentation of *bsdus grwa* called "elegant description" (*bsDus grwa'i rnam bzhag legs par bshad pa*)

(2) A summary of the advanced presentation of *prasaṅga* (*Thal 'gyur che ba'i rnam bzhag mdor bsdus*)
(3) Advanced presentation of *bsdus grwa* called "the golden key to open the art of science" (*bsDus chen gyi rnam bzhag rigs lam gser gyi sgo 'byed*)
(4) The essence of *bsdus grwa* called "the treasury of whole presentations" in verse (*bsDus sbyor gyi snying po kun bsdus rig pa'i mdzod rtsa tshig*)

In addition to these *bsdus grwa* of 'Jam dbyangs bzhad pa, a number of other influential *bsdus grwa* texts were written as college manuals for the dGe lugs pa monastic universities.[13] Blo gsal gling College of 'Bras spungs Monastery used Paṇ chen bSod nams grags pa's (1478-1554) *bsdus grwa*. sGo mang College used not only the above-mentioned *bsdus grwas* of 'Jam dbyangs bzhad pa, but also that of Ngag dbang bkra shis, which was commonly known as the *Khri rgan tshang gi bsdus grwa* or *Sras ngag dbang bkra shis bsdus grwa* because the author was a chief disciple (*sras*) of 'Jam dbyangs bzhad pa'i rdo rje (Vostrikov: 61).[14]

Perhaps nowadays the most widely used *bsdus grwa* is the *Phur lcog bsdus grwa*, which was adopted as a school manual in the Byes pa College of Se ra Monastery (Perdue). The text is also called the *Yongs 'dzin bsdus grwa* (Onoda, 1981) because its author, Phur bu lcog Byams pa tshul khrims rgya mtsho dpal bzang po (1825-1901), was the personal teacher (*yongs 'dzin*) of the Thirteenth Dalai Lama.[15]

Sa skya pa *bsDus grwa* Literature[16]

The *bsdus grwa* of the Sa skya pa has so far hardly been studied at all. Here I will just enumerate the few such treatises known to me, without trying to indicate their relation to the dGe lugs pa *bsdus grwa* or earlier gSang phu traditions. To begin with, 'U yug pa Rigs pa'i seng ge (b.1250s or 1260s) who was a disciple of Sa skya Paṇḍita, is said to have written a (*Tshad ma'i*) *bsDus pa* which was entitled *bsDus pa rigs sgrub* (*ZNDG*: 469.3) or *bsDus don rigs pa'i sdom* (*DGPK*: 323). According to the list of the sDe dge printing house, a certain Byang chub dpal wrote a *Tshad bsdus legs bshad rig pa'i 'od zer* (*DGPK*: 145) and this may be an early Sa skya pa *tshad ma'i bsdus pa*. The outstanding scholastic gYag ston Sangs rgyas dpal (1348-1414) wrote a *rtags rigs* work (*SCNT*: 74). Likewise, mKhas grub bstan gsal (fl. fifteenth century), disciple of

Byams chen rab 'byams pa (1411-1485), is said to have written a *Tshad ma'i rtags rigs chen mo* (see van der Kuijp, 1989: 17). Go rams pa bSod nams seng ge (1429-1489) is said to have learned *bsdus grwa* in Khams using the *bsDus grwa* of dGe ba rgyal mtshan (1387-1462), who was the third abbot of Na-lendra Monastery (Jackson, 1989: 34). Go rams pa's disciple Kong ston dBang phyug grub (late 1400s), who was the second abbot of rTa nag Thub bstan rnam rgyal Monastery, wrote a *Tshad ma'i spyi don blo rtag[s]* (*SKKC*: 67). In about the same period, Glo bo mkhan chen bSod nams lhun grub (1456-1532) wrote *blo rigs* and *rtags rigs* texts entitled *Blo'i rnam bzhag sde bdun gyi snying po* and *rTags kyi rnam bzhag rigs lam gsal ba'i sgron me* (Jackson, 1987: 564). Such works continued to appear in the sixteenth and seventeenth centuries. Mang thos Klu sgrub rgya mtsho (1523-1596), for instance, is said to have written a *Blo rigs chen po* (*mo*?) (*SKKC*: 100), and the famous Sa skya pa scholar Ngag dbang chos grags (1572/3-1641/2) wrote a *blo rigs* entitled *Blo rigs gi legs bshad* (*SKKC*: 108). Within the later lineage of Go rams pa's monastery, rTa nag Thub bstan rnam rgyal, there appeared the most famous recent Sa skya pa *bsdus grwa*, the *Chos rnam rgyal gi bsdus grwa*. A copy of this text is preserved at the Library of Tibetan Works and Archives, Dharamsala. The author, Chos rnam rgyal (fl. seventeenth century) also wrote a *rtags rigs*.[17] The most recent of such works in the Sa skya pa tradition were written by Blo gter dbang po (1847-1914?), who also got his initial training at rTa nag Thub bstan rnam rgyal Monastery. The *bsdus grwa* works he composed were entitled *Blo rigs zur bkol*, *rTags rigs zur bkol* (*SKKC*: 162), and *Tshad ma rtags rigs skor gtan la 'bebs par byed pa sde bdun sgo brgya 'byed pa'i 'phrul gyi lde'u mig* (*DGPK*: 326).

Conclusion

The *bsdus grwa* logic was not just a training exercise, but was important for all levels of Tibetan philosophical studies in the gSang phu and dGe lugs pa traditions. As for the relationship to the Indian tradition, only a careful and detailed investigation and comparison of the *bsdus grwa* literature and the more Indian-based *rigs gter* tradition of the Sa skya school will enable us to discriminate meaningfully between the Indian and Tibetan elements in this system of logic. At any rate, the importance of this complex Indo-Tibetan relationship should not be underestimated. Anyone who wishes to investigate seriously the indigenous Tibetan commentaries on such key Indian texts as the *Pramāṇavārttika* is confronted immediately by the fact that much of the terminology and many of the concepts used in such commentaries owe a heavy debt to the *bsdus grwa*.

Notes

1. This article summarizes a number of points which I first discussed in my articles (in Japanese) (Onoda, 1979, 1982, 1983, 1989a and 1989b), and in my monograph (in English) (Onoda, 1992). I am gratefully indebted to Dr. David Jackson and Dr. Tom Tillemans, who kindly took the trouble to read through my original manuscript and to correct my English, and who gave me their pertinent criticisms and fruitful suggestions.

2. Originally *bsdus pa* was short for *Tshad ma'i bsdus pa* or "summarized topics of Pramāṇa"(see Jackson, 1987: 128-131). For traditional definitions, see van der Kuijp, 1989: 13-15.

3. The curriculum of study varies somewhat from college to college. Phur bu lcog Ngag dbang byams pa (1682-1762), describing the composition of the main monasteries in about the year 1744, reported that dGa' ldan Monastery had two colleges, viz., Byang rtse and Shar rtse, while 'Bras spungs had seven: Blo gsal gling, sGo mang, bDe dbyangs, Shag skor, Thos bsam gling (rGyal ba), 'Dul ba and sNgags pa. Se ra Monastery had four old colleges: rGya, 'Brom steng, sTod pa, sMad pa, and two new colleges: Byes pa and sNgags pa. Later on, only sMad pa remained among the four old colleges (*PKPB*: 46). As for bKra shis lhun po Monastery in the district of gTsang, it had four colleges: Shar rtse, Thos bsam gling, dKyil khang and sNgags pa. It should be noted, however, that all four sNgags pa colleges were meant almost exclusively for the study of Tantra, that they did not principally pursue the study of dialectics (*mtshan nyid*), and that they did not have *bsdus grwa* courses.

4. Goldberg (1985) illustrates many traditional arguments about *gcig, mtshan nyid dang mtshon bya, spyi dang bye brag* and *rdzas chos dang ldog chos*.

5. If so, Phya pa was perhaps not the true father of *bsdus grwa*. Śākya mchog ldan (*NTTR*: 451) *tshad bsdus dang/ dbu bsdus kyi srol thog mar phye*; see also Jackson (1987: 129). I am told by Dr. David Jackson that rNgog lo tsā ba himself is said to have composed an *dBu ma'i bsdus pa*—perhaps the forerunner of all *bsdus pa*. This is stated in rNgog's biography by the latter's disciple Gro lung pa (eleventh to twelfth centuries).

6. kLong rdol bla ma (*TNNG*: 663); Horváth (1987: 320) corrects a line missed in copying in the Śata-Piṭaka edition.

7. mChog lha 'od zer (*RTDG*: 68): *deng sang ni gzhung lugs gang dang yang mi mthun pa'i rdzas ldog smra ba mang du thos mod/ ...gsang phu'i nye skor bstun ma'i bshad gra rig pa rno ba 'khrul byed du byas pa las gzhung gi go ba sogs la yang mi phan pa'i ngag rgyur chag....*

8. Van der Kuijp (1989: 16) considers the spelling *mChog lha* to be preferable. *Phyogs la*, *Phyogs las* and *Phyogs lha* are also found in many texts.

9. The *Ra bstod bsdus grwa* (*RTDG*) is constituted as follows: [*Chung*:] (1) *kha dog*, (2) *gzhi grub*, (3) *ldog pa ngos 'dzin*, (4) *yin log min log*, (5) *yin gyur min gyur*, (6) *rgyu 'bras chung ba*, (7) *spyi bye brag*, (8) *rdzas ldog*. [*'Bring*:] (1) *'gal 'brel*, (2) *yod rtogs med rtogs*, (3) *bar shun*, (4) *mtshan mtshon che ba*, (5) *rgyu 'bras che ba*, (6) *rjes 'gro ldog khyab*, (7) *dgag bshags sgrub bshags*. [*Che*:] (1) *drug sgra*, (2) *bsdus tshan kun la mkho ba khas blangs song tshul*, (3) *dgag gzhi dris 'phangs*, (4) *thal 'gyur*, (5) *gzhan sel*, (6) *sel 'jug sgrub 'jug*, (7) *yul yul can*, (8) *mtshon sbyor*, (9) *rtags sbyor*.

10. According to Klong rdol bla ma's account (*TNNG*: 663) the subjects of the *bTsan po bsdus grwa* were: (1) *kha dog dkar dmar*, (2) *gzhi grub*, (3) *ldog pa ngos 'dzin*, (4) *yin log min log*, (5) *yin gyur min gyur*, (6) *rgyu 'bras chung ba*, (7) *spyi bye brag*, (8) *rdzas ldog*, (9) *'gal 'brel*, (10) *yod rtogs med rtogs*, (11) *bar shun mtshan mtshon*, (12) *rgyu 'bras 'khor lo ma*, (13) *rjes 'gro ldog khyab*, (14) *dgag gshags sgrub gshags*, (15) *drug sgra rtsi tshul*, (16) *bsdus tshan kun la mkho ba khas blangs song tshul*, (17) *thal 'gyur*, (18) *gzhan sel*, (19) *sel 'jug sgrub 'jug*, (20) *yul yul can*, (21) *mtshon sbyor rtags sbyor*.

11. *The Complete Works of 'Jam dbyangs bzhad pa'i rdo rje* (*JYSB*), vol. 3, no. 18, ff. 606-718; *MHTL* 4082.

12. The *Complete Works* (*JYSB*) has four other titles which are concerned with *bsdus grwa*. Their order of subjects is as follows:

(A) *bsDus grwa'i rnam bzhag legs par bshad pa* (vol. 3, no. 19, ff. 719-774): (1) *kha dog dkar dmar*, (2) *yod rtogs med rtogs*, (3) *yin log min log*, (4) *rgyu 'bras chung ngu 'khor lo ma*, (5) *yul yul can*, (6) *ldog pa ngos 'dzin*, (7) *gcig tha dad*, (8) *spyi dang bye brag*, (9) *thal 'gyur chung ba*.

(B) *Kun mkhyen 'jam dbyangs bzhad pas mdzad pa'i thal 'gyur che ba'i rnam bzhag mdor bsdus* (vol. 3, no. 20, ff. 775-793; *MHTL* 4084): (1) *thal 'gyur che ba*.

(C) *bsDus chen gyi rnam bzhag rigs lam gser gyi sgo 'byed lung dang rigs pa'i gan mdzod blo gsal yid kyi mun sel skal ldan dad pa'i 'jug ngogs* (vol. 15, no. 10, ff. 377-459; *MHTL* 4153): (1) *dus gsum*, (2) *spyi mtshan dang rang mtshan*, (3) *dgag sgrub*, (4) *gzhan sel*, (5) *sel 'jug dang sgrub 'jug*, (6) *brjod byed kyi sgra*.

(D) *bsDus sbyor gyi snying po kun bsdus rig pa'i mdzod rtsa tshig* (vol. 15, no. 11, ff. 461-482; *MHTL* 4154): (1) *rdzas ldog*, (2) *'gal 'brel*, (3) *spyi bye brag*, (4) *mtshan mtshon*, (5) *rgyu 'bras*, (6) *yod med rtogs*, (7) *yin min log*, (8) *rjes 'gro ldog*, (9) *dgag gzhi rtsi tshul*, (10) *snga phyi btsan*, (11) *skor 'begs*.

13. Phur lcog Ngag dbang byams pa (*PKPB*) informs us that many *blo rigs* and *rtags rigs* were used in those monastic colleges. In Blo gsal gling College of 'Bras spungs Monastery, bSod nams grags pa's (1478-1554) *blo rigs* and *rtags rigs* were used. sGo mang College used 'Jam dbyangs bzhad pa's (1648-1721) *blo rigs* and *rtags rigs*. In the sMad pa College of Se ra Monastery, the monks study Grags pa bshad sgrub's (1675-1748) *rTags rigs rgyas pa* and *rTags rigs bsdus pa*, dByangs can dga' ba'i blo gros's *rTags rigs kyi sdom* and *Blo rigs kyi sdom*, and Chu bzang bla ma Ye shes rgya mtsho's *blo rigs* and *rtags rigs*. Byes pa College relied upon Phur lcog yongs 'dzin's (1825-1901) *blo rigs* and *rtags rigs*, while Shar rtse College of dGa' ldan used bSod nams grags

pa's works, and Byang rtse took sByin pa Chos 'phel rgya mtsho's *blo rigs* and *rtags rigs*.

14. The full title is: *Tshad ma'i dgongs 'grel gyi bstan bcos chen po rnam 'grel gyi don gcig tu dril ba blo rab 'bring tha gsum du ston pa legs bshad chen po mkhas pa'i mgul rgyan skal bzang re ba kun skong*, and it expounds the following subjects: (1) *dbyibs dang kha dog*, (2) *yod rtogs med rtogs*, (3) *yin log min log*, (4) *ldog pa ngos 'dzin*, (5) *gcig dang tha dad*, (6) *rgyu 'bras chung ngu*, (7) *yul dang yul can*, (8) *spyi dang bye brag*, (9) *'gal 'brel*, (10) *mtshan mtshon*, (11) *cha pa'i lugs kyi rdzas ldog*, (12) *rang lugs kyi rdzas ldog*, (13) *khyab mtha' 'god tshul*, (14) *khyab pa sgo brgyad*, (15) *khas len song tshul*, (16) *drug sgra*, (17) *thal 'gyur chung ngu*, (18) *dus gsum*, (19) *rang mtshan dang spyi mtshan*, (20) *sel 'jug dang sgrub 'jug*, (21) *rigs brjod dang tshogs brjod*, (22) *dgag sgrub*, (23) *gzhan sel*, (24) *'gal 'brel che ba*, (25) *thal 'gyur che ba*, (26) *rgyu 'bras che ba*. The Peking edition of *Sras bsdus grwa* (*SNDG*) contains *Sras bsdus grwa*'s summary in verse entitled *bsDus grwa'i rtsa tshig dwangs gsal me long*.

15. The full title is *Tshad ma'i gzhung don 'byed pa'i bsdus grwa'i rnam bzhag rigs lam 'phrul gyi lde mig*. Its subjects are: [*Chung*:] (1) *kha dog dkar dmar*, (2) *gzhi grub*, (3) *ldog pa ngos 'dzin*, (4) *yin log min log*, (5) *rgyu 'bras chung ngu*, (6) *spyi dang bye brag*, (7) *rdzas ldog*. [*'Bring*:] (1) *'gal 'brel*, (2) *yod rtogs med rtogs*, (3) *mtshan mtshon*, (4) *rgyu 'bras che ba*, (5) *rjes 'gro ldog khyab*, (6) *dgag gshags sgrub gshags*. [*Che*:] (1) *thal 'gyur chung ba*, (2) *thal 'gyur che ba*, (3) *gzhan sel dgag sgrub*, (4) *sel 'jug sgrub 'jug*.

16. Much of this section is derived from Jackson (1987: 128-131), from van der Kuijp (1989: 17) and from information personally received from Dr. David Jackson.

17. According to *SKKC*: 113, *rTags rigs las rigs lam che 'bring chung gsum gyi yig cha sogs mang du bzhugs*.

References

A khu chin Shes rab rgya mtsho

MHTL *dPe rgyun dkon pa 'ga' zhig gi tho yig: Materials for a History of Tibetan Literature*. Part 3, pp. 503-601. Śata-Piṭaka Series 30. New Delhi: International Academy of Indian Culture, 1963.

bKra shis rdo rje, Ko btso

DGPK *sDe dge'i par khang rig gnas kun 'dus gzhal med khang chos mdzod chen mo bkra shis sgo mang gi dkar chag rdo rje'i chos bdun ldan pa'i lde'u mig*. Si khron: Si khron mi rigs dpe skrun khang, 1983.

Goldberg, Margaret E.

1985 "Entity and Antimony in Tibetan *bsdus grwa* Logic." Parts I and II. *Journal of Indian Philosophy* 13: 153-199, 273-304.

Horváth, Zoltán

1987 Review of van der Kuijp (1983). *Indo-Iranian Journal* 30/4: 314-321.

Jackson, David P.

1987 *The Entrance Gate for the Wise.* Vienna: Wiener Studien zur Tibetologie und Buddhismuskunde 17, Parts 1 and 2.

1989 *The Early Abbots of 'Phan po Na-lendra: The Vicissitudes of a Great Tibetan Monastery in the 15th Century.* Vienna: Wiener Studien zur Tibetologie und Buddhismuskunde 23.

'Jam dbyangs bzhad pa'i rdo rje

JYSB *The Collected Works of 'Jam-Dbyaṅs-Bźad-Pa'i-Rdo-Rje, Reproduced from prints from the Bkra-śis-'khyil blocks.* Ed. by Ngawang Gelek Demo. 15 vols. Gedan Sungrab Minyam Gyunphel Series, vols. 40-54. New Delhi: 1972-74.

'Jam dbyangs mChog lha 'od zer

RTDG *Tshad ma rnam 'grel gyi bsdus gzhung shes bya'i sgo 'byed rgol ngan glang po 'joms pa gdong lnga'i gad rgyangs rgyu rig lde mig, Rwa stod bsdus grwa.* Dharamsala: Library of Tibetan Works and Archives, 1980.

Klong rdol bla ma Ngag dbang blo bzang

TNMG *Tshad ma rnam 'grel sogs gtan tshig rig pa las byung ba'i ming gi grangs.* Śata-Piṭaka Series 100, pp. 660-712. New Delhi: 1973.

van der Kuijp, Leonard

1979 "Phya-pa Chos-kyi seng-ge's Impact on Tibetan Epistemological Theory." *Journal of Indian Philosophy* 5: 355-369.

1983 *Contributions to the Development of Tibetan Buddhist Epistemology.* Alt- und Neu-Indische Studien 26. Wiesbaden.

1989 *An Introduction to Gtsang-nag-pa's Tshad-ma rnam-par nges-pa'i ti-ka legs-bshad bsdus-pa, An ancient Commentary on Dharmakirti's Pramāṇaviniścaya.* Otani University Collection No. 13971. Kyoto: Otani University Tibetan Works Series II.

Kun dga' grol mchog

SCNT *Paṇḍita chen po Śākya mchog ldan gyi rnam par thar pa zhib mo rnam par 'thag pa.* In *Collected Works of Śākya mchog ldan*, vol. 16, pp. 1-233. Thimphu: 1975.

mKhan po A pad et al., compilers

SKKC *dKar chag mthong bas yid 'phrog chos mdzod bye ba'i lde mig: A Bibliography of Sa skya pa Literature.* New Delhi: Ngawang Topgyal, 1987.

Onoda Shunzo

1979 "Chibetto no sōin ni okeru mondō no ruikei" [Pattern of the Tibetan Monacal Debate]. *Bukkyō Shigaku Kenkyū* [The Journal of the History of Buddhism] 22/1: 1-16.

1981 *The Yoṅs 'Dzin rTags Rigs: A Manual for Tibetan Logic.* Studia Asiatica 5. Nagoya University.

1982 "Chibetto ni okeru ronrigaku kenkyū no mondai" [Primary Course in Tibetan Monastic Universities]. *Tōyō Gakujutsu Kenkyū* [The Journal of Oriental Studies] 21/2: 193-205.

1983 "rJes 'gro ldog khyab ni tsuite" [On rJes 'gro ldog khyab]. *Indogaku Bukkyōgaku Kenkyū* [Journal of Indian and Buddhist Studies] 32/1: 437-434.

1986 "Phya pa Chos Kyi Seng Ge's Classifications of Thal 'Gyur." *Berliner Indologische Studien*, Band 2: 65-85.

1988 "On the Tibetan Controversy Concerning the Various Ways of Replying to Prasaṅgas." *The Tibet Journal* 13/2: 36-41.

1989a "Chibetto no Gakumonji" [Tibetan Monastic Universities]. *Iwanamikoźa Tōyōshiso* [Oriental Thoughts]. Series 11, chapter 3.1, pp. 352-373. Iwanami Shoten: Tokyo.

1989b "bsDus grwa sho no keifu" [Genealogy of *bsdus grwa* literature]. *Indogaku Bukkyōgaku Kenkyū* [Journal of Indian and Buddhist Studies] 37/2: 825-819.

1989c "The Chronology of the Abbatial Successions of the Gsaṅ phu sne'u thog Monastery." *Wiener Zeitshrift für die Kunde Südasiens* 33: 203-213.

1991 "Abbatial Successions of the Colleges of gSang phu sNe'u thog Monastery." *Bulletin of the National Museum of Ethnology* 15/4: 1049-1071.

1992 *Monastic Debate in Tibet—A Study on the History and Structures of Bsdus Grwa Logic*. Wiener Studien zur Tibetologie und Budddhismuskunde 27. Vienna.

Perdue, Daniel Elmo

1976 *Introductory Debate in Tibetan Buddhism*. Dharamsala: Library of Tibetan Works and Archives, 1976.

Phur bu lcog Ngag dbang byams pa

PKPB *Grwa sa chen po bzhi dang rgyud pa stod smad chags tshul pad dkar 'phreng ba: Three Karchacks*. Gedan Sungrab Series 13, pp. 46-169. New Delhi: 1970.

Śākya mchog ldan

ZNDG *Chos kyi 'khor lo bskor ba'i rnam gzhag ji ltar grub pa'i yi ge gzu bor gnas pa'i mdzangs pa dga' byed*. In his *Collected Works*, vol.16, pp. 457-482. Thimphu: 1975.

NTTR *rNgog lo tstsha ba chen pos bstan pa ji ltar bskyangs pa'i tshul mdo tsam du bya ba ngo mtshar gtam gyi rol ma*. In his *Collected Works*, vol.16, pp.443-456. Thimphu: 1975.

Smith, Gene

1969 *Tibetan Catalogue*. Seattle: University of Washington.

Stcherbatsky, Th.

1932 *Buddhist Logic*. Leningrad; reprint Tokyo: Meicho-Fukyū-kai, 1977.

Su dhi pra sha ka and Sras Ngag dbang bkra shis
SNDG *Tshad ma'i dgongs don rtsa 'grel mkhas pa'i mgul rgyan*. Ed. by dMu dge bSam gtan. Beijing: Mi rigs dpe skrun khang, 1987.

Tillemans, Tom J. F.
1989 "Formal and Semantic Aspects of Tibetan Buddhist Debate Logic." *Journal of Indian Philosophy* 17: 265-297.

Vostrikov, A.
1935-37 "Some Corrections and Critical Remarks on Dr. Johan van Manen's Contribution to the Bibliography of Tibet." *Bulletin of the School of Oriental and African Studies* 8: 60-62.

Chapter 11

Debate Manuals (*Yig cha*) in dGe lugs Monastic Colleges[1]

Guy Newland

Yig cha are the required textbooks in the curriculum of Tibetan Buddhist monastic colleges (*grwa tshang*). They may be called "debate manuals" because they are often structured around a series of debates which provide rich fodder for the oral debates characteristic of Tibetan monastic education. The word *yig cha* literally means "record" or "notes." Debate manuals have value both as explicit doctrinal records of the evolution of Buddhist thought and as implicit social records of attitudes among educated monks toward faith, reason, education, and tradition. The genre can be traced back almost a millennium, with new works still appearing in this century.

Often composed by distinguished scholars at the invitation of their colleges, many debate manuals are actually Tibetan sub-sub-commentaries pertaining to Indian Buddhist treatises (*śāstras*) such as Dharmakīrti's *Pramāṇavārttika*, Maitreya's *Abhisamayālaṃkāra*, and Candrakīrti's *Madhyamakāvatāra*. Thus, while debate manuals are by definition pedagogical works, intended to inform and to stimulate debate, the most noteworthy examples of the genre also involve elements of creative exegesis, polemic, and/or philosophical synthesis. If we believe that earlier formulations of a religious view are somehow more pure or more authentic—and therefore more worthy of academic concern—then we may dismiss debate manuals, along with Tibetan doxography (*grub mtha'*) and "grounds and paths" (*sa lam*) literature, as derivative, synthetic, post-classical scholasticism. However, if our interest is the life of Buddhist philosophy across generations of Tibetan scholars, and if we seek to know not just where tradition began but how it is remembered (and thus reshaped), then we must give debate manuals their due.

In the monastic colleges of the dGe lugs school debate manuals have been the primary focus of intellectual life for the last five or six centuries. This is certainly not to depreciate the enormous importance of Tsong kha pa Blo bzang grags pa (1357-1419) as the preeminent scholar and revered founder of the order, nor to imply a lack of reverence for Śākyamuni and the authors of the Mahāyāna treatises. Tibetan scholars do rely upon debate manuals for exegetical guidance through the "great books" of their tradition. The present Dalai Lama has reminded monks that they should not neglect to study Tsong kha pa's own writings. Yet the issuance of such a reminder, unnecessary for the best scholars, is indicative of the typical student's tendency to acquire Tsong kha pa's system in a secondhand way, relying heavily on the convenient and precise formulations of the debate manuals. Insofar as the colleges traditionally regard their manuals as ideal reformulations of the essential points of the treatises and commentaries, the focus on the manuals has tended to displace scholastic attention to the "great books."[2]

Monastic debate manuals bridge both historical and stylistic gaps by explicating the content of classical treatises in language patterned after and readily (re)assimilated to the scholastic oral debate tradition. Debate manuals, or substantial portions from them, are memorized by students and serve as the basis for (1) commentary by the teacher during class, and (2) debate among the students in the monastery courtyard after class. Thus, these manuals link the philosophy of the classical treatises to the living philosophy of courtyard debate, creating a shared universe for discourse among teachers and students of the same college. In Tibetan monastic debate, arguments must be framed as syllogisms (*prayoga, sbyor ba*) or consequences (*prasaṅga, thal 'gyur*), and the respondent must either challenge the sign (*liṅga, rtags*) (i.e., the minor premise), or the pervasion (*vyāpti, khyab pa*) (i.e., the major premise), or else accept the opponent's point. The same rules structure the debates in the manuals. Most manuals break down the material into a series of topics, covering each topic in a tripartite schema: (1) debates refuting opposing systems (*dgag pa*), (2) a presentation of the author's own system (*rang lugs bzhag pa*) of definitions (*mtshan nyid*), etc., and (3) further debates dispelling objections (*rtsod spong*) posed by actual or hypothetical critics. This format allows authors to sharpen their arguments while creating text that their debate-trained readers find relatively easy to memorize for use in the courtyard. Conversely, debate manual authors must have derived some of their written debates from oral debates current in their respective colleges and generations.

Monastic Colleges

Goldstein (21) estimates that twenty-six percent of traditional Tibet's male population were monks. Although Tibetans generally regard monks as superior to laymen, this high percentage is one reason that the official charisma of the robes was not potent enough to mark monks as an exclusive élite. In the dGe lugs, the dominant order of Tibetan Buddhism since the seventeenth century, scholarly achievement has been one of the most important paths into the élite circles of leadership. To understand this fact, we must reflect on the relationship between reason and liberation in Tsong kha pa's philosophy.

Like other Buddhists, Tsong kha pa and his dGe lugs pa followers contend that liberation from beginningless cycles of suffering is reached through non-dualistic (*advaya, gnyis med*) and trans-conceptual insight (*nirvikalpajñāna, rtog med ye shes*) into reality (*dharmatā, chos nyid*). However, for the dGe lugs pa this insight is not a spontaneous, naturally arising, objectless intuition. Rather it is something that must be gradually and systematically cultivated, and it has a specific, rationally comprehensible object—emptiness (*śūnyatā, stong pa nyid*). Although emptiness is the very nature of the mind, realization (*rtogs pa*) of this natural emptiness is a hard-won accomplishment. Realization of emptiness depends not only upon prior training in ethics, but upon conceptual mastery of what "emptiness" is and how logic can be used to approach it.

This philosophical stance reinforced the religious and political authority of those who controlled educational institutions equipped to provide the requisite training in logic and philosophy.[3] Traditionally, much of dGe lugs education was controlled by large monasteries near Lhasa, especially 'Bras spungs, Se ra and dGa' ldan.[4] Each major monastic university comprised a number of colleges, each college having its own support personnel, its own temples, its own debate manuals, its own faculty, and its own abbot (*mkhan po*). Some colleges focused on tantric studies, while others existed only in theory or in vestigial forms; the major colleges that concern us here are sGo mang and Blo gsal gling at 'Bras spungs, sMad and Byes at Se ra, and Shar rtse and Byang rtse at dGa' ldan. While education was a major function of these institutions, at any given time most of the monks at the monastic universities were not students. Goldstein (24) reports, for example, that at the middle of this century the monks at the sMad college of Se ra monastery numbered 2,800; of these only 800 were students. Few of these students could expect to complete the entire monastic curriculum; most would find other vocations within the monastery. Thus, degree-holders were, and today remain, a small élite within the monastic community.

An education at a big monastery is not presumed necessary for spiritual development, but there is an implication that study at these monasteries represents a rare and invaluable spiritual opportunity for those who can withstand its rigors. Advancement through the curriculum and academic hierarchy of these institutions is presumed to reflect the attainment of (at *least*) the conceptual knowledge and analytical skills prerequisite to yogic realization. The colleges of 'Bras spungs, Se ra and dGa' ldan monasteries give the title *dge bshes* to scholars passing exams at the end of twenty to twenty-five years of study. The charismatic valence of this title is apparent when one considers that the Sanskrit equivalent of the title *dge bshes*—*kalyāṇamitra*, usually translated "spiritual friend"—is a standard epithet of a *guru*, i.e., a spiritual master.

Traditionally, considerable wealth and power accumulated in the hierarchies of these prestigious institutions; they played important religious, political, economic, and even military roles in the history of Tibet. Far-flung networks of affiliated monasteries not only provided a feeder system for promising students and appropriate sinecure for graduates, but also offered channels for political intercourse. The abbots of the major colleges were among the most important figures in Tibetan politics. Because the abbots were always selected from the ranks of the *dge bshes*, mastery of the monastic syllabus—including expert knowledge of the debate manuals—was an important path "out of the ranks" into charismatic office and political power. While incarnate lamas (*sprul sku*) achieved their status otherwise, they were at least in principle expected to pass through the same educational system.

Intercollegiate solidarity within the large monasteries tends to be weak. Each functioning college has its own chapel (*'du khang*), staff, and debate manuals. As Goldstein (26-29) notes, when monks at Se ra Byes revolted against the central government in 1947, Se ra sMad did not help them; when 'Bras spungs Blo gsal gling quarrelled with the Dalai Lama in 1921, 'Bras spungs sGo mang did not take their side. A monk's strongest loyalties are to his college and his regional house (*khang tshan*), a sub-collegiate unit with membership traditionally based on natal province. Some colleges have traditional regional affiliations based on the provinces represented by their constituent houses; thus, rivalries between colleges within a monastery may have a regional flavor. Each college maintains the hagiographical tradition of its most important author and, to a certain extent, takes his assertions as orthodoxy. Rivalries still rage between contiguous colleges using different textbooks. At 'Bras spungs, doctrinal disputes between Blo gsal gling and sGo mang turn on differences so thin that one hesitates to call them "philosophical." Yet analytical debate of such differences plays an enormous role in the manuals and the lives of those who use them. In debate with other colleges (during the winter session and at *sMon lam*) each monk is expected to uphold, insofar as possible, the assertions of his college's manuals. Outside the context of debate with other colleges, dGe lugs monks differ greatly in their attitudes toward "debate manual orthodoxy." Many regard their teachers and manuals as sources of unassailable truth, using their definitions as absolute reference points. On the other hand, there are always those who "consider the knowledge imparted to them as a tool...accepted provisionally in order to advance" on a quest that is at once philosophical and spiritual (Dreyfus: 10-12).

The dGe lugs Curriculum

The outline of the curriculum varies only slightly from college to college, and always includes five main phases (see also Onoda, in this volume):

(1) study of logic, epistemology and psychology, based on Tibetan "Summarized Topics" (*bsdus grwa*) debate manuals deriving their content from Dharmakīrti's *Pramānavārttika* and other sources (three to six years)
(2) study of the bodhisattva path and related topics in Prajñāpāramitā (*phar phyin*) literature, based mainly on Maitreya's *Abhisamayālaṃkāra*, its Indian and Tibetan commentaries, and the related debate manuals (five to seven years)
(3) study of Mādhyamika (*dbu ma*) philosophy, based mainly on Candrakīrti's *Madhyamakāvatāra*, Tsong kha pa's *dGongs pa rab gsal* and *Legs shes snying po*, and the related debate manuals (four years)
(4) study of Abhidharma, based especially on Vasubandhu's *Abhidharmakośa* (*mNgon par mdzod*) and its commentaries (four years)
(5) study of monastic discipline (*vinaya*, *'dul ba*), based especially on Guṇaprabha's *Vinayasūtra* and the associated debate manuals (four years)

Geshe Sopa (41-42) reports that the curriculum at the Byes college of Se ra includes three years for the first phase, five years for the second, and four years for each of the other three phases. At the sGo mang college of 'Bras spungs, six years are dedicated to the first phase and six or seven years to the second phase (Hopkins: 15; Klein: 220). Once a day classes meet with a teacher for about two hours of text-study; twice daily they meet in the courtyard for sessions of oral debate among students. Five or six weeks out of every year are set aside for an inter-monastic session of debate and study of Dharmakīrti's *Pramāṇavarttika* and related texts. Those who complete the five phases of the curriculum normally spend additional years reviewing and sharpening their debate skills before undergoing examination for the *dge bshes* degree at the Prayer Festival (*sMon lam*) celebrated during the first three weeks of the new year.

In this limited space we will mention some of the debate manuals used in the third (*dbu ma*) phase of this curriculum.

Mādhyamika Debate Manuals

Many of the most important Mādhyamika debate manuals are subcommentaries on Tsong kha pa's *dGongs pa rab gsal*, his commentary on Candrakīrti's *Madhyamakāvatāra*.[5] These manuals also include relevant citations of *sūtra* and other Indian Mādhyamika texts, along with references to Tsong kha pa's *Rigs pa'i rgya mtsho*, *Legs bshad snying po*, *Lam rim chen mo*, and *Lam rim 'bring*, mKhas grub dGe legs dpal bzang po's *sTong thun chen mo* and rGyal tshab's *sPyod 'jug rnam bshad*. The authors of extant debate manuals on Madhyamaka include: Śānti pa Blo gros rgyal mtshan (fifteenth century), who wrote for the 'Khyil gang College of bKra shis lhun po Monastery; mKhas sgrub bsTan pa dar rgyas (1493-1568) and Grags pa bshad sgrub (1675-1748), authors for the sMad College of Se ra; rJe btsun Chos kyi rgyal mtshan (1469-1546), author for the Byes college of Se ra and the Byang rtse College of dGa' ldan;[6] sGom sde shar pa Nam mkha' rgyal mtshan (1532-1592), a student of rJe btsun Chos kyi rgyal mtshan and an author for the Byes College of Se ra as well as the Byang rtse College of dGa' ldan; Khyung phrug Byams pa bkra shis (sixteenth century), another student of rJe btsun Chos kyi rgyal mtshan and an author for the Byang rtse College of dGa' ldan; Paṇ chen bSod nams grags pa (1478-1554), author for the Blo gsal gling College of 'Bras spungs and the Shar rtse College of dGa' ldan; and 'Jam dbyangs bzhad pa Ngag dbang brtson 'grus (1648-1721), author of the texts of the sGo mang College of 'Bras spungs as well as the bKra shis 'kyil Monastery, which he founded.[7]

Paṇ chen bSod nams grags pa, rJe btsun Chos kyi rgyal mtshan, and 'Jam dbyangs bzhad pa are the best known and most influential of the Mādhyamika debate manual authors. In their textbooks on Madhyamaka, these writers share two main goals: (1) to provide a basis for instruction in the fundamentals of Madhyamaka philosophy, and (2) to confirm the fundamental coherence of Tsong kha pa's system by refuting contrary interpretations and rebutting critics. Born in the same century during which Tsong kha pa and his immediate disciples died, and flourishing prior to the sect's attainment of political supremacy, rJe btsun pa and Paṇ chen see the founder and his early followers in the light of a charisma slightly less magnificent than that appreciated by later generations. Paṇ chen, in particular, boldly overthrows the assertions of mKhas grub and rGyal tshab when they conflict with his own conclusions (see *BZSG*: 61a and *BJGL*: 47a-47b). The work of rJe btsun pa and Paṇ chen seems quite terse when compared to 'Jam dbyangs bzhad pa's elaborate grappling with myriad doctrinal complications. 'Jam dbyangs bzhad pa's Mādhyamika manual is more ambitious than others in its attempts (1) to demonstrate the fidelity of Tsong kha pa to his Indian sources and (2) to reconcile apparent contradictions among Tsong kha pa, mKhas grub, and rGyal tshab. Thriving in the heyday of dGe lugs power, 'Jam dbyangs bzhad pa is also more deferential to Tsong kha pa's spiritual "sons" (*sras*)—mKhas grub and rGyal tshab. When he cannot reconcile a literal (*tshig zin*) reading of mKhas grub or rGyal tshab with his own understanding of Tsong kha pa, he works to reconcile the intentions (*dgongs pa*) behind their words.[8]

Excerpt from 'Jam dbyangs bzhad pa's *dBu ma chen mo*

The following brief excerpt from 'Jam dbyangs bzhad pa's Mādhyamika debate manual illustrates how instruction, polemic, and exegesis can be finely woven on the framework of the debate format. We find the author citing Candrakīrti's *Prasannapadā* and *Madhyamakāvatāra* in order to rebut attacks by Tsong kha pa's Sa skya pa critic, sTag tshang lo tsā ba Shes rab rin chen (b. 1405). 'Jam dbyangs bzhad pa attempts to show that sTag tshang, in his critique of the dGe lugs presentation of valid cognition (*tshad ma, pramāṇa*) of conventional phenomena, adopts a position that Candrakīrti specifically refutes. At the same time, 'Jam dbyangs bzhad pa implicitly offers a solution to an exegetical problem in the *Prasannapadā*.

In his discussion of the term *lokasaṃvṛti* (*'jig rten gyi kun rdzob;* worldly conventionality" or "worldly concealer"), Candrakīrti (*PP*: 493) first seems to say that the word *loka* ("world") does not imply a contrasting *aloka* ("non-world"). Yet Candrakīrti then appears to reverse himself, writing (*PP*: 493), "Yet, in one way there is such a non-world. Those who have erroneous vision because their senses have been impaired by opthalmia, blue eye-film, jaundice, etc. are not worlds." Many scholars ignore or gloss over Candrakīrti's initial denial. 'Jam dbyangs bzhad pa thinks he can explain the intent of the initial denial, but he embeds his answer in a refutation of sTag tshang. A key feature of sTag tshang's presentation of conventionalities (*saṃvṛti, kun rdzob*) is the distinction between worldly conventionalities and yogic conventionalities (*GTKN*: 266). By citing Candrakīrti's denial of non-worldly conventionalities in refutation of sTag tshang, 'Jam dbyangs bzhad pa suggests that Candrakīrti's initial denial is intended to rule out a special category of non-worldly, yogic conventionalities.

'Jam dbyangs bzhad pa then uses a hypothetical objection as an opportunity to reconcile his reading of the *Prasannapadā* with earlier comments on the *Madhyamakāvatāra*. Confident that in a few brief strokes he has unravelled a passage in the *Prasannapadā*, aligned it with the *Madhyamakāvatāra*, and refuted sTag tshang, 'Jam dbyangs bzhad pa cannot resist concluding on a self-congratulatory note. He writes (*BMC*: 541-542):

> *Incorrect Position* held by sTag tshang the Translator: [Candrakīrti's] use of the word *loka* ["world"] in the phrase *lokasaṃvṛti* (*'jig rten gyi kun rdzob*) precludes Superiors having in their continuums conventional valid cognitions (*tha snyad pa'i tshad ma*) that perceive conventional truths (*saṃvṛtisatya*, *kun rdzob bden pa*).[9]
>
> *Correct Response*: It follows that this is incorrect because [Candrakīrti's] statement of *loka* [in "*lokasaṃvṛti*"] is descriptive; it is not [made] for the sake of applying analyses such as [yours]. This is because Candrakīrti's *Prasannapadā* (493) says:
>
> > Is there also a *saṃvṛti* that is *not* worldly from which a worldly *saṃvṛti* could be thus distinguished? This [word "worldly"] describes how things are. That analysis [which assumes that since *saṃvṛti* is sometimes modified by "worldly," there must also be an unworldly *saṃvṛti*] does not apply here.
>
> *Incorrect Position* with regard to this: It [absurdly] follows that worldly conventionalities (*lokasaṃvṛti*, *'jig rten gyi kun rdzob*) are not divided into conventionalities that are real for the world (*'jig rten gyi yang dag pa'i kun rdzob*) and conventionalities that are unreal for the world (*'jig rten gyi log pa'i kun rdzob*) because [according to you] "world" (*loka*, *'jig rten*) is stated [merely] for descriptive purposes [and not in order to differentiate two types of conventionalities].[10] If you accept the consequence, it follows that your explanation that in Candrakīrti's *Madhyamakāvatāra* (104) worldly conventionalities are of two types—those that are real from a worldly perspective and those that are unreal from a worldly perspective—is incorrect.
>
> *Correct Response:* The original reason [—that "world" is stated for descriptive purposes in the *Prasannapadā*—] certainly does not entail the consequence [—that worldly conventionalities are not divided into conventionalities that are real for the world and conventionalities that are unreal for the world—] because, since the erroneous—i.e., false—consciousnesses of one whose sense powers have been impaired by jaundice, etc., are not the world in relation to whose perspective something is posited as

real, Candrakīrti says "*worldly* conventional truth" (*loka-saṃvṛtisatya*) in order to make that point understood.[11] This is because Candrakīrti's *Prasannapadā* (493.2-4) says:

> Yet in one way there is [such a non-world]. Those who have erroneous vision because their senses have been impaired by opthalmia, blue eye-film,[12] jaundice, etc. are not worlds. That which is a conventionality for them is not a worldly conventional truth (*lokasaṃvṛtisatya*).[13] Therefore, a worldly conventional truth is distinguished from that.

Since it seems that even many former scholars did not explain[14] this, I have written a little clearly.

Conclusion

From a dGe lugs religious perspective, debate manuals engender analytical skills and lay the foundations of right view, thus providing a solid conceptual basis from which yogic inquiry into the nature of reality can proceed. We may also observe that (1) minor differences among the manuals are focal points for the intellectual expression of collegial solidarity and intercollegiate tensions, while (2) their far broader commonalities in structure and content contribute to the socialization of the monastic élite within a shared worldview.

Notes

1. Some ideas and sentences in this article are revisions of material published in my book *The Two Truths* (1992).

2. This situation is not peculiar to dGe lugs. In the colleges of the Sa skya school (and in the Sa skya College now located in Rajpur, India) the primary focus is on the work of Go ram pa bSod nams seng ge (1429-1489) rather than on the work of Sa skya Paṇḍita Kun dga' rgyal mtshan (1182-1251/2) and the other early luminaries of the order. The Sa skya pa monks use the word *yig cha* to refer to the required texts by Go ram pa bSod nams seng ge.

3. The following paragraphs describe the general situation in the monastic universities, considering both the traditional context (pre-1959) and the contemporary context of the dGe lugs monasteries reestablished in exile near Mundgod and Bylakuppe, India.

4. Tsong kha pa established dGa' ldan in 1409; his student Byams chen chos rje founded 'Bras spungs in 1416 and Se ra (spelled *Se rwa* by some authorities) in 1419. Each held several thousand monks. Other major dGe lugs monastic universities include bKra shis lhun po, bKra shis 'kyil, and sKu 'bum.

Established in 1445 in gZhis ga rtse by dGe 'dun grub pa (who was posthumously entitled "First Dalai Lama"), bKra shis lhun po became the seat of the Paṇ chen Lama in the seventeenth century. bKra shis 'kyil was founded in eastern Tibet by the dGe lugs scholar 'Jam dbyangs bzhad pa Ngag dbang brtson 'grus, and sKu 'bum was founded in the sixteenth century at Tsong kha pa's birthplace.

5. There is also a class of Mādhyamika debate manuals based on Tsong ka pa's *Legs bshad snying po*. Many of the authors are the same as those mentioned in this paragraph.

6. An excerpt from rJe btsun Chos kyi rgyal mtshan's debate manual on Madhyamaka is translated and explicated in Newland, 1984.

7. No longer extant are Mādhyamika debate manuals by Blo gros rin chen seng ge (fifteenth century) and Shes rab dbang po (fifteenth century?), both formerly used in the Byes College of Se ra. My translation of the *satyadvaya* section from 'Jam dbyangs bzhad pa's Mādhyamika debate manual is forthcoming from Snow Lion.

8. For examples, see *BMC*: 268b, 275b, and 290a. In the section dealing with the two truths, we find mKhas grub quoted eight times in eighty-six sides. By comparison, Nāgārjuna is also cited eight times; only Tsong kha pa, Candrakirti, and *sūtra* are cited more often. rGyal tshab is cited four times.

9. The Sa skya scholar sTag tshang lo tsā ba Shes rab rin chen criticizes the dGe lugs position on conventional valid cognition (*tha snyad pa'i tshad ma*). He writes (*GTKN*: 269):

> [T]he presentation of valid cognition that is well known in the world ... [may be] asserted in a way that indulges the perspective of the world. However, a so-called "valid cognizer comprehending conventionalities" is completely non-existent [not only in terms of the thorough analysis into emptiness but even] in terms of the normal analysis of our own system.

Thus, even Superiors in states subsequent to meditative equipoise (*pṛṣṭhalabdhajñāna*) cannot have valid knowledge of conventional phenomena. Nevertheless, their "yogic" mode of apprehension is distinct from the non-analytical perspective of the world. sTag tshang (*GTKN*: 266) uses this distinction to make a twofold division of conventionalities:

> In general, it is said that there are two types of conventionalities: worldly conventionalities and yogic conventionalities. . . . With regard to illustrations, coarse phenomena of a mistaken perspective that does not investigate or analyze are worldly conventionalities. Subtle impermanence—an object found by a conventional awareness with normal analysis—and the appearances in states subsequent to meditative equipoise of Superiors . . . are yogic conventionalities.

10. This incorrect position challenges a shift in 'Jam dbyangs bzhad pa's manner of reading the word "world." When the phrase "of the world" (*'jig rten gyi*) is added to the phrase "real conventionality" (*yang dag pa'i kun rdzob*) or "unreal conventionality" (*log pa'i kun rdzob*), 'Jam dbyangs bzhad pa under-

stands this to mean conventionalities that are real or unreal *for the worldly perspective.* (If the qualification "for the worldly perspective" were not added, then one would have to say that all conventionalities are unreal.) However, when the phrase "of the world" (*'jig rten gyi*) is added to "conventionality" (*kun rdzob*), 'Jam dbyangs bzhad pa does *not* take this to mean "conventionality in the perspective of the world." Such a reading might suggest a contrasting "conventionality in the perspective of yogis" as advocated by sTag tshang. Or else, it might suggest that worldly conventionalities are phenomena that worldly beings can recognize *as* conventionalities.

11. Conventional truths (*saṃvṛtisatya*), literally, are "truths-for-a-concealing ignorance," phenomena that are misapprehended as truths by the subtlest ignorance—a conception of inherent existence—of even ordinary, healthy persons. A person with jaundice who sees a white piece of paper as yellow may have a coarse ignorant consciousness that believes that the paper is actually yellow, just as it appears. That misconception conceals the white color of the paper. However, such a misconception is not the concealing ignorance in terms of which that paper is a concealer-truth because it is not a conception of inherent existence.

12. "Blue eye-film" (*ling thog sngon po*) does not appear in the Sanskrit.

13. Jacques May's Tibetan (432) reads: *'jig rten kun rdzob bden pa ma yin pas.* La Vallée Poussin's Sanskrit (493) reads *alokasaṃvṛti.*

14. At 542, reading *bshad* for *shod* in accordance with the sGo mang edition, 300a.

References

Candrakīrti

MA *Madhyamakāvatāra.* Tibetan translation: P no. 5261, vol. 98 in *The Tibetan Tripiṭaka* (see Suzuki).

PP *Mūlamadhyamakavṛttiprasannapadā.* In *Mūlamadhaymakakārikās de Nāgārjuna avec la Prasannapadā Commentaire de Candrakīrti.* Ed. by Louis de la Vallée Poussin. Bibliotheca Buddhica 4. Osnabrück: Biblio Verlag, 1970. Tibetan: P no. 5260, vol. 98 in *The Tibetan Tripiṭaka* (see Suzuki); and Jacques May, *Prasannapadā Madhyamakavṛtti, douze chapitres traduits du sanscrit et du tibétain.* Paris: Adrien-Maisonneuve, 1959.

Dharmakīrti

PV *Pramāṇavārttikakārika.* In *Pramāṇavārttika of Acharya Dharmakīrti.* Ed. by Swami Dwarikadas Shastri. Varanasi: Bauddha Bharati, 1968. Tibetan: P no. 5709, vol. 130 in *The Tibetan Tripiṭaka* (see Suzuki).

Dreyfus, Georges B. J.

1987 "Definition in Buddhism." M.A. thesis. Charlottesville: University of Virgina.

Goldstein, Melvyn C.
1989 *A History of Modern Tibet, 1913-1951: The Demise of the Lamaist State.* Berkeley: University of California Press.

Grags pa bshad sgrub
BMYG *dBu ma la 'jug pa'i dgongs pa yang gsal sgron me shes bya ba'i tshig 'grel spyi don mtha dpyod zung 'brel du bshad pa.* New Delhi: Lha mkhar yongs 'dzin bstan pa rgyal mtshan, 1972.

Guṇaprabha
VS *Vinayasūtra.* Tibetan translation: P no. 5619, vol. 123 in *The Tibetan Tripitaka* (see Suzuki).

Hopkins, Jeffrey
n.d. "Reflections on Reality: The Nature of Phenomena in the Mind-Only School." Unpublished ms.

'Jam dbyangs bzhad pa Ngag dbang brtson 'grus
BMC *dBu ma chen mo/ dBu ma 'jug pa'i mtha' dpyod lung rigs gter mdzod zab don kun gsal skal bzang 'jug ngogs.* In his *Collected Works,* vol. 9. New Delhi: Ngawang Gelek Demo, 1972. Also, Buxaduor: Gomang, 1967.

Khyung phrug Byams pa bkra shis
BMKN *dBu ma la 'jug pa'i rnam bshad dgongs pa rab gsal gyi dka' ba'i gnas gsal bar byed pa legs bshad skal bzang mgul rgyan.* New Delhi: Lha mkhar yongs 'dzin bstan pa rgyal mtshan, 1974.

Klein, Anne
1986 *Knowledge and Liberation.* Ithaca: Snow Lion.

Maitreya
AA *Abhisamayālaṃkāra.* In *Abhisamayālaṃkāra-Prajñāpāramitā-Upadeśa-śastra.* Ed. by Th. Stcherbatsky and E. Obermiller. Bibliotheca Buddhica 22. Osnabrück: Biblio Verlag, 1970. Tibetan: P no. 5184, vol. 88 in *The Tibetan Tripiṭaka* (see Suzuki).

mKhas sgrub bsTan pa dar rgyas
BMLG *bsTan bcos chen po dbu ma la 'jug pa'i spyi don rnam bshad dgongs pa rab gsal gyi dgongs pa gsal bar byed pa'i blo gsal sgron me.* New Delhi: Lha mkhar yongs 'dzin bstan pa rgyal mtshan, 1972.
GRTP *rNam bshad dgongs pa rab gsal gyi mtha dpyod rigs pa'i rgya mtsho blo gsal gyi' jug sgo.* New Delhi: Lha mkhar yongs 'dzin bstan pa rgyal mtshan, 1972.

mKhas grub dGe legs dpal bzang po
TTC *sTong thun chen mo/ Zab mo stong pa nyid rab tu gsal bar byed pa'i bstan bcos skal bzang mig 'byed.* Dharamsala: Shes rig par khang, n.d.

Newland, Guy
1984 *Compassion: A Tibetan Analysis*. London: Wisdom.
1992 *The Two Truths*. Ithaca: Snow Lion.

Paṇ chen bSod nams grags pa
BJGL *dBu ma la 'jug pa'i brgal lan zab don yang gsal sgron me*. In his *Collected Works*, vol. *ja*. Mundgod: Drebung Loseling Library Society, 1985.
BZSG *dBu ma'i spyi don zab don gsal ba'i sgron me*. In his *Collected Works*, vol. *ja*. Mundgod: Drebung Loseling Library Society, 1985.

Perdue, Daniel
1992 *Debate in Tibetan Buddhism*. Ithaca: Snow Lion.

rJe btsun Chos kyi rgyal mtshan
BMPD *bsTan bcos dbu ma la 'jug pa'i rnam bshad dgongs pa rab gsal gyi dka' gnad gsal bar byed pa'i spyi don legs bshad skal bzang mgul rgyan*. New Delhi: lHa mkhar yongs 'dzin bstan pa rgyal mtshan, 1973.

Roerich, George N., trans.
1979 *Blue Annals*. Delhi: Motilal Banarsidass.

sGom sde shar pa Nam mkha' rgyal mtshan
TZKN *Thal bzlog gi dka' bai gnas gtan la 'bebs pa*. New Delhi: lHa mkhar yongs 'dzin bstan pa rgyal mtshan, 1973.

Sopa, Geshe Lhundup
1983 *Lectures on Tibetan Religious Culture*, vol. 1. Dharamsala: Library of Tibetan Works and Archives.

sTag tshang lo tsā ba shes rab rin chen
GTKN *Grub mtha' kun shes nas mtha' bral grub pa zhes bya ba'i bstan bcos rnam par bshad pa legs bshad kyi rgya mtsho*. Thimphu: Kun bdzang stobs rgyal, 1976.

Suzuki, D.T., ed.
1956 *The Tibetan Tripiṭaka*. Tokyo-Kyoto: Tibetan Tripitaka Research Foundation.

Śānti pa Blo gros rgyal mtshan
GRKN *rNam bshad dgongs pa rab gsal gyi dka' ba'i gnad gsal bar byed pa'i bstan bcos dbang gi rgyal po*. New Delhi: Lha mkhar yongs 'dzin bstan pa rgyal mtshan, 1973.

Tsong kha pa Blo bzang grags pa
GPRS *dGongs pa rab gsal/dBu ma la 'jug pa'i rgya cher bshad pa dgongs pa rab gsal*. P no. 6143, vol. 154 in *The Tibetan Tripiṭaka* (see Suzuki).

LRB	*Lam rim 'bring/ Byang chub lam gyi rim pa chung ba*. P no. 6002, vols. 152-153 in *The Tibetan Tripiṭaka* (see Suzuki).
LRC	*Lam rim chen mo/ sKyes pa gsum gyi rnyams su blang ba'i rim pa thams cad tshang bar ston pa'i byang chub lam gyi rim pa*. P no. 6001, vol. 152 in *The Tibetan Tripiṭaka* (see Suzuki).
LSNP	*Legs bshad snying po/ Drang ba dang nges pa'i don rnam par phye ba'i bstan bcos legs bshad snying po*. P no. 6142, vol. 153 in *The Tibetan Tripiṭaka* (see Suzuki).
RPGT	*Rigs pa'i rgya mtsho/ dBu ma rtsa ba'i tshig le'ur byas pa shes rab ces bya bai' rnam bshad rigs pa'i rgya mtsho*. P no. 6153, vol. 156 in *The Tibetan Tripiṭaka* (see Suzuki).

Chapter 12

Polemical Literature (*dGag lan*)

Donald S. Lopez, Jr.

> Go bo rab 'byams pa bSod nams seng ge composed a textbook called *dBu ma 'jug pa'i dka' 'grel* ("Commentary on the Difficult Points of [Candrakīrti's] *Madhyamakāvatāra*") [in which] he denigrated the master Tsong kha pa without measure and offered many apparent refutations, citing for the most part [Tsong kha pa's own] great commentary [on Candrakīrti's text, entitled] *dGongs pa rab gsal* ("Illumination of the Intention"). This kind of talk, [demonstrating] that his own positions are merely a mass of internal contradictions, is not a [suitable] object of scholarly refutation. However, in general, the pure view of the profound emptiness is difficult to understand and when understood, it is of great meaning. In particular, in this range of snowy mountains, as a consequence of the shoe of the Hva shang being left in the monastery upon his defeat by the great master Kamalaśīla, there still seem to be many who hold the Hva shang's view. And now, due to the great diffusion of ruinous views,[1] many beings of inferior intelligence have heard and contemplated treatises like this [of Go bo rab 'byams]. In order to reverse the mistaken ideas of those who hold the correct path to be a view of permanence or annihilation, outside of the system of the supreme Ārya Nāgārjuna, his [spiritual] son [Āryadeva], and the glorious Candrakīrti, I will answer briefly. (*GL*: 4-5)

So opens the work of rJe btsun Chos kyi rgyal mtshan (1469-1546, more commonly referred to as Se ra rJe btsun pa or simply rJe btsun pa) known as *Go lan* ("The Answer to Go"), one of his three famous rejoinders to eminent contemporaries of other schools. Each of the three opponents, the Sa skya scholars Go bo rab 'byams pa bSod nams seng ge (1429-1489) and Śākya mchog ldan (1428-1507), and the eighth Karma pa of the Karma bKa' brgyud school, Mi bskyod rdo rje (1507-1544), had in their writings refuted, or in Se ra rJe btsun pa's opinion, attempted to refute, the views of Tsong kha pa. To their refutations (*dgag pa*), Se ra rJe btsun pa provides answers (*lan*). It is this genre of Tibetan Buddhist literature, literally "answers to refutations" (*dgag lan*) that is rendered here as "polemics."[2]

Space does not permit an adequate survey of the history of polemical literature in Tibet, a history that extends into the twentieth century and which includes all the major schools and subschools of Tibetan Buddhism, some extant, some defunct. This literature includes Buddhists writing against Bon pos, as well as the members of a single school writing against their fellow partisans. Here it will only be possible to examine Se ra rJe btsun pa's polemic as an exemplar of the genre. There will also be no opportunity to scrutinize rJe btsun pa's arguments themselves, which are concerned with issues that range from the triflingly pedantic to matters of central importance to Tibetan interpretation of Indian Buddhist philosophy. These latter encompass a constellation of questions that pivot around the category of the so-called Great Mādhyamikas (*dbu ma pa chen po*), which includes not only such expected figures as Nāgārjuna and Āryadeva, but Asaṅga, Vasubandhu, Maitreya, Dignāga, and Śāntarakṣita as well, and which excludes Candrakīrti. Here we find the questions of whether emptiness is the lack of some intrinsic quality (*rang stong*) or some extrinsic quality (*gzhan stong*), of whether there is consistency between Nāgārjuna's philosophical writings (*rigs mtshog*) and his devotional writings (*bstod mtshog*), whether there is doctrinal consistency among the five works of Maitreya, whether the second or the third turning of the wheel of Dharma is to be considered definitive, whether the *Ratnagotravibhāga* should be classified as a Mādhyamika or as a Yogācāra text, whether what Candrakīrti espouses is a nihilistic emptiness (*chad stong*), and whether the nonduality of subject and object is ontologically true (*bden grub*) and the final nature of reality.[3] Rather, we can only examine rJe btsun pa's "Three Answers" as a representative case of Tibetan polemical literature and consider here some of the strategies employed by the polemicist.

In the passage cited above, rJe btsun pa begins by dismissing Go bo rab 'byams pa's work as unworthy of serious consideration, so filled is it with contradictions. However, like the Buddha pondering whether or not to teach after his attainment of enlightenment, Se ra rJe btsun pa compassionately considers how difficult it is to understand the nature of reality and how vital that understanding can be. More specifically, he bemoans the desperate situation in his own Tibet, where wrong views are rampant. These wrong views originate, he says, from those of the infamous Hva shang Mahāyāna (Ho shang Mo ho yen), the northern Ch'an monk supposedly defeated in debate by the Indian master Kamalaśīla at the so-called Council of Lhasa. The great cloud of doubt that surrounds the historical accuracy (both as to substance and outcome) of the accounts of the debate that Se ra rJe btsun pa would have known cannot detain us here.[4] Suffice it say that the received dGe lugs pa tradition painted the Hva shang as the most dangerous of heretics, who held the view that the practice of virtue is irrelevant to the attainment of enlightenment, that enlightenment was to be attained immediately, and that wisdom consisted in placing the mind in a state of no thought. A perusal of Go bo rab 'byams pa's commentary on Candrakīrti in fact reveals none of these positions, nor does Se ra rJe btsun pa attribute them to him in his specific rebuttals. His point here, rather, is to evoke the most famous debate in Tibetan history, identifying himself with the victor Kamalaśīla and indirectly linking Go bo rab 'byams to his defeated Chinese opponent. Finally, in a standard move of Tibetan polemics, he suggests that the perverted views then current in Tibet derive from the Hva shang's shoe, ominously left behind in the arena of his defeat.[5]

Since his opponents have disputed Tsong kha pa's reading of the *Madhyamakāvatāra*, it would carry little weight were rJe btsun pa to counter with further statements from Tsong kha pa in his rejoinder. Instead, he turns to authorities outside the dGe lugs pa school for support. Thus, when he disputes the Karma pa's contention that the *tathāgatagarbha* (the buddha-nature) is a self-arisen, eternal, and autonomous awareness of the nonduality of subject and object, he cites Sa skya Paṇḍita's *sDom gsum rab dbye* ("Delineation of the Three Vows") for support:

> Some, who are like the Sāṃkhyas,
> Hold that the so-called existent virtue
> Is established in a self-arisen way.
> They call this the *tathāgatagarbha.*
> Because this Sāṃkhya system is incorrect
> It should be refuted with scripture and reasoning. (*KL*: 175-176)

Here, not only does he draw on the authority of a third party, but he is able to employ a quotation from that third party that declares the Karma pa's putative position to be quite heterodox; it is the view of the heterodox Sāṃkhya school, one of six schools of classical Hindu philosophy.

In the Tibetan tradition, which looks ever back to India, the Land of Superiors (*'phags yul*), as the unadulterated source of its Buddhism, precedent is of primary importance. Each school traces its doctrines back through the period of transmission of Buddhism from India to Tibet and back further to a lineage of Indian masters. This is especially true for those schools that claimed a historical link between the Indian and Tibetan: the visits to Tibet by Padmasambhava and Vimalamitra for the rNying ma pa, the tutelage of 'Brog mi under Virūpa for the Sa skya pa , the visit to Tibet of Pha dam pa Sang rgyas for the Zhi byed pa, the three visits to India by Mar pa the Translator, where he studied under Maitrīpa and Nāropa, for the bKa' brgyud. Even for the dGe lugs pa, the only major school without a direct historical link to India (although their appellation as the "new bKa' gdams pa" implies an appropriation of Atiśa), lineage is of vital importance. The dGe lugs lineage is established not through travel between India and Tibet, however, but through certain visionary experiences of Tsong kha pa, in which Nāgārjuna and his chief commentators appeared to indicate to him that it is the interpretation of Buddhapālita and, by extension, Candrakīrti that contains the true meaning of the middle way.

It would follow, then, that an appeal to precedent would serve as a potent weapon in the polemicist's arsenal. Thus, when Se ra rJe btsun pa questions Mi bskyod rdo rje's assertion that the knowledge of the nonduality of subject and object appears to be dependently arisen objectively but subjectively it is dependently arisen in a self-arisen way, rJe btsun pa asks from which text this category of the "dependently arisen self-arisen" derives, "because it is difficult to value terminology fabricated in Tibet" (*KL:* 136).

But the appeal to precedent must be considered most devastating when the opponent is confronted with the words of the founders of his own school. The various bKa' brgyud sub-schools all look back to a common lineage that begins with the buddha Vajradhara and then goes through the Indian *mahāsiddhas* Tilopa and Nāropa, to the Tibetan masters Mar pa, Mi la ras pa, and sGam po pa. In his *Answer to Kar*, rJe btsun pa writes:

> This assertion that the knowledge of the nonduality of subject and object is the truly established final mode of being is not the assertion of the earlier adepts. The Lord of Yogins, the master Mi la ras pa, says that all phenomena, from form to omniscience,[6] lack ultimate existence [and] that that is the final mode of being. And [he says that] if one is unable to posit the existence of all phenomena conventionally, one becomes like a nihilist. [He then quotes Mi la ras pa's "Instructions to Tshe ring ma," in a long passage which says that from the ultimate perspective, nothing, not even the Buddha, exists.] Thus, when [Mi la ras pa] says that the body and knowledge of the fruitional state [that is, buddhahood] do not ultimately exist, how are you able to hold that knowledge of the nonduality of subject and object truly exists? On the functioning of conventional existence, the master Mi la says:
>
> E-ma! If sentient beings did not exist,
> Where would the buddhas of the three times come from?
> Because effects do not exist without causes
> The Buddha said that everything,
> *Saṃsāra* and *nirvāṇa,*
> Exists from the perspective of conventional truth.
> The two, the existent—the appearance of things—
> And the non-existent—the empty reality—
> Are indivisible and of one taste.
> Thus, there is no subjectivity and no objectivity;
> The union of all is vast.
> The wise who understand this
> Don't see consciousness, they see wisdom.[7]
> They don't see sentient beings, they see buddhas.
> They don't see things, they see reality.
>
> Thus, Nāgārjuna and his [spiritual] son [Āryadeva], the master Mi la, and the master Tsong kha pa have the same thought and the same voice. (*KL*: 83-84)

Elsewhere, in his effort to rescue Candrakīrti from Mi bskyod rdo rje's charge of being a proponent of a nihilistic emptiness, Se ra rJe btsun pa finds laudatory statements about Candrakīrti in the works of such revered ancestors of the eighth Karma pa as Maitrīpa and Nāropa.[8]

Thus, we see the polemicist executing a range of maneuvers in an effort to defeat, or at least discredit, his adversary. In the case of the three works examined here, the attack seems motivated not so much by the desire to correct errors but by the fact that Śākya mchog ldan, Go bo rab 'byams pa, and Mi bskyod rdo rje took exception with Tsong kha pa. Because his school eventually became politically dominant in Tibet, we often forget what a controversial and, in some ways, idiosyncratic thinker Tsong kha pa was. That his readings of the great Indian *śāstras*, in which he also disputed the interpretations of others, should have provoked discussion is therefore in no way surprising (see Williams). And within dGe lugs pa literature, especially the monastic textbooks (*yig cha*), where Tsong kha pa is often referred to simply as "the omniscient master" (*rje thams cad mkhyen pa*), one finds numerous disagreements with Tsong kha pa on a variety of points, although the master is rarely named explicitly as the opponent.[9] But such disputation seems to be regarded differently when it originates outside the fold.[10] Se ra rJe btsun pa wrote against his bKa' brgyud pa and Sa skya pa opponents a century after the death of Tsong kha pa, ample time for the mystification of the master, the century during which the dGe lugs star was ascending toward the fateful meeting of the third Dalai Lama and the Altan Khan in 1578. This was the period following the decline of Sa skya hegemony in central Tibet, a period of constant strife and occasional warfare between the Karma pa patrons of gTsang and the dGe lugs patrons of dBus.[11] It is not insignificant that it is at this moment, with Tsong kha pa being transformed from one of the brilliant thinkers of a particularly vibrant period in Tibetan Buddhist thought into an iconic founder of a school poised on the brink of political power, that we discern the formation of orthodoxy, of which *dgag lan* literature is a certain sign.[12]

Notes

1. Ruinous views (*dṛṣṭikaṣāya, lta ba'i snyigs ma*) are one of the five ruinations (*pañcakaṣāya, snyigs ma lnga*), the other four being ruinous lifespan (*āyuḥkaṣāya, tshe'i snyigs ma*), ruinous afflictions (*kleśakaṣāya, nyon mongs pa'i snyigs ma*), ruinous sentient beings (*sattvakaṣāya, sems can gyi snyigs ma*), and ruinous time (*kalpakaṣāya, dus kyi snyigs ma*). These are described, among other places, in Vasubandhu's *Abhidharmakośabhāṣyam* in the commentary on III.94ab. According to the last testament of the thirteenth Dalai Lama, composed in 1932, communism, the "red ideology," is a form of ruinous view. For Lobsang Lhalungpa's translation of this important document, see Michael: 171-174.

2. The transfer of scholastic vocabulary from the West to the Buddhist context is always an imprecise science. The question here is whether *dgag lan* should be rendered as "polemics" or "apologetics." The fact that the Tibetan term includes the notion of an answer suggests that the more appropriate

term may be "apology," from the Greek *apologia*, meaning "answer" or "speech in defense." However, in the Christian tradition, apologetics are often directed, at least rhetorically, to an audience outside of the Christian faith. Furthermore, apologetics is usually concerned with laying out the fundamental points of religious belief rather than with more technical analysis of doctrine. Because in Tibet *dgag lan* is almost always confined to a Buddhist audience and, as is clear from the most cursory perusal of Se ra rJe btsun pa's three "Answers," is very often concerned with highly arcane points of scholastic philosophy, "apologetics" may not be the most felicitous translation. Here, we might follow the distinction drawn by Schleiermacher in his *Brief Outline on the Study of Theology*, in which he says that apologetics is directed outward in an effort to ward off hostility toward the community through seeking to make truth recognizable, while polemics takes place exclusively within the community, seeking to expose error, what he calls "diseased deviations within the community." Although this distinction is obviously problematic in application, in the case of Tibetan *dgag lan* literature it would seem that what we are dealing with is more closely rendered as polemics. See Schleiermacher (31-38) and Bernabeo.

3. All of these questions are debated in the "Answer to Kar." For a discussion of many of these issues, see Ruegg, 1988: 1250-1278.

4. The classic studies of the debate remain Demiéville and Tucci. The most useful study and analysis of the debate is that by Luis O. Gómez, 1987. Gómez's extensive notes contain references to his previous work as well as the wealth of Japanese scholarship on the subject. See also Karmay: 86-106; Snellgrove: 430-436; and especially Ruegg, 1989.

5. The range of symbolism surrounding the Hva shang's shoe remains to be adequately explored. Tucci has noted the parallel to the famous legend of someone encountering Bodhidharma carrying (or wearing) one shoe on his way back to India after his apparent death, precipitating an investigation in which his tomb is opened to reveal a single shoe in an otherwise empty coffin. This legend occurs in an early Ch'an text discovered at Dunhuang, the *Li tai fa bo chi*, which Yanagida (46, n. 7) dates between 774-781 and which seems to have been known in Tibet at the time of the debate. For a study of Chinese renditions of the story of Bodhidharma's shoe, see Sekiguchi Shindai: 205-210. A somewhat garbled version of the Bodhidharma story occurs in the *bLon po bka'i thang yig* section of the Tibetan history *bKa' thang sde lnga*, a *gter ma* text discovered by O rgyan gling pa (1329-1367) that contains passages identical to the Dunhuang fragment Pelliot 116. A portion of this text, including the Bodhidharma story, has been edited and translated by Tucci (see 81-82). But in the Bodhidharma story, the shoe seems less significant than the absent corpse, indicating that he is immortal, a *sheng*, or *āryan*. The meaning of the Hva shang's shoe is far more ambiguous. According to the *rGyal rabs gsal pa'i me long* (for a study of which, see Sørenson), the Hva shang said upon leaving his shoe, "Now in Tibet there are some followers of my doctrine" (see Tucci: 44). This is certainly part of the meaning taken by rJe btsun pa, although he also sees it as a malignant portent. A single shoe left in a monastery is matter out of place. Combining this with the strong Indian and

Tibetan association of shoes with filth, leaves us with the sense of Hvā shang's shoe as a pollutant that cannot be expunged, the eternal return of the suppressed.

6. The term "from form to omniscience" (*gzugs nas rnam mkhyen gyi bar*) is a stock expression used to describe all phenomena in the universe. It derives from what is considered to be an inclusive list of all phenomena encompassed by 108 categories of the impure and the pure, which begins with form (*rūpa, gzugs*), the first of the five aggregates, and ends with a buddha's knowledge of all aspects, or omniscience (*sarvākarajñātā, rnam pa thams cad mkhyen pa*). For an English translation of the 108 categories, see Hopkins: 201-212.

7. rJe btsun pa glosses this line to mean that those who have seen emptiness directly do not see what appears to a mistaken consciousness; they see what appears in unmistaken wisdom (*KL*: 85).

8. The passage he cites from Maitrīpa requires substantial exegesis to reveal an endorsement of Candrakīrti. Maitrīpa writes in his *Tattvadaśaka*:

> Those who desire to understand reality [should know that]
> Not Aspectarians, not Non-Aspectarians,
> Even Mādhyamikas who are not adorned
> With the guru's speech are only mediocre.

rJe btsun pa sees the quote (which he cites in *KL*: 87) as eliminating the Yogācāra and Yogācāra-Mādhyamika, leaving only Nāgārjuna, Āryadeva, and Candrakīrti. lCang skya rol pa'i rdo rje (1717-1786) claims in his *Grub mtha'* that Sahajavajra, whom he describes as an actual student of Maitrīpa, identifies the "guru's speech" alluded to in the quotation as the speech of Candrakīrti alone. See *GTNZ*: 298. However, Sahajavajra does not name only Candrakīrti, but mentions Nāgārjuna and Āryadeva as well. See his *Tattvadaśakaṭīkā*, 299.1.

Nāropa's endorsement of Candrakīrti seems to be of the "tantric Candrakīrti" of the *Pradīpodyotana*. rJe btsun pa (*KL*: 93) quotes Nāropa without identifying the source:

> I have written [this text]
> Based on the stages of instructions
> Of the master Nāgārjuna, Āryadeva,
> Nāgabodhi, Śākyamitra,
> Candrakīrti, etc.

(lCang skya (*GTNZ*: 248) cites the same passage and identifies it as coming from Nāropa's commentary on the *Continuation of the Tantra* (*rGyud phyi ma*), that is, the eighteenth chapter of the *Guhyasamāja*. No such text is attributed to Nāropa in the sDe sge edition of the canon and Nāropa's only work that deals specifically with the *Guhyasamāja*, the *Pañcakramasaṃgrahaprakāśa*, does not contain the passage.)

rJe btsun pa poses the question to Mi bskyod rdo rje as to whether or not Candrakīrti sets forth a nihilistic emptiness in his *Pradīpodyotana*. If he does not, this contradicts Mi bskyod rdo rje's statement that a nihilistic emptiness is set forth in Candrakīrti's works. If he does, then the emptiness described by Nāropa must also be a nihilistic emptiness since Nāropa holds Candrakīrti to be as valid as Vajradhara. Mi bskyod rdo rje might counter that Candrakīrti was wrong about emptiness in his exoteric works, like the *Madhyamakāvatāra*, but gave up the idea of a nihilistic emptiness after entering the path of Secret Mantra. But rJe btsun pa rejects this as well, citing a passage from the *Pradīpodyotananāmaṭīkā* that accords with Candrakīrti's delineation of emptiness in the *Madhyamakāvatāra*:

> If it is asked whether the mind and things are different,
> It is said, "There are no phenomena."
> That is, there is no entity of things.
> If it is asked whether there is some reality,
> It is said, "There is no reality."

See *KL*: 92-94.

9. For example, all of Tsong kha pa's major commentators dispute his contention in his *Legs bshad ser phreng* that *saṃsāra* will never end. For a discussion and analysis of their arguments see Lopez, 1991.

10. A notable and recent exception to tolerance of opposing views within a school is to be found in the case of *Klu sgrub dgongs rgyan* by dGe 'dun chos 'phel (1903-1951). In this work, dGe 'dun chos 'phel, a former monk of 'Bras spungs, strongly criticizes a number of Tsong kha pa's key positions, especially on the role of valid knowledge (*tshad ma*) in the path. The work elicited a strong polemical response from a number of dGe lugs scholars, including dGe 'dun chos 'phel's former teacher, Shes rab rgya mtsho, and shortly after its composition, dGe 'dun chos 'phel was arrested on the fabricated charge of counterfeiting currency and placed in prison. This is not to suggest that the composition of this work was the sole or even primary reason for his imprisonment; dGe 'dun chos 'phel was highly critical of the Tibetan government. However, the content of the work, combined with the fact that it was derived from teachings given to a rNying ma lama, Zla ba bzang po, and was published by the rNying ma hierarch bDud 'joms rin po che, made the work particularly unpalatable to many dGe lugs pas.

Although there has been an appreciation and practice of certain rNying ma teachings by dGe lugs monks, most notably the fifth Dalai Lama, there has also been a virulently anti-rNying ma strain in much dGe lugs literature, especially in the present century under the influence of Pha bong kha pa (1871-1941). To dGe lugs pas of such sentiments, the possibility that an admittedly brilliant scholar such as dGe 'dun chos 'phel, trained in the dGe lugs academy, would compose a work highly critical of the foundations of dGe lugs scholasticism, going so far as to question the authority of Tsong kha pa, and then that such a work be published by a prominent rNying ma lama, is anathema. Some dGe lugs scholars have claimed that *Klu sgrub dgongs rgyan*, therefore, does not represent the position of dGe 'dun chos 'phel at all, but rather is the work of his student, Zla ba bzang po, and can thus be dismissed, often without being read, as partisan anti-dGe lugs polemic. Such an argument allows these dGe lugs pas to retain dGe 'dun chos 'phel as one of their own, especially in his current incarnation since the Tibetan diaspora, as a prescient culture hero, while dismissing his most important work. And it is noteworthy that even those dGe lugs scholastics who have gone to the trouble of writing responses to the contents of the work, such as Shes rab rgya mtsho, also seek to discredit it by attributing much of *Klu sgrub dgongs rgyan* to the rNying ma disciple, as if who makes a particular philosophical point is more important than what is said.

I am currently preparing a translation and study of *Klu sgrub dgongs rgyan.* On the life of dGe 'dun chos 'phel, see Stoddard.

11. Indeed, Lhasa was under the control of the Karma pa patron Don yod rdo rje from 1498-1517 and monks from 'Bras spungs and Se ra (where rJe btsun pa was in residence) were prohibited from participating in the sMon lam festival during much of that period.

12. With the ascension of the fifth Dalai Lama to political power under the patronage of the Gushri Khan, polemical literature was to be put to a more overtly political use, as in the case of the suppression of the Jo nang pas and the conversion of their monasteries in gTsang to dGe lugs institutions in the mid-seventeenth century.

References

Bernabeo, P.

1987 "Apologetics." In *Encyclopedia of Religion*, vol. 1, pp. 349-353. Ed. by Mircea Eliade. New York: Macmillan.

Demiéville, Paul

1952 *Le concile de Lhasa.* Bibliothèque de l'Institut des Hautes Études Chinoises 7. Paris: Imprimerie Nationale de France.

Gómez, Luis O.

1987 "Purifying Gold: The Metaphor of Effort and Intuition in Buddhist Thought and Practice." In *Sudden and Gradual: Approaches to Enlightenment in Chinese Thought*, pp. 67-165. Ed. by Peter N. Gregory. Studies in East Asian Buddhism 5. Honolulu: University of Hawaii Press.

Hopkins, Jeffrey

1983 *Meditation on Emptiness.* London: Wisdom.

Karmay, Samten G.

1988 *The Great Perfection: A Philosophical and Meditative Teaching of Tibetan Buddhism.* Leiden: E. J. Brill.

lCang skya rol pa'i rdo rje

GNTZ *Grub pa'i mtha'i rnam par bzhag pa gsal bar bshad pa thub bstan lhun po'i mdzes rgyan.* Sarnath, India: Pleasure of Elegant Sayings Press, 1970.

Lopez, Donald S.

1991 "Paths Terminable and Interminable." In *Paths to Liberation: The Mārga and its Transformations in Buddhist Thought*, pp. 147-192. Ed. by Robert Buswell and Robert Gimello. Honolulu: University of Hawaii Press.

Michael, Franz

1982 *Rule by Incarnation: Tibetan Buddhism and Its Role in Society and State*. Boulder, Colorado: Westview Press.

Ruegg, D. S.

1988 "A Karma Bka' Brgyud Work on the Lineages and Traditions of the Indo-Tibetan Dbu Ma (Madhyamaka)." In *Orientalia Iosephi Tucci Memoriae Dicata*, pp. 1249-1280. Ed. by G. Gnoli and L. Lanciotti. Serie Orientale Roma 56/3. Rome: Istituto Italiano per il Medio ed Estremo Oriente.

1989 *Buddha-nature, Mind and the Problem of Gradualism in a Comparative Perspective: On the Transmission and Reception of Buddhism in India and Tibet*. Jordan Lectures in Comparative Religion 13. London: School of Oriental and African Studies.

Sahajavajra

Tattvadaśakaṭikā. P no. 3099, vol. 68 in *The Tibetan Tripiṭaka* (see Suzuki).

Schleiermacher, Friedrich

1977 *Brief Outline on the Study of Theology*. Trans. by Terrence N. Tice. Atlanta: John Knox Press.

Se ra rJe btsun pa (rJe btsun chos kyi rgyal mtshan)

GL *Zab mo stong pa nyid kyi lta ba la log rtog 'gog par byed pa'i bstan bcos lta ba ngan pa'i mun sel zhes bya ba bshes gnyen chen po go bo rab 'byams pa bsod nams seng ge ba la gdam pa*. The work has been published in India under the abbreviated title *lTa ngan mun sel*, vol. 2. New Delhi: Champa Chogyal, 1969.

KL *gSung lan klu sgrub dgongs rgyan*. New Delhi: Champa Chogyal, 1969.

SL *Zab mo stong pa nyid kyi lta ba la log rtog 'gog par byed pa'i bstan bcos lta ba ngan pa'i mun sel zhes bya ba bshes gnyen chen po shākya mchog ldan pa la gdams pa*. The work has been published in India under the abbreviated title *lTa ngan mun sel*, vol. 1. New Delhi: Champa Chogyal, 1969.

Sekiguchi S.

1967 *Daruma no Kenkyō*. Tokyo: Iwanami.

Snellgrove, David

1987 *Indo-Tibetan Buddhism: Indian Buddhists and Their Tibetan Successors*. 2 vols. Boston: Shambhala.

Sørenson, Per

1986 *A Fourteenth Century Tibetan Historical Work: Rgyal-rabs gsal-pa'i me-loṅ: Author, Date, and Sources—A Case Study*. Copenhagen: Akademisk Forlag.

Stoddard, Heather

1985 *Le Mendiant de l'Amdo*. Recherches sur la Haute Asie 9. Paris: Société d'Ethnographie.

Suzuki, D. T., ed.

1956 *The Tibetan Tripiṭaka*. Tokyo-Kyoto: Tibetan Tripitaka Research Foundation.

Tucci, Giuseppe

1958 *Minor Buddhist Texts. Part 2: First Bhāvanākrama of Kamalaśīla*. Serie Orientale Roma 9/2. Rome: Istituto Italiano per il Medio ed Estremo Oriente.

Williams, Paul

1983 "A Note on some Aspects of Mi skyod rdo rje's Critique of dGe lugs pa Madhyamaka." *Journal of Indian Philosophy* 11: 125-145.

Yanagida, S.

1983 "The *Li-tai fa-pao chi* and the Ch'an Doctrine of Sudden Awakening." In *Early Ch'an in China and Tibet*, pp. 13-49. Ed. by Whalen Lai and Lewis R. Lancaster. Buddhist Studies Series 5. Berkeley: Asian Humanities Press.

Chapter 13

The *bsTan rim* ("Stages of the Doctrine") and Similar Graded Expositions of the Bodhisattva's Path[1]

David Jackson

The Tibetan *bstan rim* ("Stages of the Doctrine") genre consists of works that expound the general Mahāyāna Buddhist doctrine—i.e., the bodhisattva's path—following a graded series of topics that leads from the spiritual status of the beginning bodhisattva to the final goal of a buddha's perfect awakening. A *bstan rim* (short for *bstan pa'i rim pa*) can be classified within Tibetan Buddhist literature as a separate genre allied to the *lam rim* ("stages of the path") type. Or, it can be considered the second main literary sub-type of the *lam rim* as more generally conceived, with the *lam rim* proper as the first sub-type.

A *lam rim* proper is a work that expounds the stages of the path of the three individuals (*skyes bu gsum gyi lam gyi rim pa*), i.e., it aims at being a complete introduction to spirituality, leading the student through the stages of the two lower spiritual orientations or "individuals" (who aspire for a better rebirth and for individual liberation), before reaching the highest level, that of the Mahāyāna "great individual" (who aspires to attain buddhahood for the benefit of all living beings). Treatises of this type normally conclude with a brief introductory mention of Tantra. The genre is primarily associated with Atiśa Dīpaṃkaraśrījñāna (ca. 982-1054) and the followers of his bKa' gdams order. Its prototype and main textual base was the *Byang chub lam sgron* (*Bodhipathapradīpa*) of Atiśa himself. The series of smaller and larger *lam rims* by Tsong kha pa (1357-1419) are now the best-known examples.

The related *bstan rim* genre should, for the sake of precision, be classified as distinct from the *lam rim* proper. The best-known early examples of the *bstan rim* were written by teachers from the school of rNgog Blo ldan shes rab (1059-1109) and his followers at gSang phu Ne'u thog, such as Gro lung pa (fl. late 1000s to early 1100s), but varieties of this basic type seem to have been composed in the 1100s and early 1200s also by scholars of the bKa' brgyud and Sa skya orders. It seems likely that both the *Thar pa rin po che'i rgyan* of sGam po pa (1079-1153) and the *Thub pa'i dgongs gsal* of Sa skya Paṇḍita (1182-1251) are either the direct descendants of earlier examples of this genre or were heavily influenced by them. In the following pages I will describe the structure and contents of several important examples of this type of treatise.

The *bsTan rim chen mo* of Gro lung pa

Within the Tibetan tradition, the best-remembered early example of the *bstan rim* is that of Gro lung pa Blo gros 'byung gnas (fl. second half of the eleventh century to the early twelfth century). Thu'u bkwan Chos kyi nyi ma (1737-1802) (*GSM*, vol. kha: 7b), for instance, mentions both a greater and lesser *bstan rim* in his account of Gro lung pa's studies and writings,[2] concluding with the remark:

> Because the *bsTan rin chen mo* is a matchless explanation of the intended purport of [Atiśa's] *Byang chub lam sgron* ("Lamp on the Path of Awakening"), Tsong kha pa too when he studied it began his reading with worship through various offerings, and he wrote his own *Lam rim chen mo* largely in conformity with it.

The work of Gro lung pa survived down to the present time in part, no doubt, because Tsong kha pa had valued it so highly.[3] But one of the more tangible reasons for its present accessibility is that certain early- or mid-nineteenth-century dGe lugs pa teachers commissioned its carving onto blocks at the Zhol printing-house near Lhasa. Those printing blocks were reportedly destroyed in the

1960s during the Cultural Revolution, but at least two prints survived outside Tibet—one in a Mongolian temple and one at the Bihar Research Society, Patna (cat. no. 1289; Jackson 1989: 164-165).

The full title of the work is *bDe bar gshegs pa'i bstan pa rin po che la 'jug pa'i lam gyi rim pa rnam par bshad pa* (*TRCM*) ("Exposition of the Stages of the Path for Entering the Jewel of the Sugata's Doctrine"). The treatise is monumental in its length and scope, being a veritable encyclopedia of Buddhism in the early "later-propagation period" (*phyi dar*) on a scale probably never before attempted by the Tibetans—and it is an important source for understanding the particular doctrinal and scholastic developments that occurred within the school of rNgog Blo ldan shes rab by the early twelfth century (though no doubt reflecting some mainstream bKa' gdams pa influences too). The work has a rambling, discursive style of presentation and is not structured according to a minutely detailed subject outline. Nevertheless, its chapters present ten main topics in a practical order:

(1) How to study under a religious teacher (8a-37a)
(2) How to cultivate an awareness of the value of a human life that is free from the conditions that obstruct the practice of religion (37a-47a)
(3) How to cultivate an awareness of death and impermanence (47a-55a)
(4) How to cultivate an understanding of the working of moral causation (55a-152a)
(5) How to cultivate an awareness of the faults of cyclic existence (152a-183a)
(6) How to cultivate the "thought of awakening" (183a-213a)
(7) How to engage in the conduct of the bodhisattva (213a-345a)
(8) How to cultivate meditatively a realization of ultimate reality (345a-447a)
(9) How to cultivate the "levels" (*bhūmi, sa*) of the bodhisattva (447a-507a)
(10) How one attains the fruit, the level of buddhahood (507a-546a)

It also contains numerous scriptural quotations, which is another reason it should one day be carefully studied and indexed.

The *Thar pa rin po che'i rgyan* of sGam po pa

Another treatise of this sort is the famed *Thar pa rin po che'i rgyan* ("Jewel Ornament of Liberation") of Dwags po lha rje sGam po pa bSod nams rin chen (1079-1153), well known among English readers thanks to the translation by H. V. Guenther (1959). Like Gro lung pa's work, it too is an exposition of the bodhisattva path, and it probably was written in the next few decades after Gro lung pa completed his own *bstan rim*. In its overall structure, the *Thar pa rin po che'i rgyan* is more penetratingly and broadly conceived, though in its individual chapters it omits none of the former's main topics. Its structure thus may represent an original plan conceived by sGam po pa himself. Nevertheless, since it also does not follow the typical organization of the teachings according to the three spiritual individuals, it can provisionally be classified here as more of a *bstan rim* than a *lam rim*. Thus, when 'Gos lo tsā ba mentions in his *Blue Annals* (*DN*: *nya* 25b) that sGam po pa composed a "*bstan rim* treatise of the bKa' gdams tradition" (*bka' gdams kyi bstan pa'i rim pa' bstan bcos*), he probably is referring to this work.

The treatise is divided into six main topics:

(1) The motivating cause for attaining highest awakening: the "buddha nature" (*tathāgatagarbha, bde gshegs snying po*)
(2) The corporal basis for achieving awakening: the precious human existence
(3) The contributing condition that impels one to achieving it: the religious teacher
(4) The means for achieving it: the instructions of the religious teacher
(5) The fruit that is so achieved: the "bodies" (*kāyas*) of buddhahood
(6) The enlightened activities that follow the attainment of buddhahood, i.e., the benefitting of living beings through the buddha's activities free from conceptual thought

When sGam po pa actually expounds these in more detail, he divides his treatise into twenty-one chapters, one chapter for each main section except for section four, to which sixteen chapters are devoted. That arrangement is quite understandable, because it is this section that contains the instructions on the general preparations, the bodhisattva's perfections, etc. Thus, sections three through nine of Gro lung pa would fit into section four of the *Thar pa rin po che'i rgyan*, each comprising a chapter or more.

Particularly noteworthy here is sGam po pa's exposition of the "motivating cause," a subject missing as a separate chapter topic in Gro lung pa's work. (It remains for future investigation to determine how Gro lung pa treats the subject of the "buddha nature" [*tathāgatagarbha*] or the theory of *gotra* [*rigs*] in the body of his treatise.) sGam po pa also includes at the end a section that is lacking in Gro lung pa's work as a separate section. It has to do with the nature of the enlightened activities of buddhahood that manifest themselves spontaneously and without conceptual thought.[4]

The *bsTan rim* of Phag mo gru pa

The author of this next *bstan rim* was Phag mo gru pa rDo rje rgyal po (1110-1170), one of sGam po pa's most influential disciples and the father of eight sub-schools within the Dwags po bKa' brgyud school. Phag mo gru pa had studied under various teachers before meeting sGam po pa, including Sa chen Kun dga' snying po (1092-1158) and the bKa' gdams pa *dge bshes* Dol pa. Thu'u bkwan records (*GSM, vol. kha*: 6b-7a) that Phag mo gru pa also wrote a treatise of the *bstan rim* type, implying that it was influenced by Dol pa's teachings.[5]

Like Gro lung pa's work, this treatise is divided into ten main sections. Yet by including a section on what kind of individual can act as a suitable recipient and on the necessary qualities such as faith, Phag mo gru pa shifts the emphasis, perhaps reflecting the teachings of sGam po pa, who similarly devoted a chapter to these topics.[6]

Phag mo gru pa treats these stages more as the essential preparation for meditation practice. The bodhisattva's discipline is included within chapter nine, which deals with the production of "the thought of awakening," and the tenth chapter is remarkably inclusive since it contains not only an exposition of the final meditation on ultimate reality through integrated wisdom and compassion, but also a discussion of the attainment of the fruit of buddhahood. The wording of the treatise's title is perhaps also of significance: *Sangs rgyas kyi bstan pa la rim gyis 'jug pa'i tshul* (*STRJ*), "How to Enter into the Buddha's Doctrine by Stages." Does the phrase "by stages" reflect a "gradual" versus "simultaneous" (*rim gyis pa/ cig char ba*) distinction Phag mo gru pa may have learned from sGam po pa? Also noteworthy are the appearance in the final chapter of decisive quotations from songs of realization (*dohās*), e.g., by Saraha (*STRJ*: 46, 47b), many of which sGam po pa had cited. The work thus probably dates to sometime after Phag mo gru pa's meeting with sGam po pa (i.e., to the period ca. 1150-1170).

The ten chapters of Phag mo gru pa's work are:

(1) The individual who practices this path, and faith (1b-2b)
(2) The defining characteristics of the teacher (3b-8a)
(3) The difficulty of obtaining a human life that is free from the conditions that obstruct the practice of religion (8a-11b)
(4) The awareness of death (11b-14a)
(5) The cultivation of an awareness of the faults of cyclic existence (14a-17b)
(6) The taking of refuge (17b-21a)
(7) Moral causation and the *prātimokṣa* (monastic) vows (21a-25b)
(8) The cultivation of benevolence and compassion (25b-30b)
(9) Producing the "thought of awakening" (30b-45b)
(10) The fruit, i.e., the three "bodies" of buddhahood (45b-52a)

Phag mo gru pa lists eleven sub-sections for chapter nine, in which the six perfections (39b) and the four means of attraction (*bsdu ba'i dngos po bzhi*) (42b) occur as subsidiary topics. Chapter ten has two main sections: (a) the cultivation of emptiness and compassion as inseparable and (b) the teaching of the fruit as being the attainment of the three "bodies" of buddhahood (47a). The first can be established in three ways, according to Phag mo gru pa: (1) through reasoning, (2) through the instructions of the guru, and (3) through scriptural quotation. The first two are not to be taught here, he says, only the last. Still, he utilizes concepts from the Pramāṇa tradition of reasoning to reject the first and establish the necessity of the second, namely the guru's instructions (46b):[7]

> Since a theory derived from learning and reflection is [merely conceptual] understanding of the "object universal" (*don spyi*), in order directly to understand the cognitive object as an "own

> mark" [or "particular"] (*rang mtshan*) one needs to cultivate in meditation the orally transmitted practical instructions of the noble guru.

Then there appear the quotations from the *dohās*.

The second part of the final chapter describes the "bodies" (*kāya*, *sku*) of buddhahood (47a), including descriptions of the Dharma Body (48a) and the Enjoyment Body (49a). It concludes with a discussion of the opposing views on whether gnosis exists for the buddha (50b) or does not (51b), an almost compulsory subject in such Tibetan treatises of the twelfth and thirteenth centuries.

In sum, this work is certainly a *bstan rim* of the early bKa' brgyud tradition, and it represents the sort of adaptation one might expect of the basic *bstan rim* structure to the demands of a more strictly practice- and meditation-oriented tradition, namely rJe sGam po pa's Mahāmudrā.

The *Thub pa'i dgongs gsal* of Sa skya Paṇḍita

Sa skya Paṇḍita Kun dga' rgyal mtshan (1182-1251) was one of the key figures in the religious and intellectual history of Tibet. Among his five major works, the one that contains his most complete presentation of Mahāyāna doctrine and philosophy was the *Thub pa'i dgongs pa rab tu gsal ba* (*TGS*) ("Elucidating the Intention of the Sage") (Jackson, 1987: 46-47, 58). This step-by-step exposition of the bodhisattva's path is a work of crucial importance not only for the study of the Sa skya tradition but also for any attempt to trace the general development of Buddhist doctrines and thought in Tibet from the eleventh century onward. It continues to be an important work within the Sa skya tradition—serving, for instance, as the text of every new Sa skya khri 'dzin's first sermon at his enthronement—and though it has no full-scale commentary, it inspired a number of ancillary works for the benefit of its expositors (Jackson, 1983: 4-5). A much-abridged modern English adaptation exists (see Wangyal and Cutillo).

In its general structure, the *Thub pa'i dgongs gsal* was not directly or primarily an outgrowth of the main bKa' gdams traditions stemming from Atiśa. Instead—in its main topical arrangement at least—it continued a *bstan rim* tradition of the rNgog pa school that Sa paṇ's uncle Slob dpon bSod nams rtse mo (1142-1182) had received at gSang phu Ne'u thog from Phywa pa Chos kyi seng ge (1109-1169). This tradition expounded the stages of the bodhisattva path in accord with two verses from the *Mahāyāna-sūtrālaṃkāra* (*MSA*: ch. 19, v. 61-62). bSod nams rtse mo had taught the general Mahā-yāna path thus in his general exposition of tantric doctrine, the *rGyud sde spyi'i rnam gzhag* (*GPN*). He also had taught it to his younger brother Grags pa rgyal mtshan (1147-1216), who in due course became the main teacher of this way of presenting the bodhisattva path, as of so much else, to his nephew Sa paṇ.

The exposition of these verses by bSod nams rtse mo differs somewhat from that of Sa paṇ. As he explained them in the *rGyud sde spyi'i rnam gzhag* (*GPN*: 13a-b), they teach these stages:

(1) At the very first there is mentioned "spiritual lineage," which is the motivating cause of possessing the spiritual endowments or capacities.

(2) Then being motivated by the cause, compassion, having gone for refuge in the three jewels, there is mentioned "devoted adherence to religion."

(3) Then there is mentioned the generation of the "thought of awakening," which is the basis for entering the [bodhisattva's] conduct.

(4) Then there is mentioned the actual conduct practicing the six perfections. These four are called "the level of devoted application."

(5) Then there is the bodhisattva's "entering the faultless [attainment]," which is the occurrence of the attainment of the first level (*bhūmi*).

(6) Then with "bringing sentient beings to maturity," there is mentioned the [attainment of] up to the seventh level (*bhūmi*).

(7) Then the two phrases "purified field" and "non-entered-into *nirvāṇa*" refer to the three irreversible levels. Those are the path.

(8) Then comes awakening—i.e., the "full awakening" and "great *nirvāṇa*"—the working of benefits for sentient beings, which is the fruit.

There is some doubt about whether the ordering of these topics and the corresponding chapter divisions found in the standard sDe dge edition of Sa paṇ's *Thub pa'i dgongs gsal* are correct. In any case, the verse as it now appears at the start of Sa paṇ's treatise is slightly different:

> Spiritual lineage, devotion to religion, the generation of the thought [of awakening], accomplishing generosity and the rest, maturing sentient beings, entering upon the stainless [paths], the pure fields, non-entered-into *nirvāṇa*, the highest awakening and demonstration.

According to the present chapter organization, these ten things are understood as referring to the following seven main topics:

(1) Spiritual lineage (*gotra*), which is the basis for the disciple's religious capacity
(2) The taking of refuge
(3) Generating the thought of awakening
(4) The six perfections (*pāramitās*, *phar phyin*)
(5) The four means of attraction
(6) The five paths and the ten levels
(7) The fruit of buddhahood

Topic four, the six perfections, makes up the bulk of the treatise. The last five phrases from the *MSA*, viz., "entering upon the stainless [paths], the pure fields, non-entered-into *nirvāṇa*, the highest awakening and demonstration," are thus said to refer to the final two main topics. The paths and levels are thus treated as one main section, as are the attainments and qualities of buddhahood, which are mentioned through the final three phrases.

The indebtedness of the Sa skya pas to the rNgog lineage—especially as passed down through Gro lung pa and Phywa pa—for this way of teaching the general Mahāyāna through these verses of the *MSA* is acknowledged by Go rams pa bSod nams seng ge (1429-1489) in one of his minor works. This work was a reply to a doctrinal question from the fifteenth-century meditator or "practicer" (*sgrub pa*) Tshul khrims bzang po, who was a disciple of their mutual teacher Mus chen sems dpa' chen po dKon mchog rgyal mtshan (1388-1469). In his question, Tshul khrims bzang po had mentioned hearing that the system of Pāramitāyāna stages of the path taught in bSod nams rtse mo's *rGyud sde spyi'i rnam gzhag* did not come down from Sa chen Kun dga' snying po (1092-1158) through the lineage of the Indian siddha Birwapa, but rather was the system of the stages of the path based on the *MSA* as transmitted through the lineage of rNgog lo tsā ba and Phywa pa. In his reply written in 1481 at Thub bstan rnam rgyal, Go rams pa (*DPZ*: 326) mentions the likelihood of influences both from Sa chen and from Phywa pa through the *rGyal sras 'jug ngogs* of Gro lung pa (compare van der Kuijp: 268, n. 69).

But if it is true for bSod nams rtse mo (who was very close to Phywa pa and his school) that this rNgog pa lineage was not to be considered the sole source of his general Pāramitāyāna teachings, the same could be said even more strongly for Sa paṇ, who otherwise opposed Phywa pa and some of his successors on many doctrinal points (though especially in the field of epistemology and dialectics). In other words, the outer structure of the *Thub pa'i dgongs gsal* and its detailed contents probably reflect the Sa skya pas' and in particular Sa paṇ's own special integration of this rNgog pa formulation into a basic body of doctrine received from other traditions.

One point that does emerge very clearly from Go rams pa's account is the importance of the work *rGyal sras 'jug ngogs,* which Go rams pa mentioned as being Gro lung pa's composition and as having been taught by Phywa pa. This, then, was the source for the tradition of arranging the topics following the two verses in the *MSA* (ch. 19, vs. 61-62) that bSod nams rtse mo had also adopted in his very brief exposition of the general Mahāyāna path in the *rGyud sde spyi'i rnam gzhag* (12b-13b). But there remain many questions about this crucial work of the rNgog pa tradition—questions that probably will not be satisfactorily answered until the work itself becomes available. On the one hand, Go rams pa asserts that it was Gro lung pa's work. It is said that Gro lung pa wrote two *bstan rims,* one longer and one shorter. This cannot have been the longer one, but could it have been the shorter? On the other hand, Śākya mchog ldan (1428-1507) (*SGNT*: 307), who was well-schooled in the tradition of rNgog, asserts in his biography of Rong ston Shes bya kun rig (1367-1449) that Rong ston received the "teachings belonging to the doctrinal realm of the [bodhisattva's] conduct, including the *rGyal sras 'jug ngogs* that had been transmitted through the lineage from rNgog lo tsā ba." This would seem to mark the tradition as originating at least with rNgog Blo ldan shes rab (1059-1109), he perhaps having learned it during his seventeen years of study in Kashmir. Though the existence of such a work is not recorded in rNgog's biography by Gro lung pa or in other lists of rNgog's writings, rNgog is said by Thu'u bkwan (*GSM*: *bka' gdams* chapter: 7b) and the bibliophile A khu chin Shes rab rgya mtsho (*MHTL* 11107) to have written his own *bstan rim.* Could this have been the *rGyal sras 'jug ngogs*?

Still other puzzling references to this or a similar work exist: it is recorded for instance that the great abbot (*mkhan chen*) bSod nams grags pa (1273-1345) had studied a text entitled the *rGyal sras lam 'jug* from the mKhan chen bKa' bzhi pa Grags pa gzhon nu (see Khetsun Sangpo, 5: 457). Could this be a misspelling or an alternative title of the same *rGyal sras 'jug ngogs* of rNgog or Gro lung pa? Or is it a similar mistaking of the popular alternative title of the *Thub pa'i dgongs gsal*, namely, the *rGyal sras lam bzang*? Or is it yet another independent work?

In the present state of Tibetan Buddhist studies—i.e., in the absence of definitive and exhaustive catalogues, bibliographies and histories—such questions cannot be easily answered. Nevertheless at least one thing is clear: the traditions of doctrine and literature that the *lam rim*, *bstan rim*, and similar works embodied were already complex and highly developed by the twelfth century. Future scholarly studies of individual works belonging to these genres must each try to clarify further where a particular work stands structurally and doctrinally in relation to the others.

The *bsTan rim* of Nag tsho and Other Unavailable Examples

In addition to the four surviving works briefly described above and such presumably lost works as the *rGyal sras snang ba* of rNgog's tradition, several other *bstan rims* are mentioned in bibliographical sources but are thought to be no longer extant. One such case is the *bstan rim* composed by Atiśa's translator Nag tsho lo tsā ba Tshul khrims rgyal ba (b. 1011), the so-called *Nag tsho'i bstan rim*. Though this work survived and was taught at least as late as the fourteenth century (it was studied for instance by mKhan chen bSod nams grags pa [1273-1345], according to Khetsun Sangpo, vol. 5: 459), its exact contents and structure are unknown. According to Thu'u bkwan (*GSM*: 112), these teachings were an independent line of *lam rim* instructions which, through the lineage coming down from Nag tsho's disciple Lag sor ba, resulted in the composition of other written manuals. A much earlier source, the *Deb ther dmar po* ("Red Annals") of Tshal pa Kun dga' rdo rje (composed 1346), states that Nag tsho's disciple Rong pa Phyag sor pa [*sic*] (fl. mid-eleventh century) stayed his whole life in meditative retreat, only coming out to mediate a violent dispute. At that time he was invited to 'U shang rdo, where he gave a religious discourse to some five hundred monks. Among those present, four assistant teachers each took notes of his sermons, and from them, four *bstan rim* came into being, namely those by the so-called "Four sons of Rong-pa": (1) Zul bya 'Dul ba 'dzin pa, (2) Rog sTag can pa, (3) gTsang na Zhu ldan pa, and (4) rNam par ba. The last of the four founded the temples of rNam pa and Ram pa Lha lding, and served for seven years as monastic leader of gSang phu Ne'u thog. The tradition of these masters was the Rong pa'i bka' brgyud, and it became known also as the "Lower bKa' gdams" because Rong pa's temple of bCom chung ba was situated below Rwa sgreng (Tshal pa Kun dga' rdo rje, *DM*: 65-66).

Still another unavailable but perhaps similar treatise was the so-called *Lam mchog* of Gro ston bDud rtsi grags (fourth abbot of sNar thang, fl. early thirteenth century), which is listed by A khu chin Shes rab rgya mtsho (1803-1875) among the *lam rim* works proper (*MHTL* 11117). Also listed there is its commentary by mChims Nam mkha' grags (1210-1285, seventh abbot of sNar thang) that became known to the later tradition as "mChims Nam mkha' grags's *bsTan rim*" (*MHTL* 11118).[8]

I have not mentioned here such important introductory manuals of Mahāyāna practice as the *sNang gsum* manuals of the Sa skya pa *Lam 'bras* or the *Kun bzang bla ma'i zhal lung* for the *rDzogs chen nying thig*, because, though they too contain Tibetan expositions of Mahāyāna practice, they are primarily appendages to other teaching cycles—in these cases, systems of tantric instructions. Thus, although in content and even topical arrangement they are sometimes similar, such preparatory manuals (*sngon 'gro'i 'khrid yig*) should be distinguished, since a true *lam rim* or *bstan rim* sets out to teach the general Mahāyāna as a path in itself sufficient for reaching the highest goal of buddhahood. Against this view some might argue that *lam rims*—including Tsong kha pa's, Bo dong Paṇ chen's, and even Atiśa's *Byang chub lam sgron* itself—presuppose the supremacy of Tantra, and assume that the disciple will choose that path after training him- or herself in every stage of the general Mahāyāna. The *lam rims* typically do include at the end a brief introductory mention of Tantra. Still, there is sufficient reason to classify and treat the introductory manuals (*sngon 'gro*) to the tantric practices separately from the *lam rim* and *bstan rim* types, just as one should also keep separate such general Mahāyāna teachings as the briefer "mind-training" (*blo sbyong*) instructions and their commentatorial literature (see Sweet, in this volume), though topically they sometimes cover almost the same ground as the *lam rims* and *bstan rims*.

Conclusions

Much of current knowledge about the *bstan rim* as a literary type thus remains very sketchy. More definitive comparisons and conclusions must await the results of careful studies on the individual surviving instances of the genre and of related literary types. Such future investigations will also have to take into account the works of other closely related Tibetan and Indian types to which there exist literary references or for which the texts themselves still survive.

The genre classifications proposed above, moreover, are only provisional, having been based on just a preliminary comparison of a few examples. One cannot exclude the possibility, for instance, that examples of works called *bstan rim* existed which explained the path of the three individuals, or that there existed treatises called *lam rim* which expounded exclusively the Mahāyāna path. For instance, it is said that the bKa' gdams master sNe'u zur pa (1042-1118), who was a principal *lam rim* teacher, taught the "stages of the doctrine" (*bstan pa'i rim pa*) in great detail, and that many notes of his sermons set down by his students existed (Khetsun Sangpo, vol. 5: 113). Until such works can be examined or until some work closely modelled after them turns up, there is no way to classify them definitively, and any speculations about them will remain just that.

Notes

1. I would like to acknowledge with gratitude the support received through research fellowships from the Alexander von Humboldt-Stiftung while at Hamburg University, 1988-89, and from the Japan Society for the Promotion of Science while at Kyoto University, 1990-91, which made possible the writing of this article. Final revisions were made while at the Austrian Academy of Sciences, Vienna.

2. Don grub rgyal mtshan, ed., *LKS*: 8, mentions what would also appear to be a briefer version of this great work: *Gro lung pa'i bstan rim rtsa tshig*.

3. See also Dung dkar Blo bzang 'phrin las, who in his annotations to Tshal pa Kun dga' rdo rje's *Deb ther dmar po* (*DM*: 374, n. 338) mentions Tsong kha pa's respect for the *bsTan rim chen mo*, but who also seems wrongly to identify all *bstan rims* with Gro lung pa's work.

4. The *Thar pa rin po che'i rgyan* was apparently not the only such work that sGam po pa wrote. A khu chin Shes rab rgya mtsho, in his bibliographical compilation, after listing this work together with other "*lam rims*" (*MHTL*

11120), mentions two related works by sGam po pa: the *Lam mchog rin chen 'phreng ba* (*MHTL* 11121) and the *bsTan bcos lung gi nyi 'od* (*MHTL* 11122).

5. Tib. text: ...*dge bshes dol pa las bka' gdams gsan cing bstan rim gyi bstan bcos kyang mdzad*. A 52-folio copy of this rare work turned up in India in the 1970s and was reproduced from a manuscript copy of an original xylograph edition in 1977 (*STRJ*).

6. This subject (and the teaching of the importance of faith as a key prerequisite) occurs also in the Sa skya tradition as the first section in the introductory instructions for the *Lam 'bras*, known as the *sNang ba gsum* ("Three Visions").

7. The Tibetan text: *thos bsam gyi lta bas don spyi'i go ba yin pas/ don rang gi mtshan nyid mngon sum du rtogs pa la bla ma dam pa'i snyan brgyud kyi gdams ngag sgom dgos te/*.

8. These works are also mentioned in Don grub rgyal mtshan, ed., *LKS*: 11: *sNar thang pa gro ston gyi lam mchog rtsa ba'i nyer mkho* and *mChims kyi lam mchog 'grel pa*. Other rare sources mentioned here are: p. 9, *sNe'u zur pa'i bstan rim mnon pa'i gsung gros*, and p. 11, *Bya yul ba'i dpe bstan rim*, *Lo pa sangs rgyas sgom pa'i bstan rim*, and *Lo tshul dar ma'i bstan rim*. I am indebted to Dr. Dan Martin for drawing my attention to this source.

References

A khu chin Shes rab rgya mtsho

MHTL *dPe rgyun dkon pa 'ga' zhig gi tho yig*. In *Materials for a History of Tibetan Literature*, part 3. Śata-Piṭaka Series 30, pp. 503-601. New Delhi: International Academy of Indian Culture, 1963. Reprint Kyoto: Rinsen, 1981.

bSod nams rtse mo

GPN *rGyud sde spyi'i rnam gzhag*. In *Sa skya pa'i bka' 'bum*, vol. 2, pp. 1.1-36.3 (vol. *ga:* 1a-74a). Tokyo: Tōyō Bunko, 1968.

Don grub rgyal mtshan, ed.

LKS *Legs par bshad pa bka' gdams rin po che'i gsung gi gces btus nor bu'u bang mdzod*. Delhi: D. Tsondu Senghe, 1985.

Go rams pa bSod nams seng ge

DPZ *Dris lan pad mo bzhad pa*. In *Sa skya pa'i bka' 'bum*, vol. 14, pp. 321.2-334.2 (vol. *tha:* 28a-72a). Tokyo: Tōyō Bunko, 1969.

'Gos lo tsā ba gZhon nu dpal

DN *Deb ther sngon po. The Blue Annals*. New Delhi: International Academy of Indian Culture, 1974. Śata-Piṭaka Series 212.

Gro lung pa Blo gros 'byung gnas

TRCM *bDe bar gshegs pa'i bstan pa rin po che la 'jug pa'i lam gyi rim pa rnam par bshad pa*. Blockprint. Bihar Research Society, Patna. See Jackson, 1989: 164-165.

Guenther, Herbert V., trans.
1959 *sGam-po-pa: The Jewel Ornament of Liberation*. London: Rider.

Jackson, David
1983 "Commentaries on the Writings of Sa-skya Paṇḍita: A Bibliographical Sketch." *The Tibet Journal* 8/3: 3-23.
1987 *The Entrance Gate for the Wise (Section III): Sa-skya Paṇḍita on Indian and Tibetan Traditions of Pramāṇa and Philosophical Debate*. Wiener Studien zur Tibetologie und Buddhismuskunde, vol. 17. 2 parts. Vienna: Arbeitskreis für Tibetische und Buddhistische Studien, Universität Wien.
1989 *The "Miscellaneous Series" of Tibetan Texts in the Bihar Research Society, Patna: A Handlist*. Tibetan and Indo-Tibetan Studies, vol. 2. Stuttgart: Franz Steiner Verlag.

Khetsun Sangpo
BDT *Biographical Dictionary of Tibet and Tibetan Buddhism*. Completed in 14 vols.? Dharamsala: Library of Tibetan Works and Archives, 1973-?

van der Kuijp, Leonard W. J.
1983 *Contributions to the Development of Tibetan Buddhist Epistemology from the Eleventh to the Thirteenth Century*. Alt- und Neu-Indische Studien 26. Wiesbaden: Franz Steiner Verlag.

Phag mo gru pa rDo rje rgyal po
STRJ *Sangs rgyas kyi bstan pa la rim gyis 'jug pa'i tshul*. Bir: Zogyam and Pema Lodoe, 1977.

Sa skya Paṇḍita Kun dga' rgyal mtshan
TGS *Thub pa'i dgongs pa rab tu gsal ba*. In *Sa skya pa'i bka' 'bum*, vol. 5, pp. 1.1-50.1 (*vol. tha:* 1a-99a). Tokyo: Tōyō Bunko, 1968.

Śākya mchog ldan, gSer mdog paṇ chen
SGNT *rJe btsun thams cad mkhyen pa bshes gnyen shākya rgyal mtshan gyi rnam thar ngo mtshar dad pa'i rol mtsho*. In *Collected Works*, vol. 16, pp. 299-377. Thimphu: Kunsang Topgyay, 1975.

Thu'u bkwan Chos kyi nyi ma
GSM *Grub mtha' thams cad kyi khungs dang 'dod tshul ston pa legs bshad shel gyi me long*. In *Collected Works*, vol. 2, pp. 5-519. New Delhi: 1969.

Tshal pa Kun dga' rdo rje
DM *Deb ther dmar po rnams kyi dang po lu lan deb ther*. Dung dkar Blo bzang 'phrin las, editor and annotator. Beijing: Mi rigs dpe skrun khang, 1981.

Wangyal, Geshe and Brian Cutillo, trans.
1988 *Illuminations: A Guide to Essential Buddhist Practices*. Novato, CA: Lotsawa.

Chapter 14

Mental Purification (*Blo sbyong*): A Native Tibetan Genre of Religious Literature[1]

Michael J. Sweet

The revival of Buddhism during the eleventh century C.E. known to Tibetan historiography as the "latter dissemination of the Doctrine" (*bstan pa'i phyi dar*; see *BA*: 63-101) was motivated, to a large extent, by revulsion against the general breakdown of religious practice, discipline, and conduct which had prevailed during the preceding two centuries (Th'u bkwan: 96; Stein: 70-72). Consequently, in order to reestablish the faith on a firmer foundation, the reformist bKa' gdams pa sect founded by the followers of Atiśa (982-1054) undertook as one of its more important missions the presentation of the fundamentals of Buddhism in a manner easily accessible to the clergy and educated laity. One of the means by which this was accomplished was the development of succinct and useful guides to the essentials of Buddhist practice—the uniquely Tibetan literary genre of "Mental Purification" (*blo sbyong*). After an examination of the meaning of the term *blo sbyong*, and a general survey of the early history and sources of this genre, this paper will examine two of its most noteworthy examples: the *Blo sbyong don bdun ma* ("Seven-Topic Mental Purification") (*LBDDM*) originating in the bKa' gdams pa tradition, and the *bLo sbyong mtshon cha 'khor lo* ("Wheel Weapon Mental Purification") (*LBTCK*), whose provenance will be discussed below.

The Term "Mental Purification"

As a named genre the mental purification literature appears to be a genuinely Tibetan innovation, although its contents are firmly anchored in Indian Buddhist tradition. The Tibetan compound *blo sbyong*, translated here as mental purification, means literally "[the] purifying [i.e. , purification] (*sbyong [ba]*) of the mind (*blo*)." As a stereotyped phrase this does not, however, appear in the standard Tibetan-Sanskrit lexicon of Buddhist terminology, the *Mahāvyutpatti* (*MVYT*), nor apparently is it to be found in the translation of any text with a confirmed Sanskrit original. In addition, none of the texts with *blo sbyong* in their title found in the earliest collection of such works, the fifteenth-century *Blo sbyong glegs bam* ("Mental Purification Collection") (*LBLB*), [2] bears a Sanskrit title along with the Tibetan one, the standard practice for texts actually or purportedly translated from an Indian original.

Nevertheless, even if this compound is not, strictly speaking, a loan translation, its meaning is quite clear in light of the compounds and phrases in which its components and their analogues appear. Tibetan *blo* is used primarily to render the Sanskrit *buddhi*, which in a non-technical sense has the meaning of "mind" in general; as a technical term it means the intellectual faculty, a sense that Buddhism shares with the other religio-philosophical systems of India. *sByong* is the present root of the Tibetan verb whose primary signification is "to purify" or "cleanse." As such it is used in rendering the action noun derivative (*śodhana*) of the Sanskrit root *śudh*, "to purify," and so we find it at *MVYT* 600 where it translates the Sanskrit [*pari*] *śodhana* as [*yongs su*] *sbyong ba.* The Sanskrit and Pāli *citta* (*sems*), which is virtually synonymous with *buddhi*, is often met with in analogous compounds and phrases throughout Indian Buddhist literature. A very close parallel appears in the most important source for the mental purification literature, Śāntideva's *Bodhicaryāvatāra* ("Introduction to *Bodhisattva* Practice") (*BCA*). In *BCA* 5, v. 97 we find the compound *sems sbyong ba*[3] (*cittaśodhana*; "mental purification") in the line "One should always observe the practice [leading to] the purification of the mind."[4] Similar compounds are found elsewhere, such as the Sanskrit *cittapariśuddhi*, "purification [or purity] of the mind" (*Abhidharmakośa* 8:1; Vasubandhu: 130), and Pāli phrases such as "to purify the mind" (*cittam parisodheti*) are common in the Theravāda literature (see *PTSD*, *PTC*). Many further examples might be cited.[5]

Moreover, such compounds and phrases are expressive of their origins in the earliest and most fundamental Buddhist practices, all of which "aim(s) at purifying the *citta*" (Johansson: 23). As an important Mahāyāna scriptural quotation puts it: "Beings become soiled by the soiling of the mind; they are purified by the purification of the mind."[6] Perhaps most importantly, the generation of universal love and compassion through empathic identification with all living beings, which similarly belongs to the most ancient stratum of Buddhist teachings (e.g., the *Aṅguttara* and *Majjhima nikāyas*, quoted in Vetter: 26-28; Buddhaghosa: 321-353), is, according to the great philosopher-saint sGam po pa (1079-1153), the very means by which the purification of the mind (*sems sbyang ba*) is brought about (Guenther: 144-146; sGam po pa: 92a2-94a6).

The Tibetan Background

The earliest texts considered by Tibetan tradition to belong to the mental purification genre (*RSBT*: 1286-1287) include the various "Stages of the Doctrine" (*bstan rim*) texts by disciples of Atiśa and his pupil, the layman 'Brom ston pa (1005-1064), the most important being the *bsTan rim chen mo* ("Great Stages of the Doctrine") of Gro lung pa Blo gros 'byung gnas, which served as a model for Tsong kha pa's *Lam rim* texts (Thu'u bkwan: 104; Chattopadhyaya: 393; and D. Jackson, in this volume). The *dPe chos* ("The Dharma Through Examples"), a collection of religious instructions given by Po to ba Rin chen gsal (1027-1105), one of the chief disciples of 'Brom ston pa,[7] teaches the basics of Buddhism through the use of folk sayings, stories, and analogies, and is representative of many of the earliest texts[8] in its adaptation of pre-Buddhist Tibetan tales and folklore to the task of explaining Buddhist doctrine to a wide audience (Stein: 266-268). Religio-moral teaching through stories, aphorisms, and analogies was a staple of Indian Buddhist literature as well, from the early *Dhammapada* onwards (Sternbach: 59, n. 297). In this connection, it is interesting to note that tradition regards Atiśa as having introduced into Tibet the well-known Indian collection of vampire (*vetāla, ro langs/ ro sgrung*) stories in their Buddhist version (MacDonald: 14-16). Such writings are comparable, as folkloristic elucidations of religious doctrine, to the Jewish *Midrash* (Silver: 193-196).

Although a folk homiletic tradition did continue in Tibet,[9] the later mental purification literature is characterized by a more abstract and systematic presentation of its subject matter, and it is these texts which have constituted the basis for study and practice down to the present day. Although this essay is mainly concerned with the bKa' gdams pa and dGe lugs pa traditions, it should be noted that the mental purification genre figures importantly in all of the Tibetan Buddhist schools.

Indian Models

Of the major Indian sources for this genre, clearly the most important is Śāntideva's epitome of the Mahāyāna, the *Bodhicaryāvatāra*, one of the so-called "Six Basic Texts of the bKa' gdams pas" (*bKa' gdams gzhung drug*; Thu'u bkwan: 106; *BA*: 268),[10] which formed the foundation for the non-Tantric teaching of that school. Atiśa's own synoptic work, the *Byang chub lam sgron* ("A Lamp for the Path to Enlightenment"; *Bodhipāthapradīpa*) (*BCLG*) is also considered an important source (Thu'u bkwan: 106; Tucci, 1949, vol. 1: 99), as are such other frequently cited works as Nāgārjuna's *Ratnāvalī* (Hahn) and Candrakīrti's *Madhyamakāvatāra* (Huntington).

The influence of the *BCA* on the mental purification literature is obvious. As a practice-oriented synthesis of the *bodhisattva* path it provided a model for mental purification texts, and it is often quoted in these texts and their commentaries to elucidate key ideas. The Tibetan tradition is quite clear about this influence, crediting Śāntideva as a major figure in the transmission of the mental purification teaching (dNgul chu mThogs med: 210; Thu'u bkwan: 109). Of the nine chapters of the *BCA*, the one of most significance for the mental purification texts is the eighth, on the perfection of contemplation (*dhyānapāramitā*).

The central conception of the eighth chapter of the *BCA*, which is developed more fully in the mental purification literature, is "exchanging oneself and others" (*parātmaparivārtana, bdag dang gzhan du brje ba*; see *BCA* 8: 120-131). This involves a thorough effort to realize the distress inherent in pride and self-centeredness, and the happiness and virtue which come from valuing others as strongly as one values oneself. This exchanging of oneself and others is closely related to "equality of oneself and others" (*parātmasamatā, bdag dang gzhan du mnyam pa*), an attitude of complete empathic identification with other sentient beings (*BCA* 8: 90-119; Buddhaghosa: 334). These are ideas that are fundamental to Buddhism as a whole (see Collins: 190-191), but which were given new emphasis and refinement of expression by Mahāyāna authors like Śāntideva.

Atiśa's *BCLG* is a précis of the entire Buddhist path, and the prototype for the "Stages of the Path" (*lam rim*) literature. The mental purification texts are often indistinguishable, even by Tibetan commentators, from works on stages of the path (*TCKZB*: 466), except in their succinct presentation, practical orientation, and concentration on one portion of the path, i.e., generation of an enlightenment-directed attitude (*bodhicittotpāda, byang chub sems skyed*; see Dayal: 58-64). The stages of the path contain the mental purification teachings within them,[11] and the full stages of the path themselves can be presented within the structure of mental purification, as in a work by Tsong kha pa (the *Tshig sbyor phun sum tshogs pa'i snyan ngag gi lam nas drangs pa'i blo sbyong* in *TKSB*, vol. 22: 406-411).

A number of key points relevant to mental purification are mentioned in the *BCLG*; for example, in verse 5, Atiśa affirms the exchanging of self and other, stating that *bodhisattvas* seek to extirpate others' sufferings because of their total empathic identification with them (see also *BCLG*, v. 32, on mental purification). Another work by Atiśa, the *Byang chub sems pa'i nor bu'i phreng ba* (*Bodhisattvamaṇyāvalī*, Toh. no. 3951; "Jewel Rosary of the *Bodhisattva*"; see Rabten and Ngawang Dhargyey), which stands at the beginning of the *LBLB* collection (7-11), does not explicitly deal with the meditative praxis essential to the mental purification tradition, but is, rather, a homiletic exhortation to *bodhisattva* conduct in general, and much of its subject matter is included as supplementary material in the mental purification texts, e.g., in the instruction (*bslab bya*) section of the *LBDDM*.

All the above lends support to the Tibetan tradition (dNgul chu mThogs med: 207; Chattopadhyaya: 85) that mental purification, as a specific arrangement of Mahāyāna teachings in a form suitable for meditation, was an oral instruction (*upadeśa, man ngag*) originally given by Suvarṇadvīpi-Dharmakīrti[12] to his pupil Atiśa, who in turn handed it down to his disciples as a private teaching (*lkog chos*) until it was publicly lectured upon by [Bya] mChad kha ba (1101-1175) and others (Thu'u bkwan: 109-110).

The Lineage of Mental Purification

The generally accepted lineage for the mental practice teaching (Smith: 68-69; Kelsang Gyatso: 13) commences with Atiśa and continues with 'Brom ston pa, the founder of the bKa' gdams pa school, and his student Po to ba Rin chen gsal. The author of the first mental purification text actually called a *blo sbyong* was gLang ri Thang pa (1054-1123), author of the *Blo sbyong tshigs brgyad ma* (*LBTG*; "The Eight Stanza Mental Purification"; see text and translation in Dalai Lama XIV and in Rabten and Ngawang Dhargyey). This is still an important text, one that presents in brief the theme of subordinating one's own welfare to that of others, upon which later authors were to expand. Glang ri Thang pa was followed by his student Shar ba pa (1070-1141) who was in turn the teacher of [Bya] mChad kha ba, the author of the *Blo sbyong don bdun ma* (*LBDDM*; "Seven-Topic Mental Purification"). This work was commented upon both by Tsong kha pa (1357-1419) and his disciple dGe 'dun grub (1391-1474; see Mullin: 57-105), and it has always been considered to be one of the most important of the mental purification texts by the dGe lugs pas.[13] In addition, commentaries by such important non-dGe lugs pa scholars as the Sa skya pa [rGyal sras] dNgul chu mThogs med (1295-1369) and the rNying ma/bKa' brgyud Eclectics (*Ris med pa*) 'Jam dbyangs mkhyen rtse'i dbang po (1820-1892) (*DNDZ*, vol. 3: 153-180) and 'Jam mgon kong sprul (1813-1899) (*DNDZ*, vol. 3: 181-213), attest to the significance of this work for Tibetan Buddhism as a whole. According to tradition, mChad kha ba was inspired to study *blo sbyong* by reading the fifth verse of the *LBTG* (*BA*: 273-275; Rabten and Ngawang Dhargyey: 11, 153):

> When others, out of envy,
> Unjustly revile and belittle me,
> May I take the defeat upon myself
> And give the victory to others.

He was also said to have originated the "custom of teaching the Blo sbyoṅ to a class (of monks)" (*BA*: 275), i.e., to have publicly taught this previously privately transmitted teaching. The earliest commentary on the *LBDDM* was the *Blo sbyong khrid yig* ("A Manual of Mental Purification") by dNgul chu mThogs med, which is still widely studied.

The seven topics of the *LBDDM* consist of: (1) "preliminary practices which teach the support for the Dharma," (2) "the actual mental purification through the enlightenment-directed attitude (*bodhicitta*), (3) "transformation of unfavorable conditions into the enlightenment path," (4) "the distillation of the entire doctrine into a practice [realizable in] a single lifetime," (5) "the criteria for the completion of mental purification," (6) "the commitments of mental purification," and (7) "the instructions for mental purification" (dNgul chu mThogs med: 207-208; *DNDZ*, vol. 3: 185).[14] The core of the text is in the second topic, the actual purification through the enlightenment-directed attitude, comprising the conventional (*kun rdzob*) and the ultimate (*don dam*) attitude, a division based on whether one is regarding the objects of compassion from the viewpoint of conventional or ultimate truth (Wangyal: 134-136).

In keeping with the emphasis of the mental purification texts on practice, only four lines in the *LBDDM* are devoted to the ultimate attitude, beginning with the second line ("Consider all phenomena to be like a dream"); it is the conventional attitude that is central to this text. The practice of "giving and taking" (*gtong len*) is described; this is a practical technique for actualizing Śāntideva's "exchanging of self and other." Giving and taking involves synchronizing one's breathing with the intention to take upon oneself the misdeeds and sufferings of all sentient beings (inhaling) and the resolve to promote the happiness and liberation of beings (exhaling) (dNgul chu mThogs med: 210-212). The remainder of the text describes meditation and behavior that facilitate the development of an enlightenment-directed attitude.

Stylistically, the *LBDDM* is a straightforwardly didactic, mnemonic text. Although it is written in the most usual form of Tibetan verse, the seven-syllable line (with some lines of irregular length), it has little else in the way of the use of metaphor or other embellishment to distinguish it from prose. Its use of colloquial language and the Tibetan proverb "Don't put a *mdzo*'s burden on an ox" (line 41), recalls the vernacular origins of this genre. The work's clarity of meaning and expression doubtless accounts for its enduring popularity among Tibetan Buddhist contemplatives.

"The Wheel Weapon Mental Purification"

The *Blo sbyong mtshon cha 'khor lo* (*LBTCK*: "The Wheel Weapon Mental Purification")[15] presents a striking contrast to the *LBDDM* in content and style. Whereas the *LBDDM* advocates exoteric

(Sūtrayāna) techniques in order to generate the enlightenment-directed attitude, the *LBTCK* uses esoteric (Tantrayāna) imagery and method to enable the practitioner to purify his or her mind from egocentricity (*bdag 'dzin, ātmagraha*), which Buddhism regards as the root of all mental impurity and suffering (Sopa and Hopkins: 38, 52, 118). As a tantric work, it has a presiding deity, in this case Yāmāntaka (literally "The Killer of Yāma [the Lord of Death]").[16] The text is attributed to the Indian teacher Dharmarakṣita, of whom little is known,[17] and its translation to his disciple Atiśa working in collaboration with Brom ston pa (*DNDZ*: 598). However, the work carries no Sanskrit title; it is not mentioned in the many biographies of Atiśa (see Eimer), nor is it included among the standard lists of works in whose translations Atiśa is held to have participated (Chattopadhyaya: 442-498). While it is found in the fifteenth-century *LBLB* collection, its transmission lineage is not clear (*TCKZB*: 466; Ngawang Dhargyey et al.: 41), and its only known commentary (*TCKZB*) dates to 1813 (Taube: 922). The strongest evidence of this work's Tibetan authorship lies in its culturally specific allusions to divination (*mo*) and the Bon religion (v. 70) and to the temptations of non-Buddhist magical practices (vv. 32, 68-69).

The text begins by comparing the *bodhisattva* to a peacock, and this simile is extended through the initial verses: Just as a peacock is believed able to consume poisonous medicinal herbs and to thrive upon them[18] the *bodhisattva* can transform the passions into the means for emancipation (vv. 1-6; see n. 10, above). The *LBTCK*'s advocacy of transmuting the passions is an indication of this work's essentially tantric character (Conze, 1964: 221). A long section (vv. 11-48) enumerates the various illnesses and misfortunes of life, concluding in each case with the resolve to accept these willingly, as they are, in the words of the refrain "the weapon of bad actions returning upon oneself" (see *Ratnāvalī* III, 71 in Hahn's ed. and *BCA* 6: 42-43). The final section of the text begins with v. 49:

> As that's the way it is, I seize the Enemy,
> I capture the deceitful bandit who ambushed me,
> The lying deceiver who has impersonated me,
> Aha! There is no doubt that he is egocentricity!

In vivid language, egocentricity is personified (see *BCA* 8: 145-154) as one "who leads me and others to ruin, who hurls the weapon of [sinful] actions, making me run, without volition, in the jungle of cyclic existence" (v. 51), and Yāmāntaka is beseeched to utterly destroy this enemy, in a series of stanzas (vv. 52-89) with the refrain:

> Crash! Bam! Dance on the head which plots my destruction,
> Mortally strike at the heart of the butcher, the Enemy, Ego!

The conclusion of this work (vv. 90-118) consists of a series of reflections on egocentricity, compassion, the *bodhisattva* vow to save all living creatures, and the ultimate emptiness of all phenomena. The text consists generally of quatrains of seven-syllable lines, and has a driving rhythmic force and vivid imagery that make it a genuine work of religious poetry. The violent attack and dismemberment of one's conventional egocentric self suggests the sacrifice of self in the early Tibetan Buddhist (rNying ma) *gcod* ritual, which was rooted in even earlier shamanistic practices (Evans-Wentz: 277-334; Tucci and Heissig: 126-132).

Conclusion

The mental purification literature is a native Tibetan practical synthesis of Buddhist doctrine which had its origin in the teachings of Atiśa, his disciples, and earlier Indian works. The major objective of the mental purification texts is to enable the practitioner to generate an attitude which combines universal compassion (the major subject of the *LBDDM*) with freedom from egocentricity (the focus of the *LBTCK*). This goal recalls contemplative manuals in the Christian tradition in particular, such as Thomas à Kempis' *Imitation of Christ* and Erasmus' *Manual of Arms for the Militant Christian* (Dolan: 24-93). The mordant critique of human egotism by the authors of the mental purification texts bears a resemblance to some of Pascal's *pensées* (e.g., on vanity and pride: 203-206).

The technique of systematic cognitive and attitudinal change propounded in these works is similar to that espoused for secular purposes by many contemporary psychotherapists, especially those of the cognitive behavioral school (see Beck et al.). While maintaining a focus on generating the enlightenment-directed attitude, mental purification texts differ widely in their content and style, and in their focus on exoteric (Sūtrayāna) or esoteric (Tantrayāna) practices. The historical and textual study of these works, which are prominent in the bKa' gdams pa, dGe lugs pa, and other Tibetan sectarian traditions, has scarcely begun; such research can be expected to add much to our knowledge of Buddhism and Tibetan literature.

Notes

1. I would like to express my gratitude to Dr. Leonard Zwilling for his editorial and bibliographic assistance with this paper, and especially for his advice on philological matters. Appreciation is also due to Prof. Geshe Sopa and to the late Geshe Wangyal, for their inspired teachings on *blo sbyong* and related subjects. All translations in this article are by the author, unless otherwise indicated.

2. This collection, also known as the *Blo sbyong rgya tsha* (in *DNDZ*, vols. 2-3), was compiled and edited by the Sa skya pa scholars [Mus chen] dKon chog rgyal mtshan (1388-1471) and [Sems dpa' chen po] gZhon nu rgyal mchog (ca. 1350-ca. 1400).

3. The form *sbyong* follows the readings in the *BCA* commentaries by Kun bzang dpal ldan (=Kun bzang chos grags; *PJTG*: 146b) and [mKhan po] gZhan dga' (1871-1927; *PJCG*: 36b), both noted students of the eclectic (*Ris med pa*) scholar 'Jam mgon 'Ju Mi pham rnam rgyal rgya mtsho (1846-1912), who was renowned for his philological expertise. In light of *MVYT* 600 this should be the correct form, yet it is *sbyang* which appears in the canonical translations of the *BCA* (*sems sbyang*) and its commentaries, probably as a result of an early misreading, since the more correct perfect form would be *sbyangs*. It is interesting that at this place in his edition Bhattacharya has *spyod* (i.e., *sems spyod*) suggesting that what he had before him was *sbyong*, as both *pa/ba* and *nga/da* can be easily misread for each other.

4. *Sems sbyong ba yi spyod pa ni/ nges par de srid spyad par bya; Cittaśodhanam-ācāram niyataṃ tāvadācaret.*

5. Compare terms such as "pure mind" (*pariśuddha-manaḥ*) in *MVYT* 194, "purity of mindfulness" (*smṛtipariśuddhi*), as a descriptor of the fourth meditative absorption (*dhyāna; Abhidharmakośa* 8: 8; Vasubandhu: 149) and its Pāli equivalent *satiparisuddhi* (Buddhaghosa: 171).

6. *"Cittasaṃkleśāt sattvāḥ saṃkliśyante cittavyavadānād viśudhyante."* This quotation, whose original source is unknown, is found in many *sūtras* and commentaries, including the *Ratnagotravibhāga* and the *Vimalakīrtinirdeśa* (see Lamotte: 52-53, 174).

7. This was commented upon by sTod lung pa Rin chen snying po, better known as gZhon nu 'od (1032-1116; see Tucci, 1949, vol. 1: 98-99). See also the *bKa' gdams thor bu*, translated by Wangyal (119-169).

8. For example, works by Shar ba Yon tan grags (1070-1141, see *BA*: 272) and sNe zur pa Yon bstan grags [?=sNeu sur pa Ye shes 'bar, 1042-1118]; *RSBT*: 1287.

9. For example, the popular *Subhāṣitaratnanidhi* ("Treasury of Aphoristic Jewels") of Sa skya Paṇḍita (1182-1251) and the *Bya chos rin chen 'phreng ba* ("Precious Garland of the Dharma Among the Birds"; Conze, 1955). For further examples see Stein: 266-269.

10. In addition to the *BCA* these are: the *Bodhisattvabhūmi* ("The Stages of the *Bodhisattva*") and the *Mahāyānasūtrālaṃkāra* ("An Ornament for the Mahāyāna Scriptures") by Asaṅga/Maitreya; Śāntideva's anthology of selections from the Mahāyāna *sūtras* and complement to the *BCA*, the *Śikṣāsamuccaya* ("Collection of Religious Instructions"); the *Jātakamāla* ("Garland of Buddha's Birth Stories") by Āryasura; and the *Udānavarga* ("Inspired Sayings"), the Sanskrit counterpart of the Pāli *Dhammapada*.

11. See, for example, the commentary on the mental purification teachings in Tsong kha pa's *Lam rim chen mo* ("Great Stages of the Path") cited in Smith (76). Klong rdol bla ma also presents stages of the path and mental purification teachings as complementary, analyzing both in the same work (*LRCB*), and another text uses Tsong kha pa's *Lam gyi gtso bo rnam gsum* ("Three Principal Aspects of the Path") as a basis for mental purification practice (Taube: 923).

12. For the little presently known about this important figure, see Eimer (vol. 1: 167-169, 194-196) and Chattopadhyaya (84-95).

13. A number of translations and studies of the *LBDDM* and related texts have appeared under dGe lugs pa auspices in recent years (e.g., Kelsang Gyatso, Rabten and Ngawang Dhargyey, Dalai Lama XIV, Mullin). I believe that the translation of *blo sbyong* in these works as "mental training" reflects the influence of modern colloquial Tibetan. In the spoken language, the root *sbyong* is used with another root, *bdar*, to form the verb "to train" (Goldstein: 808). While this is appropriate in contemporary usage, it should be noted that the primary sense of the root *bdar*, as with *sbyong*, is "to polish or clean," and the combination suggests nothing so much as the English idiom "to polish up," which even in colloquial contexts preserves the essential metaphor. Consequently, the translation of *blo sbyong* as "mental training," while appealing as a description in a contemporary idiom of Buddhist practice, obscures what the authors of these works saw as their purpose: instruction in the purification of the mind, the traditional goal of Buddhist practice.

14. Tibetan: *sngon 'gro rten gyi chos bstan pa / dngos gzhi byang chub kyi sems sbyang ba / rkyen ngan byang chub kyi lam du bsgyur ba / tshe gcig gi nyams len dril nas bstan pa / blo 'byongs pa'i tshad / blo sbyong gi dam tshig / blo sbyong gi bslab bya.*

15. Sendai no. 7007. The title contains a double meaning: Mental purification itself is like a discus or "wheel weapon" (*mtshon cha 'khor lo*) which cuts through the vitals of the enemy of egocentricity (*LBTCK*: 128); it is also a counter-weapon against the discus-boomerang of bad *karma*, referred to in the refrain to vv. 11-48. The only published translation of this work is a loose rendering with interpolated material, published in India (Ngawang Dhargyey et al.). Its commentary, the *TCKZB*, consists of lecture notes (*zin bris*) on the oral explanation of [Rwa sgreng A chi tu no mon han; Blo bzang ye shes]

bsTan pa rab rgyas (1759?-1816) (Ngag dbang chos 'byor: v; and see Smith: 104). A more exact translation of the *LBTCK*, along with part of the *TCKZB*, is found in Kirtz. The present writer and Geshe Sopa are preparing a new translation and study of the *LBTCK*, along with the *rMa bya dug 'joms*.

16. Yāmāntaka is a major deity in both the bKa' gdams pa (*BA*: 374) and dGe lugs pa schools (Lessing: 75-76, 91; Tucci, 1936: 78-82). He is the fierce form of Mañjuśrī, the embodiment of wisdom.

17. This teacher of Atiśa is described in various places as both a strict non-Mahāyānist and a devoted practitioner of *bodhicitta* (Eimer: 130, 153; dNgul chu mThogs med: 207; Chattopadhyaya: 80-81). He is also given as the author (Thu'u bkwan: 109) of the companion piece to the *LBTCK*, the *rMa bya dug 'joms* ("The Peacock's Conquest of Poison"; in *LBLB*: 145-157), which elucidates the course of mental purification in the form of an extended commentary on the opening lines of the *LBTCK*.

18. The peacock is important in Tibetan culture; it is represented in religious folklore and dance (Conze, 1955: 31-32, 60) and is associated with magical charms against snake bite (see Panglung). The peacock's protective quality against poison apparently derives analogically from its ability to kill snakes and its immunity from snake venom, as expressed in a verse of unknown provenance quoted in Prajñākaramati's commentary to the *BCA* (*BCAP*: 240): "The snake is born for the purpose of the peacock's happiness; because [the peacock] has become accustomed to poison, poison is an elixir [for him] (*ahirmayūrasya sukhasya jāyate / viṣaṃ viṣābhyāsavato rasāyanam*)." The earliest Tibetan reference to black aconite being the peacock's nourishment that I have found is in Sa skya Paṇḍita's autocommentary to *SBRN* v. 152 (*LSDG*: 138): "Its food is the very fearful great poison, black aconite (*bstan dug*)."

The peacock is to some extent conflated with the *garuḍa*, which is also known for its poison-destroying qualities (Hopkins: 21-22; Wayman: 65-68). Eating peacock flesh is also said to confer immortality (Fausbøll: 80-84). Hindu lore considers the peacock to be immune from all disease (Mani: 498-499), and its bile is regarded as an antidote against poison in the Buddhist medical literature (Filliozat: 31).

References

Atiśa

BCLG *Lamp for the Path and Commentary*. Trans. by Richard Sherburne. London, George Allen and Unwin, 1983.

[Rwa sgreng A chi tu no mon han; bLo bzang yes shes] bsTan pa rab rgyas

TCKZB *Kyab bdag rdo rje 'chang chen po nas blo sbyong mtshon cha 'khor lo'i bshad lung stsal skabs kyi gsung bshad zin bris gzhan pan myu gu bskyed ba'i bdud rtsi*. In *Khri-Chen Bstan-Pa-Rab Rgyas Collected Works*, reproduced from the bZhi sde edition, vol. 3, 463-595. Dharamsala: Library of Tibetan Works and Archives, 1985.

Beck, Aaron et al.
1979 *Cognitive Therapy of Depression*. New York: Guilford Press.

Buddhaghosa
VM *The Path of Purification—Visuddhimagga*. Trans. by Bhikkhu Ñyaṇamoli. Second ed. Colombo: A. Semage, 1964.

Chattopadhyaya, Alaka
1967 *Atiśa and Tibet*. Calcutta: Indian Studies Past and Present.

Collins, Steven
1982 *Selfless Persons: Imagery and Thought in Theravada Buddhism*. Cambridge: Cambridge University Press.

Conze, Edward
1955 *The Buddha's Law Among the Birds*. Oxford: Bruno Cassirer.
1964, ed. *Buddhist Texts Through the Ages*. New York: Harper & Row.

Dalai Lama XIV, Tenzin Gyatso
1982 *Four Essential Buddhist Commentaries*. Dharamsala: Library of Tibetan Works and Archives.

Dayal, Har
1932 *The Bodhisattva Doctrine in Buddhist Sanskrit Literature*. Reprinted 1970. Delhi: Motilal Banarsidass.

[Mus chen] dKon chog rGyal mtshan and Gzhon nu rgyal mchog, eds.
LBLB *Blo sbyong glegs bam*. Reprinted from the Lhasa bZhi sde blocks. Bir, India: The Bir Tibetan Society, 1983.

dNgul chu mThogs med [dPal ldan ye shes]
LBKY *Blo sbyong khrid yig*. In *rGyal sras 'phags pa dNgul chu mthogs med kyi rnam thar dad pa'i shing rta dang gsung thor bu*, pp. 206-234. Thimphu: Kun bzang stobs rgyal, 1975.
DNLC *Dharma rakṣa tas a ti sha la gnang ba'i blo sbyong mtshon cha 'khor lo*. Dharamsala: Tibetan Cultural Printing House, 1990.

Dolan, John P., ed.
1964 *The Essential Erasmus*. New York: New American Library.

Eimer, Helmut
1979 *Rnam Thar Rgyas Pa: Materialien zu einer Biographie des Atiśa (Dipamkāraśrījñana)*. In *Asiatische Forschungen* 67. Wiesbaden: Otto Harrassowitz.

Evans-Wentz, W. Y., ed.
1958 *Tibetan Yoga and Secret Doctrines*. Second ed. Oxford: Oxford University Press.

Fausbøll, V., ed. and trans.
1872 *Ten Jātakas*. Copenhagen: H. Hagerup.

Filliozat, Jean, ed. and trans.
1979 *Yogaśataka: texte médical attribué à Nāgārjuna.* Pondicherry: Institut Français d'Indologie.

'Gos Lotsāwa
BA *The Blue Annals.* Ed. and trans. by George Roerich. 1949. Reprint Delhi: Motilal Banarsidass, 1976.

Goldstein, Melvyn
1975 *Tibetan-English Dictionary of Modern Tibetan.* Kathmandu: Ratna Pustak Bhandar.

Guenther, H. V., trans.
1971 *Jewel Ornament of Liberation.* Berkeley: Shambhala.

Hahn, Michael, ed. and trans.
1982 *Nāgārjuna's Ratnāvalī,* vol. 1. Bonn: Indica et Tibetica Verlag.

Hopkins, E. Washburne
1915 *Epic Mythology.* Reprint Delhi: Motilal Banarsidass, 1974.

Huntington, C. W.
1989 *The Emptiness of Emptiness: An Introduction to Early Indian Mādhyamika.* Honolulu: University of Hawaii Press.

'Jam mgon Kong sprul bLo gros mtha' yas
DNDZ *gDams ngag mdzod,* vols. 2-3. Compiled by 'Jam mgon Kong sprul. Reproduced from a xylograph from the dPal spungs blocks. Delhi: N. Lungtok and N. Gyaltsan, 1971.

Johansson, Rune E. A.
1970 *The Psychology of Nirvana.* Garden City, NJ: Anchor Books.

Kelsang Gyatso, Geshe
1988 *Universal Compassion.* London: Tharpa.

Kirtz, William
1973 "Wheel Weapon of Mind Practice." Unpublished M. A. thesis. Madison: University of Wisconsin-Madison.

Klong rdol bla ma
RSBT *Bka' Gdams dang Dge Lugs Bla Ma Rag Rim gyi Gsung 'Bum Mtshan Tho.* In *The Collected Works of Longdol Lama,* Parts 1 & 2: 1285-1413. Śata-Piṭaka Series 100. New Delhi: International Academy of Indian Culture, 1973.

[mKhan chen] Kun bzang dpal ldan
PJTG *Byang chub sems dpa'i spyod pa la 'jug pa'i tshig 'grel.* Junbesi (Nepal): Serlo Gompa, 1972.

Lamotte, Étienne
1962 *L'Enseignement de Vimalakīrti.* Louvain: Publications Universitaires.

LBTCK *Theg pa chen po'i blo sbyong mtshon cha 'khor lo*. In *Blo sbyong glegs bam*, pp. 127-143. Comp. and ed. by dKon chog rGyal mtsan. Bir: Bir Tibetan Society, 1983.

Lessing, Ferdinand D.

1942 *Yung-Ho-Kung, An Iconography of the Lamaist Cathedral in Peking*. Stockholm: Report of the Sino-Swedish Expedition.

LRCB *Lam rim chung ba dang lam rim spyi 'gro blo sbyong bcas kyi sa bcad*. In *Collected Works of Longdol Lama*, Parts 1 & 2: 58-90. Sata-Pitaka Series 100. New Delhi: International Academy of Indian Culture, 1973.

MacDonald, Alexander W.

1967 *Materiaux pour l'étude de la litterature populaire tibetaine*, vol. 1. Paris: Presses Universitaires de France.

Mani, Vettam

1979 *Purāṇic Encyclopaedia*. Delhi: Motilal Banarsidass.

[Bya] mChad kha ba [sKal bzang rgya mtsho]

LBDDM *Blo sbyong bdun dun ma*. In *gDams ngag mdzod*, compiled by 'Jam mgon Kong sprul, vol. 2: 8-11. Delhi: N. Lungtok and N. Gyaltsan, 1971.

Mullin, Glenn, ed. and trans.

1985 *Selected Works of the Dalai Lama I: Bridging the Sutras and Tantras*. Ithaca: Snow Lion.

MVYT *Mahāvyutpatti*. Fourth edition. Ed. R. Sakaki. Tokyo: Tōyō Bunko, 1971.

Nam mkha' dpal [Hor ston pa]

LNO *Blo sbyong nyi ma'i 'od gser*. Reproduction of a xylograph carved in Lhasa, ca. 1950.

Ngag dbang chos 'byor

1984 *Six Preparatory Practices Adorning the Buddha's Sublime Doctrine*. Trans. by Losang Gangchenpa and Karma Lekshe Tsomo. Dharamsala: Library of Tibetan Works and Archives.

Ngawang Dhargyey, Geshe et al., trans.

1981 *The Wheel of Sharp Weapons*. Dharamsala: Library of Tibetan Works and Archives.

Panglung, Jampa

1980 "Zwei Beschwörungsformeln Gegen Schlangenbiss im Mūlasarvāstivādin-Vinaya und ihr Fortleben in der Mahāmāyūrīvidyārājñī." *Asiatische Forschungen* 71: 66-71.

Pascal, Blaise

1982 *Les Penseés de Pascal*. Ed. by Francis Kaplan. Paris: Les Éditions du Cerf.

Po to ba Rin chen gsal
PC *dPe chos rin chen spungs ba*. Sarnath: Mongolian Lama Guru Deva, 1965.

Prajñākaramati
BCAP *Bodhicaryāvatārapañjikā*. In *Bodhicaryāvatāra of Śāntideva*. Ed. by P. L. Vaidya. Darbhanga (India): Mithila Institute, 1960.

PTC *Pali Tipitakam Concordance*. E. M. Hare. London: Luzac, 1952.

PTSD *The Pali Text Society's Pali-English Dictionary*. Ed. by T. W. Rhys Davids and W. Stede. London: Pali Text Society, 1921-25. Reprinted 1972.

Rabten, Geshe and Geshe Ngawang Dhargyey
1984 *Advice from a Spiritual Friend*. Trans. and ed. by Brian Beresford. London: Wisdom.

Sa skya Paṇḍita Kun dga' rgyal mthsan
SBRN *A Treasury of Aphoristic Jewels: The Subhāṣitaratnanidhi of Sa skya Paṇḍita in Tibetan and Mongolian*. Trans. by J. Bosson. Bloomington: Indiana University Press, 1969.
LSDG *Legs bshad 'dod dgu 'byung ba'i gter mdzod ces bya ba*. Kalimpong: Saskya Khenpo Ven. Sangey Tenzin, 1974.

Śāntideva
BCA *Bodhicaryāvatāra*. Ed. by V. Bhattacharya. Calcutta: The Asiatic Society, 1960.

sGam po pa [Dvags po Lha rje]
DYTR *Dam chos yid bzhin nor bu thar pa rin po che'i rgyan*. Rumtek: Karma'i chos sgar, 1972.

Silver, Daniel J.
1974 *A History of Judaism*, vol. 1. NewYork: Basic Books.

Smith, E. Gene
1969 *University of Washington Tibetan Catalogue*. 2 vols. Seattle: University of Washington.

Sopa, Geshe Lhundup and Jeffrey Hopkins
1976 *Practice and Theory of Tibetan Buddhism*. New York: Grove Press.

Stein, Rolf A.
1972 *Tibetan Civilization*. Trans. by J. E. Stapleton Driver. London: Faber and Faber.

Sternbach, Ludwik
1974 *Subhāṣita, Gnomic and Didactic Literature*. Wiesbaden: Otto Harrassowitz.

Taube, Manfred

1966 *Tibetische Handschriften und Blockdrucke*, vol. 3. Wiesbaden: Franz Steiner Verlag.

Thu'u bkwan [bLo bzang chos kyi nyi ma]

GTSM *Grub mtha' thams cad kyi khungs dang 'dod tshul ston pa legs bshad shel gyi me long*. In *Collected Works*, vol. 2: 5-519. New Delhi reprint of the Lhasa Zhol ed.

Tsong kha pa [bLo bzang grags pa]

TKSB *The Collected Works (Gsung 'Bum) of Rje-Tshon-Kha-Pa Blo-Bzan-Grags-Pa*. Reproduced from the Bkra shis lhun po edition. New Delhi: Ngawang Gelek Demo, 1978.

Tucci, Giuseppe

1936 *Indo-Tibetica*, III, parte 2. Rome: Reale Accademia d'Italia.

1949 *Tibetan Painted Scrolls*. 3 vols. Rome: Libreria dello Stato.

Tucci, Giuseppe and Walther Heissig

1973 *Les Religions du Tibet et de la Mongolie*. Paris: Payot.

Vasubandhu

AK *L'Abhidharmakośa de Vasubandhu*. Ed. and trans. by Louis de la Vallée Poussin. Paris: Paul Geuthner, 1923-32.

Vetter, Tilmann

1988 *The Ideas and Meditative Practices of Early Buddhism*. Leiden: Brill.

Wangyal, Geshe

1973 *The Door of Liberation*. New York: Girodias.

Wayman, Alex

1987 "Researches on Poison, Garuḍa-Birds, and Nāga-Serpents Based on the *Sgrub thabs kun btus*." In *Silver on Lapis: Tibetan Literary Culture and History*, pp. 63-76. Ed. by Christopher L. Beckwith. Bloomington, IN: Tibet Society.

[mKhan po] gZhan dga' [gZhan pan chos kyi snang ba]

PJCG *Byang chub sems dpa'i spyod pa la 'jug pa'i mchan 'grel*. Blockprint, n.p., n.d.

Chapter 15

Metaphors of Liberation: Tibetan Treatises on Grounds and Paths

Jules B. Levinson

In the literature and associated oral traditions presenting the grounds (*bhūmi, sa*) and paths (*mārga, lam*) of the Hīnayāna, or Low Vehicle, and the Mahāyāna, or Great Vehicle, Buddhist poets, philosophers, and yogins from India and Tibet describe a journey from bondage and ignorance (*avidyā, ma rig pa*) to liberation (*mokṣa, thar pa*) and enlightenment (*bodhi, byang chub*). Here I want to introduce the story that emerges in the literature on grounds and paths. I will begin with a few words about the origin and development of this literature, and then consider some of its prominent themes.

Tibetan Literature

The authors of the Tibetan literature on grounds and paths include scholars working in many parts of Tibet and also in Mongolia from as early as the eleventh century until contemporary times. The earliest literature on grounds and paths that I have found is the presentation of the five paths and the Mahāyāna grounds in sGam po pa's (1079-1153) *Thar pa rin po che'i rgyan* ("Ornament for Precious Liberation"); the most recent is a text by Blo bzang rta dbyangs (1867-1937) setting forth the grounds and paths of the hearer, solitary realizer, and bodhisattva vehicles from the point of view of Prāsaṅgika Madhyamaka as interpreted by Tsong kha pa and some among his many followers. Studies of grounds and paths composed during the intervening centuries include treatments by mKhas grub dge legs dpal bzang po (1385-1438), rJe btsun chos kyi rgyal mtshan (1469-1546), 'Jam dbyangs blo bzang bshes gnyen (dates unknown), the eighth Karma pa, Mi bskyod rdo rje (1507-1554), lCang skya rol pa'i rdo rje (1717-1786), 'Jam mgon kong sprul blo gros mtha' yas (1813-1899) and 'Ju Mi pham rgya mtsho (1846-1912). Other scholars have applied the presentation of grounds and paths to the Vajrayāna, and at least two Bon po writers have written texts on grounds and paths. The proliferation of such literature indicates widespread and persistent interest in the topics of grounds and paths, the study of which continues to occupy an important place in the curriculum of contemporary monastic colleges.

Indian Origins

Tibetan scholars say that the Buddha himself initiated the discussion of grounds and paths when he taught a set of discourses known as the Prajñāpāramitā *sūtras* ("*Sūtras* on the Perfection of Wisdom") to an assembly of students at Rājagṛha. In that collection of *sūtras*, the Buddha presented the emptiness that is the profound nature of all phenomena. He indicated also the paths that three types of students—hearers (*śrāvaka, nyan thos*), solitary realizers (*pratyekabuddha, rang sangs rgyas*), and bodhisattvas—follow to the liberations they seek, but left it for others to explain those paths in an open and complete way.

The Buddha's teachings on emptiness were clarified by Nāgārjuna (first to second century C.E.) in commentaries known collectively as the Rigs tshogs drug ("Six Collections of Reasonings"). His teachings on the paths of the three *sūtra* vehicles were elaborated in a treatise (*śāstra*) by Maitreya known as the *Abhisamayālaṃkāra* ("Ornament for the Clear Realizations"). The treatises by Nāgārjuna and Maitreya inspired further discussion among many generations of Indian Buddhist scholars. That conversation eventually migrated to Tibet and continues even now in the monastic universities that the Tibetans have established outside their homeland.

In other literature, the Indo-Tibetan Buddhist tradition describes spiritual development as a series of grounds. Tibetan authors writing about the grounds of the Mahāyāna frequently use the *Daśabhūmika* ("Ten Grounds *Sūtra*") as an authoritative and inspirational source. Nāgārjuna plays an important role here too, for Tibetan authors regularly quote the verses in his *Ratnāvalī* ("Precious Garland") celebrating the bodhisattva and buddha grounds. Usually they refer also to Maitreya's verses on the Mahāyāna grounds, found in his *Mahāyānasūtrālaṃkāra* ("Ornament for the Mahāyāna *Sūtras*"). If they look to a fourth Indian source, it is frequently to Candrakīrti's (seventh century C.E.) *Madhyamakāvatāra* ("Entrance into the Middle"), a text in which the ideals of the Mahāyāna tradition are expressed in terms of the ten bodhisattva grounds and the buddha ground. One might expect Asaṅga's *Yogācaryabhūmi* ("Levels of Yogic Practice"), which contains long and elaborate discussions of the grounds of hearers and bodhisattvas, to play an important role in the Tibetan literature on grounds. To my surprise, I have found that Asaṅga's texts are mentioned only rarely in the literature on grounds and paths with which I am familiar.

Representative Texts

The Tibetan texts in which grounds and paths are discussed vary both in format and in point of view. Nevertheless, a close look at the structure of two dGe lugs pa texts gives a sense of the style of such literature and of the topics with which it is concerned. Let us consider a presentation of grounds and paths composed by dKon mchog 'jigs med dbang po, called *Sa lam gyi rnam bzhag theg gsum mdzes rgyan* ("Presentation of Grounds and Paths, Beautiful Ornament for the Three Vehicles") and another composed by Blo bzang rta dbyangs, called *Sa lam gyi rnam bzhag zab don rgya mtsho'i snying po* ("Presentation of Grounds and Paths, Essence of the Ocean of Profound Meaning").

dKon mchog 'jigs med dbang po's text opens with an outline of the paths of three types of religious practitioners. The first is those who seek rebirth in a favorable situation rather than liberation from rebirth altogether. These are called "special beings of small capacity" (*skye bu chung ngu khyad par can*). The second aim merely to accomplish their own welfare by achieving liberation from cyclic existence. They are called "beings of middling capacity" (*madhyamapuruṣa, skyes bu 'bring*). Those of the third type seek highest enlightenment themselves so as to help all other sentient beings find a genuine and enduring happiness. They are called "beings of great capacity" (*mahāpuruṣa, skyes bu chen po*). dKon mchog 'jigs med dbang po defines and illustrates the paths of each, indicates areas where the paths of the three types of practitioners overlap one another, and discusses the ways in which individual practitioners enhance their ability to consider the long-term welfare of themselves and others.

The second section of dKon mchog 'jigs med dbang po's text identifies the grounds of the Hīnayāna and then provides a detailed explanation of the paths of all three Sūtra vehicles. This includes a discussion of the various names and synonyms for the five paths, the definitions and divisions of each path, and the points at which each path begins and ends.

The final major topic is the ten grounds of bodhisattva superiors (*ārya*). dKon mchog 'jigs med dbang po explains the names given to the individual grounds, the obstructions that are abandoned over the course of the ten grounds, and the extraordinary qualities that bodhisattvas develop as they journey to complete enlightenment. These qualities are grouped into seven categories: (1) perfections (*pāramitā*), (2) magical abilities, (3) fruitional rebirths, (4) the trainings in discipline (*śīla*), meditatve stabilization (*samādhi*), and wisdom (*prajñā*), (5) the way in which reality is understood in the periods subsequent to nonconceptual realization of emptiness, (6) thorough purification, and (7) the signs of achieving a ground.

Blo bzang rta dbyangs was a Mongolian scholar who wrote prolifically both on Sūtra and on Tantra. His treatise on the grounds and paths of the *sūtras* is unusual in that it presents the Prāsaṅgika Madhyamaka school's point of view, for most texts, including dKon mchog 'jigs med dbang po's, present the views of the Yogācāra-Svātantrika Madhyamaka school. Blo bzang rta dbyangs's text is divided into two major sections that are approximately equal in length. The first section explains the grounds and paths of the Hīnayāna and Mahāyāna. The second section analyzes controversial points on which various scholars and schools disagree. In that latter section, Blo bzang rta dbyangs is particularly interested in distinguishing the Prāsaṅgika Madhyamaka school's position from that of the Yogācāra-Svātantrika Madhyamaka.

The section on the grounds and paths of the three Sūtra vehicles begins with a description of the eight Hīnayāna grounds. It then presents the five paths of the Hīnayāna in detail, with definitions, divisions, and illustrations of each. This occupies roughly six pages of a thirty-four page section. The remainder—twenty-eight pages—is devoted to a discussion of the grounds and paths of the Mahāyāna. The number of pages alloted to the Hīnayāna and the Mahāyāna, six and twenty-eight, respectively, indicates the author's relatively greater interest in Mahāyāna topics.

The portion concerned with the grounds and paths of the Mahāyāna begins with a presentation of the five Mahāyāna paths, and includes definitions, divisions, and illustrations of each. This is followed by a discussion of the ten grounds of bodhisattva superiors. Each of the ten grounds is described in terms of (1) the magical abilities that bodhisattvas achieve on that ground, (2) the practice of a perfection that has been brought to a superlative level on that ground, (3) the power to advance further that is achieved on that ground, and (4) the fruitional rebirths that are taken on that ground. Blo bzang rta dbyangs cites liberally from works by Nāgārjuna and Maitreya in describing these ten grounds. The citations help to give the reader a sense of the literature on which the Tibetan presentations are based.

After outlining the ten grounds of bodhisattva superiors, bLo bzang rta dbyangs describes the ground of a buddha. His discussion begins with a vivid and eloquent description of the way in which bodhisattvas pass from the tenth bodhisattva ground to the buddha ground. This is followed by a clarification of the nature of a buddha's three bodies, i.e., Truth Body (*dharmakāya, chos sku*), Complete Enjoyment body (*saṃbhogakāya, longs spyod rdzogs pa'i sku*), and Emanation Body (*nirmāṇakāya, sprul sku*).

The presentation of Hīnayāna and Mahāyāna grounds having been completed, Blo bzang rta dbyangs presents thirty-four pages of dialectical discussion in which he differentiates the Prāsaṅgika Madhyamaka school's view from that of other schools, and offers extensive support, both scriptural and logical, for the radical positions taken by the Prāsaṅgika Madhyamaka school. The topics explored include the ignorance that serves as the root of cyclic existence, the selflessness (*nairātmya, bdag med*) that hearers, solitary realizers, and bodhisattvas must realize in order to achieve the goals they seek, the difference between the afflictive obstructions (*kleśāvarana, nyon mongs pa'i sgrib pa*) and the obstructions to omniscience (*jñeyāvaraṇa, shes bya'i sgrib pa*), and the difference between *nirvāṇas* with remainder and those without remainder.

Imagination

Grounds and paths are presented as keys to liberation from a prison. The prison, called cyclic existence (*saṃsāra, 'khor ba*), extends both spatially and temporally. Transmigrators (*gati, 'gro ba*) stumble from one lifetime to another within the limitless prison of cyclic existence, but generally know little about the past from which they have emerged or the future that they are creating. Buddhist literature therefore describes the types of lifetimes that sentient beings (*sattva, sems can*) experience within cyclic existence and the actions (*karma, las*) that lead to particular types of rebirths.[1]

Having visualized cyclic existence, a practitioner considers how to respond to such confinement. As dKon mchog 'jigs med dbang po's text makes clear, one might respond by seeking to ensure a comfortable position within the prison, or one might seek liberation from prison for oneself alone, or one might seek the means to liberate not only oneself but also all others from prison. The literature on grounds and paths outlines the journeys toward freedom as well as the freedom that is achieved. In such literature, one is studying a map of areas that one has never visited. For that reason, the study of grounds and paths, like the study of cyclic existence itself, requires a reader to imagine unknown territory. We find in such literature a carefully crafted set of meaningful images that enable students to imagine areas of progressively greater freedom, to become inspired by the world they have imagined, and to set forth on the journey toward freedom in the very act of imagining an alternative to endless and oppressive confusion. Let us consider three images that are central to the transmission of the Buddhist vision.

Three Metaphors

To dispel the ignorance that creates and sustains cyclic existence, those who desire liberation generate consciousnesses (*jñāna, shes pa*) that realize selflessness. The selflessness that they realize is the opposite of the self that is conceived by ignorance. Through realizing selflessness, those consciousnesses uproot the ignorance that conceives self, whereupon the gates of cyclic existence fall open. In the literature on spiritual development, those consciousnesses are called "grounds" (*bhūmi, sa*) and "paths" (*mārga, lam*). Moreover, the consciousnesses that lead to realization of selflessness and those that, subsequently, are both deeply marked by that realization and centrally involved in strengthening it further are also called "grounds" and "paths."

The first point to realize is that "ground" and "path" are metaphors. The grounds and paths of hearers, solitary realizers, and bodhisattvas are not material highways, and the map of their development does not describe a physical geography. Grounds and paths refer, rather, to consciousnesses. Although only some consciousnesses are grounds and paths, all grounds and paths are consciousnesses.[2] Some of those grounds and paths realize selflessness; the others either lead to or arise from such realization. In that sense, we might say that the grounds and paths of the Sūtra vehicles are the study of selflessness.

It is important to realize that all of the grounds and paths of the three vehicles are just consciousnesses. That they are consciousnesses means that they are clear and immaterial awareness, without color, shape, sound, odor, taste, or texture. Although engraved upon the personality of the practitioner, they cannot be seen with the eye or touched with the hand. The presentation of spiritual development in the Buddhist tradition is, in that sense, a careful survey of an invisible, inaudible, and intangible world. As such, it could easily become an uninviting abstraction. That would defeat what must be one of the central purposes of the discussion, which is not only to inform but also to inspire, and that may be why the literature on spiritual development has attracted metaphors that arouse both curiosity and longing.

Why are these consciousnesses called "paths"? dKon mchog 'jigs med dbang po characterizes paths as consciousnesses serving as passageways to the enlightenments that are their fruits (428). He then explains that they are called "paths" because they cause one to progress to the rank of liberation (428). Similarly, Blo bzang rta dbyangs says that such consciousnesses are called "paths" in that they cause one to progress to the city of liberation (74). Both authors use the causative form of the verb, *bgrod,* here translated as "progress," indicating that these consciousnesses do not merely allow practitioners to achieve liberation but actually impel them toward it.

How do consciousnesses move practitioners toward liberation? In speaking about paths generally, Blo bzang rta dbyangs observes that, although "ground" and "path" are interchangeable terms, in usage, "path" refers mainly to the factor of wisdom (*prajñā, shes rab*) and "ground" refers mainly to the factor of method (*upāya, thabs*) (74). As becomes apparent in his text, the discussion of spiritual development as a series of five paths presents mainly the development of wisdom, which means the genesis and maturation of the wisdom realizing selflessness. Thus, it is through realizing selflessness that paths drive practitioners toward liberation.

The name "ground" is applied to many different types of consciousnesses. For instance, an intention to emerge from cyclic existence (*niḥsaraṇa, nges 'byung gi bsam pa*), compassion (*karuṇā, snying rje*), generosity (*dāna, sbyin pa*), realizations of selflessness, and other such consciousnesses are all called "grounds." In explaining the reason for this, sGam po pa says:

> They serve as the basis for the qualities that are the good qualities of that ground and the occasion of that ground, or, they cause higher grounds to develop, whereby they are called grounds....One dwells in and enjoys that wisdom, whereby they are called grounds; for example, like an enclosure for oxen. One travels on that wisdom, whereby they are called grounds; for example, like racing horses. That wisdom is the basis of all good qualities being born, whereby they are called grounds; for example, like fertile soil. (279)

Similarly, dKon mchog 'jigs med dbang po says:

> As for calling these grounds, just as earth serves as the basis for plants, trees, and so forth, so these serve as the basis for the many good qualities of one who has entered a path, whereby they are called such. (426)

Also, Blo bzang rta dbyangs says:

> In the world, the ground serves as a basis of production and abiding of fruit trees, forests, and so forth. Similarly, these perform the similar function of serving as the basis of the production and abiding of worldly qualities and qualities that are beyond the world. (74)

These scholars see wisdom, compassion, generosity, and so forth as bases that both nourish and enable further growth, and so they call such consciousnesses "grounds." Just as trees, mountains, lakes, animals, humans, farms, cities, and so forth all depend on the earth, so the beneficial qualities of body, speech, and mind developed by hearers, solitary realizers, and bodhisattvas all depend upon the consciousnesses from which they grow. Like the earth that is the basis for fruit trees and forests, such consciousnesses are the foundation for (1) the increase of beneficial qualities and (2) the release of a limitless number of sentient beings from mistaken conceptions and mistaken appearances. As we read, we are invited to regard such minds as fertile points of departure, like good earth in which grow magnificent, shade-giving trees, beautiful flowers, luxurious green grass, and a rich harvest of corn.

In describing the internal structure of the Hīnayāna and Mahāyāna, the literature on grounds and paths creates a basis for discussing both the significant features of each and their differences. In that context, the grounds or paths of any one person's journey are individually distinct. In general, however, "ground" and "path" are synonyms: any consciousness that is one is also the other (*ZGN*: 74). Generally speaking, then, the names "ground" and "path" point to further extension of the Hīnayāna or Mahāyāna disciplines. As a ground, a consciousness serves as the basis for an increase of one's own good qualities and, in the Mahāyāna, for the liberation of others from suffering. Thus, "ground" suggests the further development both of oneself and of others. As a path, a consciousness invites further steps, and itself carries one part of the way. In brief, grounds and paths encourage motion and expansion.

dKon mchog 'jigs med dbang po gives "vehicle" (*yāna, theg pa*) as one of six synonyms for "path" (428). Since all paths are also grounds, "ground," "path," and "vehicle" are mutually inclusive: whatever is one is also the other two. However, the terms are used differently and suggest different aspects of the consciousnesses to which they refer. Consciousnesses are called "vehicles" when they are able to bear the welfare of sentient beings. The grounds and paths that carry practitioners to the liberations of *arhats* and buddhas are vehicles in that they bear sentient beings to the states of well-being that those practitioners seek. The final paths that practitioners achieve at the end of their journeys are also called vehicles because they themselves are the vessel for such well-being.

In each case, the image—ground, path, vehicle—connects one experience to another. Saying that a consciousness realizing emptiness is a "path" leading to liberation connects an extraordinary experience with an ordinary experience. Calling compassion a "ground" associates the fertility of the heart with the fertility of the earth. The metaphor enables a practitioner to think about compassion in a new way. Similar purposes have led Buddhist writers to cast the literature of spiritual development in the terms of agriculture, ocean voyages, and warfare, which is to say, in the terms of the ordinary world.

Conclusion

From several points of view, the literature on grounds and paths provides a general environment for study and meditation in the Tibetan Buddhist tradition. In it are described the initial steps in the direction of liberation, the obstructions to further progress toward liberation, and the landmarks along the paths to liberation. This literature describes also the qualities that develop as practitioners approach liberation, the nature of the liberations that are achieved, and the varieties of journeys that different kinds of practitioners make toward liberation. However, except for texts that are specifically concerned with the paths of the Vajrayāna, the literature of grounds and paths explains the Sūtrayāna rather than the Vajrayāna. For this reason it does not describe the entirety of Tibetan Buddhist practice and omits in particular the ritual, the vision of sacredness, and the *yoga* to which Tibetan Buddhists have been overwhelmingly dedicated. Nevertheless, the grounds and paths of *sūtra* are studied, taught, debated, and have been written about repeatedly since the introduction of this body of knowledge to the people of Tibet. Moreover, the texts that present the grounds and paths of the Vajrayāna correlate the practices and realizations of that vehicle with the grounds and paths of the Sūtrayāna, and speak of Vajrayāna accomplishments in terms of the outline set down in the literature on the grounds and paths of the Sūtrayāna. This indicates that the Sūtra presentation has sufficient authority that the more powerful Vajrayāna of which it is a subset does not render it irrelevant or quaint. On the contrary, the presentation made in the *sūtras* and *śāstras* informs and directs Vajrayāna practice to a significant degree, in that the network of metaphors and analogies redefines and enlarges the perspectives of those who bring such a visualization into their own lives, in somewhat the way that remarkable people alter and extend the outlooks of those who meet them. These images reveal a territory that lies beyond the futility of cyclic existence, whereby they also invite and orient a personal exploration of the unknown ground.

Notes

1. For traditional discussions of cyclic existence, see Dalai Lama XIV: 24 ff., Lati Rinbochay et al.: 23-47, and Kalu Rinpoche: 23-28.

2. There is the exception that three of the eight branches of the eightfold path—correct speech, correct ends of actions, and correct livelihood—are not consciousnesses.

References

Asaṅga

NPS *rNal 'byor spyod pa'i sa/ Sa'i dngos gzhi* (*Yogacaryābhūmi/ Bhūmivastu*, "Levels of Yogic Practice/ Actuality of the Levels"). P nos. 5536-5538, vols. 109-110.

Blo bzang rta dbyangs

ZGN *Phar chen theg pa'i lugs kyi theg pa gsum gyi sa dang lam gyi rnam par bzhag pa mdo tsam du brjod pa zab don rgya mtsho'i snying po* ("Brief Expression of the Presentation of the Grounds and Paths of the Three Vehicles According to the System of the Great Perfection Vehicle, Essence of the Ocean of Profound Meaning"). In *The Collected Works (Gsuṅg 'Bum) of Rje-Btsun Blo-Bzang-Rta-Mgrin*, vol. 4, pp. 65-139. New Delhi: Mongolian Lama Gurudeva, 1975.

Candrakīrti

UJ *dBu ma la 'jug pa* (*Madhyamakāvatāra*, "Supplement to [Nāgārjuna's] 'Treatise on the Middle'"). P nos. 5261, 5262, vol. 98. Edited Tibetan in Louis de la Vallée Poussin's *Madhyamakāvatāra par Candrakīrti*. Bibliotheca Buddhica 9. Osnabruck: Biblio Verlag, 1970. English translation of Chapters One through Five in Tsong ka pa, Lekden, and Hopkins, *Compassion in Tibetan Buddhism*, pp. 95-230. Valois, NY: Gabriel/ Snow Lion, 1980, pp. 95-230. English translation of Chapter Six by Stephen Batchelor in Geshé Rabten, *Echoes of Voidness*, pp. 47-92. London: Wisdom, 1983.

Dalai Lama XIV, Tenzin Gyatso

1975 *The Buddhism of Tibet and the Key to the Middle Way*. Translated by Jeffrey Hopkins and Lati Rimpoche. New York: Harper & Row.

DB *mDo sde sa bcu pa* (*Daśabhūmikasūtra*, "Ten Grounds *Sūtra*"). P no. 761.31, vol. 25. Translated by M. Honda in "An Annotated Translation of the 'Daśabhūmika.'" In *Studies in Southeast and Central Asia*, pp. 115-276. Ed. by D. Sinor. Śata-Piṭaka Series 74. New Delhi: 1968.

dByangs can dga ba'i blo gros

KZJN *dPal gsang ba 'dus pa 'phags lugs dang mthun pa'i sngags kyi sa lam rnam gzhag legs bshad skal bzang 'jug ngogs* ("Presentation of the Grounds and Paths of Mantra According to the Superior Nāgārjuna's Interpretation of the Glorious Guhyasamāja, A Good Explanation Serving as a Port for the Fortunate"). Blockprint, n.p., n.d.

dKon mchog 'jigs med dbang po

TSDG *Sa lam gyi rnam gzhag theg gsum rdzes rgyan* ("Presentation of Grounds and Paths, Beautiful Ornament for the Three Vehicles"). In *The Collected Works of dKon-mchog-'jigs-med-dbang-po*, vol. 7. New Delhi: Ngawang Gelek Demo, 1972.

GT *Shes rab kyi pha rol tu phyin pa brgyad stong pa'i mdo* (*Aṣṭasāhasrikāprajñāpāramitāsūtra*, "Eight-Thousand-Stanza Perfection of Wisdom *Sūtra*"). P no. 734, vol. 21. Translated by E. Conze, *Aṣṭasāhasrikāprajñāpāramitā*. Asiatic Society Bibliotheca Indica 284. Calcutta, 1958; reprint Bolinas, CA: Four Seasons Foundation, 1962.

Hopkins, Jeffrey

1992 "A Tibetan Perspective on the Nature of Spiritual Experience." In *Paths to Liberation: The Mārga and its Transformations in Buddhist Thought*. Ed. by Robert E. Buswell, Jr., and Robert M. Gimello. Studies in East Asian Buddhism 7. Honolulu: University of Hawaii Press.

'Jam dbyangs blo bzang bshes gnyen

KZMP *Sa lam gyi rnam bzhag skal bzang mig phyed* ("Presentation of Grounds and Paths, Opener of the Eyes of the Fortunate"). Blockprint, n.p., n.d.

'Jam mgon kong sprul blo gros mtha' yas

SBD *bGrod bya sa dang lam gyi rim par phye ba* ("Distinguishing the Stages of Those That Are to Be Traversed, the Grounds and Paths"). In *Shes bya mdzod/ Theg pa'i sgo kun las btus pa gsung rab rin po che'i mdzod bslab pa gsum legs par ston pa'i bstan bcos shes bya kun khyab* ("Treasury of Knowledge/ Treasury of Precious High Speech Gathered from All the Doors of Vehicles, Treatise Pervading All That Is to Be Known and Teaching Well the Three Trainings"). Lhasa: Mi rigs dpe skrun khang, 1983.

'Ju Mi pham rgya mtsho

KJ *mKhas pa'i tshul la 'jug pa'i sgo zhes bya ba'i bstan bcos* ("Treatise Called, 'Door of Entry into the Way of the Learned'"). Blockprint, n.p., n.d.

Kalu Rinpoche

1986 *The Dharma that Illuminates All Beings Impartially Like the Light of the Sun and the Moon.* Edited by The Kagyu Thubten Choling Translation Committee. Albany: State University of New York Press.

Lati Rinbochay et al.

1983 *Meditative States in Tibetan Buddhism.* London: Wisdom Publications.

Karma pa VIII, Mi bskyod rdo rje

DGGS *dBu ma la 'jug pa'i rnam bshad dpal ldan dus gsum mkhyen pa'i zhal lung dwags brgyud sgrub pa'i shing rta* ("Explanation of [Candrakīrti's] *'Supplement to [Nāgārjuna's] "Treatise on the Middle",'* Sacred Speech of the Glorious Knower of the Three Times, Chariot Establishing the Dak po Lineage"). Blockprint, n.p., n.d.

lCang skya rol pa'i rdo rje

TLDG *Grub pa'i mtha'i rnam par bzhag pa gsal bar bshad pa thub bstan lhun po'i mdzes rgyan* ("Clear Exposition of the Presentations of Tenets, Beautiful Ornament for the Meru of the Subduer's Teaching"). Varanasi: Pleasure of Elegant Sayings Press, 1970.

Maitreya

MTG *mNgon par rtogs pa'i rgyan* (*Abhisamayālamkāra*, "Ornament for the Clear Realizations"). P no. 5184, vol. 88. Sanskrit edition by Th. Stcherbatsky and E. Obermiller, *Abhisamayālaṃkāra-Prajñāpāramitā-Updeśa-Śāstra.* Bibliotheca Buddhica 21. Osnabruck: Biblio Verlag, 1970. English translation by Edward Conze, *Abhisamayālaṃkāra.* Serie Orientale Roma 6. Rome: Istituto Italiano per il Medio ed Estremo Oriente, 1954.

DDG *Theg pa chen po'i mdo sde rgyan gyi tshig le'ur byas pa* (*Mahāyāna-sūtrālaṃkārakārikā*, "Ornament for the Mahāyāna Sūtras"). P no. 5521, vol. 108.

mKhas grub dge legs dpal bzang po

KYP *Sa lam gyi rnam gzhag mkhas pa'i yid 'phrog* ("Presentation of Grounds and Paths, Captivating the Minds of the Learned"). In *The Collected Works (gsuṅ 'bum) of Mkhas-grub Dge-legs Dpal*, vol. 9, pp. 309-337. New Delhi: Ngawang Gelek Demo, 1983-1985.

Nāgārjuna

RP *rGyal po la gtam bya ba rin po che'i 'phreng ba* (*Rājaparikathā-ratnāvalī*, "Precious Garland of Advice for the King"). P no. 5658, vol. 129. Translated by Jeffrey Hopkins and Lati Rimpoche in

The Precious Garland and The Song of the Four Mindfulnesses. London: George Allen and Unwin, 1975. Partial translation by G. Tucci, *Journal of the Royal Asiatic Society* 1934, pp. 307-325; 1936, pp. 237-252, 423-435.

Ngag dbang dpal ldan

GZSB *gSang chen rgyud sde bzhi'i sa lam gyi rnam bzhag rgyud gzhung gsal byed* ("Illumination of the Texts of Tantra, Presentation of the Grounds and Paths of the Four Great Secret Tantra Sets"). Blockprint, n.p., n.d.

Rig 'dzin rgyal mtshan

BTCSL *Bon theg pa chen po'i sa lam* ("Grounds and Paths of the Bon Mahāyāna"). Blockprint, n.p., n.d.

rJe btsun chos kyi rgyal mtshan

KGG *mKhas pa'i mgul rgyan ces bya ba sa lam rnam bzhag* ("Presentation of Grounds and Paths, Necklace for the Learned"). Blockprint, n.p., n.d.

sGam po pa

TRG *Dam chos yid bzhin gyi nor bu thar pa rin po che'i rgyan zhes bya ba theg pa chen po'i lam rim gyi bshad pa* ("Explanation of the Stages of the Paths of the Mahāyāna, Called 'The Excellent Dharma, the Wish-Fulfilling Jewel, the Ornament for Precious Liberation'"). Thimphu: National Library of Bhutan, 1985. Translated by Herbert V. Guenther, *The Jewel Ornament of Liberation*. Berkeley: Shambhala, 1971.

Shes rab rgyal mtshan

PGM *Sa lam 'phrul gyi sgron me* ("Magical Lamp for the Grounds and Paths"). Blockprint, n.p., n.d.

Tsong-ka-pa

1977 *Tantra in Tibet: The Great Exposition of Secret Mantra*. Introduced by Tenzin Gyatso, His Holiness the Fourteenth Dalai Lama. Translated and edited by Jeffrey Hopkins. London: George Allen and Unwin.

Tsong-ka-pa, Kensur Ngawang Lekden, and Jeffrey Hopkins

1980 *Compassion in Tibetan Buddhism*. Valois, NY: Snow Lion.

Chapter 16

gDams ngag: Tibetan Technologies of the Self

Matthew Kapstein

The Tibetan terms *gdams ngag* (Skt. *upadeśa*) and *man ngag* (Skt. *āmnāya*, but sometimes also *upadeśa*) refer broadly to speech and writing that offer directives for practice, whether in the general conduct of life or in some specialized field such as medicine, astronomy, politics, yoga or meditation. In any of these areas, they may refer to "esoteric" instructions, i.e., advice not usually found in theoretical textbooks but derived from the hands-on experience of skilled practitioners, and thus intended primarily for those who are actually engaged in the practice of the discipline concerned. *Man ngag* seems often to connote a higher degree of esotericism than does *gdams ngag*, particularly where both terms are employed together contrastively, and despite their essential synonymity.[1]

In this short essay I shall focus on the category of *gdams ngag*, "instruction," as understood in connection with meditational and yogic practice. In this context, *gdams ngag* refers essentially to the immediate, heartfelt instructions and admonitions of master to disciple concerning directly liberative insight and practice. *gDams ngag* in this sense is, in the final analysis, a product solely of the interrelationship between master and disciple; it is the non-repeatable discourse event in which the core of the Buddhist enlightenment comes to be manifestly disclosed. It is in this sense, for instance, that we find the term used in narrating a signal event in the life of the famed rNying ma pa master Mi pham Rin po che (1846-1912):

> One time, Mipham went into Khyentse Rinpoche's presence. "How did you apply yourself to experiential cultivation when you stayed in retreat?" he was asked.
>
> "While pursuing my studies," Mipham answered, "I made conclusive investigations, and while performing the ritual service of the meditational deity in retreat I have taken care to see that I have reached the limits of the stage of creation."
>
> "Those are difficult. The great all-knowing Longcenpa said, 'Not doing anything, you must come to rest right where you are.' I have done just that. By so resting I have not seen anything with white flesh and a ruddy complexion that can be called the 'face of mind.' None the less, if I were to die now it would be all right. I do not even have a grain of trepidation." So saying, Khyentse Rinpoche laughed aloud. Mipham [later] said that he understood that to be the guru's instruction (*gdams ngag*).
>
> (Dudjom Rinpoche, 1991: 876-877)

gDams ngag, then, is the articulation of the dynamic interaction between master and disciple; it expresses the essentially hermeneutical movement in which the disciple is reoriented in the depth of his or her being to the goal of the teaching. Insofar as the Buddha's entire doctrine is held to be directed to that goal, the achievement of perfect enlightenment on behalf of oneself and all creatures, all expressions of Buddhadharma may be in a certain sense termed *gdams ngag* (cf. 'Jam mgon, *DNgDz*, vol. 12: 626-630). Nevertheless, the term has been thematized in Tibetan Buddhist discourse to refer above all to those meditational and yogic instructions that most frequently form the basis for systematic salvific practice. One must include here also the innumerable writings on *blo sbyong*, "spiritual training/purification," and the entire genre of *khrid yig*, "guidebooks," i.e., practical manuals explicating particular systems of meditation, yoga and ritual. It is in this context that *gdams ngag* has come to form the basis for an important set of distinctions among Tibetan Buddhist traditions, corresponding in general to distinctions of lineage, while crosscutting distinctions of sect.[2] These systematic approaches to liberation through meditation and yoga, which will be our concern here, may be thought to be the quintessential Tibetan "technologies of the self."[3]

There is no single classification of the many traditions of *gdams ngag* that is universally employed by Tibetan Buddhist doxographical writers. From about the thirteenth century onwards, however, the preeminence of certain particular traditions gave rise to a characteristic scheme that we encounter repeatedly, with small variations, throughout Tibetan historical, doctrinal and bibliographical literature.[4] According to this, there are eight major *gdams ngag* traditions, which are referred to as the "eight great conveyances that are lineages of attainment" (*sgrub brgyud shing rta chen po brgyad*). The paradigmatic formulation of this classificatory scheme is generally attributed to 'Phreng bo gTer ston Shes rab 'od zer (Prajñāraśmi, 1517-1584), whose verses on this topic are widely cited by Tibetan authors ('Jam mgon, *DNgDz*, vol. 12: 645-646). The "eight great conveyances" as he enumerates them may be briefly explained as follows:[5]

(1) The sNga 'gyur rnying ma, or "Ancient Translation Tradition," derives its special *gdams ngag* primarily from the teachings of Padmasambhava and Vimalamitra, eighth-century Indian Buddhist masters who visited Tibet, and from the great Tibetan translators who were their contemporaries, especially Pa gor Bai ro tsa na. Of the tremendous body of special *gdams ngag* belonging to the rNying ma tradition, most widely renowned are those concerned with the meditational teachings of rDzogs chen, the Great Perfection.[6]

(2) The bKa' gdams, or "Tradition of [the Buddha's] Transmitted Precepts (*bka'*) and Instructions (*gdams*)," is traced to the activity of the Bengali master Atiśa (982-1054) and his leading Tibetan disciples, notably 'Brom ston rGyal ba'i 'byung gnas (1104-1163). It is owing to its special role in maintaining the vitality of teachings derived from the bKa' gdams tradition that the dGa' ldan or dGe lugs order, founded by rJe Tsong kha pa Blo bzang grags pa (1357-1419), is often referred to as the New bKa' gdams school (bKa' gdams gsar ma). The bKa' gdams tradition specialized in *gdams ngag* relating to the cultivation of the enlightened attitude (*bodhicitta, byang chub kyi sems*), the union of compassion and insight that is characteristic of the Mahāyāna.[7]

(3) Lam 'bras bu dang bcas pa, the "Tradition of the Path with its Fruit," is derived ultimately from the teachings of the Indian *mahāsiddha* Virūpa, and was introduced into Tibet by 'Brog mi lo tsā ba Śākya Ye shes (992-1072). This tradition of esoteric practice, emphasizing the *Hevajra Tantra*, became from early on a special concern of the Sa skya pa school, and so has been primarily associated with Sa skya and the several Sa skya pa suborders, such as the Ngor pa and Tshar pa.[8]

(4) The Mar pa bKa' brgyud, or "Succession of the Transmitted Precepts of Marpa," has as its particular domain the teachings of the Indian masters Tilopa, Nāropa and Maitrīpa as transmitted to Mar pa Chos kyi blo gros (1012-1097), the translator of lHo brag. His tradition of *gdams ngag* stresses the Six Doctrines (*chos drug*) of yogic pratice—inner heat, the apparitional body, lucid dreaming, inner radiance, the transference of consciousness at death, and the teachings of the intermediate state (*bar do*)—as well as the culminating meditations of the Great Seal (*mahāmudrā, phyag rgya chen po*).

The proliferation of lineages adhering to the teachings of Mar pa, those of his foremost disciple, Mi la ras pa (1040-1123), and those of the latter's main students Ras chung rDo rje grags (1083-1161) and sGam po pa bSod nams rin chen (a.k.a. Dwags po Lha rje, 1079-1153) was very widespread, and the many teaching lineages that arose among their followers almost all created their own distinctive formulations of the bKa' brgyud *gdams ngag*. The four "great" bKa' brgyud orders (bKa brgyud che bzhi) were founded by sGam po pa's immediate disciples, among whom Phag mo gru pa rDo rje rgyal po's (1110-1170) leading disciples founded eight "lesser" orders (*chung brgyad*). (The terms "great" and "lesser" refer solely to their relative proximity to sGam po pa, and imply neither quantitative nor qualitative judgment.) The first Karma pa hierarch, Dus gsum mkhyen pa (1110-1193), is numbered among the four "greats," while 'Bri gung skyob pa 'Jig rten gsum mgon (1143-1217) was prominent among the founders of the eight "lesser" orders. Among the eight is also counted Gling rje ras pa Padma rdo rje (1128-1188), whose disciple gTsang pa rGya ras (1161-1211) founded the 'Brug pa bKa' brgyud order, which in turn gave rise to several major suborders. (The 'Brug pa later established itself as the state religion in Bhutan, a position it retains at the present time.) Mar pa bKa' brgyud teachings have been widely transmitted among non-bKa' brgyud pa orders, for instance among the dGe lugs pa, a considerable portion of whose esoteric *gdams ngag* originated in the Mar pa bKa' brgyud tradition.[9]

(5) The Shangs pa bKa' brgyud, the "Succession of the Transmitted Precepts of Shangs Valley," is traced back to Khyung po rnal 'byor Tshul khrims mgon po of Shangs (d. ca. 1135), a master whose foremost teacher was the *ḍākinī* Niguma, said to have been the sister or wife of Nāropa. The special teachings of the Shangs

pa tradition, which are similar to those of the Mar pa bKa' brgyud tradition, differing primarily in points of emphasis, were widely influential. Despite the almost complete absence of distinctive Shangs pa institutions, they were transmitted within the Mar pa bKa' brgyud, dGe lugs, Jo nang and rNying ma orders. The Shangs pa teachings have aroused considerable interest among Buddhists in the West owing to the widespread activity of their leading contemporary proponent, the late Kalu Rinpoche Rang byung kun khyab (1905-1989).[10]

(6) The closely related teachings of Zhi byed, "Pacification," and gCod yul, "Object of Cutting," originated respectively with the enigmatic Indian yogī Pha Dam pa Sangs rgyas (d. 1117) and his remarkable Tibetan disciple, the yoginī Ma cig Lab kyi sgron ma (ca. 1055-1143). Though schools specializing in Pacification were very widespread from the twelfth to fourteenth centuries, the teaching all but disappeared in later times. The Object of Cutting, however, permeated the entire Tibetan Buddhist tradition and is today preserved by all orders. Both of these systems of *gdams ngag* seek to bring about the realization of liberating insight as it is understood in the "Perfection of Wisdom" (Prajñāpāramitā) *sūtras* by means inspired by esoteric Buddhist practice. This takes particularly dramatic form in the traditions of the Object of Cutting, whose exquisite liturgies involve the adept's symbolic offering of his or her own body as food for all beings throughout the universe.[11]

(7) rDo rje'i rnal 'byor, the "Yoga of Indestructible Reality," refers to the system of yoga associated with the *Kālacakra Tantra*, as transmitted in Tibet initially by Gyi jo lo tsā ba Zla ba'i 'od zer during the early eleventh century. Later traditions that were particularly influential include those of Zhwa lu and Jo nang. The former came to be favored in the dGe lugs pa school, and continues to be transmitted in that order today, above all by H. H. the Fourteenth Dalai Lama. The latter fell into decline in the wake of the suppression of the Jo nang pa sect during the seventeenth century, but was later revived in eastern Tibet, particularly by the proponents of the so-called Eclectic Movement (*Ris med*), during the nineteenth century.[12]

(8) rDo rje gsum gyi bsnyen sgrub, the "Service and Attainment of the Three Indestructible Realities," represents an extremely rare tradition, closely allied with the *Kālacakra Tantra*, and stemming

from the teaching of the divine Vajrayoginī, as gathered by the Tibetan *siddha* O rgyan pa Rin chen dpal (1230-1309) during his travels in the northwestern quarters of the Indian subcontinent. The teaching was popularized by O rgyan pa's successors during the fourteenth century, when several commentaries on it were composed, but subsequently seems to have lapsed into obscurity. O rgyan pa also figures prominently as a transmitter of several of the major bKa' brgyud lineages, notably the 'Brug pa and Karma pa traditions.[13]

During the nineteenth century this scheme of the "eight great conveyances" provided the basis for the great Tibetan anthology of *gdams ngag*, the *gDams ngag mdzod* ("The Store of Instructions"), compiled by 'Jam mgon kong sprul Blo gros mtha' yas (1813-1899), one of the leaders of the Eclectic Movement.[14] "The Store of Instructions" provides encyclopedic and balanced treatment of all of the major Tibetan Buddhist *gdams ngag* traditions and several of the more important minor ones, and preserves scores of instructional texts by some of the most famous Tibetan authors as well as by many who are less well-known. It includes in its compass entire previous collections of *gdams ngag* materials, such as the *Blo sbyong brgya rtsa* ("The Hundred [Teachings on] Spiritual Training and Purification"), representing the essential *gdams ngag* of the bKa' gdams traditions ('Jam mgon, *DNgDz*, vols. 2-3), and the *Jo nang khrid brgya dang brgyad* ("The Hundred and Eight Guidebooks of the Jo nang pas"), an eclectic compilation by Jo nang rje btsun Kun dga' grol mchog (1507-1566) that is in certain respects a precursor to "The Store of Instructions" itself (*DNgDz*, vol. 12).

Because all of the traditions mentioned above have generated abundant literature devoted to their own distinctive *gdams ngag*, including both texts immediately concerned with the details of practical instruction and systematic treatises that attempt to formulate the distinctive perspective of a particular *gdams ngag* tradition in its relation to Buddhist doctrine broadly speaking, it will not be possible to attempt to survey here the extraordinary volume of materials that are illustrative of these many differing traditions. Indeed, one may well wonder at this remarkable proliferation of the Tibetan technologies of the self: if, after all, the goal is in any case the achievement of buddhahood here and now, then why complicate matters by providing those who wish to follow the path with such a dizzying array of road maps? The traditional view is that, like a well-equipped pharmacy, the Buddha's teaching provides appropriate remedies for the many different afflictions of living beings; the myriad *gdams ngag* of Tibetan Buddhism may thus be seen to constitute a spiritual pharmacopeia. The medical analogy, however, by suggesting that, to a certain degree at least, eclecticism and pluralism are to be welcomed for the therapeutic enrichment they provide, points to a complicated cluster of problems: briefly, how is one to form a comprehensive vision of the totality of possible approaches to the path, that remains sufficiently critical to exclude false paths, without at the same time undermining the positive values of pluralism? Kong sprul's eclectic and even unitarian approach to the difficulties that arise here finds its complement in the attempt to elaborate and defend favored systems of *gdams ngag* through doctrinal apologetics, whether these be relatively catholic in outlook, or narrowly sectarian. *gDams ngag*, essentially the pithy expressions of contemplative experience, thus become the basis for renewed dogmatic system-building. This occurred very prominently in certain of the schools of Tibetan Buddhism—consider in this regard the massive philosophical elaboration of the Great Perfection (rDzogs chen) teachings of the rNying ma school,[15] or of the Great Seal (Mahāmudrā, Phyag chen) precepts of the several bKa' brgyud orders,[16] or of the originally bKa' gdams pa Path Sequence (Lam rim) instructions among rJe Tsong kha pa and his successors.[17] The products of these and other similar doctrinal syntheses certainly represent some of the most creative developments in the field of Tibetan Buddhist thought. The exploration of the many ramifications of such system-building, however, lies beyond the scope of this small contribution.

In order to provide the reader with a concrete example of the teaching of a particular tradition of *gdams ngag*, I give below, in the manner of an appendix, some short translated excerpts from "The Hundred and Eight Guidebooks of the Jo nang pas," concerning the history and the actual teaching of the practical dimension of the approach to Madhyamaka thought known as *dBu ma chen po* ("The Great Middle Way"). It is important to recall that *gdams ngag* traditions are not thought of ahistorically in Tibet: each such tradition has its unique origin, history of transmission, and relevance to a special historical setting. Thus, even a very terse historical note, such as the one given here, helps to situate a given *gdams ngag* for the Tibetan reader or auditor. The equally terse presentation of the teaching itself reflects what is in fact a series of rubrics, intended to guide an expanded course of oral explanation. The strictly maintained correlation between history and doctrine reinforces the role played by these instructions as the practical technologies of the self, for in a tradition's history we find the concrete exemplifications of the human ideals that are to be realized by one's submission to the course of training imposed by that same tradition's *gdams ngag*.[18]

I have chosen this particular extract to honor Geshe Lhundrup Sopa, to whom the present volume is dedicated, for Geshe-la has been a preeminent exponent of Madhyamaka thought throughout the nearly three decades that he has graced Buddhist Studies in the special setting of our own time and place. Those who have had the good fortune to study with him will no doubt supplement the topics briefly enumerated here with their own recollections of Geshe-la's learned expositions of related subject matter.

From the "History of the Hundred and Eight Guidebooks":

> Concerning the *dBu ma chen po'i khrid* ["The Guidance on the Great Middle Way"]: it was received by the bodhisattva Zla ba rgyal mtshan from the Newar Pe nya pa, one who belonged to the lineage of Nāgārjuna, father and son [i.e., Nāgārjuna and Āryadeva]. He taught it to rDzi lung pa 'Od zer grags pa, and he to Gro ston, who propounded it widely. There are some who hold that this was the lineage of the *dBu ma lta khrid* ["The Guidance on the View of the Middle Way"] that came to the venerable Re mda' ba from mNga' ris, in West Tibet, but that is uncertain. This is [also] called the *gZhung phyi mo'i dbu ma* ["The Middle Way according to the Original Texts," i.e., of Nāgārjuna and Āryadeva], and so is the ancient tradition, not yet divided into Prāsaṅgika and Svātantrika. That which is distinguished as the special doctrine of Red mda' ba, however, is the unblemished adherence to the Prāsaṅgika tradition, that follows the texts of the glorious Candrakīrti.[19]

From the "Text of the Hundred and Eight Guidebooks":

> *dBu ma chen po'i khrid yig* ["The Guidebook of the Great Middle Way"]: Concerning "The Guidance on the Great Middle Way": One begins by going for refuge and cultivating the enlightened attitude [*bodhicitta*]. Then, investigating the abiding nature of appearance and emptiness, appearance is [determined to be] just this unimpeded and ever-varied arising. As for the understanding of emptiness, however, it is neither the emptiness that

follows after a pot has been shattered, nor is it the emptiness that is like the pot's emptiness of being a blanket, nor is it the emptiness of sheer nothingness, like that of a hare's horn. It is, rather, self-presenting awareness's emptiness with respect to substantial essence at the very moment of appearance. And that, because it is empty of veridicality in terms of the relative, is apparition-like, and, because it is absolutely empty of essence, is sky-like. In brief, whatever the manner of appearance, there is not even so much as the tip of a hair that is veridically established. This is not the emptiness of [appearance's] cessation, nor the emptiness of the fabricated. It is precisely the emptiness that has reference to appearance itself.

When cultivating this experientially, you adopt the bodily disposition of the meditational posture. First you consciously strive somewhat [to recall and to concentrate upon the understanding of appearance and emptiness taught above]. In the end you relax [that deliberate striving]. Beginners should practice frequently in short sessions.

When you have thus cultivated the meditation, the three spiritual experiences of clarity, bliss and nonconceptuality arise. It will come about that mind will not grow excited about that at all, but will remain at ease, like the hand resting just where you place it. Your awareness becomes absorbed in simplicity, in the simple disposition of reality. (1) The inception of one-pointedness that remains unexcited with respect to [both] untarnished clarity of mind and circumstantial objects is called "tranquility" (*śamatha, zhi gnas*) while (2) its nonconceptual nature, like the circle of the sky that is free from apprehended referent, is called "insight" (*vipaśyanā, lhag mthong*). (3) Complete absorption is untouched by the intellect that apprehends objectives, and (4) your course of conduct involves the awareness of the qualities of dream and apparition in the aftermath [of meditative absorption]. You experientially cultivate [this teaching] in these four ways. When hairline discriminations of being and nonbeing forcefully arise, you gradually develop your skill, and it is said that in this way you will come to meet the face of that abiding nature that is unpolluted by the taints of the conceptual elaborations of the eight limitations.[20]

> The heart of all [*kun*] doctrines is the Great Middle Way:
> To delight [*dga'*] the wise, it is completely free [*grol*]
> From the range of unreflective and foolish meditations;
> It is the great path of supreme [*mchog*] freedom from
> limitations.[21]

This was compiled from the guide[book] of the bodhisattva Zla [ba] rgyal [mtshan].[22]

Notes

1. In Zhang (1985), vol. 2: 1343, *gdams ngag* is defined as *man ngag gam phan pa'i ngag, "man ngag*, or beneficial speech," while on p. 2056 *man ngag* is defined as *thabs kyi snying po'am thabs zab mo*, "the essence of a method, or a profound method." For examples of the use of *man ngag* to indicate a particularly esoteric instruction, in contrast to *gdams ngag*, note the special conventions of the rNying ma and bKa' gdams traditions, the first of which refers to its most esoteric teachings as forming the *man ngag gi sde*, "the class of esoteric precepts," while the latter distinguishes between *gdams ngag pa*, "the instructional tradition," and *man ngag pa*, "the esoteric precept tradition."

2. On the distinction between "sect" and "lineage," I have attempted to provide some clarification in Kapstein, 1980: 139. "By *sect*, I mean a religious order that is distinguished from others by virtue of its institutional independence; that is, its unique character is embodied outwardly in the form of an independent hierarchy and administration, independent properties and a recognizable membership of some sort. A *lineage* on the other hand is a continuous succession of spiritual teachers who have transmitted a given body of knowledge over a period of generations but who need not be affiliated with a common sect."

3. This phrase is, of course, borrowed from Foucault. Though this is not the place to explore the rich possibilities for comparative interpretation that are opened up by Foucault's analysis of the technologies for the care of the self in the West, readers of the present volume who are interested in such comparison may wish to consult Martin, et al., 1988. While East-West comparisons are not examined in this work, the broad range of Western spiritual disciplines that are discussed will be found to be highly suggestive.

4. Consider, for instance, the arrangement of the major sections of Roerich, 1976, in comparison with Kong sprul's approach. For different but overlapping approaches to the lineages and sects of Tibetan Buddhism, compare also: Jo nang rJe btsun Kun dga' grol mchog, et al., *Jo nang khrid brgya'i skor*, in 'Jam mgon, *DNgDz*, vol. 12; and Thu'u bkwan, 1984.

5. It should be noted that a great many representative *gdams ngag* texts have been translated into English in recent years, and have often been published privately or by small presses in popular editions for the use of English-speaking Buddhists. I have made no attempt in the notes that follow to treat this literature comprehensively. Interested readers are advised to consult the catalogues of the publishers that have been most active in this area: Dharma Publishing (Emeryville, California), The Library of Tibetan Works and Archives (Dharamsala), Rangjung Yeshe Publications (Hong Kong/Kathmandu), Shambhala (Boston), Snow Lion (Ithaca), Station Hill Press (Barrytown, New York), and Wisdom Publications (Boston). Those seeking a single, useful anthology of *gdams ngag* in English may wish to consult Stephen Batchelor, 1987. A somewhat dated but still interesting collection is Evans-Wentz, 1950. Brief surveys of some of the major traditions will be found in Tucci, 1980.

6. See also Roerich, 1976, Book II; *DNgDz*, vol. 1; *ShK*, vol. 1: 508-516; vol. 3: 276-296. Dudjom Rinpoche, 1991, provides, in vol. 1, thorough accounts of

rNying ma history and doctrine from a traditional perspective; and the bibliographies in vol. 2 document much of the Western language work on the rNying ma tradition, and also editions of original rNying ma texts.

7. See also Roerich, 1976, Book V; *DNgDz*, vols. 2-3; *ShK*, vol. 1: 516-520; vol. 3: 296-305; Chattopadhyaya, 1981; Eimer, 1982; Sherburne, 1983.

8. See also Roerich, 1976, Book IV; *DNgDz*, vol. 4; *ShK*, vol. 1: 520-526; vol. 3: 305-332; Davidson, 1981; Inaba, 1963.

9. Refer to Roerich, 1976, Book VIII; *DNgDz*, vols. 5-7; *ShK*, vol. 1: 526-533; vol. 3: 321-394. Among many works on the Mar pa bKa' brgyud traditions now available in English, see also: Chang, 1962, 1982; Douglas and White, 1976; Evans-Wentz, 1928, 1950; Guenther, 1963, 1971, 1973; Hanson, 1977; Kapstein, 1985; Karma Thinlay, 1978; Khenpo Rinpoche Konchog Gyaltsen, 1986; Lhalungpa, 1977, 1985; Nālandā Translation Committee, 1980, 1982; Stein, 1972.

10. See Roerich, 1976, Book IX; *DNgDz*, vol. 9; *ShK*, vol. 1: 533-538; vol. 3: 394-407: Kapstein, 1980, 1991; Mullin, 1985.

11. Roerich, 1976, Book IX; *DNgDz*, vol. 9; *ShK*, vol. 1: 538-548; vol. 3: 407-429. See also: Aziz, 1979, 1980; Gyatso, 1985. Allione, 1984, ch. 2, provides a popular introduction to the *gCod* tradition and its founder, Ma cig.

12. Roerich, 1976, Book X; *DNgDz*, vol. 10; *ShK*, vol. 1: 548-552; vol. 3: 429-457. Useful introductions to the Kālacakra traditions include: Sopa, et al., 1985; and The Dalai Lama and Hopkins, 1988. On the Zhwa lu and Jo nang pa traditions, see especially Ruegg, 1963, 1966.

13. Roerich, 1976: 696-702; *DNgDz*, vol. 10; *ShK*, vol. 1: 552-554; vol. 3: 457-461. On the life and travels of the *siddha* O rgyan pa, see also Tucci, 1940.

14. The finest introduction to the Eclectic Movement and its leaders remains Smith, 1970.

15. This is best exemplified in the work of Kun mkhyen Klong chen rab 'byams pa Dri med 'od zer (1308-1363), on whom see especially Dudjom Rinpoche, 1991: 575-596; Guenther, 1975-76; Thondup Rinpoche, 1989.

16. Scholastic systematization within the bKa' brgyud schools is well-exemplified by sGam po pa, translated in Guenther, 1971; and Dwags po bKra shis rnam rgyal, translated in Lhalungpa, 1985. Note that the general framework for the first mentioned is in fact derived from the *lam rim* traditions of the bKa' gdams tradition, in which sGam po pa was ordained. The syncretic tendencies of bKa' brgyud scholasticism are further discussed in Kapstein, 1985.

17. Refer to D. Jackson's article on *bsTan rim* literature in the present volume.

18. Cf. Dorje and Kapstein, Translators' Introduction to Dudjom Rinpoche, 1991, vol. 1, book 2.

19. Jo nang rJe btsun Kun dga' grol mchog, *Khrid brgya'i brgyud pa'i lo rgyus*, plates 320-321, in *DNgDz*, vol. 12. Zla ba rgyal mtshan, from whose teaching this tradition is derived, is best known among Tibetans for his contributions to the development of the traditions pertaining to the worship and meditation of the bodhisattva Avalokiteśvara. Red mda' ba (1349-1412) was a noted

scholar of the Sa skya pa sect, who was among the foremost teachers of rJe Tsong kha pa, and whose insistence on the authority of the Prāsaṅgika school of Madhyamaka interpretation was sometimes regarded as standing in complete opposition to those traditions that claimed adherence to the Great Middle Way.

20. Being, nonbeing, permanence, annihilation, arising, cessation, self and nonself.

21. The syllables given in Tibetan together form the author's name, which he has encoded in the closing verses of each of the 108 instructional texts of the *Jo nang khrid brgya* in this fashion.

22. Jo nang rje btsun Kun dga' grol mchog, *Zab khrid brgya dang brgyad kyi yi ge*, plates 389-390, in *DNgDz*, vol. 12.

References

Allione, Tsultrim

1984 *Women of Wisdom*. London: Routledge and Kegan Paul.

Aris, Michael, and Aung San Suu Kyi, eds.

1980 *Tibetan Studies in Honour of Hugh Richardson*. Warminster: Aris and Phillips.

Aziz, Barbara Nimri

1979 "Indian Philosopher as Tibetan Folk Hero." *Central Asiatic Journal* 23/ 1-2: 19-37.

1980 "The Work of Pha-dam-pa Sangs-rgyas as revealed in Ding-ri Folklore." In Aris and Aung, 1980: 21-29.

Aziz, Barbara Nimri, and Matthew Kapstein, eds.

1985 *Soundings in Tibetan Civilization*. New Delhi: Manohar.

Batchelor, Stephen, ed.

1987 *The Jewel in the Lotus*. Boston/London: Wisdom.

Chang, Garma Chen Chi

1962 *The Hundred Thousand Songs of Milarepa*. 2 vols. New Hyde Park, New York: University Books.

1982 *Esoteric Teachings of the Tibetan Tantra*. York Beach, Maine: Samuel Weiser.

Chāttopadhyāya, Ālakā

1981 *Atiśa and Tibet*. Second ed. Delhi: Motilal Banarsidass.

Dalai Lama [XIV] and Jeffrey Hopkins

1988 *Kalachakra Tantra: Rite of Initiation*. London: Wisdom.

Davidson, Ronald M.

1981 "The Ṅor-pa Tradition." *Wind Horse* 1: 79-98. Berkeley: Asian Humanities Press.

Douglas, Nik and Meryl White
1976 *Karmapa: The Black Hat Lama of Tibet*. London: Luzac.

Dudjom Rinpoche, Jigdrel Yeshe Dorje
1991 *The Nyingma School of Tibetan Buddhism: Its Fundamentals and History*. Trans. by Gyurme Dorje and Matthew Kapstein. Boston: Wisdom.

Eimer, Helmut
1982 "The Development of the Biographical Tradition Concerning Atiśa." *The Journal of the Tibet Society* 2: 41-51.

Evans-Wentz, W.Y., ed.
1928 *Milarepa*. Trans. by Kazi Dawa-Samdup. London: Oxford University Press.
1950 *Tibetan Yoga and Secret Doctrines*. London: Oxford University Press.

Guenther, Herbert V.
1963 *The Life and Teaching of Nāropa*. Oxford: Clarendon Press.
1971 *The Jewel Ornament of Liberation*. Berkeley: Shambhala.
1973 *The Royal Song of Saraha*. Berkeley: Shambhala.
1975-76 *Kindly Bent to Ease Us*. 3 vols. Emeryville, CA: Dharma Publishing.

Gyatso, Janet
1985 "A Preliminary Study of the Gcod Tradition." In Aziz and Kapstein, 1985: 320-341.

Hanson, Judith, trans.
1977 *The Torch of Certainty*. Boulder: Shambhala.

Inaba, Shoju
1963 "The Lineage of the Sa skya pa, A Chapter of the Red Annals." In *Memoirs of the Research Department of the Tōyō Bunko* 22: 106-123.

'Jam mgon kong sprul Blo gros mtha' yas
DNgDz *Gdams ṅag mdzod: A Treasury of Instructions and Techniques for Spiritual Realization*. 12 vols. Delhi: N. Lungtok and N. Gyaltsan, 1971.

Kapstein, Matthew
1980 "The Shangs-pa bKa'-brgyud: An Unknown Tradition of Tibetan Buddhism." In Aris and Aung, 1980: 138-144.
1985 "Religious Syncretism in 13th Century Tibet: The Limitless Ocean Cycle." In Aziz and Kapstein, 1985: 358-371.
1991 "The Illusion of Spiritual Progress." In *Paths to Liberation*. Ed. by Robert Buswell and Robert Gimello. Honolulu: University of Hawaii Press.

Karma Thinlay [Karma phrin las]
1978 *The History of the Sixteen Karmapas of Tibet*. Boulder: Shambhala.

Khenpo Rinpoche Konchog Gyaltsen with Katherine Rogers
1986 *The Garland of Mahamudra Practices*. Ithaca: Snow Lion.

Kong sprul Yon tan rgya mtsho ['Jam mgon kong sprul Blo gros mtha' yas]
ShK *Shes bya kun khyab*. 3 vols. Beijing: Mi rigs dpe skrun khang.

Lhalungpa, Lobsang, trans.
1977 *The Life of Milarepa*. New York: E. P. Dutton.
1985 *Mahāmudrā: The Quintessence of Mind and Meditation*. Boston: Shambhala.

Martin, Luther H., Huck Gutman, and Patrick Hutton, eds.
1988 *Technologies of the Self: A Seminar with Michel Foucault*. Amherst, MA: The University of Massachusetts Press.

Mullin, Glenn H.
1985 *The Tantric Yogas of Sister Niguma: Selected Works of the Second Dalai Lama*. Ithaca: Snow Lion.

Nālandā Translation Committee
1980 *The Rain of Wisdom*. Boulder: Shambhala.
1982 *The Life of Marpa the Translator*. Boulder: Prajñā Press.

Roerich, George, trans.
1976 *The Blue Annals*. Second ed. Delhi: Motilal Banarsidass.

Ruegg, David Seyfort
1963 "The Jo naṅ pas: A School of Buddhist Ontologists according to the Grub mtha' sel gyi me loṅ." *Journal of the American Oriental Society* 83: 73-91.
1966 *The Life of Bu ston Rin po che*. Rome: Istituto Italiano per il Medio ed Estremo Oriente.

Sopa, Geshe Lhundub, Roger Jackson and John Newman
1985 *The Wheel of Time: The Kalachakra in Context*. Madison, WI: Deer Park.

Sherburne, Richard, S. J., trans.
1983 *A Lamp for the Path to Enlightenment*. London: George Allen and Unwin, 1983.

Smith, E. Gene
1970 Introduction to *Kongtrul's Encyclopedia of Indo-Tibetan Culture*. New Delhi: Sarasvati Vihar.

Stein, Rolf A.

1972 *Vie et chants de 'Brug-pa Kun-legs le yogin.* Paris: Adrien-Maisonneuve.

Tatz, Mark

1987 "The Life of the Siddha-Philosopher Maitrīgupta." *Journal of the American Oriental Society* 107/4: 695-711.

Thondup Rinpoche, Tulku

1989 *Buddha Mind: An Anthology of Longchen Rabjam's Writings on Dzogpa Chenpo.* Ed. by Harold Talbott. Ithaca: Snow Lion.

Thu'u bkwan Blo bzang chos kyi nyi ma

1984 *Thu'u-bkwan grub-mtha'.* Lanzhou, Gansu: Mi rigs dpe skrun khang.

Tucci, Giuseppe

1940 *Travels of Tibetan Pilgrims in the Swat Valley.* Calcutta.

1980 *The Religions of Tibet.* Trans. by Geoffrey Samuel. Berkeley: University of California Press.

Zhang Yisun, ed.

1985 *Bod-rgya tshig-mdzod chen-mo.* 3 vols. Beijing: Mi rigs dpe skrun khang.

Chapter 17

Literature on Consecration (*Rab gnas*)[1]

Yael Bentor

Introduction

Indian and Tibetan works on consecration (*pratiṣṭhā, rab gnas*) of sacred objects such as stūpas and images are included by Tibetan authors within the general category of *cho ga* (*vidhi*), a term which might be very broadly translated "ritual" or "ritual method." Ritual texts constitute a significant part of nearly every Tibetan library. Furthermore, in the majority of Tibetan monasteries the performance of rituals is the principal undertaking of most monks. Even in monastic educational institutions monks devote part of their time to rituals. It should be emphasized that almost all forms of Tibetan meditation are highly ritualized and therefore fall within this category as well. Western scholarship, however, has not yet adequately reflected this Tibetan preoccupation with ritual.[2] The present study attempts to help fill this gap through a brief overview of the Tibetan consecration ritual and its literature.[3] Not only are consecrations one of the rituals most frequently performed by reincarnate lamas and abbots, they are also the means by which religious objects are made sacred or holy.

The Objects To Be Consecrated

Consecrated objects are classified, following one of the most fundamental Tibetan Buddhist classifications, into receptacles of the Buddha's body, speech and mind. The receptacles of the Buddha's body are images and *thang kas*; the receptacles of the Buddha's speech are books and *dhāraṇīs* (sacred formulae); and the receptacles of the Buddha's mind are stūpas and *tsha tshas* (see Tucci, 1932). Here, the word "receptacle" (*rten*) will be used, as the most general term, for all of these sacred objects.[4] Tibetan temples usually contain all three categories of receptacles. Laypeople usually try to have at least some representation for each of the three receptacles on the family altar, as well. In addition, there are also various minor objects which are consecrated in similar rituals.[5]

The Structure of the Consecration Ritual

The consecration ritual as such is not an autonomous entity, but constitutes a part of a larger system. In its elaborate version the consecration ritual is typically a matrix of five complete rituals. Some of the rituals in this matrix serve as frames within which the others are enclosed.[6] The largest frame consists of the *sādhana* (*sgrub thabs*, "means of accomplishment") (see Cozort in this volume, Kloppenborg, etc.) of the deity (*lha*)[7] invited into the receptacle. Only as a deity can the performers accomplish the ritual of inviting a deity into the receptacle in a consecration, or effect the purposes of most other Tibetan rituals. The *sādhana* is accompanied by the ritual of entering into a *maṇḍala* (*bdag 'jug*). The propitiation (*bskang gso*) (Ellingson: 677-775; Canzio) is performed as a smaller frame of the concluding rituals, while the fire offering (*homa, sbyin sreg*) (Sharpa, 1987; Skorupski, 1983b) is enclosed by the other rituals. Thus, a study of the consecration ritual requires reference to many others as well.

The Core of the Consecration

Not only is the consecration performed within the frame of the *sādhana*, it is, in fact, a special application of the *sādhana*. Having completed the generation process (*utpatti, bskyed pa*), one can apply one's powers to the generation of a receptacle as a deity (*rten bskyed*) through a similar method.

The main components at the core of the consecration ritual, common to almost all consecration manuals I have been able to examine, are as follows:[8]

(1) Visualizing the receptacle away (*mi dmigs pa*), always performed in conjunction with meditation on emptiness (*stong pa nyid*).

(2) Generation of the receptacle as the *dam tshig sems dpa'* (*samayasattva*) of one's *yi dam* (*rten bskyed*).
(3) Invitation of the *ye shes sems dpa'* (*jñānasattva*) into the receptacle (*spyan 'dren*), and its absorption (*bstim*) into the *dam tshig sems dpa'* (*dam ye gnyis su med pa*).
(4) Transformation of the receptacle back into its conventional appearance of an image, stūpa, book, etc. (*rten bsgyur*).
(5) Requesting the *ye shes sems dpa'* to remain in the receptacle as long as *saṃsāra* lasts (*brtan bzhugs*) (cf. Cabezón, in this volume).

The mode of transformation which renders the receptacle sacred in the first three steps is none other than the principal tantric ritual—the basis of the generation process, which is also variously applied according to the specific circumstances of each ritual. It is the tantric ritual *par excellence*.[9] Thus, in a process parallel to that of transforming oneself into one's chosen deity by means of a *sādhana* practice, or to that of generating a deity in front of oneself, or in a vase, the receptacle is transformed into the nature of *ye shes sems dpa'*. Through the fourth step, the deity invited to abide therein takes the appearance of that receptacle. It is no longer a conglomerate of profane substances but an embodiment of the deity. This process provides a very concise parallel to the perfection process (*saṃpannakrama, rdzogs rim*) of dissolution into nondual emptiness or clear light, and to the concluding step of *sādhana* practice, in which the practitioners emerge once more in the world as emanations of a buddha. 'Dul 'dzin Grags pa rgyal mtshan (1374-1434) explains this step as follows:

> ...think that the form of that deity [invited into the receptacle] is transformed completely and turns into the appearance of that cast image, painting and so forth.... With regard to books, think that sNang ba mtha' yas and his consort, having dissolved into light, transform into the form of letters. (378)[10]

The fifth step, which is specific to consecrations, does not involve a transformation in the receptacle.

The most crucial aspect of the consecration, as well as of most other tantric rituals—the nature of the *ye shes sems dpa'* invited into the receptacle—remains elusive. The tradition seems to be deliberately vague about this point. Usually the sets of terms used in relation to tantric practices are different from those employed in philosophical deliberations. While in the latter case there can be a thorough analysis of each element, many aspects of tantric practices are not treated in an analytical way. Any insight into the nature of the *ye shes sems dpa'* is assumed to be available only through demanding meditational practices. Even though the great majority of Tibetan monastic and lay people do not consider themselves capable of apprehending the exact nature of that which is embodied in a receptacle after consecration, they do possess some intuition that there is something sacred present there.[11] Like written works and the oral explanations of eminent teachers, ordinary people as well are not explicit about the nature of this presence. Some admit that they do not know. Yet, most Tibetan people act as if something is present in a consecrated receptacle, something which may bring blessings (*byin rlabs*) and good fortune (*bkra shis*).

The extent of the effects of this sacred presence is not everywhere uniform. A major stūpa such as Bodhanath in the Kathmandu Valley is considered more sacred than a private receptacle kept in the family home. This is due to the fact that Bodhanath Stūpa has served as a major pilgrimage site for many generations of Tibetan people and due to the large number of rituals performed at that locality by innumerable high lamas. These activities serve to augment the sacred nature of the stūpa. Furthermore, when one of two identical receptacles is consecrated by a lama of higher esteem it would be considered superior. Thus, that which is present in a receptacle does not depend solely on the consecration ritual in and of itself. The powers of high lamas or of the devotion of generations of pilgrims are also considered to be transmitted into specific receptacles.

Even though most Tibetan works are not very explicit with regard to the nature of the *ye shes sems dpa'*, they do characterize it by apparently contradictory qualities. On the one hand the *ye shes sems dpa'* is said to be similar (*'dra*) to the visualized *dam tshig sems dpa'*. In the very fundamental tantric process, practitioners first visualize the *yi dam*. Into this visualized deity, called the *dam tshig sems dpa'*, the *ye shes sems dpa'*, which is similar to it, is invited. The two are then fused into nonduality (*gnyis su med pa*). This process indicates that the *ye shes sems dpa'* resembles the *yi dam* which is visualized in one's mind. On the other hand, the *ye shes sems dpa'* is described as pervading the entire universe down to the tiniest particle with its presence (see below). Therefore, the meditator should realize that the invited *ye shes sems dpa'* is more than the visualized *yi dam*. Moreover, that which embodies the receptacle is not only the nonduality of the *ye shes sems dpa'* but the nonduality formed by the absorption of the *ye shes sems dpa'* into the *dam tshig sems dpa'*. Any use of concrete terms for that which is present in the receptacle would place limits on its sacred nature.

These two aspects of the *ye shes sems dpa'*, which correspond to the Form Body (*rūpakāya, gzugs sku*) and Dharma Body (*dharmakāya, chos sku*), are parallel also to the two major concepts, central to our understanding of consecrated receptacles, to be discussed under the two following headings.

The Receptacle as an Emanation of a Buddha

The entity invited to the receptacle is seen as one of the Form Bodies of a buddha. The following verse from the *Rab tu gnas pa mdor bsdus pa'i rgyud* ("Consecration Tantra"; *RNDG*) is recited in almost every consecration.

> As all the buddhas, from [their] abodes in Tuṣita heaven, entered the womb of Queen Māyā, likewise may you enter[12] this reflected image (*gzugs brnyan*). (*RNDG* sDe dge: 293-294)

A buddha is invited to abide in a receptacle in a manner reflecting the periodic birth of an Emanation Body (*nirmāṇakāya, sprul sku*) of the buddhas in the samsaric world according to the Mahāyāna conception. (This verse alludes also to the notion that a new receptacle is not created but "born.") Similarly, in the consecration work by Brag phug dGe bshes (b. 1926) the ritual master requests:

> May these receptacles consecrated by me, the *vajra* holder, having become receptacles of worship and loci of prostration for all beings, actually perform the actions of the Emanation Body of a buddha. (299-300)

Guru bKra shis distinguishes three types of Emanation Bodies.

> The supreme Emanation Bodies (*mchog gi sprul sku*) are those appearing in the world in the manner of the twelve deeds [of the Buddha]. The born Emanation Bodies (*skye ba sprul sku*) are those appearing as sentient beings in the manner of *āryas*, ordinary people, etc. Made Emanation Bodies (*bzo sprul sku*) are those appearing in an unanimated manner, such as stūpas, boats and bridges. (vol. 1: 128-129)

Here stūpas are classified as Emanation Bodies of the buddhas. Likewise most of the residents around Bodhanath Stūpa in Nepal consider that stūpa as a reincarnation. As an emanation of a buddha in its Form Bodies the receptacle acts for the sake of sentient beings. It "looks with a compassionate eye on the trainee (*gdul bya*) until the end of *saṃsāra*" (Gung thang: 102). It will create faith and devotion in those who see it and induce them to generate the mind of enlightenment (*bodhicitta, byang chub sems*) (*RNDG* sDe dge: 294). The presence of an emanation will be a source of blessing (*adhiṣṭhana, byin rlab*) for that locality, a cause of auspicious events (*maṅgala, bkra shis*) (rMor chen Kun dga' lhun grub: 537). As an emanation the receptacle not only acts for the sake of beings but also serves as a base for the accumulation of merit.

> As long as a king has not appeared in the capital, he does not possess any political power. Similarly, as long as the consecration is not completed, [the receptacle] is unworthy of worship.[13]

In sum, a receptacle serves to localize a certain emanation of one of the buddhas and bodhisattvas currently present in the world according to the Mahāyāna, thereby making them available for interaction with human beings.[14] It supplies a rather metaphysical Mahāyāna idea with a concrete sense.

Consecrations and the Ultimate Truth

Regarding the deity invited to embody the receptacle only as an Emanation Body would not pose problems of the kind discussed below. Yet, the entity invited and absorbed into the receptacle is conceived also in terms of the Dharma Body. A process of establishing the *ye shes sems dpa'* in a receptacle contradicts iṭs nature, something which cannot be established. This may be clarified in the following explanations of sDe srid Sangs rgyas rgya mtsho (1635-1705):

> The indivisible, secret and naturally immaculate *ye shes sems dpa'* of the body, speech and mind of all buddhas is as vast as space. The *ye shes* of the buddhas pervades everything, down to each of the countless particles, with holy nature. Therefore, there is nothing to invite from the outside. However, ordinary people [beginners] whose minds are inferior do not know it. (156)

And

> Everything compounded as *dharmas*, which are comprised of both the grasped and the grasper, the entire animated and unanimated three worlds, has from the very beginning reached the nature of clear light. The *ye shes sems dpa'*, which is not conditioned by another, abides pervading itself, as does the sesame oil in the sesame [seed]. This is known as naturally arrived-at establishing/consecration (*rab gnas*). (157)

The paradox of inviting the *ye shes sems dpa'*, which is omnipresent without ever being established, is dealt with in a number of consecration works. The following dialogue contained in the *RNDG* is an especially noteworthy example.

> The bodhisattvas asked: "O Blessed One! How do the Victorious Ones establish/consecrate (*rab gnas*) all the unestablished/unconsecrated (*rab tu mi gnas pa*) *dharmas*?"
>
> The Blessed One replied: "All the buddhas firmly abide without any establishing/consecration. [They] abide, as space does, in everything. The alternative viewpoint is false imputation (*rab tu brtags*). In the case of relative worldly truth there is the false imputation of establishing/consecration. When examined from the point of view of ultimate truth, who blesses what how? From the beginning [it was there] unproduced. So how could it be established/consecrated? This has been taught only as a basis for comprehension by sentient beings who have just set foot on the path." (*RNDG* sDe dge: 292-293)

The answer is given here in terms of the two truths. The notion of establishing a buddha in a receptacle exists only in relative truth. In ultimate truth, consecration is an impossibility. The theory of the two truths is applied here in order to harmonize ritual practice with certain theoretical positions. Since these answers are offered also by ritual manuals, it is likely that they would serve the point of view of ritualists, as will become evident below.

This position of the *RNDG* is taken up also by several renowned authors of consecration manuals. Grags pa rgyal mtshan (1147-1216) says:

> In ultimate truth, by performing consecration of the *tathāgata* image one does not make any improvement on it; by not performing it there is no impairment. Still, consecration was taught as a mere designation in conventional truth for the sake of increasing the virtue of the faithful. (*GKNT*: 53.2)

Thus, in ultimate truth the consecration has no effect. Its value is only for the devotee who perceives it in conventional truth. The standpoint of the *RNDG* with regard to the notion of establishing a buddha or a deity is not limited to this *tantra* alone. The consecration chapter of the *Dākārṇava Tantra* (*KGGT*) has the following:

> All the deities including the resident[s] of the *maṇḍala*, the holy Dharma, etc., are in the place of origination of all *dharmas*. In whatever abode they reside they are well established/consecrated at all times. (*KGGT* sDe dge: 395)

Similarly, the consecration chapter in the *Saṃvarodaya Tantra* (*DPBB*) says,

> The abiding of the established/consecrated deity should be in a manner free of conceptualization (or alternation, *nirvikalpa*) for the sake of the merit of a disciple who sincerely requests it. (*DPBB* sDe dge: 582-583)

According to these *tantras*, then, the purpose of a consecration is not the establishing of a deity in a receptacle, but accumulation of merit of the patron (*DPBB*) and development of religious realization by the beginners (*RNDG*). The latter point is made also by Atiśa (982-1054) who, in his frequently quoted consecration text in the bsTan 'gyur, says,

> The consecration is both necessary and unnecessary. When examined from the point of view of ultimate truth, who blesses what how? From the beginning [it was there] without birth and cessation; how could it be established/consecrated? Those who realize all *dharmas* as clear light do not need consecrations of objects of worship. Neither is it for those who have not realized emptiness but have realized that stūpas, books, images and so forth arise from blessing of emanations of the buddhas, and do no arise otherwise. If they have strong faith, a consecration is not necessary. For the beginners, the untrained, in relative truth, in worldly labels, for beings who do not know the real essence, the teacher taught consecration. (*KVCS* sDe dge: 510)

Similar arguments apply not only to consecration rituals but to any tantric ritual in which the *ye shes sems dpa'* is absorbed in the *dam tshig sems dpa'*, as the Bhutanese scholar Brag phug dGe bshes maintains:

> Now, if everything is of the nature of the *dharmakāya*, what absorbs into what? There is no objective sphere to be absorbed into. Therefore, if one asks: Is ritual also unnecessary? In ultimate truth that is just it. (254)

This view may be extended to any religious practice or concept, as Sa skya Paṇḍita (1182-1251) says in his *sDom gsum rab dbye*:

> Therefore, in ultimate truth, all phenomena being without mental elaborations, there is not any ritual there; when there is not even the Buddha himself, there is no need to mention any other ritual. All the classifications of the cause, the path and the result are relative truth. Individual liberation, mind of enlightenment, initiation and so forth, and to that extent also ritual and meditative visualization, as well as the whole profound interdependent origination, the classification of the ground and the path, and even obtaining perfect buddhahood, are relative truth and not ultimate truth. (307.1)

On the other hand, religious practice is possible only on the level of conventional truth. Furthermore, it is on the basis of such conventional practices that the ultimate truth can be attained.

> The absolute cannot be understood independently of general [Buddhist] practice (*vyavahāra*). Without the ladder of genuine relativity a wise man cannot ascend to the top of the palace of reality (*tattva*). (*Satyadvayāvatāra* 20, translated in Lindtner: 195)

This verse of Atiśa relies not only on Bhāvaviveka,[15] but also on Candrakīrti's *Madhyamakāvatāra* (VI, 80): "The relative truth functions as the means, the absolute truth functions as the goal" (Lindtner: 173), as well as on Nāgārjuna's *Mūlamadhyamakakārikā* (XXIV, 10): "The absolute cannot be taught unless one relies upon convention" (Lindtner: 187).

sDe srid Sangs rgyas rgya mtsho summarizes such positions with special reference to consecration:

> For people who realize the condition of ultimate truth which is without mental elaborations, for those who have completely passed beyond this great ocean of *saṃsāra*, any rituals such as consecration are definitely unnecessary. For beginners who have not realized this, the definite necessity of rituals and so forth should be made known. With regard to the two truths consecration is both necessary and not necessary. (158)

Thus, consecration is explained as a process of the localization of the omnipresent "divine power" for the sake of those who do not realize its true nature. It is not an easy matter to perceive the omnipresent nature of the Dharma Body, or to regard the entire universe as sacred. One prefers to confine the ultimate powers in certain identifiable places. The consecration ritual serves this purpose. For the great majority of the Tibetan Buddhist community who have not achieved enlightenment and, in fact, do not consider themselves to be close to that goal, the implication of these theoretical positions is that consecrations *are* necessary. Therefore, having explained the consecration on both levels, the *tantras* and writers quoted above proceed to discuss the consecration ritual in detail.

In conclusion, since the consecration ritual suggests the possibility of making the *dharmakāya* available on a mundane level, this raises questions about its congruency with theoretical conceptions of reality as it is, in which actions such as establishing or transforming do not occur. Nonetheless, the application of the theory of the two truths not only serves to solve the apparent contradiction between the main purpose of consecration and the true nature of reality, it even underlines the need for performing consecrations.[16] Such theoretical considerations serve to justify not only the view of receptacles benefiting the believer on the level of relative truth, by serving as basis for realization of Buddhist ideas and accumulation of merit, but also the idea of the actual presence of a buddha in stūpas or images, since this may serve the same purpose for the believer.

The Consecration Literature

The consecration ritual derives its scriptural authority from the *RNDG*, preserved only in Tibetan, from chapters on consecration in the *Saṃvarodaya* (ch. 22), *Hevajra* (ch. II, i), *Ḍākārṇava* (ch. 25), *Caturyoginī* (ch. 5), and *Abhidhānottara* (ch. 48) *Tantras*, from a short reference in the *Vajra Pañjara Tantra* (ch. 9 and in the concluding part), as well as from the consecration chapter of the *Heruka gal po* (*HGPC*) (ch. 21) found in the *rNying ma'i rgyud 'bum*. Even though *tantras* are not ritual manuals, most of the components of the Tibetan consecration ritual do appear in some form at least in the *RNDG*, and in the consecration chapters in the *Saṃvarodaya* and *HGPC Tantras*. Additional scriptural authority for the Tibetan consecration is derived from some thirty Indian works contained in the Tibetan bsTan 'gyur wholly or partly devoted to consecration.[17]

There are over two hundred Tibetan works on consecration, which belong mostly to two major groups. The majority are ritual manuals containing prescriptions (but very few explanations) composed since the twelfth century. To a second group belong more than a dozen explanatory works on consecration, a relatively late genre which developed during the Tibetan "renaissance" of the seventeenth century. A few works combine both prescriptions and explanations. This high number of consecration works composed by Tibet's most revered lamas is a good indication of both the prevalence and importance attached to this ritual. Most of these works were composed for a particular consecration performed by its author. Later these would also be used by their disciples. In composing consecration works, authors relied closely on previous works of the same sort, the result being that most of these works, especially those of a certain lineage, are quite similar. However, it is important to note that this system also leaves a small door open for innovations based on reasoning (*rtogs*).[18]

Neither the consecration manuals nor the explanatory works are concerned with the meaning of ritual actions. These actions derive their *raison d'être* from their occurrence in the scriptures. Even a vague allusion will suffice for such an authority. Only on very rare occasions is a rationale for a certain action suggested. Consecration in its elaborate form includes an explanation for the sake of the patron, and some of the explanatory works were written for such occasions.[19] The audience for these works, therefore, are not only ritual masters, but also the majority of lay and monastic people present at the consecration. The explanatory works emphasize the merit accumulated through the erection and consecration of receptacles, and, likewise, the faults of not doing so. Following a short reference in the *RNDG*, they discuss the qualities required of the ritual master, the proper time and place for consecrations, and the receptacles worthy of consecration. They frequently contain histories of images and stūpas, especially the first images and stūpas in India and Tibet. Certain explanatory works[20] also discuss the origin of consecration, that is to say, their occurrence in the scriptures and accounts of the first consecrations in Tibet, especially that of bSam yas, the first Tibetan monastery. Some speak of the essence (*ngo bo*) of consecration, its etymology (*nges tshig* and *sgra don*), etc. Such discussions are useful for our understanding of the Tibetan presentation of the consecration ritual.

Consecration manuals are written for an audience of ritual specialists who are intimately familiar with both ritual theories and their fine details. They contain a large number of special and technical terms. Since performers have memorized a considerable number of ritual recitations, the manuals often mention only the first few words of a set of verses or *mantras*.

Ancillary Rituals

So far, only the core of the consecration ritual has been discussed. To the rituals of establishing the *ye shes sems dpa'* in the receptacle are appended various ancillary rituals, some of which seem to be earlier independent forms of consecration that lost their prominence when the tantric ritual became prevalent. Among these are the eye opening (*spyan dbye*), bathing (*khrus gsol*), enthronement offerings (*mnga' 'bul*) and recitation of the verse of interdependent origination.[21] Rather then being supplanted, they were incorporated into the tantric ritual of consecration, but with a secondary importance.

The Place of the Consecration Among the Rituals Performed for Receptacles

A number of rituals accompany the construction of Tibetan receptacles. These open, prior to the beginning of the construction of the receptacle, with a ground ritual (*sa chog*) for procuring and blessing the site (Gyatsho; mKhas grub rje: 278-285). During the construction, the ritual of depositing the relics or *dhāraṇīs* is performed (*gzungs gzhug* or *gzungs 'bul*) (Gyalzur, Kalsang, Dagyab). Only upon the completion of the receptacle does the consecration ritual (*pratiṣṭhā, rab gnas*) per se take place. Consecration may by repeated on an annual basis or upon the visit of a high lama, who is often requested to reconsecrate existing receptacles. When a receptacle requires considerable restoration a ritual called *arga*[22] is performed in which the deity that was invited to abide in the receptacle through the consecration ritual is requested to reside temporarily in a specially prepared mirror for the duration of the restoration (Gyatsho, Manen).

The Deposition of Relics

Space does not allow me to discuss here this manifold of ancillary and accompanying rituals.[23] Instead, I would like to comment on the relation between the insertion of relics and the final consecration of a receptacle.

In his discussion of consecration, Tucci says:

> It [consecration] takes the place of that 'life' (*jīvita*, say the pāli sources) which introduced into the *mc'od rten* either some part

> of the Master's body, like his nails or hair, or an object which had come in contact with him, like a piece of his dress, or relics which, becoming transformed into a magic replica of the Saint himself bound his mysterious presence to that monument or that image. (1949: 313)

It is unlikely that the consecration would "take the place" of a cult so deeply rooted in Buddhism as the relic cult,[24] and, indeed, it does not. Earlier consecration manuals, such as those by Abhayākaragupta (1064?-1125?) or Grags pa rgyal mtshan (*RNDS*), include rituals of both deposition of relics and consecration. Later manuals are usually devoted to only one of these subjects. Tucci, basing his discussion on a consecration work by the first Paṇ chen Lama (1570-1662) which treats only the final consecration, overlooked the literature on the deposition of relics. During my field work in Nepal in 1987-89 I saw instances in which the consecration was neglected or postponed,[25] but the deposition of relics was never omitted.

Very rarely do Tibetan rituals completely supplant their earlier forms. Typically, Tibetan rituals are an assemblage of various rituals of different ages with the more recent tantric version assuming a central position. Among such ritual assemblages are initiations (Snellgrove, 1987: 228-235), fire offerings (which include Vedic elements), ground rituals, consecrations, etc.[26] Thus, although the insertion of relics historically preceded the consecration ritual as it is described here, it is still incorporated, and in a more elaborate form, in the ritual as it has been practiced until today by Tibetans. It is precisely this historical dimension that has yet to receive the attention it deserves. As Blondeau and Karmay have said on investigations of Tibetan rituals:

> No study has been published until now on the historical origins of a rite, its transformation in time, and its variations from one tradition to another. If such a study would be carried out, it would allow us, perhaps, to uncover the process of assimilation and the successive additions which build rituals such as those observed nowadays.[27] (122)

Conclusions

Through the consecration ritual a receptacle is transformed into an embodiment of one's chosen deity. Like a buddha the receptacle is endowed with the nondual emptiness of *dharmakāya*, while functioning in the world as a Form Body. The consecration ritual complements, and does not replace, the infusion of a receptacle with "divine power" or the presence of the buddha through the insertion of relics. Even though on the theoretical level the *dharmakāya* cannot be localized, through the employment of the theory of the two truths such a process of localization becomes indispensable. Indeed, on the practical level consecrations are among the most popular rituals for both lay and monastic people. The dichotomy frequently made between "official" and "popular" religion enters a different dimension here. Consecrated receptacles are viewed both as actual emanations of buddhas and as bases for realization of Buddhist ideas and accumulation of merit on the level of relative truth. Both concepts coexist in practice as well as in theory.

Notes

1. I would like to thank Gregory Schopen and Dan Martin for their valuable comments on earlier versions of this paper; and the Fulbright-Hays Doctoral Dissertation Research Abroad Program, the William and Flora Hewlett Foundation and Henry Luce Foundation (administrated through the Social Science Research Council) for their generous support of my research in Nepal during 1987-89.

2. The most comprehensive study of Tibetan ritual is that of Beyer. Previous inquiries were undertaken by Snellgrove (1957) and Lessing. For recent works see Blondeau and Karmay, Buffetrille, Ellingson, Kohn, Kvaerne, Skorupski (1986), etc.

3. It is interesting to note that almost all the literature on consecration that exists in Western languages is written by Tibetans. Such are the works by Paṇchen Ötrul, Dagyab, Sharpa Tulku, Gyatsho, Gyalzur (in collaboration with Verwey) and Manen (translation of Phun tshog). The only extended discussion by a non-Tibetan is by Tucci (1949). There is also a dissertation on this subject by Schwalbe, although he did not directly utilize Tibetan literary sources. Finally, A. David-Neel wrote on the consecration ritual mainly in order to demonstrate that, in fact, it is not nearly so "primitive" as it may seem.

4. This classification of receptacles is found also in works which seem to be of Indian origin contained in the Tibetan bKa' 'gyur, for example, in Atiśa's consecration work.

5. Such as amulets (see Skorupski, 1983a), which also are receptacles of relics, paintings of deities, *dhāraṇīs*, protective wheels (*srung 'khor*), etc. Also, *vajra* and bell, counting rosaries, victory banners (*rgyal mtshan*), etc. may be

consecrated. Some works, such as those by Nag po pa (559-560), Abhayākaragupta (129-131) and the First 'Jam dbyangs bzhad pa mention also consecrations of pools, wells, groves, etc. (671). However, these consecrations seem to be confined to recitation of verses of auspiciousness and the verse of interdependent origination (see Bentor, 1992). A deity cannot be invited to abide in ordinary objects (Ngag dbang blo gros: 494). There is also a Tibetan text for the consecration of a bridge by dByangs can grub pa'i rdo rje; unfortunately, it is not yet available to me.

6. Witzel and Minkowski have suggested that the origin of the "frame story" common in the Indian epic may be found in such ritual structures.

7. For one, but not the only, view on the concept of deity in Tibetan Buddhism see Tsong kha pa, 1977 and 1981, etc. It should be emphasized that the word *deity* is an inadequate translation of *lha* or *deva*.

8. The first three and the last steps outlined below appear in almost every manual consulted. The fourth step is, however, occasionally absent.

9. Kohn: 152. Still, a distinction should be made between transformations brought about through one's chosen deity in *sādhana* practice or in rituals such as initiation, consecration etc., on one hand, and between empowering offerings and substitutes (*glud*) on the other.

10. According to the lower *tantras* when images are consecrated, Akṣobhya (or Vajrasattva) is established therein; when books are consecrated, Amitābha; and when stūpas and temples are consecrated, Vairocana. See Abhayākaragupta, sDe dge: 126-127; 'Jam dpal bshes gnyen, sDe dge: 72; *HGPC*: 329; Kun dga' snying po, 47.4; Grags pa rgyal mtshan, *RNDS*: 159; Paṇ chen Lama I: 825; sDe srid: 241-242; Kong sprul: 119; Brag phug: 237; Ngag dbang blo gros: 489-494. There are, of course, variations among these works. The lords (*gtso bo*) of the three families, the *tathāgatas* Akṣobhya (Mi 'khrugs), Amitābha ('Od dpag med), and Vairocana (rNam par snang mdzad), correspond to the aspects of body, speech and mind respectively. Akṣobhya and Vairocana, however, often interchange. Consecration rituals may have belonged to the lower *tantras* before they were adopted by the Highest Yoga Tantra. In recent centuries, however, the *yi dam* invited to abide in the receptacle belongs to the Highest Yoga Tantra, such as rDo rje sems dpa' (Vajrasattva), rDo rje 'jigs byed (Vajrabhairava), Kye rdo rje (Hevajra), and bDe mchog (Cakrasaṃvara). In a number of consecration works Śākyamuni Buddha is invited to abide in the receptacle and in some of these instances the ritual is designated by the controversial term "*sūtra*-style consecration" (*mdo lugs rab gnas* or *pha rol tu phyin pa'i lugs rab gnas*) (see Bentor, 1992).

11. For a succinct description of the "presence" in images see Cabezón and Tendar (138).

12. While the sTog Palace edition has "may you enter (*zhugs*) this reflected image" (745), the sDe dge and Peking (122.3) editions give "may you abide (*bzhugs*)."

13. This is cited by Grags pa rgyal mtshan (*RNDS*: 246.1) (Sa skya pa). Similar passages are found in gTer bdag gling pa (*LSRT*: 16) (rNying ma pa) and Brag phug dge bshes (242) (bKa' brgyud pa).

14. Compare to Hindu images which are considered to be *avatāras* of Hindu deities (Eck: 35 and passim).

15. The statement of Bhāvaviveka that gave rise to this verse is the central theme of Eckel's *To See the Buddha* (1992).

16. Such passages articulating the point of view of ultimate truth are not limited to Tibetan sources. For similar passages found in Mahāyāna *sutras*, see, for example, Snellgrove, 1987: 37 and Lancaster: 289.

17. A bibliography of these works, as well as a selected bibliography of Tibetan works on consecration, deposition of relics, and *arga* rituals is included in Bentor, 1991.

18. An example for such an innovation is found in the consecration work by Brag phug dge bshes (265-292) who, like other Tibetan scholars, was puzzled by the necessity to initiate the deity invited to the receptacle as if it were a disciple.

19. See rMor chen (Sa skya pa); gTer bdag gling pa, *YDGB* (rNying ma pa); Dad pa mkhan po (dGe lugs pa); Phrin las rgya mtsho (bKa' brgyud pa/ Ris med), etc.

20. Such as Padma phrin las; sDe srid Sangs rgyas rgya mtsho; and gTer bdag gling pa, *LSRT*.

21. *Ye dharmā hetuprabhavā hetuṃ teṣāṃ tathāgato hy avadat teṣāṃ ca yo nirodha evaṃ vādī mahāśramaṇaḥ.*

22. This *arga* ritual should not to be confused with the offering of *argha* water (*mchod yon* or *yon chab*), the first water offered to an invited deity.

23. For further details on these rituals see Bentor, 1991.

24. The relic cult plays a very important role in Buddhism as was noted, for example, by Snellgrove: "There were certainly pure philosophical doctrines propounded during the early history of Buddhism, just as there have been ever since, but there is no such thing as pure Buddhism per se except perhaps the cult of Śākyamuni as a supramundane being and the cult of the relic stūpa" (1973: 411).

25. This was for a variety of reasons. The rationale allowing it is based on the fact that an already consecrated image is deposited inside the larger receptacle (see Kong sprul: 104).

26. This topic is further discussed in Bentor, 1991 and 1992.

27. My translation. In Bentor, 1992 I have attempted to trace the historical development of one aspect of the consecration ritual.

References

Abhayākaragupta

VNMU *Vajrāvalīnāmamaṇḍalopāyikā* (*dKyil 'khor gyi cho ga rdo rje phreng ba zhes bya ba*). Toh. no. 3140; P. no. 3961; sDe dge, vol. 75, esp. pp. 113-131.

Atiśa

KVCS *Kāyavākcittasupratiṣṭhānāma (Sku dang gsung dang thugs rab tu gnas pa zhes bya ba)*. Toh. no. 2496; P. no. 3322; sDe dge, vol. 53, pp. 508-519.

Bentor, Yael

1988 "The Redactions of the *Adbhutadharmaparyāya* from Gilgit." *The Journal of the International Association of Buddhist Studies* 11/2: 21-52.

1991 "The Indo-Tibetan Buddhist Consecration Ritual for Stūpas, Images, Books and Temples." Ph.D. dissertation. Bloomington: Indiana University.

1992 "*Sūtra*-style Consecration in Tibet and Its Importance for Understanding the Historical Development of the Indo-Tibetan Consecration Ritual for *Stūpas* and Images." *Tibetan Studies: Proceedings of the 5th Seminar of the International Association for Tibetan Studies, Narita, 1989*, pp.1-12. Narita: Naritasan Shinshoji.

Beyer, Stephan

1973 *The Cult of Tārā: Magic and Ritual in Tibet*. Berkeley: University of California Press.

Blondeau, Anne-Marie and Samten G. Karmay

1988 "'Le cerf à la vaste ramure': en guise d'introduction." In *Essais sur le rituel*, pp. 119-146. Ed. by Anne-Marie Blondeau and Kristofer Schipper. Louvain-Paris: Peeters.

Brag phug dGe bshes dGe 'dun rin chen

RNGP *bDe mchog bcu gsum ma dang sbyar ba'i rab gnas shin tu rgyas pa rgyud lung man ngag gi bang mdzod (rab gnas rgyas pa)*. In *Rituals of the Thirteen Deity Maṇḍala of Cakrasamvara of the Bhutanese Tradition*, vol. 1, pp. 187-361. Thimphu: 1978. Also in his *Collected Works*, vol. 5, pp. 453-627. Mandi, H.P.: 1985.

Bu ston Rin chen grub

NBRN *rNal 'byor rgyud dang mthun ba'i rab gnas kyi cho ga bkra shis rab tu gnas pa*. In *Collected Works*, vol. 12, pp. 479-541. New Delhi: 1968.

Buffetrille, Katia

1987 "Un rituel de mariage tibétain." *L'Ethnographie* 83/100-101: 35-62.

Cabeźon, José and Geshe Thubten Tendar

1990 "The Thangka According to Tradition." In *White Lotus*, pp. 133-138. Ed. by Carole Elchert. Ithaca: Snow Lion.

Canzio, Riccardo

1988 "Etude d'une ceremonie de propitiation Bonpo: Le *Nag-zhig bskang-ba*: structure et exécution." In *Essais sur le rituel*, pp. 159-

172. Ed. by Anne-Marie Blondeau and Kristofer Schipper. Louvain-Paris: Peeters.

Dad pa mkhan po Blo bzang thugs rje
RNSP *Rab gnas chen mo'i skabs kyi bshad pa bya tshul 'dod rgu'i dpal ster.* In *Collected Works*, pp. 65d-73d. New-Delhi: 1976.

Dagyab, Loden Sherap
1977 *Tibetan Religious Art.* 2 vols. Wiesbaden: Otto Harrassowitz.

The Ḍākārṇava Tantra: Śrīḍākārṇavamahāyoginītantrarājanāma (chapter 25)
KGGT Toh. no. 372, sDe dge, vol. 78, pp. 394-397; P. no. 19, vol. 2, pp. 174.3.1-175.1.4. sTog Palace, no. 337, vol. 93, pp. 160-164.

David-Neel, Alexandra
1945 "The Tibetan Lamaist Rite Called Rab Nes Intended to Cause Inanimate Objects to Become Efficient." *Journal of the West China Border Research Society* [Chengdu] 16: 88-94.

dByangs can grub pa'i rdo rje
ZPRN *Zam pa rab gnas bya tshul 'gyur med rdo rje'i lhun po.* In *Collected Works*, vol. *ga*, 5 fols. [found in the Tōhoku University Collection of Tibetan Works].

'Dul 'dzin grags pa rgyal mtshan
RNZB *Rab gnas rgyas ba'i zin bris.* In *Collected Works of Tsong kha pa*, vol. 13, pp. 337-407. New Delhi: 1979.

Eck, Diana L.
1981 *Darśan: Seeing the Divine Image in India.* Chambersburg: Anima Books.

Eckel, Malcolm David
1992 *To See the Buddha.* San Francisco: HarperSanFrancisco.

Ellingson, Terry Jay
1979 "The Maṇḍala of Sound: Concepts and Sound Structures in Tibetan Ritual Music." Ph.D. dissertation. Madison: University of Wisconsin-Madison.

Grags pa rgyal mtshan
GKNT *rGyud kyi mngon par rtogs pa rin po che'i ljon shing.* In *The Complete Works of the Great Masters of the Sa Skya Sect of the Tibetan Buddhism*, vol. 3, pp. 1.1-70.1. Tokyo: Tōyō Bunko, 1968.
RNDS *Arga'i cho ga dang rab tu gnas pa don gsal ba.* In *The Complete Works of the Great Masters of the Sa Skya Sect of the Tibetan Buddhism*, vol. 4, pp. 237-252. Tokyo: Tōyō Bunko, 1968.

gTer bdag gling pa 'Gyur med rdo rje
LSRT *sKu gsung thugs kyi rten rab tu gnas pa'i cho ga rgyud dang man ngag gi don rab tu 'char bar byed pa'i 'grel byed legs par bshad pa'i*

rol mtsho. In *Methods for the Consecration and Vivification of Buddhist Icons, Books and Stūpas*, pp. 1-36 [first text]. Tashijong, Palampur: 1970.

YDGB *Rab gnas dge legs 'dod 'jo'i yon bdag bsgo ba'i stong thun nyer mkho*. In *Methods for the Consecration and Vivification of Buddhist Icons, Books and Stūpas*, pp. 1-19 [second text]. Tashijong, Palampur: 1970. Also in the *Rin chen gter mdzod*, vol. 66, pp. 329-352 (Paro: 1976), and in *rNying ma bka' ma rgyas pa*, vol. 2, pp. 125-153 (Darjeeling: 1982-83) .

Gung thang pa, dKon mchog bstan pa'i sgron me

RNLG *Rab gnas kyi lo rgyus gtso bor gyur pa'i bshad pa*. In *Collected Works*, vol. 8, pp. 95-109. New Delhi: 1975.

Guru bKra shis

NTRM *bsTan pa'i snying po gsang chen snga 'gyur nges don zab mo'i chos kyi 'byung ba gsal bar byed pa'i legs bshad mkhas pa dga' byed ngo mtshar gtam gyi rol mtsho* (*Chos 'byung ngo mtshar gtam gyi rol mtsho*.) 5 vols. Delhi: 1986.

Gyalzur, Losang Paldhen and Antony H. N. Verwey

1983 "Spells on the Life-wood: An Introduction to the Tibetan Buddhist Ceremony of Consecration." In *Selected Studies on Ritual in the Indian Religions*, pp. 169-196. Ed. by Ria Kloppenborg. Leiden: E. J. Brill.

Gyatsho, Thubten Legshay

1979 "Chos kyi dus ston bya stangs las rab gnas bya tshul." In *Gateway to the Temple*, pp. 73-75. Trans. by David Paul Jackson. Kathmandu: Ratna Pustak Bhandar.

Heruka'i gal po chen po

HGPC *dPal khrag 'thung gal po che (Śrī Heruka-tanadu)*. In *rNying ma'i rgyud 'bum*, vol. 25, ch. 21. Thimphu: 1973.

'Jam dbyangs bzhad pa I, Ngag dbang brtson 'grus

RNSP *Rab gnas kyi bshad pa kun mkhyen chen po 'Jam dbyangs bzhad pa'i rdo rjes mdzad par grags pa*. In *Collected Works*, vol. 4, pp. 667-680. New Delhi: 1972.

'Jam dpal bshes gnyen

JPPB *Āryamañjuśrīnāmasaṃgīticakṣuvidhi ('Phags pa 'Jam dpal gyi mtshan yang dag par brjod pa'i spyan dbye pa'i cho ga)*. Colophon title: "'Phags pa 'Jam dpal gyi mtshan yang dag par brjod pa'i rab tu gnas pa'i cho ga." Toh. no. 2573; P. no. 3400; sDe dge, vol. 65, pp. 68-74.

Kalsang, Jampa

1969 "Grundsätzliches zur Füllung von Mc'od rten." *Zentralasiatische Studien* 3: 51-53.

Kloppenborg, Ria and Ronald Poelmeyer

1987 "Visualizations in Buddhist Meditation." In *Effigies Dei: Essays on the History of Religions*, pp. 83-95. Ed. by Dirk van der Plas. Leiden: E. J. Brill.

Kohn, Richard Jay

1988 "Mani Rimdu: Text and Tradition in a Tibetan Ritual." Ph.D. dissertation. Madison: University of Wisconsin-Madison.

Kong sprul Blo gros mtha' yas, 'Jam mgon

TNZB *rTen la nang gzhug 'bul ba'i lag len lugs srol kun gsal dri bral nor bu chu shel gyi me long*. In *Collected Works*, vol. 12, pp. 97-148. Paro: 1975.

Kun dga' snying po

KDKG *dPal Kyai rdo rje'i rtsa ba'i rgyud brtag pa gnyis pa'i dka' 'grel man ngag don gsal*. In *The Complete Works of the Great Masters of the Sa Skya Sect of the Tibetan Buddhism*, vol. 1, pp. 66-78. Tokyo: Tōyō Bunko, 1968.

Kvaerne, Per

1988 "Le rituel tibétain, illustré par l'evocation, dans la religion Bon-po, du 'Lion de la parole'." In *Essais sur le rituel*, pp. 147-158. Ed. by Anne-Marie Blondeau and Kristofer Schipper. Louvain-Paris: Peeters.

Lancaster, Lewis R.

1974 "An Early Mahayana Sermon about the Body of the Buddha and the Making of Images." *Artibus Asiae* 36: 287-291.

Lessing, Ferdinand D.

1976 *Ritual and Symbol: Collected Essays on Lamaism and Chinese Symbolism*. Taipei: The Chinese Association for Folklore.

Lindtner, Chr.

1981 "Atiśa's Introduction to the Two Truths, and its Sources." *Journal of Indian Philosophy* 9: 161-214.

van Manen, Johan

1933 "On Making Earthen Images, Repairing Old Images & Drawing Scroll-pictures in Tibet." *Journal of Indian Society of Oriental Art* 1: 105-111.

Minkowski, C. Z.

1989 "Janamejaya's Sattra and Ritual Structure." *Journal of the Oriental American Society* 109: 401-420.

mKhas grub rje

1968 *Mkhas Grub Rje's Fundamentals of the Buddhist Tantras*. Translated by Ferdinand D. Lessing and Alex Wayman. The Hague: Mouton.

Nag po pa

Pratiṣṭhāvidhi (Rab gnas kyi cho ga'i tshul). Toh. no. 1257; P. no. 2386; sDe dge, vol. 9, pp. 559-564.

Ngag dbang blo gros snying po gzhan phan mtha' yas pa'i 'od zer

PBGT *dPal kye rdo rje'i rnal 'byor la brten pa'i rab gnas mdor bsdus pa dpal 'byor rgya mtsho srub skyes lha'i bcud len.* In *rGyud sde kun btus,* vol. 29, pp. 577-615. Ed. by bLo gter dbang po. Delhi: 1972. Also in *Lam 'bras tshogs bshad,* vol. 6, pp. 483-521. Dehra Dun, H.P.: 1985.

Ötrul, Paṇ chen Rinpoche

1987 "The Consecration Ritual (Rabney)." *Chö Yang* 1/2: 53-64.

Padma 'phrin las rDo rje brag rig 'dzin

GDGT *Rab tu gnas pa'i rnam par nges pa rgyud don rgya mtsho gsal bar byed pa nor bu'i snying po.* In *Rituals of rDo rje brag,* vol. 1, pp. 1-285. Leh: 1973.

Paṇ chen Lama I, Blo bzang chos kyi rgyal mtshan

GLGT *Rab tu gnas pa'i cho ga lag len du dril ba dge legs rgya mtsho'i char 'bebs.* In *Collected Works,* vol. 4, pp. 813-874. New Delhi: 1973.

Phrin las rgya mtsho, sGrub sde sprul sku

YGTT *Rab gnas yon bsgo'i skabs kyi stong thung (gtong thun) 'jug bde phun tshogs bkra shis cha brgyad.* In *Rab gnas rgyas bshad,* pp. 63-88. Tashijong, Palampur: 1970.

Rab tu gnas pa mdor bsdus pa'i rgyud (Supratiṣṭhātantrasaṃgraha)

RNDG Toh. no. 486; P. no. 118; sDe dge, vol. 85, pp. 292-299; sTog Palace, vol. 98, pp. 742-752.

rMor chen Kun dga' lhun grub

YGSP *Rab gnas kyi yon bsgo'i bshad pa legs bshad 'od kyi snye ma.* In *sGrub thabs kun btus,* vol. 13, pp. 535-545. Dehradun, U.P.: 1970.

Sa skya Paṇḍita Kun dga' rgyal mtshan

DSRY *sDom pa gsum gyi rab tu dbye ba.* In *The Complete Works of the Great Masters of the Sa Skya Sect of the Tibetan Buddhism,* vol. 5, pp. 297.1-320.4. Tokyo: Tōyō Bunko: 1968. (Also published separately.)

The Saṃvarodaya Tantra: Śrīmahāsambarodayatantrarājanāma (chapter 22)

DPBB Toh. no 373; sDe dge, vol. 78, pp. 581-583; P. no. 20, vol. 2, p. 213.3.3-5.3. sTog Palace, no. 338, vol. 93, pp. 400-402.

Schwalbe, Kurt J.

1979 *The Construction and Religious Meaning of the Buddhist Stūpa in Solo Khumbu, Nepal.* Ph.D. dissertation. Berkeley: Graduate Theological Union.

sDe srid, Sangs rgyas rgya mtsho

JLGC *Rab tu gnas pa'i skor brjod pa'i sgra.* In *Mchod sdong 'jam gling rgyan gcig rten gtsug lag khang dang bcas pa'i dkar chag thar gling rgya mtshor bgrod pa'i gru rdzing byin rlabs kyi bang mdzod*, vol. 2, pp. 151-356. New Delhi: 1973.

Sharpa, Tulku and Michael Perrot

1985 "The Ritual of Consecration." *The Tibet Journal* 10/2: 35-45.

1987 *A Manual of Ritual Fire Offerings.* Dharamsala: Library of Tibetan Works and Archives.

Skorupski, Tadeusz

1983a *Tibetan Amulets.* Bangkok: White Orchid Press.

1983b "Tibetan homa rites." In *Agni: The Vedic Ritual of the Fire Altar*, pp. 403-417. First ed., 1983; reprint Delhi: Motilal Banarsidass: 1986.

1986 "Tibetan Marriage Ritual." *Journal of Asian and African Studies* 31: 76-95.

Snellgrove, David L.

1957 *Buddhist Himalaya.* Oxford: Bruno Cassirer.

1959 *The Hevajra Tantra: A Critical Study.* London: Oxford University Press.

1973 "Śākyamuni's Final Nirvāṇa." *Bulletin of the School of Oriental and African Studies* 36: 399-411.

1987 *Indo-Tibetan Buddhism: Indian Buddhists and Their Tibetan Successors.* 2 vols. Boston: Shambhala.

Tsong kha pa

1977 *Tantra in Tibet: The Great Exposition of Secret Mantra, Volume 1.* Trans. by Jeffrey Hopkins. London: George Allen and Unwin.

1981 *The Yoga of Tibet: The Great Exposition of Secret Mantra, Volumes 2 and 3.* Trans. by Jeffrey Hopkins. London: George Allen and Unwin.

Tucci, Giuseppe

1932 *'Mchod rten' e 'tsha tsha' nel Tibet indiano ed occidentale.* Indo-Tibetica 1. Rome: Reale Accademia d'Italia. Translated into English by Uma Marina Vesci under the title *Stūpa*. Ed. by Lokesh Chandra. Śata-Piṭaka Series. New Delhi: 1988.

1949 *Tibetan Painted Scrolls.* Vol. 1, pp. 308-316. Rome: La Libreria dello Stato. Reprinted Kyoto: Rinsen Book, 1980.

Witzel, Michael

1987 "On the Origin of the Literary Device of the 'Frame Story' in Old Indian Literature." In *Festschrift U. Schneider*, pp. 380-414. Ed. by H. Falk. Freiburg.

Chapter 18

Offering (*mChod pa*) in Tibetan Ritual Literature

John Makransky

Offering as a Religious Practice in Indian and Tibetan Buddhism

The Tibetan word *mchod pa* means "to offer"; as a substantive it also means "offering." During the early period of translation of Indian Buddhist texts into Tibetan (eighth-ninth century C.E.), *mchod pa* was made the standard translation for Sanskrit terms whose semantic field encompassed making offerings, honoring, venerating, and pleasing.

Mahāvyutpatti 6107 gives *mchod pa* as the Tibetan translation of *pūjā*, a Sanskrit noun whose verbal root *pūj* means to honor, worship, reverence, venerate (Monier-Williams: 641). Importantly, *Mahāvyutpatti* 6107-6133 lists the names of common substances for *pūjā*, those being offering substances: flowers, lamps, incense, perfumes, oils, parasols, banners, etc. The early translators, then, apparently understood *pūjā* in Indian Buddhist texts to mean honoring or venerating through a presentation of offerings. *Mahāvyutpatti* 6131 also identifies *mchod pa* as a translation for the Sanskrit verb *mahīyate*, meaning "to be glad or happy," "to prosper," or "to be honored" (Monier-Williams: 803; Apte: 1255). *mChod pa* as a translation of *mahīyate* would connote being pleased or gladdened, with the implication that the pleasure is brought about through a presentation of offerings (cf. *BGTD*: 856). The word *mchod pa* as a Tibetan Buddhist term, then, means to make offerings in a ritually prescribed context to sacred or powerful beings in order to honor, venerate and please them (*NGLC*, fol. 72b3).

Offering has had a central place in Indian Buddhist practice from earliest times. Laity were enjoined where possible to offer to the religious order, to assist travellers with material needs, and to give to the needy (Lamotte: 72). Monks and nuns were leading donors of sacred objects and monuments (Schopen, 1985: 23-28). Such activity was motivated by the Buddhist doctrine of karmic merit (*puṇya*), according to which beneficial karmic results accrue from positive acts such as generosity. Offerings to sacred beings were thought to accrue greater merit. Hence offering in all its forms to the Buddha and his religious order was singled out as a special religious act with great karmic results.

Pūjā as an offering rite in Indian Buddhism constituted a special form of giving, which magnified its merit through a ritualized structure and by designating supreme fields of merit (*puṇyakṣetra*) as the beneficiaries: the Buddha, his religious order (*saṃgha*), and the reliquaries (*stūpa*) holding the earthly remains of such beings (Lamotte: 633; Hirakawa, 1990: 273). Images of the Buddha increasingly served as the focus of such offering rituals from the turn of the first millennium C.E. (Lancaster: 289; Kern: 50-52). Incense, flowers, food, lamps, banners, clothing, and music were typically offered to *stūpas* and Buddha images (Hirakawa, 1963: 92-93). With the development of Mahāyāna Buddhism, *sūtras* as expressions of Buddha knowledge were viewed as more significant "remains" of the Buddha than his ashes, hence even more important as objects of offering (Schopen, 1975: 164-165). In Mahāyāna milieus, offering rites were performed in contexts where meditation focusing on enlightened beings was also becoming prominent, sometimes involving visualization of buddhas whose presence and inspiration were felt.[1] Mahāyāna texts described bodhisattvas who yogically generated infinite offering substances, emanating them as offerings to buddhas in pure realms whose transforming power, envisioned as infinite radiance, then blessed the world.[2] With the development of tantric forms of Mahāyāna practice, *pūjā* constituted both a material offering ritual and a structured meditative visualization of boundless offerings to Buddhist deities whose presence was invoked and from whom blessings in the form of light and nectar were received. All such elements of Indian Buddhist practice were incorporated into Tibetan Buddhist offering practice and literature.

Some Indologists have noted that the term *pūjā* in Hindu *sūtras* and epic literature referred primarily to a ritual for venerating guests through offerings (Falk: 83). The structure of ancient Indian customs for entertaining esteemed guests is retained throughout the history of Buddhist *pūjā* practice in India and Tibet, where the "guests," as noted above, are sacred beings or their representations. I-tsing, a seventh-century Chinese scholar and pilgrim, described the offering rites he observed in north India. Noteworthy is his description of royal ablution rituals for Buddha statues in seventh-century Indian monasteries. The Buddha image was bathed in perfumed water, anointed with scented oils, dried with a white cloth, then set up in the temple where offerings of incense and flowers were made to it (I-tsing: 147-152). This bathing ritual, transmuted into a visualization practice with the same order of elements that I-tsing described, became a standard part of Tibetan offering literature (as described in the section below on *mngon 'gro*, "preliminary practices"). The "outer offerings" in Tibetan rituals (also discussed below) are those that were offered to royal guests in ancient India.

Of critical importance in understanding the motivation behind Tibetan offering is the concept of karma and merit (*puṇya*) which Tibet inherited from Indian Buddhism. According to this doctrine, a person's virtuous actions bear fruit in future lives as pleasurable or spiritually beneficial experiences, while his or her non-virtuous actions bear fruit as painful experiences. In a sense, then, from a Tibetan point of view, all pleasurable and painful experiences in life were "given" to oneself through one's own actions in past lives. And every action now undertaken "gives" a future result determined by the moral content of its motivation. Karma and its fruition, understood broadly as the giving and receiving of experience, are the pivotal operations of *saṃsāra* and *nirvāṇa*. Hence giving and receiving also lie at the heart of religious practice. Formal rituals of offering generate tremendous karmic merit (*puṇya*) by providing the ritual structure through which giving obtains its most powerfully beneficial karmic form. By following the ritual format, a practitioner generates the purest motivation to give the very best substances to the highest object: the supreme field of karmic merit (*puṇyakṣetra*, *tshogs zhing*), the buddhas.

Again, with karmic merit in mind, Tibetans understand offering (*mchod pa*) in its widest sense to include all religious practices, not just formal rituals of offering per se. Prostrations before sacred images, recitations of *mantra*, and circumambulations of sacred sites, for example, are routinely tallied and the total presented as an offering to the buddhas.

Thus, offering in general and formalized ritual offering in particular powerfully reaffirm all the dimensions of the Indian Buddhist worldview that Tibet inherited. As Beyer notes (1973: 29-36), Tibetan practice ritualizes the moral attitudes and metaphysics of Indian Buddhism, embodying doctrine in a concrete form which is experienced as a powerful psychological reality. The offerings, purified by their dissolution into emptiness and mentally reconstructed in pure form, are real. The buddhas to whom they are offered are present. The blessing received from the buddhas is felt. The aspiration to manifest enlightenment for the sake of others, and the actual capability of doing so by such practices, is confirmed.

While the elements above were inherited from Indian Buddhism, Tibetans have also understood ritual offering in relation to their own cultural norms. As Robert Ekvall notes,

> Gift-giving in Tibetan society is not primarily a social amenity or an expression of personal liking .... Basically, it is the key or pivotal act in a succession of moves that establish a web of interlocking claims and obligations between the giver and the recipient. The giver has made a deposit in the bank; in one way or another, the one who has received the gift must honor checks drawn on that deposit....
>
> On the occasion of initial presentation of a gift, an immediate return of items of value may or may not take place. If it does take place, some of the credit to the giver has been expended. The value of the return, however, is always less than the original deposit, and some credit for the intangibles is left. This, in any case, is only the beginning of the exchange. From that point on, the two parties are involved in a never ending trading of gifts and realization of mutual responsibilities by means of patronage, aid, moral support, and loyalty. (156-157).

Although, doctrinally speaking, Tibetan masters often say that buddhas have no need for offerings and that offering is therefore done only for the practitioner's own spiritual development, the structure of offering rituals fits into established Tibetan cultural patterns of giving and obligation. When the giver of offerings is a

Tibetan Buddhist, and the recipients are powerful Buddhist deities ritually invoked, the giver receives an "immediate return" of blessing or empowerment (*byin rlabs*). This does not expend the full "credit" of the giver. A greater return of continued spiritual and mundane help comes from an ongoing relationship with the deities. Such a continuing relationship, like any other in Tibetan culture, is maintained through giving, in this case through ritual offering. The same basic principle applies to Tibetan offering rites from pre-Buddhist times which are made to local spirits of lands, waters, and sky. Common examples of such rites are the offering of burnt juniper twigs to the local gods (*bsang gsol*), or the addition of a stone to a cairn at the top of a mountain pass as a thanksgiving offering to the god of the pass (Ekvall: 168, 173-174). Giving enjoins an obligation upon human and god for reciprocation. It is the act which establishes and maintains helping relationships in all realms.

It is also quite possible, however, to think of Tibetan Buddhist offering ritual as a particular expression of what may be a cross-cultural religious principle: profound spiritual empowerment requires giving much.

Tibetan offering ritual is a performance learned by oral instruction, by memorizing texts and studying their meanings, by imitating ritual gestures and recitations, and by training in the appropriate crafts and musical instruments. Offering literature in written form is just one of the means used to transmit what is primarily a tradition of practice learned by example.

Virtually all Tibetan ritual texts (of which there are many thousands) include offering as a significant component, many giving it an extended treatment, including ritual texts of preliminary practices (*mngon 'gro*), *guru pūjās* (*bla ma mchod pa*), *maṇḍala* offerings, litanies of praise (*bstod pa*), fasting rites (*smyung gnas*), festival rites, manuals of tantric practice (*sgrub thabs*), initiation rites (*dbang*), consecrations (*rab gnas*), fire offerings (*sbyin sreg*), and ritual applications of divine power.

Where a ritual text gives offering central prominence, the text may (or may not) carry the explicit title "offering ritual," *mchod pa'i cho ga* (e.g., *bla ma'i mchod pa'i cho ga*, *maṇḍal bzhi pa'i mchod pa'i cho ga*), but in any case, such a text always includes performative elements in addition to descriptions of offering per se, elements which contextualize, structure and give purpose to the explicit actions of offering. Commonly included, for example, would be descriptions of the assembly of holy beings to whom one offers, recitations expressing the altruistic motivation for the offering practice, its soteriological aims and its metaphysical basis in emptiness, vivid descriptions of empowerment by the holy beings, etc.

"Offering literature," then, might be viewed less as a distinct genre than as a basic literary component of many ritual genres, a component which has sometimes been prominently attended to in its own right and expanded into autonomous texts which themselves contain elements beyond descriptions of offering per se. In any case, whether offering appears as a component of a ritual text or constitutes the primary focus of the text, offering rituals contain a number of distinct performative elements which appear repeatedly in various forms throughout ritual literature. A brief synopsis of such elements can provide a window into the offering sections of a fairly wide range of ritual genres. As an example, we will focus on performative elements of "preliminary practice" texts (*mngon 'gro*), a ritual genre in which offerings figure prominently.

Ritual Components of Offering in Tibetan Literature: *mNgon 'gro* as Example

Preliminary practices (*mngon 'gro*) are rituals and ritualized meditations whose explicit purpose is to generate karmic merit, purify mental and physical obstructions, and receive blessing from guru lineages so as to empower the practitioner for success in higher meditations and tantric practice. Preliminary practice texts are structured around offering. Among such texts are those which prescribe the following six "preparatory practices" (*sbyor chos drug*):

(1) Clean the meditation area and set up a statue, a sacred text and a reliquary (*mchod rten*) as representations of the body, speech and mind of the buddhas. Cleaning signifies the removal of mental obstructions, clearing the way for yogic realization. Also, the reality of the buddhas' presence is psychologically reinforced by cleaning the place before formally invoking them, as when inviting guests to one's home (*NGLC*: 66b1-72a2).

(2) Arrange beautiful offerings properly procured. Offering substances are arranged on the altar, the most fundamental being: water for drinking (*arghaṃ*), water for washing (*pādyaṃ*), flowers (*puṣpe*), incense (*dhūpe*), butter lamps (*āloke*), perfume (*gandhe*), food

(*naivedye*) and music (*śabda*). Anything pleasant to the senses may be multiplied in imagination and offered in pure form by multiplying imagined emanations of oneself. These are "outer offerings," substances of the physical world suitable as offerings for royal or divine guests. Leading scholars of all Tibetan sects composed elegant verses expressing the imaginative presentation of such offerings:

> From expansive well-fashioned vessels, radiant and precious,
> Flow gently forth four streams of purifying nectars.
> Beautiful flowers and trees in blossom with bouquets and
> garlands
> Exquisitely arranged fill the earth and sky.
> The heavens billow with blue summer clouds
> Of lazulite smoke from sweet fragrant incense.
> Light from suns and moons, glittering jewels,
> And scores of flaming lamps frolicking joyfully
> Dispel the darkness of a thousand million billion worlds.
> ...Music from an endless variety of various instruments
> Blends into a symphony filling the three realms....
> (Paṇ chen Lama I, *DTBM*: 11-13).

It is said that the eleventh-century Indian master Atiśa sanctioned water offerings (*mchod yon*) especially for Tibet as a substitute for other offerings that were difficult to obtain there (*NGLC*: 74b5). Generally, then, bowls of water are offered in lieu of or in addition to the eight basic outer offerings above, seven bowls representing the first seven offerings, with music represented by an instrument or by the sound of the ritual performance itself.

(3) Sitting in correct posture on a comfortable seat, one takes refuge (*skyabs 'gro*) in Guru, Buddha, Dharma and Saṅgha, receives their blessing envisioned as light and nectar, and generates the thought of enlightenment for the sake of all beings (*sems bskyed*) (*NGLC*: 76a6-92b3). That thought is the highest possible motivation for action (*karma*) of any kind. It directs all the ritual activity which follows toward the highest soteriological ends.

(4) One then recollects the field of karmic merit (*tshogs zhing gsal gdab pa*). A vast array of lineage gurus, tantric deities, buddhas, bodhisattvas, *pratyekabuddhas*, *śravakas*, *ḍākas*, *ḍākinīs*, and protector deities is visualized and their presence invoked by ritual procedures (*NGLC*: 92b3-102b2; Dalai Lama XIV: 62-91). Each element of the visualization has levels of signification based on Tibetan

systematizations of Sūtra and Tantra, the whole array being viewed as a manifestation of enlightened mind, the gnosis of bliss and void, the inseparability of *bla ma* (*guru*) and *yi dam* (*iṣṭadevatā*). Offering one's practices to that "field" is said to generate enormous karmic merit, to purify, and to bless, the three fundmentals of spiritual progress. In fact, from a Tibetan perspective, no meditator is ever actually alone. A practitioner in "solitary" retreat not only visualizes the field of deities, but feels their presence, repeatedly entreating them for inspiration and blessing.

A ritual ablution is often offered. The Indian custom of offering a bath to royal guests is transmuted into a ritual conducted with a mirror, washing flask, basin, and fine cloth (*kha btags*) using gestures, mantra and visualization, interpreted to signify purification and spiritual empowerment. While reciting the following verse and *mantra*, the practitioners visualize a luminous bathhouse of crystal and jewels into which offering goddesses are emanated who bathe the deities in heavenly nectar:

> Just as the gods offered a bath at the birth [of the Buddha],
> So I offer a bath of pure heavenly water for your bodies.
> *oṃ sarva tathāgata abhiṣekata samaye śrīye āh hūm*
> ["*oṃ* all *tathagātas* consecrate in glorious assembly *āṃ hūṃ*"]

While reciting the *mantra*, the master holds the mirror so as to reflect the Buddha image on the altar, then pours water in front of the mirror into the basin. This ritualizes the two-truth ontology of Buddhism. The reflection of water pouring over the reflection of the Buddha image effects ablution on a transactional level (*saṃvṛti satya*). Yet since the rite is performed through mirror reflection, its lack of ultimate reality is affirmed (*paramārtha satya*). The implications are to be applied to all things.

In visualization, the bath water condenses into five spots on the deities' bodies: forehead, throat, chest, and two shoulders. The practitioners visualize the offering goddesses patting the deities dry there while the master applies the cloth to the mirror in the five corresponding places:

> Their bodies are dried with finest cloth, clean and fragrant
> *oṃ hūṃ traṃ hrīḥ āḥ kāya vishodhanaye svā hā*
> ["*oṃ hūṃ traṃ hrīḥ āḥ* cleansing body *svā hā*"]

While one visualizes the offering goddesses applying scented oils to the deities' bodies, the following verse is recited:

> With the finest oils scented with fragrances pervading the three thousand universes, I anoint the bodies of the Śākyendras shining luminous, as though polishing purified gold.

As the goddesses offer fresh garments, the following verse makes the soteriological significance of the rite explicit:

> To obtain the Vajra Body indestructible, I offer fine smooth ethereal garments with faith indestructible. May I too obtain the Vajra Body.

As the goddesses offer jewelled ornaments to the deities:

> Though the Victors, intrinsically adorned with marks and signs [of enlightenment] need no further adornment, still, by my offering exquisite jewelled ornaments, may all beings obtain the Body adorned with marks and signs.

The rite concludes:

> I pray that you remain [in the world] for as long as I continue to make offerings, out of your great love for me and all beings and through the power of your supernatural manifestations.

At the termination of the visualization, the goddesses dissolve into the hearts of the practitioners, who visualize the remaining bath water, now consecrated by contact with the deities, pouring into all realms of beings to purify their sufferings. The deities' old clothing dissolves as an empowering golden light into each practitioner's forehead (*NGLC*: 101b-102b. See also Lessing, 1959: 159-171; Beyer, 1973: 336-338).

(5) The seven-limb offering is to be performed (*saptāṅgā pūjā, yan lag bdun pa'i mchod pa*) (see also Cabezón, in this volume) together with the *maṇḍala* offering. The seven-limb offering is said to distill all merit-making and purifying disciplines into seven basic practices. Its inclusion in a variety of Mahāyāna texts at an early stage indicates its centrality to Indian Mahāyāna cult practice.[3] The ritual remains fundamental to Tibetan practice. The seven parts of the ritual are: (1) prostration, (2) offering, (3) confession, (4) rejoicing in the merit of others, (5) asking the buddhas to teach the Dharma, (6) requesting them to continue to manifest in the world without passing away, and (7) dedicating the merit from these practices to the enlightenment of all beings. Although as *pūjā* all seven practices are offered to the buddhas, the second practice involves the explicit offering of material and mentally created substances.

Here the offering substances, water bowls, etc. which were set up on the altar earlier are formally offered to the deities with the recitation of verses like those above by the first Paṇ chen Lama, Blo bzang chos kyi rgyal mtshan. Using the offering substances on the altar as a material basis, the practitioner visualizes boundless pure offerings, filling the sky with exquisite flower garlands, incense, perfumes, canopies, butter lamps, incense, heavenly garments, music, etc. Offering goddesses emanated from the practitioner's chest present the offerings to the deities in the field of merit. Such practices appear to be modelled on Mahāyāna *sūtra* descriptions of bodhisattvas who emanate infinite offerings to the buddha fields.

The offering of accomplishment (*sgrub mchod*) involves the practitioner's visualization of all virtues and merit that he or she has ever accumulated in the past and will ever accumulate in the future, in the form of vast, pure offering substances that are presented to the field of merit (*NGMT*: 81a-84a; *DTBM*: 15).

A *maṇḍala* must be offered to the field of merit. The basic sense of the Sanskrit word *maṇḍala* is "circle," but the semantic range of related meanings is wide. Geographically, *maṇḍala* can refer to a surrounding area, sphere or realm. In tantric practice, it refers to the abode or realm of the tantric deity. Here it refers to the most inclusive of all offerings: the practitioner's entire psycho-physical universe taken as a whole. As the practitioner drops heaps of grain containing precious stones onto metal discs, using rings to build up tiers, he or she visualizes each heap as a component of the Indic universe: the golden ground, Mount Meru, ocean, mountains, continents, sun, moon, seven royal symbols, eight offering goddesses, together with all possessions of gods and men. Holding the disc overflowing with grain in both hands, the practitioner reenvisions it as the whole universe transformed into a pure realm, and offers it to the buddhas with this verse:

> The earth anointed with incense and strewn with flowers,
> Adorned with Mt. Meru, the four continents, sun and moon,
> Visualized as a pure buddha realm: I offer it.
> May all beings partake in the pure realm.

This is the "outer *maṇḍala*," the offering of the external world. The practitioner may also offer the "inner *maṇḍala*," his or her own body. Visualizing one's skin as the golden ground, one's blood as nectar, one's flesh as the flowers, one's trunk as Mt. Meru, one's four limbs as the continents, one's eyes as the sun and moon, one's internal organs as the wealth of gods and men, one envisions it all as a pure realm, and offers it to the buddhas:

> The objects of my desire, anger and ignorance,
> Enemies, friends and strangers, my body and wealth
> I offer without any sense of loss. Accept them and
> Please bless me for spontaneous release from the three poisons.

Such practices cultivate the psychology of gladly giving up all for enlightenment (*NGLC*: 106a6-109a6. See also *NGMT*: 80a-80b; *NDGM*: 93-116; Tharchin: 63-79; Lessing, 1976: 13-24). Literary models for this practice include the Bodhisattva Sadāprarudita of the *Aṣṭasāhasrikā Prajñāpāramitā Sūtra*, who enthusiastically offers his own heart, blood and marrow to venerate his guru Dharmodgata (Conze: 284-285), and the Mahāsiddha Nāropa who, lacking any offering materials, is reported in his hagiography to have cut up his own body as a *maṇḍala* offering to his *guru* Tilopa (Guenther: 83).

(6) The last of the preparatory practices involves requesting and receiving blessing or empowerment from the deities in the field of merit. Having offered all to the deities, the practitioner's psyche is now open to receive all. Blessings to accomplish the path to enlightenment are envisioned as colored lights and nectars pouring from the field of merit into the psycho-physical energy centers (*cakra, rtsa 'khor*) of the practitioner's body and mind. Finally, the field of merit dissolves into the principal guru-deity, which dissolves into the practitioner. The practitioner meditates on the inseparable oneness of the guru's enlightened mind with his or her own. Manuals of *guru yoga* (*bla ma'i rnal 'byor*) focus especially on this rite as preparation for tantric practice.

Offering Paradigms in Tantric Literature

Tantric ritual texts include the practices discussed above, but have other essential features as well. Buddhist tantric practice involves the identification of oneself with buddhahood as the key method to its attainment. Tantric texts often include, then, not only a mental creation of deities in front of the practitioner (*mdun skyed*) like the field of merit above, but also the mental creation of the practitioner him or herself as enlightened deity (*bdag skyed*). Offerings are made to a guru-deity generated in front (*mdun skyed*) for merit and purification as above, but especially to receive the deity's power and blessing, visualized as nectar and light emitted from the mantra at its heart. Such divine power may be directed to mundane purposes, such as curing disease, bringing wealth, long life, etc., all ideologically subserved in the tantric literature to spiritual objectives. But the main purpose of the divine blessing is to empower the development of the practitioner through the stages of meditative realization. Offerings are also made to oneself as self-generated deity (*bdag skyed*) in manuals of tantric practice (*sādhana, sgrubs thabs*) whose purpose is to effect the total transmutation of one's body, speech and mind into those of the enlightened *guru*-deity. The Buddhist principle of nonduality, internalized and empowered by all preparatory ritual elements, now takes form in the identification of deity as cognitive object with deity as cognitive subject.

In tantric rites, all ritual elements are envisioned as pure appearances of the *guru*-deity's mind, characterized, in essence, as the gnosis directly cognizing voidness, or in Highest Yoga Tantras (*rnal 'byor bla med rgyud*), as the gnosis of voidness and bliss inseparable (*bde stong dbyer med ye shes*). Four general types of offering are basic to tantric practice: outer offering (*phyi mchod*), inner offering (*nang mchod*), secret offering (*gsang mchod*) and thatness offering (*de kho na nyid mchod*). The outer offerings mentioned above (water, flowers, incense, lamps, etc.) are offered in ways ritually prescribed by tantric theory, involving special modes of *mantra* recitation, hand gesture and visualization (*sngags, phyag rgya, ting nge 'dzin*). What follows is a general description of tantric offering formulas commonly found in generation stage (*bskyed rim*) manuals of Highest Yoga Tantra.

All offerings in Highest Yoga Tantra must be consecrated as manifestions of the bliss-void gnosis (*bde stong dbyer med ye shes*) of the buddhas. Only a buddha (i.e., a tantric deity) has the power to do this. Hence, prior to offering, the practitioner first generates him or herself as deity (*bdag skyed*) in both mind and body (see Cozort, in this volume). Ordinary appearances are dissolved into the blissful gnosis of voidness. That gnosis projects a manifestation of the practitioner as deity. As deity, he or she is now ready to consecrate the offerings. First the "inner offering" is consecrated, which, in the practice of fierce deities, involves the transmutation of five meats (*sha lnga*) and five bodily fluids (*bdud rtsi lnga*) into an ocean of pure gnosis nectar, symbolizing the transmutation of the psycho-physical components of *saṃsāra* (the senses, aggregates and elements) into those of enlightenment (*tathāgatas*, consorts, the five gnoses). The inner offering, represented by a cup of wine (*chang*) or tea, is cleared (*bsang ba*) of harmful influences by recitation of a fierce mantra and the projection of wrathful protectors, purified (*sbyang ba*) of the appearance of self-existence by meditative dissolution into voidness with recitation of the mantra: *oṃ svabhāva śuddāḥ sarvadharmāḥ svabhāva śuddho 'ham* ("*oṃ* all phenomena are intrinsically pure, I am intrinsically pure"), and then generated (*bskyed pa*) into the appearance of samsaric fleshes and fluids. The body, speech and mind of enlightenment, in the form of the syllables *oṃ*, *āḥ*, and *hūṃ*, bless (*byin gyis brlab*) these substances, transmuting them into a pure ocean of nectar of tremendous potency, which is used for further ritual applications (*DNKD*: 8b-10a; *NGMT*: 35a-36b; cf. Beyer, 1973: 158-159).

The outer offerings (flowers, incense, butter lamps, etc.) can now be consecrated. A drop of inner offering substance, envisioned as the potent nectar of bliss-void gnosis, is sprinkled over the outer offering substances with recitation of *mantra* and visualization as above to clear away harmful influences. The outer offerings are purified of their appearance of self-existence by dissolution into voidness as above. From that bliss-void gnosis is projected the appearance of boundless offering substances (water, flowers, incense, lamps, perfumes, foods, music). Though appearing as manifold offerings, their essence is gnosis and their effect when enjoyed is to elicit highest yogic bliss. With this in mind, the offerings are blessed as the body, speech and mind of the buddhas by the recitation of "*oṃ*" (Vajra Body); the name of each offering substance (*arghaṃ*, *pādyaṃ*, *puṣpe*, *dhūpe*, *āloke*, *gandhe*, *naivedye*, *śabda*); "*āḥ*" (Vajra Speech); "*hūṃ*" (Vajra Mind). Ritual hand gestures (*mudrā*, *phyag rgya*) symbolize each offering mimetically as it is blessed (*DNKD*: 10a-10b; *NGMT*: 36a-37b).[4]

The outer offerings, having been consecrated as the appearance of bliss-void gnosis, are now ready to be offered to the tantric field of merit, with the appropriate *mantra* and hand gesture for each. As the practitioner makes the hand gesture for each offering substance and says its *mantra*, offering goddesses are visualized emanating from the heart to present the offering to the field of merit in elegant dance. With hand gestures that represent the dancing movements of the goddesses, they are then visualized as returning and reabsorbing into the heart: *oṃ* [name of deity] *arghaṃ pādyaṃ puṣpe dhūpe āloke gandhe naivedye śabda praticcha hūṃ svāhā* ("*oṃ* [name of deity] accept this water for drinking, water for your feet, flowers, incense, light, perfume, food, and music, *hūṃ svāha*"). Visualizations of the varieties and methods of offering can be highly intricate (*NGMT*: 68a-73b). All space is filled with exquisite flowers, lights, smells, foods; the universe resonates with wonderful sounds. Sometimes the practitioner, using appropriate *mantras* and hand gestures, also emanates goddesses of the six senses to offer ritual representations of each sense to the field of merit: *oṃ āḥ vajra ādarśe hūṃ, oṃ āḥ vajra viṇe hūṃ, oṃ āḥ vajra gandhe hūṃ, oṃ āḥ vajra rāse hūṃ, oṃ āḥ vajra sparśe hūṃ, oṃ ah vajra dharme hūṃ* ("*oṃ āḥ* Vajra Mirror, Lute, Perfume, Taste, Touch, Mental Object, *hūṃ*"). Next the inner offering is presented. Reciting *oṃ āḥ hūṃ*, the practitioner sprinkles the liquid toward the field of merit with the fingers while visualizing its presentation to the deities by goddesses (*DNKD*: 13a-14a; *NGMT*: 64b-74b, 85a-b; *SDKR*: 7a-7b). The presentation of outer and inner offerings to the practitioner as self-generated deity is done in much the same manner as above, with offering goddesses projected from his or her own heart presenting the offerings to the practitioner as deity with entourage.

The secret offering (*gsang mchod*) involves the visualized presentation of divine consorts to the principal deity. Their union generates a gnosis of highest yogic bliss, constituting the offering. The blissful gnosis induced by the secret offering, in its capacity of nondually cognizing voidness (*bde stong dbyer med ye shes*), constitutes the offering of thatness (*de kho na nyid mchod pa*) (*DNKD*: 14a; *NGMT*: 89b-90a, 93a).

Some early scholars, profoundly misunderstanding the sexual imagery found in Tibetan tantric art and literature, described it as the "debasement" of Buddhism (e.g., Waddell: 15). The Tibetan holocaust and subsequent diaspora, which has been a tragedy of profound dimensions for Tibetans, has helped us to clarify questions of this kind, for it has provided us with far greater access to Tibetans' own perspectives on their practices than had earlier been the case. It is now generally known that Tibetan tantric symbolism represents not, as was once thought, the triumph of animal instinct over spirituality, but precisely the opposite: a remarkable system for subordinating sexual imagery and instinct to the requirements of spiritual practice. Traditional Tibetan culture has never shared the West's obsessive concerns about sexuality. What Tibetan *tāntrikas* are very much concerned about, on the other hand, is Buddhist enlightenment, and it is here that the imagery of psycho-sexual yoga is so highly valued: as the quintessential symbol of the nonduality of compassionate means and wisdom, and as a yogic method capable of generating the subtlest realization of voidness at the deepest stratum of human consciousness.

Often at the beginning of a tantric ritual, a ritual cake known as a *gtor ma* is offered to malevolent spirits in order to appease them, or to Dharma protectors (*chos skyong*) for protection from harms and interferences. At the conclusion of the ritual, *gtor ma* are again usually offered to some or all of the following: the principal tantric deities (*yi dam*) who embody all gurus, buddhas, etc., *ḍākinīs* (*mkha 'gro ma*) who are powerful guides on the tantric path, Dharma protectors, local spirits of all kinds, and sentient beings of the six realms. The *gtor mas*, made of barley flour dough decorated with colored butter, are consecrated by the same four-step procedure as for the outer and inner offerings above. The purpose of the offering is made clear upon its completion, when the practitioner recites verses of praise and makes supplications for protection, health, long life, success in all things mundane and supramundane, and for the enlightenment of all beings (*DNKD*: 40a-41a; Beyer, 1973: 219-222).

Another important tantric offering is a celebratory feast called a *tshogs mchod* (assembly offering). Delicious foods, beautifully arranged on the offering table, are consecrated by the four steps outlined above, offered to the merit field of deities, local spirits, and sentient beings, and then consumed as sacramental food by the assembled practitioners. This is a party, a thanksgiving celebration to which all mundane and supramundane beings are invited. At its conclusion, celebratory songs of tantric *mahāsiddhas* are joyfully sung (*DTBM*: 25-39). This ritual is of special importance to tantric practitioners who must perform it twice a month or more to maintain their precepts, to maintain a good relationship with the *ḍākinīs*, to receive powerful blessings from the deities, and to quickly realize the higher reaches of the tantric path (*NGMT*: 87a).

There are far too many Tibetan offering rituals, most of considerable complexity and multiple layers of meaning, to do them justice in this short space. Above are brief summaries of a few common offering formulas found in Tibetan Buddhist ritual literature. The reader interested in further study may want to consult Stephan

Beyer's book, *The Cult of Tārā*, the most comprehensive account of Tibetan offering rituals presently available in English, though it too is far from exhaustive.

Notes

1. For a few examples, see Harrison: 37-52; Williams: 26-33, 217-224; Beyer, 1974: 121-124.

2. E.g., Bendall and Rouse: 276-280, 291-292, 299-306; Kern: chs. 2, 6, 7, 16, 20, 22.

3. E.g., *Bhadracaripraṇidhānagāthā*, *Triskhandhaka Sūtra*, *Ratnāvalī* of Nāgārjuna, *Praṇidhānāsaptatināmagāthā* ascribed to Āryaśūra.

4. See Beyer, 1973: 147 for drawings of the hand gestures.

References

Apte, Vaman Shivaram

1957 *The Practical Sanskrit-English Dictionary*. Revised and enlarged edition. Poona: Prasad Prakashan.

Bendall, Cecil and W. H. D. Rouse

1971 *Śikṣā-Samuccaya: A Compendium of Buddhist Doctrine*. Second edition. Delhi: Motilal Banarsidass.

Beyer, Stephan

1973 *The Cult of Tārā: Magic and Ritual in Tibet*. Berkeley: University of California Press.

1974 *The Buddhist Experience: Sources and Interpretations*. Encino: Dickenson.

Bod rgya tshig mdzod chen mo

BGTD Beijing: Zang-Han daicidian, 1985.

Conze, Edward

1973 *The Perfection of Wisdom in Eight Thousand Lines and Its Verse Summary*. Bolinas: Four Seasons Foundation.

Dalai Lama XIV, Tenzin Gyatso

1988 *The Union of Bliss and Emptiness: A Commentary on the Lama Choepa Guru Yoga Practice*. Ithaca: Snow Lion.

dGe legs dpal bzang po (mKhas grub rje)

rGyud sde spyi'i rnam par gzhag pa. Ed. and trans. by F. D. Lessing and A. Wayman as Mkhas grub rje's *Fundamentals of the Buddhist Tantras*. Motilal Banarsidass: Delhi, 1978.

Dharma bhadra dpal bzang po

DNKD *rJe btsun rdo rje rnal 'byor ma'i bskyed rdzogs kyi zin bris mkha' spyod bgrod pa'i gsang lam snying gi thig le.* In his *gSung 'bum* (Collected Works), reprint of a sDe dge edition, vol. ca, ff. 1-59.

Ekvall, Robert B.

1964 *Religious Observances in Tibet: Patterns and Function.* Chicago: University of Chicago Press.

Falk, Nancy E. Auer

1987 "Hindu Pūjā." In *Encyclopedia of Religion.* Ed. by Mircea Eliade. New York: Macmillan.

Gling ras pa Pad ma rdo rje

bLa ma mchod pa'i cho ga yon tan kun 'byung. Blockprint. Chemre: Hemis rGod tshang Hermitage.

Guenther, Herbert V.

1963 *The Life and Teaching of Nāropa.* New York: Oxford University Press.

Harrison, Paul

1978 "Buddhānusmṛti in the *Pratyutpanna-Buddha-Saṃmukhāvasthita-Samādhi-Sūtra.*" *Journal of Indian Philosophy* 6: 35-57.

Hirakawa, Akira

1963 "The Rise of Mahāyāna Buddhism and its Relationship to the Worship of Stūpas." *Memoirs of the Research Department of the Tōyō Bunko* [Tokyo] 22: 57-106.

1990 *A History of Indian Buddhism.* Trans. and ed. by Paul Groner. Honolulu: University of Hawaii Press.

I-tsing

1896 *A Record of the Buddhist Religion as Practised in India and the Malay Archipelago, AD 671-695.* Trans. by J. Takakusu. London: Clarendon Press.

'Jam mgon kong sprul Blo gros mtha' yas

NDGM *Nges don sgron me.* Trans. by Judith Hanson as *The Torch of Certainty.* Boulder: Shambhala, 1977.

Kern, H.

1884 *Saddharma-Puṇḍarīka or The Lotus of the True Law.* Oxford: Clarendon Press.

Lamotte, Etienne

1988 *History of Indian Buddhism: From the Origins to the Śaka Era.* Trans. by Sara Webb-Boin. Louvain: Institut Orientaliste Louvain-la-Neuve.

Lancaster, Lewis

1974 "An Early Mahāyāna Sermon about the Body of the Buddha and the Making of Images." *Artibus Asiae* 36: 287-291.

Lessing, Ferdinand D.

1942 *Yung-Ho-Kung: An Iconography of the Lamaist Cathedral in Peking*. Stockholm: Reports from the Scientific Expedition to the Northwestern Provinces of China under the Leadership of Dr. Sven Hedin, XVIII.

1959 "Structure and Meaning of the Rite Called the Bath of the Buddha According to Tibetan and Chinese Sources." *Studia Serica Bernhard Karlgren Dedicata*. Copenhagen: Ejnar Munksgaard.

1976 *Ritual and Symbol: Collected Essays on Lamaism and Chinese Symbolism*. Taipei: Orient Cultural Service.

Monier-Williams, Monier

1899 *A Sanskrit-English Dictionary*. London: Oxford University Press.

Mullin, Glenn H.

1983 *Meditation on the Lower Tantras*. Dharamsala: Library of Tibetan Works and Archives.

Paṇ chen Lama I, bLo bzang chos kyi rgyal mtshan

DTBM *Zab lam bla ma mchod pa'i cho ga bde stong dbyer med*. Translated as *The Guru Pūjā* by Alexander Berzin et al. Dharamsala: Library of Tibetan Works and Archives.

Pha bong kha bDe chen snying po

NGLC *rNam grol lag bcangs su gtod pa'i man ngag zab mo tshang la ma nor ba mtshungs med chos kyi rgyal po'i thugs bcud byang chub lam gyi rim pa'i nyams khrid kyi zin bris gsung rab kun gyi bcud bsdus gdams ngag bdud rtsi'i snying po*. Blockprint. Dharamsala: Bod gzhung shes rig dpar kang.

Schopen, Gregory

1975 "The Phrase 'sa pṛthivīpradeśaś caityabhūto bhavet' in the *Vajracchedika*: Notes on the Cult of the Book in Mahāyāna." *Indo-Iranian Journal* 17: 147-181.

1985 "Two Problems in the History of Indian Buddhism: The Layman/Monk Distinction and the Doctrines of the Transference of Merit." *Studien zur Indologie und Iranistik* 10: 9-47.

Tharchin, Sermey Geshe Lobsang

1987 *A Commentary on Guru Yoga and Offering of the Maṇḍala*. Ithaca: Snow Lion.

Tsong kha pa bLo bzang grags pa

SDKR *gSang 'dus bskyed rim gyi zin bris*. In his *gSung 'bum* (Collected Works). Reprint of bKra śis lhun po ed., vol. *ca*, ff. 1a-40a. New Delhi: Ngawang Gelek Demo.

Tulku, Sharpa and Michael Perrott

1987 *A Manual of Ritual Fire Offerings*. Dharamsala: Library of Tibetan Works and Archives.

Waddell, L. Austine

1895 *The Buddhism of Tibet, or Lamaism*. London: W. H. Allen.

Williams, Paul

1989 *Mahāyāna Buddhism: The Doctrinal Foundations*. New York: Routledge.

Ye shes rgyal mtshan

NGMT *Bla ma mchod pa'i krid yig gsang ba'i gnad rnam par phye ba snyan rgyud man ngag gi gter mdzod*. Blockprint. Dharamsala: Bod gzhung shes rig dpar kang.

Chapter 19

Sādhana (*sGrub thabs*): Means of Achievement for Deity Yoga

Daniel Cozort

Let us share the imaginative vision of a Buddhist meditator who performs the esoteric practice of the *Kālacakra Tantra.*[1] To begin: we imagine that the Buddha Akṣobhya, residing at the center of the cosmos, manifests himself as Kālacakra, an impressive black or dark blue man with three necks of black, red, and white, and four faces of black, red, white, and yellow, a third eye at the center of each brow. His open mouths reveal fine, sharp teeth. Surrounding the bound bundle of his long hair is a crown ornamented with a thunderbolt (*vajra, rdo rje*), a half moon, and an image of the Buddha Vajrasattva. Heavy gold circles dangle from his ears, and golden bracelets, arm bands, and anklets adorn his many arms and legs. He displays twenty-four black, red, and white arms, which end in long fingers and red palms. His hands grasp a multitude of deadly weapons such as a sword, a trident, and an axe, and peaceful emblems such as a bell, a jewel, and a lotus. He balances himself on red and white legs as he embraces his yellow consort, Viśvamātā, whose three-eyed faces are yellow, white, blue, and red. Her eight arms also hold weapons and emblems.

Kālacakra and Viśvamātā stand on a huge lotus at the center of a great pyramid-like palace built in five tiers, flanked by four elaborate gates, and surrounded by extensive grounds. Their mansion is populated by over seven hundred other marvelous beings (who are actually emanations of Kālacakra and Visvamātā). The surrounding mountains and hills sparkle with streams, are shaded by trees, and resound with bird songs. Their world is protected by fierce beings and a diamond fence.

Kālacakra is one of the principal buddha-forms (called *lha*, "deities") that are the focus of esoteric Tibetan Buddhist rituals based on the canonical texts called *rgyud* (*tantra*). These tantric rituals are, in turn, conducted according to meditational liturgies known widely by their Sanskrit name, *sādhana* (*sgrub thabs*), literally "means of achievement."[2] *Sādhanas* guide one's efforts to imagine magnificent panoramas and beings (such as those described above) and to perform appropriate ritual utterances (*mantra*, *sngags*), gestures (*mudrā*, *phyag rgya*) and other activities with the aim of achieving buddhahood oneself. The complex physical, verbal, and mental practice that they prescribe is called "deity *yoga*" (*devatā yoga*, *lha'i rnal byor*), for one practices a discipline (*yoga*) aimed at causing one's own mind to appear as one or more enlightened beings in exalted *sambhogakāya* form. In short, a *sādhana* is the handbook that deity *yogīs* recite, in solitude or with others,[3] as they vividly imagine the divine environment, its occupants, their speech, and their transformations.

Sādhanas and the Tantras

Sādhanas are only one type of tantric literature. The tantric corpus, the history of which is difficult to determine with any precision,[4] includes the "root" *tantras* (attributed to the historical buddha), explanatory *tantras*, commentaries on specific *tantras*, works on the general philosophy and structure of Tantra,[5] *sādhanas*, songs (*dohā*, *nyams mgur*), and a variety of ritual texts. However, because the *sādhana* contains guidelines for the actual performance of rituals, it is the type of text that has the greatest practical importance for *sādhakas*, those who have ritually received the permission and empowerment to practice a specific *tantra*.[6] *Tantras* themselves are ill-suited to be recited as the basis of a rite: they are arranged unsystematically; they contain deliberately obscure language; and they do not extensively describe preliminary practices typically considered essential in a *sādhana*, such as rousing in oneself an attitude of renouncing the cycle of rebirth, generating compassion, and ascertaining that phenomena are empty (*stong pa*) of inherent establishment (*rang bzhin gyis grub pa*).

A useful *sādhana* will guide one through each phase of the preliminary and main services of the liturgy in a clear and precise fashion. Even so, it cannot stand alone. Further oral instruction from a competent *guru* (*bla ma*) is considered crucial. Indian *sādhanas*, in particular, tend to be mere outlines;[7] those composed in Tibet frequently are much more detailed and some are, in fact, elaborations of the Indian texts.[8] Even the most elaborate *sādhanas* may give only a sketchy description of the environment and deities to be visualized. One is expected to rely on oral instruction and on icons (which are created with rigorous adherence to *sādhana* depictions). Indeed, much Tibetan religious art depicts the deities of tantric Buddhism and is produced not merely to pay homage to deities or to inspire the pious, but to facilitate deity *yoga*.

From a given *tantra* can come countless *sādhanas*, differing greatly in length and intricacy. The Sanskrit sense of *tantras* as "threads" suggests a material from which many *sādhanas* may be woven; similarly, the Tibetan translation, *rgyud* ("stream" or "continuum"), suggests a flow that can be channeled in many different ways. The generation of new *sādhanas* may be attributed to factors such as the differences among lineages of explanation (as they might be embodied, for instance, in different explanatory *tantras*) or a teacher's decision to tailor a *sādhana* to the needs of specific students or to modify it in a manner that reflects his or her preferences and experience.[9] Consequently, although several hundred *sādhanas* are contained in the Tibetan Buddhist canon—the sDe dge bsTan 'gyur alone has four *sādhana* collections[10] comprising over 560 items—there are far more to be found in the works of indigenous Tibetan scholars and *yogīs*.[11] One prominent non-canonical collection is the *sGrub thabs kun btus* ("Collection of All *Sādhanas*") compiled in fourteen volumes by 'Jam dbyangs blo gter dbang po; the rNying ma collections of the "old" tantras of the first dissemination of Buddhism in Tibet and of "discovered" (*gter ma*) texts also contain many *sādhanas*.[12] Only a few *sādhanas* have been translated into Western languages.[13]

Each of the four principal orders of Tibetan Buddhism has placed more emphasis on certain deities than others, which in turn is reflected in the proportion of *sādhanas* that have been written for those deities. For instance, Vajrakīla and Hayagrīva are particularly important for the rNying ma order, Heruka Cakrasaṃvara for the bKa' brgyud, Hevajra for the Sa skya, and Yamāntaka and Guhyasamāja for the dGe lugs.

Sādhanas and Deity Yoga

As stated earlier, a *sādhana* is literally a "means of achievement." What is achieved may be mundane, such as the eight great feats (flying or recovery of youth, etc.) (Tsong kha pa: 59) or the four activities of pacification (of demons, etc.), increase (of lifespan, etc.), subjugation, and ferocity (Dalai Lama XIV, 1984: 98). The aim of most *sādhanas*, however, is the greatest of all achievements, the attainment of buddhahood. The principal means to this end is the work of deity *yoga*, which mainly involves the construction of *maṇḍalas* (*dkyil 'khor*), literally "circles." The *maṇḍalas* are of two types, a residence (a divine mansion) and residents (deities) that together represent the entire cosmos and its occupants.[14] To visualize these complex images requires great concentration and, at least initially, great effort, for one must build up the image, revivify those aspects of it that become hazy or dull, and envision its transformation during the course of the *sādhana*. In addition, one may simultaneously be imagining oneself to be the deity that is visualized.

Nevertheless, one is called upon to realize (or at least imagine) that this image is not merely one's fabrication, for the marvelous *maṇḍalas* that appear in space are really nothing less than the progressive manifestation of *one's own mind* that realizes emptiness, appearing in form. That is, one is to regard oneself as a buddha;[15] on this basis, one imagines that one's omniscient consciousness that never wavers from absorption on emptiness (one's Truth Body [*dharmakāya, chos sku*]) manifests visibly as the divine residence and residents (one's Form Body [*rūpakāya, gzugs sku*]).[16] Moreover, one imagines that this manifestation in form occurs without deliberation, being the spontaneous display of compassion.[17] In short, one is to live proleptically in one's future buddhahood by pretending that one's own wisdom appears as the *maṇḍala*.

The particular *sādhana* one practices, and hence, the deity one achieves, is related to the guidance one receives in the choice of a type of Tantra—from the classes of Action (*bya*), Performance (*spyod*), Yoga (*rnal byor*) or Highest Yoga (*rnal 'byor bla med*)[18]—and in the choice of the deity that is its focus,[19] which may very well be affected by the religious order to which one belongs, as noted earlier. One's choice also is, in principle, linked to one's psychic makeup. A striking feature of tantric icons is that they may be either peaceful or wrathful in aspect; identification with one or the other through creative visualization affords one the opportunity to use productively even one's negative emotions, such as lust or hatred, in the service of the spiritual path. For instance, as a deity *yogī*, one may take on the fierce aspect of a deity such as Kālacakra. However, that fierceness will be directed not against others, but rather, it will ravage one's own inner adversaries of ignorance, desire, and hatred. Or, one may experience the bliss of Kālacakra's sexual union with Viśvamātā, but that bliss will be used to energize the wisdom that realizes emptiness.

Significantly, aggressive action need not indicate harmful intent; as the fourteenth Dalai Lama notes (1984: 98), the tantric practitioner's motivation should always be that of compassion for others. It may seem paradoxical to embody anger or lust when these are what one is committed to oppose; however, this "embodiment" is analogous to the way in which, in the context of meditating on emptiness, one deliberately appropriates the "I" of a deity by thinking of oneself as that deity (known as having "divine pride"). Despite this apparent regression into dualistic awareness, seemingly the very opposite of what one ought to be doing, the substitution of the deity's "I" for one's own undermines one's ordinary false sense of "I" and thus facilitates one's discernment of selflessness (Dalai Lama XIV, 1977: 64). So too, here the experience of aggression or bliss, which occurs within thinking of oneself as a deity, undermines one's ordinary anger and lust, which arise through trying to protect and enhance one's ordinary ego.

The Structure of a *Sādhana*

As Gómez has noted (378), the tantric ritual is modeled after, and contains elements from, both pre-Mahāyāna and non-tantric Mahāyāna liturgies. Thus, we find the tantric practitioner going for refuge to the Three Jewels (Buddha, Spiritual Community, and Doctrine), generating compassion, and meditating on emptiness as well as performing the unique tantric practice of deity *yoga*. As an example, let us consider a recently composed *sādhana* (Dalai Lama XIV, 1985: 383-424) of the Kālacakra stage of generation (*utpattikrama, bskyed rim*).[20] It exhibits the typical structure of a *sādhana*, with preliminaries, an "actual" *sādhana* that rehearses the entire process of transformation into a buddha, and concluding acts. Although not all *sādhanas* are so constructed, many are, and this one admirably suggests the complex dynamism of a deity *yoga* practice.

In this Kālacakra *sādhana*, one begins as one would in most non-tantric meditation, by contemplating death and impermanence and one's precious opportunity to attain enlightenment in this life. Then one begins the visualization, imagining the field of buddhas, bodhisattvas, and teachers,[21] and, declaring that one takes refuge in them, practices with the altruistic intention to highest enlightenment and cultivates the sublime states of love, compassion, sympathetic joy, and equanimity with regard to all sentient beings.

Having completed these motivational preliminaries, one performs a seven-branched ceremony (*pūjā*) of honoring Kālacakra while visualizing a simpler version of the scene depicted earlier: one imagines that the mind that realizes emptiness appears as Kālacakra (who is felt to be undifferentiable from one's own teacher, in this particular *sādhana*); that he and his consort, who are sexually united, stand on discs of sun, moon and planets set in a lotus that is itself mounted on a throne; and that they are surrounded by fierce protectors who emanate from Kālacakra's heart. Then, as in many Mahāyāna Buddhist rituals, one performs a seven-step offering: one (1) pays homage to Kālacakra and his consort; (2) makes offerings of a multitude of pleasant objects, including one's own body, speech and mind, to them; (3) confesses one's faults; (4) expresses admiration for the good deeds of others; (5) asks them to turn the Wheel of Dharma; (6) asks them to remain in Form Bodies to teach others; and (7) dedicates one's merit to others (see Makransky, in this volume).

One follows this ritual by again recalling one's teacher and affirming his or her undifferentiability from Kālacakra, and by recalling the initiation that gave one permission to perform this *sādhana*. One imagines that Kālacakra dissolves into one's crown and that one now *is* Kālacakra in the brilliant circle of mansion and deities, emanating fierce protective deities from one's heart and uttering the divine speech associated with all the deities. The deities melt, dissolving into oneself; oneself also dissolves, but then re-forms as Kālacakra, whereupon one renews one's vows and pledges.

In this *sādhana,* one concludes by rehearsing, in a highly condensed way (which itself indicates that this *sādhana* is developed mainly for beginners), the entire practice of the two stages of generation and completion (*niṣpannakrama, rdzogs rim*).[22] These two stages are the "actual" *sādhana* that is required in order to bring about one's transformation into a buddha. In the stage of generation one imagines the construction of the residence circle and its population with deities. One imagines that sexual union with one's consort causes an inner heat (*gtum mo,* the "Fierce Woman") that melts a subtle substance called a "drop" (*bindu, thig le*) so that it flows through a subtle central channel in the body;[23] this drop is imagined to bless all sentient beings. Again, one generates the deities and again the drop melts and flows. One imagines that all the *actual* deities descend and dissolve into the imaginary ones and that one receives initiations and blessings from them. Again, one imagines the melting and flowing of the drop, this time downward from the crown through the central channel, past channel-intersections called "wheels" (*cakra, 'khor lo*), causing one to experience different degrees of bliss. Then one imagines the upward flow of the drop, experiencing bliss of an even more sublime nature. Although this concludes the *yogas* of the stage of generation, one ends by further repetition of *mantra* and by making offerings to the assembled deities.

Then, the stage of completion is rehearsed by imagining the sort of practice one would perform in that stage: one focuses attention on a tiny drop at the midpoint of the brows, which brings about the appearance of eleven mental images such as the appearance of smoke, of a mirage, and of specks of light like fireflies; one observes that the reverberations of the breath are *mantra* sounds; one holds all subtle energies in a pot-like configuration below the navel, causing great inner heat; one has sexual union with a consort to cause the drops to flow in the channels; one observes that the collection of those drops causes the body to dematerialize, leaving only a body of "empty form"; and simultaneously, one experiences the destruction of all the obstructions to liberation and buddhahood. The *sādhana* ends with sincere wishes for its success for oneself and for all other sentient beings.

Conclusion

Although there are many variations, great and small, within the *sādhana* literature, *sādhanas* are basically similar in terms of their structure, motivating factors and use of deity *yoga*. In brief, one establishes one's motivation and establishes oneself in the view of emptiness, which is reality. Then one practices the visualization of the divine realm, honoring the buddha whose form one sees. One thereby experiences a merging of that realm with oneself. Finally, one experiences bliss and imagines a process of bodily transformation through the various practices of the stages of generation and completion. Thus, the *sādhana* is a rehearsal of the entire spiritual path, but also is the living of a new life, a divine life, with the eventual goal of exchanging or transforming the present dim-witted, limited, and corrupt personality for the crystalline, spacious, and altruistic state of supreme enlightenment.

Notes

1. The description of Kālacakra is a condensed version, based on the introduction by Jeffrey Hopkins, of the elaborate description in Dalai Lama XIV, 1984: 75-91. A scroll painting (*thang ka*) of Kālacakra can be found on the cover of that book as well as in the center of the Kālacakra initiation book from the 1981 Madison, Wisconsin initiation. Plates showing the details of the Kālacakra *maṇḍala* are also included in the former.

2. The practitioner, a *sādhaka,* is also a *siddha* (who may also be called a *sādhu*, though this word is commonly used for all manner of Indian holy persons), one who has (or, less technically, at least seeks) power (*siddhi*).

3. The chanting itself can be extraordinary, as demonstrated by the monks of the dGe lugs tantric colleges. Hear, for instance, the 1989 Ryodisc recording of the Gyuto (rGyud stod) Monks, *Freedom Chants from the Roof of the World*, which includes a *sādhana* of Yamāntaka.

4. As Wayman (1987: 473) has noted, the tantric tradition probably developed orally from around the third century C.E., leaving textual evidence only by way of chapters appended to other works which are concerned with *dhāraṇī*, and thus with evocation of a deity by means of *mantra*. Hirakawa Akira (526-527) finds evidence for a dating of the sixth or seventh century for first texts of the Kriyā, Caryā, and Yoga Tantra type (to use the fourteenth-century scholar Bu ston's classification). It appears that the oldest extant tantra of the Anuttarayoga type is the *Guhyasamāja Tantra*, produced no later than the end of the eighth century. Inasmuch as the very essence of tantra is ritual performance, *sādhanas* or *sādhana*-like texts must have have been produced

right along with root tantras. The Indian *sādhanas* collected in the *Sādhanamālā*, the oldest extant manuscript of which is dated to 1165 C.E. (D. C. Bhattacharyya: 3), may have been composed over many centuries. The authors to whom these *sādhanas* are attributed range from Saraha, the "tantric" Nāgārjuna, and Lūyipa, all of whom may have lived as early as the seventh century, to Abhayākaragupta, who flourished in the twelfth century. Many of them, however, are anonymous. Most of these short *sādhanas* are found in Tibetan translation in the bsTan 'gyur of the Tibetan Buddhist canon.

5. A number of indigenous Tibetan treatises describe the general procedure for tantric practice. For instance, Tsong kha pa's vast *sNgags rim chen mo* synthesizes many *tantras*, commentaries, and *sādhanas*; however, since even it makes somewhat broad generalizations, it lacks the specific, detailed visualization instructions required for practice, although it is true that some *sādhanas* could easily be constructed from it. Similarly, there are also works that set forth in great detail the way to practice the stage of generation of a given *tantra*, but do not contain all the elements of a *sādhana*.

6. One is empowered to perform a *sādhana* only if one has been "purified" and "enhanced" by initiation. It is also through the initiation that one really learns the *sādhana*, since the initiation is as much a rehearsal of the *sādhana* as the *sādhana* is a rehearsal for buddhahood.

7. See, for instance, the hundreds of short Indian *sādhanas* in the *Sādhanamālā* (Bhattacharya, 1968), an extra-canonical compilation that includes *sādhanas* from virtually the entire history of Indian Buddhist tantrism.

8. There are *sādhanas* in the bsTan 'gyur of the Tibetan canon that are virtually identical to the Indian *sādhanas* in the *Sādhanamālā*. However, as Wayman (1973: 55) notes, most of the subsequent Tibetan *sādhanas* based on Indian originals are superior in terms of completeness.

9. An excellent example of this among those deity *yoga* manuals translated into English are the three versions of the Kālacakra practice included in Dalai Lama XIV, 1985: 381-433—a simple, general practice formulated in the seventeenth century by the first Paṇ chen Lama, Blo bzang chos kyi rgyal mtshan (1567?-1662); a much more elaborate practice formulated by the present Dalai Lama, Tenzin Gyatso, and versified by Gling Rin po che (1903-1983); and a very short practice by Blo bzang bstan 'dzin.

10. The collections are *Pa tshab sgrub thabs brgya rtsa, Ba ri sgrub thabs brgya rtsa, sGrub thabs rgya mtsho*, and *Lha so so sna tshogs kyi sgrub thabs*.

11. A desideratum, but a task beyond the scope of this chapter, is a survey of all of the collected works (*gsung 'bum*) of major writers in each of the principal orders to determine which deities they chose for *sādhana* composition, how long were their works, and to what degree they depended upon Indian *sādhanas*. We would expect to see numbers in proportion to the attention given those deities in the respective traditions, but it would be interesting to see how emphases may have shifted over time. One difficulty with that task is that not all *sādhanas* are clearly labelled as such by title and there are a great many "branch" texts, such as short works on the stage of generation

(*utpattikrama, bskyed rim*) of particular deities, empowerment texts, ritual texts for fire offerings, or works on the *maṇḍalas* of various deities, such as the *Niṣpannayogāvalī* of Abhayākaragupta, that are similar to *sādhanas*. Thus, one would have many individual texts to examine.

For example, in the catalogue of works for authors of the dGe lugs tradition who composed a quantity of texts large enough to have "Collected Works" (the catalogue's name is *gSung 'bum dkar chag*), there are between 10,000 and 15,000 individual titles. The lists of dGe lugs founder Tsong kha pa Blo bzang grags pa and his two principal disciples, rGyal tsab dar ma rin chen and mKhas grub dge legs dpal bzang, show several Guyhasamāja, Vajrabhairava (a form of Yamāntaka), and Kālacakra works and a smaller number for Cakrasaṃvara, Hevajra, and others. Mullin (1983: 44), who has analyzed the works of the Dalai Lamas, notes that several composed dozens of *sādhanas*. The fifth Dalai Lama is famed for *sādhanas* he composed for twenty-five deities.

12. The rNying ma scholar Tulku Thondup Rinpoche (1986) provides schema of the categories of texts in two non-canonical rNying ma collections, the *rNying ma rgyud 'bum* (182-183), the original collection of tantras used by the rNying ma order, and the *Rin chen gter gyi mdzod* (186-188), a major collection of "discovered" (*gter ma*) texts. Both contain many *sādhanas*.

13. English translations of *sādhanas* can be found, inter alia, in Beyer (1973 and 1974), Mullin (1983 and 1991), Dalai Lama XIV (1985 and 1988), Willis, Willson (1984, 1985, and 1986), Yeshe, Blofeld, and Conze (1956 and 1964). Davidson discusses a number of important Sa skya *sādhanas* for the Hevajra cycle, including a detailed summation of dKon mchog lhun grub's *mNgon rtogs yan lag drug pa'i mdzes rgyan* with elaborations from Ngor chen Kun dga' bzang po's *dPal kye rdo rje'i sgrub pa'i thabs kyi rgya cher bshad pa bskyed rim gnad kyi zla zer*. The rNying ma scholar Tulku Thondup Rinpoche (1986: 177-181) summarizes *Rig 'dzin 'dus pa*, a model *sādhana* of the *kLong chen snying thig* cycle discovered by 'Jigs med gling pa (1729-1798). In an earlier work (1982) he translated the same author's *rNam mkhyen lam bzang*, called a "preliminary" (*sngon 'gro*), but really, as he notes, a complete *sādhana*.

14. Gómez (378) notes concisely that the *maṇḍala* is at once a chart of the present human being, a plan for liberation, and the representation of a transfigured body; that is, the parts of the *maṇḍala* can be homologized to the personal aggregates, it is the context for liberation, and it may be homologized to the body of the buddha one is to become.

15. Although all supramundane deities in the tantric *maṇḍalas* are forms of buddhas, some take the form of bodhisattvas of high attainment such as sPyan ras gzigs (Avalokiteśvara) or sGrol ma (Tārā); see Dalai Lama XIV, 1984: 96.

16. In most *tantras*, the particular Form Body would be an Enjoyment Body (*longs sku, sambhogakāya*), but since this is not the case for the *Kālacakra Tantra*, the less specific term is used.

17. Buddhas are said to have transcended the need for conceptual awareness; all of their actions occur spontaneously, without deliberation, in reaction to the needs of sentient beings.

18. The rNying ma religious order recognizes six sets, a result of dividing the latter category into three sets.

19. Each set of *tantras* has many deities associated with it. Some deities, such as Tārā, have both lower tantra and Highest Yoga Tantra *sādhanas*. There are differences in the structure of such *sādhanas*, as will be discussed below, but there is also the difference that practitioners of Action and Performance Tantras are not required to take special tantric vows. Also, it should be noted that a *sādhana* does not necessarily have only *one* main deity. The *guru yoga* instructions of the Dalai Lama (1988: 11) combine visualizations of Yamāntaka, Guhyasamāja, and Heruka in the *guru's* body.

20. The Tibetan text, composed by H. H. the Fourteenth Dalai Lama and versified by Gling Rin po che, can be found in the Deer Park Kālacakra Initiation manual (51-69). *Sādhanas* associated with *tantras* of the Highest Yoga Tantra class are mainly concerned with the procedure of the first stage, the stage of generation (this is noted by Jackson [119], who provides an extensive summation of mKhas grub rje's *sādhana* in a chapter that begins on that page). Why are most *sādhanas* restricted to the generation stage? I would speculate that this is mainly because although many people receive initiations into a Highest Yoga Tantra stage of generation (thousands at a time, for instance, are initiated into Kālacakra), only the relative few who succeed in completing it require *sādhanas* for the stage of completion. Those persons can receive further instruction—and perhaps only oral instruction is necessary or sufficient—when appropriate.

The *sādhana* to which I refer in the next several paragraphs concludes with a brief summation of the occurrences of the stage of completion, but since this is little more than an outline it would be insufficient to use as the basis of a completion stage practice.

21. As this can be done in various ways, one would need additional instructions from a teacher.

22. John Newman (personal communication) noted that Kālacakra texts seem to prefer the term *saṃpannakrama*, occasionally *utpannakrama*.

23. Tantric physiology assumes the existence of a somatic system of channels, energy currents, and drops that are "subtle" (supersensory).

References

Akira, Hirakawa

1987 "Buddhist Literature." In *Encyclopedia of Religion*. Ed. by Mircea Eliade. New York: Macmillan.

Beyer, Stephan

1973 *The Cult of Tārā*. Berkeley: University of California.

1974 *The Buddhist Experience: Sources and Interpretations*. Belmont, CA: Dickenson.

Bhattacharya, Benoytosh

1958 *Indian Buddhist Iconography.* Second edition. Calcutta: Mukhopadhyay.

1968 *Sādhanamālā.* Baroda: Oriental Institute.

Bhattacharyya, Dipak Chandra

1973 *Tantric Buddhist Iconographical Sources.* New Delhi: Munshiram Manoharlal.

Blofeld, John

1987 *The Tantric Mysticism of Tibet.* Boston: Shambhala.

Conze, Edward

1956 *Buddhist Meditation.* New York: Harper & Row.

1964 *Buddhist Texts Through the Ages.* New York: Harper & Row.

Davidson, Ronald M.

1992 "Preliminary Studies on Hevajra's *Abhisamaya* and the *Lam-'bras Tshogs-bshad.*" In *Tibetan Buddhism: Reason and Revelation.* Ed. by Steven D. Goodman and Ronald M. Davidson. Albany: State University of New York Press.

Dalai Lama XIV, Tenzin Gyatso

1977 "Introduction" to *Tantra in Tibet.* London: George Allen and Unwin.

1981 *Kalachakra Initiation.* Madison, Wisconsin: Deer Park.

1984 *Kindness, Clarity and Insight.* Ithaca: Snow Lion.

1985 *Kalachakra Tantra: Rite of Initiation.* London: Wisdom.

1988 *The Union of Bliss and Emptiness.* Ithaca: Snow Lion.

Gómez, Luis

1987 "Buddhism: Buddhism in India." In *Encyclopedia of Religion.* Ed. by Mircea Eliade. New York: Macmillan.

Jackson, Roger

1985 "The Kalachakra Generation Stage Sādhana." In Geshe Lhundub Sopa, Roger Jackson, and John Newman, *The Wheel of Time.* Madison: Deer Park. Reprinted Ithaca: Snow Lion, 1991.

'Jam dbyangs blo gter dbang po

1970 *sGrub thabs kun btus.* 14 vols. Dehra Dun: G. T. K. Lodong, N. Lungtok, and N. Gyaltsen.

Mullin, Glenn

1983 *Meditations on the Lower Tantras.* Dharamsala: Library of Tibetan Works and Archives.

1991 *The Practice of Kalachakra.* Ithaca: Snow Lion.

Rawson, Philip
1991 *Sacred Tibet*. London: Thames and Hudson.

Thondup, Tulku
1982 *The Dzog-Chen Preliminary Practice of the Innermost Essence*. Dharamsala: Library of Tibetan Works and Archives.
1986 *Hidden Teachings of Tibet*. London: Wisdom.

Tsong kha pa Blo bzang grags pa
1981 *Yoga of Tibet*. Trans. by Jeffrey Hopkins. London: George Allen and Unwin.

Wayman, Alex
1973 *The Buddhist Tantras*. New York: Samuel Weiser.
1987 "Esoteric Buddhism." In *Encyclopedia of Religion*. Ed. by Mircea Eliade. New York: Macmillan.

Willis, Janice
1972 *The Diamond Light of the Eastern Dawn*. New York: Simon and Schuster.

Willson, Martin
1984 *Cittamani Tārā: An Extended Sādhana*. London: Wisdom.
1985 *Rites and Prayers: An FPMT Manual*. London: Wisdom.
1986 *In Praise of Tārā*. London: Wisdom.

Yeshe, Lama Thubten
1984 *Sādhana and Ritual Feast (Ts'ok) of Heruka-Vajrasattva*. London: Wisdom.

Chapter 20

Firm Feet and Long Lives: The *Zhabs brtan* Literature of Tibetan Buddhism[1]

José Ignacio Cabezón

Woe unto us, Master, when thou shalt depart from the world.

—*Zohar* II, 193b[2]

The Death of the Buddha

All Buddhists believe that Śākyamuni, the historical Buddha, attained the state of immortal bliss known as *nirvāṇa*. According to some Abhidharma literature, however, the Buddha's *body* is a conditioned phenomenon, since it is something he possessed before he became enlightened. It is therefore subject to decay and death (see Cabezón, 1987: 34; and *LSSP*: 126b). But despite the fact that the Buddha's death was seen as inevitable, because of his extraordinary accomplishments it was maintained that the Buddha could prolong his life for an enormous period of time, even for an eon, if he so wished. In the *Mahāparinibbāna Sutta* (*Dīgha Nikāya* III, 103), for example, the Buddha hints to his disciple Ānanda that this is the case. Ānanda fails to pick up on the hint and makes no attempt to encourage the Buddha to remain as long as possible in the world. The demon Māra then appears and reminds the Buddha of a statement he had made shortly after his enlightenment, in which he claimed that he would not pass away until his order and his teachings had been established in the world. Māra points out to the Buddha that this has now occurred and encourages him to pass away. The Buddha agrees that after three months he will do so. The earth quakes and Ānanda asks the Buddha why this has occurred. He is told that there are eight causes of earthquakes and that the eighth is that of a *tathāgata*'s imminent passing. He relates to Ānanda in this way the news that he will die within three months. Ānanda, overwrought by the news, thrice requests the Buddha to remain, but his requests are to no avail. Having missed his cue, Ānanda is unable to overturn the Buddha's decision. The Buddha continues (*Digha Nikaya* II,115):

> Then, O Ānanda, thine is the fault, thine is the offense—in that when a suggestion so evident and a hint so clear were thus given thee by the Tathāgata, thou wast yet incapable of comprehending them, and thou besoughtest not the Tathāgata, saying: "Vouchsafe, Lord, to remain during the aeon for the good and happiness of the multitudes, out of pity for the world, for the good and the gain and the weal of gods and men." If thou should then have so besought the Tathāgata, the Tathāgata might have rejected the appeal even unto the second time, but the third time he would have granted it. Thine, therefore, O Ānanda, is the fault, thine is the offense! (Rhys Davids: 122)

Rhys Davids (126) believes that in the oldest core of the canon, this idea of the Buddha's ability to remain for an eon is missing and that instead the Buddha's passing away was simply seen as a lesson in impermanence and the inevitability of death.[3] Be that as it may, it is clear that, based upon this incident, the idea of requesting the Buddha to live for as long as possible is an old and influential one which has gained wide acceptance in both the Theravāda and Mahāyāna traditions.

The Idea of Supplication

In the *Bhadracaripraṇidhāna*, a very early Mahāyāna work, we find incorporated into a seven-part (*saptāṅga, yan lag bdun*) prayer that became the basis of much later Tibetan ritual a verse that supplicates the buddhas in the different world systems to remain in the world for the benefit of sentient beings:

> With folded hands I beseech those of you
> Who have the intention of demonstrating the action of

passing away
To remain for as many eons as there are atoms in the universe
So as to benefit and bring happiness to all beings.
(*TS*: 13)[4]

The verse clearly presupposes the earlier Pāli account of the Buddha's passing away and Ānanda's negligence in failing to ask him to remain, but its overtly Mahāyāna flavor allows it to go in directions unknown to Pāli sources. Taking for granted a vast cosmos populated by buddhas, the novelty of the *Bhadracari*'s approach lies in the implicit assumption that there are many—indeed infinite numbers—of buddhas throughout the universe whose long lives are to be requested. What is more, it assumes that the responsibility for preserving the lives of enlightened beings throughout the universe has passed onto each individual adept. The lesson to be learned from Ānanda's error is that it is incumbent upon every Buddhist practitioner to supplicate the buddhas that remain within the various realms of the universe, requesting them to continue to live for as long as possible.

One other point should be mentioned in passing, and that is that this particular type of supplication, beseeching the buddhas not to pass into *nirvāṇa* but to remain in the world (*zhugs gsol*), is a specific example of the more general category of supplication (*gsol ba*), which also includes beseeching the buddhas and bodhisattvas for their blessings (*byin rlab gsol ba*),[5] inciting them to teach (*chos kyi 'khor lo 'khor bar bskul ba*),[6] and, in the later Tibetan tradition, requesting spiritual masters who have recently passed away to return in new incarnations (*myur gsol*).

The *Zhabs brtan* Literature in Tibet

Tibetan Buddhism is, of course, tantric in character. As such, it places tremendous emphasis on the role of the spiritual master (*guru, bla ma*). It is one of the fundamental axioms of Buddhist tantrism that the spiritual master is to be viewed as a fully enlightened being, that is, as a buddha. In the *lam rim* literature, a proper relationship to the spiritual master, both mentally (in terms of one's attitude[7]) and physically (demonstrating one's respect for him or her through proper action and service), is considered the "root of the path" (*lam gyi rtsa ba*). Given the fact that the spiritual master was to be viewed as a buddha and that all buddhas were to be supplicated to remain within the world and not to pass on, it is only natural that at some point in the history of Tibetan religious literature prayers requesting the longevity of various spiritual masters should have developed. Such a genre of literature in fact evolved into a separate type of Tibetan religious poetry called *zhabs brtan* (literally, "firm feet").

It is taboo in Tibetan culture to give one's masters shoes as offerings, for fear that they might misinterpret it as a sign of one's desire that they "pass on," never to return. The idea is that as long as their feet are firm on the ground and close to one, spiritual teachers will be able to guide one on the path. Hence, anything that could even hint at their departure (e.g., a new pair of shoes) is considered inappropriate.

Despite its rather comical name, the *zhabs brtan* is one of the most beautiful genres in all of Tibetan religious literature. Always in the form of verses with fixed meter, it is usually undertaken only by the great masters of Tibetan verse (*snyan ngags*) (see R. Jackson, in this volume). Its beauty, however, is not the stark beauty of the Zen verse, but the beauty of a rococo adornment or a baroque period High Mass: it is the beauty of the extreme elaboration of symbol within rigidly controlled limits set by tradition that is so typical of Buddhist scholasticism. For this reason, the *zhabs brtan* is not only representative of indigenous Tibetan religious poetry, indeed it stands as one of its high points.

Stylistically, we find in *zhabs brtan* numerous pan-Indian mythological motifs (often having to do with creation myths) employed as metaphors for Buddhist concepts. In one particularly fine example of the genre composed by the Junior Tutor of the fourteenth Dalai Lama for mKhan zur Lhun grub thabs mkhas, the former abbot of the Byes College of Se ra Monastery and one of Geshe Sopa's principal teachers, we find mention of "a Mount Meru of precious and vast exegesis." The metaphor compares the former abbot's learning to Meru, the highest of mountains, situated at the center of the universe. Other verses praise his qualities through metaphors devoted to specific themes. The third verse, for example, develops the metaphor of a great ocean; the fourth, the motif of the onset of spring; and the fifth, that of the moon as the source of cooling rays in summertime. Throughout, the imagery creates an atmosphere of renewal and freshness designed to counteract the master's intention to allow his body to proceed toward decay and death:

May he be protected by the immortal nectar of the captivating Tārā,
The true immutable *vajra*, the essence of life,
Who acts out the illusory role revealed as the amazing major and minor marks,
Endowed with qualities, like a rainbow over Mt. Tise.

Your glory has accomplished the knowledge which can continuously bear up under the weight
Of a veritable Mt. Meru of precious and vast exegesis;
Perfectly skilled in incomparable and supreme method and wisdom,
I beseech you, treasury of the qualities of firmness and sagacity.

You are the dance of a string of waves of valid scripture and reasoning
On an expanse of golden sands, the pure purport of the Conqueror.
Please remain with us, ocean the likes of which has never before been seen;
Who makes pale the Ganges, Dignāga and Dharmakīrti.

The female cuckoo, your three vows, beckons purification and liberation
In a forest of *yongs 'du'* trees, you are the entity who, in the spring of true happiness,
Spreads the never-degenerating power of contentment.
Please remain with us as the supreme of preaching guides.
(*TDBN*: 1b-2a)

It is common in the tantric tradition of the Mahāyāna for adepts to meditate on one of a number of peaceful divinities known as "long-life deities" (*tshe lha*). *Zhabs brtan* often begin with an invocation of one or another of the various long-life deities, such as Amitāyus, or, as in this case, the goddess Tārā. Implicit here is the assumption that the deity will act to intercede on the master's behalf. It seems, however, that this form of initial invocation occurs more often in cases where the spiritual master whose long life is being requested is not a recognized incarnation. Since the time of the fifth Dalai Lama certain masters and their subsequent incarnations came to be considered the actual manifestations of fully enlightened deities. The Dalai Lamas have themselves, since this time, been considered to be the manifestation of Avalokiteśvara, the embodiment of compassion. This being the case, we find that the *zhabs brtan* of these masters, themselves considered buddhas, vary stylistically from the norm. What need, for example, is there to invoke the intercession of another deity when the master in question is himself considered to be a manifestation of an enlightened being?[8]

Another interesting and unique feature of most *zhabs brtan* is the interweaving of the syllables of the master's name into the prayer itself. Of course, since Tibetan personal names are almost always religious names, and since the content of the prayer is itself religious in nature, this is actually a less formidable feat than it might seem at first glance. The effect is almost impossible to capture in translation, however, since the individual syllables of the name are often by themselves meaningless and since they are interwoven within the verses to create new words which at times bear no resemblance to the meaning of the words in the original name of the master. In the above example each line of the second verse contains one syllable of the former abbot's name, Lhun grub thabs mkhas.

Finally, we find that *zhabs brtan* often end with "a prayer of truth" (*bden pa'i smon lam*). This again is a very ancient tradition going back to the Pāli sources, and is present even in non-Buddhist works. The idea, in a Buddhist context, is that the truth of the Buddha or his doctrine, or sometimes one's own pure intentions, themselves have the power to bring about desired goals within the world, such as long life or even that of peace and happiness in the world (see *DSMT*).

A great deal more could be said from a historical and literary-critical point of view concerning the stylistic features of the *zhabs brtan*. This, however, would mean examining many different examples from different periods of time, which of course is impossible within the present context. I content myself, therefore, with having pointed out a few prevalent motifs and structural features, and turn now to some historical and sociological aspects of the *zhabs brtan* and its recitation.

The Early History of the *Zhabs brtan* in Tibet

We have seen that the idea of there being a need to request the long life of enlightened beings is very old. We have also seen that when this became amalgamated with the notion inherent in tantric Buddhism that the spiritual master was himself or herself a buddha, it was natural for there to arise a ritual literature whose function it was to beseech the spiritual master—as an enlightened being—to remain in the world and not to pass away. We find, however, that despite the fact that tantric Buddhism originated and existed in India for centuries, no such literature seems to have existed there.[9] In fact, the *zhabs brtan* as a genre did not exist in Tibet until early in the eighteenth century, about a millennium after the introduction of Buddhism.

We find no mention of any *zhabs brtan* in any of works of the early masters of the Sa skya school[10] (eleventh to thirteenth centuries), or even in the works of the founders of the dGe lugs pa school, Tsong kha pa and his two chief disciples. Indeed, my research on this question has shown that the first works identified specifically as *zhabs brtan* are in the *Collected Works* of the first Rwa sgreng Rin po che, Ngag dbang chos ldan, also known as A chi thu no mon han (1677-1751).[11] Given the popularity of the genre today, this is indeed surprising. Also, given that it is now a pan-sectarian phenomenon, popular among almost every school of Tibetan Buddhism, it is surprising to find that the *zhabs brtan* seems to have developed almost exclusively within the dGe lugs school until very recent times.[12]

This is not to say that the *zhabs brtan* did not have precursors. As early as the sixteenth century, in the works of the first Paṇ chen Lama, Blo bzang chos kyi rgyal mtshan (1569-1662), we find several works identified as *brtan zhugs*[13] (literally, "abiding with stability" or "remaining stable"; it is sometimes a contraction of *zhabs brtan zhugs pa*, literally, "abiding with firm feet"). From this time forward we find works called *brtan zhugs* among the writings of most of the major figures of the dGe lugs school: in the *Collected Works* of the fifth Dalai Lama, in that of the first lCang skya rin po che, Ngag dbang blo bzang chos ldan (1642-1714),[14] and in that of the A kya sprul sku, Blo bzang bstan pa'i rgyal mtshan, a contemporary of lCang skya Rol pa'i rdo rje. How do these *brtan zhugs* compare with the later *zhabs brtan*? For one thing, at least in the earliest versions, they do not show all of the stylistic features of the later fully developed *zhabs brtan*. They lack the initial invocation and usually the final prayer based on "words of truth."

Consider, for example, the "Supplication to Remain Stable, In One Verse" (*brTan zhugs śloka gcig*) of the first Paṇ chen Lama, written most likely for the fifth Dalai Lama:

> O Lord of Speech, who are the supreme moon that outshines all
> other orators,
> The great ocean of doctrine, the scriptures and realizations, of

Blo bzang [Tsong kha pa],
May the excellence of your virtuous name, triumphant in every direction,
Not wane for a hundred eons.
(Blo bzang chos kyi rgyal mtshan, 1973: 33a)

Another example of early *brtan zhugs*, the "Supplication and Request to Remain Stable called 'The Spread of the Buddha's Teachings,'" is perhaps closer still to the *zhabs brtan* genre:

Namo guru Mañjughoṣāya.

O Protector of the day, who are the glory of the teachings of the Buddha,
You are the crown jewel who has gathered beneath it
The great ocean that is the source of all desires, the scriptures and spiritual realizations.
I beseech you to accept my request and live a lengthy life.

I request the long life [*zhabs brtan*] of you, the holy one, who dispels the darkness from beings,
Who is so skilled at making swell the ocean of the *sūtra* and *tantra* teachings
Of the second Buddha, the conqueror, Tsong kha pa,
With the millions of rays of your enlightened activity.

May you remain for a long time, O holy spiritual friend,
Who seeks to increase the happiness of the beings of this fortunate age
By exhibiting the gem of the two stages and three trainings
That emerges from the ocean of the Buddha's teachings.
(Blo bzang chos kyi rgyal mtshan, 1973: 6b)

It is clear from these various examples of *brtan zhugs* that this genre is the direct precursor of the *zhabs brtan*. Although not as elaborate, and though the name *zhabs brtan* is not used to specify the genre until almost two hundred years later, it is clear that the latter is the direct descendant of the former.

Whether we ask the question of the *brtan zhugs* or of the more developed *zhabs brtan* literature, however, there is still the quandary of what historical circumstances led to the sudden and exponential increase in the popularity of this genre as a distinct literary form.

E. Gene Smith has conjectured that the sudden popularity of a related genre of liturgical works, the *myur gsol* ("prayers for the quick reincarnation of deceased masters"), is due to the fact that "the eighteenth century saw a sudden mushrooming of incarnate lama lineages in the Mongol lands" (3). This might explain the sudden popularity of the specifically *zhabs brtan* form of liturgical work (which is roughly contemporaneous with the *myur gsol*) but, as we have seen, the *zhabs brtan* have an antecedent in the *brtan zhugs* literature, which predates it by almost two hundred years. Hence, the real problem is to explain the sudden rise in popularity of the *brtan zhugs*.

The answer to the question comes from noticing that the *brtan zhugs* begins to gain popularity during the time of the first Paṇ chen Lama, who is the tutor of the fifth Dalai Lama. In fact, the earliest examples we have of this literature are *brtan zhugs* of the fifth Dalai Lama himself. What is the significance of the fact that the *brtan zhugs* originates during the time of the fifth Dalai Lama? The Great Fifth (lNga pa chen po), as he is known in the tradition, is renowned for having consolidated power over Central and Western Tibet (dBus gTsang) during his reign. As is well known, he simultaneously elevated the status of his incarnation lineage by declaring that he, and indeed all of the previous Dalai Lamas, were the incarnation of Avalokiteśvara, the manifestation of compassion. The *brtan zhugs* could have been yet one more method to accomplish the goal of distinguishing this particular incarnation lineage as unique. Perhaps the implication was that it was not the long life of everyone that was worth supplicating. This is not, of course, to say that the first Paṇ chen Lama wrote the Great Fifth's *brtan zhugs* simply for political reasons; this would be reductionism in the extreme. Nonetheless, that his actions had certain repercussions in the political sphere seems unquestionable. Of course, it is natural that a ritual/poetical device that was found to be successful in consolidating the self-identity and glory of one lineage should have spread, and within a few generations the popularity of the *zhabs brtan* as an independent genre was guaranteed.

The Place of the *Zhabs brtan* in Tibetan Ritual Practice

Today, the *zhabs brtan* is an essential part of Tibetan ritual. In the dGe lugs school it is customary to recite the *zhabs brtan* of the fourteenth Dalai Lama and (until their deaths) of his two tutors, at the end of almost every major ritual event or doctrinal discourse. Especially during the performance of the "Offering to the Spiritual Master" (*Bla ma mchod pa*) (see Makransky, in this volume), one of the most popular rituals within the tradition, it is customary to break in the midst of the ceremony to recite the *zhabs brtan* of the master to whom the ritual is being dedicated and/or that of other masters in the tradition. Often, the monks of a monastery will be commissioned to recite the *zhabs brtan* of a certain spiritual master a certain number of times, or more commonly, the recitation of the *zhabs brtan* is an addendum to a number of repetitions of the *gNas brtan phyags mchod* (*NTPC*), a ritual of supplication and offering to the sixteen *arhants* that is also related to the establishment of long life. In short, the recitation of *zhabs brtan* has become so popular in modern times that the word has almost become a synonym for ritual itself.[15]

Zhabs brtan are usually chanted with a special melody, which may be used in other settings as well, but infrequently. In addition, it has become a fairly common practice to perform elaborate rituals to request the long lives of great masters of the tradition. These are called *brtan zhugs* (after the precursor of the *zhabs brtan* literature), and involve not only the recitation of *zhabs brtan* and related works, but also an elaborate presentation of money, precious substances, and symbolic offerings of various sorts. The popular belief is that such ceremonies ensure the longevity of the master to whom the ritual is dedicated.

Conclusion

Despite *brtan zhugs, zhabs brtan* and other ritual devices, spiritual masters continue to die. Does this require explanation or justification? Not for Tibetan Buddhists. According to the tradition, an enlightened being will always be engaged in the actions that are most beneficial for sentient beings, whether asked to do so or not. The death of a master is the ultimate lesson in impermanence for the disciple, a point made by Rhys Davids above. If impermanence plagues even the bodies of the enlightened, how much more our own!

The *Saddharmapuṇḍarīka Sūtra* ("Lotus Sūtra") adduces other reasons.[16] *Tathāgatas* die, the text states, because they wish to emphasize that they are not to be taken for granted. If humans were to think that buddhas would be present forever, they would never exert themselves in spiritual practice. It is held that by "feigning" death buddhas create a longing in the hearts of humankind for the appearance of other enlightened beings (this longing itself being a source of merit), but what is most important is that it creates within human beings the will to practice the doctrine and engenders within disciples an attitude of awe that appreciates the rarity of the appearance of a buddha within the world (Vaidya: 190).

Is the fact that spiritual masters die in spite of the disciple's prayer for their long life sufficient reason for abandoning the recitation of *zhabs brtan*? The answer, extrapolated from the *Saddharmapuṇḍarīka Sūtra*, is clearly no. As with all forms of Tibetan ritual, *zhabs brtan* are believed to act as vehicles for the adept's own mental transformation. What is most important is that adepts desire the continued presence of their master, not that the master actually remain. In the end, Ānanda's greatest fault did not lie in the fact of the Buddha's premature death but in the fact that Ānanda himself may not have sufficiently appreciated the presence of his master.

Notes

1. Portions of this paper were presented before the Minnesota South Asia Consortium and the 1989 meeting of the International Association for Tibetan Studies in Narita, Japan.

2. As translated by Fine: 312.

3. The *Saddharmapuṇḍarīka Sūtra* makes it clear that the Tathāgata play-acts death so that his disciples will not take him (or his coming) for granted and so continue to practice with ardor, realizing that the teachings are rare and precious. The Mahāyāna notion that the Tathāgata was enlightened eons ago is made clear, as is the idea that the Tathāgata could not only live for an eon, but forever, if he so chose:

> *tāvaccirābhisaṃbuddho 'parimitāyuṣpramāṇastathāgataḥ sadā sthitaḥ/ aparinirvṛtastathāgataḥ parinirvāṇam ādarsayati vaineyavasena* (Vaidya: 190)
>
> Thus, having attained complete enlightenment so long ago, the Tathāgata has an infinite lifespan. He remains forever. But although he does not actually die, he play-acts death for the sake of his disciples.

In other passages, however, it seems that the infinity (*aparimita*) of his lifespan is not taken literally but refers instead to an extremely long but finite period of time [*me kalpakoṭīnayutaśatasaharāṇi bhaviṣyanti ayuṣpramāṇasya-āparipūrṇatvāt* (Vaidya: 190)].

4. A similar verse, found in the setting of a different seven part prayer, is the famous verse in the *Bla ma mchod pa* ("Ritual of Offering to the Spiritual Master"):

Though your vajra body has no birth or death
You have taken on the vessel of the king of the power of union.
I request that you, in accordance with my prayers,
Remain forever and not pass away until the end of existence.
(*LC*: 53)

5. See, for example, *LC*: 58 and *YT*: 109-112 for two renowned examples of this type of prayer in the dGe lugs pa school.

6. Here, the word *bskul ba* ("inciting") almost has the same connotation as *gsol ba* ("supplicating" or "beseeching"). See *TS*: 13.

7. Consider the words of Ngag dbang blo bzang rgya mtsho, the fifth Dalai Lama (*JPZL*: 16a): "To whatever extent one can bring an end to the misperception that (spiritual masters) have even the most subtle of faults, and to the extent that one can increase the faith in the fact that they possess even the most minute good qualities, to that extent will this (attitude) become for one the root of the accumulation of all goodness and of all spiritual attainment."

8. As an example of this, see the renowned *zhabs brtan* composed for the fourteenth Dalai Lama by his two tutors, called "A Melody to Establish Immortality" (*CGBN*: 144). This work has been memorized by almost every Tibetan in exile, and by those who have access to the work in Tibet itself.

9. There are, to my knowledge, no such works translated into Tibetan from the Sanskrit. Taube's (685) Sanskrit equivalent of *sthirāsana*, though not identified as such, seems to be a reconstruction from the Tibetan.

10. Although we find "praises" (*bstod pa*) and "homages" (*bskur ba*) in the *Sa skya bka' 'bum* (bSod rnams rgya mtsho, *SK*) there is no mention of any *zhabs brtan* literature.

11. Moreover, he has two later contemporaries who are also known for their composition of *zhabs brtan* literature. These are the famous Thu'u bkwan Blo bzang chos kyi nyi ma (1737-1802) and the second lCang skya rin po che, Rol pa'i rdo rje (1717-1786). The A chi thu no mon han works are listed in Taube's catalogue of German manuscripts (685 passim), but I have yet to obtain copies. In *CWTK*, vol. 3 (*ga*): 703-727, we find a very interesting work which is a commentary by Blo bzang 'jig med on the *Zhabs rtan gsol 'debs dge legs 'dod 'jo*, a *zhabs brtan* written by lCang skya Rol pa'i rdo rje for Thu'u bkwan.

12. Besides the *gSung 'bum* of the early Sa skya masters, I have also searched, in vain, for examples of *zhabs brtan* in the works of Tāranātha (b.1575), 'Brug pa Pad ma dkar po (1526-1592), Jaya Paṇḍita (b.1642), and 'Ju Mi pham rgya mtsho (1846-1914).

13. Blo bzang chos kyi rgyal mtshan (1973), vol. *ca*, no. 4 (*gSol 'debs brtan zhugs sangs rgyas bstan dpal ma*), no. 5 (*Sems dpa' chen po la bstod pa brtan zhugs dang bcas pa*), no. 32 (*Thams cad mkhyen pa'i sprul sku'i brtan zhugs*) and no. 33 (*brTan zhugs śloka gcig*).

14. All of them are to be found in vol. *ja* of his *gSung 'bum* (see Lokesh Chandra: 184-192).

15. Hence, despite the fact that monks often are invited to the homes of lay persons to perform other rituals, it is common to say that they have "gone to *zhabs brtan*."

16. The notion that the Buddha's death is a mere *upāya*, an example of skillful means, to teach his disciples a lesson in impermanence is to be found in chapter 15 ("Tathāgatāyuṣpramāṇaparivartaḥ") of the *Saddharmapuṇḍarīka Sūtra* ("Lotus Sūtra") (Vaidya: 189-195; see also Kern: 298-310).

References

bSod rnams rgya mtsho, ed.

SK *Collected Works of the Masters of the Sa skya Sect [Sa skya pa'i bka' 'bum]*. Tokyo: Tōyō Bunko.

Cabezón, José Ignacio

1987 *The Development of a Buddhist Philosophy of Language and its Culmination in Tibetan Mādhyamika Thought*. Ph.D dissertation. Madison: University of Wisconsin-Madison.

Dalai Lama V, Ngag dbang blo bzang rgya mtsho

JPZL *Byang chub lam gyi rim pa'i khrid yig 'Jam dpal zhal lung*. Bylakuppe, India: undated blockprint.

Dalai Lama XIV, bsTan 'dzin rgya mtsho

DSMN *bDen gsol smon tshig*. In *bLa ma'i rnal sbyor*, pp. 557-559. Dharamsala: Shes rig par khang, 1979.

Fine, Lawrence

1984 "Kabbalistic Texts." In *Back to the Sources*. Ed. by Barry W. Holtz. New York: Summit Books.

Gling Rin po che, Thub bstan lung rtog rnam rgyal phrin las and Khri byang Rin po che, Blo bzang ye shes

CGBN *Chi med grub pa'i dbyangs snyan*. In *Bla ma'i rnal sbyor*. Dharamsala: Shes rig par khang, 1979.

gNas brtan phyags mchod

NTPC In *Bla ma'i rnal sbyor*, pp. 157-171. Dharamsala: Shes rig par khang, 1973.

Kern, H.

1963 *Saddharmapuṇḍarīka or Lotus of the True Law*. Sacred Books of the East, vol. 21. New York: Dover.

Khri byang rin po che, Blo bzang ye shes

TDBN *Zhabs brtan gsol 'debs rtag brtan grub pa'i dbyangs snyan*. Lhasa: blockprint, n.d.

Lokesh Chandra

1981 *Materials for the Study of Tibetan Literature.* First edition, Delhi: Śata-Piṭaka Series 28. Reprinted Tokyo.

Paṇ chen Lama I, Blo bzang chos kyi rgyal msthan

1973 *Collected Works of the First Panchen Lama.* Delhi: Mongolian Lama Gurudeva.

LC *Bla ma mchod pa.* In *Bla ma'i rnal sbyor.* Dharamsala: Shes rig par khang, 1979.

Rhys Davids, C. A. F.

1966 *Dialogues of the Buddha.* [Translation of *Dīgha Nikāya*] London: Luzac and Co.

Smith, E. Gene

1969 "Introduction" to the *Collected Works of Thu'u kwan.* Delhi: Ngawang Gelek Demo.

Taube, Manfred

1966 *Tibetische Handschriften.* Teil 3. Wiesbaden: Franz Steiner Verlag.

Thu'u bkwan Blo bzang chos kyi nyi ma

CWTK *Collected Works of Thu'u bkwan.* Delhi: Ngawang Gelek Demo, 1969.

Tsong kha pa, Blo bzang grags pa

LSSP *Legs bshad gser phreng.* Bylakuppe, India: blockprint n.d.

YT *Yon ten gzhir gyur ma.* In *sByor chos* of dBen sa pa. In *Bla ma'i rnal 'byor.* Dharamsala: Shes rig par khang, 1979.

TS *lTung bshags, sPyi bshags, bZang spyod.* Chushi Kangdrug, 1984.

Vaidya, P. L., ed.

1960 *Saddharmapuṇḍarīkasūtram.* Buddhist Sanskrit Texts 6. Darbhanga: Mithila Institute.

Chapter 21

The Gesar Epic of East Tibet

Geoffrey Samuel

King Ge sar of Gling (*Gling Ge sar rgyal po*) is the hero of one of the major epic cycles of Central and East Asia, known throughout and beyond the Tibetan and Mongolian cultural regions.[1] There may well have been a historical King Ge sar in East Tibet in the tenth or eleventh century but he probably was just one of a number of sources for the epic (*sgrung*) as we know it today (Samuel, 1992). The Ge sar epic constitutes the principal repertoire of professional epic bards (*sgrung mkhan*) who are found especially in the nomadic areas of Tibet. The epic is also performed by amateurs, particularly in East Tibet. Ge sar is regarded as an ancestor-hero by the people of Khams, and the epic is felt to express the martial and heroic spirit of the Khams pa people. Wealthy Khams pa families often own manuscripts of the epic, and several episodes were printed in woodblock editions in the nineteenth century under monastic patronage.

Although Ge sar is known throughout Tibet, the most elaborate tradition of the epic is found in the East Tibetan manuscript and printed versions. The full extent of the East Tibetan Ge sar cycle has only become clear over the last few years, as texts of the major episodes have been published in India, Bhutan and the People's Republic of China. Numerous individual episodes have been printed in the Tibetan refugee community, and a 31-volume collected edition has appeared in Bhutan. In the People's Republic of China, an extensive "Save the Gesar Epic" campaign has been underway for some years, and so far about sixty versions of various episodes have been published in Tibetan, mostly from blockprint and manuscript sources, but some on the basis of oral performances by contemporary epic bards.

In English-speaking countries, the Tibetan Ge sar stories have become known mainly through summaries of the main episodes by Alexandra David-Neel and Lama Yongden, first published in French in 1931 and translated into English in 1933 (see David-Neel and Yongden). While reasonably faithful to the outline of the story, this version gives no real idea of the literary and musical qualities of the epic. In particular, it includes only one (unrepresentative) song (117-119; cf. 117, n. 1). In fact, the core of a performance of the epic is a series of songs sung by the various characters in the story. An average episode in manuscript contains 5000 to 10,000 lines of verse (50 to 100 songs) linked by a spoken narration, although some episodes are considerably longer (see Wang). These songs, which are performed without instrumental accompaniment, are the most characteristic part of the epic, and, after surveying the main episodes of the epic, I shall devote most of this article to describing them.

The Main Episodes of the Epic

The East Tibetan epic as it is known today consists of a number of separate episodes. The principal ones, using the numbering of Wang Yinuan (q.v.), are as follows (see also Stein, 1959):[2]

(1) *Lha gling* ("The Gods and Gling"). The people of the land of Gling, which is identified by Eastern Tibetans with the territory of Gling tshang near sDe dge, appeal to the gods for help against the demons who are troubling their land. The gods agree to send one of their number to be born on earth to rescue Gling from the four great demon kings (of the North Country, Hor, Mon and 'Jang). Padmasambhava visits the underwater land of the *nāgas* to obtain a *nāga* princess who will be Ge sar's mother.

(4) *'Khrungs gling* ("The Birth"). Ge sar is born on earth as the son of the *nāga* princess and Seng blon, a chief of the tribes of Gling. His wicked uncle, Khro thung, attempts to kill him, but is unsuccessful.

(8) *rTa rgyugs* ("The Horse-Race"). Ge sar tricks his wicked

uncle Khro thung into arranging a horse-race, the winner to become ruler of Gling and husband to 'Brug mo, daughter of the chief of sKya lo. Ge sar wins the race, ascends the throne and marries 'Brug mo.

(10) *bDud 'dul* ("Defeating the Demon-King of the North"). Another wife of Ge sar's, Me bza' 'Bum skyid, is abducted by Klu btsan, the demon king of the North and the first of Ge sar's four great enemies. With the aid of Me bza' and of Klu btsan's sister, the female warrior A stag lha mo, Ge sar kills Klu btsan, and the people of the demon-realm become converts to Buddhism and allies of Gling. However, Me bza' drugs Ge sar so that he forgets his mission, and he remains with her in the demon-realm of the North.

(11) *Hor gling g.yul 'gyed* ("The War of Hor and Gling"). Meanwhile the three demon-kings of Hor, led by Gur dkar, overcome Gling and abduct 'Brug mo, who becomes the mother of Gur dkar's child. Ge sar is eventually aroused from his drugged state, returns to Gling and leads a successful campaign to defeat Hor, which becomes an ally of Gling.

(13, 14) *'Jang gling g.yul 'gyed* ("The War of 'Jang and Gling"); *Mon gling g.yul 'gyed* ("The War of Mon and Gling"). These are the two further demon-king episodes, in which King Sa tham of the 'Jang (a people identified with the Naxi of present-day Yunnan) and King Shing khri of Mon are defeated, and their peoples become allies of Gling.

(18) *Nag po rgya gling kyi le'u* ("The China Episode"). Ge sar goes on a (peaceful) visit to China, where he wins the hand of a Chinese princess through his wisdom and magical ability.

(106) *dMyal gling* ("Hell and Gling"). Ge sar goes to the underworld to rescue his mother (or, in some versions, A stag lha mo; Wang lists this separately as no. 19). After Ge sar's return, he declares his mission at an end and departs to the realm of the gods.

As Wang's numbering implies, there are many other episodes. Most of these follow a standard pattern. Conflict arises between Gling and some neighboring people, usually non-Buddhist. The allies of Gling are assembled and, after a series of battles and magical tricks which occupies most of the episode, Ge sar and the heroes of Gling defeat the warriors and subdue the fortress or administrative center (*rdzong*) of the enemy ruler, whose subjects become converted to Buddhism and allied to Gling. Among the better-known of these episodes are the *sTag gzig nor rdzong* ("Iranian Cattle Fortress," Wang's no. 16), *Sog stod rta rdzong* ("Upper Mongolian Horse Fortress," no. 20) and *Sog smad khrab rdzong* ("Lower Mongolian Armor Fortress," no. 21), *Kha che g.yu rdzong* ("Turquoise Fortress of Kashmir," no. 26; Kaschewsky and Tsering, 1972), *Gru gu'i go rdzong* ("Weaponry Fortress of the Turks," no. 30), *Sum pa mdzo rdzong* ("Dzo [bull-female yak hybrid] Fortress of Sum pa," no. 35; Kaschewsky and Tsering 1987a) and *Ri nub* (or *Mi nub*) *dar rdzong* ("Silk Fortress of Burma," no. 103). In each case a particular "treasure" (of horses, arms, turquoises, pearls, etc.) is opened and brought back to Gling.

These episodes exist both in oral performance and as written texts. The tradition of oral performance undoubtedly predates the existence of written texts. Many of the professional bards are still illiterate and perform independently of the textual tradition. There is, in any case, no standard text of the epic. Although particular written versions of some episodes have gained wide currency, there are several entirely different written versions of the major episodes, and even the "same" version may vary considerably between different manuscripts. New episodes are still being performed and written down, mostly following the standard pattern outlined above. According to a widespread idea, these new episodes are not new creations, but memories of a previous life in which the singer or author was one of Ge sar's followers. The idiom is similar to that of the discovery of "treasure" literature (*gter ma*) (see Gyatso, in this volume) and as in that case there is a strong "shamanic" element present (cf. Samuel, 1993).

We now turn to the core of the epic: the songs sung by the various characters.

The Structure of the Songs

The style and language of the songs have been discussed extensively by Helffer (381-460). While her study is confined to the 56 songs in the Gling tshang version of the *rTa rgyugs* episode, the style of these songs does not differ significantly from that of other episodes available in written form. The same body of tunes is used for all Ge sar songs, so only a limited degree of stylistic variation is possible in any case.

The epic songs are written in the seven-syllable line used by Tibetan translators to render Sanskrit verse (*pāda*). This line is frequently found in religious verse, including many of the songs of Mi la ras pa. As used in the epic, it falls into three or four segments (| •• | •• | ••• | or | •• | •• | •• | • |), as in these lines from the opening song of the Gling tshang "Horse-Race," a song for the goddess Ma ne ne (Gung sman rgyal mo).

de-nas jo-rus lha-yi sras
ne-ne nga-yi glu-la gson
Now, Jo ru [Ge sar], divine son,
listen to your aunt's song.
(My translation; cf. Stein, 1956: 278; Helffer: 10-11)

The first segment is very frequently extended to three syllables (| ••• | •• | •• | • |):

mtho nam-mkha' mthing-gi gur-khang na
dpung-mang skar-ma'i bkrag-mdangs te
On the blue tent of the high heavens,
when the many hosts of stars shine out.
(ibid.)

Standard epithets and phrases are very common in the epic, as might be expected in a form still closely linked to extemporaneous verbal performance. Verbal repetitions, standard lists, and extended images and analogies are also features suggestive of the oral epic (see Herrmann). The songs have a standard plan, which is followed quite closely in most manuscripts (Helffer: 400):

(1) The tune is stated, using two or four lines of syllables without lexical meaning (*glu a la tha la tha la red*).
(2) The character invokes one or more protective deities.
(3) The locality is introduced: "If you don't know where this is, it is...."
(4) The character singing is introduced: "If you don't know who I am, I am..."; this may be extended for several lines.
(5) The main body of the song follows.
(6) The songs ends with a concluding formula: "If you understand this song, let it remain in your mind; if you don't understand, there's no explanation."

Words, Music and Meaning

What, though, are the songs about? Ge sar is undoubtedly a Buddhist hero. The central theme of the epic is the triumph of Buddhism over Bon, Hinduism, sorcery, demonic power and plain human selfishness and evil. However, while Ge sar's Buddhist identity is made clear in the *lHa gling* and reinforced by the constant appearances of and references to Padmasambhava and other Buddhist deities, the central Buddhist goal of enlightenment is only implicitly present in the epic. Much more salient is Buddhism as a source of magical or shamanic power (Samuel, 1991 and 1994). Essentially, the songs of the epic form a dialogue among different sources of power, Buddhist and non-Buddhist. It is no accident that epic songs begin with an invocation to one or another set of patron deities (normally preceded in performance by the mantra of Avalokiteśvara, *oṃ maṇi padme huṃ hrīḥ*). The central issue in the epic is the conflict between the protective and morally just power of Buddhism and the destructive and demonic power of egoism in its various forms.

The songs play a key role in articulating this conflict. Here the musical aspects of epic performance should be recalled. The songs are performed to short tunes which cover two or three (occasionally four or more) lines of verse, and these tunes repeat over and over again until the song is finished, without regard to the syntactic structure of the song as a whole. The variety of song melodies used depends on the performer. Many skilled performers employ different melodies for each major character or character type. Ge sar and other central characters may have several melodies, depending on the occasion and type of song.

The songs themselves fall into a variety of types, but typically involve an attempt to predict or control subsequent events in the story. They are, in other words, an exercise of magical power, normally on behalf of the speaker and of the spiritual forces at his or her command.

In some cases, a song is a direct exercise of magical power. The Gling tshang *rTa rgyugs* has several songs of this kind, including two in which Ge sar magically transforms 'Brug mo into an ugly old woman, and back again (songs 15 and 17; Helffer: 92, 98-101) and another in which he overcomes three mountain-gods (song 40; Helffer: 280-281). More often, the exercise of power is indirect, as in the frequent songs of prophecy and advice (*lung bstan*). An example is the song of the goddess Ma ne ne from which I quoted above. In this song, Ma ne ne, Ge sar's heavenly guardian, tells him that it is time for him to seize the throne of Gling, to capture his magic horse and to marry 'Brug mo, and explains how he must do this. Such songs are especially common at the beginning of an episode, but may occur at any time.

A prophecy may also be retold: in the *Kha che g.yu rdzong*, Ge sar receives a prophecy from Padmasambhava (song 6) and then narrates it to the leaders of Gling (song 7, cf. Kaschewsky and Tsering, 1972: 294-298, 365-166; Samuel, 1991). Prophecies are not necessarily true, and Ge sar, in particular, frequently adopts magical disguises in order to convey false prophecies and advice to his enemies. Thus, in song 2 of the Gling tshang *rTa rgyugs*, Ge sar, disguised as Hayagrīva, persuades Khro thung to arrange the horse-race by telling him that he or his son will win it and so gain 'Brug mo and the throne of Gling (Helffer: 12-15).

Similar to the song of prediction is the song of divination. Divination of various kinds is a frequent theme in the epic, including the arrow-divination technique (*mda' mo*) which is specially associated with Ge sar (for examples in the *lHa gling* and *'Khrungs gling* see Stein, 1956: 34, 46). In the *rTa rgyugs*, the diviner consults the divining-threads (*ju thig*) at Ge sar's request and foretells his victory (song 47):

> Behold! As a presage of greatness
> [The thread] falls first on the life-knot of the heavens;
> You will have dominion like the blue sky covering all.
> The second falls on the life-knot of the earth;
> An omen that you will be established on a firm, unshakeable foundation,
> An omen, that if you take the throne, you will occupy the leading place,
> An omen, that you will be enthroned for the good of all beings.
> (My translation; cf. Helffer: 308-309)

Related are the songs of good omen (*rten 'brel*), of words of truth (*bden tshig*), and of blessings (*bkra shis*), intended to set a particular series of events in motion through karmic connectedness. Frequently an "auspicious" character is asked to sing a song of this kind. In the Gling tshang *lHa gling*, when tea is made, sPyi dpon, the chief of the tribes of Gling, asks the cooks to offer some of the tea to the gods and to sing a song of good omen (song 16; Stein,

1956: 24, 180). In the *Kha che g.yu rdzong* (song 8), Ge sar asks the same sPyi dpon to sing a song of the defeat of the Kashmiri army, since sPyi dpon is a *ṛṣi* whose words will be fulfilled (*bden tshig grub pa'i drang srong*).

> The red of Chinese coral and of rose-hips
> May seem alike in being red;
> As time passes, they are unlike and separate.
> The yellow of gold and brass
> May seem alike in being yellow;
> As time passes, they are unlike and separate.
> The army of Kashmir and that of white Gling
> May seem alike in force and ability to win;
> As time passes, they are unlike and very different.
>
> (My translation; cf. Kaschewsky and Tsering, 1972: 303-304, 367-368)

Most episodes end with one or more songs of blessings (*bkra shis*) or good omen.

Another kind of expression of power over future events may be found in the battle scenes which take up a large part of most of the later episodes. Warriors typically sing songs in which they boast about their strength and valor in battle and the might of their fellow warriors, general or king. Usually two combatants exchange songs, after which a fight takes place in which one is defeated — and the other's song has therefore proved true. Here, from the *Kha che g.yu rdzong*, is the Kashmiri hero gYu lag thog lce singing as he draws his bow against Ge sar's general, 'Dan ma:

> Guardians of the teachings of Kashmir:
> Watch over me and direct my hero-song.
> ... ...
> I am gYu lag, the leader of the army.
> Armies that come, I throw into the depths.
> I am a hero who can grasp the Garuda bird!
> ... ...
> You can chase away little dogs with stones,
> But it won't work with the red tiger.
> You can catch little birds with a sling,
> But it won't work with the high-flying Garuda.
> You can despise weak little princes,
> But it won't work with the King of Kashmir.
>
> (Kaschewsky and Tsering, 1972: 330, 376)

Not all songs fall into these categories. A few are concerned with the straightforward delivery of a message or a request. In general, however, a high proportion of the songs can be interpreted in terms of the exercise of shamanic power.

Conclusion

The Gesar epic undoubtedly shares many features, including elements of the plot, with the epic traditions of other societies. What is striking, however, is the way in which this material has been transformed into a peculiarly Tibetan narrative dealing with specifically Tibetan concerns. If the Buddhism of the epic is not, by and large, that of the literary and philosophical tradition of the great monasteries, it is not fundamentally incompatible with it.[3] Ge sar's supporters see him not simply as a pro-Buddhist hero but as an earthly representative of Padmasambhava and other tantric deities.

Notes

1. I have given a brief survey of Western research on Ge sar in Samuel (1992). The principal studies are those of Francke, Roerich (1942, 1958), Stein (1956, 1959), Damdinsuren, Hermanns, Helffer, and Kaschewsky and Tsering (1972, 1987).

2. All of these episodes have been published in modern editions within the People's Republic; for references see Samuel (1992). Most are also included in the Bhutanese edition (Tobgyel and Dorji, 1979 onwards). Stein (1956) includes Tibetan text and abridged French translations of the Gling tshang versions of nos. 1, 4 and 8.

3. Thus the Gling tshang blockprint versions were edited and printed under the direction of the great rNying ma pa scholar 'Ju Mi pham rgya mtsho (1846-1912), and many other masters (or *bla mas*), especially of the Ris med schools of eastern Tibet, have used the epic as a vehicle for Buddhist and particularly rDzogs chen teachings (see Samuel, 1992).

References

Damdinsuren, Ts.
1957 *Istoricheskie Korni Geseriady*. Moskow: Izdatel'stvo Akademii Nauk SSSR.

David-Neel, Alexandra and Lama Yongden
1987 *The Superhuman Life of Gesar of Ling*. Boston and London: Shambhala.

Francke, A. H.

1905-41 *A Lower Ladakhi Version of the Kesar Saga*. Calcutta: Royal Asiatic Society of Bengal.

Helffer, Mireille

1977 *Les chants de l'épopée tibétaine de Ge-sar d'après le livre de la Course de Cheval*. Paris and Geneva: Librairie Droz.

Hermanns, Matthias

1965 *Das National-Epos der Tibeter Gling König Ge sar*. Regensburg: Verlag Josef Habbel.

Herrmann, Silke

1988 "Possibilities for New Perspectives in Epic Research on the Tibetan *Gesar*." In *Tibetan Studies*. Ed. by H. Uebach and Jampa L. Panglung. Munich: Bayerische Akademie der Wissenschaften.

Kaschewsky, Rudolf and Pema Tsering

1972 "Gesars Anwehrkampf gegen Kaschmir." *Zentralasiatische Studien* 6: 273-400.

1987 *Die Eroberung der Burg von Sum-pa*, 2 vols. Wiesbaden: Otto Harrassowitz.

Samuel, Geoffrey

1991 "Music and Shamanic Power in the Gesar Epic." *Metaphor: A Musical Dimension*, pp. 89-108. Ed. by Jamie Kassler. Sydney: Currency Press.

1992 "Gesar of Ling: the Origins and Meaning of the East Tibetan Epic." *Tibetan Studies: Proceedings of the 5th Seminar of the International Association for Tibetan Studies, Narita, 1989*, pp. 711-722. Ed. by Shōren Ihara and Zuihō Yamaguchi. Narita, Japan: Naritasan Shinshoji.

1993 *Civilized Shamans: Buddhism in Tibetan Societies*. Washington, D.C.: Smithsonian Institution Press.

1994 "Gesar of Ling: Shamanic Power and Popular Religion." In *Tantra and Popular Religion in Tibet*. Ed. by G. Samuel et al. New Delhi: Aditya Prakashan.

Stein, R. A.

1956 *L'épopée tibétaine de Gesar dans sa version lamaïque de Ling*. Paris: Presses Universitaires de France.

1959 *Recherches sur l'épopée et le barde au Tibet*. Paris: Presses Universitaires de France.

Tobgyel, Kunzang and Mani Dorji

1979 *The Epic of Gesar*, in 31 volumes. Thimphu, Bhutan: Kunsang Tobgyel.

Wang Yinuan

1985 "Incomplete Statistics of Sections and Lines in the Tibetan *King Gesar*." *Gesar Yanjiu* [Gesar Research] 1: 184-211. [In Chinese.]

Chapter 22

"Poetry" In Tibet: *Glu, mGur, sNyan ngag* and "Songs Of Experience"[1]

Roger R. Jackson

Introduction: Genres and Their Parameters

Despite a literary tradition going back thirteen centuries, Tibet generally has had a culture in which many important types of knowledge—not just of personal experience, but of history, philosophy and science, too—were transmitted orally. It is well known that "verse"—metrically regulated composition—is an excellent mnemonic device, and so it should not surprise us that a tremendous amount of Tibetan literature is in verse. From among the vast number of versified works found in their language, Tibetans have separated out certain pieces because of their greater concentration of rhythm, image and meaning, their heightened "imagery" (*gzugs*), "vitality" (*srog*) and "ornamentation" (*rgyan*) (see B. Newman, in this volume). These works are designated in Tibetan by at least three separate terms: *glu* (songs), *mgur* (poetical songs) and *snyan ngag* (ornate poetry).[2]

It is, of course, impossible to specify that these three genres amount to that formulation of "a concentrated imaginative awareness of experience in language arranged to create a specific emotional response through meaning, sound, and rhythm" (*Webster's*: 887a) that in the West we call "poetry," but they probably are as close as we are likely to come to a Tibetan equivalent. This is so especially if we accept that—problems of cultural translation aside—Western "poetry" is set off from other forms by its heightened rhythm, imagery, meaning, vitality and ornamentation, while Tibetan *glu, mgur* and *snyan ngag* are set off from other verse forms by their arrangement of rhythm, sound and meaning to create a specific emotional response to someone's experience.

Glu, mgur and *snyan ngag* are interrelated in subtle and important ways, but they are distinguishable. Indeed, one may see the movement from *glu* to *mgur* to *snyan ngag* as reflecting both the evolution of "poetry" in Tibet from ancient to more recent times and the spectrum of poetic styles, from that of popular, oral, indigenously rooted works, to that of monastic, literary, Indian-inspired compositions. In what follows, we will briefly consider the historical and stylistic parameters of *glu, mgur* and *snyan ngag;* analyze some examples of a sub-genre of *mgur* ("songs of experience": *nyams mgur*) that seems particularly comparable to the highly personalized "poetry" of the modern West; and conclude with some reflections on the relation between "poetry" (Western or Tibetan) and experience (religious or otherwise).

Glu, mGur and *sNyan ngag*

Thousands upon thousands of examples of *glu, mgur* and *snyan ngag* are scattered throughout the corpus of Tibetan literature, in ancient chronicles, edict collections (*bka' thang*), documents from Dunhuang, Treasure texts (*gter ma*), rituals, biographies, and the collected works (*gsung 'bum*) of the great masters of the various lineages. Only rarely have the works of multiple authors been anthologized,[3] and rarer still are analytical works that seek to make sense of the sources, contents and forms of the Tibetan poetic tradition.[4] Still, as indicated above, *glu, mgur* and *snyan ngag* (along with the Gesar epic corpus) together roughly comprise the Tibetan poetic canon. *Glu,* which remains in Tibetan as a general term for "song," is the earliest, most indigenous, most secular, and most orally and musically oriented of the genres. *mGur,* which originally was either a synonym or a subdivision of *glu,* came eventually to denote a more Buddhistic type of "song," and might be either Tibetan or Indian in its inspiration, oral or written in its style. *sNyan ngag,* "speech [agreeable] to the ear," is an ornate, written, Indian-inspired type of Buddhist (and occasionally secular) poetry that did not appear until the thirteenth century, well after the other two genres. The three genres are not absolutely distinguishable—*glu* and *mgur* often are used synonymously even in later periods, and the aesthetic theories behind *snyan ngag* often influenced post-thirteenth-century *mgur*, but they are distinct enough that we may isolate them and briefly consider the sources, themes and styles of each of them in turn.

Glu

As in many cultures, poetry in Tibet almost certainly had its origins in connection with ritual, music and dance. It is not surprising, therefore, that the oldest form of Tibetan poetry bears the name for "song"—*glu*.[5] *Glu* are found scattered widely in both the documents found in the caves at Dunhuang[6] and in later texts, especially the Treasure (*gter ma*) literature, that preserve authentically ancient material. Among the most important sources are the *bTsun mo'i bka' thang*, the *Padma'i bka' thang* and the *Maṇi bka' 'bum*. The *glu* found in these texts are broadly divisible into royal songs (*rgyal po'i glu*) and popular songs (*'bangs kyi glu*). The latter are generally not very well attested in the earliest sources, since it was royal rather than popular culture that was likely to be committed to writing at that time. On the other hand, reasonable inferences about the nature of such songs may be made from the ways in which they were utilized by later poets, especially Mi la ras pa (twelfth century), 'Brug pa kun legs (sixteenth century) and the sixth Dalai Lama (seventeenth century), as well as by the forms in which they have survived to the present day. They include love and marriage songs in dialogue form, planting and harvest songs, songs of advice (*legs bshad*), riddle songs and songs connected with religious ceremonies, such as consecrations (*rab gnas*).

Royal songs included two major sub-categories, *mgur*, which emphasize "positive personal experience, exalting either the singer's own exploits or those of his acquaintances...[and] express the singer's joy at having overcome an obstacle, hopes for future success, or praise for another person's deeds" (Ellingson: 67), and *mchid*, which are "usually songs of provocation and dispute...[which combine] vivid, sophisticated symbolic imagery with more direct insults to create sung verbal combat" (Ellingson: 68-69). As Ellingson notes, both *mgur* and *mchid* "were essential to the political functioning of the Tibetan kingdom. . . .[A] *mchid* might furnish the spur to upset a precarious alliance and provoke a war, and *mgur* [be] used to cement an alliance and enhance the prestige of a leader" (69-70). Still another type of royal song recorded administrative policy (*lugs kyi bstan bcos*). Advice on how to rule, formulations of official policies, and even matters as prosaic as a census were preserved in the form of songs, probably for reasons more connected with mnemonics than aesthetics.

Both popular and royal songs had associated with them both a performative context and specific melodies (*dbyangs* or *'debs*; see Ellingson: 247) that gave them a distinctness not conveyed by their written form. In strictly rhythmic terms, however, they tended to be somewhat alike, most often being set in straightforward six-syllable dactylic lines often arranged into stanzas. Frequently, they relied upon imagistic and semantic parallelisms from stanza to stanza, as well as certain emphatic particles (such as *ni*) and reduplicated or trebled onomatopoetic phrases, such as *kyi li li*, *me re re*, etc. An example that illustrates all of these stylistic features is the following:

Nearer, ah, nearer yet Yarpa, ah, near the sky Sky-stars, ah, *si-li-li.*	*je nye ni je nye na* *yar pa ni dgung dang nye* *dgung skar ni si li li*
Nearer, ah, nearer yet Lakar, ah, near the stone Stone-stars, ah, *si-li-li.*	*je nye* [*ni*] *je nye na* *gla skar ni brag dang nye* *brag skar ni si li li*
Durwa, ah, near the stream Otter, ah, *pyo-la-la.*	*sdur ba ni chab dang nye* *gyur sram ni pyo la la'*
Nyenkar, ah, near the earth All fruits, ah, *si-li-li.*	*nyen kar ni dog dang nye* *'bras drug ni si li li*
Maltro, ah, near to Lum Cold winds, ah, *spu-ru-ru.*	*mal tro ni* [*klum*] *dang nye* *syi bser ni spu ru ru*

(Bacot et al.: 116; cf. trans. at ibid.: 157-158; Stein, 1972a: 254; and Beyer, 1992: 149)[7]

The strong use of stanza-to-stanza parallelism, the theme of "nearness," the invocation of place-names, the references to natural phenomena, the repeated use of the emphatic "ah" (*ni*) and the utilization of trebled phrases (*si li li*, etc.) all are quite evident here; somewhat subtler, perhaps, is the way in which the song is saved from mechanical predictability by shifts in the placement of place-names and trebled phrases. The essential structure is maintained, but variations add an element of grace that elevates the song above the commonplace.

mGur

We have already seen that in the earliest period, *mgur* probably referred to a sub-genre of *glu* in which singers boasted either of their own or others' accomplishments. Ellingson, for instance, cites the following *mgur* celebrating a Tibetan victory over the Chinese:

> Labong, he, with his clans
> Hero's deeds performed:
> Chinese forts (high): destroyed
> Chinese people (many): controlled
> Of lands there with their tribes
> Tibet, ah, he made the capital
> Above, ah, sky rejoiced
> Below, ah, earth enjoyed.
>
> (Bacot et al.: 113-114; cf. trans. at ibid.: 151-152 and Ellingson: 68)

Such secular *mgur* continued to be preserved and composed, but with the growth of Buddhism in Tibet, especially in the eleventh and succeeding centuries, the period of the later diffusion (*phyi dar*) of the Dharma, "*mgur*" came increasingly to refer to *religious* songs with an experiential component: they might be either reports of spiritual realization or instructions based upon such realizations, or a combination of the two. Religiously oriented *mgur* do occur in the period of Buddhism's early diffusion (*snga dar*): Padmasambhava is said to have originated the tradition by singing of his accomplishments for King Khri srong lde'u btsan, and his disciple Vairocana is credited by the historian dPa' bo gtsug lag phreng ba with being the first great composer of Tibetan-language *mgur*, in songs combining Buddhist and popular themes for the purpose of propagating the Dharma (Ellingson: 230).

The categorization of *mgur* as a primarily religious genre, however, dates chiefly from the time of the greatest of all Tibetan poets, Mi la ras pa (1040-1123). Though his hundreds of *mgur*—the traditional number is a hundred thousand—were not given their definitive written form until several centuries after his death,[8] their influence on Tibetan culture seems to have been widespread from Mi la's time onward, through their preservation in various oral versions and written recensions, and through the importance Mi la quickly assumed as a Tibetan Buddhist culture-hero. Mi la's greatness lay in his ability to compose songs—and they were "songs," with *dbyangs* or *'debs* melodies (Ellingson: 247-249)—that combined the imagery, structural parallelism and expressive directness of ancient *glu* with distinctively Buddhist themes and Indian-inspired metrical schemes. In particular, Mi la ras pa—and thus the classical tradition of *mgur*—can be seen as inheriting two major influences: (1) the early diffusion traditions of songs of "positive personal experience," primarily secular in orientation and distinctly Tibetan in style, and (2) the tradition—brought to Tibet by Mi la's guru Mar pa—of tantric songs, those often spontaneous, always richly symbolic *dohās, caryāgīti* or *vajragīti* sung by Indian *mahāsiddhas* to express their spiritual realizations.[9] The themes, moods and styles of Mi la's *mgur* range widely: though the Dharma almost always is the real subject, it is expressed in verses at various times simple or complex, devout or wrathful, puritanical or ribald, humorous or stern, intensely autobiographical or impersonally didactic. For now, one brief extract, which demonstrates his combination of sensitivity to nature, unashamed expression of personal achievement and ability to promulgate Buddhist doctrine, will have to suffice:

> This hermitage, fort of awakening:
> Above it: high snow peaks, abode of gods
> Below it: my many benefactors
> Behind it: mountains curtained off by snow.
> ... ...
> The yogī who sees all that
> Is atop the Clear Jewel Rock.
> For transient appearances, I draw analogies:
> Pleasures I contemplate as mirages
> This life I see as a dream, a reflection.
> ... ...
> Myriad things, whatever appears to the mind:
> Ah, cyclic events of the triple world,
> Nonexistent, yet appearing—how wondrous![10]
> (*MLGB*: 66-67; cf. trans. Chang I: 64-65)

The success of Mi la ras pa's songs in helping to popularize Buddhism, combined with the innate Tibetan love of poetry and song, helped assure that in the centuries after Mi la, *mgur* composition came to be a widely practiced art. Its composers ranged from "crazy" (*smyon pa*) Mi la ras pa-style yogis like 'Brug pa kun legs, to great polymaths like Klong chen rab 'byams pa, Tsong kha pa and Padma dkar po, to Dalai and Paṇ chen Lamas, to modern figures such as Geshe Rabten, Dilgo Khyentse Rinpoche and Chögyam Trungpa Rinpoche.[11] With such a range of *mgur*, it is difficult to generalize about the genre's themes and prosody. Don grub rgyal, who has written the most comprehensive study to date, lists seven major types of *mgur*, those that (1) remember the guru's kindness, (2) indicate the source of one's realizations, (3) inspire the practice of Dharma, (4) give instructions on how to practice, (5) answer disciples' questions, (6) admonish the uprooting of evil and (7) serve as missives to gurus or disciples (194-195). Obviously, many *mgur* will combine more than one of these approaches. Stylistically, *mgur* show an even greater variety, ranging from straightforward, rhythmically simple personal reports (most often in seven- or nine-syllable lines, mixing trochees and dactyls, that became as central to Tibetan verse as iambic pentameter to English) to complex, ingeniously constructed, highly ornamented verses (of up to twenty-one syllables) whose sophistication rivals that of Sanskrit ornate poetry, *kāvya*. Indeed, because of the influence of Indian aesthetics from the thirteenth century onward, it is difficult sometimes to determine whether a particular composition should be classed as *mgur* or *snyan ngag*. Don grub rgyal insists (31ff.) that *mgur* are distinguished by their shorter and more unpredictable metrical styles, their greater simplicity and directness and their incorporation of popular Tibetan images and phrases (Don grub rgyal, ch. 8). Nevertheless, most later *mgur* bear at least some influence from the Indian aesthetic tradition, and this places the genre squarely between *glu* and *snyan ngag*, in terms of both its historical development and its place in the culture, as a bridge between earlier, more popular, and later, more belleletristic modes of poetic expression.

sNyan ngag

The term *snyan ngag* first appears during the period of Buddhism's early diffusion as a translation for the Sanskrit term *kāvya*, a complex, highly rule-governed type of versification in which much of the greatest Indian classical poetry was written. As Buddhist Sanskrit texts, some of which employed *kāvya*, were translated into Tibetan beginning in the ninth century, Indian prosody began slowly to influence poetry in Tibet. In the early period, Sanskrit prosody could have been known by only a few, whose response to it probably did not go much beyond experimentation with different metrical schemes. In the period of the later diffusion, Mi la ras pa's primarily trochaic verse clearly has been influenced by translations of Indian texts (especially *vajra* songs), but Mi la displays no knowledge of Sanskrit prosody—if his *mgur* are guided by an aesthetic, it is that of the spontaneous, inspired utterances of Indian tantric adepts or, in his own tradition, shamanic bards who draw their songs from the "sky-treasury" (*nam mkha' mdzod*) (Stein, 1972: 272-276). As with so many innovations in Tibetan intellectual life, it is to Sa skya Paṇḍita Kun dga' rgyal mtshan (1182-1251) that the real influence of *kāvya* on Tibetan poetry can be traced. In his *mKhas pa la 'jug pa'i sgo*, Sa paṇ "took upon himself the task of translating into Tibetan poems and verses of early Indian poets together with the structural and rhythmic rules of writing poetry" (Tsering: 8).[12] Sa paṇ's enthusiasm for Sanskrit verse and prosody was not widely shared by Tibetans, but another Sa skya pa scholar, Shong ston rDo rje rgyal mtshan, continued his work, championing in particular the poetic and theoretical works of the Indian scholar, Daṇḍin (seventh century). By the end of the thirteenth century, Sanskrit aesthetic theories were having a significant effect upon the Tibetan intelligentsia, and Daṇḍin's *Kāvyādarśa* (Tib. *sNyan ngag gi me long*) was on its way to becoming the most important source of such theories—a position it has enjoyed until the present day.[13]

As noted earlier, the theory and practice of *snyan ngag* influenced the composition of *mgur*—and perhaps even *glu*—from the thirteenth century onward. However, its influence upon the tradition of *glu* was slight, and among *mgur* composers it influenced most those who received a classical monastic education, and least those whose sphere was less academic. *sNyan ngag* itself was composed almost entirely by those with an academic background—but as the monastic university system took hold in Tibet, this came to include many of the nation's greatest thinkers and, for that matter, saints. Examples of *snyan ngag* are scattered widely throughout the collected works of such figures as Tsong kha pa, the fifth Dalai Lama, Khams sprul bsTan 'dzin chos kyi nyi ma, A mdo dGe 'dun chos 'phel (who, in typically contrarian fashion, preferred Kālidāsa to Daṇḍin as an Indian model) and Dudjom Rinpoche. Quite apart from purely poetic compositions (especially in such genres as long-life prayers and *pūjās*; see Cabezón, Makransky in this volume), some of the finest examples of *snyan ngag* will be found in the verse forewords, invocations and afterwords of independent treatises or commentaries.

There is not the space here to detail all the themes and principles of the *snyan ngag* tradition. Unsurprisingly, its imagery is largely borrowed from Indian models. Its metrical and semantic patterns tend toward the complex, with lines as long as twenty-one syllables and the poet's meaning played out across a stanza of four or more lines (or even multiple stanzas), rather than the single line-units of more popular poetry. In principle, *snyan ngag* are supposed to evoke one or more of the traditional affect-states (*bhāva, nyams 'gyur*) of Sanskrit aesthetics: charm, heroism, disgust, merriment, wrath, fear, pity, wonderment and peace, and to display the formal and verbal ornaments (*alaṃkāra, rgyan*) that help to produce those states. In practice, of course, the considerable differences between the Sanskrit and Tibetan languages limits the types of ornamentation that can be transmitted transculturally, nor do Tibetans seem to have been intent on evoking particular affect-states with quite the rigor that Sanskrit tradition demanded (see Don grub rgyal, chs. 7: 1 and 8). A brief excerpt from Tsong kha pa's *rTen 'brel bstod pa* ("Praise of Dependent Origination") will suffice to give the flavor of *snyan ngag*:

> The lily garden of the words of Nāgārjuna—
> Prophesied to expound as it is
> The method of your [the Buddha's] matchless vehicle,
> Which abandons extremes of "is" and "isn't"—
> Is lit by the white-light rosary
> Of the sayings of the glorious moon [Candrakirti],
> Whose expanding circle of stainless wisdom
> Moves unimpeded through the sky of scripture,
> Clearing the darkness of the heart that grasps extremes,
> Its brilliance obscuring the stars produced by falsehood.[14]
>
> (Namdol and Samten: 49-51; cf. trans. ibid. and Thurman: 105-106)

As Stein notes (1972a: 269-270), since the absorption into Tibetan culture of Sanskrit prosody, "there has strictly speaking been no development or innovation. . . . From that [time] onwards, we find side by side one style that is nearer to the indigenous tradition, in spite of adaptation, and another more learned and pedantic one of Indian inspiration." Thus, from the late thirteenth century to the present day, Tibetan poetry has consisted primarily of the overlapping genres of *glu, mgur* and *snyan ngag*. *gLu* is the most "indigenous," the most direct, the most connected to its musical, oral and secular roots. *sNyan ngag* is the most "learned and pedantic," the most ornate, the most élite and purely literary. *mGur* falls somewhere in between: highly "popular" examples of *mgur* are virtually indistinguishable from *glu*, highly literary examples could as easily be considered *snyan ngag*, but most *mgur* maintain, in varying degrees, a balance of elements—Tibetan and Indian, secular and religious, oral and literary, personal and universal—that make it the most appealing of the genres to modern readers, and one worth exploring, at least briefly, in more depth.

Nyams mgur: "Songs of Experience"

Whether secular or religious, ancient or classical, *mgur* are songs of "positive personal experience," but most of them do not display the intensely concentrated expression of subjectivity that has been a hallmark of Western (and Western-inspired) poetry at least since the rise of Romanticism. Indeed, we should not expect to find subjectivity conceived or expressed in exactly the same way in cultures so vastly different. At the same time, neither the Buddhist doctrine of "no self" nor some mythical "Oriental" subjugation of ego has entailed the elimination of a distinctly subjective, autobiographical point of view from at least some poetic forms. Thus, both early Tibetan *mgur* and Indian tantric *vajragīti*, not to mention the words of the Buddha as recorded in the bKa' 'gyur, often involve direct, personal reports of experience and claims to attainment, whether secular or religious, physical or psychological. The personal, subjective strain in the Tibetan poetic tradition is found in its most intensive form in the subgenre of classical *mgur* described by Don grub rgyal (194) as "songs about the way in which experiential realizations arise from one's having meditated on the guru's instructions," or, for short, "songs of experience"—*nyams mgur*.[15] Like their Tibetan and Indian forerunners, *nyams mgur* express "joy at having overcome an obstacle [or] hopes for future success" (Ellingson: 67), especially in terms of the struggle for enlightenment. Their tone, therefore, is primarily positive and celebratory. However, the recollection of obstacles or the intention to overcome them introduces in some cases a note of uncertainty, providing a spiritual and artistic tension that heightens the poem's effectiveness—especially on an audience whose members are themselves hopeful, but not yet spiritually accomplished. Here, we will briefly examine poems about spiritual experience from six authors. They range in time from the eleventh to the twentieth century, in tone from boastful to pessimistic, and in style from popular, *glu*-like songs to ornate instances of *snyan ngag*—but they all focus as a *theme* on personal spiritual experience, and thus, I would argue, are instances of "songs of experience," *nyams mgur*.

As we already have seen, Mi la ras pa is generally considered the greatest Tibetan poet, as well as the most important figure in the tradition of religious *mgur* composition—not to mention one of the pivotal figures in the lineage of the bKa' brgyud order. He is also perhaps the most straightforwardly personal of all Tibetan poets, singing again and again of his personal struggles and attainments. His life story, marked by an early flirtation with black magic and back-breaking ordeals at the hands of his guru, Mar pa, is known to virtually every Tibetan, and the background knowledge of the severity of his trials makes his frequent celebrations of spiritual triumph that much more satisfying to his audience. Here is one such celebration:

> My mind turned away from cyclic events,
> To the wilderness of Lashi snow-peak
> Came I, Mila, who long to be alone.
> ... ...
> The sky was wrapped in mist. Then
> Through nine whole days and nights snow fell
> Then a further eighteen days and nights it fell:
> Fell huge, huge as clumps of wool
> Like feathered birds fell flying
> Fell small, small as a spindle-wheel
> Like swarming bees fell swirling.
> ... ...
> I, the yogi Mila, clad in triple cotton garb
> Struggled in the desolation of icy peaks
> The falling snow I conquered, melted it into streams
> And the great roaring wind I stilled back to its source—
> My cotton cloth blazing like a fire.
> ... ...
> Wrestling like an athlete in mortal combat
> Clashing as a sword that conquers spears
> By conquest in that struggle bravely faced
> I set a model for Buddhists of all kinds
> Especially for great contemplatives.
>
> (*MLGB*: 29-31; cf. trans. Chang, I: 26-27)

Here is a second example from Mi la ras pa, illustrating something of the outcome of his meditation, the great yogic ease that is entailed by the sort of struggle and victory described above:

> I, the yogi Milarepa:
> Gazing nakedly, I see the essential
> Uncomplicated, I see as through the sky
> Settling at leisure, I realize the actual
> As essentially void, I realize all things
> Easing into relaxation, I reach my source
> In the stream of awareness, clear and muddy interchange.
> ... ...
> Recognizing Buddha as my mind
> I do not desire accomplishment.
> When realization rises within
> The host of afflictive thoughts
> Naturally disperse to their source
> Like darkness before the dawning sun.
>
> (*MLGB*: 460; cf. trans. Chang, II: 406)

Tsong kha pa Blo bzang grags pa (1357-1419), best known as the founder of the now-dominant dGe lugs school of Tibetan Buddhism, was a virtuous, charismatic saint, too, but in almost every other way, he was Mi la ras pa's opposite: he was a scholar, commentator and lecturer, who lived at the heart of the Tibetan monastic establishment. Perhaps because of his scholarly emphasis, his writings are far less personal than Mi la's. His visionary experiences (especially his famous encounter with Mañjuśrī) are recorded in biographies, not in texts directly attributable to him. Still, there are a number of texts by Tsong kha pa that might be considered *nyams mgur*, and they are made all the more interesting by their paucity. One of them, the *Lam rim bsdus don* ("Summary Meaning of the Stages of the Path") or *Lam rim chung ngu* ("Short Text on the Stages of the Path"), actually is referred to in some dGe lugs pa traditions by the alternative title of *Lam rim nyams mgur ma* ("Song of Experience of the Stages of the Path") (see Dalai Lama, 1988: 27). It does, in fact, summarize the dGe lugs version of the *lam rim* meditation sequence, running systematically—and in *snyan ngag*-influenced style—through such topics as guru devotion; the value of a human rebirth; impermanence, death and karma; the altruistic aspiration to enlightenment; the six perfections; and the tantric path. What makes the text a *nyams mgur* is the refrain, found after each of the last fifteen verses, where

Tsong kha pa actually seems to make a realization-claim, albeit modestly:

> Meditate as the holy gurus [did];
> You who desire liberation—I, too, have sought to practice thus.
>
> (*LRDD*: 55b-58a; cf. trans. Thurman: 59-66)

A second text in which Tsong kha pa speaks of his own experiences is the *Rang gi rtogs pa brjod pa mdo tsam du bshad pa*, in which he gives an account of his education and training, alluding to the difficulties he had to overcome in understanding various points of Mādhyamika and tantric doctrine. The account is interspersed with the refrain, addressed to Mañjuśrī:

> I thought in this way, and my plan was well fulfilled.
> How great your kindness, O holy wisdom treasure!
>
> (*RTJS*: 52b-55b; cf. trans. Thurman: 40-46)

Again, the claim is modest, but in the context of Tsong kha pa's autobiographical reticence, it stands as a clear indication that he does, indeed, occasionally sing of his own experience.

'Brug pa Padma dkar po (1527-1592) was a bKa' brgyud pa who looked back to Mi la ras pa for inspiration, yet he, like Tsong kha pa, was a great scholar and commentator, many of whose treatises remain definitive for bKa' brgyud pas today. As a recipient of the bKa' brgyud lineage, he was well acquainted with the tradition of *mgur* composition; indeed, his collected writings include a 78-folio selection of "*vajra* songs" (*rdo rje'i glu*). However, Padma dkar po was a citizen of a world far more intellectually and politically complex than Mi la ras pa's, so his *mgur* reflect a degree of doctrinal systematization, aesthetic influences from *snyan ngag*, and a certain ambivalence about the world that we see little of in Mi la. The following selection does seem to celebrate spiritual victory, but it is neither easily won nor, perhaps, incorruptible:

> The thirst for delight and pain were long my companions.
> My enemy was defilement, skilled at distraction:
> His army, thoughts, savage and many,
> His spies—sinking and scattering—perceptive and persistent.
> (My allies, mindfulness and alertness, wander off;
> My apathetic mind knows how to limit progress;
> My babbling thoughts delight in straying.)
> There's danger he may breach the borders of my calm:
> Look within, Padma dkar;
> Don't bind the mind, don't bind, release it:

The bound mind begins to stray in all directions
But set it wandering and it comes to rest.
(*DJL*: 350-351; cf. trans. Beyer, 1974: 78)

Most of Padma dkar po's *nyams mgur* do reflect the celebratory style of the genre, but, as Beyer correctly notes (1974: 74), it is "tempered by an all too acute awareness of the ways of the crowded world and the unsteadiness of the human heart, including his own." If Padma dkar po is not exactly modern in his ambivalence, he nevertheless displays a frankness that, in the inevitable context of *nyams mgur*—reporting one's experience so that it may inspire others—would be attractive to those who have known and continue to struggle with the same sort of ambivalence.

The sort of ambivalence hinted at in Padma dkar po is a central theme of the songs (*mgul glu*) of the sixth Dalai Lama, Tshangs dbyangs rgya mtsho (1683-1706), whose short, tragic life and popular way of expressing himself have endeared him to Tibetans nearly as much as Mi la ras pa. As a Dalai Lama, he was formally a monk and a member of the dGe lugs lineage, but his attraction to fleshly temptations beyond the Potala, and his interest in rNying ma pa doctrines, are well-attested. His songs are written primarily in quatrains of six-syllable lines evocative of ancient *glu* traditions. Their repeated references to lovers and love affairs have proven an embarrassment to the monastic establishment, and the argument sometimes is made that they reflect a symbolic, tantric type of discourse that refers to inner accomplishments. There is at least one song that does seem to contain tantric references:

Pure glacial water of Crystal Mountain
Dew of nāgavajra grass
Down-stream of healing ambrosia:
If it's drunk, then by the pure vow
Of the barmaid Vajraḍākinī
No need to experience lower realms!
(Dondhup: 82; cf. trans. ibid.: 83)

This almost could be a *vajra*-song of the sort encountered in the Mother *tantras*, but it is obscure and atypical, and cannot establish the Sixth as a tāntrika posing as a libertine. The opposite argument, however, that he was simply a rake and hypocrite , with no interest at all in spirituality, seems no more persuasive. Indeed, it is probably safest to see the sixth Dalai Lama as a man torn between spiritual and sensual inclinations, as expressed in the following song:

Contemplated, my guru's face
Comes not at all to mind;
Uncontemplated, my lover's face
Comes again and again to mind.
(Dondhup: 78; cf. trans. ibid.: 79)

This may not exactly be a celebration of spiritual victory, but it certainly is a song about spiritual experience, expressed honestly in a popular idiom; as such, different as it may be from a song of Mi la or Tsong kha pa, and however it may stretch the boundaries of the genre, it does serve an example of *nyams mgur*.

The composition of *nyams mgur* is not confined to the ancient and medieval past; modern Tibetans have written them as well. Geshe Rabten (1920-1986) was a learned dGe lugs pa-trained monk who escaped from Tibet in 1959, and eventually settled in Switzerland. He has written of his retreat experiences in a twelve-verse *mgur*, to which he has appended a commentary. The outlook with which he enters his retreat is prompted by his guru's analysis of the illusory nature of a rather modern "basis of imputation," a hundred-rupee note, but in what follows, Geshe Rabten's language and viewpoint remain traditionally dGe lugs:

The old monk: seemed so real before
When examined: like bird tracks in the sky.
The apparent bird: just circling in the mind
Its tracks, when sought: ineffable—naturally void.
(Rabten: 24; cf. trans. ibid.: 25)

This could easily have been written by Tsong kha pa, and this demonstrates that, even in the modern era, traditional Tibetan views and modes of expression may still hold sway.

Chögyam Trungpa Rinpoche (1939-1987) was a bKa' brgyud pa lineage-holder who also fled Tibet in 1959, settling in India, then Scotland, then Boulder, Colorado, and finally Halifax, Nova Scotia. He received an Oxford education to go with his Tibetan training, and explained Tibetan Buddhism to Westerners in language that often was couched in their own psychological and aesthetic categories. Very self-consciously an inheritor of Mi la ras pa's tradition of spontaneously expressing realization through *mgur*, Trungpa was an active and imaginative poet all his life, writing in both Tibetan and English. The latter are beyond our purview, but a brief sample of his Tibetan *mgur*, entitled *Zur ze yi ge* ("Cynical Letter") should suffice to demonstrate his verbal dexterity, strong sense of irony, and mastery of both traditional bKa' brgyud pa and modernist styles:

> The laughing poet
> Has run out of breath and died.
> The religious spin circles, in accordance with religion;
> If they had not practiced their religion, they could not spin.
> The sinner cannot spin according to religion;
> He spins according to not knowing how to spin.
> The yogis spin by practicing yoga;
> If they don't have cakras to spin, they are not yogis.
> Chögyam is spinning, watching the spinning/samsara;
> If there is no samsara/spinning, there is no Chögyam.
>
> (Trungpa, 1983: 22-23 [his trans.])

Particularly notable here is Trungpa's ironic invocation of traditional Buddhist images of wheels, which may be either saṃsāric or transcendental, and his sense that he himself is a product of his "spinning," whether for better or worse.

It should be evident from the *nyams mgur* reviewed here that although Stein is right to maintain that most Tibetan poetic *forms* became fixed by the end of the twelfth century, the tradition has by no means stood still, and that constantly changing circumstances—Tibetan history is no more static than any other—have led to a rich diversity of content, tone and style, that only can be multiplied by the increasing contact Tibetan poets—especially those of the diaspora—are having with non-Tibetan culture. If it is argued that, in fact, there is *such* diversity of content, tone and style in these poems that we cannot reasonably subsume them under a single genre, I would simply reiterate what I suggested before: *nyams mgur* are above all united by a common *theme*, personal spiritual experience; all of the poems we have cited refer to this, so all of them are *nyams mgur*.

Conclusion: Experience, Religion and Poetry

Nyams mgur obviously represent only a small portion of the Tibetan poetic tradition: they are not even the majority among *mgur*, let alone among *glu* and *nyan ngag*. At the same time, they include a disproportionate number of the greatest poems, and they probably are the most popular of the genres—no doubt because they speak to their audience, whether illiterate nomad or learned monk, of real and personal experience, in a way that permits a certain level of psychological identification, even communion. We saw at the outset that poetry in the modern West is "writing that formulates a concentrated awareness of *experience*," and, indeed, simply within the American tradition of the past two centuries, the poets generally considered greatest *are* those that seem to concentrate their experience most intensely and imaginatively: Dickinson, Whitman, Pound, Eliot, W. C. Williams, Stevens, Lowell.

Does this mean that *nyams mgur* fulfill a modern definition of poetry? They are, after all, songs (*mgur*) of experience (*nyams*). *Nyams* is a rich, multivalent term in Tibetan, connoting experience, thought, mind-state—indeed, much of what we would consider the inner dimension of a human being. However, in its primary usage, *nyams* means inner *spiritual* experience or realization, and, indeed, when we analyze the inner dimension expressed in *nyams mgur*, we see that it is essentially "religious," i.e., related to experiences on the Buddhist path to enlightenment. Tibetan poets, even the most "confessional," have tended to expose their sentiments largely within the context of their progress—or lack of it—along that path. They do not—as Western poets often do—report the minutiae of their inner states, or even speak much of the great non-religious passions that—sometimes, at least—must animate them. In this sense, *nyams mgur* as a whole would appear more closely to parallel the Western subgenre of "religious poetry," i.e., poetry that places front and center the poet's relation to what we might call "the transcendent." This genre, of course, includes the work of many great pre-modern poets, including Dante, Donne, Milton and St. John of the Cross, as well as a fair number of moderns, including (among writers in English) Shelley, Swinburne, Yeats and Eliot.

The comparison between *nyams mgur* and Western "religious poetry" has a certain appropriateness, but it is misleading in several important ways. First, and most importantly, the comparison may conceal an implicit denigration of Tibetan poetry, on the basis of its representing only a fairly narrow range of human experience, i.e., the "religious." This notion is woefully misplaced, for it fails to account for the considerable differences in what counts as "experience" from culture to culture. Tibetans were not and are not lacking in a complex range of "psychological states," but those states only partially overlap those of modern Westerners. Just as modern poets faithfully reflect the central, if not universal, concerns of their culture, e.g., the individual's quest for meaning and certainty in an ambiguous world, so Tibetan poets have faithfully reflected their culture's normative, if not universal, concern: the individual's relationship to the attainment of enlightenment. Thus, though their concerns might strike a modern Westerner as "medieval," Tibetan poets reflect the important "experiences" of their culture as faithfully as do their Western counterparts.

Further, it might be argued that *nyams mgur* actually contain a wider spectrum of human experience than just the "religious"—especially with the dogmatic connotations that the term sometimes bears in the West. After all, (a) many Tibetan poets describe their obstacles as well as their achievements, so "deluded" states of mind receive their due, too. Also, (b) the practice by many poets of nondualistic meditations like *rdzogs chen* or *mahāmudrā,* or their realization of the leveling of all phenomena in the ultimate reality of emptiness, should open their poetry to their reporting, without discrimination, of whatever appears—very much as in Zen poetry nonduality becomes the basis for the positive valuation of all experience and phenomena, no matter how conventionally insignificant. Further, (c) the spontaneous, "mad" (*smyon*) style in which at least some *mgur* (notably those of Mi la ras pa and his bKa' brgyud pa successors) are composed should entail an unfettered mode of expression, in which traditional stylistic and thematic limits are transcended.

Indeed, Allen Ginsberg argues that the bKa' brgyud poetic tradition is a repository "of millennial practical information on the attitudes and practices of mind speech & body that Western poets over the same millennia have explored individually, fitfully, as far as they were able—searching thru cities, scenes, seasons, manuscripts, libraries, backalleys, whorehouses, churches, drawing rooms, revolutionary cells, opium dens, merchant's rooms in Harrar, salons in Lissadell" (Trungpa, 1983: 11). Thus, *nyams mgur* connect—if not with the mainstream of Western poetry or religiosity—at least with a significant alternative visionary and spiritual tradition, embodied in the modern era by Blake, Whitman, Rimbaud, Apollinaire, Williams and Robert Creeley—as well as Jack Kerouac, Gary Snyder and Ginsberg himself.

Ginsberg is almost certainly right when he speaks of the *mgur* of Chögyam Trungpa in this vein, and he may well be right that the aesthetic and philosophical traditions of Tibetan Buddhism can be the basis for an aesthetic of "first thought, best thought," as in Zen and the Western poets he cites. However, Trungpa Rinpoche is, so far, an exception, since he was explicitly influenced both by Zen and by Western modernism. A reconsideration of the other *mgur*-composers we have discussed makes it clear that (a) while obstacles are described by almost all *nyams mgur* composers, and may even be dominant in some (like the sixth Dalai Lama) their main focus remains "positive personal experience" of a religious type recognizable to most Tibetans, not the sort of introspective cataloguing known to Western readers, (b) whatever thematic freedom might in principle be entailed by meditation on emptiness, virtually no pre-modern Tibetan poet has paid much attention to exalting conventionalities, à la Basho or Williams—unless natural descriptions qualify, which is debatable, since nature seldom is described for its own sake;[16] and (c) despite the spontaneity and freedom with which many *mgur* were composed, they have tended to fall fairly comfortably within stylistic and metrical parameters that were hallowed by tradition. Whether the poetic path followed by Trungpa Rinpoche will be followed by others as Tibetans increasingly interact with modern cultures remains to be seen, but for now, more traditional notions of poetic theme and style continue to hold sway.

Notes

1. I would like to thank Carleton College for a 1990 summer grant that enabled me to write the first draft of this article. I also wish to acknowledge the advice and encouragement of the late A.K. Ramanujan, who is deeply missed by all who knew him, but whose work and example continue to inspire all who love Asian literature.

2. One also could include the tradition of the Gesar epic (*sgrung*), which is outside the parameters of this essay: I am here concerned with shorter poetic forms. On the epic, see the contribution by Geoffrey Samuel in this volume.

3. The most notable exception is the *bKa' brgyud mgur mtsho*, initially compiled by the eighth Karma pa, Mi bskyod rdo rje (1507-1554); an updated version has been ably translated by Trungpa (1980). The great rNying ma pa master, Klong chen rab byams pa (1308-1363), also undertook an anthology of *mgur*, which remained incomplete at his death (Tsering: 11).

4. Some exceptions in Western languages are Stein, 1959 (on epic poetry); Stein, 1972a: 252-276; Ellingson (passim); and, most recently, Beyer, 1992, whose Tibetan grammar includes a wealth of examples drawn from Tibetan

poetry, as well as a separate chapter on metrics. For a concise overview, with a useful bibliography, see Tulku Thondup and Kapstein. In Tibetan, Don grub rgyal's recent (1985) *mGur glu'i lo rgyus dang khyad chos* is one of the few such analyses. (I would like to thank Dr. Leonard van der Kuijp for drawing my attention to, and making available to me, Don grub rgyal's text.)

5. As Ellingson notes (67), the original term probably was *klu*, which transformed into the homophonous *glu* at a relatively early period.

6. The best sources for these are Bacot et al. and Lalou. Both Stein (1972a) and Ellingson draw the majority of their examples from these collections.

7. With the exception of the passage from Chögyam Trungpa, below, all translations are mine; alternative translations are indicated parenthetically for those who may wish to compare.

8. The most important single collection is the *Mi la ras pa'i mgur 'bum* (*MLGB*; translated in Chang), which, like Mi la's biography, was compiled by gTsang smyon Heruka (1452-1507).

9. On Indian tantric songs in general, see Templeman. On *dohās*, see Shahidullah, Thaye and Guenther, 1993. On *caryāgīti*, see Kvaerne. *Vajragīti* have been rather less studied. Though they eventually came to refer primarily to independent "poetic" compositions, their original function seems to have been ritual, as part of the celebration at tantric feasts (*gaṇacakra*, *tshogs [kyi 'khor]*) and initiations (*abhiṣeka*, *dbang bskur*), in the texts of which many songs still are to be found. An especially beautiful example is the "Song of the Spring Queen," included in the *tshogs* section of the popular dGe lugs pa liturgy, the "Offering to the Spiritual Master" (*Bla ma mchod pa*), compiled by the first Paṇ chen Lama, Blo bzang chos kyi rgyal mtshan (1570-1662) (*LMC*: 73-77; see trans. at, e.g., Gyatso: 310-312). For tantric songs composed in Tibet at the same time as Mi la ras pa's, see Trungpa, 1982 (Mar pa) and Aziz, vol. 1 (Pha dam pa sangs rgyas).

10. I include the Tibetan here for those who wish to get some sense of the sound and rhythm of Mi la ras pa's *mgur*: *byang chub rdzong gi dben gnas 'di / phu na lha btsan gangs dkar mtho / mda' na yon bdag dang ldan mang / rgyab ri dar dkar yol bas bcod / . . . de la lta ba'i rnal 'byor pa / kun gsal rin chen brag stengs na / snang ba mi rtag dpe ru 'dren / 'dod yon mig yor chu ru bsgom / tshe 'di rmi lam sgyu mar blta / . . . sna tshogs nyams la ci yang 'char / e ma khams gsum 'khor ba'i chos / med zhing snang ba ngo mtshar che / /.*

11. For translations of 'Brug pa kun legs, see Stein, 1972b; Dowman. For Klong chen pa, see Longchenpa, 1989. For Tsong kha pa, see Thurman: 40-46, 59-66. For Padma dKar po, see Beyer: 77-79. For the sixth Dalai Lama, see, e.g., Dhondup. For the second and seventh Dalai Lamas, see Mullin, 1985 and 1994. For the first Paṇ chen Lama (most of whose *nyams mgur* are found in *AFPL*), see Guenther, 1975: 118-124; and Jackson, n.d. For Rabten, see Rabten. For Trungpa, see, e.g., Trungpa, 1983. I do not know of any translations yet of Dilgo Khyentse Rinpoche's poetry.

12. It should be noted that Sa paṇ also was arguably the greatest Tibetan exponent of the style of aphoristic verse known as *legs bshad* (*subhāṣita*, "well

explained"), which had antecedents both in earlier Tibetan tradition and in India; see Stein, 1972a: 258-259, 268-269.

13. On Daṇḍin and the *Kāvyādarśa*, see, e.g., Gupta, Eppling. The latter is certainly the definitive work to date, and includes a superb discussion of the *Kāvyādarśa*'s influence on Tibet (1435-1545). See also van der Kuijp and B. Newman, in this volume.

14. To give a sense of the sound and rhythm of a "simple" *snyan ngag*, I include the Tibetan: *kyod kyi bla med theg pa'i tshul / yod dang med pa'i mtha' spangs te / ji bzhin 'grel par lung bstan pa / klu sgrub gzhung lugs ku nda'i tshal / dri med mkhyen pa'i dkyil 'khor rgyas / gsung rab mkha' pa thogs med rgyu / mtha' 'dzin snying gi mun pa sel / log smra'i rgyu skar zil gnon pa / dpal ldan zla ba'i legs bshad kyi / 'od dkar 'phreng bas gsal byas pa / /*. Rhythmically, this is very similar to the *mgur* of Mi la ras pa cited above; in this case, the differences between the genres are more evident on the level of imagery and metaphor, which in Tsong kha pa's verse are typically elaborate and Indic.

15. *Nyams mgur* also is the Tibetan translation of the Sanskrit term *dohā*, a particular form of *vajragīti*. Not all instances of Tibetan *nyams mgur* are *dohās*, since the latter entail particular metrical schemes that Tibetan writers may not employ in reporting their "experience." For an interesting recent discussion of *nyams mgur*, by one of the most skillful Western translators of Tibetan poetry, see Mullin, 1994: 20-25.

16. Though it would take a lengthy essay to demonstrate how and why, I would argue that there is a significant difference between Indo-Tibetan and Sino-Japanese Buddhist poetic treatments of the natural world. In the former, conditioned by a cosmology in which nature is a part of *saṃsāra*, hence, finally, to be transcended, mountains, rivers, trees and animals tend to be treated either as pleasant backdrops to meditation or as symbols for items of the Buddhist Dharma. In the latter, shaped by a cosmology in which nature defines our limits, and so cannot and should not be transcended, features of the non-human world tend to be regarded as valuable in and of themselves, or to serve as examples that humans ought to emulate.

References

Aziz, Barbara, ed.

1979 *The Tradition of Pha-dam-pa-saṅs-rgyas*. 5 vols. Thimphu: Druk Sherik Parkhang.

Bacot, J., F. W. Thomas and Ch. Toussaint, eds.

1940-46 *Documents de Touen-houang relatifs à l'histoire du Tibet*. Paris: P. Geuthner.

Beyer, Stephan

1974 *The Buddhist Experience: Sources and Interpretations*. Belmont, CA: Dickenson.

1992 *The Classical Tibetan Language*. Albany: State University of New York Press.

Chang, Garma C. C., trans.

1989 *The Hundred Thousand Songs of Milarepa*. 2 vols. Boston and Shaftesbury: Shambhala.

Dalai Lama XIV, Tenzin Gyatso

1988 *The Union of Bliss and Emptiness: A Commentary on the Lama Choepa Guru Yoga Practice*. Trans. by Thubten Jinpa. Ithaca: Snow Lion.

Dhondup, K., ed. and trans.

1981 *Songs of the Sixth Dalai Lama*. Dharamsala: Library of Tibetan Works and Archives.

Don grub rgyal

1985 *Bod kyi mgur glu byung 'phel gyi lo rgyus dang khyad chos bsdus par ston pa rig pa'i khye'u rnam par rtsen pa'i skyed tshal: mGur glu'i lo rgyus dang khyad chos*. [Lhasa:] Mi rigs dpe skrun khang.

Dowman, Keith, trans.

1980 *The Divine Madman: The Sublime Life and Songs of Drukpa Kunley*. Clear Lake, CA: The Dawn Horse Press.

Ellingson, Terry Jay

1979 "The Mandala of Sound: Concepts and Sound Structures in Tibetan Ritual Music." Ph.D. dissertation. Madison: University of Wisconsin-Madison.

Eppling, John

1989 "A Calculus of Creative Expression: The Central Chapter of Daṇḍin's Kāvyādarśa." Ph.D. dissertation. Madison: University of Wisconsin-Madison.

Guenther, Herbert V.

1976 *Treasures on the Tibetan Middle Way*. Second edition. Berkeley: Shambhala.

1993 *Ecstatic Spontaneity: Saraha's Three Cycles of Dohā*. Nanzan Studies in Asian Religions 4. Berkeley: Asian Humanities Press.

Gyatso, Geshe Kelsang

1992 *Great Treasury of Merit: A Commentary to the Practice of* Offering to the Spiritual Guide. London: Tharpa.

Gupta, D. K.

1970 *A Critical Study of Daṇḍin and His Works*. Delhi: Meharchand Lachhmandas.

Jackson, Roger
n.d. *Mind Illumining Mind: Mahāmudrā and the dGe lugs Tradition of Tibetan Buddhism*. [In progress.]

Kvaerne, Per
1977 *An Anthology of Buddhist Tantric Songs: A Study of the Caryāgīti*. Oslo-Bergen-Tromso: Universitetsforlaget.

Lalou, Marcelle, ed.
1939-61 *Inventaire des manuscrits tibétains de Touen-houang conservés à la Bibliothèque Nationale*. I-III. Paris: Bibliothèque Nationale.

Longchenpa [Klong chen pa]
1989 *A Visionary Journey*. [*Nags tshal kun tu dga ba'i gtam*]. Trans. by Herbert V. Guenther. Boston: Shambhala.

Mi la ras pa
MLGB *Mi la ras pa'i mgur 'bum: The Collected Songs of Spiritual Experience of Rje-btsun Mi-la-ras-pa*. Ed. by Gtsaṅ-smyon He-ru-ka. Gangtok: Sherab Gyaltsen, 1983.

Mullin, Glenn H., trans.
1985 *Selected Works of the Dalai Lama VII: Songs of Spiritual Change*. Ithaca: Snow Lion.
1994 *Mystical Verses of a Mad Dalai Lama*. Wheaton, IL: Theosophical Publishing House.

Namdol, Gyaltsen and Ngagwang Samten, ed. and trans.
1982 *Pratītyasamutpādastutisubhāṣitahṛdayam of Ācārya Tsoṅkhāpā*. Sarnath: Central Institute of Higher Tibetan Studies.

Pad ma dkar po
DJL *dPal Padma dkar po'i rdo rje'i glu phreng ba nga ma zhes bya ba*. Manuscript copy, n.p.

Paṇ chen Lama I, Blo bzang chos kyi rgyal mtshan
AFPL *The Autobiography of the First Panchen Lama bLo-bzang-chos-kyi-rgyal-mtshan*. Ed. Ngawang Gelek Demo. Gedan Sungrab Minyam Gyunphel Series 12. Delhi: 1969.
LMC *Bla ma mchod dang tshogs 'khor bcas*. In *Bla ma'i rnal 'byor dang yi dam khag gi bdag bskyed sogs zhal 'don gces btus*. Dharamsala: Tibetan Cultural Printing Press, 1978.

Rabten, Geshe
1989 *Song of the Profound View*. Trans. and annot. by Stephen Batchelor. London: Wisdom.

Shahidullah, M., ed., trans. and annot.
1928 *Les chants mystiques de Kāṇha et Saraha: Les Dohā-koṣa et les Caryā*. Paris: Adrien-Maisonneuve.

Stein, R. A.

1959 *Recherches sur l'épopée et le barde au Tibet*. Paris: Presses Universitaire de France.

1972a *Tibetan Civilization*. Trans. by J. E. Stapleton Driver. Stanford: Stanford University Press.

1972b *Vie et chants de 'Brug pa kun legs le yogin*. Paris: Paris: G.-P. Maisonneuve et Larose.

Templeman, David

1994 "Dohā, Vajragīti and Caryā Songs." In *Tantra and Popular Religion in Tibet*. Ed. by Geoffrey Samuel, Hamish Gregor and Elisabeth Stutchbury. New Delhi: International Academy of Indian Culture and Aditya Prakashan.

Thaye, Jampa

1990 *A Garland of Gold: The Early Kagyu Masters in India and Tibet*. Bristol: Ganesha Press.

Thurman, Robert A. F., ed.

1982 *Life and Teachings of Tsong Khapa*. Dharamsala: Library of Tibetan Works and Archives.

Trungpa, Chögyam

1980 *The Rain of Wisdom*. Translated by the Nālandā Translation Committee under the direction of Chögyam Trungpa. Boulder: Shambhala.

1982 *The Life of Marpa the Translator*. Translated by the Nālandā Translation Committee under the direction of Chögyam Trungpa. Boulder: Shambhala.

1983 *First Thought, Best Thought: 108 Poems*. Boulder and London: Shambhala.

Tsering Tashi

1981 "Tibetan Poetry Through the Ages." *The Tibet Society Newsletter* 10 (Summer 1981): 8-12. [Originally printed in *Lotus Fields* 2 (Spring 1979)].

Tsong kha pa Blo bzang grags pa

LRDD *Byang chub lam gyi rim pa'i nyams len gyi rnam gzhag mdor bsdus*. In *gSung thor bu*. In *The Collected Works (gsuṅ 'bum) of the Incomparable Lord Tsoṅ-kha-pa Blo-bzaṅ-grags-pa*, reproduced from prints from the 1897 Lha-sa Old Zol (Dga'-ldan-phun-tshogs-gliṅ) blocks, vol. 2, 55b-58a. New Delhi: Mongolian Lama Gurudeva, 1978.

RTJS *Rang gi rtogs pa brjod pa mdo tsam du bshad pa*. In *gSung thor bu*. In *The Collected Works (gsuṅ 'bum) of the Incomparable Lord Tsoṅ-kha-pa Blo-bzaṅ-grags-pa*, reproduced from prints from the 1897 Lha-sa Old Zol (Dga'-ldan-phun-tshogs-gliṅ) blocks, vol. 2, 52b-55b. New Delhi: Mongolian Lama Gurudeva, 1978.

Tulku Thondup and Matthew T. Kapstein
1994 "Tibetan Poetry." In *The New Princeton Encyclopedia of Poetry and Poetics*. Ed. by Alex Preminger and T. V. F. Brogan. Princeton: Princeton University Press.

Webster's
1977 *Webster's New Collegiate Dictionary*. Springfield, MA: G. & C. Merriam Co.

Chapter 23

Tibetan Belles-Lettres: The Influence of Daṇḍin and Kṣemendra

Leonard W. J. van der Kuijp

The *locus classicus* for the Indian Buddhist classification of the five domains of knowledge (*vidyāsthāna, rig gnas*), or sciences, is the quatrain of the chapter of the fifth century *Mahāyānasūtrālaṃkāra* XI, 60 (a taxonomy of scientific fields of endeavor already found in the probably earlier *Yogācārabhūmi*) in which a total of five are enumerated:

(1) Science of language
(2) Science of medicine
(3) Technology
(4) Logic and epistemology
(5) Inner science (Buddhism proper)

The first of these, the so-called *śabdavidyā* (*sgra rig pa*), includes not only (Sanskrit) grammar, but also its ancillary sciences of poetics, prosody, lexicography and dramaturgy. Tibetan belles-lettres is preeminently based on the science of poetics.[1] In this preliminary survey we shall mainly concern ourselves with the Tibetan transmissions of Daṇḍin's *Kāvyādarśa* (Tib. *sNyan ngag me long*), the treatise which formed the necessary precondition for the development of Tibetan ornate poetry, as well as with Kṣemendra's *Bodhisattvāvadānakapalatā*, a major collection of Indian poetry that, upon its translation into Tibetan, exerted a profound influence on Tibetan poetry (and Tibetan Buddhist iconography). First, a few introductory remarks are in order.

Tibetan poetry and poetics are among the least developed areas in modern Tibetology which, so far, has been largely concentrated on the Tibetan counterparts of the Indian, and in some cases Chinese, Buddhist texts that found their way into the massive Tibetan Buddhist canon. In fact, this canon, of which the first prototypes can be dated to the beginning of the ninth century, and which achieved its most complete form only around the middle of the eighteenth century in the sDe dge edition of eastern Tibet, constitutes the cornerstone and model for virtually every genre of Tibetan literature as such. As the most authoritative corpus of texts, it formed a continuous source of inspiration for many of Tibet's finest men of letters, so that one may say that, by and large, the literary genres of India all have a Tibetan counterpart and that, as a consequence, Tibet's literature is, with a few very important exceptions, a continuation of that of India and as permeated with the religious sentiment that is so characteristic of much of India's traditional literature. While it is therefore undeniable that Tibetan literature depends to a large measure on that of India, much like Roman literature was inspired by the Greeks, this does not mean that we do not find indigenous forms.

Aside from inscriptions, the earliest witnesses of indigenous Tibetan writing were only unearthed during the beginning of this century in a cave-depot of the Buddhist cave monastery of Dunhuang in Gansu Province in the People's Republic of China. These include translations and adaptations from Indic and Chinese sources—the latter includes the classics of the *Shangshu* or *Shujing* (see Huang, Coblin), the *Zhanguoce* (see Imaeda) and the *Shiji* (see Takeuchi)—as well as independent compositions, including the very first specimen of heroic poetry. While most of these are religious in nature, a good portion of the manuscripts contain works that are more of a secular order. The Dunhuang cave also elicited several fragments of imaginative adaptations from the *Rāmāyaṇa*, the famous Indian epic of the story of Rāma and Sītā (see de Jong, 1989). A subsequent revival of interest in this tale may have been brought about through the eleventh-century translation of Prajñāvarman's commentary on the *Viśeṣastava* (where Rāma and Sītā are mentioned several times), the *Rāmajātaka*, and foremost, by Daṇḍin's *Kāvyādarśa* ("The Mirror of Poetics"), the seventh-century Indian textbook on poetic theory, in which the author refers several times to their story in connection with the illustrations he provides for the poetic figures that are discussed.

The Tibetan Versions of Daṇḍin's *Kāvyādarśa*

Daṇḍin's *Kāvyādarśa*, "The Mirror of Poetics," a classic treatment of Indian poetic theory, was first made known to the Tibetan scholarly world by Sa skya Paṇḍita Kun dga' rgyal mtshan (1182-1251), who translated major portions of its first and second chapters in his unprecedented treatise on the principles of learned discourse, the *mKhas pa rnams la 'jug pa'i sgo*, the title of which can be paraphrased as "An Introduction to Scholarship," composed between ca. 1220 and 1230 (see Jackson). The text of the *Kāvyādarśa* is divided into three chapters, the first of which delineates the general characteristics of ornate poetry and the features that distinguish the so-called southern from the eastern schools of literary composition. The second chapter catalogues and discusses those poetic figures that are based on the semantic relationships within a verse, and the third does the same for the poetic figures that have their origin in the phonological relations within a verse. It became the model against which Tibetan literary critics, such as there were, measured the poetic accomplishments of their fellow writers, after it was translated into Tibetan by Shong ston lo tsā ba rDo rje rgyal mtshan and Lakṣmīkara under the patronage and support of 'Phags pa Blo gros rgyal mtshan (1235-1280), Sa skya Paṇḍita's nephew, and grand-governor (*dpon chen*) Shākya bzang po (d. 1270?), sometime between 1267 and 1270. In course of time, new Sanskrit manuscripts of Daṇḍin's work found their way into Tibet, which resulted in improvements on, or variations of, the earlier translations. An example of this already appears in the first stanza of the *Kāvyādarśa*, which reads in Sanskrit (Shastri and Potdar: 1) [reduplication of consonants has been elided]:

> *caturmukhamukhāmbhojavanahaṃsavadhūrmam /*
> *mānase ramatāṃ nityaṃ sarvaśukla sarasvatī //*

> May the all-white, the goose,
> Among the lotus[-like] mouths of the four-faced [god
> Brahma],
> Sarasvatī, dwell forever
> In my mind.

Some Sanskrit manuscripts of the text have, in the third foot, the variant reading *dirghaṃ*, "long," for *nityaṃ*, "forever." The Tibetan translation of this stanza in each of the four canonical prints is:

> *gdong bzhi gdong gi pad tshal gyi //*
> *ngang pa'i bu mo thams cad dkar //*
> *dbyangs can ma ni kho bo yi //*
> *yid la ring du gnas par mdzod //*

It thus follows those Sanskrit texts that have *dirghaṃ*. However, the reading of *nityaṃ* is attested in the exegesis of sNar thang lo tsā ba of the year 1408 (see *DGE*: 25), for there the last two feet read:

> *dbyangs can ma ni kho bo yi //*
> *yid mtshor rtag par gnas par mdzod //*

To be noted also is the variant *yid mtshor* for *yid la*, which can to some extent also reflect Sanskrit *mānase*.

This process of successive reevaluation may be said to have culminated in the text-critical work on, and exegesis of, the text by the great linguist and Sanskritist Si tu Paṇ chen bsTan pa'i nyin byed (1699-1774) and his disciple the fourth Khams sprul bsTan 'dzin chos kyi nyi ma (1734-1779) of, respectively, 1772 and 1770 (see *SI* and *KHAMS*). In all, one can isolate some seven phases of its transmission in Tibet under the following Tibetan Sanskritists:

(1) Sa skya Paṇḍita
(2) Shong ston lo tsā ba / Lakṣmīkara
(3) dPang lo tsā ba Blo gros brtan pa (1276-1342)
(4) sNar thang lo tsā ba dGe 'dun dpal (ca. 1400), alias Saṃghaśrī
(5) sNye thang lo tsā ba Blo gros brtan pa (mid-fifteenth century)
(6) Zhwa lu lo tsā ba Rin chen chos skyong dpal bzang po (1441-1528)
(7) Si tu Paṇ chen and the fourth Khams sprul

Each of these phases is thus characterized by a renewed appraisal of earlier translations, one that was often undertaken in conjunction with the availability of new Sanskrit manuscripts. Not all of these ended up in subsequent editions of the canon, however. Of the four editions that are available, the Beijing and sNar thang recensions contain the text edited by dPang lo tsā ba, whereas the sDe dge and Co ne have the edited text of sNye thang lo tsā ba. Moreover, the bilingual Sanskrit-Tibetan version published in Bhutan is the one that resulted from Zhwa lu lo tsā ba's studies of the text (see *ZHWA*).

The *Kāvyādarśa* was also the object of numerous lengthy commentaries which, commencing with a series of glosses by Shong ston lo tsā ba himself, reached their zenith, from a philological point of view, in the magnificent commentary of the fourth Khams sprul. The earliest extant exegesis—the published manuscript is unfortunately incomplete—is owed to dPang lo tsā ba (see *DPANG*). The enormous impact of Daṇḍin's text on Tibetan letters in general is also apparent from the fourteenth century onward, where one can discern a conscious use of its poetic figures—these fall into two classes: poetic figures based on semantic considerations and those based on phonological ones—in virtually every literary genre, whether it be in eulogies, biographies, chronicles or dissertations on medicine, astrology and so on. Several important exegeses of the text were written during the present century, and we may mention here the one by Mi pham rNam rgyal rgya mtsho (1846-1912) of 1909, and those by the contemporary scholars bSe tshang Blo bzang dpal ldan and Dung dkar Blo bzang 'phrin las (see *MI*, *BSE* and *DUNG*). All of the writers mentioned thus far are Buddhist, but this does not mean that only Tibetan Buddhist scholars were interested in poetry and poetics. An example of a Bon po writer on this subject is the late Tshul khrims rgyal mtshan (1898-?), although his work, virtually a précis of the *Kāvyādarśa*, is indistinguishable from its Buddhist counterparts (see *TSHUL*).

Already the earliest Tibetan commentaries on the *Kāvyādarśa* provide evidence that two Indian commentaries, namely those by Ratnaśrī and Vāgīśvarakīrti, had penetrated into Tibet's literary consciousness (see van der Kuijp, 1986). It was in these glosses that further information on the fate of Rāma and Sītā came to be transmitted to Tibet. And it is essentially with this state of affairs in mind that we must view the first prose adaptation of a portion of their story by dMar ston Chos kyi rgyal po, a disciple of Sa skya Paṇḍita, in his commentary on a gnome (number 321) in the eighth chapter of his master's *Legs bshad rin po che'i gter* ("A Treasury of Elegant Sayings"), a work Sa skya Paṇḍita completed sometime between 1215 and 1225 (see *DMAR*: 190-196).[2] However, the most famous author of a Tibetan adaptation of this story is arguably Zhang zhung Chos dbang grags pa (1404-1469), whose work of 1438 is written in highly ornate poetry, using a great variety of Daṇḍin's poetic figures (see *ZHANG*). There is no doubt that Zhang zhung emulates the poetic style for which his master mKhas grub dGe legs dpal bzang po (1385-1438) has become notorious, for his diction is at times rather obscure and turgid, and always extremely intellectual. A commentary on this work, written by Ngag dbang bstan pa'i rgya mtsho of bKra shis 'khyil Monastery, was also recently published (see *NGAG*). It includes an identification of the poetic figures employed by Zhang zhung as well as a number of text-critical comments anent the corruptions that had crept into manuscripts and blockprints of Zhang zhung's work. To give an idea of the text and its exegesis, we have translated the first verse with which Zhang zhung begins his actual poem, together with Ngag dbang bstan pa'i rgya mtsho's comment (see *NGAG*: 90-91). It depicts rNga yab (Cāmara), the land of the demons, ruled by king Daśagriva, the abductor of Sītā, and contrasts it with 'Dzam gling (Jambudvīpa), the world as we know it.

> The one following the goose *Jambudvīpa,
> Is *Cāmara, the leader of gander[s].
> Desiring the rising red one (*dmar ba*),
> The one who followed it is Adi's [read: Ādi's]
> youngster.

> The meaning: *Cāmara and *Dvicāmara (or: Paracāmara) are associate isles of *Jambudvīpa and, insofar as the demons live in Cāmara, the leader of gander[s] who follow after the goose *Jambudvīpa, the great continent, that is, chase after it, is *Cāmara, the associate isle which is the demon abode. That very item is likened to this [scenario]: For instance, [propelled] by the force of desiring the beauty of the red lustre of the rising sun, Adi's [read: Ādi's] youngster, that is, Adi's [read: Ādi's] son, who followed or follows it, has the same quality as the sun. "Aditya" [read: Āditya], that is, *Mi sbyin skyes* [in Tibetan] is said to be the name given to [his] mother. In this [verse, the author] set up *Jambudvīpa and *Cāmara as metaphors for a goose and gander, and then set up their corresponding similes, namely the rising red hue is a simile of the former and the sun a simile for the latter. In this fashion, the stanza is a comparison-metaphor (*upamārūpaka, dpe'i gzugs can*), because it is similar to the statement in the *Kāvyādarśa* [II: 89],

> This moon-like countenance suffused,
> With a reddishness through intoxication,
> Vies with the moon,
> Rising and of excellent redness.

Although there is, in this [verse], no explicit word indicating similarity in the last foot, by implication [we] consider the reading [of the third foot] in the gTsang blockprint [= the bKra shis lhun po xylograph of Zhang zhung's work, see *ZHANG*: 2a] of his text,

> Desiring the rising speech (*smra ba*),

to be corrupt.

Apart from Zhang zhung's epic poem, there are at least two pieces in prose that were equally inspired by the *Rāmāyaṇa*. Both of these date from the eighteenth century. The first is a work on the ten incarnations of Viṣṇu—Rāma is the sixth of this series—by the fourth Khams sprul (see *KHAMS1*: 709-715), composed after his commentary on the *Kāvyādarśa*. The second constitutes a brief chapter in the commentary on a versified autobiography of Ngag dbang brtson 'grus (1648-1722) which his subsequent reembodiment dKon mchog 'jigs med dbang po (1728-1791) completed in 1777 (see *DKON*: 641-648). Contrary to the prevailing opinion that the *Rāmāyaṇa* was translated into Tibetan by Tāranātha (1575-1635)—this was based on a misreading of a passage in his autobiography which merely relates that he had read the text with Paṇḍita Purṇānanda and Pryamānanda (*sic*) in the year 1603[3]—the first complete Tibetan version is owed to the labors of dGe 'dun chos 'phel (1903-1951), whose manuscript copy in four volumes has survived and is currently being prepared for publication in Lhasa. Motifs from the *Rāmāyaṇa* sometimes turn up in the most unexpected places. A case in point is an occurrence in a work on epistemology and logic by gSer mdog Paṇ chen Shākya mchog ldan (1429-1507), where a philosophical issue is likened to the epic's twin brothers, Bha li (= Vālin) and mGrin bzangs (= Sugrīva) (*GSER*: 552). In connection with further influence exerted by the Indian epic literature on Tibetan belles-lettres, we should also mention the late reworking of the ordeal of the five Paṇḍava brothers of the *Mahābhārata* epic by Dza sag lHa smon Ye shes tshul khrims, who flourished during the second half of the nineteenth century (see *DZA*). His primary source (or sources) still need to be ascertained.

Very common experimental writings among the educated elite were those in which each of the poetic figures relating to the semantic, and not the phonological, make-up of the Tibetan version of the *Kāvyādarśa* was given an illustration. A huge number of such compositions survive and these are representative of the best in Tibetan ornate poetry.[4] Outstanding early published examples of this genre are the writings of Klong chen Rab 'byams pa Dri med 'od zer (1308-1364), the second Zhwa dmar mKha' spyod dbang po (1350-1405) and Bo dong Paṇ chen Phyogs las rnam rgyal (1375-1451).[5] Two of Klong chen pa's longish poems were recently translated into English (see Guenther), and both are inconceivable without Daṇḍin. Bo dong Paṇ chen, himself also a commentator on the *Kāvyādarśa*, was one of the greatest poets of his time, and the indigenous catalogues of his writings list a substantial number of original compositions, manuscripts of which the vast majority still remain to be located. The ones that have been published to date are his magnificent allegory entitled *sNyan dngags gi bstan bcos yid kyi shing rta* ("A Treatise of Ornate Poetry, A Vehicle of the Mind") (according to his biographer dKon mchog 'bangs, he wrote it in 1397 at the age of twenty-two), the *dNgul dkar me long* ("The White-Silver Mirror"), and the *Phun tshogs bcwo brgyad* ("The Eighteen Excellences"), an ornate eighteen-verse eulogy-*cum*-biography of his patron, Rab brtan kun bzang 'phags (1389-1442), the ruler of the principality of rGyal mkhar rtse in Central Tibet, located between Lhasa and gZhis ka rtse (see *BO, BO1, BO2*). This work later served as the poetic framework for the prose of the so-far anonymous biography of this enlightened ruler (see *DNT*). A biography written along mixed lines, stylistically speaking, was not the first of its kind, however. Already in 1387, Tsong kha pa Blo bzang grags pa (1359-1419) wrote a poetically conceived, ornate biography of his patron and teacher sPyan snga Grags pa byang chub (1356-1386) that belongs to the so-called mixed literary genre in that was written in alternating poetry and prose (see *TSONG*). The all-pervasive influence of Daṇḍin's dicta is abundantly apparent in each and every one of these writings.

Literary Forms

The genres Tibetan writers worked with in terms of compositional structure essentially fall into four separate categories: prose, verse, a mixture of prose and verse, and a unique type of continuous poetry which, consisting of one enormous metric foot, is characterized by an absence of such Tibetan punctuation markers as the single or double *shad* (/, //) (see van der Kuijp, 1986a). This kind of composition does not have an Indian counterpart—it is possible that so-called hypermetric texts in Sanskrit may have stimulated it, however—and therefore seems indigenous to Tibetan literature. The first to experiment with the latter genre were rJe btsun Grags pa rgyal mtshan (1147-1216) and his nephew Sa skya Paṇḍita; other exponents of this form of literature were, *inter alia*, 'Phags pa, dGe 'dun grub pa (1391-1474) (posthumously styled the first Dalai Lama), and gSer mdog Paṇ chen. Another form of poetry for which there are Indic parallels is what is variously called *ka phreng*, *ka rtsom*, or *ka bshad*. These compositions, of which the first known to me is attested in 'Phags pa's oeuvre (see *'PHAGS*), consist of thirty lines, the first beginning with *ka*, the first letter of the Tibetan alphabet, and each subsequent line beginning with the next letter (a very useful collection of large number of these may be found in Wen). An Indian canonical example of such a text is Saraha's *Kakhasyadohā*, on which an autocommentary is also extant.

The Tibetan version of the *Bodhisattvāvadānakalpalatā*

Another major event in the history of Tibetan poetry and poetics was the monumental translation of Kṣemendra's *Bodhisattvāvadānakalpalatā* (eleventh century) by Shong ston lo tsā ba and Lakṣmīkara, again under the patronage of 'Phags pa and grand-governor Shākya bzang po (see de Jong, 1979 and Mejor). As with Daṇḍin's text, this translation would therefore also date from around 1267 to 1270. This work, in which Kṣemendra recreated in elegant and highly stylized poetic form the lives of various bodhisattvas, played a vital role in the literary and artistic life of Tibet, for not only did it give rise to an enormous number of literary recreations, but its motifs soon began to appear as frescoes in monasteries and homes of the landed aristocracy. It was included in the Tibetan canon both in a bilingual Sanskrit-Tibetan version and its Tibetan rendition alone. One recension of the latter was based on a manuscript of the text that was prepared with the financial support of Ta'i si tu Byang chub rgyal mtshan (1302-1364) (see van der Kuijp, 1994). The original translation underwent a series of revisions of which the bilingual Sanskrit-Tibetan edition that was issued under the patronage of the fifth Dalai Lama Ngag dbang blo bzang rgya mtsho (1617-1682) in the year 1665 is but one instance. We learn from his autobiography that the fifth Dalai Lama, an outstanding poet in his own right, was himself in part responsible for this revision and he writes that the finished manuscript, accompanied with a printer's colophon, was sent to his residence in the beginning of March of that year. Apart from the fifth Dalai Lama's own glosses on certain passages, the first to attempt a revision of the earlier translation was dPang lo tsā ba, who also ventured to write some comments on those places in the text which he thought presented particular difficulties. Other revisions that followed were those initiated by So ston 'Jigs med grags pa (fourteenth century) and the ruler of the house of Rin spungs, Ngag dbang 'jig rten dbang phyug grags pa (1542-?1625), himself also the author of an excellent commentary on the *Kāvyādarśa* (completed in 1586) and a host of other pieces of ornate poetry. These are known respectively as the black and red annotations, presumably because of the color of the ink used. Kṣemendra's work inspired the latter to write a series of poems each of which summarized one chapter of the text. The sixth Zhwa dmar Gar dbang chos kyi dbang phyug (1584-1630), too, is recorded as having written a poetic composition taking the *Kalpalatā* as his model (see *SI-'BE*: 266). And, lastly, Lo chen Chos dpal (1654-1718), alias Dharmaśrī, another excellent poet and linguist, also composed a series of one-hundred-and-eight verses, each of which deals with one chapter.

The Tibetan translation of this work continued to be studied from a philological point of view, however, at least until well into the eighteenth century. For example, dBal mang dKon mchog rgyal mtshan (1764-1853) relates an oral account in his biography of his teacher and friend Gung thang pa dKon mchog bstan pa'i sgron me (1762-1823) of 1831 to the effect that the latter had made corrections to the Tibetan version of the text (*DBAL*: 71).[6] It is sometimes held that the scion of the house of Rin spungs was also responsible for a prose version of the *Kalpalatā*, but this appears to be incorrect, for the colophon of the only published prose rendition refers to the fifth Dalai Lama's bilingual edition (for various prose versions, see Mejor: 29-31).

Concluding Remarks: The Use of Poetry and Literary Criticism

We have seen that ornate poetry and the *Kāvyādarśa* occupy an important place in Tibetan literature. Some of the poems written according to Daṇḍin's canon were so abstruse as to elicit exegetical remarks which, at times, could be very elaborate indeed. A case in point would be the enormous commentary written by Yongs 'dzin Ye shes rgyal mtshan (1713-1791) on the opening verses of one of mKhas grub's treatises on epistemology and logic (see *YE*).[7] In spite of the large volume of Tibetan poetry, when reading through Tibet's rich literary legacy, one cannot help but be struck by the virtually complete absence of literary criticism; that is to say, there is really no evidence of a conscious reflection on the creative process in literature by means of a fully articulated and explicit set of criteria. Though the earliest guidelines as to what constitutes literature were to some extent provided by Sa skya Paṇḍita in the first chapter of his *mKhas pa rnams la 'jug pa'i sgo* ("Introduction to Scholarship")—this section of the text deals with grammar and the principles of literary composition—his remarks remained a relatively isolated phenomenon and evidently fell dead from his pen. Literary criticism in Tibet, such as it was, appears to have been by and large confined to the making of text-critical and philological remarks, including commenting on unusual diction, and to identify the kind of poetic figure from Daṇḍin's treatise used by a given author. It is only rarely that Tibetan authors of the pre-modern period, that is before the 1950s, give critical appraisals of the literary merit of the writings of their predecessors or contemporaries, and when they do, these are usually unsupported by an explicit mention of the criteria with which they are working.

Tibet, too, knew of the power of the pen, for one of the alleged causes of the outbreak of the civil war of 1614 was an ambiguous poem written by the sixth Zhwa dmar at the occasion of the formal installation on the throne of 'Bras spungs Monastery of the fourth Dalai Lama Yon tan rgya mtsho (1588-1616). The poem is quoted in the fourth Dalai Lama's biography by the fifth Dalai Lama (see *DAL*: 276-278).[8] In an allusion to *Mahāyānasūtrālaṃkāra* XI, 60, one of its quatrains begins:

> "If one has not become learned in the domains of knowledge,
> Even a supreme noble one would not attain omniscience."
> Because such has been said, without the force of [your] intelligence being distracted,
> May you make the most supreme effort in the domains of knowledge!

The fourth Dalai Lama, the great-grandson of Altan Khan (1505/07-1582/83) of the Tümed Mongols, had been living away from Tibet until the year 1614. The point made in this quatrain was that his scholarship and learning left something to be desired, an observation that may very well have contained a kernel of truth. The sixth Zhwa dmar himself was the first son of the head of the 'Bri gung pa sect of the bKa' brgyud pa, and, some twenty-five years earlier, his younger brother dKon mchog rin chen (1590-1655), later the twenty-third abbot of 'Bri gung Monastery, had been the primary (and only Tibetan) candidate for the reembodiment of the third Dalai Lama bSod nams rgya mtsho (1543-1588). After some deliberation, he was passed over by Seng ge, the financial secretary (*phyag mdzod*) of the recently deceased third Dalai Lama, who then with the support of the Tümed Mongols was able to determine his master's successor to be Yon tan rgya mtsho. The poem and its tenor should be read with this in mind, as well as with the militant rivalry that existed between the financial supporters of the dGe lugs pa in dBus and the house of the gTsang pa, which mainly supported the bKa' brgyud pa and the Sa skya pa (including the Jo nang pa) schools. No friend of the bKa' brgyud pa, the fifth Dalai Lama characterizes the sixth Zhwa dmar's poem as not being very successful when compared with compositions of other poets, which he styles as "mellifluous and forceful," but it is interesting that he does not even attempt to come to the defense of the fourth Dalai Lama's scholarly abilities, because, basically, there were none. Lastly, in 1647, the fifth Dalai Lama composed his own commentary on the *Kāvyādarśa* which he used inter alia as a vehicle to make a number of political, philosophical and religious statements. One example of this should suffice. Illustrating the so-called poetic figure of corroboration (*arthāntaranyāsa, don gzhan bkod pa*) of what is unsuitable and suitable from the *Kāvyādarśa* II, 176, he writes (see *DAL1*: 125):

If a bad explanation of followers of the Sa skya teachings
were to be explicated,
Wherefore not mention the stupid tales of the bKa' brgyud's
great meditators?
Much learning must beget eloquence,
Little learning constitutes nonsensical chatter.

Notes

1. Tibetan and Chinese scholars in the People's Republic of China have done excellent work in Tibetan literature and belles-lettres. Among many works that have been published in recent years, we may mention the outstanding survey of Tibetan literature found in the large volume edited by Zhou Jiesheng and Luo Runcang (1985) and in the three-volume selection of belles-lettres, together with copious annotations, in Blo bzang chos grags and bSod nams rtse mo (1989).

2. A Chinese translation of this story can be found in He (1987: 112-118).

3. This was first proposed by Roerich (1963). Tāranātha writes in his autobiography—see the passage in *TAR* 143—that he suspected that, despite them being self-declared Buddhists, they were Hindus at heart, and that he therefore did not request any initiations or teachings from them. He did, however, consult them on grammatical questions and did some translations. In addition to having heard from them the *Rāmāyaṇa*, he also listened to their exposition of the *Mahābhārata*.

4. Among the earliest instances of these would be the texts by the contemporaries Thar pa gling lo tsā ba Nyi ma rgyal mtshan (ca.1270-1320) and Lo tsā ba mChog ldan legs pa'i blo gros dpung rgyan mdzes pa'i tog, manuscripts of which are housed in the China Nationalities Library, Cultural Palace of Nationalities, Beijing, under catalogue numbers 002383 and 002382.

5. Four such texts by nineteenth- and early twentieth-century eastern Tibetan scholars may be found in the collection edited in Thub bstan nyi ma.

6. The same passage also has it that Gung thang pa did the same for what he considered to be infelicitous renderings in the translations of the Sārasvata and Pāṇini Sanskrit grammars by 'Dar lo tsa ba mGag dbang phun tshogs lhun grub (1633/34-?).

7. Another exegesis of verses of the same text was written by 'Jam dbyangs 'phrin las at the request of the third (or sixth) Paṇ chen Lama Blo bzang dpal ldan ye shes (1738-1780), although, for some reason, it was included in the collected writings of dKon mchog 'jigs med dbang po (see *'JAM*).

8. A more explicitly anti-dGe lugs pa establishment poem by the sixth Zhwa dmar is referred to in Chab spel Tshe brtan phun tshogs and Nor brang O

rgyan (546-547), who cite as their source a handwritten manuscript of the early nineteenth-century chronicle of Rag ra Ngag dbang bstan pa'i rgyal mtshan. The first four lines of this poem read:

> *brag tig zhag gsum gyi grong khyer na //*
> *kho rwa gan tshogs pa'i ru rnon tsho //*
> *rje chos dbyings ri dwags thang bzhugs la //*
> *ra rno rtul 'gran pa ci rang yin //*

The tenor of this quatrain is unmistakable, for the dGe lugs pa are likened to yaks, whereas the Kar ma bKa' brgyud are put on par with the lion. Interestingly, this poem is not found in the published version of the chronicle, where the passage the two authors had in mind occurs in *RAG*: 266-267.

References

Blo bzang chos grags and bSod nams rtse mo, eds.

1989 — *Gangs ljongs mkhas dbang rim byon gyi rtsom yig gser gyi sbram bu*. 3 vols. Xining: Qinghai minzu chubanshe.

Bo dong Paṇ chen Phyogs las rnam rgyal

BO — *Grub pa'i slob dpon dpal dbyangs can dga' ba'i zhabs kyis mdzad pa'i snyan ngag gi bstan bcos yid kyi shing rta*. In *Kāvya Texts from Bhutan*, pp. 597-687. Thimphu, 1976

BO1 — *dNgul dkar gyi me long*. In *The Literary Arts in Ladakh*, vol. 1, pp. 41-56. Darjeeling: Kargyud sungrab nyamso khang, 1972.

BO2 — *Phun tshogs bcwo brgyad*. In *The Literary Arts in Ladakh*, vol. 1, pp. 91-106. Darjeeling: Kargyud sungrab nyamso khang, 1972.

bSe tshang Blo bzang dpal ldan

BSE — *Tshangs sras bzhad pa'i sgra dbyangs*. Lanzhou: Gansu minzu chubanshe, 1984.

Chab spel Tshe brtan phun tshogs and Nor brang O rgyan

1990 — *Bod kyi lo rgyus rags rim g.yu yi phreng ba*, bar cha. Lhasa: Bod ljongs bod yig dpe rnying dpe skrun khang.

Coblin, W.S.

1991 — "A Study of the Old Tibetan *Shangshu* Paraphrase, pt. I." *Journal of the American Oriental Society* 111/2: 303-322; "A Study of the Old Tibetan *Shangshu* Paraphrase, pt. 2." *Journal of the American Oriental Society* 111/3: 523-539.

Dalai Lama V, Ngag dbang blo bzang rgya mtsho

DAL — *'Jig rten dbang phyug thams cad mkhyen pa yon tan rgya mtsho dpal bzang po'i rnam par thar pa nor bu'i 'phreng ba*. [Biographies of the third and fourth Dalai Lamas.] Solon, 1982.

DAL1 — *sNyan ngag me long gi dka' 'grel dbyangs can dgyes pa'i glu dbyang*. Ed. by Khenpo Thupten Tshondu. Varanasi, 1966.

dBal mang dKon mchog rgyal mtshan

DBAL *'Jam dbyangs bla ma rje btsun dkon mchog bstan pa'i sgron me'i rnam par thar pa brjod pa'i gtam dad pa'i padmo bzhad pa'i nyin byed*. In *Collected Works*, vol.7, pp. 1-407. New Delhi, 1974.

dKon mchog 'jigs med dbang po

DKON *gSol 'debs kai ta ka'i 'phreng mdzes kyi rnam bshad tshig don rab gsal*. In *Collected Works*, vol. 7, pp. 625-675. New Delhi, 1972.

dMar ston Chos kyi rgyal po

DMAR *Legs par bshad pa rin po che'i gter dang 'grel pa*. Lhasa, 1982.

Dharma Rā dza'i rnam thar

DNT *Dharma rā dza'i rnam thar dad pa'i lo thog rgyas byed dngos grub kyi char 'bebs*. Dharamsala: Library of Tibetan Works and Archives, 1978.

dPang lo tsā ba Blo gros brtan pa

DPANG *sNyan ngags* (sic) *me long gi rgya cher 'grel pa gzhung don gsal ba*. In *Rig gnas phyogs sdebs, a Collection of Miscellaneous Works on Tibetan Minor Sciences*, pp. 281-502. Dharamsala: Library of Tibetan Works and Archives, 1981.

Dung dkar Blo bzang 'phrin las

DUNG *sNyan ngag la 'jug tshul tshig rgyan rig pa'i sgo 'byed*. Xining: Qinghai minzu chubanshe, 1982.

Dza sag lHa smon Ye shes tshul khrims

DZA *sKya seng bu lnga'i byung ba brjod pa blo ldan yi dbang 'dren byed rmad byung 'phrul gyi shing rta. Rare Tibetan Historical and Literary Texts from the Library of Tsepon W.D. Shakabpa*, series 1, pp. 209-227. New Delhi, 1974.

gSer mdog Paṇ chen Sākya mchog ldan

GSER *Tshad ma rigs gter gyi dgongs rgyan rigs pa'i 'khor los lugs ngan pham byed*. In *Collected Works*, vol. 10. Thimphu, 1975.

Guenther, Herbert V.

1989 *A Visonary Journey. The Story of The Wildwood Delights, The Story of The Mount Potala Delights*. Boston: Shambhala.

He Wenxuan

1987 *Zangzu geyen gushi xuan*. Lhasa: Xizang renmin chubanshe.

Huang Bufan

1981 "'Shangshu' sipian gu zangwen yiwende chubu yanjiu." *Yuyan yanjiu* 1: 203-232.

Imaeda, Y.

1980 "L'identification de l'original chinois du Pelliot tibétain 1291—traduction du *Zhanguoce*." *Acta Orientalia Hungarica* 34: 53-68.

Jackson, David P.

1987 *The Entrance Gate for the Wise (Section III). Sa-skya Paṇḍita on Indian and Tibetan Traditions of Pramāṇa and Philosophical Debate*, vols.1-2. Wiener Studien zur Tibetologie und Buddhismuskunde, Heft 17, 1-2. Vienna: Arbeitskreis für Tibetische und Buddhistische Studien Universität Wien.

'Jam dbyangs 'phrin las

'JAM *rNam 'grel gyi rnam bshad rigs pa'i rgya mtsho'i mgo mjug bar gsum gyi snyan ngag gi tshig 'grel rin po che'i sgron me*. In *The Collected Works of dKon mchog 'jigs med dbang po*, vol. 7, pp. 533-569. New Delhi: 1972.

de Jong, J. W.

1979 *Textcritical Remarks on the Bodhisattvāvadānakalpalatā*. Studia Philologica Buddhica, Monograph Series 2. Tokyo: Reiyukai Library.

1989 *The Story of Rāma in Tibet. Text and Translation of the Tun-huang Manuscripts*. Tibetan and Indo-Tibetan Studies 1. Stuttgart: Franz Steiner Verlag Wiesbaden, GMBH.

Khams sprul IV, bsTan 'dzin chos kyi nyi ma

KHAMS *rGyan gyi bstan bcos me long pa chen bla ma'i gsung bzhin bkral ba dbyangs can ngag gi rol mtsho legs bshad nor bu'i 'byung khungs*. Thimphu, 1976.

KHAMSa *Lha chen po khyab 'jug gi 'jug pa bcu'i gtam rgya bal mkhas pa'i ngag rgyun gangs can rna ba'i bdud rtsi*. In *Khams sprul snyan 'grel*, vol. 2, pp. 705-722. Tashijong: The Sungrab nyamso junphel parkhang Tibetan Craft Community, 1969.

van der Kuijp, Leonard W. J.

1986 "Bhāmaha in Tibet." *Indo-Iranian Journal* 28: 31-39.

1986a "Sa-skya Paṇḍita on the Typology of Literary Genres." *Studien zur Indologie und Iranistik* 11/12: 41-52.

1994 "Studies in Fourteenth-Century Tibetan Cultural History I: Ta'i si tu Byang chub rgyal mtshan as a Man of Religion." *Indo-Iranian Journal* 37: 139-149.

Mejor, M.

1992 *Kṣemendra's Bodhisattvāvadānakalpalatā. Studies and Materials*. Studia Philologica Buddhica, Monograph Series 7. Tokyo: The International Institute for Buddhist Studies.

Mi pham rNam rgyal rgya mtsho

MI *sNyan dngags me long gi 'grel pa dbyangs can dgyes pa'i rol mtsho*. Lhasa: Xizang renmin chubanshe, 1984.

Ngag dbang bstan pa'i rgya mtsho

NGAG *rGyal po rā ma ṇa'i gtam rgyud las brtsams pa'i snyan ngag gi bstan bcos dri za'i bu mo rgyud mang gi sgra sbyangs kyi rnam bshad dri med shel gyi 'bab stegs*. Chengdu: Sichuan minzu chubanshe, 1981.

'Phags pa Blo gros rgyal mtshan
'PHAGS *Ka sogs sum cu la spel ba*. In *Sa skya pa'i bka' 'bum*, vol. 7, p. 231/2/4-3/5. Ed. by bSod nams rgya mtsho. Tokyo: Tōyō Bunko, 1968.

Rag ra Ngag dbang bstan pa'i rgyal mtshan
RAG *rGyal rabs chos 'byung shel dkar me long mkhas pa'i mgul rgyan*. Ed. Bre srang. Gangs can rig mdzod 9, pp. 195-397. Lhasa: Bod ljongs bod yig dpe rnying dpe skrun khang, 1990.

Roerich, George
1963 "The Story of Rāma in Tibet." In *XXIV Int. Congress of Orientalists. Papers presented by the delegation of the USSR*, pp. 184-189. Moscow.

Sa skya Paṇḍita kun dga' rgyal mtshan
mKhas pa rnams la 'jug pa'i sgo. In *Sa skya pa'i bka' 'bum*, vol. 5, pp. 81/1-111/3. Ed. by bSod nams rgya mtsho. Tokyo: The Tōyō Bunko, 1968.

Shastri, Vidyabhusana Pandit Rangacharya Raddi and K. R. Potdar
1979 *Kāvyādarśa of Daṇḍin*. Government Oriental Series Class A, no. 4. Poona: Shandarkar Oriental Research Institute.

Si tu Paṇ chen bsTan pa'i nyin byed, ed.
SI *Slob dpon dbyug pa can gyis mdzad pa'i snyan ngag me long zhes bya ba skad gnyis shan sbyar*. In *Collected Works*, vol. 6, pp. 629-731/732. Sansal: Palpung sungrab nyamso khang sherab ling Institute of Buddhist Studies, 1990.

Si tu Paṇ chen bsTan pa'i nyin byed and 'Be lo Tshe dbang kun khyab
SI-'BE *sGrub brgyud karma kaṃ tshang brgyud pa rin po che'i rnam par thar pa rab 'byams nor bu zla ba chu shel gyi phreng ba*, vol. 2. New Delhi, 1972.

sNar thang lo tsā ba dGe 'dun dpal
DGE *sNyan ngag me long gi rgya cher 'grel pa*, 2 vols. Thimphu, 1976.

Takeuchi, T.
1985 "A Passage from the *Shih Chi* in the *Old Tibetan Chronicle*." In *Soundings in Tibetan Civilization*, pp. 135-145. Ed. by Barbara N. Aziz and Matthew Kapstein. New Delhi: Manohar.

Tāranātha
TAR *rGyal khams pa tā ra nā thas bdag nyid kyi rnam thar nges brjod pa'i deb gter shin tu zhib mo ma bcos lhug pa'i rtogs brjod*. In *Collected Works*, vol. 1, pp. 1-654. Leh, 1982.

Thub bstan nyi ma, ed.

1987 *Khams khul mkhas dbang rnams kyi snyan ngag dper brjod phyogs sgrig*. Chengdu: Sichuan minzu chubanshe.

Tshul khrims rgyal mtshan

TSHUL *sNyan ngag gi bstan bcos rin chen lde mig*. *Bon po'i dag yig skor*, pp. 631-744. Solan, 1985.

Tsong kha pa Blo bzang grags pa

TSONG *Byang chub sems dpa' sems dpa' chen po grags pa byang chub dpal bzang po'i rtogs pa brjod pa'i snyan dngags byin rlabs kyi lhun po*. In *Collected Works* (Bkra shis lhun po print), vol. 3, pp. 288-335. New Delhi, 1976.

Wen Guogen, ed.

1986 *Ka bshad gces sgrig me tog phreng mdzes*. Chengdu: Sichuan minzu chubanshe.

Yongs 'dzin Ye shes rgyal mtshan

YE *Ṭik chen rigs pa'i rgya mtsho'i mchod brjod dang rtsom par dam bca'i don rnam par bshad pa rigs lam gsal byed*. In *Collected Works*, vol. 21, pp. 1-213. New Delhi: Tibet House, 1976.

Zhang zhung Chos dbang grags pa

ZHANG *rGyal po rā ma ṇa'i gtam rgyud las brtsams pa'i snyan ngag gi bstan bcos dri za'i bu mo'i rgyud mang gi sgra dbyangs*. In Nepal-German Manuscript Preservation Project, reel no. L 30/29: 16 folios.

Zhou Jiesheng and Luo Runcang, eds.

1985 *Zangzu wenxue shi*. Chengdu: Sichuan minzu chubanshe.

Zhwa lu lo tsā ba Rin chen chos skyong bzang po

ZHWA *sLob dpon dbyug pa can gyis mdzad pa'i snyan dngags me long*. In *Kāvya Texts from Bhutan*, pp. 1-98. Thimphu, 1976.

Chapter 24

The Tibetan Novel and Its Sources

Beth Newman

Like other civilizations, Tibet has belles-lettres (*kāvya*). Yet, despite much recent study of Tibetan literature and culture, the prevailing view continues to be that Tibet never developed a genre of literature whose primary purpose is aesthetic enjoyment (Hoffman: 193-212; Snellgrove and Richardson: 59-63; Stein: 251-252; Tucci: 94-96). The purpose of this essay is to show that the Tibetans, as inheritors of Indian literary culture, produced numerous works in an ornate style meant to be appreciated as displays of verbal virtuosity. While in general it cannot be denied that Tibetan culture is pervaded by Buddhist thought and sensibilities, it is going too far to contend that there is no literature outside of religion.

Most of the authors in the Tibetan belles-lettres tradition strove to give their readers pleasure from their craft of style, and in addition impart religious instruction and moral edification through their choice of subject matter (often the life of the Buddha, *jātaka* stories, *avadānas*, etc.). Yet there is at least one work with aesthetic pleasure as its *raison d'être*: the eighteenth-century Tibetan novel *gZhon nu zla med kyi gtam rgyud* ("The Tale of the Incomparable Prince"), by mDo mkhar zhabs drung Tshe ring dbang rgyal (1697-1763). Because the novel's use of ornate poetry and prose to tell a fictional story in a Buddhist context can only be understood within the context of Tibetan belles-lettres a brief history of that genre precedes our discussion of the novel.

Tibetan Belles-Lettres

There are two traditions of Tibetan artistic composition: literature in an indigenous stylistic genre, and literature (*kāvya, snyan ngag*) that follows a canon of expression derived from Indian stylistic prescriptions (*alaṃkāraśāstra*) (see van der Kuijp and R. Jackson, in this volume).

The Tibetan term *snyan ngag* is used with two closely related but distinct meanings: it signifies both the science of poetics (*alaṃkāraśāstra*), and the products of the poetic process—belles-lettres itself (*kāvya*) (*KJG*: 5; *SKK*, vol. 2: 298; Klong rdol: 391; Smith, vol. 3: 1; Tucci: 626). Indo-Tibetan poetics is devoted solely to the mechanics of composition; its primary concerns are the components of literature, such as comparative structures or figures of speech (*alaṃkāra*). Poetics describes the expressive apparatus that gives rise to aesthetic pleasure through a systematization of the figures, their relationship to content, and their poetic application (Gerow: 14).

The foundation of the study of poetics in Tibet can be attributed to Sa skya Paṇḍita [or Paṇ chen] Kun dga' rgyal mtshan (1181-1251), and his nephew and successor 'Phags pa 'gro dgon chos rgyal Blo gros rgyal mtshan (1235-1280) (*BG*: 57). These early Sa skya masters set the course for the later development of literature in Tibet through commissioning translations of the major Sanskrit works on poetic theory, and the poetry and dramas which make up almost the entire contents of the *sGra mdo* and *sKye rabs* sections of the canon (Smith: 6; Tucci: 104).

The Sa skya masters were interested in poetics as part of the process of propagating Buddhism in Tibet rather than as art for art's sake. These scholars wanted to maintain the accuracy of doctrine (*'dzin*), preserve it in its purity and entirety (*skyong*), and spread it to others (*spel*). In addition, expertise in composition was required in order to structure clear explanations of doctrine (*'chad*), to dispute with opponents (*rtsod*), and to compose lucid treatises (*rtsom*). Thus, every composition necessitated a knowledge of poetics (*KJG:* i-ii).

To aid in the transmission of Buddhism to Tibet Sa skya Paṇḍita wrote works on composition, prosody and lexicography.[1] His primer on composition, the *mKhas pa rnams 'jug pa'i sgo*, drew heavily upon the *Kāvyādarśa* of Daṇḍin.[2] Through Sa skya Paṇḍita's work, and later translations and commentaries on Daṇḍin, the

Kāvyādarśa became the authoritative manual on the composition of belles-lettres in Tibet. In addition, at the request of the Sa skya ruler dPon chen Shākya bzang po and 'Phags pa, Shong ston rDo rje rgyal mtshan, his disciple dPang Lo tsā ba Blo gros brtan pa (1276-1342), and the Nepalese pandit Lakṣmīkara translated various works that became the basis for all future Tibetan work on poetics.[3]

Other early Sa skya writing, while not composed with the intention of influencing Tibetan literary style, had considerable impact on the thematic content of belles-lettres. Pithy expositions of ethical issues often included a brief exposition of the Indian epics, the *Rāmāyaṇa* and *Mahābhārata*. The *Rāmāyaṇa* was used more frequently, for the story could illustrate lay ethics compatible with Buddhism.[4] The most influential Tibetan account of the *Rāmāyaṇa* is found in dBus pa dMar ston chos rgyal's commentary on the *Sa skya legs bshad*. Most later commentaries and independent works on the epic follow his version of the stories.[5]

Traditional Buddhist themes were of course the subjects of full-length Tibetan poetic compositions and used as illustrations in poetic manuals. In the *rTag tu ngu yi rnam thar*, rJe Tsong kha pa (1357-1419), the founder of the dGe lugs pa school, composed an elegant rendering in verse of the story of the bodhisattva Sadāprarudita found in the eight-thousand-line *Prajñāpāramitā Sūtra* (Conze: 277-299). Later writers, notably Jo nang Tāranātha Kun dga' snying po (1575-1634), 'Jam dbyangs bzhad pa (1648-1721) and the second Paṇ chen Blo bzang ye shes dpal bzang (1663-1737) used themes from the *avadānas* in their poetic writing.

After the mid-fifteenth century the adaptation of Indian themes and styles into Tibetan literature slowed. There were no new developments until renewed contact between India and Tibet in the sixteenth century revived interest in the study of Sanskrit stylistics (Tucci: 13-14, 137).

The study of poetics was formalized in Tibet under the fifth Dalai Lama, Ngag dbang blo bzang rgya mtsho (1617-1682). He established a government school for lay and ecclesiastic officials where all would-be government officials were required to master the rules of poetics (Shakabpa: 123; Smith, vol. 3: 9), and he was an author and patron of literature (Tucci: 146). Although some scholars have said that a number of the works attributed to the fifth Dalai Lama and his regent sDe srid Sangs rgyas rgya mtsho were written by others (Smith, vol. 3: 19),[6] we can safely say that the fifth Dalai Lama and his court presided over a period of cultural efflorescence.

In the eighteenth century a new phase of poetic scholarship began with Si tu Paṇ chen Chos kyi 'byung gnas (1700-1774), and his main student of poetics, Khams sprul bsTan 'dzin chos kyi nyi ma (1730-1779).[7] These two scholars were the chief representatives of a new school analyzing poetry in terms of three qualities: (1) the body (*lus*) or subject matter (*brjod bya*), (2) ornamentation (*rgyan*) as the employment of the canons of *kāvya*, and (3) the life (*srog*) or aim (*don*) which is the intent (*dgong, gshad 'dod*), or motivation (*brjod 'dod*). This threefold analysis contrasts with an earlier systematization found in the fifth Dalai Lama's work *dByangs can dgyes pa'i glu* and the treatises of his followers. This school discusses only two categories: the subject matter and the figures of speech. The dispute over which system to follow resulted in two separate traditions of commentarial literature on poetics.[8]

The Tibetan Novel

It is within the context of the eighteenth-century belles-lettres that we can examine the poetic work of one of the great men of Tibetan letters, mDo mkhar zhabs drung Tshe ring dbang rgyal.[9] His mixed poetry and prose novel, *gZhon nu zla med kyi gtam rgyud* ("The Tale of the Incomparable Prince"), is an illustration of the fully developed *kāvya* style in Tibet.

Tshe ring dbang rgyal clearly intended *gZhon nu zla med* to fit into the Indo-Tibetan poetic tradition: the style and virtually all the thematic influences on the novel are of Indian origin. A synopsis of the plot of the novel will help contextualize our subsequent detailed discussion of work's style and content.

Plot Synopsis

The king and queen of a kingdom find that they are unable to have a child. Their ministers advise them to make offerings to the gods and ask for progeny as a boon. In response to their prayers, the couple has a miraculous son, Prince gZhon nu zla med.

After much controversy, the elders of the realm decide to bring up the prince in a secular fashion. They plan for him to rule the realm rather than take up a religious life. When it is time for the prince to marry, the only suitable girl is Yid 'ong ma, a princess already betrothed to the vicious, unprincipled Prince Lha las phul byung. Prince gZhon nu zla med attempts to win the princess by diplomacy, and, failing that, by subterfuge. A clever kidnap attempt fails, and Yid 'ong ma and Prince gZhon nu zla med's best friend, dPa' bo srid pa gzhon nu are taken captive by their enemy, Prince Lha las phul byung.

While Prince gZhon nu zla med gathers a large army and prepares to rescue them, Yid 'ong ma is forced to marry the evil lHa las phul byung. But, she tricks him into postponing the marriage's consummation. dPa' bo srid pa gzhon nu convinces his captors that he has turned traitor and joined their cause. He then causes dissension in the court and seriously weakens the defenses of the enemy kingdom.

Prince gZhon nu zla med's army arrives and wins a bloody battle. The prince is united with Yid 'ong ma but doubts her virtue. Finally he is convinced of her purity and they are happily married.

Meanwhile, Prince gZhon nu zla med's father has fallen in love with a lower class girl. To obtain her, the king promises that if she bears a son the boy will inherit the kingdom. The main queen, the court, and all the upper nobility are aghast but powerless to intervene. The new queen, mDzes sdug me tog, conceives and delivers a boy. Prince gZhon nu zla med and Yid 'ong ma return and befriend the child.

When Yid 'ong ma goes to visit her parents, Prince gZhon nu zla med is made regent until his younger half-brother comes of age. He attempts to rule the realm religiously by perfecting the practice of charity. The prince's charity nearly bankrupts the realm and the old king must quell the unrest led by mDzes sdug me tog's father.

The second queen has become infatuated with Prince gZhon nu zla med. But when he rejects her amorous advances, she fears that he will expose her impropriety. Playing into her father's plans, mDzes sdug me tog convinces the old king to banish the prince. gZhon nu zla med's loyal friend dPa bo srid pa gzhon nu follows him into exile.

Yid 'ong ma returns from her journey and finds her husband gone. Although the court tries to dissuade her, she decides to follow her husband into exile. She loses her way in the forest, where her maidservants are devoured by wild animals. She gives up hope, but finally manages to join the two men in religious retreat in the forest hermitage.

After Prince gZhon nu zla med fulfills the terms of his exile, he decides to return to civilization to share the joy of his spiritual knowledge. En route, he saves dPa' bo srid pa gzhon nu's life by making a salve from the marrow of his own bones. This selfless act brings the prince to the spiritual plane of a bodhisattva. He preaches the Buddhist message to his family and court. His friends, family, and former enemies are all brought to happiness.

Discussion of the Novel in the Context of Poetics

The two major thematic sources of material for this novel are the *Rāmāyaṇa* and the corpus of *avadāna* literature.[10] These have approximately equal importance as a source for themes, plot and metaphors. The plot of *gZhon nu zla med* is clearly indebted to the *Rāmāyaṇa*. Yid 'ong ma's capture by the evil prince and the subsequent questioning of her virtue parallel the trials of Sītā. dPa' bo srid pa gzhon nu's destruction of the enemy is modeled after Hanuman's assistance to Rāma. His later devotion to his ruler in exile is an adaptation of the role of Lakṣmaṇa. The sub-plot of the second queen mDzes sdug me tog, the forest exile, and the glorious return of the prince also reflect the Rāma story.

The second half of the novel focuses upon the religious conscience and actions of the prince. Here the author drew heavily from the *avadāna* literature. His generosity, to the point of giving away parts of his realm, and his healing of a wounded follower by sacrificing his own body, are common themes in Buddhist *jātakas*. In addition, many minor incidents and images show clear links to the *avadānas*.

The novel *gZhon nu zla med* is meant to "accord with the texts of epic drama (*mahākāvya, snyan ngag chen po*)" (ZZ: 533). According to the canons of Daṇḍin's poetics, an epic must produce an understanding of all four aims of life: virtue or duty (*dharma, chos*), wealth and power (*artha, nor*), love and pleasure (*kāma, 'dod pa*), and renunciation and liberation (*mokṣa, tharpa*) (*Kāvyādarśa*, I: 14-15; Warder, vol. 1: 170). Tshe ring dbang rgyal indicates in the novel's colophon the specific sections of his work that illustrate these aspects of human experience (ZZ: 528-531). The love story and war in the first half of the novel portray the three mundane facets of human experience. The second half of *gZhon nu zla med* is devoted to a poetic description of renunciation and liberation from cyclic existence.

An epic must have more than vague references to these four aims: it must portray life by describing the following topics: cities, oceans, mountains, seasons, moonrise, sunrise, sport or play in a garden, park, or water, festivals of lovemaking and drinking, frustration due to separation from a lover, weddings, the birth and maturation of a prince, political debate or counsel, embassies or emissaries, expeditions, battles and war, and the triumph of a hero (*Kāvyādarśa*, I: 16-17; Warder, vol. 1: 171). Again, Tshe ring dbang rgyal takes pains to leave no doubt that he covered all of these topics: in the colophon he lists point by point how he treated each one (*ZZ:* 529-531).

In the novel's colophon Tshe ring dbang rgyal states that he also followed all Daṇḍin's stylistic prescriptions for a work of poetry. The first chapter of the *Kāvyādarśa* describes the types and general qualities of *kāvya* literature (*Kāvyādarśa*, I: 31). Following these prescriptions we label *gZhon nu zla med* a standard *campū*: a mixed verse and prose composition. Prose conveys the plot, short descriptions, and brief dialogues. In contrast, poetry is employed for lengthy speeches, longer descriptive passages, and recapitulations of prose. The meter of the verses varies from seven to twenty-one syllables per foot, with nine- or eleven-syllable feet most common. The usual length of a verse is four feet, but three, six or even more feet to a verse are occasionally found.

Tshe ring dbang rgyal follows the second chapter of the *Kāvyādarśa* very closely. He employs all the poetic ornaments, or figures of speech (*alaṃkāra*, *rgyan*). Indeed, he borrows many metaphors from other works of Indian *kāvya*. For example, the loving affinity of the moon and night lilies (Newman: 393) can be found in Āryaśūra's *Jātakamālā* (IX: 47), and a swoon compared to a vine or tree cut down at its root (Newman: 483) appears in the *Jātakamālā* (IX: 47).[11]

Conclusion

Tshe ring dbang rgyal's novel *gZhon nu zla med kyi gtam rgyud* is a Tibetan work with strong roots in the Indian belles-lettres tradition. Although Tshe ring dbang rgyal's composition is a *campū* and his themes are from the *avadānas* and the *Rāmāyaṇa*, the novel is more than a transposition of Indian poetry and poetics into Tibetan. While it fulfills all the requirements of the genre, *gZhon nu zla med kyi gtam rgyud* transforms traditional themes into a new and creative work.

This novel continues to be the most popular work of Tibetan fiction. *gZhon nu zla med* has a religious theme, but it is a work meant for enjoyment. Tshe ring dbang rgyal defends his composition with the rationale that poetry has long been used to sweeten the taste of what might otherwise be didactic works (ZZ: 531-532; 'Jam mgon kong sprul, vol. 2: 296-297). This Tibetan work is an excellent example of *kāvya* used to describe human experience in beautiful language that only secondarily aims to edify the reader.

Notes

1. His work on scholarly composition is titled *mKhas pa rnams 'jug pa'i sgo*. The work on prosody is the *sDeb sbyor sna tshogs me tog gi chen po*, and his lexicographical work is the *Tshig gi gter*.

2. The *mKhas pa rnams 'jug pa'i sgo* contains almost all of the second chapter of the *Kāvyādarśa*. Modern Tibetan scholars say that Sa skya Paṇḍita chose Daṇḍin's work from among the other textbooks of Indian poetics because it summarizes the essentials of Bhāmaha's earlier *kāvya* work and is philosophically neutral, so its examples are suitable for Buddhists and non-Buddhists alike. However, according to Warder (vol. 4: 169 and 173) Daṇḍin was a religious Vaiṣṇava. It is possible that Sa skya Paṇḍita relied upon the *Kāvyādarśa* simply because it was the only work on poetics available.

3. Lakṣmīkara translated the entire *Kāvyādarśa*. Shong ston wrote a short but seminal commentary on it, the *dByangs chen mgu rgyan zhes pa*. dPang Lo tsā ba wrote the most famous and authoritative commentary on the *Kāvyādarśa*, the *sNyan ngags me long gyi rgya cher 'grel gzhung don gsal ba*, commonly known as the *dPang ṭig*.

Shong Blo gros brtan pa is also known as mKhas pa'i dbang po. It is difficult to identify any particular Blo gros brtan pa of this period because three roughly contemporary Sa skya pa translators held the name. In Roerich (786) dPang is identified as Shong ston's brother. However, according to Klong rdol (392), followed by Smith (vol. 3: 5), the Shong brothers, Shong ston rDo rje rgyal mtshan and Shong Blo gros brtan pa, both taught poetics to dPang Blos gros brtan pa.

4. According to the late Venerable Geshe Blo bzang rnam rgyal, the *Mahābhārata* never became popular in Tibet because its characters and content are too closely related to Hindu doctrines to be adapted to a Buddhist frame-

work. He further explained that Tibetan versions of the *Rāmāyaṇa* are not as pervaded by Hindu ideology as later Indian versions. Some Western scholars tend to agree with this explanation (Stein: 266).

5. See, for example, the *Rama na'i rtogs brjod* by Zhang zhung ba Chos dbang grags pa (1404-1469).

6. Smith cites different attributions than those found in Lokesh Chandra, 1963: vol. 3, Klong rdol number 16267, and A khu number 10973.

7. Si tu Paṇ chen's work, *Yul gangs can pa'i brda yang dag par sbyor ba'i bstan bcos kyi bye brag sum cu pa dang rtags kyi 'jug pa'i gzhung gi rnam par bshad pa mkhas pa'i mgul rgyan mu tig 'phreng mdzes*, based on Sanskrit commentaries by Ratnaśrijñāna and Vāgīśvarakirti, was a return to primary source works. Tibetan scholars after Shong ston had utilized only secondary Tibetan commentaries (van der Kuijp: 32).

Khams sprul's commentary is called *rGyan gyi bstan bcos me long paṇ chen bla ma'i gsung bzhin bkral ba dbyangs can ngag gi rol mtsho legs bshad nor bu'i 'byung khungs*.

8. There were other minor differences in the two schools: those following the fifth Dalai Lama's work placed more emphasis on the third chapter of the *Kāvyādarśa*, treating acrostics and other such puzzles, than Si tu's school. They also disagreed about the number of verses in the first chapter of the *Kāvyādarśa*; dGe lugs pa commentators counted 125 verses, whereas those following Si tu's commentary counted 105 verses. In general, later dGe lugs pa scholars followed the fifth Dalai Lama's work while bKa' rgyud and rNying ma scholars followed Si tu's text.

9. Tshe ring dbang rgyal composed seven works, and an additional two are incorrectly attributed to him. The following list is arranged chronologically, insofar as that is possible.

(1) *gZhon nu zla med kyi gtam rgyud*, extant, a poetry and prose novel composed between 1718 and 1723.

(2) *Bla ma yi dam dbyer med la bstod pa*, not extant, a versified praise composition written between 1728 and 1732.

(3) *dPal mi'i dbang rtogs brjod pa 'jig rten kun tu dga' ba'i gtam*, extant, the mixed poetry and prose biography of Mid dbang Pho lha nas bSod nams stob rgyas, completed in 1733.

(4) A short treatise on Sanskrit grammar, title unknown, not extant, completed in 1737 or 1738.

(5) *Dirghayurindra dzi na'i byung ba brjod pa zol med ngag gi rol mo asti*, extant, prose autobiography completed in 1762 or 1763.

(6) *Nye bar mkho ba'i legs sbyar gyi skad bod kyi brda' ka li'i phreng ba sgrigs ngo mtshar nor bu'i do shal*, extant, a Tibetan-Sanskrit lexicon, date of composition unknown.

(7) *Sangs rgyas kyi rtogs pa brjod pa mda brgya bskad gnyis shan sbyar*, not extant, probably identical to the work entitled *sTon pa'i rnam thar*, not extant, date of composition unknown.

(8) *Ja chang lha mo'i rtsod gleng bstan bcos*, extant, prose, date of composition unknown. Incorrectly attributed to the author (Newman: 119).

(9) A commentary on the Tibetan grammatical treatises *Sum cu pa* and *rTags 'jug pa*. Incorrectly attributed to the author (Newman: 121).

10. Some Western scholars have repeated statements in the Chinese press regarding the novel's realism and accurate descriptions of Tibetan society. In particular, they assert that the novel is a thinly disguised description of a political marriage alliance between the son of lHa bzang Khan and the daughter of the Dzungar ruler Cewang Arabten. A comparison of the events related to this 1714 Mongol marriage (Petech: 33) and the novel shows that they are totally dissimilar. The events of the novel are pure fiction, without any basis in reality and the descriptions of court life are not at all reflections of life in Tibet.

11. For additional examples see Newman: 134ff.

References

Āryaśūra *See* Speyer, J.S.

Chos dbang grags pa
RTJ *Ramana'i rtogs brjod (rGyal po ra ma na'i gtam rgyud las brtsans pa'i snyan ngag gi bstan bcos dri zi bu mo rgyud mang)*. Lhasa: Si khron mi rigs dpe skrun khang, 1981.

Conze, Edward
1973 *The Perfection of Wisdom in Eight Thousand Lines*. Bolinas, CA: Four Seasons Foundation.

Dalai Lama V, Ngag dbang blo bzang rgya mtso
BG *Early History of Tibet. Gong sa rgyal dbang lnga pa chen po mchog gis mdzad pa'i bod kyi rgyal rabs rdzongs ldan gzhon nu'i dga' ston*. New Delhi, 1967.

Gerow, Edwin
1971 *A Glossary of Indian Figures of Speech*. The Hague: Mouton.

Hoffmann, Helmut
1975 *Tibet: A Handbook*. Bloomington, IA: Research Center for the Language Sciences, Indiana University Press.

'Jam mgon kong sprul Blo gros mtha' yas
SKK *Shes bya kun hhyab*. Beijing: Mi rigs dpe skrun khang, 1982.

Kāvyādarśa
Kāvyādarśa of Daṇḍin. Ed. by S.K. Belvalkar. Poona: The Oriental Book-Supplying Agency, 1924.

Klong rdol bla ma Ngag dbang blo bzang
Tibetan Buddhist Studies. Ed. by Ven. Dalama. Mussoorie: Ven. Dalama, 1963.

van der Kuijp, Leonard W.J.
1986 "Bhāmaha in Tibet." *Indo-Iranian Journal* 29/1: 31-39.

Lokesh Chandra, ed.
1963 *Materials for a History of Tibetan Literature*. Vol. 3. New Delhi: International Academy of Indian Culture.
1968 *The Autobiography and Diaries of Si-tu Pan-chen*. New Delhi: International Academy of Indian Culture.

Newman, Beth E.
1987 Solomon, Beth Ellen. "The Tale of the Incomparable Prince: A Study and Translation of the Tibetan Novel *gZhon nu zla med kyi gtam rgyud* by mDo mkhar zhabs drung Tshe ring dbang rgyal." Ph.D. dissertation. Madison: University of Wisconsin-Madison.

Petech, L.
1972 *China and Tibet in the Early XVIIIth Century*. Leiden: E. J. Brill.

Roerich, George N.
1949 *Blue Annals*. New Delhi: Motilal Banarsidass.

Sa skya Paṇ chen [Paṇḍita], Kun dga' rgyal mtshan
KJG *mKhas pa rnams 'jug pa'i sgo*. New Delhi: T. G. Dhong thog Rinpoche, 1967.

Shakabpa, W.D.
1967 *Tibet: A Political History*. New Haven: Yale University Press.

Smith, E. Gene
1969 Introduction to *Encyclopedia Tibetica*, vol. 3: 2. Edited by S.T. Kazi. New Delhi: Tibet House Library Publications.

Snellgrove, David and Hugh Richardson
1980 *A Cultural History of Tibet*. Boulder, CO: Prajñā Press.

Speyer, J.S.
1982 *Jātakamālā*. New Delhi: Motilal Banarsidass.

Stein, R.A.
1972 *Tibetan Civilization*. London: Faber and Faber.

Tshe ring dbang rgyal
ZZ *gZhon nu zla med kyi gtam rgyud*. Dharamsala: Shes rig par khang, 1964.

Tucci, Guiseppe
1980 *Tibetan Painted Scrolls*. Kyoto: Rinsen Book Co.

Warder, A.K.
1972 *Indian Kāvya Literature*. New Delhi: Motilal Banarsidass.

Chapter 25

Influence of Indic *Vyākaraṇa* on Tibetan Indigenous Grammar[1]

P. C. Verhagen

The production of the enormous Indo-Tibetan translation literature, mainly incorporated in the two canons commonly known as bKa' 'gyur and bsTan 'gyur, but also contained in other corpora of translations such as the *rNying ma'i rgyud 'bum*, required of Tibetan scholars a high degree of expertise in the intricacies of Sanskrit grammar.

The tutelage in Sanskrit grammar that the Tibetans received at the hands of their Indian masters, as well as the instruction on this subject within the Tibetan scholastic traditions, was based on the Indic indigenous systems of *vyākaraṇa* (the collective term for the traditional Indic science of grammar). The textbooks that we find employed most frequently here are the so-called *Cāndra* (henceforth abbreviated as C) and *Kātantra* (K) grammars (See Verhagen, 1991b: 47-49, 51).

These two systems of Sanskrit grammar were developed (and became particularly popular) in the Buddhist traditions in India. They are in fact simplified, more practical versions of the extremely sophisticated and involved system of Pāṇini (ca. fourth century B.C.E.), as laid down in his *Aṣṭādhyāyī* and in the enormous subsequent literature in that tradition. The *Cāndra* and *Kātantra* grammars distinguish themselves from the Pāṇinian system particularly in their restriction to the main rules, avoiding going into details on obscure exceptions, and omitting altogether rules dealing with Vedic Sanskrit. Moreover, particularly in *Kātantra*, the rules are presented in a topical, subjectwise ordering which is markedly different from that in Pāṇini's grammar (See Scharfe: 162-167; Verhagen, 1991a: 34-35).

Structures, devices and techniques found in Indic *vyākaraṇa* strongly influenced grammatical science in Tibet; they often served as models for the description of linguistic phenomena as found in the traditions of indigenous Tibetan grammar (see, e.g., Inaba, 1955 and Miller, 1976: ix-x; 1987: 85ff.).

Here I will briefly list some example of this influence that can be detected in the two earliest Tibetan grammatical treatises, *Sum cu pa* (henceforth referred to as *SCP*) and *rTags kyi 'jug pa* (*TKJ*), as well as in the subsequent commentaries on these basic texts that form the vast majority of the subsequent Tibetan indigenous grammatical literature.

(1) The use of numerous technical terms which are evidently translations of terms from *vyākaraṇa*, e.g., the phonological terms for places and modes of articulation, the majority of the syntactic-semantic terms for the meanings of the nominal cases and for the verbal tenses *casu quo* modes.

In this connection, it should be mentioned that untranslated Sanskrit grammatical terminology is only very rarely used (see Miller, 1963: 492 [1976: 8]). The only instances of this are the terms *āli* and *kāli* (in *SCP* 1, on which more below) and the terms *pu(ṃ) liṅga* and *strī liṅga*, "masculine gender" and "feminine gender" in *SCP* 22 and 23 respectively (see Miller, 1988: 270). The interpretation of the element *pu* in *pu(ṃ) liṅga* as put forth in the early nineteenth-century commentary *Si tu'i zhal lung* by dNgul chu Dharmabhadra (1772-1851) (see Miller, 1963: 492 [1976: 8]; Tillemans and Herforth: 33) does not seem admissible. This commentator take *pu* to be a technical term indicating the *p-varga* ("*p*-group") (i.e., the homorganic group in the alphabet beginning with *p*, i.e., the labial stops). He bases this interpretation on *Cāndra sūtra* 1.1.2, which he actually quotes in the commentary.[2] However, to my knowledge, the combination of *pU* (in the sense of "*p*-group), or similar terms, with *liṅga* is not found in Indic indigenous grammatical literature. On the other hand, the use of the terms *pu(ṃ) liṅga* and *strī liṅga*, together with *napuṃsaka liṅga* ("neuter gender"), indicating the three grammatical genders in Sanskrit, is extremely common in Indic indigenous grammar (see Abhyankar: 214, 252, 333 [s.v. *liṅga* (3)], 434; Renou, I: 170, II: 12, 72, 150). This would seem to make dNgul chu Dharmabhadra's interpretation of the term *pu liṅga* so unlikely as to be inadmissible unless further corroboration can be found. However farfetched the interpretation may be, it remains remarkable that even at such a late stage in the history of Tibetan indigenous grammar (he wrote his commentary in 1806; see Tillemans and Herforth: 33), awareness of the Indic origins of a great many aspects of these grammatical traditions was keenly enough felt that the commentator quotes the *Cāndra* rule as his authority.

We should also briefly mention the fact that in our received text *SCP* and *TKJ* both bear a Sanskrit version of their title alongside the Tibetan. These Sanskrit titles are of course secondary and most probably represent later accretions to the texts (see Miller, 1990b: par. 5).

(2) The use of extremely succinct, condensed basic rules. The brevity and terseness of the rules [mnemonic principle!] regularly makes their full and correct interpretation highly problematic without consulting the explanatory commentarial literature, the use of which should however be approached with due caution, considering the speculative nature of a considerable part of the comments (see Miller, 1990a: 189-191). The same holds true for the basic texts in *vyākaraṇa* and to a certain extent also for the Indic commentaries. In the Indian systems of grammar, the basic rules, termed *sūtra*, are generally not in metrical form. In *SCP* and *TKJ* the rules do have a metrical form; they have a seven-syllable line, with varying numbers of lines per verse. As a result, the use of the term *śloka* for the "verses" of *SCP* and *TKJ* has become common practice. It has recently been suggested that the term *sūtra* might be more apt here (Miller, 1987: 109, n. 6; 1988: 263, n. 3). It may be useful to note that, as an exception to the general rule, in two sections (*pāda*) of the second book of *Kātantra*, viz. 2.5 (on nominal compounds) and 2.6 (on secondary nominal derivatives) [as well as 2.7, on derivation of feminine nouns, only found in the latest versions of the text], the basic *sūtras* do have a metrical form; they can be read together forming stanzas (see Verhagen, 1991a: 40, n. 74; Belvalkar: 85; Scharfe: 162). The two (or three) sections in question in fact represent later accretions to the text to which, inter alia, their verse-form stands proof.

(3) Certain aspects of the ordering of the rules, e.g., the introduction of the set of phonemes at the beginning of the text, immediately followed by the identification of functional subsets within that set (*SCP* 1-6; however see also *TKJ* 1-3; see Miller, 1990b: par. 2.4, 3.2).

This could to a certain extent be likened to the *śiva sūtras* as found, e.g., at the beginning of the basic texts of Pāṇini and Cāndra (see Miller, 1987: 87, 91, 95). In the opening verses of *SCP*, I would rather prefer to see a parallel with the phonological statements at the beginning of the *Kātantra Sūtra* text (which in their turn closely resemble and have presumably been derived from models in the Vedic *Prātiśākhyas*) (see below).

Another typically Indic aspect in the rule ordering is the use of interpolations in the textual structure for reasons of descriptive economy. A striking example of this is *SCP* 12, describing the particle with the alternate forms *kyang/'ang/yang*, which seems to be an interpolation in the description of the case particles (in *SCP* 8-11 and 15-17), but which is conveniently placed after the rules on the genitive (*SCP* 9-10) and instrumental (*SCP* 11) particles, thus avoiding the necessity of repeating the morphophonemic details on initial alternation that these three particles have in common (Miller, 1987: 105).

(4) Certain aspects of method and technique, e.g., the method of referring to specific phonemes by means of a numerical indication and the use of rudiments of the traditional method of case attribution in *vyākaraṇa* (on both of which more below).

This is by no means an exhaustive enumeration of all points where the Tibetan grammatical traditions are evidently influenced by Indian linguistics. It is rather intended to give some impression of the wide range of aspects that have Indian antecedents. In the following two subsections I would like to make some observations on two of the above-mentioned points where a modelling after *vyākaraṇa* can be supposed.

Numerical Reference to Phonemes

The method of referring to specific phonemes by means of a numerical indication is based on a grid of the traditional alphabet where for this purpose the vowels are simply numbered and the consonants are divided into groups (or classes: *varga*, *sde*) of consonantal phonemes with the same point of articulation. *SCP* 3 defines the groups of consonants within the alphabet, namely as seven and a half groups of four phonemes each (*kā li phye dang brgyad sde ni/bzhi bzhi dag tu phye ba las/*; see also Miller, 1990a: 266). For instance, in the subsequent verse in *SCP*, reference is made by means of this grid to individual phonemes in the following manner: "the last two (elements) in the first, third and fourth (*sde*)" (*dang po gsum pa bzhi pa yi/mas gnyis*), i.e., *g* and *ng* (from the first group consisting of *k*, *kh*, *g*, and *ng*), *d* and *n* (from the third group *t*, *th*, *d* and *n*) and *b* and *m* (from the fourth group *p*, *ph*, *b* and *m*), and "the seventh (*sde*) except *sh*" (*bdun pa la ni sha ma gtogs*), i.e., *r*, *l* and *s* (from the seventh group *r*, *l*, *sh* and *s*). It is important to note that this method of reference is used in *SCP*, but not in *TKJ*. In the latter treatise, we find a method of phoneme inventory employing covert categories quite different from that in *SCP* (see Miller, 1990b: par. 2.4).

It has been proposed (Miller, 1966: 138-141 [1976: 46-49]) that this method as found in *SCP* derives from mnemonic phonological jargon in exegetical Vajrayāna literature, where the same practice is met with regularly in the analytical description of *mantras*. This seems not necessarily to have been the case. The same method of referring to consonantal phonemes by place-number within the "classes" in the alphabet is the standard procedure in the *Kātantra* system of grammar. The basic text of *Kātantra* grammar opens with the statement that the traditional alphabet will serve as basis for reference to phonemes in this grammar.[3] This seemingly self-evident statement must be seen in light of the fact that most major systems of *vyākaraṇa* (e.g., Pāṇinian and *Cāndra* grammar) use a particular system of reference to phonemes by means of so-called *śiva sūtras*, where the phonemes are arranged in an order different from the classical alphabet.

In *Kātantra*, references to individual phonemes (or groups of phonemes) then generally take a form very similar to those in *SCP*. The vowels are simply numbered.[4] The first 25 consonants in the traditional alphabet are arranged in groups (*varga*)[5]; in Sanskrit, of course, each *varga* consists of five elements (as opposed to Tibetan, which omits voiced aspirated stops) (see Miller, 1988: 266). References to consonants in these groups are made by the place-number within the *varga*.[6] The *Kātantra* has evidently adopted this method of reference from the so-called *Prātiśākhyas*,[7] the phonological auxiliary treatises to the *Vedas*, belonging to the later Vedic period, probably last three centuries B.C.E.

Considering the numerous forms of influence from Indic grammatical traditions that are evident in Tibetan indigenous linguistics, it would seem that the derivation of this method from the *Kātantra* is at least as probable as from tantric literature. In this context, it should be noted that so far in my investigation of the Indo-Tibetan canonical literature on Sanskrit grammar (as mainly laid down in Verhagen, 1991a), I have not found a single instance of the technical terms *āli* and *kāli* being used in that literature to denote "vowel" and "consonant." This is a strong corroboration for the assumption (as proposed by Miller, 1966 [1976: 33-56]; see also 1988: 275) that these terms have not been derived from a model in *vyākaraṇa*, but, rather, from tantric literature. To the one instance in Indic grammatical literature of the use of *kādi* "*k*, etc." (which might be related to the term *kāli*, lit. "*k*-row") for "consonant" that Miller mentions (1966: 147 [1976: 55]), namely in the *Vājasaneyi Prātiśākhya*, one more should be added: *Kātantra* 1.1.9, *kādīni vyañjanāni*, defines the consonants (*vyañjana*) as "*k*, etc." (*kādi*). However, as no instances of the term **ādi* (for "vowel"), nor of *āli* and *kāli*, have been found in Sanskrit grammatical literature thus far, it would seem that the tantric background of these terms cannot reasonably be doubted.

At this point, it is appropriate to note that recently the Vajrayāna origin of another salient feature of the phonological terminology in Tibetan grammar has come to light. The phoneme-identification in terms of gender (*pho*, "male"; *mo*, "female"; *ma ning*, "neuter"; *shin tu mo*, "very female"; and *mo gsham*, "barren female") as found in *TKJ*[8] is most probably modelled on the practice of describing the phonemes in *mantras* by means of a classification in three genders (*pho*, *mo* and *ma ning*), which is found in Indo-Tibetan exegetical tantric literature.[9]

The Case for *Kāraka* in Tibetan Indigenous Grammar

Here, I would like to make a few observations on the influence (partly evident, partly hypothesized) of the system of case attribution in Sanskrit *vyākaraṇa* on the indigenous description of certain phenomena in Tibetan grammar.

The description of case-grammar in *vyākaraṇa* involves the introduction of the so-called *kārakas*. The *kārakas* constitute a set of six syntactic-semantic relations, comparable to the concept of underlying cases in modern Western linguistics. The six *kārakas* are:

"agent" (*kartṛ*), "direct object" (*karman*; in *C*, *āpya* or *kriyāpya*), "instrument" (*karaṇa*), "indirect object" (*saṃpradāna*), "point of departure (etc.)" (*apādāna*; in *C*, *avadhi*) and "location" (*adhikaraṇa*; *C* has *ādhāra*). On the one hand, the *kārakas* are defined in semantic terms; on the other hand, they are expressed by certain suffixes, the actual case-endings. Thus they form an intermediate level between the semantic and morphological levels, allowing for an elegant description of a variety of syntactical and morphological phenomena, notably the argument-structure of active and passive sentences, but also relating to primary and secondary nominal derivation, infinitive constructions, nominal composition, etc. A notable feature of this *kāraka* system is the fact that certain *kāraka* roles are attributed not only to (and hence expressed by) nouns but also to verbal forms.[10]

Miller has convincingly argued for an interpretation of the statements on case semantics in *SCP* and *TKJ* in light of this Indic *kāraka* system, namely as based on "the same conceptualization of the correlations between grammatical forms and their syntactic functions" as found in the Indic *kāraka* system (1990a: 194; also 1987: 102-104; however see also Tillemans, n.d.: n. 13; unfortunately, I have not yet been able to consult Tournadre). Not only have the Tibetan grammarians adopted (and, naturally, adapted) this system of syntacto-semantic categories, but in many instances they also used direct translations of Sanskrit technical terms for individual categories[11] (see Inaba, 1954: 14-15; Miller, 1990a: 196-198; Verhagen, 1992).

The *bDag/gZhan* Dichotomy

I would now like to turn to a notion in Tibetan indigenous grammar that has posed (and still poses) considerable difficulties, and which consequently has led to a variety of interpretations among both the Tibetan palaeogrammarians and Tibetological specialists in this field. This is the so-called *bdag/gzhan* dichotomy. Of the two basic Tibetan grammatical treatises, only *TKJ* deals with this concept, and that only in four extremely terse references (viz. *TKJ* 12-15). However, the subsequent commentarial literature elaborates extensively on this notion, a number of authors presenting a wide variety of interpretations of the specific details and ramifications of this system. Following the recent study of Tillemans and Herforth (1989), we might characterize the *bdag/gzhan* opposition as a categorization relevant only for the interpretation of transitive clauses, and applying to both nominal as well as verbal syntactical arguments. Here the nominal argument "agent" and the verbal argument which is (as termed by Tillemans and Herforth) "agent-prominent" (*in casu* the present and imperative forms) are labelled as *bdag*, "self," while the nominal argument "direct object" and the "object-prominent" (or as Tillemans and Herforth have it, "patient-prominent") verb forms (i.e., future and—according to some authors—perfect tense) receive the designation *gzhan*, "other."

Some early Tibetologist proposed a derivation of *bdag* and *gzhan* from the pair of Indic grammatical terms *ātmanepada* ("middle voice") [lit. "syntactic word form (expressing action) for one's self"] and *parasmaipada* ("active voice") [lit. "syntactic word form (expressing action) for another"] respectively (Laufer: 543; note that his rendering of *ātmanepada* as "das Passiv" is inaccurate). This supposition cannot be maintained. Perhaps the mere terms *parasmaipada* and *ātmanepada* have played a role, but the denotations and uses of the *parasmaipada/ātmanepada* and *bdag/gzhan* pairs bear far too little resemblance to suppose a case of integral concept borrowing here (Inaba, 1954: 184; Tillemans, 1988: 494, and 1991: final paragraph; Tillemans and Herforth: 11-13).

In spite of the fact that at the present moment in Tibetology a great number of the puzzling problems surrounding the notions of *bdag* and *gzhan* have not yet been solved satisfactorily, I would like to venture a working hypothesis on the origin of these notions. The attribution of identical labels to both nominal and verbal arguments, which we observe in the Indic *kāraka* system as well as in the *bdag/gzhan* dichotomy in Tibetan grammar, I take to be the key feature here. This has led me to suppose that the *bdag/gzhan* attribution may very well have been modelled orginally on the *method* of the *kāraka* system, without however borrowing the *terms* used in that system (see Verhagen, 1991c: 209). Specifically, the functioning of the *kāraka* system in the case-attribution to agent and direct object in active and passive clauses (see n. 10) would then have served as model. Considerable further research will be needed to test the hypothesis tentatively proposed here. For instance, an important corroboration would be to find statements in the (preferably early) commentarial literature in some way attesting to this origin of the *bdag/gzhan* categorization; so far such attestations have not been found. In the light of this hypothesis, of course, the choice of the precise terms *bdag* and *gzhan* must still be explained. As mentioned earlier, it might be that the mere terms *parasmaipada* and *ātmanepada* were adopted (or rather paraphrased) by the Tibetan grammarians as *gzhan* and *bdag* respectively, but the terms were given a wholly different meaning. Or were the *terms* perhaps not based on Indian models at all?[12] Were they innovations—within the framework of the Tibetans' reworking of the *kāraka* system—to express an intuition that a closer relation exists between agent and transitive verb (hence "self," *bdag*) than between direct object and transitive verb (hence "other," i.e., "more alien," "more remote," *gzhan*)? Was the agent, in a somewhat unsophisticated fashion, described as the "I" (*bdag*) of the transitive clause, while the direct object is called "the other," i.e., "the other than I?"

It seems evident that the dichotomy at least indicates a particularly close relation existing on the one hand between the future (and possibly also perfect) tense of a transitive verb and its direct object, as well as between present and imperative tenses of a similar verb and its agent (see Tillemans and Herforth's characterization in terms of "argument-prominence," *scil*, "agent-prominent" and "patient-prominent," passim, particularly 80-81).

Another question that should be addressed is exactly in what aspects the *kāraka* and *bdag/gzhan* models correspond and differ; precisely, how are they related? What shifts of function and meaning have taken place in the transition from the Indic context to the Tibetan?

It is my intention to pursue these lines of investigation, focusing on the concepts of Indic origin in Tibetan grammatical description in general, particularly on the reworking of the *kāraka* system. However, the early stage of the research does not yet allow drawing definite conclusions concerning the relationship between the *kāraka* and *bdag/gzhan* schema.

In connection with the *kāraka* terms proper, another Indic grammatical technical term should be mentioned here, viz. *bhāva*. This concept, in the present context best translated as "(verbal) action per se," plays a role in the verbal component of the *kāraka* system, namely as the syntactic-semantic role attributed to a verbal form when no *kāraka* can be "expressed" by the verb, i.e., in impersonal passive. The notion of *bhāva* found its way into Tibetan grammar; translated as *dngos po,* it is regularly employed by the Tibetan commentators. Recently, Miller has hinted at a relation between the notion of *bhāva,* particularly the two types that are distinguished (viz. *ābhyantara* and *bāhya-bhāva,* "internal" and "external") and the *bdag / gzhan* dichotomy in Tibetan indigenous grammar (1990a: 201 and n. 12).

Finally, it should be noted that *vyākaraṇa* is not only relevant for early Tibetan grammatical literature, but also for that of later periods. For instance, in the extensive commentary on *SCP* and *TKJ* by Si tu paṇ chen Chos kyi 'byung gnas (1699?-1774) numerous quotations from and references to Sanskrit grammatical treatises can be found. So far I have been able to trace the following:

(1) *K* 2.4.26 quoted in commentary ad *SCP, maṅgala-śloka* (ed. Das: 3, line 19)
(2) *K* 2.6.16 quoted [and see *K* 2.6.21 (!)] in commentary ad *SCP* 7 (ed. Das: 11, line 1)
(3) reference to case-attribution according to *K* in commentary ad *SCP* 8 (e.g., ed. Das: 15, line 15) and in commentary ad *TKJ* 31 (e.g., ed. Das: 76, line 9)
(4) *Cāndra Varṇa Sūtra* quoted in commentary ad *SCP* 27 (ed. Das: 33, line 15; see Inaba, 1955: 438)
(5) *K* 1.1.23 quoted in commentary ad *TKJ* 27 (ed. Das: 70, line 10; see Inaba, 1955: 439-440)
(6) *Cānda uṆādi-sūtra* referred to in commentary ad *TKJ* 27 (ed. Das: 71, line 17; see Inaba, 1955: 438-439)
(7) reference to a.o. Sanskrit suffixes *Ktvā, tavya* and *tumUN* (ed. Das: 81, line 24) and Sanskrit indeclinables *ca, vā, eva, svạr, śīghram, tūrṇṇam, kartavyam, svasti, mithyā, uccais* (ed. Das: 81, lines 1-3) in the interesting exposé on the difference between Sanskrit *nipāta,* "indeclinable particle," and Tibetan *tshig phrad,* "enclitic particle" (ed. Das: 79, line 23 to 82, line 2) in commentary ad *TKJ* 31.

I hope to return to these passages at a later occasion, as they merit a far more detailed study than the space available for the present contribution allows. The quotation from *Cāndra* grammar, namely *sūtra* 1.1.2, found in the commentary briefly called *Si tu'i zhal lung,* by dNgul chu Dharmabhadra (1772-1851), has already been mentioned above.

Concluding Observations

This paper is by no means intended as an exhaustive survey of the Indian influences to be detected in the work of the Tibetan grammarians. It is a mere first tentative step towards exploration of the Indian antecedents of a great number of elements in the Tibetan indigenous science of grammar. Thorough understanding of these elements of Indic origin no doubt is a *sine qua non* for the correct interpretation and full appreciation of many of the intricate subtleties in the indigenous Tibetan grammatical literature.

Notes

1. The research for this essay has been made possible by a fellowship of the Royal Netherlands Academy of Arts and Sciences.

2. Even if this interpretation were accepted it would not "provide a datable point of reference at least for the particular layer of the *SCP* text represented by these two ślokas" (Miller, 1963: 492 [1976: 8]), where the data of *Cāndra* grammar then would be considered as this point of reference. This is not the case because the method of indicating a consonantal homorganic group by the first element of the group combined with technical marker *U* is already used by Pāṇini (ca. fourth century B.C.E.) (see *Aṣṭādhyāyī* 1.1.69), the date of Pāṇini of course being much too early to be of any significance in the dating of Tibetan grammatical treatises.

3. *K* 1.1.1 *siddho varṇasamāmnāyaḥ*, *vṛtti*-commentary: *siddhaḥ khalu varṇānāṃ samāmnāyo veditavyaḥ / na punar anyathopadeṣṭavya ity arthaḥ //* (...) *varṇā akārādayaḥ / teṣāṃ samāmnāyaḥ pāṭhakramaḥ*. Liebich: 14: "'Das Alphabet wird (in meiner Grammatik) in der normalen Reihenfolge (verwendet)', (d. h. also nicht in künstlicher Umbildung wie in den Śivasūtra's Pāṇini's)." [*sūtra*:] "The enumeration of phonemes has been well-established [in the traditional alphabet]." [*vṛtti*:] "The enumeration of the phonemes [as employed in the present grammar] must be considered as [the one which is] truly well-established [*scil.* the traditional alphabet]; the meaning (by implication) is that [this traditional ordering of the phonemes] need not again [or: separately] be rearranged [*scil.* in a set of *śiva-sūtras*]. (...) The phonemes are [the elements] *a* etc.; their enumeration is the [traditional] order of recitation." See *Taittirīya Prātiśākhya* 1.1: *atha varṇasamāmnāyaḥ*.

4. The classification of the vowels is given in *K* 1.1.2-8; e.g., 1.1.2 *tatra caturdaśādau svarāḥ*, "Here [i.e., in the traditional alphabet] the fourteen [elements] at the beginning are the vowels [*svara*]" (i.e., *a, ā, i, ī, u, ū, ṛ, ṝ, ḷ, ḹ, e, ai, o,* and *au*); 1.1.3 *daśa samānāḥ*, "The ten [at the beginning] are called simple [vowels] [*samāna*] ," (i.e., *a, ā, i, ī, u, ū, ṛ, ṝ, ḷ, and ḹ*); 1.1.4 *teṣāṃ dvau dvāv anyonyasya savarṇau*, "Of these [ten] two by two [the elements] are mutually homogenous [*savarṇa*]," etc.

5. *K* 1.1.10 *te vargāḥ pañca pañca pañca*, "These [consonants] [i.e., the first twenty-five of these consonants] are [arranged in] five groups [*varga*] of five [elements] each" [i.e., *k, kh, g, gh* and *ṅ*; *c, ch, j, jh* and *ñ*; *ṭ, ṭh, ḍ, ḍh* and *ṇ*; *t, th, d, dh* and *n*; *p, ph, b, bh* and *m*].

6. Instances of *K* referring to consonantal phonemes by means of this numerical indication, strongly resembling the method in *SCP*, are, e.g., 1.1.11, *vargāṇāṃ prathamadvitīyāḥ śaṣasāś cāghoṣāḥ*, "The first and second [element] of [each of] the *vargas* and [the phonemes] *ś*, *ṣ* and *s* are [termed] voiceless [*aghoṣa*]"; 1.4.1, *vargaprathamāḥ padāntāḥ svaraghoṣavatsu tṛtīyān*, "The first [elements] of [any of] the *vargas*, when at the end of a *pada*, and when followed by a vowel or a voiced consonant, are changed into the third [elements of that respective *varga*]." See also 1.4.2-4 and 1.4.16, *varge tadvargapañcamaṃ vā*, "When followed by [any elements from a] *varga* [final *m*] optionally is changed into the fifth [element] of that *varga*."

7. The four main *Prātiśākhyas*, viz. *Ṛk-*, *Taittirīya-*, *Atharva-* and *Vājasaneyi-Prātiśākhya*, all use this method of reference; see the terms *prathama*, *dvitīya*, *tṛtīya*, *caturtha* and *pañcama* in Renou III: 63, 69, 73, 88, 105; Böhtlingk: 660.

8. A threefold division into *pho*, *mo* and *ma ning* for syllable-final phonemes in *TKJ* 16-17, 22-23 and 27, a fourfold division into *pho*, *mo*, *ma ning* and *shin tu mo* for prescript phonemes in *TKJ* 3, 6, 10, 12-15, and a fivefold division into *pho*, *mo*, *ma ning*, *shin tu mo* and *mo gsham* for radical phonemes in *TKJ* 1.

9. E.g., in the *Legs sbyar klog tshul gyi bstan bcos blo gsal kun dga' ba* by the Sa skya pa scholar Ngag dbang kun dga' bsod nams grags pa rgyal mtshan (1537-1601), kept in the Van Manen collection, Kern Institute, Leiden University, reg. nr. Br. 79 / H 177, particularly in the second part of this pronunciation manual where a summary is given of the systems of phoneme-categorization as expounded by sNar thang lo tsā ba Saṅghaśrī (fourteenth century). Here we find one system employing terms of gender (*pho*, *mo* and *ma ning*) and one with the names of the five elements (*sa*, "earth"; *me*, "fire"; *chu*, "water"; *rlung*, "air"; and *nam mkha'*, "ether"). I have touched on these matters in a paper entitled "Mantras and Grammar. Observations on the study of the linguistical aspects of Buddhist esoterical formulas in Tibet," presented at the International Symposium "The Language of Sanskrit Buddhist Texts," Central Institue for Higher Tibetan Studies, Sarnath, 1-5 October 1991 (and forthcoming in the proceedings of that Symposium). I intend to return to this terminological derivation in a separate study in the near future.

10. For example, the Sanskrit grammarians label the verb in an active sentence as indicating the *kāraka kartṛ*, "agent," but in a passive construction as indicating *karman*, "direct object." As a consequence of this, in these sentences the nouns expressing the *kāraka* that is already indicated by the verb (i.e., the agent in the active, and the direct object in the passive construction) are attributed the case that does not express a *kāraka* itself, namely the nominative. For more details on the system of *kārakas* see, e.g., Cardona, Kiparsky and Staal, Renou I: 127, and Abhyankar: 118.

11. The terms in question are *las* (*SCP* 8, *TKJ* 28; Skt. *karman*), "direct object"; *byed pa po* (*SCP* 11; Skt. *kartṛ*), "agent"; *byed pa* (see *TKJ* 28; Skt. *karaṇa*), "in-

strument"; *ched* (*SCP* 8; see Skt. *tādarthya*, *C* 2.1.79, *K* 2.4.27) and *sbyin* (*TKJ* 28; comp. Skt. *saṃpradāna*), "indirect object" [see Miller, 1990b: par. 2.8); *'byung khungs* (*sa*) (*SCP* 15, *TKJ* 28; comp. Skt. *avadhi*? [as in the Tibetan translations of *Vibhaktikārikā*, Peking bsTan 'gyur, vol. *le*, 59r8 and *Subanta-ratnākara*, Peking bsTan 'gyur, vol. *no*, 448r7-8; I do not agree with the categoric identification with Skt. *apādāna* by Inaba, 1954: 15, Miller, 1987: 100-101; *apādāna* is generally translated by *nges par kun tu sbyin pa*; see Verhagen, 1991a: 255; 1992: 837]), "point of departure/ origin"; and (*rten*) *gnas* (*SCP* 8, *TKJ* 28; Skt. *ādhāra*), "location." Relevant in connection with the *kāraka* system, though strictly speaking not *kāraka* terms, are: *chos-dngos* (*TKJ* 28), particularly important as perhaps the most evident remnant of the *kāraka* system, comparable to various Indic designations of the function of the nominative case (see Verhagen, 1992: 837); *'brel pa* (*'i sa*) (*SCP* 10, *TKJ* 28; Skt. *saṃbandha*), "relation/connection"; and *bod pa* (*'i sgra*) (*SCP* 17, *TKJ* 28; Skt. *saṃbodhana*), "vocative."

12. Tillemans (1988: 494-495), hypothesizing that the terms might not have an Indic origin at all, suggested a possible relation of this term *bdag* with the technical term *bdag po* (as in *bdag po'i sa* alias *bdag* [*po'i*] *sgra*) in *SCP* 22, roughly speaking a technical term for "agent," or more precisely the deverbal nomen agentis and the denominal possessive noun.

References

Abhyankar, K. V. and J. M. Shukla

1977 *A Dictionary of Sanskrit Grammar*. Second revised edition. Gaekwad's Oriental Series 134. Baroda: Oriental Institute.

Belvalkar, S. K.

1915 *An account of the different existing systems of Sanskrit grammar, being the Vishwanath Narayan Mandlik gold medal prize essay for 1909*. Poona: the author.

Böhtlingk, O.

1887 "Über die Grammatik *Katantra*." *Zeitschrift der deutschen Morgenländischen Gesellschaft* 41: 657-666.

Candragomin

C *Cāndra-vyākaraṇa*. Ed. by B. Liebich in *Cāndra-Vyākaraṇa. Die Grammatik des Candragomin. Sūtra, Uṇādi, Dhātupāṭha*. Abhandlungen für die Kunde des Morgenlandes 4 (Leipzig: Deutsche Morgenländische Gesellschaft u. F. A. Brockhaus, 1902) and *Cāndra-Vṛtti. Der Original-Kommentar Candragomins zu seinem grammatischen Sūtra*. Abhandlungen für die Kunde des Morgenlandes 14 (Leipzig: Deutsche Morgenlandische Gesellschaft u. F. A. Brockhaus, 1918).

Cardona, G.

1967 "Pāṇini's syntactic categories." *Journal of the Oriental Institute M.S. University of Baroda* 25/3: 201-215.

Das, Sarat Chandra

1915 *An Introduction to the Grammar of the Tibetan Language with the texts of Situ Sum-tag, Dag-je Sal-wai Melong and Situi Shal lung.* Darjeeling. [Book II is editio princeps of *Mkhas pa'i mgul rgyan mu tig phreng mdzes* by Si tu paṇ chen Chos kyi 'byung gnas].

Inaba, S.

1954 *Chibettogo koten bunpōgaku.* Kyoto: Hōzōkan.

1955 "The Influence of Indian Grammar on the Development of Classical Tibetan Grammar." [In Japanese.] *Indogaku Bukkyōgaku Kenkyū* 3/2 [= 6]: 432-440.

Kātantra

K Ed. J. Eggeling, *The Kātantra with the Commentary of Durgasimha,* fasc. I-VI. Bibliotheca Indica New Series nos. 297-298, 308-309, 396-397. Calcutta: Asiatic Society of Bengal, 1874-1878.

Kiparsky, P. and J. F. Staal

1969 "Syntactic and semantic relations in Pāṇini." *Foundations of Language* 5: 83-117.

Laufer, B.

1898 "Studien zur Sprachwissenschaft der Tibeter. Zamatog." *Sitzungsberichte der philos.-philol. und hist. Classe der k.b. Akademie der Wissenschaften z. München* I: 519-594.

Liebich, B.

1919 *Zur Einführung in die indische einheimische Sprachwissenschaft I: Das Kātantra.* Sitzungsberichte der Heidelberger Akademie der Wissenschaften 4. Heidelberg: Carl Winter.

Miller, Roy Andrew

1963 "Thon-mi Sambhota and his Grammatical Treatises." *Journal of the American Oriental Society* 83: 485-502. [Reprinted with addenda et corrigenda in Miller, 1976: 1-18].

1966 "Buddhist Hybrid Sanskrit *āli, kāli* as Grammatical Terms in Tibet." *Harvard Journal of Asiatic Studies* 26: 125-147. [Reprinted with addenda et corrigenda in Miller, 1976: 33-56].

1976 *Studies in the Grammatical Tradition in Tibet.* Amsterdam Studies in the Theory and History of Linguistic Science III, 6. Amsterdam: John Benjamins.

1987 "Text Structure and Rule Ordering in the First Tibetan Grammatical Treatise." In *Silver on Lapis: Tibetan Literary Culture and History,* pp. 81-110. Ed. by C. I. Beckwith. Bloomington: The Tibet Society.

1988 "The First Two Tibetan Grammatical Treatises as Known to the Sa skya Pandita." In *Tibetan Studies. Proceedings of the 4th Seminar of the International Association for Tibetan Studies, Schloss Hohenkammer, Munich 1985,* pp. 263-278. Ed. by H. Uebach and J. L. Panglung. Studia Tibetica 2. Munich: Kommission für Zentralasiatische Studien Bayerische Akademie der Wissenschaften.

1990a "Case-grammar in the First Two Tibetan Grammatical Treatises." In *Reflections on Tibetan Culture: Essays in Memory of Turrell V. Wylie*, pp. 187-204. Ed. by L. Epstein and R. F. Sherburne. Lewiston, NY: Edwin Mellen Press.

1990b "Prolegomena to a Reading of the Second Tibetan Grammatical Treatise." *Inner Asian Buddhist and Tibetan Studies. Papers read at the Bicentenary Csoma de Körös Symposium Visegrád 1984. Acta Orientalia Hungarica* 44/1-2: 67-88.

Renou, Louis

1942 *Terminologie grammaticale du Sanskrit*. Bibliothèque de l'École des Hautes Études, Sc. Historiques et Philologiques, fasc. 280-281. Paris: Librairie Ancienne Honoré Champion.

rTags kyi 'jug pa

TKJ *Lung du ston pa rtags kyi 'jug pa*. Peking bsTan 'gyur, mDo 'grel, vol. *ngo*, 39r8-40v5 (ed. Suzuki 1955-1961, # 5835), Co ne bsTan 'gyur, mDo 'grel, vol. *co*, 161v5-162v7.

Scharfe, H.

1977 *Grammatical Literature*. A History of Indian Literature 5, Fasc. 2. Ed. by J. Gonda. Wiesbaden: Otto Harrassowitz.

Sum cu pa

SCP *Lung du ston pa rtsa ba sum cu pa* or *Byā ka ra ṇa rtsa ba'i ślo ka sum cu pa zhes bya ba*. Peking bsTan 'gyur, mDo 'grel, vol. *ngo*, 38r3-39r8 (ed. Suzuki 1955-1961, # 5834), Co ne bsTan 'gyur, mDo 'grel, vol. *co*, 160v1-161v4.

Tillemans, Tom J. F.

1988 "On *bdag*, *gźan* and Related Notions of Tibetan Grammar." In *Tibetan Studies. Proceedings of the 4th Seminar of the International Association for Tibetan Studies, Schloss Hohenkammer, Munich, 1985*, pp. 491-502. Ed. by H. Uebach and J. L. Panglung. Studia Tibetica 2. Munich: Kommission für Zentralasiatische Studien Bayerische Akademie der Wissenschaften.

1991 "A Note on *Bdag don phal ba* in Tibetan Grammar." *Études asiatiques* 45/2: 311-323.

Tillemans, Tom J. F. and D. D. Herforth

1989 *Agents and Actions in Classical Tibetan: The Indigenous Grammarians on Bdag and Gźan and Bya byed las gsum*. Wiener Studien zur Tibetologie und Buddhismuskunde 21. Vienna: Arbeitskreis für Tibetische und Buddhistische Studien Universität Wien.

Tournadre, N.

1990 "Présentation de la grammaire traditionnelle et des cas du tibétain. Approche classique et analyse moderne." In: *Tibet, civilisation et société. Colloque organisé par la Fondation Singer-Polignac à Paris, les 27, 28, 29 avril 1987*. Paris.

Verhagen, P. C.

1991a "Sanskrit Grammatical Literature in Tibet: A study of the Indo-Tibetan canonical literature on Sanskrit grammar and the development of Sanskrit studies in Tibet." Ph.D. dissertation. Leiden. [Slightly revised version forthcoming: *A History of Sanskrit Grammatical Literature in Tibet. Volume I. Transmission of the Canonical Literature*. Handbuch der Orientalistik, Abt. 2, Bd. 8. Leiden: E. J. Brill, 1994.]

1991b "Sanskrit Grammatical Literature in Tibet: A First Survey." In *Panels of the VIIth World Sanskrit Conference, Kern Institute, Leiden: August 23-29, 1987. Vol. VII. Sanskrit Outside India*, pp. 47-63. Ed. by J. G. de Casparis. General Editor J. Bronkhorst. Leiden: E. J. Brill.

1991c Review of Tillemans and Herforth, *Bulletin of the School of Oriental and African Studies* 54/1: 208-210.

1992 "A Ninth-century Tibetan Summary of the Indo-Tibetan Model of Case-semantics." In *Tibetan Studies: Proceedings of the 5th Seminar of the International Association for Tibetan Studies, Narita 1989. Volume 2: Language, History and Culture*, pp. 833-844. Ed. by S. Ihara and Z. Yamaguchi. Narita.

Chapter 26

Tibetan Legal Literature: The Law Codes of the dGa' ldan pho brang[1]

Rebecca R. French

From the time of the early empire, there is substantial evidence that Tibetan governments employed complex legal procedures as part of a law system incorporated into their administrative bureaucracies. By the late seventeenth century, the structure of this legal system had taken the form of several levels of courts staffed by monk and lay officials who received petitions, conducted investigations and issued formal decision documents employing standardized legal procedures.

Tibetan law appears to be a unique and intrinsic product of the culture without substantial influence from external legal systems. The official law which comes to us encoded in a narrow documentary trail beginning in the eighth century is an ancient amalgam of the royal laws of the early kings, folk law customs, Tibetan social structure, Buddhist ethical teachings and Buddhist forms of reasoning. These documents are essentially secular in the sense that they were written for the lay population and did not mimic the Vinaya or any other religious text. Storehouses of legal thought, they also depict the politics, history and ethnography of Tibet in previous centuries.

Types of Legal Literature in Tibet

An investigator into the topic of legal literature in pre-1959 Tibet is confronted with an initial conundrum: how does one go about determining and categorizing what was "legal"?[2] Tibetans don't strictly demarcate the semantic zone of the "legal" or have precise standards for what can and cannot be considered "legal literature." The best guide is to look at the use of the term for "moral rules or law," *khrims*, a polyseme which can be modified by the addition of an initial or final morpheme to form a semantic compound. Compounds created by the addition of an initial morpheme often describe general categories of rules or law, the most significant of which, for our purposes, is *rgyal khrims*, the law of the kings, official or state law.[3] Compound words created with the addition of a final morpheme to *khrims* are a good indicator of the sphere of the "legal" in Tibet, for these compound words are almost invariably descriptive of particular aspects of the secular law system: *khrims khang, khrims sa* (official court); *khrims shu ba* (petitioning or going to a law official); *khrims pun, khrims bdag* (official judge); *khrims kyi yig cha* (an official judicial decree); and *khrims yig* (official law codes, documents).

From the Tibetan point of view then, law is the province of the state, and legal literature consists of the written pronouncements, decisions and documents of the official government. The Western use of the term "law" is much broader and can encompass both oral and written evidence of a wide range of transactions, agreements and decision-making activities of both a private and public nature.

Sources of Tibetan Legal Literature

There are at least five major sources for Tibetan legal literature:

(1) *Religious source material*: Vinaya, religious texts with discussion relating to law, etc.

(2) *Written and oral statements on the legal system in both Tibetan and other languages*: novels, autobiographies and biographies,[4] travellers' accounts of cases or punishments, oral statements and histories, letters, written histories, etc.

(3) *Extant official government documents for both internal and external use*: edicts,[5] passports, decision-documents for law cases, treaties, receipts, legal sentencing papers, government contracts, appointments to positions, real estate record books, tax record books, tax documents, deeds to land, constitutions, written advice to officials, administrative rule books, letter writing manuals, advice to official administrators, letters of advice to foreign states such as Bhutan and Sikkim, etc.

It should be noted here that Dieter Schuh's collection of and contribution to Tibetan legal literature has been immense. His publications in the *Monumenta Tibetica Historica*, Abteilung III, have reproduced facsimiles of many of the Tibetan documents in this category with transliteration, synoptic translation and contextual analysis.

(4) *Documents issued by non-governmental institutions*: monastic constitutions, leases, deeds to land, decision-documents, oral and written contracts and agreements, etc. The work of Ter Ellingson and Krystyna Cech in the area of monastic constitutions has been particularly interesting.

(5) *Law codes*: in addition to the several law codes that will be discussed here, there are other law codes that are pertinent to this inquiry. For example, Michael Aris has rendered an excellent translation of the Bhutanese Legal Code of 1729 composed by bsTan 'dzin chos rgyal for the Tenth King (Aris). Finally, it must be noted that all work on Tibetan law codes follows in the footsteps of Meisezahl's pioneering article, "Die Handschriften in den City of Liverpool Museum."

It is important to notice what this list does not include. The Tibetan legal system seems not to have relied on casebooks similar to the vast compendia of legal cases available to Chinese officials when searching for precedents (see Bodde and Morris). Research into the techniques of legal document storage indicates that an indexing system in each courtroom allowed knowledgeable clerks to find copies of old cases for reference, but the indexes only coordinated them chronologically by court (French, 1990: 388-391). There were separate court cost schedules attached to the end of some codes (*KDK*), there were letters of advice written at various times throughout Tibetan history to outlying provinces and countries answering legal questions (*BLB*) and there were separate books written giving advice to government officials. However, no separate books of court procedure, no commentaries, no interpretations of the code and no supplements to the code[6] appear to have been written.

When is a Law Code a Law Code?

What is it about the documents, here being called law codes, that entitles them to that appellation? To begin, Tibetans refer to them as their law codes and understand them as a set of required rules organized into coordinated sections, similar to their religious codes. Secondly, in some of the introductory sections and colophons, these documents describe their origin and production pointing to their status as codified compilations of legal rules. Third, there are structural and substantive features that signal their status as law codes: division into sections, coverage of criminal matters, discussion of procedures, court costs sections, etc.

On the other hand, these codes lack many features present in the law codes of most Western and Asian (particularly Chinese and Japanese) legal systems. Their style, at times, is profoundly precatory and hortatory instead of definitive; it is suggestive and admonitory instead of commanding. For example, the entire dGa' ldan pho brang Law Code of Twelve Sections (*GDPB 12*) is strewn with statements that decision-makers should, after investigating and weighing the evidence, decide for themselves according to the truth. The systematic feature of a law code is lacking: many of the sections lapse into discussions of issues pertinent to previous sections, some include apparently irrelevant material; also a particular subject is often spread throughout the code rather than confined to a single section. Most of these codes are not exclusive instruments, that is, they did not supersede all earlier laws. Indeed, it was quite common to find wealthier households that had copies of several different law codes from different periods.[7] Myriad questions of textual history, authenticity, use, and accuracy, perhaps not all entirely answerable, also confront the reader of these law codes. Finally, aspects of promulgation and the formal enactment of the law codes are problematic in the Tibetan setting. Many Tibetans report having heard the "reading of the laws" that occurred every year prior to 1959 in most districts. The fact that the formal governmental decree that was annually recited on this occasion, the Mountain-Valley Decree (*ri lung rtsa tshig*), was related to but not part of the law codes, further compounds the problem of promulgation.

Given these extensive caveats, the most compelling reason for a detailed study of these law codes is their resonance with Tibetan culture. They are filled with information about ways-of-doing things and points-of-view—ranked social hierarchies, marriage and divorce patterns, barter equivalencies, proverbs and sayings—which will be new to Tibetologists, anthropologists and historians alike. The degree of absorption of the ideas from these law codes into the general population appears to have been extensive, as most of the law cases that have been collected from interviews with Tibetans include concepts and language from these codes.[8] In this sense, the codes sitting on the desks of law courts such as the High Court of Tibet (*gsher khang*) until 1959 were not dead letter law but vibrant compendia of Tibetan life.

The Early Law Texts

Texts from the period of the early empire which have been analyzed by Professor Geza Uray of Budapest, Hugh Richardson, and others demonstrate the existence of a system of legal rules as early as the ninth century in Tibet.

The first historical law texts of King Srong btsan sgam po, which come to us in fragments from different documents, have been analyzed by Professor Geza Uray.[9] As reconstructed by Professor Uray, there appear to be at least four separate parts to the code, some of which are additions dating well beyond Srong btsan sgam po's time. The earliest code has a beginning passage in which the king proclaims the granting of laws to Tibet, explains the purpose of this act and advertises the benefits it will bring to his subjects. This form of self-aggrandizing introduction became a standard for the later codes with the addition of the appropriate words of Buddhist prostration and several paragraphs giving some history and the name of the humble compiler(s). In this earliest code, it has the simple format of a statement that the king did these acts.

These passages revel in numerical lists. For example, there are the first group of Six Institutions, the second group of Thirty-Six Institutions (including the Six Great Principles, the Six Symbols of the Heroes and the Six Codes), excerpts from the Six Codes and the Four Catalogues of Different Ranks. These stand as an outline for later elaboration.

Through a very detailed examination and comparison of several early texts from different dates, Professor Uray has elucidated at least three different types of rules propounded during the first royal dynasty:

(1) The Four Fundamental Laws prohibiting murder, thievery, lechery and bearing false witness
(2) The Ten Non-Virtuous Acts from the Buddhist scriptures
(3) The Sixteen Pure Human Moral Rules

These legal fragments are strongly rooted in Buddhist doctrine. The four fundamental laws, for instance, come directly from the first four of the Ten Non-Virtuous actions, namely murder, theft, sexual misconduct and lying. These four remained as part of the legal rules of Tibet over the next thirteen hundred years; the law codes used in the first half of the twentieth century in Tibet had prominent sections on murder, theft, adultery and oath-taking for lies and false accusation. The emphasis on enumeration in these early passages was carried into the sNe'u gdong Code of the fourteenth century (*ZBKB*). By the seventeenth century, all that was left of this style was the reference to the previous codes in the title and the division of the code into sections.

Hugh Richardson's work (1952) on early Tibetan political treaties is well known. He has also written on some of the fascinating legal documents of this early period—namely Pelliot Tibetain 1071, 1072 and 1073—in two of his more recent articles (1989 and 1990). With regard to the question of an original law code, he states:

> The Tibetan Chronicle from Tunhuang shows that by the eighth or ninth century Srong brtsan sgam po was regarded as having established 'a great code of supreme law'—*gtsug lag bka' grims ched po* (p. 118); and the Annals record that six years after Srong brtsan's death the Chief Minister Mgar stong bstan yul zang wrote the text of the laws—bka' grims gyi yi ge bris (p. 13[6]). There is no contemporary evidence about their content but in later tradition the sixteen laws attributed to Srong brtsan sgam po are no more than a series of moral precepts. However, documents from Tunhuang reveal the existence of several specific legal codes and regulations. One long document in the India Office Archive collection of the Stein mss (10 no. 740) gives details of the proper decision, according to a new set of regulations, in cases concerning such matters as loans, taxation, marital disputes and so on. Many other Tunhuang documents refer to the law regarding contracts, sales, taxes, land-holding etc. and often mention the judge, *zhal ce pa*, who decides the cases. (1989: 7)

In these two recent articles, Richardson translates and analyzes the elaborate rules covering dog bites, the yak hunt and injury by yak in the empire period. One can discern in his work on these early documents several features characteristic of the later law codes; for example, (1) nine recognized ranks in society, (2) "great difference in social status" as indicated by graduated penalties according to rank, (3) the importance of bravery and the "stern standard of honour in a warlike society," and (4) "elaborate provisions for the disposition of land and possessions . . . [which] underline the importance attached to property."

He concludes his second article with the following comments:

> This long and elaborately detailed document gives an unusual view of Tibetan life and manners. Scholars such as Rolf Stein, the doyen of Tibetan studies, have shown the extent to which early Tibetan thought and practice in literature, religion and the vocabulary of royal ceremonial were subject to Chinese influences, but these codes of law, especially shameful punishment of the fox's tail, seem to be purely Tibetan in character. (1990: 20)

What can we say in general about these early works? In the empire period, Tibet had judges, legal fora and detailed legal rules divided into distinct categories by subject matter. These rules, though related to and reputedly based on Buddhist principles, were primarily addressed to the problems of secular imperial rule. Most interesting, they delineated social classes and structure and regulated in detail an important ceremonial ritual of that period, namely the yak hunt. There is, however, no evidence that these legal writings were widely disseminated in Tibet in their original form either during this period or later.

Sa skya Law Codes

There is very little information about the changes or advances in the legal system during the period of decentralization following the empire's collapse by 866 C.E., although the smaller states undoubtedly preserved and adapted many of the administrative and legal rules of the former central government to their own localities. With respect to the period of consolidation by the Sa skya, which followed, Guiseppe Tucci has stated that the Sa skya probably used a Mongolian code:

> Probably at that time the Mongol penal code was introduced into Tibet, either the Yasa of Gengis Khan or more probably its successive elaborations and adaptments, incorporated into Yuan laws. (...) They were introduced into Tibet by the Yuan and found the Sa sKya Pa ready to accept and enforce them. (1949: 37)

Corroborating his conjecture is the statement in the 1960s by the two sons of the Sa skya royal family that a Sa skya code has been used by the Sa skya government officials to provide standards and guidelines for legal judgments (see Cassinelli and Ekvall). There are also other older sources, such as the 1894 Gazetter of Sikkim, which states that "Kung ga gyal tsan of Sa skya pa who was born in 1182" and was the "king of 13 provinces in Tibet" produced a law code that came in "two sets, one containing 13 laws and the other 16," which were later revised and used by the Dalai Lamas (see Gazetter: 46; White: 311).

Unfortunately, without actual examples of these codes, it is difficult to assess either Tucci's conjecture that Mongolian-influenced codes existed during this period or to judge the degree to which these codes might have influenced later codes. Other evidence suggests that Tucci might have been wrong. For example, a very knowledgeable older Tibetan who had worked in Sa skya as a legal representative and also been chosen to represent the state of Sa skya and its citizens in the courts of Lhasa in the 1940s has stated repeatedly in interviews that there was no distinct Sa skya code when he practiced and there never had been one historically.[10] Lamas from the Sa skya sect now living in India and those in Tibet responded in the same way. The Sa skya law codes thus remain one of the more interesting puzzles in Tibetan legal literature.

The sNe'u gdong Law Code

Several scholars have credited Byang chub rgyal mtshan, founder of the Phag mo gru dynasty in 1354, with drafting a new code of laws as part of his efforts to restore Tibet to its previous imperial glory (Tucci; Uray; Snellgrove; Michael). Although this is certainly a reasonable presumption, none of the codes cited by these scholars and none that I have collected or translated appear to date from his reign. Indeed, the available codes date from the reign of his successors, sometime during the fourth, fifth or sixth king of the Phag mo gru dynasty. Although composed later, the codes that we have could have been based on one written during the time of this first king but not as yet discovered.

Composed perhaps in the first half of the fifteenth century, the Phag mo gru or sNe'u gdong Law Code (*ZBKB*; *NDLC*) is a full-length code of law that both preserves links to the past (in the poetical numerical form of the empire period) and looks ahead to the more modern and functional styles of later eras. The code itself can be easily divided into two parts that illustrate these separate modes of expression.

The introductory part of the code is quite long and divided into a short initial "general" statement followed by a long "specific" statement. Both of these statements appear to be compilations of accumulated wisdom and proverbs on subjects such as the proper attributes of a good witness, judge or guarantor, the proper and improper forms of speech in court, and the best qualities for a party to a suit. Following the style of the early codes, these attributes are arranged in numerical sets. For example, the "Five Types of Speech" are (1) Black-eyed Speech, (2) Evil Speech in Eight Forms, (3) Twenty-five Forms of Glorious Speech, (4) Sharp-response Speech and (5) High Victorious Speech.[11] The last category outlines the attributes of a good party to a suit capable therefore of "high victorious speech."

Although the style of the writing in this part is at times elliptical and at times discursive, there is much to be learned about the social customs of Tibet in the fourteenth century from these enumerations and proverbs. For example, a party to a suit will be in an advantageous position in court if it can demonstrate "high victorious speech" with any of the following twelve attributes divided into three subcategories:

> ...greatness in the heritage of one's paternal ancestors, greatness in the acts for the country, greatness in learning and great wealth [the "Four Great Causes"]; presenting tea and beer, wearing silk, lynx and fox, using a yak-cow crossbreed and having important guests from a long distance [the "Four Great Symbols"]; and taking on a guru, taking care of one's parents, taking care of one's relatives and servants and vanquishing enemies easily [the "Four Great Qualities"]. (*ZBKB*)

Passages such as these have both a pleasing lyrical rhythm and a straightforwardness that tells the reader directly which factors are positive and which negative in the consideration of a case. This is an important stylistic point because this method of giving the factors or criteria for consideration but not, given those factors, how to rule in a case, shows up repeatedly later. These are signs of the prudential or admonitory style of writing which so distinguishes sections of the later Tibetan codes.

The second part of the sNe'u gdong law code is completely different in style; it begins with a plain list of fifteen substantive laws and then proceeds to elaborate rather pedantically, one at a time, the factors and rules for each subject. The list covers murder, theft, oath-taking, adultery, family separation, selling and buying goods, accounts, loans of animals, rules for the chief of the army, rules for those who retreat and rules regarding the payment of court costs. Gone is the whimsical, old-fashioned style; these are rules for the operation of an official bureaucracy.

This second half of the code is so sophisticated and so replete with exceptions and finely tuned distinctions that it points to a long history of legal elaboration rather than to the brilliance of a contemporaneous legal scholar.[12] This observation is based on the sheer weight of the evidence: the murder section, for example, covers almost twenty different elaborations and exceptions to the basic rule.[13] It seems most likely that these rules were developed *ab intra* over several hundred years prior to the fourteenth century but only the discovery of earlier codes of manuscripts referring to the laws and comparisons with external sources will elucidate this conjecture.

gTsang Law

The first modern law code, the gTsang code, remained widely distributed throughout Tibet right up until the mid-twentieth century, and comes in the widest variety of forms of any Tibetan law code. Eight different versions are presently in my collection, ranging from eleven to sixteen sections each.

After the prostrations and historical introduction, a central core of twelve sections appears in most versions of the gTsang and later codes, whether in full or abridged form. Four additional sections can be added to these twelve, to make up codes of thirteen, fifteen and sixteen sections.[14] These four include the "Brave Tiger" and "Fearful Fox" sections on military administration, "Rules for Officers" and "Barbarians on the Border."[15]

The gTsang law codes appear to have been drafted during the reign of the fourth gTsang king, Karma bstan skyong dbang po (r.

1623-1642), who was keenly concerned with legal administration. The codes state that he sent out edicts (*rtsa tsig*) to elicit responses and information for an official compilation of legal rules. In one version of the gTsang code (*BKKY*), the king appointed a compiler (referred to in the text as "the donkey with a leopard skin on its back") because, as the text states, each region still had its own rules and there was no unified legal system in Central Tibet. This scholar then collected from many sources: ancient law books, legal texts kept by lamas, oral statements from old men, observations of the operation of the laws of the different regions, including Tibet, Mongolia, Bhutan and Monpa, and the word of the gTsang king on law. From these multifarious sources, the compiler goes on to say, the legal rules were assembled, compared and categorized into sixteen sections.[16]

The gTsang codes are truly modern, administrative codes by Tibetan standards. Their format is functional, their style is generally simple, their content is primarily secular and their purpose is administrative coordination and control. Although it is quite possible that the rules in this compilation predated the time of the fourth king, there is presently no method for accurately proving this. For this reason, the gTsang period must be our starting point for any discussion of modern Tibetan law codes.

The Law Codes of the dGa' ldan pho brang

Within only a few years of the compilation of the gTsang codes, the Mongolian Gushri Khan swept into Tibet, putting his religious preceptor, the fifth Dalai Lama of the dGe lugs pa sect, in control of the country. The law codes of the Dalai Lama period were compiled after the installation of the new ruler and were then used, without major changes, for the rest of the three-hundred-year reign of the dGe lugs pas.

I distinguish two basic types of Dalai Lama codes: (1) the first, which I have called the dGa' ldan pho brang Law Code of Twelve Sections (*GDPB 12*), dates to approximately 1650[17] and was written by a local governor under the guidance of two people — the first regent, bSod nams chos 'phel, and the Mongolian benefactor of the fifth Dalai Lama, Gushri Khan (bsTan 'dzin chos rgyal)[18]; (2) the second, which I have called the dGa' ldan pho brang Law Code of Thirteen Sections (*GDPB 13*), was written less than three decades later in approximately 1679 by Sangs rgyas rgya mtsho,[19] the regent of the fifth Dalai Lama.

Other scholars have followed Professor Tucci's lead in citing the Phag mo gru or sNe'u gdong law code as the template for the dGa' ldan pho brang law codes. Tucci states, "...but the Phag Mo Gru's code prevailed and after being revised by the fifth Dalai Lama and the sDe.Srid, Sangs.rGyas.rGya.mTsho, is still used in Tibet" (37). A close analysis of the codes reveals, however, that these later codes took their structure, form and a large part of their content from the codes of the gTsang kings rather than the sNe'u gdong. In every passage of the text, the gTsang code is the template from which the regents were working to alter, adjust or add; perhaps as much as one third to one half of the older gTsang codes were imported unchanged into the new codes. It is interesting to ask why the new leader and his regents chose the previous code of the secular kings of gTsang as their paradigm rather than either the sNe'u gdong code or some more religious work, but it is a question that remains to be answered by historians knowledgeable about the social structure and religious institutions of these periods.

A further presumption among the scholarly communities, both Western and Tibetan, namely that these codes were exclusively criminal in nature, is also controverted by their contents. While the criminal sections are substantial, the 1,336 lines of the basic law code cover an enormous number of other subjects: the amount of pay to be given to government messengers on official journeys, the barter equivalents of volumes of barley, what to do with borrowed animals that die the day after they are returned to their owners, the division of male and female children in a divorce, the proper method for a judge or mediator to interrogate a witness, victim compensation for injury, and hundreds of other topics (see *GDPB 12*).

Although these codes are arranged into sections with subject headings, the dGa' ldan pho brang law codes are not tightly organized documents. The gTsang codes were reproduced in large chunks within the body of the new codes in only a partially systematic way. The style of the paragraphs also varies widely throughout the code; some are very specific and descriptive; others are discursive, prolix, vague or abstruse. The result is a mosaic organized into fields of substantive rules with several underlying themes (e.g., judicial reasoning and legal procedure) and interspersed segments (historical comments, barter equivalents, proverbs). The code written during the time of the first regent has twelve sections, arranged as follows:

Introduction

Prostration passage, lines 1-32
History of the Commission and Production of the Text; with Praise for the Fifth Dalai Lama, Gushri Khan and the Regent, 33-197[20]
Officers' Rules, 198-267[21]

Main Body of the Text

(1) Truthful and Untruthful Petitions, 268-289
(2) Arrest Procedures, 289-305
(3) Major Crimes, 306-336
(4) Punishments to Promote Mindfulness, 337-453
(5) Government Emissaries, 454-593
(6) sTong Compensation for Murder, 594-823
(7) Injury Compensation, 824-883
(8) Oath-taking, 884-1073
(9) Theft Compensation, 1074-1094
(10) Separation of Relatives, 1095-1147
(11) Adultery Compensation, 1148-1206
(12) Before and After Midnight, 1207-1330

Conclusion

Poetic Verses and Prostration, 1317-1330
Dedication, 1331-1336

There is a standard format for the prologue of each section that consists of the number and name of the section and four lines or more of verse relating to the subject matter of the section. Commonly, there are then a few introductory or historical comments followed by the corpus. To give some feel for the content and style of these codes I include here a draft translation of the beginning of section ten, lines 1095-1122 of the dGa' ldan pho brang Law Code of Twelve Sections. It is a passage that, although representative of the whole, was adopted entirely from the gTsang code and therefore gives us a glimpse of that older code as well. (My comments or additions are included in brackets.)

No. Ten, The Section on the Separation of Relatives [is here explained] as follows:

When the time comes to divide a fighting family,
It is necessary to thoroughly investigate,

What the two sides did, male and female differences, etc.
and then decide suitably and honestly,
according to the legal system.

As an initial point, the mediator to a family dispute should do a thorough and honest investigation of the marriage arrangements and the root cause of the breakup.

First, in the early law codes [it was stated] that eighteen *zho* [weight of gold coin] were charged for the symbol of the tiger [wife throws the husband out of the house] and twelve *zho* were charged for the spot of the leopard [husband throws the wife out].

However, in actuality, if the husband is thrown out but he was innocent, the wife owes eighteen *zho* payable in three installments plus a sorry payment of clothes or ornaments and blankets [to the husband]. For a big mistake by the wife, she owes . . . [excluded for the sake of brevity].

If the wife is thrown out but she is innocent, the husband owes twelve *zho* and three *bre* [measurement of grain] for every day and [three *bre*] for every night spent with him. In another system, he owes one gold *se ba* [money equivalent to seven *bre*] for the day wage and three *bre* for the night wage. [However,] these amounts should be determined according to the wealth of the family. (*GDPB 12*, lines 1095-1122)

This section goes on, in the next few lines, to discuss the division of clothes and articles of marriage, the division of children with men getting male offspring and women getting female offspring and payment by the husband of the "value of mother's milk" to the wife for feeding the child in its infancy.

Conclusion

Tibet had a long history of law code drafting culminating in the dGa' ldan pho brang codes of the seventeenth century that remained in use until the mid-twentieth century. As Richardson has pointed out, they were a "purely Tibetan" product, more so perhaps than any of the other aspects of Tibetan culture that have been studied.

With the texts presently available, it is possible to sketch out four basic law-code drafting periods—the empire period, the sNe'u gdong period, the gTsang period and the dGa' ldan pho brang period. The Sa skya period may have produced a code but none are presently extant.[22] In general, these documents tax present comparative law definitions of law codes as they are not overly systematic, exclusive, or definitive, and many serious questions remain about their use, accuracy and promulgation. In contradiction to several hypotheses, the gTsang rather than the sNe'u gdong law codes were the template for the later codes and none of the law codes were purely criminal in subject matter. Other questions for further investigation include: Why were new codes introduced and was a new code expected from a new ruler? What is the relationship between Tibetan law codes and the law codes of other Buddhist legal systems? How do the codes reflect the historical reality? How were they actually "compiled"? Were the law codes simply obsolete documents?

Based in Buddhism but secular in nature, these law codes are compilations of customary practices, proverbs, phrases, examples, songs, cases, rules and administrative requirements which influenced the entire Himalayan region. They provided the immense area of the Tibetan plateau with unifying concepts of legal procedure and legal rules which acted as a remarkable means of social control—flexible, durable, pervasive and reinforcing—because they were embedded in Tibetan culture itself. As such, they constitute a rich storehouse of material for Tibetologists, Asian specialists and lawyers alike and serve as a window into the operation of Tibetan society over the last thousand years.

Notes

1. The translation and investigation of the Tibetan law codes was undertaken initially in India and Nepal between 1983 and 1987. Kungo Thubten Sangye, formerly of the Library of Tibetan Works and Archives, was the primary source for every aspect of the translation and understanding of these texts. His contribution to both this project and to all Tibetan scholarship was immeasurable. Funding was provided by the National Science Foundation, Yale East Asian Concillium, Wenner-Gren Foundation, Social Science Research Council, Berkeley Scholar in India Program, Charlotte Newcomb Fund and American Association of University Women. Many thanks to Gyatso Tsering, Tashi Tsering and Lobsang Shastri of LTWA for their support and assistance. I would also like to thank the many others who have aided this research, including P. Richardus and Josef Kolmas for providing me with copies of law codes from their collections and Michael Aris for our initial discussions of this paper.

2. Tibetan legal literature has been one of the least known areas of Tibetan literature due to the dearth of research and the general obscurity of Tibetan bureaucratic and legal vocabulary.

3. Other compounds are: *yul khrims* (local law); *chos khrims* (religious law); *tshul khrims* (moral law and monastic rules); *rang khrims* (self-law or regulation). Exceptions to this general rule include words like *bka' khrims* (commandments, commandments of law). Within this group, the strongest contrast for Tibetans is between *chos khrims* and *rgyal khrims*, the former representing the word of the Buddha in its purest form, including the rules of the monastic community; the latter the rules of the historic kings based on the foundation of the teachings of the Buddha. Although Tibetans depict the political, religious, administrative and legal functions of their former society as an interconnected and interpenetrable whole, this dichotomy between religious and king law remains at the foundation of their structure of government and constitutes the demarcation of their legal system.

4. An excellent example here is the beginning of the *rnam thar* of Mi la ras pa, which concerns his familial struggles over an oral will by his father.

5. Several of these edicts are available; for example, see "The Edict of the C'os rGyal of Gyantse" in Tucci: 714.

6. For example, many supplements were available in the Yuan period (1271-1368) in China. See Ch'en: 90.

7. Some Tibetans interviewed even reported codes from multiple nationalities. In the northeast of the plateau, the tenthold of one nomadic leader had two Tibetan law codes that were consulted and viewed as authoritative, in addition to copies of both Chinese and Mongolian law codes.

8. See extensive case citation in French. Note that it is also likely that the law codes merely reproduced what was already customary and acceptable among the population.

9. His two primary sources here are the *Royal Annals* and the *mKhas pa'i dga' ston*.

10. Private communications, Tsewang Tamdin, Dharamsala, India, 1986-87.

11. The Tibetan for this in the law code is *che thabs mtho gyal gyi gshags la.*

12. Or perhaps, though less likely, it points to borrowing from other cultures.

13. It gives a history of the law of murder, the social classes that distinguish the victim, compensation payments (these categories were already present in the empire period), exceptions in the case of killing a woman or killing by a child, murder during a theft, murder by mob or multiple persons, attempted murder, payments in land instead of money or goods, mitigation in payments, merit payments for the purification of the dead body, payments in the case of cremation and for religious ceremonies, numerous allowances to be paid to all the relatives, reductions due to early payment and then a very long passage on the form that the payments can take.

14. For a discussion of this aspect of the law codes (with charts), see Meisezahl.

15. Other codes, particularly the sNe'u gdong law code, have a further variant section entitled "Behind the Pass," which is a type of hot-pursuit law.

16. Also, the number sixteen was chosen to correspond with the original Six-

teen Pure Human Moral Rules cited by Uray. For another version of a gTsang code, see *gTshang pa rgyal po'i khrims yig zhal lce bcu gsum pa,* The Code of Thirteen Sections of the Tsang Kings, LTWA Ta.5 13546.

17. This date is from Kungo Thubten Sangye's research into this code. Concerning what is presented as a Dalai Lama code, R.O. Meisenzahl states the following, citing Yamaguchi (nos. 443-444): "In Yamaguchi's opinion this text was written during the term of the regent Sonam Choephel of Tibet (1595-1658). In the colophon, Folio 52b, however, the date 1631 is documented, which date is before the above regency" (my translation from the German). See Meisezahl: 222. This could be a gTsang law code if the above date of 1631 is correct.

18. This law code has no official name in Tibetan and is found in several versions. The one particularly cited here is in *Tibetan Legal Materials,* LTWA Ta.5 13550, pages 35-95 (Delhi: Dorjee Tsering at M. M. Offset Press). The numbers cited in the text from this work correspond to the line numbers of the interlinear translation of this text done in 1985-1987 with Kungo Thubten Sangye.

19. This work comes in a sixteen-section version as well. The fifth regent is also credited with authorship of a text entitled "Twenty-one Rules for the Government Officer," an unpublished manuscript I was given in Tibet.

20. This section also includes the following subsections: a history of the commission and production of the text by the author, a history of the Dalai Lama lineage and its relationship with the Mongols, the history of Gushri Khan with prostrations and a quasi-history of Mongolia, the previous secular kingdoms and their lamas, the high lineage of the first regent bSod nams chos 'phel, the fame of the priest-patron relationship between the Dalai Lama with his first regent and Gushri Khan, and an enumeration of the good acts of the dGe lugs pa sect.

21. Although this section begins with the dedication lines and poetry verses of the Officers' Rules section, it does not actually contain much in the way of rules for officials to follow. Instead there is a melange of topics analogous to those of the previous section (see preceding note). In addition, the Five Heinous Crimes in Buddhism (*pham pa*) are mentioned in line 213, a discussion of limb severage and death punishments, other miscellaneous rules about wild animals, loans, market taxes, the existence of the ancient Sixteen Code of Rules and the names of some of the sections eliminated from the gTsang codes.

22. There may also be other decades that will become important law code periods as more documents become available. In the early twentieth century, for example, an Army Code (which I have in my collection) was drafted during the ascendancy of Tsarong.

References

Aris, Michael

1979 *Bhutan: The Early History of a Himalayan Kingdom.* Wiltshire, England: Aris and Phillips.

BKKY *Bod kyi khrims yig chen mo zhal lce bcu drug gi 'grel pa* ("The Great Tibetan Law Code of Sixteen Sections"). Thimphu,Bhutan: Kunsang Topgyel and Mani Dorji, Class II Shop No. 3. Ballimaran, Delhi: M. M. Photo-Offset Press.

BLB *'Bras ljong bstran bsrung rnam rgyal gyis sde srid sang rgyas rgya mtshor khrims skor dogs gcod shu ba.* Seventeenth-century manuscript acquired in Tibet.

Bodde, Derk and Clarence Morris

1967 *Law in Imperial China; Exemplified in 190 Ch'ing Dynasty Cases.* Philadelphia: University of Pennsylvania Press.

Cassinelli, C.W. and Robert Ekvall

1969 *A Tibetan Principality: The Political System of Saskya.* Ithaca, New York: Cornell University Press.

Cech, Krystyna

1988 "A Bonpo bCa'-yig: the Rules of the sMan-ri Monastery." In *Tibetan Studies.* Ed. by Helga Uebach and Jampa Panglung. Munich.

Ch'en, Paul

1979 *Chinese Legal Tradition under the Mongols.* Princeton: Princeton University Press.

Ellingson, Ter

1980 "Tibetan Monastic Constitutions: the bCa'-Yig." Paper presented at the Ninth Wisconsin South Asia Conference. Revised version published in L. Epstein and R. Sherburne, eds., *Reflections on Tibetan Culture: Essays in Memory of Turrell V. Wylie.* Lewiston, New York: Edwin Mellen Press, 1990.

French, Rebecca

1990 "The Golden Yoke: A Legal Ethnography of Tibet Pre-1959." Ph.D. dissertation. New Haven, Connecticut: Yale University.

1995 *The Golden Yoke: The Legal Cosmology of Buddhist Tibet.* Ithaca: Cornell University Press.

The Gazetter of Sikkim

1894 "Sikkim Laws." *The Gazetter of Sikhim.* Calcutta: The Gazetter of Sikhim Press.

GDPB 12 The dGa' ldan pho brang Law Code of Twelve Sections. In *Tibetan Legal Materials*, pp. 35-95. Ballimaran, Delhi: Dorjee Tsering at M.M. Offset Press, 1985.

GDPB 13 The dGa' ldan pho brang Law Code of Thirteen Sections. Unpublished seventeenth-century manuscript in Tibetan. Library of Tibetan Works and Archives, Ta.5 13547.

KDK *Khrims 'degs kyi ang rims*. In *Tibetan Legal Materials*, pp. 131-135. Ballimaran, Delhi: Dorjee Tsering at M.M. Offset Press.

Meisezahl, R. O.
1973 "Die Handschriften in Den City of Liverpool Museum (I)." *Zentralasiatische Studien* 7: 221-284.

Michael, Franz
1982 *Rule by Incarnation*. Boulder, CO: Westview Press.

NDLC *sNe'u gdong Law Code*. In *Tibetan Legal Materials*, pp. 15-35. Ballimaran, Delhi: Dorjee Tsering at M. M. Offset Press.

Richardson, Hugh
1952 *Ancient Historical Edicts*. London: Royal Asiastic Society of Great Britain and Ireland.
1989 "Early Tibetan Law concerning Dog-bite." *Bulletin of Tibetology*, new series 3: 5. Gangtok, India: Sikkim Research Institute of Tibetology.
1990 "Hunting Accidents in Early Tibet." Unpublished manuscript obtained from Michael Aris.

Schuh, Dieter and L. S. Dagyab
1978 *Urkunden, Erlasse und Sendschreiben aus dem Besitz sikkimeisischer Adelshauser und des Kolsters Phodang*. Monumenta Tibetica Historica, Abt. 3, Band 3. St. Augustin: VGH Wissenschaftsverlag.

Schuh, Dieter and J. K. Phukhang
1979 *Urkunden und Sendschreiben aus Zentraltibet, Ladakh und Zanskar*. Monumenta Tibetica Historica, Abt. 3, Band 4. St. Augustin: VGH Wissenschaftsverlag.

Snellgrove, David and Hugh Richardson
1980 *A Cultural History of Tibet*. Colorado: Prajñā Press.

TPGP *gTshang pa rgyal po'i khrims yig zhal lce bcu gsum pa*. The Code of Thirteen Sections of the gTsang Kings. Dharamsala, India: Library of Tibetan Works and Archives, Ta.5 13546.

Tucci, Guiseppe
1949 *Tibetan Painted Scrolls*. Rome: Istituto Italiano per il Medio ed Estremo Oriente.

Uray, Geza
1972 "The Narrative of Legislation and Organization of the mKhas pa'i dga' ston: The Origins of the Traditions concerning Srong brcan sgam po as First Legislator and Organizer of Tibet." In *Acta Orientalia Academiae Scientarium Hungaricae.* 26/1: 11-68. Tomus.

White, John Claude
1909 *Sikkim and Bhutan: Twenty-one Years on the Northeast Frontier 1887-1908.* London: Edward Arnold.

Yamaguchi, M.
1970 *Catalogue of the Tōyō Bunko Collection of Tibetan Works on History.* Tokyo: Tōyō Bunko.

ZBKB *Zin bris kyi bod rgyal sne'i gdong 'pa'i khrims yig zhal bce bco lnga pa.* Manuscript in the Library of Tibetan Works and Archives, Ta.5 13550.

Chapter 27

The Origin of the *rGyud bzhi:* A Tibetan Medical Tantra

Todd Fenner

Introduction

The *rGyud bzhi* is the principal textbook of Tibetan medicine. It is cited frequently in almost all Tibetan medical literature and is the text Tibetan medical students must master before becoming physicians. At the Medical and Astrological Institute in Dharamsala, all medical students are expected to commit the text to memory; it is the foundation of their education.

The *rGyud bzhi* is also the most featured work in what little Western literature there is concerning Tibetan medicine.[1] It was Csoma de Körös who introduced the book to the West through his extensive analysis of it in the January 1835 issue of the *Journal of the Royal Asiatic Society*. Since then, at least four partial translations of the book have appeared in the West: one in Russian, by Peter Badmaev (1903); and three in English, by Rechung Rinpoche (1973), Jampa Kelsang (Alan Wallace) (1976) and Terry Clifford (1984).

While the *rGyud bzhi* is well known in the West among those interested in Tibetan medicine, little is known of its history. All Tibetan writers have accepted the tradition that the *rGyud bzhi* is a translation of a Sanskrit medical book entitled the *Amṛtahṛdayā-*

ṣṭaṅgaguhyopadeśa Tantra ("The Essence of Nectar: The Manual of the Secret Teachings of the Eight Limbs") and have said no more, except for Rechung Rinpoche, who has given a fuller account of the general history of medicine in Tibet. This essay, then, examines the book's place in Tibetan medical literature, the traditional history of the book, the history of medicine at the time it was introduced, the work's style, and something about its contents, with a view to attempting an assessment of its origin. Although we cannot treat all these topics in detail, some pertinent and interesting points can be made.

The Place of the *rGyud bzhi* in Tibetan Medical Literature

Defining the range of Tibetan medical literature depends directly on how one defines Tibetan medical practice. If medical practice encompasses those practices which are designed to improve or maintain mental and physical health, then the range of literature is quite vast. One needs to include a wide assortment of religious, ritual, and yogic practices as well as various practices of divination, amulet and talisman making, astrology and the like, in addition to the practices and theories that modern Western culture normally associates with the science of medicine.

The practice of medicine in Tibet is fully integrated with Tibetan religious views and practices. Healing is a major task asked of many lamas, and the different lineages each have rituals designed to accomplish this task. These rituals usually involve the deities Bhaiṣajyaguru, White Tārā, and Amitāyus (associated most closely with medicine and long life), but may include other deities as well, such as Vajrasattva, usually associated with the purification of negative karma. In a popular divination manual, now in English translation (Mipham, 1990), the author usually recommends making offerings to a class of deities known as dharma protectors whenever an unfavorable prognostication for illness results after a toss of the dice.

However, it would be a mistake to think that the Tibetan religious literature which pertains to healing is concerned only with ritual. There are, scattered throughout tantric literature, sections treating physiological theory, physical culture, and pharmacology as well. This is true of both canonical and post-canonical literature. The second chapter of the *Kālacakra Tantra*, for instance, is entirely devoted to physiology and medicine. Medicine in the *tantras*, however, is always secondary to the ultimate aim of achieving buddhahood. If it is addressed at all, medicine in the root *tantras* is clearly only a part of the whole.

The purpose of medicine in the genre of literature that is termed *gso ba rig pa* (the science of medicine), though, is not enlightenment, but the treatment of disease and the maintenance of health through physical means. Ritual, the collection of merit, the power of the lama, etc. are never discounted, but the approach emphasizes therapies such as taking medicine, eating properly, getting exercise or rest, and making lifestyle changes.

The *rGyud bzhi* can be considered as both the best-known work of this genre, and its archetype. It is encyclopedic in scope, whereas other works of the genre tend to amplify one or more of the subjects it covers in briefer form. Works on pharmacology, pediatrics, physiology, diagnostics, etc., share with the *rGyud bzhi* the same general theory of medicine, and to my knowledge there are no works that dispute its premises.

Until the seventeenth century, Tibetan medicine was taught in monasteries as part of the worldly sciences, and in lineages from individual physician to disciple. The dominant lineages stemmed from the second gYu thog (eleventh century), a namesake of the first gYu thog (786-911?), who was closely connected with the transmission of the *rGyud bzhi* to Tibet. The second gYu thog wrote extensive commentaries on the *rGyud bzhi* and was responsible for giving the text its initial preeminence. In the fourteenth century two physicians, Byangs pa and Zur mkhar pa, each founded a medical lineage based on that started by the second gYu thog. The *rGyud bzhi* became the principal text in each lineage, and was the subject of a major commentary by each founder. In the late seventeenth century, sDe srid Sangs rgyas rgya mtsho, the regent to the fifth Dalai Lama, and holder of the lineages of both Byangs and Zur, founded the first formal medical college in Tibet, lCags po ri, in Lhasa. He also wrote what is probably the most influential commentary on the *rGyud bzhi*, the *Vaiḍūrya ngon po* ("Blue Lapis Lazuli"). Physicians trained at lCags po ri were sent to every district in Tibet. In this way the *rGyud bzhi* came to have a lasting and major effect on Tibetan medicine.[2]

The Origins of the *rGyud bzhi*

There is a specific section in the bsTan 'gyur devoted to the translation of several Indian medical and pharmaceutical texts (*gSo ba rig pa*). The *rGyud bzhi*, however, is not found in the medical section of the bsTan 'gyur, nor, for that matter, anywhere in the bKa' 'gyur or bsTan 'gyur. The text does not belong to the canon because it is a *gter ma* (see Gyatso, in this volume). According to 'Dud 'joms Rinpoche, Grva pa mngon shes (1012-1090) discovered the text in a pillar of the middle story of the dBu rtse Temple of bSam yas Monastery, at three a.m. on the full moon night of the seventh month of the year 1038 ('Dud 'joms, 1977: 95). Its status as a *gter ma* may have influenced the editors of the canon to question its authenticity as a translation of an Indic original. This fact, however, did not deter any school from accepting the text as a basis for medical practice. In fact, the text is accepted as such by all lineages, regardless of the disparaging remarks about *gter ma* in general that some of them may make.

There are a great many differences between the *rGyud bzhi* and the medical books in the canon. The canonical books consist of the *Yogaśataka*, the *Jīvasūtra*, and the *Avabheśajakalpa*, all attributed to the sage/adept Nāgārjuna, and the *Aṣṭaṅgahṛdaya* by Vāgbhata, his autocommentary to it, and two other commentaries to that work by Candranadana. These works all have human authors, and fit the mold of classical Āyurvedic texts in style and content. In fact, the *Aṣṭaṅgahṛdaya*, written in the early seventh century by Vāgbhata at Nālandā Monastic College, is considered to be one of the four most important texts of classical Indian medicine, along with the *Cāraka*, the *Sūśrūta* (also attributed to Nāgārjuna[3]), and the *Mādhavanidāna*.

Classical Āyurvedic texts are manuals consisting of aphorisms and formulae grouped under different headings, each heading being a unit unto itself that bears no necessary relation to the next one. They are also secular works. The names of sages and yogīs may be mentioned on occasion, but there is no religious position or flavor to them. The *Cāraka* and *Sūśrūta*, both redactions of earlier works, are organized in a manner that appears almost haphazard to the Western reader, being collections of aphorisms containing both prose and verse. Their authors and editors seem more concerned about preserving the integrity of an original aphorism than in reworking them to fit into a more uniform whole. The *Aṣṭaṅgahṛdaya* and the *Mādhavanidāna*, on the other hand, are much more consistent in style: one can read them without concern that the same subject might suddenly be dropped, only to be taken up again some fifty to a hundred pages later.

In terms of content, the classics are similar. The *Sūśrūta* adds chapters on surgery and the *Mādhavanidāna* is concerned only with nosology and diagnosis, but all agree on a general theory of medicine and physiology. This theory, in a nutshell, is as follows. The human body has three humors—wind, bile, and phlegm[4]—which cause both physical and mental disease if one or a combination of them gets out of balance with the others in a particular part of the body. This balance is maintained or lost principally by a combination of lifestyle, climate and the foods one eats, while treatment consists of making adjustments in these factors. In Āyurveda, prescriptions (with the exception of purgatives and emetics) do not act as drugs, but rather as food supplements meant to restore balance. Diagnosis consists primarily of taking a history and observing symptoms such as the color of the patient and so on.

The *rGyud bzhi* is distinguished from classical Āyurvedic texts in several important ways. Perhaps the first thing one notices about the *rGyud bzhi* is that it is not a secular medical text at all. After a few standard opening phrases, the text begins: "Thus have I heard, at one time...," etc. In other words, the text begins in the style of a Buddhist *sūtra*. The work is set in "Medicine City" (lTa na sdug), in the midst of a palace made from the five gems. This city is free of all types of diseases and is situated in the midst of a veritable medicine jungle of fruits, herbs, roots and minerals, while being pervaded by fragrant perfumes. In the center of the palace, seated on a throne of lapis lazuli, is the buddha Bhaiṣajyaguru (lit. "Medicine Teacher"), surrounded by a retinue of gods, sages, Buddhists and non-Buddhists. Before teaching, Bhaiṣajyaguru enters into the *samādhi* (concentration state) called "the king of medicines which pacifies the four hundred and four diseases." Then, rays of light, shining in hundreds of thousands of colors, emanate from his heart to the ten directions. First they clear away faults from the minds of beings, then they gather back and re-emanate as the sage Rig pa'i ye shes. Rig pa'i ye shes begins to speak to the assembly, first telling of the importance of the study of medicine and then starting a question-and-answer period, the contents of which make up the substance of the *rGyud bzhi*.

This opening is standard for most Mahāyāna *sūtras*. First, a witness states what has been heard (a reaffirmation of the oral lineage), describes those present and the locale of the teaching, and describes the various concentrations entered into prior to the dissemination of the teaching. Here is also the clear identification of the sage Rig pa'i ye shes as Bhaiṣajyaguru. The different retinues of Bhaiṣajyaguru heard different lectures, each according to their tradition, faith, and understanding. The gods heard the text of the *gSo dpyad 'bum pa*; the Hindu sages heard the eight parts of the *Cāraka*; non-Buddhists heard the *dBang phyug nag po'i rgyud*; the Buddhists heard the *Rigs gsum mgon pa'i skor*.[5] Also, for the benefit of beings, in India the mixing of medicines was taught; in China, moxabustion and the taking of pulse; in Dol po, bleeding; in Tibet, the examination of urine and pulse. All this was transmitted without distinction by Rig pa'i ye shes, but again, the teaching was heard differently by beings of different propensities. Only one sage, Yid las skyes, heard the text the way it was really preached; he heard the "Essence of Nectar" in 5900 verses, the four *tantras*, i.e., the *rGyud bzhi*.

Yid las skyes, however, did not make his knowledge very accessible. Rather, after writing it down in lapis on a shield of solid gold, he stored it with *ḍākinīs* in the land of Uḍḍiyāna. For the future welfare of beings, however, copies of the work were placed in leather boxes and put in several places. The forest of Vajrāsana (Bodhgaya) was one such place; also included were the secret rock cave of the demi-gods, Svayambhu in Nepal, and a cave in Go de shan in China.

The text is alleged to have arrived in Tibet during the reign of Khri srong lde'u btsan, where it was translated by the scholar Vairocana. After learning Sanskrit from Padmasambhava and Śāntarakṣita, Vairocana went to Kashmir, where he studied under several scholars, including Candranandana, the commentator of the *Aṣṭāṅgahṛdaya*, from whom he learned the *rGyud bzhi*. Vairocana returned to Tibet and offered the translation of this text to the king. The *rGyud bzhi* was not propagated at this time, however, because Padmasambhava decided it would be more beneficial to hide the text. This, according to legend, he did in the *bum pa can* ("vase-shaped") pillar of the middle story of the dBu rtse Temple of bSam yas, where it remained hidden until Grva pa mngon shes found it two hundred and fifty years later.

The *rGyud bzhi*, then, is considered a divine work, the original version of all medical texts. This is important to consider when hearing or reading traditional accounts of the text or the history of Tibetan medicine, which place the work in a category with the other *sūtras* and *tantras*. Yet the *rGyud bzhi* does not read like a *sūtra* (or *tantra*), except in a few parts, such as the beginning. The Medicine Buddha *sūtras*, which one could rightfully claim as the sacred predecessors of the *rGyud bzhi*, read like most Mahāyāna *sūtras*, in which the order of the sections has little if any importance, and each new idea is embedded in a sort of repeating chorus, which was essential to the text's meditative or mnemonic purposes. Also, while many *sūtras* appear to be redactions and collections of oral traditions and visions occurring at different times, the *rGyud bzhi* is precisely organized and carefully scripted, more like a traditional *śastra*.

The first *tantra* of the *rGyud bzhi*, the *rTsa rgyud* ("Root Manual") briefly sets forth a basis upon which an entire system can be built. It gives essential phrases that cover the medical system in brief and gives a mnemonic device which provides a structure for all that follows: the simile of a fig tree, with its roots, branches and leaves. The second *tantra*, the *bShad rgyud* ("Manual of Explanation"), expands and elucidates the principles laid down in the *rTsa rgyud*. The third *tantra*, the *Man ngag rgyud* ("Manual of Precepts"), provides practical advice regarding treatment, with an explanation of different diseases. Finally, the fourth *tantra*, the *Phyi rgyud* ("Appendix"), discusses different, more advanced methods of diagnosis and explains the preparation of medicines as well as such methods as bloodletting.

The text is, as I have said, structured quite differently than a normal *sūtra* or *tantra*; it is also more systematically organized than the classical Āyurvedic texts. One may contend that the *Aṣṭaṅgahṛdaya* and *Mādhavanidāna* are also quite organized; but they are manuals, whereas the *rGyud bzhi* is a textbook. The *rGyud bzhi* is not a collection, however well arranged, of medical aphorisms—it is a work that has the plan of a written text. This suggests that it was written at one time and if not by one person, then by consensus. It also suggests that it was not the product of a vision or yogic trance, but of the rational mind-set of a scholar. Even the ecstatic vision described at the beginning is formulaic.

In content the *rGyud bzhi* differs further from these Indian medical texts: its exposition of medical theory and practice reveals some unique features. The Āyurvedic texts list only four causes of disorder: wind, bile, phlegm and trauma. Thus, all diseases are classified as being either wind-born, bile-born, phlegm-born or some combination of these—"wind-bile fever," for example. The *rGyud bzhi* does not discard these categories—in fact, it uses them quite often and even relates the humors to the three poisons (lust, anger and ignorance)—but as far as disease is concerned these three are subsumed under two broader classes, hot and cold. The *rGyud bzhi* says that wind and phlegm are cold diseases, while blood and bile are hot ones. The inclusion here of blood as a humor is also interesting, for as the classes "hot" and "cold" are foreign to Āyurveda, so is the inclusion of blood among the humors. To be fair, blood is not always to be found in Tibetan lists of humors, but the fact that it is mentioned in the *rGyud bzhi* is significant.

With regard to methods of treatment and diagnosis, the *rGyud bzhi* also contains elements foreign to Āyurveda. Briefly, these methods are the taking of pulse, moxabustion, urinalysis and bloodletting. The categories of hot and cold, the identification of blood as a humor, and the practice of bloodletting are all prime marks of classical Greek medicine, whereas pulse-taking and moxabustion are prime characteristics of Chinese medicine. To be sure, the way these practices and categories are used do not correspond exactly to Greek and Chinese systems. For instance, the taking of pulse is more complex in the Chinese system than in the Tibetan. There is reason to believe, however, that these similarities are more than coincidental.

Tibet may have been known in the modern West as the "Forbidden Land," a model of isolation, but during the reigns of Srong btsan gam po and Khri srong lde'u btsan, in the seventh and eighth centuries, the capital of Tibet was almost cosmopolitan. Before Kri srong lde'u btsan committed Tibet to following an Indian cultural-religious model in preference to a Chinese one, Chinese views competed equally with the Indian. This was also true of medicine: physicians from several areas were invited to come to Lhasa to teach and translate what they knew. Srong btsan sgam po is said to have invited three physicians to his court: Bharadrāja from India, Han Wang Hang from China, and Galenos from Persia. Srong btsan sgam po's Chinese queen is also said to have brought with her from China a book entitled *sMan dpyad chen mo*, which was translated by Hva shang Mahādeva and Dharmakoṣa.

All three of these physicians taught and translated the various texts they brought, while the king had their teachings collected and disseminated. The official view was that if one did not study all three traditions, one could not be considered a great physician. After the teachings had been given, the Indian and Chinese doctors returned to their countries, but Galenos, the Persian, stayed on as Srong btsan sgam po's personal physician, and continued to teach and write. He married a local women and fathered three children, who continued his medical teachings. This type of medical eclecticism continued through the reigns of succeeding kings, who had Indian and Chinese doctors in attendance.

It also is important to remember that during the reign of King Kri srong lde'u btsan, when the *rGyud bzhi* was supposedly brought into Tibet and hidden, the situation had not changed. Lhasa had remained a melting pot of the medical traditions. At Khri srong lde'u btsan's court were Śāntigarbha from India; Guhyavajra from Kashmir; sTong gsum gang ba, Ha shab bal la, and Hang ti pa ta from China; Halashanti from Persia; Seng mdo 'od chen from Grugu; Kyal ma ruci from Dol po; and Dharmasala from Nepal. All of them taught medicine and translated texts.

Conclusion

If there was any place where a textbook blending the medical traditions of Greece, India, and China would be expected to originate, it would be Tibet. The hypothesis that the *rGyud bzhi* is a translation of a Sanskrit medical work is an unlikely one. It differs too much in both style and content from related Indian works for this hypothesis to be credible. Too, the fact that the work is not mentioned in any other Sanskrit medical text must be accounted for. Even Candranandana, who supposedly taught the text to Vairocana, seems oblivious to its existence in his commentaries to the *Aṣṭaṅgahṛdaya*. It is likely that the *rGyud bzhi* is a native Tibetan text, certainly Buddhist, mainly Indian in its influence, but with strong elements of Chinese and Greek traditions as well.

In summary, the *rGyud bzhi* appears to be a native Tibetan work, written at a time when the traditions of India, China and Greece met and blended together within a Buddhist framework.

One modern Tibetan writer (Tsarong, 1981: 93-94), reports a belief that the second gYu thog heavily revised the *rGyud bzhi,* and that this may account for the differences between it and traditional Indian works. This may be true, but the original text found by Grva pa mngon shes was presumably still in existence at least through 1959. I would assume that if it was, and the second gYu thog radically changed the work, this belief would have become far more widespread than it has. I think it far more likely that the original gYu thog wove the various traditions together using Indian works, perhaps the *Aṣṭaṅgahṛdaya,* to form the *rGyud bzhi* as it was found at bSam yas. Because of Tibetan reverence for things Indian, and perhaps because the work was written under the inspiration of Bhaiṣajyaguru, the Chinese and Greek traditions were not given credit for their part in the work. In any case, the text came to be considered a secret Indian work revealed for the benefit of sentient beings.

Notes

1. A good list of Tibetan medical works can be found in the appendix of Tsarong. A bibliography of Western books and articles (up to 1973) on the subject can be found in Rechung.

2. My primary source for the historical events mentioned in this paragraph and the next section is lDe srid Sangs rgyas rgya tsho's *History of Tibetan Medicine,* which, despite the title, is still in Tibetan. For those who do not read Tibetan, the best source I am aware of is the introduction to Rechung. The biography of the first gYu thog, which is translated in that book, is also a source.

3. It is interesting that an extant work of this stature, attributed to Nāgārjuna, does not seem to have been brought to Tibet, while some comparatively very minor works were. This fact may provide a clue as to its real date, as well as shed light on the different Nāgārjuna legends in India.

4. The role of humors in Indic medicine is similar to that in classical Western medicine; however, the humors themselves differ. In the West, there are four—blood, black bile, yellow bile, and phlegm. The Indic humors bile and phlegm correspond quite closely to the yellow bile and phlegm of Western theory. The third Indic humor, wind, has no counterpart in Western medicine.

In Indic theory, bile is reponsible for heat, digestion, the emotion of anger, and other functions. Phlegm counterbalances the heat of bile and provides the body with firmness. Wind not only refers to breath and abdominal gas, but also is seen as the vehicle of thoughts and life.

5. Except for the fairly obvious reference to the *Cāraka Saṃhitā,* the other titles refer to works I have never seen.

References

Badmaev, Peter

1903 *Glavnoe rkovodsva po vrochehnoi naukie Tibeta Zhud Zhi*. St. Petersburg.

bDud 'joms Rin po che

1977 "Hagiography of gRva pa mngon shes, the discoverer of the famous medical work *rGyud bzhi*." From *rNying ma'i chos byung*. In *The Rise of Esoteric Buddhism in Tibet*, pp. 94-96. Trans. by Eva M. Dargyay. Delhi: Motilal Banarasidass.

Cāraka

1963 *Cāraka Saṃhitā*. Edited with Hindi commentary by Jayadeva Vidhyalankara. Delhi: Motilal Banarsidass.

Clifford, Terry

1984 *Tibetan Buddhist Medicine and Psychiatry*. York Beach, Maine: Samuel Weiser.

gYu thog pa

1968 *Yuthok's Treatise on Tibetan Medicine*. Edited by Lokesh Chandra. Delhi: International Academy of Indian Culture .

Kālacakra Tantra

1958 *Paramādibuddhaśrīkālacakranāmatantrarāja*. P no. 4, vol. 1, pp. 127.4.1-175.1.1.

Kelsang, Jampa, trans.

1976 *The Ambrosia Heart Tantra*. Dharamsala: Library of Tibetan Works and Archives.

Körös, A. Csoma de

1835 "Analysis of a Tibetan Medical Work." *Journal of the Asiatic Society of Bengal* (Jan. 1835), pp. 1-20.

lDe srid Sangs rgyas rgya mthso

1975 *History of Tibetan Medicine (gSo rigs khog 'bugs legs shad bai dur ya me long)*. Leh: Tashigangpa.

1974 *gSo ba rig pa'i bstan bcos sman bla'i dgongs rgyan rgyud bzhi'i gsal byed bai dur sngon po'i ma lli ka*. 4 vols. Leh: Tashigangpa.

Mādhava

1954 *Mādhavanidāna*. Ed. by Brahmashankar Shastri. Varanasi: Chowkambha Sanskrit Series.

Mipham

1990 *MO, Tibetan Divination System*. Trans. by Jay Goldberg and Lobsang Dakpa. Ithaca: Snow Lion.

Rechung Rinpoche
1973 *Tibetan Medicine*. Berkeley: University of California Press.

rGyud bzhi
1975 *rGyud bzhi*. Leh, Tashigangpa.

Sūśrūta
1967 *Sūśrūta Saṃhīta*. Ed. by Sri Lalacandra Vaidya et al. Delhi: Motilal Banarsidass.

Tsarong, T. J.
1981 *Fundamentals of Tibetan Medicine*. Dharamsala: Tibetan Medical Centre.

Vagbhata
1959 *Aṣṭaṅgahṛdayam*. Ed. by Yaunanand Upadhyaya. Varanasi: Chowkhamba Sanskrit Series.
1962 *Aṣṭaṅgasaṃgrāha*. Ed. by Atridava Gupta. Bombay: Nirnagsagar Mudranalaga.

Chapter 28

Tibetan Literature on Art

Erberto Lo Bue

Tibetan texts dealing with art may be grouped under the following headings: iconographic sources found in religious literature; iconometric sources found in literature dealing with arts and crafts or astrology; handbooks for artists; and art historical sources found in literature dealing with the rise of Buddhism in India and its diffusion in Tibet (see van der Kuijp, in this volume). The first three categories may be regarded as both descriptive and prescriptive, whereas the fourth is merely descriptive.

Iconographic Literature

Religious literature is the basis of Tibetan iconography, and the so-called Tibetan pantheons published in the West are in fact collections of drawings illustrating *sādhanas* (Lo Bue, 1990: 185-187), that is, short texts invoking individual deities (see Cozort, in this volume). *Sādhanas* are in turn based upon the vast literature of *sūtras*, *tantras* and related commentaries that were translated into Tibetan, mostly from Sanskrit, during the second half of the eighth century and in the early ninth century, as well as during the three centuries following the renaissance of Buddhist studies in western Tibet after the year 1000. The descriptions of individual deities in *tantras* and *sūtras* are generally meant for the purpose of conjuring up a specific god, goddess or *maṇḍala* by piecing them together through a process of visual assemblage, and thus contain useful iconographic information, though they are of little use to artists for everyday practical purposes. The *Hevajra Tantra*, for example, provides iconographic details on the image of Hevajra (Snellgrove, 1976, I: 110), but its advice on how it should be executed is scarcely practicable:

> by a painter who belongs to our tradition, by a yogin of our tradition, this fearful painting should be done, and it should be painted with the five colours reposing in a human skull and with a brush made from the hair of a corpse (....) in a lonely spot at noon on the fourteenth day of the dark fortnight, in a ferocious state of mind from the drinking of some wine, with the body naked and adorned with the bone accoutrements: one should eat the sacrament in its foul and impure form, having placed one's own *mudrā* at one's left side, she who is beautiful, compassionate, well endowed with youth and beauty, adorned with flowers and beloved of her master. (1976, I: 114-115)

Such a description obviously belongs to the world of tantric literature rather than to the practice of art. However, a similar kind of visionary attitude can be observed in iconographic practice when a master decides to have a certain deity represented according to his own visions or dreams. Thus Tsong kha pa (1357-1419) had the wall paintings of a temple restored in conformity with the way the gods represented used to appear to him during meditation (Tucci, 1980: 41). Yongs dge Mi 'gyur rdo rje, an eastern Tibetan master (b. 1628), painted the images of deities exactly as they appeared to him in meditation (Stein, 1981: 246). The fifth Dalai Lama (1617-1682), who devoted a section of his treatise on astrology to images and iconography (Tucci, 1980: 136-137), had his rather orthodox visions painted in a beautiful manuscript, which was started in 1674 and completed eleven years after his death. One of the texts included in it gives instructions on how to draw the various *cakras* of the four goddesses of action (Karmay: 69, 134-135, pl. 31; 228-229, text IX).

The role of scholars has always been paramount in the choice and interpretation of the religious texts describing the deities to be represented by artists. Tāranātha (1575-1634), for example, explained the iconography and meaning of deities and symbols belonging to complex tantric cycles as portrayed in *maṇḍalas* (Tucci, 1980: 129-130). But before him, Bu ston Rin chen grub (1290-1364) played a crucial role in accelerating the process of standardization of iconography by sifting the contents of a vast mass of religious literature, following historical criteria and exegetical methods. His contribution to iconographic literature is invaluable, considering the huge editorial work which he undertook on all available collections of Buddhist texts in Tibet, whose final outcome was the compilation of the Buddhist canon, first of the bKa' 'gyur (see Harrison, in this volume), and later of the bsTan 'gyur. Furthermore, his history of Buddhism in India and Tibet (1347), the first *chos 'byung* (see van der Kuijp, in this volume) to be written in Tibet, which includes the description of the lineages of kings as well as of religious masters belonging to different schools, not only was a model for subsequent history writers (Tucci, 1980: 142), but also provided a useful chronological frame for generations of artists to come. In particular Bu ston drew and gave all the necessary instructions to paint, carve and cast images of masters, *maṇḍalas* and cycles of deities in the temples on the upper stories at the monastery of Zhwa lu, southern Tibet (Ruegg: 21a-22a; see also Tucci, 1980: 660; Vitali, 1990: 110). He prepared the *lha 'bums* ("one hundred thousand deities"), namely the iconographic descriptions of the *maṇḍalas* belonging to different tantric cycles (see Ruegg: 21b-22a) and a whole volume of his Collected Works is devoted to the description of the *maṇḍalas* painted on the walls of those temples. Bu ston is portrayed and mentioned in several inscriptions in the temples and chapels distributed on the eight floors of one of the most important artistic monuments in Tibet, the Great Stūpa erected during the second quarter of the fifteenth century at rGyal rtse. These inscriptions contain specific references to Bu ston's *lha 'bums* as well as the names of the scholars who personally planned, directed and surveyed the work of the teams of painters and sculptors that decorated the more than seventy chapels and temples of the Great Stūpa (Tucci, 1941, IV/2: 72-73, 96, 102, 109; see also 200, 216, 240, 246, 252). Their constant references to specific texts, including a detailed discussion drawn from Bu ston's guide to Zhwa lu in order to account for the choice of one iconographic source to the exclusion of others (92-93; see also 235-237), well illustrate the important role played by that great scholar in shaping the iconographic literature of Tibet.

Among religious texts, an important source of inspiration traditionally has been provided by the legendary accounts of the Buddha's past lives. In particular, the *Avadānakalpalatā* (by the eleventh-century Kashmiri poet Kṣemendra), translated into Tibetan in the thirteenth century and accessible to artists in a simplified prose version (see Tucci, 1980: 441), was illustrated in sets of painted scrolls and xylographs. Also the *mDo mdzangs blun* ("The Sūtra of the Wise and the Fool"), a popular collection of tales translated from Chinese into Tibetan by the Chinese scholar Facheng (known in Tibetan as Chos grub; fl. 770-858), was represented in wall paintings. In general, the hagiographic literature on Indian and Tibetan saints (see Robinson, in this volume), describing the more or less legendary lives of tantric adepts (*siddhas*) and other religious teachers, has traditionally provided unique sources to the painters and woodcutters entrusted to illustrate the lives of greater and smaller masters, as is shown by the captions that are often painted under each episode in biographical scrolls (see, for example, Tucci, 1980: 418-437; Snellgrove, 1967: pls. 49-45; Dollfus, 1991: 50-71).

Iconometric Literature

The bsTan 'gyur includes four Indian works specifically devoted to iconometry, but, in practice, the theory of the proportions of the image of the Buddha in Tibet is based upon three religious texts found in the Buddhist canon: chapter 30 of the *Mahāsaṃvarodaya Tantra*; chapter 5 of the *Kālacakra Tantra*; and the *Pratimālakṣaṇa Sūtra*, generally known in Tibet as *Sha ri'i bus zhus pa'i mdo*, of which four different versions have been known to Tibetan artists (Tucci, 1980: 291-292). The *Mahāsaṃvarodaya Tantra* states that the figure of the standing Buddha measures 120 digits (*aṅgula, sor mo*). However, the *Kālacakra Tantra* asserts that the figure of the Buddha measures a few more digits than 120, which led commentators to interpret this as meaning 125 digits (Peterson: 241-242, 246, table I; Jackson: 144-147). This prompted Ratnarakṣita, one of the last Indian scholars to find shelter in the Nepal Valley in the first half of the thirteenth century and the author of a commentary on the *Mahāsaṃvarodaya Tantra*, to amend the measurements of the Buddha figure contained therein, by stating that they amounted to 125 digits (Jackson: 145, 147, n. 14), thus implying that the *Tantra* was in error and should conform with the *Kālacakra Tantra* tradition. The lack of clarity of the *Kālacakra Tantra* on this point aroused discussions which lasted for centuries, but generally the theory of the five extra digits prevailed, being accepted by the great scholar and painter Padma dkar po (1526-1592) (*BKNS*: 310) and by other artists down to this century. One of the greatest scholars in Tibet, the regent Sangs rgyas rgya mtsho (1653-1705), wrote a text recording the proportions of the eight different types of stūpa (Tucci, 1980: 136-137) and attempting to solve the discrepancy between the *Kālacakra Tantra* and the *Mahāsaṃvarodaya Tantra*. In that text, which is part of the *Vaiḍūrya g.ya sel*, an encyclopedic work devoted to astrology, chronology and history, Sangs rgyas rgya mtsho tried to reconcile the two traditions by suggesting that the measurement of 120 digits ought to apply to painted figures and that of 125 to statues, thus allowing for the additional depth of three-dimensional images (Jackson: 144; Peterson: 243). The regent's suggestion was rejected by the famous artist and scholar Zhu chen Tshul khrims rin chen (1697-1769), who found out that it was the consequence of a spurious interlinear note added by a scribe or editor in a treatise written by the religious artist 'Phreng kha ba dPal blo bzang po (1543-1588) (Jackson: 145). Tshul khrims rin chen followed the tradition of allowing 125 digits to the Buddha figure, 120 to peaceful bodhisattvas, and so forth, with a decreasing number of digits for each of the four other categories of figures, according to the sixfold classification he adopted (Jackson: 50).

Tibetan scholars could not agree on the number of the categories of figures either. Bu ston and the eighth Black Hat Karma pa Mi bskyod rdo rje (1507-1554), for example, apparently divided them into eleven groups, but the Tibetan encyclopaedist Klong rdol bla ma (1719-1805) reduced them to four (Jackson: 50, 67, n. 4; Tucci, 1980: 299) and adopted the 120-digit measurement for the Buddha figure. Present-day artists, such as the eastern Tibetan painter dGe 'dun (18-19), are aware of the co-existence of two different traditions. Furthermore, later Tibetan writers on iconometry pointed out that several categories of figures could not be traced to canonical sources. In particular, Rong tha Blo bzang dam chos rgya mtsho (1863-1917) states that the measurements of the proportions of two classes of wrathful deities originated from an oral tradition which was based upon the correct measures of ancient Indian images (Jackson: 147).

Since Tibetan artists in practice resort to detailed drawing displaying the proportions of the various categories of figures rather than to textual sources (Lo Bue, 1990: 188-194), it may be suggested that iconometric texts are seldom more than displays of erudition by literati who are little concerned with their practical application by artists. They are often incomplete and tend to take for granted a great deal of knowledge from the reader, in a manner that is characteristic of their Indian models. Padma dkar po (*BKNS*: 309, 312), for example, is very helpful when he explains the Indian numerical symbols used in the *Śrīcaturpīṭha Tantra*, where the "eyes of the sky" means 20 digits; the "king," 16; the "sun," 12; and the "water treasure," namely the ocean, 4. However, his description of the measurements of the proportions of the stūpa of the Enlightenment type leaves out those of the discs making up the spire, and suffers even when compared with Klong rdol bla ma's description, however incomplete (Padma dkar po, *CTGK*: 319-322; Klong rdol bla ma, *ZDSB*: 760-761). This kind of carelessness is typical of a scholarly literature that is chiefly aimed at the accumulation of religious merit rather than at the transmission of practical information.

Handbooks for Artists

In the Tibetan cultural context, where literary production tends to be a scholarly exercise meant to accumulate religious merit, one can hardly expect to come across handbooks especially aimed at artists, such as Cennino Cennini's *Il libro dell'arte*, relating details of techniques and of the preparation of materials. Tantric Buddhist texts like Buddhaguhya's *Dharmamaṇḍala Sūtra*, which is specifically devoted to the subject of *maṇḍalas*, contain very little information on materials (see for instance Lo Bue, 1987: 795, vv. 42-44) and techniques, being more concerned with problems of classification and the explanation of symbolic meanings. Even when such texts include information on the materials to be used for painting and modelling the images of tantric deities, this betrays a strong concern for their symbolic value. The passage in the *Hevajra Tantra* giving instructions on how to obtain the pigments to paint the *maṇḍala* of Hevajra is a case in point: "Black colouring is obtained from charcoal of the cemetery, white from ground human bones, yellow from ochre, red from cemetery bricks, green from *caurya* leaves and ground human bones, and dark blue from ground human bones and cemetery charcoal."[1] The advice given to sculptors in the *Kṛṣṇa-Yamārī Tantra* is not less significant: "The image of Yamārī, with one face and two arms, should be made from clay mixed with ashes from a funeral pyre of the flesh of a brahmin" (Pal: 14).

Our first quotation from the *Hevajra Tantra*, with these two just cited, gives us the impression of facing here a tradition of tantric practitioners who were scarcely concerned with the actual practice of art. I have pointed out elsewhere how irrelevant that kind of tradition is to the artists' practice (Lo Bue, 1990). Bearing this in mind, we shall now turn our attention to the few available sources dealing with materials and techniques.

Among the scholars who wrote on the materials used in art, mention should be made of Des dmar dGe bshes bsTan 'dzin phun tshogs, an influential eighteenth-century writer.[2] The accounts on statuary metals by Padma dkar po, 'Jigs med gling pa (1729-1798) and Klong rdol bla ma contain some information on the alloys, but very little on modelling, casting and embossing techniques (see Lo Bue, 1981). A long chapter on metals and one on bells are contained in a manuscript kept at the British Museum, London.[3] Other scholars wrote on the materials used in painting, for instance Sum pa mKhan po (1704-1788), who dealt also with methods, and Mi pham rgya mtsho (1846-1912), who wrote on the preparation of colors, ink and gold for painting (Jackson: 23, n. 1; 80, 90-93). Bo dong Paṇ chen (1375-1451), along with the two last-mentioned scholars, also dealt with the theory of colors, but one of the best and most detailed accounts on pigments and their combinations was written by Rong tha Blo bzang dam chos rgya mtsho (Jackson: 92). Of late, also in connection with a renewed Western interest in Tibetan art, a few practical handbooks have been produced: Rong tha's volume on the theory of proportions (*TGLL*), along with his three volumes devoted to the creation of *maṇḍalas* (1971-73); and two volumes by an outstanding eastern Tibetan painter, dGe dga' bla ma (b. 1931),[4] who based his work (1983) on several sources, particularly the *Blo gsal dgyes pa'i rol mo* by the eighth Zhwa nag Karma pa (1983: 7). Mention also should be made of a volume (*BKRM*) by the northeastern Tibetan painter 'Jam dbyangs blo gsal (b. ca. 1913).[5]

No image may be regarded as complete unless it has undergone the *rab gnas* ritual of consecration, which is meant to establish in it the grace and wisdom of the particular deity or master represented. Special texts explain how the consecration ceremony ought to be performed (see Bentor, in this volume). But first of all, various holy articles, such as sacred invocations written on strips of paper, relics, medicinal and precious substances, coins, grains, small stūpas and other offerings are lodged inside the hollows of statues and sealed, while sacred invocations or the hand-prints of a master are drawn on the reverse side of painted scrolls. The holy contents of a statue must be placed not haphazardly, but following a special ceremony (*gzungs 'bul gyi cho ga*) as laid down in the relevant texts (Dagyab: 32-33). This kind of ritual literature may be regarded as related to art, too.

Art History

Most of the available information on the history of Tibetan art is scattered in historical and hagiographical literature, in guides to famous pilgrimage sites (*gnas bshad*), in accounts of religious pilgrimages (*lam yig*; see J. Newman, in this volume), as well as in the inscriptions found in temples or on images. There is very little literature specifically devoted to the history of art. References to foreign artists in Tibet during the monarchic period (seventh to ninth century) occur in the *sBa bzhed*, a historical account attributed to gSal snang, a minister of the sBa clan (second half of the eighth century), which underwent subsequent editing, possibly up to the thirteenth century (Stein, 1961: vi).[6] Another useful source for the history of early artistic monuments in Tibet is the *mKhas pa'i dga' ston* (1564) by dPa' bo gTsug lag 'phreng ba (1504-1566),[7] who made use of ancient records that were subsequently lost. Local histories often include detailed information on the construction and decoration of religious buildings. The history of the princes of rGyal rtse, for example, contains many references to the erection of a number of monasteries, temples, stūpas and images in the Myang (or Nyang) area of southern Tibet.[8] Also the *Myang chos 'byung*, an important text recently attributed to Tāranātha (*MYTM*: Editor's Foreword),[9] gives a wealth of historical information on a number of monasteries in Myang, including details of the statues and paintings found in the temples at rGyal rtse, the dates of their foundation, completion and consecration, as well as the names of the donors and of the masters who performed the *rab gnas* ceremonies.

Hagiographies are equally useful sources for art historians to the extent that they record the works of art commissioned by religious masters or restored on their behalf, although they hardly ever mention the names of the artists who were involved in those undertakings. The biography of Tsong kha pa and the autobiography of Tāranātha give details of the restoration work which they carried out on various old temples and stūpas (Tucci, 1980: 164, 190, 197, 200) and of the decoration they undertook in newly constructed buildings. In this connection, mention should be made of Bu ston's biography for remarks concerning Zhwa lu, of the biography of Kun dga' rin chen (1517-1584) for Sa skya (this is a very useful complement to the guide to Sa skya attributed to that master; see Tucci, 1980: 156), of the biography of the second Paṇ chen Lama (1663-1737) for bKra shis lhun po (Tucci, 1980: 133, 161), and of the fifth Dalai Lama's autobiography, where the Great Fifth recorded even the names of some artists who decorated the Potala Palace (Tucci, 1980: 278). In three volumes of his Collected Works, the fifth Dalai Lama also reported the inscriptions which he dictated on the occasion of the consecration of religious buildings and objects. These volumes constitute a precious document for the history of Tibetan art, since they mention the names of artists and donors (Tucci, 1980: 135). Interesting information relevant to art history also may be gathered from the fifth Dalai Lama's history of Tibet (*BKGR*, 1643), dealing with its princely clans, partially translated by Tucci (1980: 625-656).

A most important source for art historians is provided by the inscriptions sometimes found on images and paintings. They are generally written in the ornate style (*alaṃkāra*) based on the Indian *kāvya*, with dedicatory verses explaining the occasion for which the images were executed and giving the names of their donors. The inscriptions painted on the walls of the temples and chapels of the Great Stūpa and of the main temple at rGyal rtse give us a wealth of information on the paintings and statues, including their iconographic sources, the names and occupations of their donors, the names and places of origin of the artists, as well as the names of the scholars who supervised their work (Tucci, 1941, IV/1: passim). Similar detailed information may be gathered from the guides to monasteries listing religious items and holy relics, boasting of their miraculous powers, and recording the stays of particularly famous masters. These guides, generally called *dkar chag* ("list," "catalogue"; see Martin, in this volume) are, in fact, eulogies extolling the virtues of the institutions for which they were composed. Also, the accounts of travels and pilgrimages by famous masters can provide useful information on religious art. An interesting *lam yig* (*GJBT*) was compiled by Kaḥ thog Si tu Chos kyi rgya mtsho (1880-1925), a student of 'Jam dbyangs mkhyen brtse'i dbang po (1820-1892), the author of a famous guide to the holy places of central and southern Tibet (*HDSB*), where mention is made of the chief art works contained in the monasteries.[10] Kaḥ thog Si tu traveled in the same regions from 1918 to 1920, and described the monastic foundations he visited, including the religious enclave at rGyal rtse (*GJBT:* 392-401), to which his master devotes only a few lines (Ferrari: ff. 16b-17a; *HDSB*: 35-36).

At least three short texts may be regarded as truly art-historical, not only because they provide the names of artists and art schools in a chronological sequence, but also on account of their attempts to differentiate them on stylistic grounds. That is particularly true of two related texts dealing with Buddhist statuary in India and Tibet up to the fifteenth century. One was written in verse by Padma dkar po (*LMTP*), while the other is anonymous and, in the main, a transcription of the former with a few alterations in the wording (Tucci, 1959: 180). The anonymous manuscript is incomplete, and deals with more or less related subjects: musical instruments, silk, cups, tea, weapons. It is interesting also from a linguistic point of view, being greatly influenced by the spoken language of southern Tibet and, in the section dealing with statuary, by the Bhutanese dialect (Tucci, 1959: 179). Thus, it is a precious document of the colloquial language of those regions, which seldom finds its way into texts and dictionaries. The third text is a passage in the autocommentary written by 'Jam mgon Kong sprul (1811-1899) for the few, cryptic, ambiguous and altogether too compact verses he devotes to the origin of religious art in Tibet, with particular reference to the schools of painting. The verses and their commentary make up the fourth chapter in the fourth section of his encyclopaedic work *Shes bya kun khyab* (1970, I-III: 570-573; 1982, I; 38-39, 575-578), dealing with the origin of arts and sciences. Although Kong sprul is not a remarkable writer from a stylistic point of view, the prose of his autocommentary is usually lucid and literary in style (Smith: 37).

Conclusion

The study of Tibetan literature dealing with art is still in its infancy and a comprehensive book on the history of Tibetan art is still to be written. Tibetan literature specifically devoted to the arts and crafts is relatively scarce, and relevant information is generally scattered in texts often untranslated and belonging to different literary genres. As a rule, technical information on art is handed down in workshops from master to pupil, and it may be suggested that the bulk of Tibetan literature dealing with art is oral. Research in this particular area requires knowledge both of the Tibetan language and of the various disciplines making up the body of the culture and civilization of Tibet.

Notes

1. I follow Snellgrove's translation, except for the term *ldong ros*, which I translate as "ochre" (see Jackson: 175, "realgar"), instead of "green lac" (Snellgrove, 1976, I: 51; II: 9).

2. This master, whose initial epithet is also spelled *Dil dmar*, wrote a text on arts and crafts (*RPZY*; see Dagyab: 132, No. 288), of which an incomplete manuscript is kept at the Library of the School of Oriental and African Studies (University of London) under the access number MS177045. Another text by the same author is mentioned by Jackson: 179.

3. *Rin po che bzo yi las kyi bsgrub pa'i rgyud dang ja dang dar gos chen dang rta rgyud tshugs bzang ngan gyi thegs* (British Museum, Ms Or. 11374, 136 ff.). I am grateful to Ms. H. Helffer for drawing my attention to this text, which belongs to the Charles Bell Collection.

4. I met and interviewed this painter during my fieldwork in 1978, under the sponsorship of the Central Research Fund, University of London.

5. I met and interviewed this painter during my fieldwork in 1978, under the sponsorship of the Central Research Fund, University of London.

6. Besides Stein's edition of 1961 there exist two recent editions of this text: *TPKS* and *BZCB*.

7. Besides Lokesh Chandra's edition of this text, also known as *lHo grag chos 'byung*, there is also a recent one published in China: *CBKG*.

8. There exist apparently two editions of this text, completed in 1481, by 'Jigs med grags pa, a religious scholar who was known by the title of Phyogs thams cad rnam par rgyal ba: *DPLT*, which was published in a partial translation by Tucci (1980: 662-670) under the heading "From the Chronicles of Gyantse"; and *GTCG*, which is kept in the Tucci Fund at IsMEO, Rome. The text translated by Tucci has disappeared, whereas *GTCG* appears to be identical with *DRDN* and *RTKZ*.

9. It is not clear on which grounds this attribution is made, for the text does not appear in the list of contents of Tāranātha's Collected Works, where only his *gnas bshad* to Jo nang is mentioned (Lokesh Chandra: 21 and 91, No. 545). If this work was indeed written by Tāranātha it is strange that there is no

mention in it of the Great Stūpa of rGyal rtse, the most important artistic monument in Myang, built a century and a half before Tāranātha's time. For a discussion on the authorship and date of this text see Tucci, 1941, vol. IV/1: 41-45.

10. There exist at least three editions of mKhyen brtse's guide (Ferrari: xx-xxi).

References

Bu ston Rin chen grub

ZLTI *Zha lu'i gtsug lag khang gi gzhal yas khang nub ma byang ma shar ma lho ma rnams na bzhugs pa'i dkyil 'khor sogs kyi dkar chag*. In his gSung 'bum (Collected Works). New Delhi reprint reproduced by Lokesh Chandra: *The Collected Works of Bu-ston*, 1969, part 17 (vol. *tsa*).

Dagyab, Loden Sherap

1977 *Tibetan Religious Art*, part I. Wiesbaden: Otto Harrassowitz.

Dalai Lama V, Ngag dbang blo bzang rgya mtsho

BKGR *Bod kyi rgyal rabs rdzogs ldan gzhon nu'i dga' ston*. *Early History of Tibet*. Ed. by Ngawang Gelek Demo. Delhi: 1967.

Des dmar dGe bshes bsTan 'dzin phun tshogs

RPZY *Rig pa bzo yi gnas kyi las tshogs phran tshegs 'dod rgur bsgyur ba spra phab 'od kyi snang brnyan*. Unpublished manuscript. School of Oriental and African Studies Library, University of London.

Dollfus, Paul

1990 "Peintures tibétaines de la vie de Mi-la-ras-pa." *Arts asiatiques* 47: pp. 50-71.

dPa' bo gTsug lag 'phreng ba

KPGT *Chos 'byung mKhas pa'i dga' ston*, part 4 (*ja*). Reproduced by Lokesh Chandra. New Delhi: International Academy of Indian Culture, 1962.

CBKG *Dam pa'i chos kyi 'khor lo bsgyur ba rnams kyi byung ba gsal bar byed pa mkhas pa'i dga' ston*. 2 vols. Beijing: Mi rigs dpe skrun khang, 1986.

Ferrari, Alfonsa

1985 *mK'yen brtse's Guide to the Holy Places of Central Tibet*. Rome: Istituto Italiano per il Medio ed Estremo Oriente.

Gega Lama (dGe dga' bla ma)

1983 *Principles of Tibetan Art*, vol. 1. Darjeeling.

Jackson, David P. and Janice A.

1984 *Tibetan Thangka Painting: Methods and Materials*. London: Serindia Publications.

'Jam mgon kong sprul Yon tan rgya mtsho

RNZB *Rig gnas zhar byung dang bcas brjod pa'i skabs*. In his *Shes byung kun khyab*. New Delhi reprint reproduced by Lokesh Chandra, with an introduction by E. Gene Smith: *Kongtrul's Encyclopaedia of Indo-Tibetan Culture* (1970), parts I-III, ff. 17a-20a and 198a-224b. In the Beijing edition (1982), vol. *stod*, pp. 36-42 and 556-608.

Jamyang ('Jam dbyangs blo gsal)

BKRM *Bod kyi ri mo 'bri tshul deb gsar kun phan nyi ma. New Self-Learning Book on the Art of Tibetan Painting*. Dharamsala.

'Jam dbyangs mkhyen brtse'i dbang po

HDSB *lHa ldan sogs dbus 'gyur chos sde khag dang yar lung lho rgyud gtsang stod byang rwa sgreng rgyal ba'i 'byung gnas sogs kyi rten gnas po'i gnas yig ngo mtshar lung ston me long*. Dharamsala: Tibetan Cultural Printing Press, 1979.

'Jigs med grags pa

DPLT *Dad pa'i lo thog rgyas byed dngos grub kyi char 'bebs*. Unpublished manuscript (see note 8).

DRDN *Dharma ra dza'i rnam thar dad pa'i lho thog*.... Dharamsala: Library of Tibetan Works and Archives, 1978.

GTCG *rGyal rtse chos rgyal gyi rnam par thar pa dad pa'i lo thog dngos grub kyi char 'bebs*. Unpublished manuscript at the Istituto Italiano per il Medio ed Estremo Oriente, Rome.

RTKZ *Rab brtan kun bzang 'phags kyi rnam thar*. Lhasa: Bod ljongs mi dmangs dpe skrun khang, 1987.

Kaḥ thog Si tu chos kyi rgya mtsho

GJBT *An Account of a Pilgrimage to Central Tibet during the Years 1918 to 1920, being the text of Gangs ljongs dbus gtsang gnas bskor lam yig nor bu zla shel gyi se mo do*. Palampur reprint reproduced from the original Tibetan xylograph by Khams sprul Don brgyud nyi ma, 1972.

Karmay, Samten

1988 *Secret Visions of the Fifth Dalai Lama, The Gold Manuscript of the Fournier Collection*. London: Serindia.

Klong rdol bla ma Nga dbang blo bzang

ZDSB *bZo dang gso ba skar rtis rnams las byung ba'i ming gi grags*. In his gSung 'bum (Collected Works). New Delhi reprint reproduced by Lokesh Chandra from the collections of Prof. Raghu Vira: *The Collected Works of Longdol Lama*, 1973, parts 1-2, vol. *ma*, pp. 744-792.

Lo Bue, Erberto F.

1981 "Statuary Metals in Tibet and the Himālayas: History, Tradition and Modern Use," and "Casting of Devotional Images in the Himālayas: History, Tradition and Modern Techniques." In *Aspects of Tibetan Metallurgy*, pp. 33-86. Ed by W. A. Oddy and W. Zwalf. British Museum Occasional Papers, No. 15.

1987 "The Dharmamaṇḍala-sūtra by Buddhaguhya." In *Orientalia Iosephi Tucci Memoriae Dicata*, part 2, pp. 787-818. Ed by G. Gnoli and L. Lanciotti. Rome: Istituto Italiano per il Medio ed Estremo Oriente.

1990 "Iconographic Sources and Iconometric Literature in Tibetan and Himalayan Art." In *Indo-Tibetan Studies*. Ed. by T. Skorupski. Tring: The Institute of Buddhist Studies.

Lokesh Chandra

1981 *Materials for a History of Tibetan Literature*. Kyoto: Rinsen Book Co.

Padma dkar po

BKNS *Bris sku'i rnam bshad mthong ba don ldan*. In his *Collected Works*. Darjeeling reprint reproduced from the Byang chub gling blocks (1973), chapter VII (*ja*), pp. 307-317.

CTGK *mChod rten brgyad kyi thig rtsa*. In his *Collected Works*. Darjeeling reprint reproduced from the Byang chub gling blocks (1973), chapter VIII (*nya*), pp. 319-323.

LMTP *Li ma brtag pa'i rab byed smra 'dod pa'i kha rgyan*. In his *Collected Works*. Darjeeling reprint reproduced from the Byang chub gling blocks (1973), chapter VI (*cha*), pp. 293-306.

Pal, Pratapaditya

1974 *The Arts of Nepal*, part I. Leiden: E. J. Brill.

Peterson, Kathleen

1980 "Sources of Variation in Tibetan Canons of Iconometry." In *Tibetan Studies in Honour of Hugh Richardson*. Ed by M. Aris and Aung San Suu Kyi. Warminster: Aris & Phillips.

Rong tha Blo bzang dam chos rgya mtsho

1971-73 *The Creation of Maṇḍalas: Tibetan Texts Detailing the Techniques for Laying Out and Executing Tantric Buddhist Psychocosmograms*. 3 vols. New Delhi: Don 'grub rdo rje.

TGLL *Thig gi lag len du ma gsal bar bshad pa bzo rig mdzes pa'i kha rgyan*. New Delhi: Byams pa chos rgyal, 1967(?).

Ruegg, David Seyfort

1966 *The Life of Bu ston Rin po che*. Rome: Istituto Italiano per il Medio ed Estremo Oriente.

sBa gSal snang

BZCB *sBa bzhed ces bya ba las sba gsal snang gi bzhed pa*. Beijing: Mi rigs dpe skrun khang, 1982.

TPKS *bTsan po Khri srong lde btsan dang mKhan po slob dpon Padma'i dus mdo sngags so sor mdzad pa'i sba bzhed gtags ma*. Dharamsala: Tibetan Educational Printing Press, n.d.

sGa stod gNas bzang ba dGe 'dun

KZKT *sKu gzugs kyi thig rtsa dam pa gong ma rnams kyi man ngag mngon du phyung ba blo dman 'jug bde 'dzam bu'i chu gser: Canonical Proportions for the Representation of the Buddhas, Bodhisattvas, and Tutelary and Protective Deities*. Paro: Ngodrup and Sherab Demy, 1978.

Smith, E. Gene

See 'Jam mgon Kong sprul

Snellgrove, David

1967 *Four Lamas of Dolpo*, vol. I. Oxford: Bruno Cassirer.

1976 *The Hevajra Tantra*, parts 1 and 2. London: Oxford University Press.

Stein, Rolf A.

1961 *Une chronique ancienne de bSam-yas: sBa-bžed*. Paris: Institut des Hautes Études Chinoises.

1981 *La civilisation tibétaine*. Paris: L'Asiathèque-Le Sycomore.

Tāranātha(?)

1983 *Myang yul stod smad bar gsum gyi ngo mtshar gtam gyi legs bshad mkhas pa'i 'jug ngogs*. Lhasa: Bod ljongs mi dmangs dpe skrun khang.

Tucci, Giuseppe

1932 *Indo-Tibetica*, vol. I. Rome: Reale Accademia d'Italia.

1941 *Indo-Tibetica*, vol. IV, parts 1 and 2. Rome: Reale Accademia d'Italia.

1959 "A Tibetan Classification of Buddhist Images, According to Their Style." *Artibus Asiae* 22: 179-187.

1980 *Tibetan Painted Scrolls*. 2 vols. Kyoto: Rinsen Book Co.

Vitali, Roberto

1990 *Early Temples of Central Tibet*. London: Serindia.

Chapter 29

Itineraries to Sambhala

John Newman

Introduction

Tibetan travellers wrote accounts of their journeys called *lam yig*, which we may translate as "route descriptions," or "itineraries." Such texts are a subspecies of the genre Turrell V. Wylie appropriately designates "religious geography."[1] In the introduction to his history of Buddhism in A mdo, Brag dgon zhabs drung dKon mchog bstan pa rab rgyas (nineteenth century) lists a number of these itineraries,[2] several of which are extant and have been studied by Western scholars:

(1) *rGya gar lam yig* ("Itinerary to India") of Chag Chos rje dpal (1197-1264) (Roerich, 1959 and *LSDMG*).[3]

(2) *Bal yul gyi lam yig* ("Itinerary to Nepal") of lHa mthong bShes gnyen rnam rgyal (born 1512).[4]

(3) *rDo rje gdan gyi lam yig* ("Itinerary to Vajrāsana," i.e., Bodh Gaya).[5]

(4) *O rgyan lam yig* ("Itinerary to Uḍḍiyāna," i.e., Swat), presumably that of U rgyan pa Rin chen dpal (1230-1309) (Tucci, 1940).[6]

(5) *Sha mbha la'i lam yig* ("Itinerary to Sambhala") of Man lung Guru and Chos rje 'Byor ldan grags pa (see below).

Several well-known *lam yig* are noticeably absent from dKon mchog bstan pa rab rgyas's list, e.g.:

(1) *Po ta la'i lam yig* ("Itinerary to Potala") (Tucci, 1948-51: 179-186).
(2) *Kalāpāvatāra* (*KA*; Tib. *Ka lā par 'jug pa*, "Itinerary to Kalāpa," the capital of Sambhala) (see below).
(3) *Grub pa'i gnas chen po shambha la'i rnam bshad 'phags yul gyi rtogs brjod dang bcas pa ngo mtshar bye ba'i 'byung gnas zhes bya ba* (*NTBBN*; a.k.a. *Shambha la'i lam yig*) of Paṇ chen Blo bzang dpal ldan ye shes (see below).

Although all of the above *lam yig* are mainly concerned with pilgrimage—travel to Buddhist sacred sites—when we compare the two groups of itineraries we notice that the journeys they depict are qualitatively different. The first group describes straightforward routes open to the ordinary traveller. The latter journeys are reserved for the tantric adept (*siddha*, *grub thob*) who has the magic powers necessary to overcome natural and supernatural obstacles on the way. Both types of *lam yig* are represented among the itineraries to Sambhala.[7]

Sambhala

To understand the development of the Tibetan itineraries to Sambhala we must first examine the notions of Sambhala found in earlier Hindu and Buddhist Indian literature. The toponym "Sambhala" first appears in the Hindu prophetic myth of Kalki in the *Mahābhārata* and the *Purāṇas*. In Hindu texts Sambhala is a Brahman village, of undetermined location, that will be the birthplace of Kalki, the future messianic incarnation of Viṣṇu. At the end of the current degenerate Kali age, it is said, Viṣṇu will incarnate as the pious Brahman warrior Kalki, who will rid the earth of barbarians and unruly members of the lower castes. Kalki's apocalyptic war will purify the world, re-establish Brahman dominance of the social order, and thus institute a new age of righteousness (see, e.g., O'Flaherty: 235-237, 333).

The Vaiṣṇava myth of Kalki was borrowed and adapted by the authors of the Indian Buddhist Kālacakra ("Wheel of Time") Tantra literature. In the Kālacakra texts Sambhala is no longer a mere village—it is a mighty kingdom at the center of a vast empire consisting of ninety-six great lands and more than a *billion* villages (Newman, 1987: 289, 298, 307, etc.; cf. 1985: 54-58). This Buddhist Sambhala is the homeland of a long dynasty of bodhisattva kings known by the title *kalkin* (Tib. *rigs ldan*), an epithet which in the Buddhist literature means "chieftain." It is prophesied that at the end of the Kali age the last Buddhist *kalkin*, Raudra Cakrin, will lead the army of Sambhala in a great holy war that will obliterate the forces of Islam (Newman, 1985; 1987: 578-654; 1989a; 1989b).

We are confronted here with a case of religious syncretism: the Buddhists have appropriated a Hindu myth and refashioned it to suit their own purposes. With this sort of birthright one would expect the Buddhist Sambhala to be a mere phantasm, and any effort to locate it an exercise in futility. In fact, things are not so simple.

The Indian Kālacakra literature gives clear indications of the location of its Sambhala. Sambhala is north of India, and it is north of the Śītā River, which we may identify with the Tarim River in Eastern Turkestan.[8] Also, a passage dealing with astronomy clearly locates Sambhala relative to other identifiable countries: Sambhala is on a latitude to the north of Tibet, Khotan, and China.[9] If we combine these two pieces of information, that Sambhala is to the north of China, and is north of the Tarim River, we see that the Indian Kālacakra literature locates Sambhala in the region north of the Tian Shan.

The question arises, why did the authors of the Indian Kālacakra literature adopt the Hindu myth of Sambhala, transform it into a mighty kingdom, and locate it in Central Asia? The Kālacakra's mythic history was devised in part as a response to contemporaneous (early eleventh century) Muslim incursions into northwestern India. It displays an acute awareness of the threat the new ideology of Islam posed for Buddhists and Hindus alike. Thus, the Indian Buddhist myth of Sambhala was fashioned partly as a reaction to current religio-political conditions: the Kālacakra countered the Muslim raids on northwest India with an apocolyptic vision of a holy war to be carried out by a bodhisattva messiah from Central Asia (Newman, 1985: 78-80; 1987: 626-638; 1989a; 1989b).

Almost simultaneous with its introduction in India, Tibetans became ardent followers of the Kālacakra.[10] Given the fairly clear indications of Sambhala's geographical location in the Kālacakra literature, it is not surprising that Tibetans should be interested in the route to this holy land.[11]

The *rMi lam rdzun bshad sgyu ma'i sgra dbyangs chen mo*

The earliest datable Tibetan itinerary to Sambhala is that of Man lung Guru (born 1239).[12] We do not know what form Man lung Guru's itinerary originally circulated in—as we have it today it is embedded in the fourth chapter (ff. 15a3-17b1) of an anonymous work entitled *rMi lam rdzun bshad sgyu ma'i sgra dbyangs chen mo* (*MLDS*).[13] This *lam yig* describes the route to Sambhala in rather matter-of-fact terms: One leaves Bhaktapur, Nepal (Tib. Khu khom)[14] and travels north to the region of Khotan (Li yul). Nearby is the Tarim River (Shing rta, i.e., the Śitā), which flows from west to east, and in this region live the Uighurs (Hor). North of the Tarim lie the mountains (the Tian Shan) that make up the southern boundary of Sambhala. Sambhala is a general name for northern portions of "small Jambudvīpa," the Kālacakra designation for what we would call Central Asia (*MLDS*: 15a3-15b1).

The *lam yig* also gives an alternative route to Sambhala: From central Tibet one travels to mNga' ris Mang yul in western Tibet. From there one goes to Turkestan (sTod hor gyi yul), and on to the lands of the Mongols (Sog po'i yul), finally reaching the center of Sambhala in no more than two or three years (*MLDS*: 17a4-5).

The author of this itinerary claims personally to have seen the king of Sambhala deliver a religious sermon to a large audience (*MLDS*: 16a4-6), and he takes great offense at sceptics who would doubt the credibility of his knowledge of Sambhala (*MLDS*: 19b1-20a1). At the same time, he accuses the Sa skya hierarch 'Phags pa of having fabricated an extensive account of Sambhala in order venally to deceive (*zog 'tshong*) the Mongol emperor, presumably referring to Qubilai Khan.[15]

The *lam yig*'s description of Sambhala is a curious mélange of elements drawn from the canonical Indian Kālacakra literature (primarily the *Vimalaprabhā*), erstwhile *realia* (the architecture, diet, and clothing of the Sambhalese), and the obligatory travellers' sexology.[16] However, there is nothing extraordinary about the actual *route* to Sambhala—it is presented as though any Tibetan with sufficient yaks and roasted barley flour could go there. Things are quite different with the next *lam yig* we will examine.

The *Kalāpāvatāra*

We do not know when or where the *Kalāpāvatāra* (*KA*) was composed,[17] but the Tibetans first came to know of it when it was translated from the Sanskrit by rGyal khams pa Tāranātha (1575-1634). Tāranātha's colophon states that he translated the text from a Nepalese manuscript, and received assistance on difficult points from a Brahman pandit named Kṛṣṇa.

The *KA* is an unusual and interesting piece of literature, a sort of tantric Baedeker.[18] It begins like a Buddhist *sūtra*, describing Mañjuśrī dwelling on a mountain named *Mahendra. Avalokiteśvara goes there, and by means of a dialogue the two impart myriads of Mahāyāna teachings to the gods, demons, ghosts, dragons, and humans there. Five hundred people of Kośala, Vaiśālī, Videha, and Mithilā hear of this conversation and go to Mount *Mahendra. Since Mañjuśrī does not appear, they ask Avalokitesvara for instruction. Avalokiteśvara is pleased with their request, and he induces Ekajaṭā to request the discourse from Amoghāṅkuśa, who proceeds to describe the route to Kalāpa, the capital of Sambhala.

Amoghāṅkuśa notes that, in the future, knowledge of the Dharma will degenerate [in India], but it will be preserved in the north, in Kalāpa on Mount Kailāsa [in Sambhala]. There the people are happy and righteous, and all the *sūtras* and *tantras* of the Mahāyāna are preserved. A tantric practitioner (*sādhaka*) who seeks magical attainments (*siddhi*) both for himself and for others should propitiate his chosen deity for permission to travel to Kalāpa. Without permission he will certainly meet disaster.

Having gained authorization, the practitioner should recite one million *mantras*, and make more than one hundred thousand fire offerings to various deities. Again, without successful completion of these rites, the traveller will not reach Kalāpa, but will be punished by dragons, ghosts, and goblins on the way. The traveller then goes to the tree where the buddhas achieve enlightenment [at Bodh Gaya], worships the tree, and departs on his journey. He first goes west, takes a ship to an island, and worships a stūpa of the former Buddha Kanakamuni. Having returned to India, the pilgrim heads northeast, and then north, for six months. On a mountain named Kakari, the traveller must dig some roots while reciting the appropriate *mantra*, dry the roots, paint an image of the pig-faced goddess Mārīcī on a white slab of stone, and recite her *mantra*, requesting her to overcome obstructors and protect the practitioner. The traveller then grinds the roots and concocts a medicinal elixir. Having recited the *mantra* and worshipped the goddess, he drinks the drug, achieving freedom from hunger, thirst, and fatigue.

Further legs of the journey entail propitiation of demonesses: the bloody worship of Mandehā provides the traveller with food to cross the desert; *Vidyuccalā enables him to cross the frigid river Śītā. Additional *mantra* recitation and consumption of plant materials purify the practitioner's body, making it light and powerful. Throughout this process, it is imperative that the traveller have the right attitude of dispassionate altruism. Armed with this, and performing more rituals and overcoming more obstacles, the traveller is eventually carried to Kalāpa in the arms of sorceresses.

Kalāpa is a marvelous place, a paradise on earth. The people are free from evil, ignorance, and want, and live happy lives of at least one hundred years. Equal to its worldly delights, however, are the spiritual qualities of Kalāpa. There the accomplished practitioner will achieve transcendent and mundane *siddhis* merely by paying homage to the sacred king; less advanced adepts will receive instruction from him, enabling them quickly to attain their goals.

Having heard this wonderful discourse, the five hundred fortunate people return to their homes and teach it to others. Then they use its method to travel to Kalāpa, where they achieve *siddhi*. So ends the *Kalāpāvatāra*.

The *KA* is a very different sort of itinerary than the *MLDS*. Whereas the *MLDS* describes a route we can trace on a map, the *KA* traverses the realm of spiritual imagination. In the *KA* "real" physical geography is almost irrelevant—freezing rivers, lofty mountains, and vast wastes are for the most part unrelated to identifiable features of the earth's surface; they merely provide obstacles to be overcome through ritual purification and empowerment.[19] While the *KA* and the *MLDS* have the same goal—access to the religious teachings of Sambhala, their means are radically different. Any traveller can follow the path described by Man lung Guru; only an adept of tantric magic can hope to reach Kalāpa via the route described in the *Kalāpāvatāra*.

The *Shambha la'i lam yig* of Paṇ chen Blo bzang dpal ldan ye shes

The *Grub pa'i gnas chen po shambha la'i rnam bshad 'phags yul kyi rtogs brjod dang bcas pa ngo mtshar bye ba'i 'byung gnas* (*NTBBN*) (composed 1775), more commonly known as the *Shambha la'i lam yig*, of the third Paṇ chen Lama, Blo bzang dpal ldan ye shes (1738-1780), is the best known of the itineraries to Sambhala, no doubt due to the fact that it was the first to be translated into a European language (Grünwedel; cf. Vostrikov: 231-232; Bernbaum, 1985: 42-44 et seq.). In fact only about a fifth of the text is devoted to the actual route to Sambhala—most of it is taken up by a description of India and its political and religious history, and the remainder by an account of Sambhala and its political and religious history (cf. Vostrikov: 232). As Bernbaum (1985: 42-80) has shown, the Paṇ chen Lama's version of the journey to Sambhala is a very close, often verbatim, restatement of the *KA*'s description—thus, it contains little of independent intrinsic interest.

More interesting than the Paṇ chen's route to Sambhala, however, is his attitude toward the accessibility of this marvelous land. Subsequent to Tāranātha's translation of the *KA*, Tibetans had available two entirely different descriptions of the way to Sambhala: the "realist" itinerary of Man lung Guru, and the "spiritual" route of the *KA*. Given the choice, the Paṇ chen opted decisively for the latter. In the *NTBBN* he says: "If you wish physically to travel to [Sambhala], you must definitely have achieved the power of *mantras* and merit. Otherwise, the goblins, fierce *nāgas* and so forth will kill you on the way" (*NTBBN*: 34a2-3, cf. 34a6-35a4, 48b6-49b1; *SZKBT*: 4a5-6). Furthermore, the Paṇ chen explicitly compares the "authority" of the *KA* and the *MLDS*: he notes that Man lung Guru's *lam yig* is very easy to follow, and it contains many things that are not in accord with the "authoritative" (*tshad ldan*) itinerary, the *KA*—in brief, only the *KA* is authoritative, all other *lam yig* are false (*rdzun ma*) (*LSGK*: 5a3-5b1, 6a2-3; cf. *NTBBN*: 35a2, 50a1-2).

Why did Paṇ chen Blo bzang dpal ldan ye shes choose the metaphysical instead of the physical route to Sambhala? At least two possibilities come to mind. One is given by the fourth bTsan po No mon han sprul sku 'Jam dpal chos kyi bstan 'dzin 'phrin las (1789-1838) in his *'Dzam gling chen po'i rgyas bshad snod bcud kun gsal me long* (*NCKSML*: 202a1-203a6). The bTsan po No mon han asserts that the Sambhala taught in the Kālacakra Tantra is an "emanated city" (*sprul pa'i sgrong khyer*), and thus appears to ordinary beings in different ways. The extremely difficult route described in the *KA* is for the traveller seeking tantric *siddhi*, he says, but that does not exclude there being other ways to go there. For example, the *Po ta la'i lam yig* requires the traveller to journey under the sea and through space to reach Avalokiteśvara's palace on Potala (cf. Tucci, 1948-51: 179-187), yet Buddhagupta went there with merchants in a boat (cf. Tucci, 1931: 693). Thus, although its brevity makes it difficult to find the center of Sambhala, Man lung Guru's easy itinerary *does* provide a viable route to Sambhala. However, if non-Buddhists are given easy access to Sambhala, there is a danger that Sambhala itself could eventually be overrun by barbarians: *this*, the bTsan po No mon han says, is the reason Paṇ chen Blo bzang dpal ldan ye shes taught that one should not encourage people to travel to Sambhala.

While the Paṇ chen's concern for the sanctity of Sambhala may help us to understand his preference for the *KA* over Man lung Guru's itinerary, we may conjecture that other motives were also at work. Paṇ chen Blo bzang dpal ldan ye shes was considered by his followers, and perhaps by himself, to be a "pre-incarnation" of Kalkin Raudra Cakrin, the prophesied apocalyptic king of Sambhala.[20] By the second half of the eighteenth century the geography of the Turkic and Mongol lands was becoming more familiar to the Tibetans, and in reading the Paṇ chen's account of Sambhala one senses some uneasiness that such a vast empire was apparently nowhere to be found. Under these circumstances Man lung Guru's itinerary was something of an embarrassment. If the realistic route to Sambhala led not to a grand Buddhist empire, but to a virtual wasteland sparsely inhabited by nomads, what did this say about the Paṇ chen's future role in the Buddhist apocalypse? Better to assert that Man lung Guru's account is "false," and to protect the sacred utopia with a veil of ritual magic.[21]

Conclusion

The *lam yig* genre reflects both the religious and the geographical interests of the Tibetans. On the one hand, the Tibetans inherited a concern for sacred geography—as opposed to physical geography—along with the Indian Buddhist worldview that dominates classical Tibetan culture. The Indian itineraries in Tibetan translation (*Kalāpāvatāra* and *Po ta la'i lam yig*) treat physical geography as a virtually irrelevant backdrop for journeys of the spirit. However valuable they might be to an adept in magic, they are practically worthless for the conventional traveller.

Indigenous Tibetan *lam yig*, on the other hand, display a sense of pragmatism that is absent from the Indian texts. Tibetan itineraries are also inspired by religiosity—they describe arduous, life-threatening pilgrimages to Buddhist holy places, and they are spiced with anecdotes of strange and miraculous people and places on the way. However, there is nothing mysterious about the route descriptions they contain: they are clearly conceived as realistic accounts of actual journeys to be duplicated by other ordinary pilgrims; we can trace their routes on a map.[22] This practical concern for factuality within the context of religious endeavors (also noteworthy in the Tibetan historiographic tradition) distinguishes the Tibetan *lam yig* from its Indian antecedents. A tendency to coordinate spiritual imagination with empirical reality is an important characteristic of the Tibetan adaptation of Indian Buddhist culture.

Notes

1. "These texts are intended primarily to describe the geographical location and religious history of pilgrimage places, sacred objects, and the hermitages of former Buddhist holy men. They are devoid of specific information on physical geography per se and are better understood when thought of as *guide-books* for pilgrims visiting unfamiliar places and things" (Wylie, 1965: 17; cf. 1970: xv; Vostrikov: 217).

2. *Chag lo'i rGya gar lam yig / Bal yul gyi lam yig Lha mthong lo tsā bas mdzad pa / rDo rje gdan gyi lam yig / O rgyan lam yig / Man lung gu ru dang / Chos rje 'byor ldan grags pa'i Sha mbha la'i lam yig /* (*DTGT*: 20.4-5); cf. Vostrikov: 231. I am grateful to Dan Martin for drawing my attention to this passage.

3. We should also mention the *rGya gar gyi gnas chen khag la bgros pa'i lam yig* (first ed., Calcutta: The Mahabodhi Society, 1939) of the remarkable polymath dGe 'dun chos 'phel (1905-1951). This modern pilgrim's guide to India includes such information as train fares and mileage, as well as still valuable scholarly notes on the sacred sites he visited.

Tāranātha's account of the travels of his Indian guru Buddhagupta, the *Grub chen bu ddha gu pta'i rnam thar rje btsun nyid zhal nas gzhan du rang rtog gi dri mas ma spags pa'i yi ge yang dag pa*, studied by Tucci (1931), is not strictly speaking a *lam yig*, but it contains much interesting information on India and other regions. Tucci (1931: 684) notes that this is one of the main sources for the geographical information found in the *Sham bha la'i lam yig* of Paṇ chen Blo bzang dpal ldan ye shes, referred to below.

4. I do not know if this has any relation to the *Bal yul gnas yig* or the *Bal yul mchod rten 'phags pa shing kun dang de'i gnas gzhan rnams kyi dkar chag*, both edited by Wylie (1970: 37-48); see also Kaschewsky.

5. See Jackson: 223-224; Jackson #1510, BRS bundle no. 590: *rDo rje ldan gyi dkar chag dang lam yig*. Jackson hypothesizes that this text may be by Chag Chos rje dpal (see above), but his analysis of its contents differs markedly from the *LSDMG*.

6. In this work Tucci also studies the *Orgyan mkha' 'gro'i gling gi lam yig thar lam bgrod pa'i them skas* of sTag tshang ras pa (a.k.a. Orgyan pa) Ngag dbang rgya mtsho (seventeenth century). For further information on U rgyan pa Rin chen dpal see Roerich, 1974.

7. The Sanskrit Kālacakra literature spells this name *sambhala*; the Tibetans transliterated it as *sham bha la*. For the sake of consistency we follow the Sanskrit, except in the titles of Tibetan texts.

8. Newman, 1987: 309. The Śitā is the northern river of the four great rivers of traditional Buddhist cosmography (*Abhidharmakośabhāṣya* 3.57). Hsüan-tsang (Beal: I.12-13 and s.v.), Man lung Guru (Laufer: 404; also, see below), and the bTsan po No mon han (Wylie, 1962: 58) all describe the Śitā in ways that correspond to the Tarim, and H.W. Bailey (5) concurs with this identification.

9. *...boṭa lī ca cīnādideśesu...sambhalaviṣayāntam....*(*Vimalaprabhā*: 40a1-2).

10. Indeed, the appearance of the Tibetan word *li* ("Khotan") in the Sanskrit text of the *Vimalaprabhā* (see note 9) indicates its author was familiar with, and perhaps had contact with, Tibetans. Other passages in the *Vimalaprabhā* also support this hypothesis: see, e.g., Newman, 1987: 362.

11. The Tibetan itineraries to Sambhala have been extensively studied by Edwin Bernbaum (1980, 1985). The following discussion is indebted to his fine research, but our conclusions about the history and significance of Man lung's *lam yig* and the *Kalāpāvatāra* differ on several fundamental points, as noted below.

12. The *Blue Annals* states that Man lungs pa was born in 1239, and went to Potala in 1300 (Roerich, 1974: 790-791).

13. Bernbaum (1985: 37-38), who discovered a manuscript of the text, refers to it as the *Śambhala pa'i lam yig*, and believes the entire text is the work of Man lung Guru. In fact the title page (1a1) and the final colophon (20a1-2) of this manuscript give the title as *Sham bha la pa'i lam yig*, which we might translate as "The Itinerary of the Man [Who Went to] Sambhala"—this no doubt refers to Man lung Guru's itinerary contained in the fourth chapter. However, this title appears nowhere else in the manuscript, and the colophons to all of the five chapters (11b5, 13b1, 15a2, 17a6, 19b1) give the title as *rMi lam rdzun bshad sgyu ma'i sgra dbyangs chen mo*, "The Great Melody of Illusion, the False Account of a Dream." (This title derives from the author-redactor's view that empirical reality is illusory—thus, even the factual geo-

graphical information that makes up most of the text is, in some profound epistemological sense, false.) Also, Sambhala is not even mentioned in the other four chapters, which describe journeys to the East (China, chapter 1), the South (India and Potala, chapter 2), the West (Uḍḍiyāna, chapter 3), and the Center (Tibet, chapter 5). I believe *rMi lam rdzun bshad sgyu ma'i sgra dbyangs chen mo* is the main title of the text, and suspect *Sham bha la pa'i lam yig* is a subtitle affixed to call attention to the most rare or interesting itinerary it contains.

We can assume that Man lung Guru's *lam yig* forms the basis for the fourth chapter of *MLDS* because Paṇ chen Blo bzang dpal ldan ye shes refers to Man lung Guru's account in ways that correspond exactly to this chapter (*NTBBN*: 34a3-6; cf. 41b3-4; at 50a2 he refers to rJe Shambha la pa, apparently indicating Man lung Guru. See also *LSGK*: 5a3-5b1; *NCKSML*: 202b5-6).

However, the work as a whole is a synthesis of various travellers' accounts—it refers to journeys of Urgyan pa Rin chen dpal (1230-1309), 'Phags pa (1235-1280), and Red mda' ba gZhon nu blo gros (1349-1412). It also mentions the third Ming emperor of China, Yung-lo, who reigned early in the fifteenth century—thus it could not be the work of Man lung Guru. The name of the author-redactor is not given in the manuscript. However, dKon mchog bstan pa rab rgyas's linkage of Man lung Guru with Chos rje 'Byor ldan grags pa (see note 2) may suggest the latter's redaction of the text. This and a host of other issues raised by the *MLDS* await further study. For previous study of the Sambhala chapter of the text see Laufer: 402-407; and Bernbaum, 1985: 37-39.

14. Our manuscript reads *khu khom*, Laufer's (404) has the form *khom khom*. I assume these are both variants of the apparently more common form *kho khom*: see Wylie, 1970: 13, n. 11; Kaschewsky: 435.

15. *yul 'di'i zhib rgyas 'tshad* [read: *'chad*] *tshul ni / sa skya pa chos rgyal 'phags pas hor rgyal po la smras pa de zog 'tshong phyir yin par mngon no //* (*MLDS*: 17a3).

16. For example, the *lam yig* reports that people in a large city south of the border of Sambhala reproduce in an unusual hermaphroditic fashion. All of the citizens possess male genitals in their right thighs, and female in their left. After a mere three months gestation, the child is born from the left thigh (*MLDS*: 15a5-15b1).

In his own *lam yig* Paṇ chen Blo bzang dpal ldan ye shes, obviously following Man lung Guru, merely avers that hermaphrodites dwell on the border of Sambhala (*NTBBN*: 41b3-4). Yet in his *LSGK* (5a3-5b1) he asserts that this feature of Man lung Guru's *lam yig* is bizarre, and does not appear in the authoritative (*tshad ldan*) sources such as the *Kalāpāvatāra*, which he claims to follow. Help in the resolution of this contradiction may be found in the editor's colophon to *NTBBN* (50a4-5). There it is reported that the Paṇ chen had said the *NTBBN* needed revision, but the revision had not been carried out. It is possible that the *NTBBN* was written first, and the *LSGK* represents the Paṇ chen's later view, which further devalues Man lung Guru's account.

17. Bernbaum believes that (1) the verse sections of the *Kalāpāvatāra* are interpolated into a older prose original; (2) it contains no clear reference to the

Kālacakra tradition existing in Sambhala; (3) it probably predates the Kālacakra tradition, perhaps even predating Islam; and (4) the *KA* itself probably influenced the primary texts of the Kālacakra tradition—the *Śrī Kālacakra* and the *Vimalaprabhā* (Bernbaum, 1985: 128-133; cf. 28, 80-81, 102, 115-116).

I see no evidence to support any of these hypotheses. (1) It is extremely problematic to attempt to stratify a Sanskrit text based solely on features of its Tibetan translation. In any case, the verse sections simply frame and elaborate on the prose narrative. This is common practice in Sanskrit literature—it provides no evidence for stratification. (2) The *KA* in fact refers to the *Paramādibuddha-tantra* (*Dam pa dang po'i sangs rgyas rgyud*)—the Kālacakra *mūlatantra*—as existing in Kalāpa, the capital of Sambhala (*KA*: 317a4-5; cf. Bernbaum, 1985: 93, n.140). (3) Thus, the *KA* could not predate the Kālacakra tradition. (Given its content, if the *KA* predated Islam we would have to entirely rewrite the history of late Indian Buddhism.) (4) There is no evidence that the *KA* influenced the *Śrī Kālacakra* and the *Vimalaprabhā*; it is certainly simpler to assume the opposite to be true. (Cf. Newman, 1987: 195-206.)

Given the facts that the earlier Indo-Tibetan Kālacakra tradition exhibits no awareness of the *KA*, that it was not translated into Tibetan until the seventeenth century, and that Tāranātha specifies that it was translated from a Nepalese manuscript, it is possible that the *KA* is a product of medieval Newar Buddhism. Comparison of the deities and rituals of the *KA* with those of the Newars may support this hypothesis. On the other hand, the introduction to the *KA* (315b7-316a1) indicates that the legendary human audience of the sermon contained in the *KA* came from Kośala, Vaiśālī, Videha, and Mithilā. We know from manuscript colophons that vestiges of the Kālacakra tradition survived in this region at least into the fifteenth century, and it is possible that the *KA* originated there.

18. For a complete translation of the *KA* see Bernbaum, 1985: 44-80.

19. Although a few of the toponyms and geographical features of the *KA*'s route may be correlated with real entities, I have the impression that most are the products of literary imagination. Bernbaum (1985: 181-194) has shown that a portion of the *KA* draws on the journey to Uttarakuru episode of the *Rāmāyaṇa*.

20. See the full title of the *Shambha la'i smon lam* ("The Prayer [to be reborn] in Sambhala"): "The prayer to be reborn at the head of the entourage when in the future the supreme reverend lama himself [i.e., Paṇ chen Blo bzang dpal ldan ye shes] takes up the form of Raudra Cakrin in Sambhala and performs marvelous deeds"—*rJe btsun bla ma mchog nyid ma 'ongs dus shambha lar drag po 'khor lo'i skur bzhengs nas ngo mtshar ba'i mdzad pa ston skabs 'khor gyi thog mar skye ba'i smon tshig* (*KTKMT*). Chief among the "marvelous deeds" is the annihilation of the barbarian Muslims, as mentioned above.

21. Some contemporary Tibetans have adopted similar strategies when confronted by modern geography. They have placed Sambhala under the Arctic ice, on another planet, or in the realm of invisibility (Bernbaum, 1980: 31-39).

22. The *lam yig* section of the Paṇ chen's *NTBBN* is an exception to this rule, but even the *NTBBN* includes factual geographical information—obtained from British travellers in Tibet—elsewhere in the text (Vostrikov: 232).

References

Bailey, H. W.

1965 "A Metrical Summary of the Saddharma-puṇḍarīka-sūtra in Gostana-deśa." *Bulletin of Tibetology* 2/2: 5-7.

Beal, Samuel

1884 *Si-yu-ki: Buddhist Records of the Western World.* New York: Paragon Book Reprint Corp., 1968.

Bernbaum, Edwin Marshall

1980 *The Way to Shambhala: A Search for the Mythical Kingdom beyond the Himalayas.* Garden City, NY: Anchor Books.

1985 "The Mythic Journey and Its Symbolism: A Study of the Development of Buddhist Guidebooks to Śambhala in Relation to their Antecedents in Hindu Mythology." Ph.D. dissertation. Berkeley: University of California.

Brag dgon zhabs drung dKon mchog bstan pa rab rgyas

DTGT *Yul mdo smad kyi ljongs su thub bstan rin po che ji ltar dar ba'i tshul gsal bar brjod pa deb ther rgya mtsho zhes bya ba. The Ocean Annals of Amdo.* Ed. by Lokesh Chandra. New Delhi: International Academy of Indian Culture, 1977.

bTsan po No mon han 'Jam dpal chos kyi bstan 'dzin 'phrin las

NCKSML *'Dzam gliṅ rgyas par bśad pa thag riṅ gsal bar mthoṅ byed durba na, or 'Dzam gliṅ chen po'i rgyas bśad snod bcud kun gsal me loṅ* [1830 redaction]. Ed. by Tashi Tsering. New Delhi: Ngawang Sopa, 1980.

Chos dpal dar dpyang

LSDMG *Bla ma'i gsung dri ma med pa bsgrigs pa. The Biography of Chag lo-tsā-ba Chos rje dpal (Dharmasvāmin).* Ed. by Champa Thupten Zongtse. Śata-Piṭaka Series 266. New Delhi: International Academy of Indian Culture, 1981.

Grünwedel, Albert

1915 "Der Weg nach Śambhala des dritten Gross-Lama von bKra-śis-lhun-po bLo-bzaṅ dPal-ldan-ye-śes." *Abhandlungen der Königlich Bayerischen Akademie der Wissenschaften* 29/3.

Jackson, David P.

1989 *The 'Miscellaneous Series' of Tibetan Texts in the Bihar Research Society, Patna: A Handlist.* Tibetan and Indo-Tibetan Studies 2. Stuttgart: Franz Steiner Verlag Wiesbaden GmbH.

Kalāpāvatāra

KA *Kalāpāvatāra (Ka lā par 'jug pa).* In sDe dge bsTan 'gyur, sNa tshogs *po*, ff. 315b-327a. [Also in Peking and sNar thang; Co ne omits.]

Kaschewsky, Rudolf

1982 "Zu einigen tibetischen Pilgerplätzen in Nepal." *Zentralasiatische Studien* 16: 427-442.

Laufer, Berthold

1907 "Zur buddhistischen Litteratur der Uiguren." *T'oung pao* 8: 391-409.

rMi lam rdzun bshad

MLDS *rMi lam rdzun bshad sgyu ma'i sgra dbyangs chen mo* (a.k.a. *Sham bha la pa'i lam yig*). Manuscript, 20 fols., n.p., n.d.

Newman, John

1985 "A Brief History of the Kalachakra." In Geshe Lhundub Sopa et al., *The Wheel of Time*, pp. 51-90. Madison, Wisconsin: Deer Park Books. Reprint. Ithaca, New York: Snow Lion, 1991.

1987 "The Outer Wheel of Time: Vajrayāna Buddhist Cosmology in the Kālacakra Tantra." Ph.D. dissertation. Madison: University of Wisconsin-Madison.

1989a "The Kalki Avatāra of Viṣṇu and the Buddhist Kalkins of the Kālacakra Tantra: Myth as Polemic and Propaganda." Unpublished paper presented at the 41st Annual Meeting of the Association of Asian Studies.

1989b "Islam in the Buddhist Kālacakra Tantra." Unpublished paper presented at the Annual Meeting of the American Academy of Religion.

O'Flaherty, Wendy Doniger

1975 *Hindu Myths*. Harmondsworth, England: Penguin Books.

Paṇ chen Lama III, Blo bzang dpal ldan ye shes

KTKMT "rJe btsun bla ma mchog nyid ma 'ongs dus shambha lar drag po 'khor lo'i sku bzhengs nas ngo mtshar ba'i mdzad pa ston skabs 'khor gyi thog mar skye ba'i smon tshig." In *rJe btsun bla ma mchog nyid ma 'ongs dus shambha lar drag po 'khor lo'i sku bzhengs nas ngo mtshar ba'i mdzad pa ston skabs 'khor gyi thog mar skye ba'i smon tshig [/] shambha la'i zhing bkod bri tshul [/] dga' ldan lha brgya ma'i skabs su nye bar mkho ba'i kha tshar [/] dga' ldan lha brgya ma'i 'pho ba [/] ngag dbang lha mo dbyangs can ma la bstod pa [/] rdo rje 'jigs byed la brten nas dug zhi bar byed pa'i thabs bcas*. In *The Collected Works (gSuṅ 'bum) of the Third Panchen Lama of Tashilhunpo, Blo-bzaṅ-dpal-ldan-ye-śes*, vol. 13, *bKa' rgya*, ff. 1b1-2b5. New Delhi: Chode Tashilhunpo Society, 1978.

LSGK *Dus 'khor las brtsams te dris lan blo gsal dga' bskyed*. In *The Collected Works*, vol. 13, *bKa' rgya*, ff. 1-7.

NTBBN *Grub pa'i gnas chen po shambha la'i rnam bshad 'phags yul gyi rtogs brjod dang bcas pa ngo tshar bye ba'i 'byung gnas zhes bya ba* (a.k.a. *Shambha la'i lam yig*). In *The Collected Works*, vol. 10, *nya*, ff. 1-50.

SZKBT "Shambha la'i zhing bkod bri tshul." In *rJe btsun bla ma mchog nyid...dug zhi bar byed pa'i thabs bcas*. In *The Collected Works*, vol. 13, *bKa' rgya*, ff. 2b5-4b1.

Roerich, George

1959 *Biography of Dharmasvāmin (Chag lo tsā-ba Chos-rje-dpal) A Tibetan Monk Pilgrim*. Historical Researches Series 2. Patna: K. P. Jayaswal Research Institute.

1974 *The Blue Annals*. 1949. Reprint. Delhi: Motilal Banarsidass.

Tucci, Giuseppe

1931 "The Sea and Land Travels of a Buddhist Sādhu in the Sixteenth Century." *Indian Historical Quarterly* 7/4: 683-702.

1940 *Travels of Tibetan Pilgrims in the Swat Valley*. Calcutta: The Greater India Society.

1948-51 "Buddhist Notes." *Mélanges chinois et bouddhiques* 9: 173-220.

Vostrikov, A. I.

1970 *Tibetan Historical Literature*. Trans. by Harish Chandra Gupta. In *Indian Studies Past & Present* No. 4. Ed. by Debiprasad Chattopadhyaya. Calcutta: R. K. Maitra.

Vimalaprabhā

Asiatic Society of Bengal manuscript G.10766.

Wylie, Turrell V.

1962 *The Geography of Tibet According to the 'Dzam-gling-rgyas-bshad*. Serie Orientale Roma 25. Rome: Istituto Italiano per il Medio ed Estremo Oriente.

1965 "The Tibetan Tradition of Geography." *Bulletin of Tibetology* 2/1: 17-25.

1970 *A Tibetan Religious Geography of Nepal*. Serie Orientale Roma 42. Rome: Istituto Italiano per il Medio ed Estremo Oriente.

Chapter 30

Tables of Contents (*dKar chag*)[1]

Dan Martin

Nowadays, Tibetan language books are often printed and bound in what is nearly the universal book format, with a table of contents page listing the parts of the book with their page numbers. More often than not this table of contents page bears as its heading the Tibetan word [*d*]*kar chag*[*s*].[2] This was not always the case. In the past few centuries there were, it is true, often short, separately titled texts called *dkar chag* occurring at the beginning of a lama's collected works (*gsung 'bum*), or at the beginning of each volume, telling the title of each text enclosed, with at least a letter to indicate its place within the volume, and usually the number of leaves in that volume (each individual text, as a rule, having its own separate pagination). This might help to locate the desired text a bit more efficiently, but that was not the main function. In order to understand this point, one should know that traditional Tibetan books were only rarely bound in signatures. These "books" (which Tibetans call *dpe cha*), whether handwritten or printed from woodblocks (see Jest), are made up of long, narrow separate sheets, wrapped in cloth (*na bza'*) and then pressed between two slightly larger boards which are tied or otherwise fastened together. The entire ensemble of loose pages, cloth and "book boards" (*glegs shing*) is called a *glegs bam*. We should note also that while the cloth is being wrapped around the stack of pages, a cloth label is inserted just before the task is complete. This label extends out one of the small ends of the volume; usually, underneath a brocade flap one can discover the name of the author or some other indication of the contents, as well as a letter of the Tibetan alphabet which tells (to the initiate into this arcane system of library "call numbers") which volume of the set it is.

I do not believe it requires a degree in library science to understand how this sort of library composed of individual pages would tend to lend necessity to a "register" that would allow one to know with complete accuracy both how many texts *ought* to be in a given volume (and in which order) and, also, how many loose sheets *ought* to be in a given text. Without these "inventories," Tibetan libraries could, and in any case occasionally do, turn into a nearly unsortable jumble of shuffled pages.

We may seem to be proposing that "tables of contents" as we usually understand the term should be recognized as one of the great genres of Tibetan literature. While there may be some justification for this in the canons of modernist art criticism (cf. the shopping list in the story of lithography's origins), it must be remembered that we are here concerned with a traditional *Tibetan* literary *genre* that only corresponds in part to an English-book reader's expectations about what a "table of contents" should do, and the key question that needs to be asked is, Contents of what? These *dkar chags*, these so-called tables of contents, are among the most challenging, intriguing and fascinating documents for the historian of Tibetan culture, society, religion, politics... and they are not being used very much by researchers,[3] perhaps in part because they are still considered "just boring lists."

Contents of What?

I would first like to attempt a survey of the Tibetan *dkar chag* literature before advancing a few ideas about the meaning of the word and, finally, supplying a brief outline of one particular example. By far the most celebrated *dkar chag* is the *Shel dkar me long* ("White Crystal Mirror") written by the "Great Fifth" Dalai Lama Ngag dbang blo bzang rgya mtsho in 1645 C.E. (see Grünwedel, Vostrikov: 222-223, Waddell). It tells of the history and holy objects housed in the "Lhasa Cathedral" (best known as the Jo khang) and other temples in Lhasa. The longest of all *dkar chags* is the Great Fifth's regent Sangs rgyas rgya mtsho's exhaustive two-volume 1697 work concerning the Dalai Lama's genuinely monumental tomb *mchod rten* that looms up from the lower through the upper storeys of the Potala Palace. This latter work is in some ways completely characteristic of the genre, although its length may make it seem "overblown." Its 766 folio pages contain thirteen chapters, beginning with a cosmogony and cosmography that only gradually begins to narrow in on Tibet, then Lhasa, and finally the Potala itself. It includes a lengthy treatise on astrology/astronomy, since choosing the perfect moments for building and consecrating such a monument is considered quite important. There are elaborate descriptions of the actual layout of the *mchod rten,* the materials used, the relics and other sacred items (including an enviable library of Buddhist scriptures) that were enclosed within it, a treatise on consecration rituals in general as well as the particular one performed (see Bentor, in this volume), a discussion of the benefits of building and paying reverence to *mchod rtens,* and so forth. The chapter about the craftsmen employed in the project is especially interesting. The army of artisans—about 1500 are named—came from (besides Tibet) India, Kashmir, China, the areas north of Tibet, and most notably from Nepal; the names of most of the goldsmiths, in particular, are clearly Newari. There is a record of the offerings designated for the upkeep and compensation of the workmen, even some discussion about the tools they used. Overall, the text contains poetry, astronomy, technology, economics, geography, physics, "theology," philosophy, controversy—but also a record of the complex interactions necessary for constructing a public receptacle for "the sacred."

Both of the just-described *dkar chags* are included in the thirty-three-or-so *dkar chags* listed among the sources used in the compilation of the *Deb ther rgya mtsho* ("Ocean Annals," *DTGT*), the famous history of the A mdo region of northeastern Tibet. Of the thirty-three, twenty-five are *dkar chags* to holy places (including temples and monasteries), four are for *mchod rtens* (also, *mchod sdong,* or *gser gdung*), and one each for the following: embalming salts (a relic), the Potala Palace, an image, and a cycle of yoga instructions. This list cannot be considered representative of the entire genre. Obviously, the author of the *Deb ther rgya mtsho* only listed texts useful for his historical enterprise. My impression is that the majority of available texts bearing the word *dkar chag* in their titles are "tables of contents" to collected works (*gsung 'bum*) or other multi-volumed sets. With some exceptions, these are of little extrinsic interest. However, there are, besides these, quite a few *dkar chags* that are in effect bibliographies of bodies of Buddhist teachings, or "hand-lists" to library holdings, and these can be of considerable interest to serious students.

The most significant *dkar chag* of this latter type for students of Buddhism, but also perhaps the oldest surviving text of the genre, is one of three "hand-lists" to scriptural manuscripts housed in particular buildings during Tibet's imperial period. I refer to the *lDan dkar ma* catalogue (see Lalou). The other two catalogues, the *'Phang thang ma* (the earliest) and the *mChims phu ma*, were available to Tibetan writers of centuries past, but sadly for us have yet to come to light. Consulting the *lDan dkar ma* helps scholars to ascertain which texts were actually available in late imperial times (the early ninth century). These three texts are believed to be the forerunners of the later canon catalogues, such as the one contained in Bu ston's 1322 *Chos 'byung*, and the catalogues accompanying the various woodblock-printed editions of the bKa' 'gyur—the Lhasa, sDe dge, Co ne, and others. These latter are not simple lists of texts; they often contain discussions about the "canonicity" of certain texts, about different translations, about problems encountered in their editing, and about still other matters that contemporary textual Buddhologists would do well to utilize more fully than they have until now. They also contain much more; the Co ne catalogue, for example, has an important chapter on the history of the Co ne region. (For more on canon catalogues, see Vostrikov: 205-215.)

We should mention here also catalogues to the "alternative canons"—the Old Tantra Collection catalogues by Kaḥ thog pa written in 1797 (*NGB*, vols. 35-36) and by 'Jigs med gling pa (*NGB*, vol. 34). Both of these works are in effect lengthy histories of the rNying ma pa school and include detailed discussions about the various recensions of the collected *tantras* and issues surrounding them. We must also point out the existence of two catalogues of the Bon canonical collections, the "Word" (*bKa'*) and "Word Adhering" (*bKa' brten*) (see Kvaerne, in this volume), by Kun grol grags pa (b. 1717) and by a former abbot of sMan ri Monastery, Nyi ma bstan 'dzin (b. 1813). (*ZDGC*; Kvaerne) Such canon catalogues are terribly important for those who want to learn about, or just to locate printed versions of, scriptural texts.

What Are *dKar chags* For?

Scriptural texts are not, however, the only things that Buddhists have found holy, and in fact other holy objects might in some contexts take priority, possibly even historically speaking. Take for example this bold statement, bold in light of the fact that many still ignore or downplay the religious and devotional dimensions of Buddhism.

> ... taking carefully from the legendary elements those references that do not offend rational thought, one assumes that one has discovered an historical figure, who was the founder of a small rationally and philosophically minded community, and that this movement represents 'original Buddhism'. One then goes on to assume that this originally pure doctrine was distorted by later mythical and popular beliefs. There were certainly pure philosophical doctrines propounded during the early history of Buddhism, just as there have been ever since, but there is no such thing as pure Buddhism *per se* except perhaps the cult of Śākyamuni as a supramundane being, and the cult of the relic *stūpa*. (Snellgrove, 1973: 411)

The cults of relics and stūpas go far back into Buddhist history, most likely well before the third century B.C.E. reign of Aśoka, from whose time evidence begins to be abundant. In Tibet, there are generally three classes of things that are considered holy, and a temple lacking any one of these three things would hardly be possible. These are the Three Receptacles (*rten gsum*). The first is the Body Receptacle, meaning mainly icons of Buddhas and Buddhist saints. The second is Speech Receptacle, meaning the Word (*bka'*) of the Buddha, especially the bKa' 'gyur, but extended to other Buddhist books as well. The third is Mind Receptacle, meaning almost always and in any case primarily the stūpa (*mchod rten*). As I have pointed out elsewhere (Martin, 1994), all three of these may, and in the case of *mchod rtens* invariably do, contain relics. All three of these may, in fact, have *dkar chags* written for them, as may the temples and shrines that contain the Three Receptacles, and herein, I believe, lies the key to what we should understand as falling within the *dkar chag* genre. Stated in a simplified manner, a *dkar chag* is a text describing the construction and/or content of items which the Tibetan Buddhist traditions consider holy and capable of bestowing blessings (*byin brlabs*). In the case of temples, monastic complexes, or even *natural* holy places like

Mount Kailash, the word *dkar chag* is interchangeable with the genre term *gnas bshad* or *gnas yig* (holy place description/guide). The itinerary, or *lam yig*, is a quite distinct genre (see J. Newman, in this volume). The *gnas yig* is a guide to the holy site itself, while a *lam yig* tells the traveller how to get there.[4]

A more etymological study of the word [*d*]*kar chag*[*s*], which would explain how this particular word came to have this particular usage, might be welcome at this point. However, here I must confess myself stumped. I have heard several different explanations over the last few years, but none was given with much conviction. The following explanation is offered with equal lack of conviction, but I think that it has *some* justification. The syllable *dkar* means "white" and the syllable *chags* means, among other things, "formation" (as, for example, in the phrase *'jig rten chags tshul*, "the way the world was formed"). According to this theory, the word means "formation of white," and may be a (typical Tibetan) abbreviation for a larger phrase such as **dkar chos chags tshul*, meaning literally "how white Dharma was formed," to be further interpreted as "an account of merit making." Whether this etymology is a "true" one or not,[5] it does tell something important about at least one of the motives for writing these texts, which is just to memorialize the merit of all those who participated in or supported the construction of public objects of worship.

An Example

All these points and much more could be demonstrated by looking at any single example. I have chosen to end with one entitled *rNga yul chos grwa chen po dGe ldan legs bshad gling gi mchod rten mThong ba don ldan gyi dkar chag: Dad ldan yid kyi dga' ston* ("A Mental Festival for the Faithful: *dKar chag* of the *mChod rten* 'Significant Vision' at the Great Monastery of rNga yul called dGe ldan legs bshad gling") (Dharma'i ming can, 1987). rNga yul is rNga pa (also spelled *lNga ba*), or the area now in northern Szechuan Province which appears on modern maps as A-pa Tibetan Autonomous District (Chinese could not pronounce the initial "ng" sound, so it was just dropped). The author, who completed the work in the Fire-Hare year (1987), signs himself as "the foolish person with the name Dharma."

After verses eulogizing the Buddha, the teacher who founded the monastery, the monastery itself, and finally the *mchod rten*, the work proper begins with a discussion of the particular type of *mchod rten* built. It was a Miracle (*cho 'phrul*) *mChod rten*, also called a Delusionary Power Converting (*bdud 'dul*) *mChod rten*. This is one of a famous set of eight *mchod rtens* (on which not all texts are in agreement; see Tucci: 21-24) that commemorate particular events in the life of the Buddha. This one recalls the Buddha's display of miracles at Śrāvastī, and his conversion of the six *tīrthika* teachers. The main body of the work is divided into four parts:

(1) The origins of Body, Speech and Mind Receptacles (pp. 6-17)
(2) How the *mchod rten* in question was constructed (pp. 17-51)
(3) The benefits of constructing, prostrating or making offerings to a Receptacle (pp. 51-60)
(4) Dedication of the virtuous action of composing the work to the Enlightenment of all beings (pp. 60-63)

(1) The origins of Body, Speech and Mind Receptacles. There are brief stories told about various Body Receptacles, both sculpted and painted, of Indian origin, including those brought by the Chinese and Nepalese queens of Emperor Srong btsan sgam po in the late seventh century. The first Speech Receptacle was erected by Dharmodgata (see Conze: 288 for the story). The part on the Mind Receptacles begins with a general treatment based on scriptural sources and then a more specific discussion of the eight *mchod rtens*. This serves as background for the construction of the *mchod rten* that is the main subject of the work.

(2) How the mchod rten *was constructed.* The monastery of dGe ldan legs bshad gling was newly founded in 1870, at the request of a local ruler called rMe'u Sa dbang chen po, by the Kirti Rinpoche Blo bzang 'phrin las bstan pa rgya mtsho. This teacher was quite famous during his time, and we are fortunate to have a list of his collected works in twelve volumes with a brief biography in a recent publication from the People's Republic (*SBTD*, I: 18-45). He was born to the south of the lake Kokonor in 1849. In his fifth year he was recognized as the reincarnation of Rong po Chos rje by the third 'Jam dbyangs bzhad pa Incarnate, who gave him the name that appears above. Rong po Chos rje (=Rong po Grub chen sKal ldan rgya mtsho) lived from 1607 to 1677 and is most renowned

for his founding of the dGe lugs pa monastery Reb skong in A mdo. Kirti Rinpoche studied mainly at the monastic seminary of bKra shis 'khyil (he never travelled to central Tibet), and completed the monastery in rNga pa in 1873, where he died in 1905.

Shortly after his founding of the monastery, Kirti Rinpoche built a *mchod rten* named "Significant Vision." He composed a *dkar chag* to this *mchod rten* in no less than 108 (a significant number) folio pages. It is not, unfortunately, available to me. To return to information found in our *dkar chag*, we find that this original "Significant Vision" *mchod rten* was completely destroyed in 1967, one among the many Tibetan cultural monuments destroyed during the "Cultural Revolution." The monastery doors reopened in 1980, following the gradual liberalization policy of the PRC that had begun in 1977, shortly after the death of Chairman Mao. It was in 1983, on the fifteenth day of the seventh Tibetan month, that three monks, together with the author, laid out the chalk lines for the foundation of the new *mchod rten*, scattering flowers while chanting verses of auspiciousness. Soon afterward, about ten stoneworkers from neighboring Khro cu went to work on the foundation, the "earth-hugger" (*sa 'dzin*), which was twenty-five "Chinese cubits" (*gung khru*, i.e., meters) across, with the height of the completed structure to be at over thirty-eight of the same units.

Then, in 1984, a well-known lama visited the monastery and gave a large endowment, thirty thousand *yüan* and several pounds of silver. This was followed by an avalanche of donations both large and small of money, images, scriptures, building materials. Twenty-four smaller *mchod rtens* (to surround the main one) were each sponsored by a named individual with donations of fifteen hundred *yüan* each. Others made donations specifically for the string of prayer wheels that would encircle the *mchod rten*. Some of these donations are listed as given on behalf of deceased relatives.

Now the text (p. 30) begins to list the sacred articles that were enclosed within the *mchod rten*. Four monks and one helper were appointed to do the printing of short Sanskrit religious texts called *dhāraṇīs*, which have various purposes, and have to be produced in great numbers. For some of these, the monastery possessed the necessary woodblocks, but others had to be borrowed. Some were printed in the traditional style directly from woodblocks in the monastery's printshop, while others were machine printed. The lines of print have to form a continuous straight line, and so the already long strips of paper are pasted together end-to-end one after the other to form nearly endless ribbons that are then rolled into rolls and sewn into closely fitting cloth packages (*na bza'*). There were, in this instance, over 152,000 copies of the *Five Great Dhāraṇīs* treated in this manner. But there were as well whole books inserted into the *mchod rten*, including fifteen copies of Tsong kha pa's *Lam rim chen mo*, ten copies of his *sNgags rim chen mo*, and a silver-lettered *Ma ṇi bka' 'bum* manuscript, to give just three titles among the more than seventy listed. The *dhāraṇīs* and religious texts are all included in the first of four classes of relics, the class of Dharma Body Relics.

The second class of relics, which were also inserted, are called "mustard seed-like relics" (*yungs dkar lta bu'i ring bsrel*). I have discussed this type of relic in some detail elsewhere (Martin, 1994); here it will suffice to say that they are miraculously multiplying crystalline spheres or smooth amber-like substances that sometimes emerge from bones, hair, or other bodily constituents of saints, from icons, and from *mchod rtens*. The present list includes examples that came from the relics of the Buddha, of the previous Buddha Kāśyapa, from the Potala Palace, from the Great *mChod rten* at Bodhnath in Nepal Valley, and from the "treasure excavator" (*gter ston*, or *gter bton*) Gu ru Chos dbang (1212-1270).

The third class of relics consists of actual bodily remains of Buddhas and Buddhist saints. Bones, teeth, flesh, and blood of mostly, but not entirely, dGe lugs pa saints are listed here. Some of the bodily remains are in the form of *tsha tsha* (small clay tablets and miniature *mchod rtens* made with a metal mold, often containing cremation remains), or pellets containing water used to "wash" saintly relics. One such pellet is associated with the remains of Yongs 'dzin Gling Rinpoche (one of the Tutors to the present Dalai Lama) who died in India in 1983.

The fourth class of relics, *sku 'bal ring bsrel*, "clothing relics," here includes many images that belonged to saints, but also printed images of Padmasambhava (etc.) and painted *thang kas*. Of course it also includes clothing (but only pieces of the cloth, not usually entire garments), other personal articles (rosaries, bells, etc.), hair, and *tsha tsha* made by the hands of particular lamas. The listing of the items in this class takes up one fifth of the volume of the book.

(3) The benefits of constructing, prostrating or making offerings to a Receptacle. In the next section are quotes from scriptures telling

the benefits of constructing icons, *mchod rtens*, etc., and the benefits of prostrating to, making offerings to, and circumambulating these holy objects. Among others, there is a famous quote from the "Skillful Means" chapter of the *Saddharmapuṇḍarīka Sūtra* where the Buddha says that people who themselves draw or have others draw pictures of the Blessed One on walls become enlightened, even those who do so just in play, scratching the wall with a splinter or with their fingernails (Roth: 299; Kern: 50-51). Then there are a few citations on the benefits of building *mchod rtens*. Here we find a quote from Vanaratna, the thirteenth-century Bengali teacher, about how insects that die under the feet of the workmen or that are touched by the smoke produced while preparing food or drink for the workmen at a place where the Three Jewels dwell do not fall into the three lower realms of rebirth (see also Martin, 1988: 358).

This section ends with more quotes on the good results to be expected from prostrating, making offerings and circumambulating a *mchod rten*. Making offerings means an act of worship that includes the giving of commodities. Prostrations and circumambulations are acts of worship conceived as the giving of services. Tibetans sometimes combine the two by prostrating their way around *mchod rtens*. Although the scriptures are not very explicit on this point, Tibetans have generally aimed to perform the high round number of 100,000. Still, since this particular *mchod rten* has twenty-four lesser *mchod rtens* surrounding it, the author considers 4,500 circumambulations more than sufficient. He emphasizes the great importance of good motivations, beginning acts of worship with the idea of achieving enlightenment and ending with a dedication of the virtue and an aspiration that all sentient beings will finally achieve enlightenment.

(4) Dedication. The last section of the book dedicates the merits of its composition toward enlightenment, with extra wishes for good crops and an end to battles, famines, droughts and disease—public disasters in general. The *dkar chag* ends with an author's colophon. He was requested to write it by an incarnate lama, but protested not only that he lacked the ability, but that it would only lead to ridicule and disgrace for the monastery. Still, when the *mchod rten* neared completion the requests became persistent, so "I, the foolish person with the name Dharma, wrote it following the pattern of past *dkar chags*."

I hope that, even in this highly abridged form, the reader has caught a glimpse of the highly evolved, living pattern of Tibetan religion, something that nearly always fails to make any appearance in the high dreams of esotericists on the one hand, and in the learned publications of scriptural philologists, intellectual Buddhologists, interpreters of Madhyamaka philosophy, and so forth, on the other. Tibetan religiosity, with all its arguable rootedness in classical Buddhist scriptures, has yet taken a shape all its own. It cannot be dismissed as part of a simple dichotomy between a popular mass phenomenon and an aloof monastic hierarchy (although something like this can sometimes be detected); the "popular" phenomenon bridges the official-*versus*-popular distinction with *shared*, and not only disparate, perceptions. The world-transcending saints *need* the denizens of Everyday Land (otherwise, to whom would their compassionate activity be directed?), just as the people, both monk and lay, walking around the *mchod rtens* need humanly communicable evidence that transcendence is an ever-open option for them as well, an option embodied in the very form and content of the *mchod rten*, which serves as its "key to memory."[6] For them, the saints and believers, and for the student of human religiosity as well, a "table of contents" could prove useful for identifying and locating the holy both inside and outside the texts.

Notes

1. I am indebted to many people, but here I would especially like to thank Tashi Tsering of the Library of Tibetan Works and Archives for recommending, and procuring a copy of, the *dkar chag* from eastern Tibet used as an example at the end of this article. I must also thank Elliot Sperling for certain useful suggestions and information, as well as Gregory Schopen for his kind instigations.

2. The word may be found spelled in several different ways, the initial "d" and the final "s" being optional, but neither letter is normally pronounced in the Central Tibetan dialect. The etymology of this word is uncertain, and will be touched on later in this article.

3. The best exception to this rule is Rossi-Fillibeck (1976, 1988), who has particularly studied the *dkar chag* literature on the holy places of Yer pa and Mount Ti se (Kailash). The classics are Ferrari's (1958) study of Tibetan geography based on a *dkar chag*, Vostrikov's (1970: 205-230) general discussion of the genre and, also, Waddell (1895), Grünwedel (1919), and Schubert (1935), although this last-mentioned is a *gnas bshad*. We should note also Snellgrove's

(1979), Macdonald's (1975, 1981), Dowman's (1981) and Wylie's (1970) studies of Nepalese geography using Tibetan *dkar chags*. Antoni Huber (Christchurch) has been doing interesting research on the *dkar chags* and *gnas bshad* to the holy land of rTsā ri in the Assam border area in the southeastern part of Central Tibet inside the great bend in the Brahmaputra River (see also Martin, 1988). Helmut Eimer has done much work on canon catalogues. See, for example, Eimer, 1983.

4. As an example of a combination of both *lam yig* and *gnas bshad*, note the pilgrimage record of Central Tibet by Kaḥ thog Si tu (*BTNK*), which describes an itinerary at the same time as it describes the holy articles that may be found at each place.

5. At this point my impression is that the "true" etymology of the word will be found by considering the use of the word in the Old Tibetan inscriptions and in documents from Dunhuang. The word *dkar chag* (without the final "s") is used in some of these documents in contexts which suggest that the original meaning might have been something like "grain allotment" (*dkar* =rice, *chag* =portion). This needs further study by experts on these documents (meanwhile, see Thomas, 1935+, II: 41ff, 81, etc.). In one context (p. 81), the word is used in the sense of an official document that listed allotments of paper to scribes. Still more intriguing, an Old Tibetan legal document uses the word *dkar chags* in a context that suggests the meaning "to be proven blameless" (bSod nams skyid, *THNT*: 13, 53 n. 6).

6. Many studies of the *mchod rten* emphasize its "elemental" and "universal" symbolism. While we would not deny the importance of these types of symbolism, those bsTan 'gyur texts that are devoted to *mchod rtens* emphasize, almost exclusively, the thirty-seven "wings of enlightenment" (*bodhipakṣa*) and similar attributes of the Enlightened Ones. This is not the place to address this question with the necessary rigor or detail; my intention is only to point out the possibility that, when evidence takes precedence over creative imagination (in no way belittling the latter), the concept of the presence of the Enlightened Ones and/or enlightenment will take priority in descriptions of both the external formal symbolism and the internal content of the *mchod rten*.

References

Brag dgon dKon mchog bstan pa rab rgyas

DTGT *Deb ther rgya mtsho* (=*A mdo chos 'byung*, =*Yul mDo smad kyi ljongs su thub bstan rin po che ji ltar dar ba'i tshul gsal bar brjod pa deb ther rgya mtsho*). Delhi: A lag 'Jam dbyangs, 1974. [Also, Lokesh Chandra, New Delhi, 1975]. Composed in 1865.

bSod nams skyid and dBang rgyal, eds.

THNT *Tun hong nas thon pa'i gna' bo'i Bod yig shog dril*. Beijing: Mi rigs dpe skrun khang [1983/1985].

Conze, Edward

1975 *The Perfection of Wisdom in Eight Thousand Lines & Its Verse Sum-*

mary. Bolinas: Four Seasons Foundation.

Dharma'i ming can
1987 *rNga yul chos grwa chen po dGe ldan legs bshad gling gi mchod rten mThong ba don ldan gyi dkar chag: Dad ldan yid kyi dga' ston*. Dharamsala: Library of Tibetan Works and Archives Manuscript Collection, Class no. KA-5, Accessions no. 19265.

Dowman, Keith
1981 "A Buddhist Guide to the Power Places of the Kathmandu Valley." *Kailash* 8/3-4: 183-291.

Eimer, Helmut
1983 *Some Results of Recent Kanjur Research*. Archiv für zentralasiatische Geschichtsforschung, Heft 1. Sankt Augustin: VGH Wissenschaftsverlag.

Ferrari, Alfonsa
1958 *Mk'yen brtse's Guide to the Holy Places of Central Tibet*. Rome: Istituto Italiano per il Medio ed Estremo Oriente.

Grünwedel, Albert
1919 "Die Temple von Lhasa: Gedicht des ersten Dalailama, für Pilger bestimmt, aus dem tibetischen Texte mit dem Kommentar ins Deutsche übersetzt." *Sitzungsberichte der Heidelberger Akademie der Wissenschaften, Philosophisch-historische Klasse* 14, pp. 1-93.

Jest, Corneille
1961 "A Technical Note on the Tibetan Method of Block-Carving." *Man* [London] 61: 83-85 [article no. 102].

Kaḥ thog Si tu Chos kyi rgya mtsho
BTNK *Gangs ljongs dbus gtsang gnas bskor lam yig nor bu zla shel gyi se mo do* ["An Account of a Pilgrimage to Central Tibet during the Years 1918 to 1920"]. Palampur: Khams sprul Don brgyud nyi ma, Sungrab Nyamso Gyunphel Parkhang.

Kern, H.
1884 *Saddharma-Puṇḍarīka or the Lotus of the True Law*. Oxford: Clarendon Press. Reprint, New York: Dover Publications, 1963.

Kun grol grags pa
ZDGC *Zab dang rgya che g.yung drung bon gyi bka' 'gyur gyi dkar chag nyi ma 'bum gyi 'od zer*. A manuscript in 197 leaves [photographic copy kept at Tibetan Bonpo Monastic Centre, Dolanji], composed in 1751.

Kvaerne, Per
1974 "The Canon of the Tibetan Bonpos." *Indo-Iranian Journal* 16: 18-56, 96-144.

Lalou, Marcelle

1953 "Les textes bouddhiques au temps de Khri-sroṅ-lde-bcan." *Journal asiatique* 251 [fasc. 3]: 313-353.

Macdonald, Alexander W.

1975 "A Little-Read Guide to the Holy Places of Nepal—Part 1." *Kailash* 3/2: 89-144.

Macdonald, Alexander W., and Dwags-po Rin-po-che

1981 "Un guide peu lu des Lieux-saints du Nepal." In *Tantric and Taoist Studies in Honour of R. A. Stein*, vol. 1, pp. 237-273. Ed. by Michel Strickmann. Brussels: Institut Belge des Hautes Études Chinoises.

Martin, Dan

1988 "For Love or Religion? Another Look at a 'Love Song' by the Sixth Dalai Lama." *Zeitschrift der Deutschen Morgenländischen Gesellschaft* 138/2: 349-363.

1994 "Pearls from Bones: Relics, Chortens, Tertons and the Signs of Saintly Death in Tibet." *Numen* 41: 273-324.

NGB

rNying ma'i rgyud 'bum. 36 vols. Thimphu: Dingo Khyentse Rimpoche, 1973+.

Rossi-Filibeck, Elena de

1976 "I distretti del Tibet nel diciannovesimo secolo." *Annali* [Istituto Universitario di Napoli] 36 [=n.s. vol. 26, fasc. 4]: 507-520.

1988 *Two Tibetan Guide Books to Ti se and La phyi*. Monumenta Tibetica Historica, Abteilung 1, Band 4. Bonn: VGH Wissenschaftsverlag.

Roth, Gustav

1987 "The Physical Presence of the Buddha and Its Representation in Buddhist Literature." In *Investigating Indian Art: Proceedings of a Symposium on the Development of Early Buddhist and Hindu Iconography Held at the Museum of Indian Art Berlin in May 1986*, pp. 291-312. Berlin: Museen für Indische Kunst.

SBTD

Mi rigs dpe mdzod khang gi dpe tho las gsung 'bum skor gyi dkar chag shes bya'i gter mdzod. Vol. 1. Zhing hwa: Si khron mi rigs dpe skrun khang, 1984.

Schubert, Johannes

1935 "Der tibetische Māhātmya des Wallfahrtsplatzes Triloknāth." *Artibus Asiae* 4 [fasc. 1]: 76-78; 5 [fasc. 2-4]: 127-136.

Snellgrove, David

1973 "Śākyamuni's Final Nirvāṇa." *Bulletin of the School of Oriental and African Studies* 36: 399-411.

1979 "Places of Pilgrimage in Thag (Thakkhola)." *Kailash* 7/2: 75-170.

Thomas, F. W.

1935+ *Tibetan Literary Texts and Documents Concerning Chinese Turkestan.* London: The Royal Asiatic Society.

Three Karchacks

1970 *Three Karchacks.* Edited and reproduced by Ngawang Gelek Demo with English Introduction by E. Gene Smith. Delhi.

Tucci, Giuseppe

1988 *Stupa: Art, Architectonics and Symbolism.* Indo-Tibetica 1. New Delhi: Aditya Prakashan.

Vostrikov, A. I.

1970 *Tibetan Historical Literature.* Trans. by Harish Chandra Gupta. Calcutta: R. D. Press. Composed in 1936; first published in Russian in 1962.

Waddell, L. A.

1895 "Description of Lhasa Cathedral, Translated from the Tibetan." *Journal of the Asiatic Society of Bengal* 14: 259-283 [+plate XXVI].

Wylie, Turrell V.

1970 *A Tibetan Religious Geography of Nepal.* Rome: Istituto Italiano per il Medio ed Estremo Oriente.

About the Contributors

Yael Bentor is a Lecturer in the Department of Indian Studies at The Hebrew University of Jerusalem. She received her Ph.D. in Tibetan Studies from the Department of Uralic and Altaic Studies—now renamed the Department of Central Eurasian Studies—at Indiana University in 1991. Her major publications include "On the Symbolism of the Mirror in Indo-Tibetan Consecration Rituals," "On the Indian Origins of the Tibetan Practice of Depositing Relics and *Dhāraṇīs* in *Stūpas* and Images," and "Tibetan Tourist Thangkas in the Kathmandu Valley." Her current research focuses on Indo-Tibetan rituals.

José I. Cabezón is Associate Professor of Philosophy of Religion at Iliff School of Theology, Denver, Colorado. He received his Ph.D. in Buddhist Studies from the University of Wisconsin-Madison in 1986. His major publications include *Buddhism, Sexuality and Gender, A Dose of Emptiness,* and *Buddhism and Language.* His current research focuses on cross-cultural comparison as a method and classical Tibetan polemical literature on the doctrine of emptiness.

Daniel Cozort is Assistant Professor of Religion at Dickinson College, Carlisle, Pennsylvania. He received his Ph.D. in the History of Religions from the University of Virginia in 1989. His major publications include *Highest Yoga Tantra: An Introduction to the Esoteric Buddhism of Tibet* and *Imagination and Enlightenment: Tibetan Tantric Art.* He is revising for publication his dissertation on some dGe lugs exegeses of Prāsaṅgika-Mādhyamika texts critical of non-Prāsaṅgikas.

Todd Fenner is currently a Senior Manager at the consulting firm of Deloitte & Touche LLP. He also teaches Buddhism at the Los Angeles Drikung Kagyu Center and at Ganden Buddha Norling in San Diego. He received his Ph.D. in Buddhist Studies from the University of Wisconsin-Madison in 1979. His current research focuses on the history of doctrinal and practice differences among the Tibetan lineages.

Rebecca R. French is Associate of Law at the University of Colorado at Boulder. She has a J.D. and an L.L.M. in law and received her Ph.D. in Anthropology from Yale University in 1990. Her major publications include *The Golden Yoke: The Legal Cosmology of Buddhist Tibet*. She is currently working on an annotated translation of four Tibetan law codes.

Janet Gyatso is Assistant Professor of Religion at Amherst College. She received her Ph.D. in Buddhist Studies at the University of California at Berkeley. She edited a volume of essays on memory in Indian and Tibetan Buddhism, entitled *In the Mirror of Memory* and has published a variety of articles on the Treasure tradition, Tibetan autobiographical writing, and Tibetan religions. A translation and study of the secret autobiographies of 'Jigs med gling pa is forthcoming from Princeton University Press. Her current research focuses on Buddhist tantric ritual and literature, and the place of women therein.

Paul Harrison is Senior Lecturer in Religious Studies at the University of Canterbury in Christchurch, New Zealand. He received his Ph.D. in Buddhist Studies from the Australian National University in 1980. His major publications include *The* Samādhi *of Direct Encounter with the Buddhas of the Present* and *Druma-kinnara-rāja-paṛiprcchha-sūtra: A Critical Edition of the Tibetan Text (Recension A)*. His current research focuses on Mahāyāna *sūtra* literature, the history of Buddhism and the development of the Tibetan canon.

Paul Jeffrey Hopkins is Professor of Religious Studies at the University of Virginia, where he has taught Tibetan Studies and Tibetan language since 1973. He received a Ph.D. in Buddhist Studies from the University of Wisconsin in 1973. He has published many articles and books, the most prominent being *Meditation on Emptiness* and *Emptiness Yoga* and the most recent being *Fluent Tibetan: A Proficiency Oriented Learning System, Novice and Intermediate Levels* and *Tibetan Arts of Love*. He is currently writing an analysis of Tibetan interpretations of the Mind Only doctrine of emptiness ranging from the fifteenth to twentieth centuries.

David Jackson is Professor of Tibetan in the Institute for the Culture and History of India and Tibet at Hamburg University. He received his Ph.D. in (Tibetan) Buddhist Studies from the University of Washington in 1985. His major publications include *The Entrance Gate for the Wise, Section III, Enlightenment by a Single Means*, and *A History of Tibetan Painting* (forthcoming). His current research focuses on the biography of the late Dezhung Rinpoche (1906-1987).

Roger R. Jackson is Associate Professor of Religion at Carleton College, Northfield, Minnesota. He received his Ph.D. in Buddhist Studies from the University of Wisconsin-Madison in 1983. His major publications include *The Wheel of Time: Kalachakra in Context* (with Geshe Sopa and John Newman) and *Is Enlightenment Possible?* His current research focuses on the history of Mahāmudrā, especially in the dGe lugs tradition, and on Indian and Tibetan Buddhist religious poetry.

Matthew Kapstein is Associate Professor of the Philosophy of Religion at Columbia University in the City of New York. He received his Ph.D. in Philosophy from Brown University in 1987. His major publications include, with Gyurme Dorje, the English edition of H. H. the late Dudjom Rimpoche's *The Nyingma School of Tibetan Buddhism: Its Fundamentals and History*. His current research focuses on the interrelationships among literacy, religion and statecraft during the period of the Tibetan empire.

Leonard W. J. van der Kuijp is Associate Professor of Tibetan Language and Literature with the Department of Asian Languages and Literature of the University of Washington. He received his D.Phil. from Hamburg University, Germany, in 1983. His major publications include *Contributions to the Development of Tibetan Buddhist Epistemology* and "On the Life and Political Career of Ta'i si tu Byang chub rgyal mtshan (1302-?1364)." His current research focuses on Tibetan cultural and intellectual history of the thirteenth to fifteenth centuries.

Per Kvaerne is Professor of History of Religions and Tibetology at the University of Oslo, Norway. He received his Ph.D. in Buddhist Studies from the University of Oslo in 1973. His publications include *An Anthology of Buddhist Tantric Songs: A Study of the Caryāgīti*; *Tibet: Bon Religion. A Death Ritual of the Tibetan Bonpos* and *The Bon Religion of Tibet: Iconography of a Living Faith*. His current research is in the history of the Tibetan Bon religion.

Jules B. Levinson is Assistant Professor in the Department of Religion at Hamline University. He received his Ph.D. in Religious Studies from the University of Virginia in 1994. His current research focuses on Tibetan Buddhist soteriological literature.

Erberto Lo Bue is Lecturer in Tibetan language and literature at the Institute of Linguistics and Oriental Studies of the University of Milan and teaches Tibetan art history at Cesmeo in Turin. He received his Ph.D. in Tibetan Studies from the School of Oriental and African Studies (University of London) in 1981. His major publications include *Gyantse Revisited* and *The Great Stūpa of Gyantse*, with F. Ricca, as well as several exhibition catalogues, the most important being *Tesori del Tibet: oggetti d'arte dai monasteri di Lhasa*. His current research focuses on Buddhist Himalayan artists' traditional iconographic sources, materials and techniques.

Donald S. Lopez, Jr. is Professor of Buddhist and Tibetan Studies in the Department of Asian Languages and Cultures at the University of Michigan. He received his Ph.D. in Religious Studies from the University of Virginia in 1982. His major publications include *Elaborations on Emptiness: Use of the Heart Sūtra* (forthcoming), *Curators of the Buddha: The Study* *of Buddhism under Colonialism* (editor), and *Buddhism in Practice* (editor). He is currently serving as editor-in-chief of *The Journal of the International Association of Buddhist Studies.*

John Makransky is Assistant Professor of Comparative Theology and Buddhist Studies at Boston College. He received his Ph.D. in Buddhist Studies from the University of Wisconsin in 1990. His publications include *Toward Enlightenment: Controversy Over the Buddhakāyas in India and Tibet* (forthcoming) and "Proposal of a Modern Solution to an Ancient Problem: Literary-Historical Evidence that the *Abhisamayālaṃkāra* Teaches Three Buddha Kāyas." His current research focuses on relations between meditation practices and doctrines of enlightenment in India and Tibet.

Dan Martin is currently Visiting Scholar at the Department of Indian Studies, The Hebrew University at Jerusalem. He completed his Ph.D. in Tibetan Studies at the Department of Uralic and Altaic Studies—now renamed the Department of Central Eurasian Studies—at Indiana University in 1991. His publications include *Maṇḍala Cosmogony: Human Body, Good Thought and the Revelation of the Secret Mother Tantras of Bon.* He is interested in the history of Tibetan sectarian relations and general cultural history from the tenth century to the present.

Guy Newland is Associate Professor of Religion at Central Michigan University. He received his Ph.D. in the History of Religions from the University of Virginia in 1988. His major publications include *The Two Truths* and *Compassion: A Tibetan Analysis.*

Beth Newman is a business planner at Sarasota Memorial Hospital. She received her Ph.D. in South Asian Languages and Literature from the University of Wisconsin-Madison in 1987. Her translation of the Tibetan novel *gZhon nu zla med kyi gtam rgyud* will be published in Harper Collins' Library of Tibet series in 1996.

John Newman is John D. and Catherine T. MacArthur Assistant Professor of Asian Religions at New College, the honors college of the State University System of Florida. He received his Ph.D. in Buddhist Studies from the University of Wisconsin-Madison in 1987. His publications include "Buddhist Sanskrit in the Kālacakra Tantra" and "Buddhist Siddhānta in the Kālacakra Tantra." His current research focuses on the history and doctrines of the Kālacakra Tantra.

Shunzo Onoda is Associate Professor at Bukkyo University, Kyoto. He received his D.Lit. in Buddhist Studies from Bukkyo University in 1993. His major publications include *Monastic Debate in Tibet, the Yoṅs 'Dzin rTags Rigs: A Manual for Tibetan Logic,* and "The Chronology of the Abbatial Successions of the Gsaṅ phu sne'u Monastery." His current research focuses on Tibetan thangka paintings.

James Burnell Robinson is Associate Professor of Religious Studies at the University of Northern Iowa, Cedar Falls, Iowa. He received his Ph.D. in Buddhist Studies from the University of Wisconsin-Madison in 1975. He has published *Buddha's Lions*, as well as various articles on religious myth and symbolism. His current research focuses on recurrent symbolic patterns in the esoteric dimension of the world's religions.

Geoffrey Samuel is Professor of Religious Studies at Lancaster University, U.K. He received his Ph.D. in social anthropology from Cambridge in 1975. His major publications include *Mind, Body and Culture* and *Civilized Shamans*. His current research focuses on the Tibetan epic, shamanic aspects of Tibetan religion, and healing, shamanism and ritual in Asian societies more generally.

Jeffrey D. Schoening is a Tibetan language teacher. He received his Ph.D. in Buddhist Studies from the University of Washington in 1991. His major publication is *The Śālistamba Sūtra and Its Indian Commentaries*. His current research focuses on Buddhist *sūtras* and their commentaries and on the Sa skya school of Tibetan Buddhism.

Tadeusz Skorupski is Senior Lecturer in Buddhist Studies at the School of Oriental and African Studies, University of London. He received his Ph.D. in Indo-Tibetan Studies from the University of London in 1978. His publications include *The Sarvadurgatipariśodhana* and *The Cultural Heritage of Ladakh*.

Michael J. Sweet is a psychotherapist at the Madison VA Hospital and clinical Assistant Professor in the Department of Psychiatry, University of Wisconsin-Madison. He received Ph.D.s in Buddhist Studies and Counseling Psychology, both from UW-Madison. He has published articles on Western and Buddhist psychotherapy, and on the history of sexuality. His current research focuses on *blo sbyong* texts, and on queer identities in classical Indian culture.

Pieter Cornelis Verhagen is Research-Fellow on behalf of the Royal Netherlands Academy of Arts and Sciences at the Department of Languages and Cultures of South and Central Asia, Leiden University. He received his Ph.D. in Languages and Cultures of South and Central Asia from Leiden University in 1991. His major publications include *A History of Sanskrit Grammatical Literature in Tibet. Volume I: Transmission of the Canonical Literature*, "Royal Patronage of Sanskrit Grammatical Studies in Tibet" and "A Ninth-Century Tibetan Summary of the Indo-Tibetan Model of Case-Semantics." His current research focuses on the Tibetan literature on Sanskrit grammar, indigenous Tibetan grammar, and the applications of linguistic disciplines in Tibetan Buddhist exegesis.

Joe Bransford Wilson is Associate Professor of Asian Philosophy and Religion at the University of North Carolina at Wilmington. He received his Ph.D. in Religious Studies (specializing in Tibetan Buddhism) from the University of Virginia in 1984. He is the author of *Translating Buddhism from Tibetan,* as well as number of articles dealing with Indian and Tibetan Buddhist philosophy. His current research focuses on Yogācāra in Tibet and historiographic issues underlying Buddhist histories of philosophy.

INDEX

betan schools, 247; Tibetan and Sanskrit terms and equivalents, 245-246
mental training, as inadequate translation for *blo sbyong*, 254n
merit (*puṇya, bsod nams*): and ritual offerings, 313-314; sponsorship of bKa' 'gyur as act of, 85
Mes ag tshoms, 151
metallurgy, handbooks on, 476
metaphysics, as ritualized in offerings, 315. *See also* cosmology, emptiness, two truths.
metrical schemes, Indian, and Tibetan poetry, 373-377
mGar stong bstan yul zang, 443
mgur: as Buddhistic songs, 369; as particularly religious songs, 372; as sub-category of "royal songs," 370; seven types of, 374; tradition of influenced by *snyan ngag*, 375. *See also* poetry.
Mi bskyod rdo rje: as criticized by rJe btsun Chos kyi rgyal mtshan, 218, 220-221, 225n; *bKa' brgyud mgur mtsho*, 386n; commentary on *Abhidharmakośa*, 134; literature on grounds and paths by, 262; on iconometry, 474
Mid dbang Pho lha nas bSod nams stob rgyas, biography of by Tshe ring dbang rgyal, 419n
Midrash, Buddhist folk teachings compared with, 246
Mi la ras pa, 278, 381-382; and beginnings of chiefly religious songs, 372-373; as cited by rJe btsun pa, 220-221; Chögyam Trungpa's indebtedness to, 382; melodies of songs of, 373; *mgur* of contrasted with Tsong kha pa's *snyan ngag*, 388n; *rnam thar* of as example of law, 453n; songs of, 362, 370; straightforwardly personal poet, 378-379; trochaic verse of songs of, 375
Miller, Roy Andrew, 431
Milton, John, 384
Mīmāṃsā, 174
mind, Tibetan and Sanskrit terms and equivalents, 245-246
Minkowski, C. Z., 304n
Mi pham rNam rgyal rgya mtsho (Mi pham Rin po che), 135n, 253n, 275-276, 355n; edition of Ge sar epic by, 366n; exegesis of *Kāvyādarśa* by, 397; handbook on painting, 476; literature on grounds and paths by, 262
miracles, explanations of, 63-64
Miscellany (*sNa tshogs*) section, commentaries in, 114
missionaries, and Western encounters with Tibet, 11
mKhan chen bKa' bzhi pa Grags pa gzhon nu, 239
mKhan chen bSod nams grags pa, 239
[mKhan po] gZhan dga', 253n
mKhan po 'Jigs med phun tshogs, 163n; as *gter ston*, 148
mKhan zur Lhun grub thabs mkhas, 347, 349
mKhas grub bstan gsal, 194
mKhas grub dge legs dpal bzang po: cited by 'Jam dbyangs bzhad pa, 212n; commentaries on, 403; literature on grounds and paths by, 262; poetic style of, 398; *sādhanas* of, 340n, 341n; *sTong thun chen mo*, 208
mKhas grub rje. *See* mKhas grub dge legs dpal bzang po.
mKhas pa'i dga' ston, 453n; as source for art history, 477
mKhas pa lDe'u, 48; *chos 'byung* of, 42, 46
mKhas pa rnams la 'jug pa'i sgo, of Sa skya Paṇḍita, 395, 412, 418n; and *Kāvyādarśa*, 418n
mKhas sgrub bsTan pa dar rgyas, 208
mNga' ris, 282
mngon 'gro. See preliminary practice texts.
modernism, Chögyam Trungpa influenced by, 383
monasteries: and elaboration of *snyan ngag*, 375; curricula of, 187-198, 202-213; insignificance of in legends of *siddhas*, 59, 62; power of, 15; structure of, 188, 196n, 205. *See also* bKra shis kyil, bKra shis lhun po, bSam yas
Mon gling g.yul 'gyed, episode of Ge sar epic, 360
Mongolia: connections with sNar thang, Sa skya, 76; influence on Tibetan historiography, 44; law codes of as influencing Tibet, 444-445; relations with, 44-45
monks: as élite, literati, 15; in relation to laity, 204; most not students, 205
motivating cause, in sGam po pa's *Thar pa rin po che'i rgyan*, 233
Mūlasarvāstivādins, Tibetan Vinaya and, 87n
Mullin, Glenn, 340n
[Mus chen] dKon chog rgyal mtshan, 253n
Mus chen sems dpa' chen po dKon mchog rgyal mtshan, 237
Mu tig btsan po, 162n